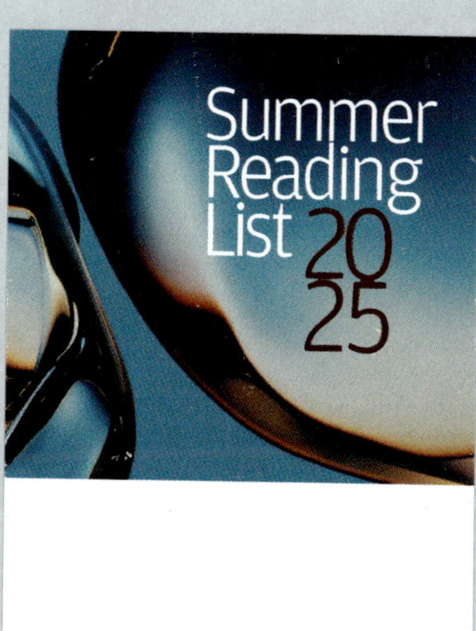
Summer
Reading
List
20
25
J.P.Morgan

MIRROR

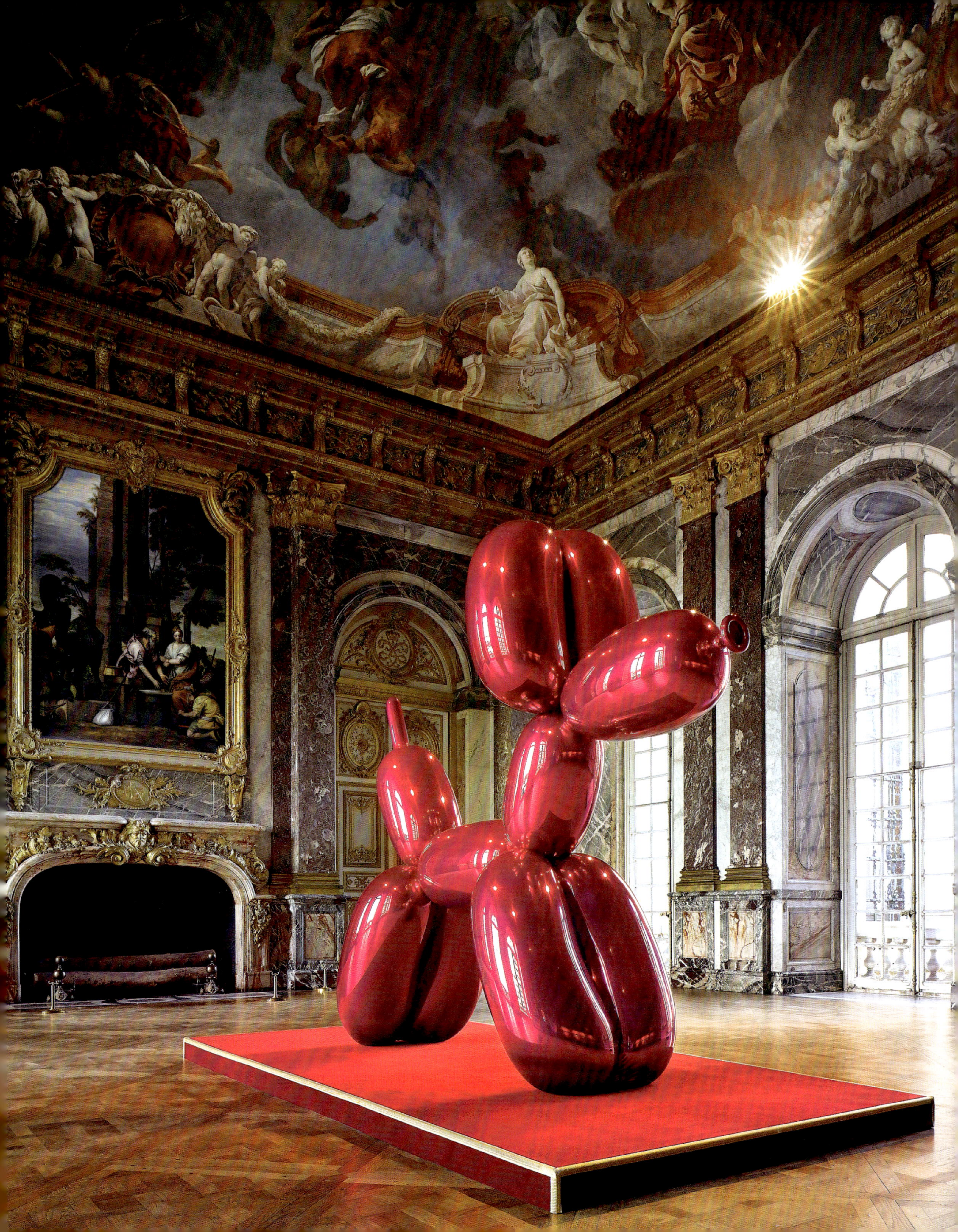

MIRROR

THE REFLECTIVE SURFACE IN CONTEMPORARY ART

MICHAEL PETRY

With 244 Illustrations

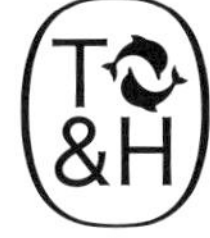

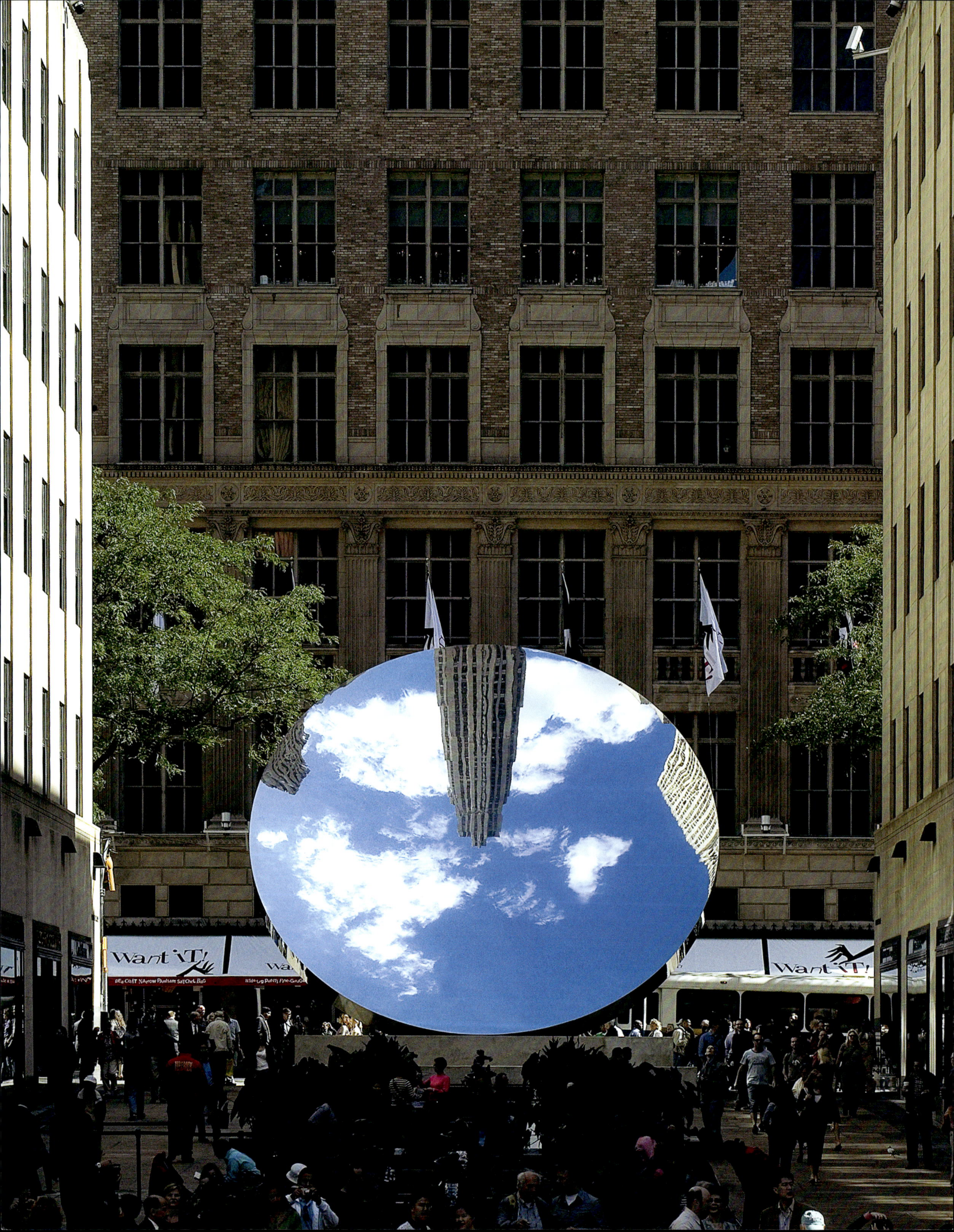

INTRODUCTION

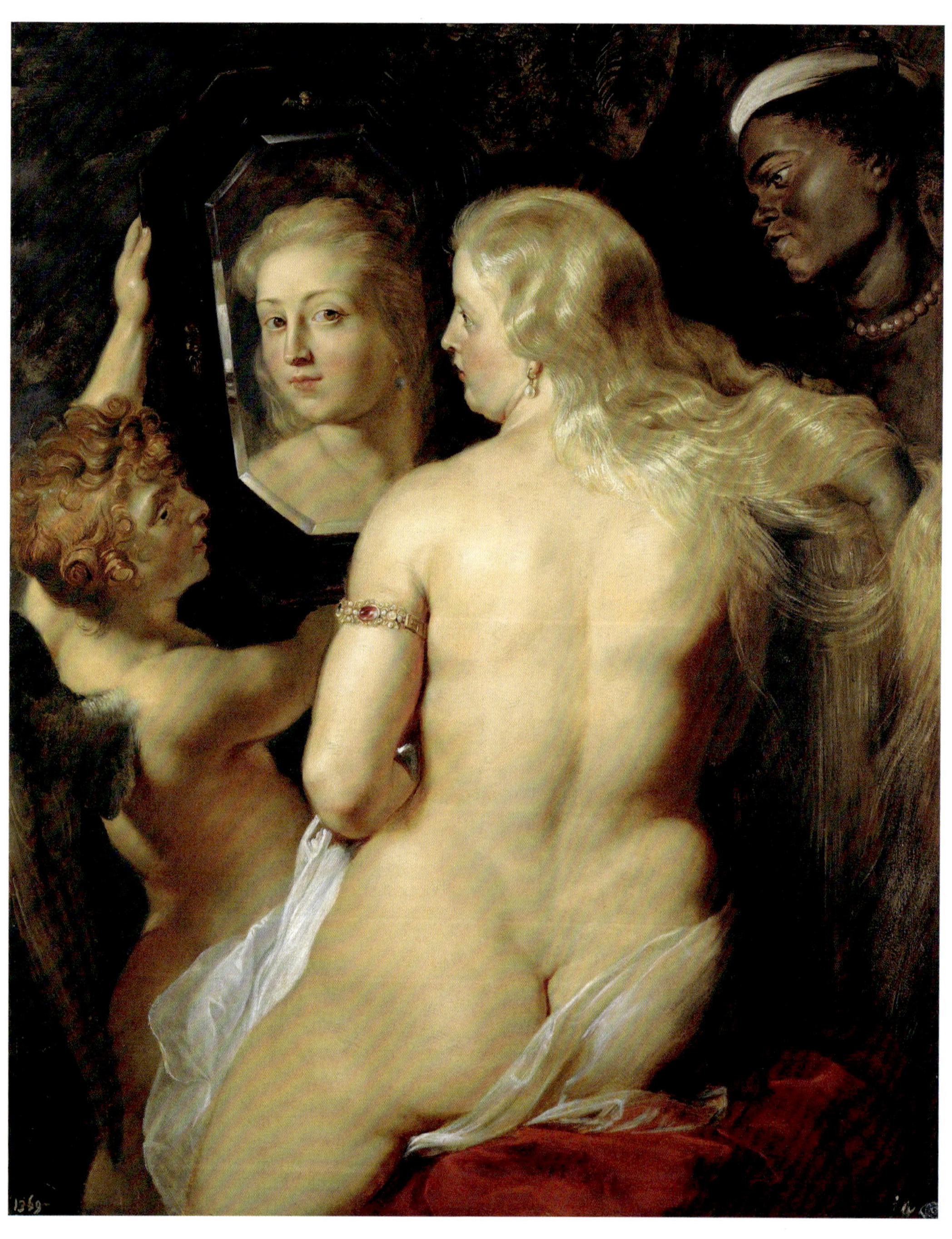

Artists have long been fascinated by mirrors and reflective surfaces that allow viewers to see themselves in direct interaction with the artwork. Looking into a mirror creates a liminal space, where reality slips between the real world and one in which the mirror reverse is presented. No matter how we look into a mirror or a shiny surface, the face we see back is not the one that others see. Left and right are reversed and what we see is at best a virtual self.

This introduction aims to present a few historical works as an introduction to concepts further developed by contemporary artists. For hundreds of years artists looked into mirrors to paint self-portraits that enabled them to see themselves, but not as others did. They painted or sculpted a version of themselves as only they saw it. To truly reach under the surface, to find the core, was impossible. Of course that did not stop artists from attempting it and giving the world incredible works. In a well-known, sensual image, Albrecht Dürer's self-portrait of 1500 shows him at the age of twenty-eight, his long, beautiful fingers playing with the fur of his coat collar. Rembrandt looked into the mirror all his life, staring into its void to show the ravages of time as he documented his ever-changing face. In the same periods Sofonisba Anguissola and Judith Leyster left fascinating self-portraits, as this was not a gendered exercise. Angelica Kauffman was a friend of Joshua Reynolds and both documented themselves as well as the elite of their times.

Holding a mirror up to yourself, be it an actual or a metaphorical one, is quite a difficult task to undertake, and one many non-artists are urged to do by society. Friedrich Nietzsche said in *On the Genealogy of Morals* (1887): 'Of necessity we remain strangers to ourselves, we understand ourselves not, in ourselves we are bound to be mistaken, for of us holds good to all eternity the motto, "Each one is the farthest away from himself" – as far as ourselves are concerned we are not "knowers".' Yet artists keep trying to know themselves and to use their search for that knowledge as a guide for others, those who might see or read their work.

Jan van Eyck's *Arnolfini Portrait* (1434) may be one of the first paintings to feature a significant mirror. The painting depicts the two newlyweds Giovanni Arnolfini, a wealthy merchant, and Giovanna Cenami. The couple are shown hand in hand, their pose framing a convex mirror on the back wall, in which they are seen from the rear, along with a doorway, the entrance to the room. There stand two men (one of whom is likely the artist himself), who, together with the reflection of the window on the left, create new spaces outside the frame of the painting. Light comes in and

is reflected in the mirror and off the surface of the brass chandelier, focusing our view not so much on the mirror but on van Eyck's extravagant signature – a Latin inscription reading 'Jan van Eyck was here' – above the mirror. He wants us to know who created these many spaces, he is the focus of the painting, he presents a conceptual self-portrait in disguise.

Artists have also depicted mirrors to open up a visual portal into the reflective world. Perhaps the best-known use of a mirror in a painting is Diego Velázquez's *Venus at her Mirror* (c. 1647–51)

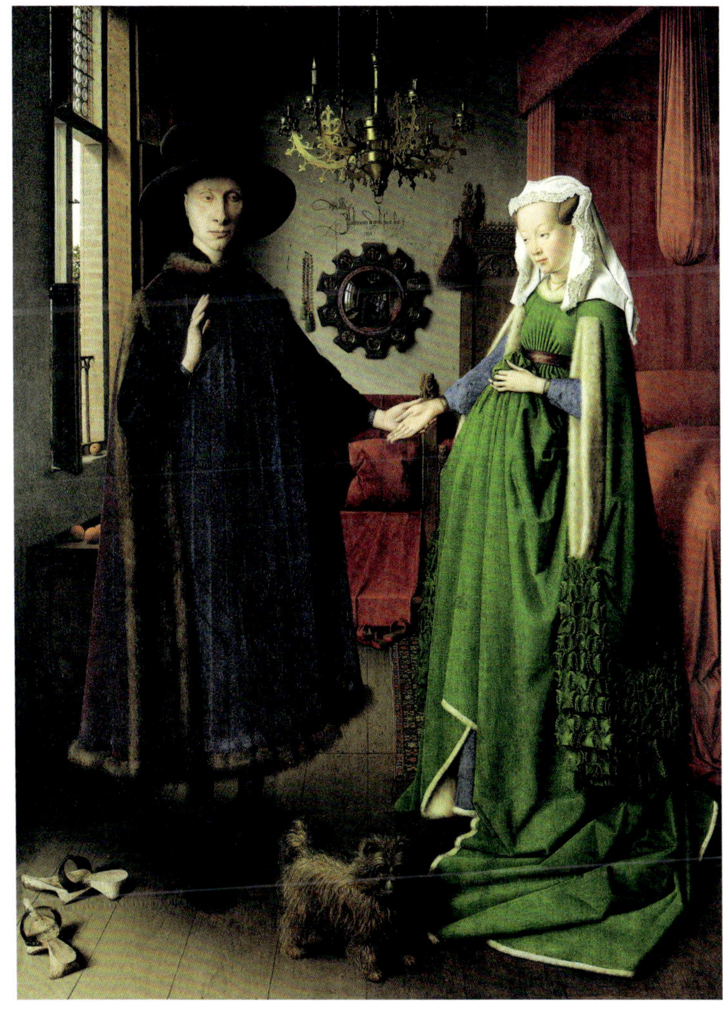

Jan van Eyck, *The Arnolfini Portrait*, 1434
Oil on oak panel, 82.2 × 60 cm (32½ × 23½ in)

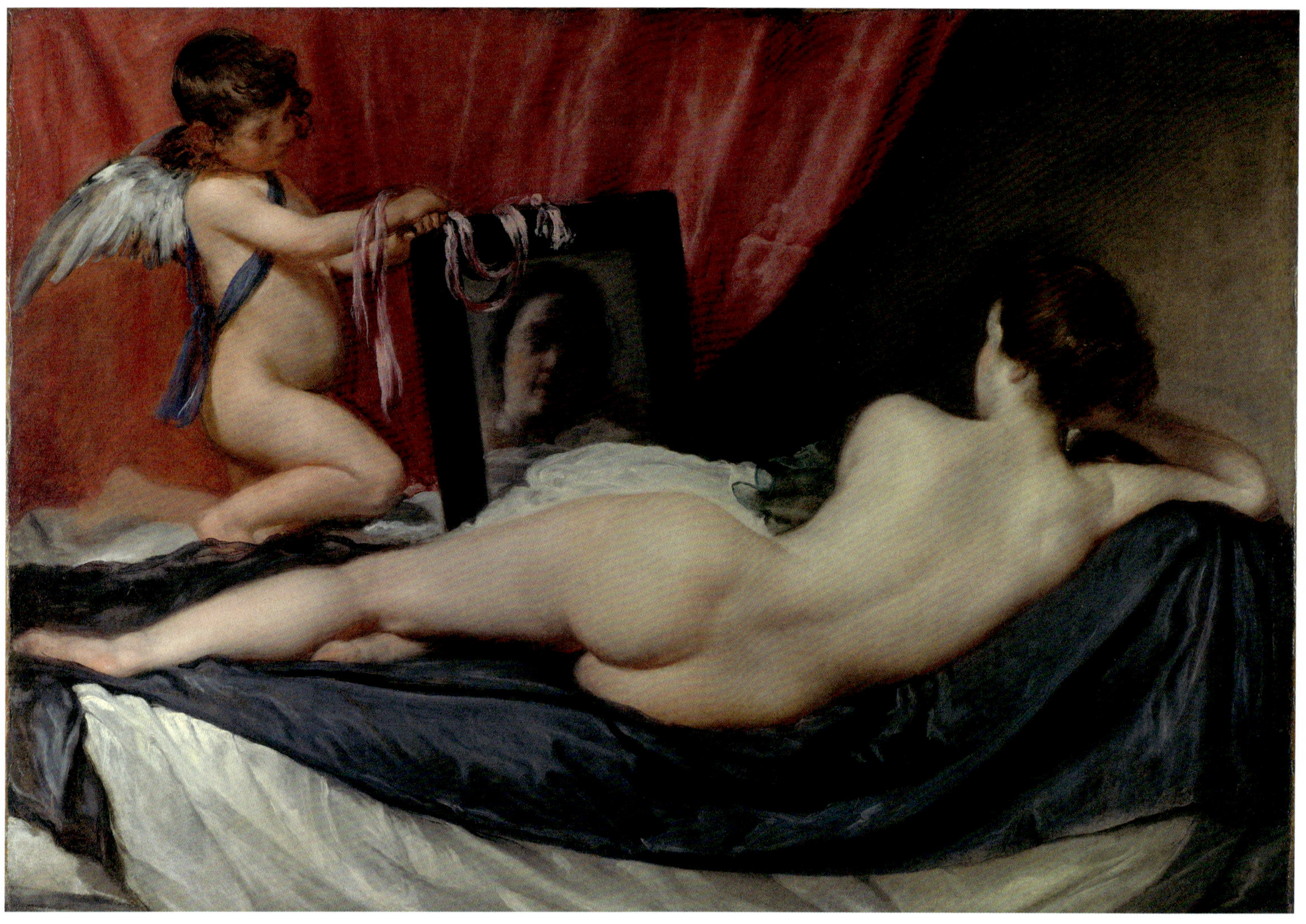

Diego Velázquez, *Venus at her Mirror* ('The Rokeby Venus'), c. 1647–51
Oil on canvas, 122 × 177 cm (48 × 69¾ in)

known as 'The Rokeby Venus'. A nude, very real woman lies on a luxurious bed, her back to the viewer, as Cupid holds up a mirror in front of her. Venus is looking into the mirror so that we see her face: in a trick of perspective, she is not looking at herself, or we would see a different view of her face, but looks directly outward, holding the viewer's gaze. She looks comfortable being naked and shows no visible sign of distress at seeing the invader of her privacy. This has led many to claim the model was Velázquez's Italian lover (it was painted in Italy), as female nudes were frowned upon in Spain at the time (the Inquisition found such images worth burning, along with the painters of them). He allows us to see the face of a woman, not a goddess, in the image in the mirror – which, however, is blurred. The whole scene is suffused with eroticism, the pale flesh exposed for the male eye to caress.

Such a painting made by a male artist today would be considered suspect, but similar scenes are common throughout art history. Peter Paul Rubens's *Venus at a Mirror* (*c.* 1615) was executed much earlier, though is less well known. Again the goddess, much more typically curvaceous than in Velázquez's version, presents her face

in a mirror held up for us to see. These works were never meant for wide distribution. Along with many more conventional nudes, these two paintings were in fact a type of erotica that was allowed in much stricter religious times, as they alluded to a classical ideal. Nude Saint Sebastians were similar images for those men who preferred to see male flesh exposed.

The Impressionist Édouard Manet's *A Bar at the Folies-Bergère* (1882) presents a different view of the erotic, one where commerce is more clearly in charge, although that is not to say that the models in the Renaissance were not paid for their flesh any the less. Here, a flush-faced young barmaid looks out directly at the viewer. However, within the realm of the painting, she is clearly looking at the top-hatted gentleman who would be directly in front of her if this was an exact representation of the real world. Playing with perspective, the painter has shifted the gentleman to the right in the long bar mirror that reflects not only him, but the barmaid's back and all the bustle of the popular bar. In the top left corner of the painting a pair of green feet hang from the ceiling, an acrobat, which speaks of performance, as much as the woman with opera glasses speaks of seeing, looking, spying on this hidden world. Here is where rich gentlemen came to see poor women flash their legs and more; this was a world for men, rich men, rich enough not to care about morality, at least not at night, or any day save Sunday. At the time of painting this work, Manet was dying from late-stage syphilis, and some suggest that the gentleman at the bar is no other than Death come for him, as well as for the viewer. All the while, viewers are reflected in the sad eyes of the barmaid, who has seen it all before.

In René Magritte's *Not to Be Reproduced* (1937), the sitter's eyes cannot be seen in his image in front of a mirror, nor in the mirror itself. The viewer is presented with the back of a man with dark hair staring at a mirror, but the reflection is exactly what the viewer sees of him – that is, his back. Two black-coated backs face the viewer. The virtual window is corrupted, broken: how is it that it is not possible to see the man's face? It is a confounding image, like a waking nightmare, a false reality where, like the man depicted, everything of the norm ceases to exist. Like the mysterious, faceless man, it suggests that viewers are also only the backs of themselves seen from behind, unable to find self-knowledge, but perhaps able to sense the moment of death overtaking from behind. Ask any ageing beauty (of any gender) if mirrors are kind, and most will disagree. If we are honest with ourselves, our own mirrors often show us things we do not want to see, from teenage spots to middle-aged hair loss and the wrinkles of old age, if we are lucky to live that long. Some rejoice in these honest depictions of our reversed selves, but few do not feel a tug of sadness. Magritte sums this up in one surreal image.

Claude Cahun's *Reflected Image in Mirror, Checked Jacket* (1928) is a seminal photograph for those whose gaze is often upon themselves. We see her looking directly out at us: she grabs our gaze as she grabs the collar of her jacket, while her reflection looks away from us, deeper into the mirror. She and the situation are liminal. Her hair is cropped short like a young man's, and her deliberate blurring of gender lines in what was then seen as a scientific if not always truthful medium (photography) posed questions of identity that contemporary artists (including Sarah Pucill; see p. 227) continue to explore. Her work can be seen as a precursor to those working with selfie culture and those critiquing what a photograph

really is. Not long previously, when audiences saw the first cinema film of a train coming towards them in a darkened theatre, legend has it that they had run screaming, thinking a disaster was about to happen. What is real, and what we know of reality, and any scientific or philosophical explanation of it are ever-changing. What then of the reality found in the reflective surface?

That leads us to the work of contemporary artists, those who often use real mirrors or polished metal so bright that it too acts as a mirror for the viewer's gaze. This book will look at the many different current uses of reflecting surfaces and also at the new mirror, the hand-held miracle that is the smartphone. The smartphone allows making self-portraits as easy as one, two, three thousand of them posted to your site every day if you so choose. But *MirrorMirror* also looks at more traditional reflective surfaces such as metal, for example in Jeff Koons's *Balloon* sculptures, Subodh Gupta's stainless-steel life-sized trees and Not Vital's mirror architecture. It documents works that use actual mirrors, including pieces by Gavin Turk, Alicja Kwade and Song Dong, and the large-scale, spectacular installations of Doug Aitken, Teresita Fernández, Olafur Elliason and Sarah Sze. In all of these new works, the concept of reflection, the notion of creating an alternative space or of opening up space within the frame of the viewer's interaction with the artwork, have a root in the past, which is also important to remember.

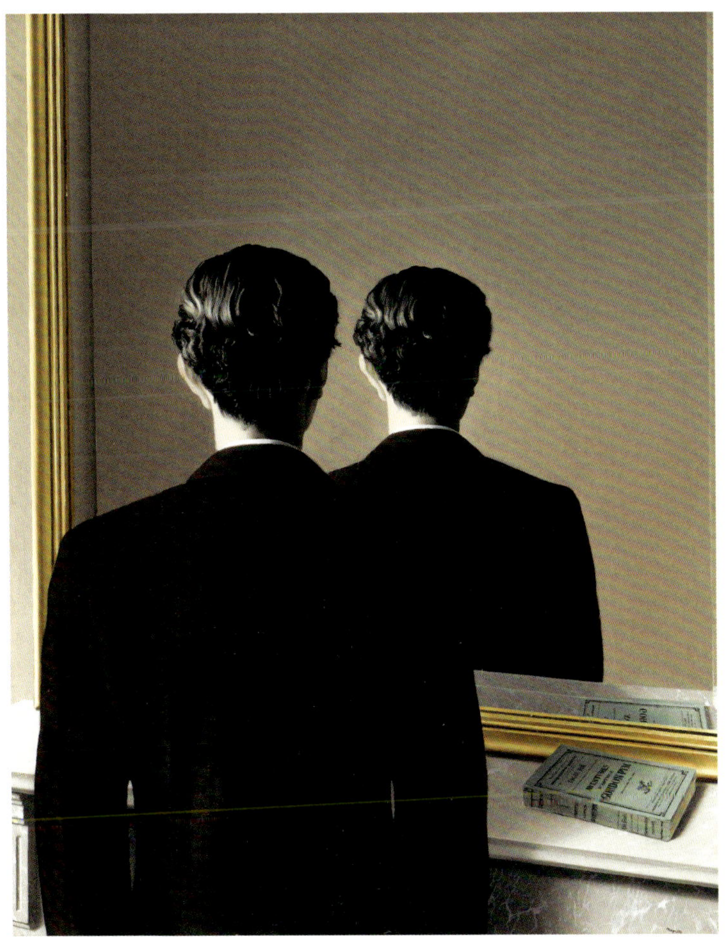

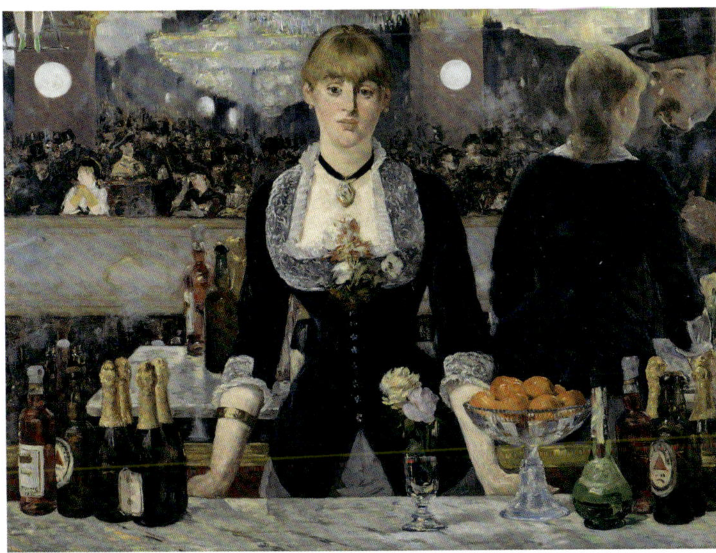

Édouard Manet, *A Bar at the Folies-Bergère*, 1882
Oil on canvas, 96 × 130 cm (38 in × 51¼ in)

René Magritte, *Not to Be Reproduced*, 1937
Oil on canvas, 81.3 × 65 cm (32 × 25½ in)

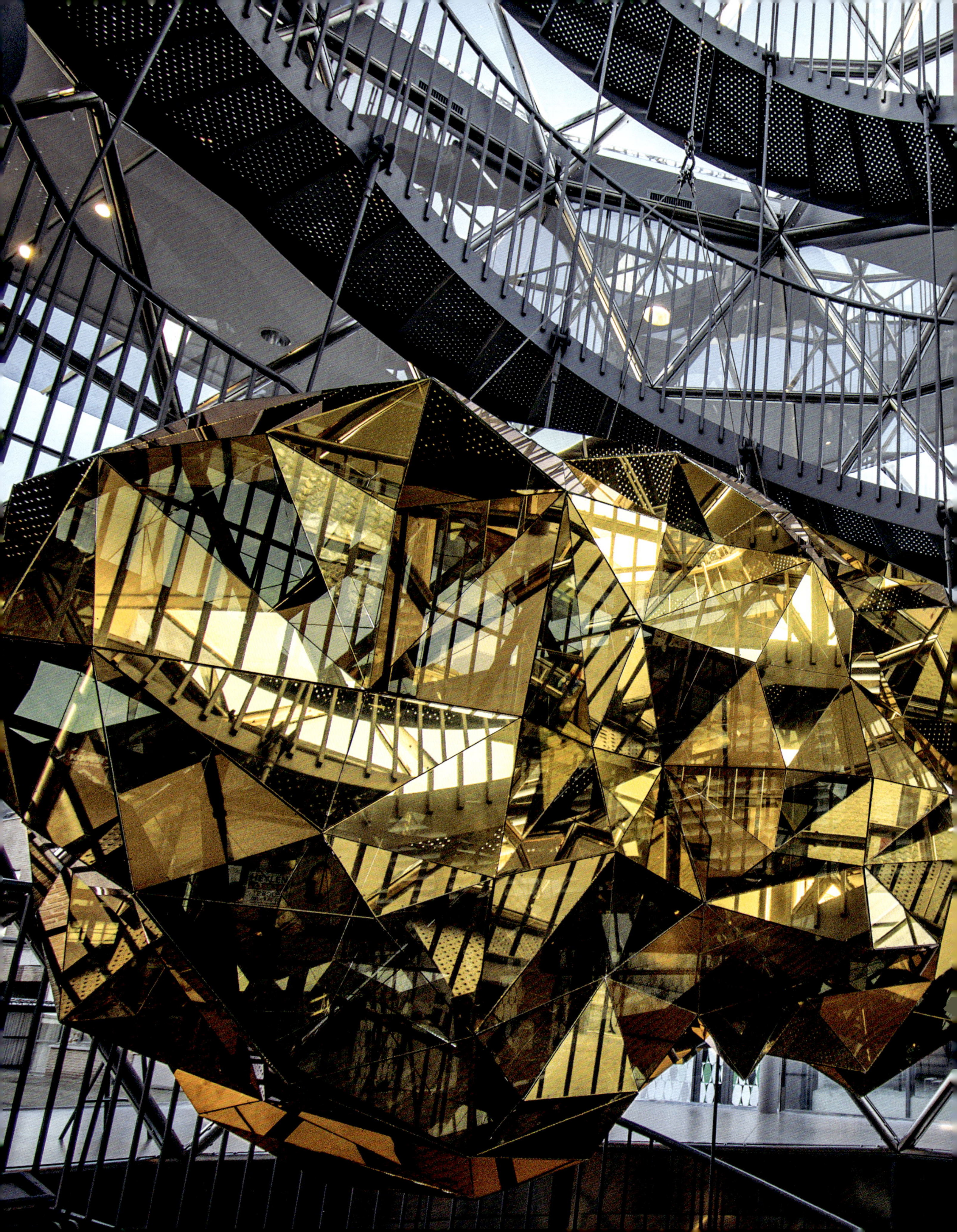

INSTALLATIONS

The way installations are made, their duration and their replicability are all subjects of great interest, as is how installations differ from large-scale sculpture. In this chapter, the installations all use a reflective surface as the centre point of the work, be it made of actual mirror, polished steel or a material such as Mylar. Whatever they are made of, the distinct difference from those works presented in the other chapters is that the works are installed and the context of the installation is a significant element of the work.

Michel François utilized the vast space of the Halle Verrière at Meisenthal in France but placed only a few works in it, to create a complete environment that needed to be seen in the context of the building and the works, with all elements understood in relation to each other. Philipp Fürhofer's positioning of a mirrored floor and ceiling in Frankfurt's Schirn Kunsthalle rotunda consumed the whole of the building and used it as raw material for a disconcerting reflective installation. Olafur Eliasson's placement of a single mirror in a yellow-lit room in Versailles transported the viewer into another space completely. The three works installed in very different buildings – a brick industrial workspace, a modern white museum and a historic palace – all used the setting as an essential constituent. The site of each exhibition was a place that the artworks engaged with, or had a conversation with, making the site itself a key element of the work for the viewer to experience. Of the three, only Fürhofer's cannot easily travel to another site, as it was temporarily built into the fabric of the Kunsthalle. But the concept for the work could see it altered in physical shape to respond to another site where the possibility of an above and below viewing was possible. Whether the artist would see that as a new work, or a work in a series, or simply another version of his piece, would not change the nature of the work as an installation.

Anish Kapoor is well known for his use of stainless steel to make large-scale mirrors that reflect clouds and sky as well as the site they are placed in (see p. 4). These large-scale works have been installed across the globe and echo his more intimate, room-sized mirrors, which often come in a variety of solid colours. The smaller works reflect the viewer as well as the room.

Nomenclature has been at the core of the study of installations but has never been the main point for the artist, or the viewer, who is the focus of such works. The works in this chapter are in a way completed only with the experience of them. Installations (on the whole) are different from sculptures and paintings in the way that those independent works exist regardless, and while it is certainly better they are seen rather than kept in storage, an uninstalled installation shifts into simply being a concept.

C. Matthew Szösz, *Study after Breugel's Landscape with the Fall of Icarus*, 2022. GlazenHuis, Lommel, Belgium. Flat golden mirrored glass, metal 3.3 × 2.2 × 2.1 m (10¾ × 7¼ × 6⁹⁄₁₀ ft)

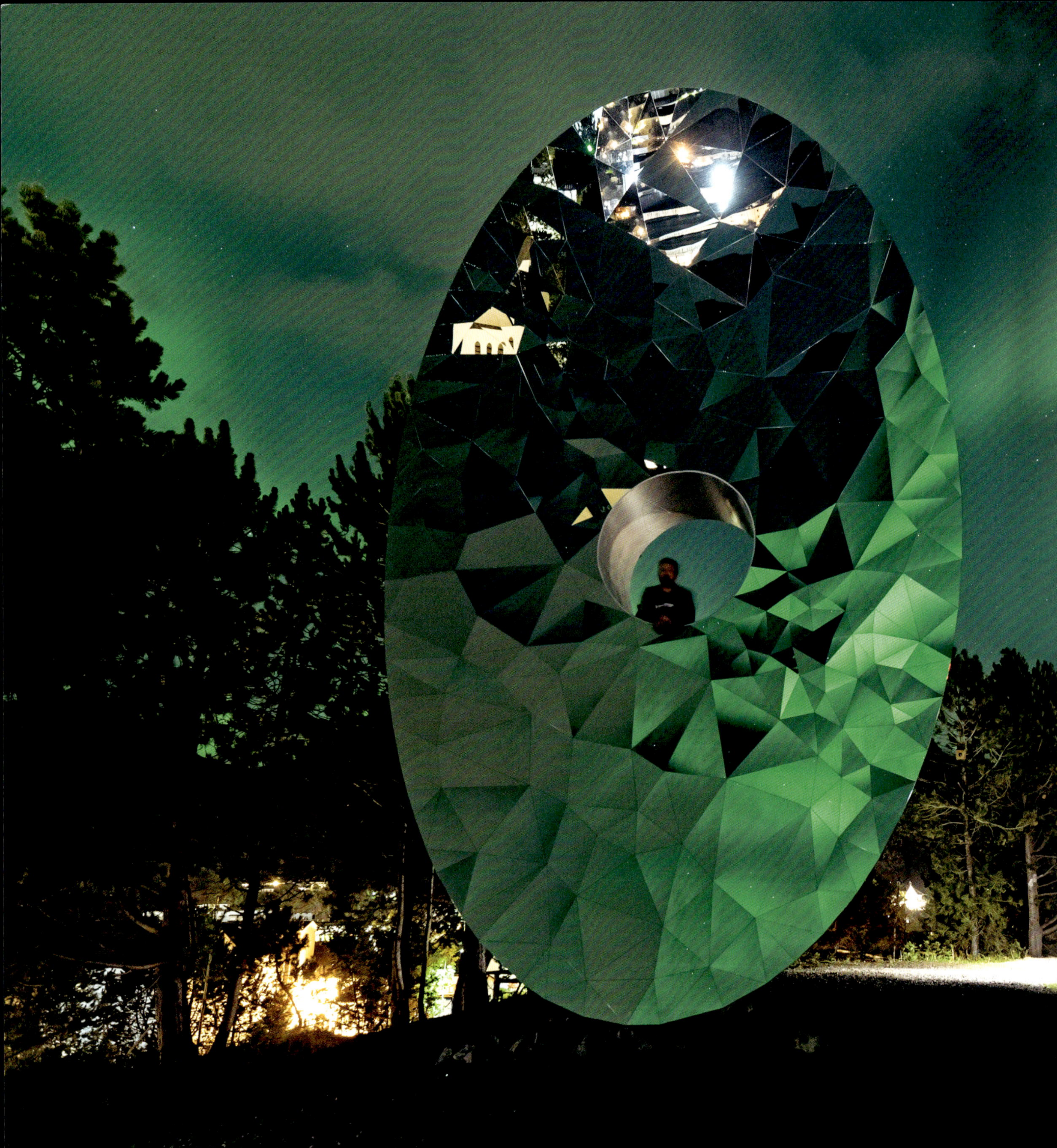

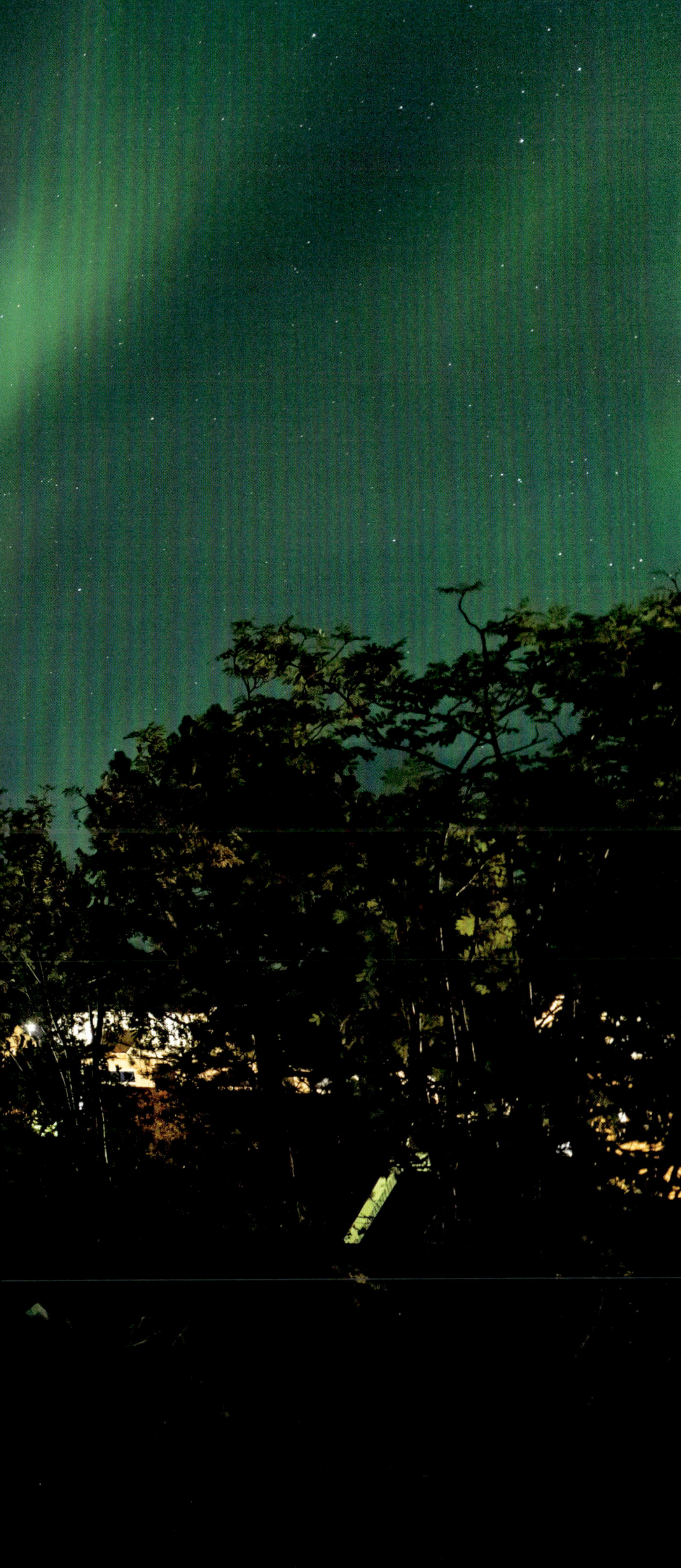

Standing on a hill in the archipelago of Lofoten, *Eye of the North* by Berlin-based Danish artist **JEPPE HEIN** (b. 1974) reflects the dramatic scenery, intense weather and ever-changing light of this northerly part of Norway. The work is a convex (rear) and concave (front) fragmented mirror made up of a series of steel triangles in a complex composition based on the stars in the night sky above Lofoten, using a projection of the northern hemisphere on the front and the southern hemisphere on the back. When the sun shines on it, the work generates heat on the concave front side, warming viewers and allowing them to physically feel the abstract concepts inherent in the work – the linkage of humans to the environment, the stars and each other. Visitors may climb the rear stairs and enter the 1.5-metre (5-foot) diameter centre of the eye, allowing them to see the world around them as the work itself disappears from view.

Eye of the North, 2020
Langåsen Natur- og Skulpturpark, Svolvær,
Lofoten, Norway
High-polished stainless steel, substructure
8 × 5 × 1.7 m (26¼ × 16½ × 5½ ft)

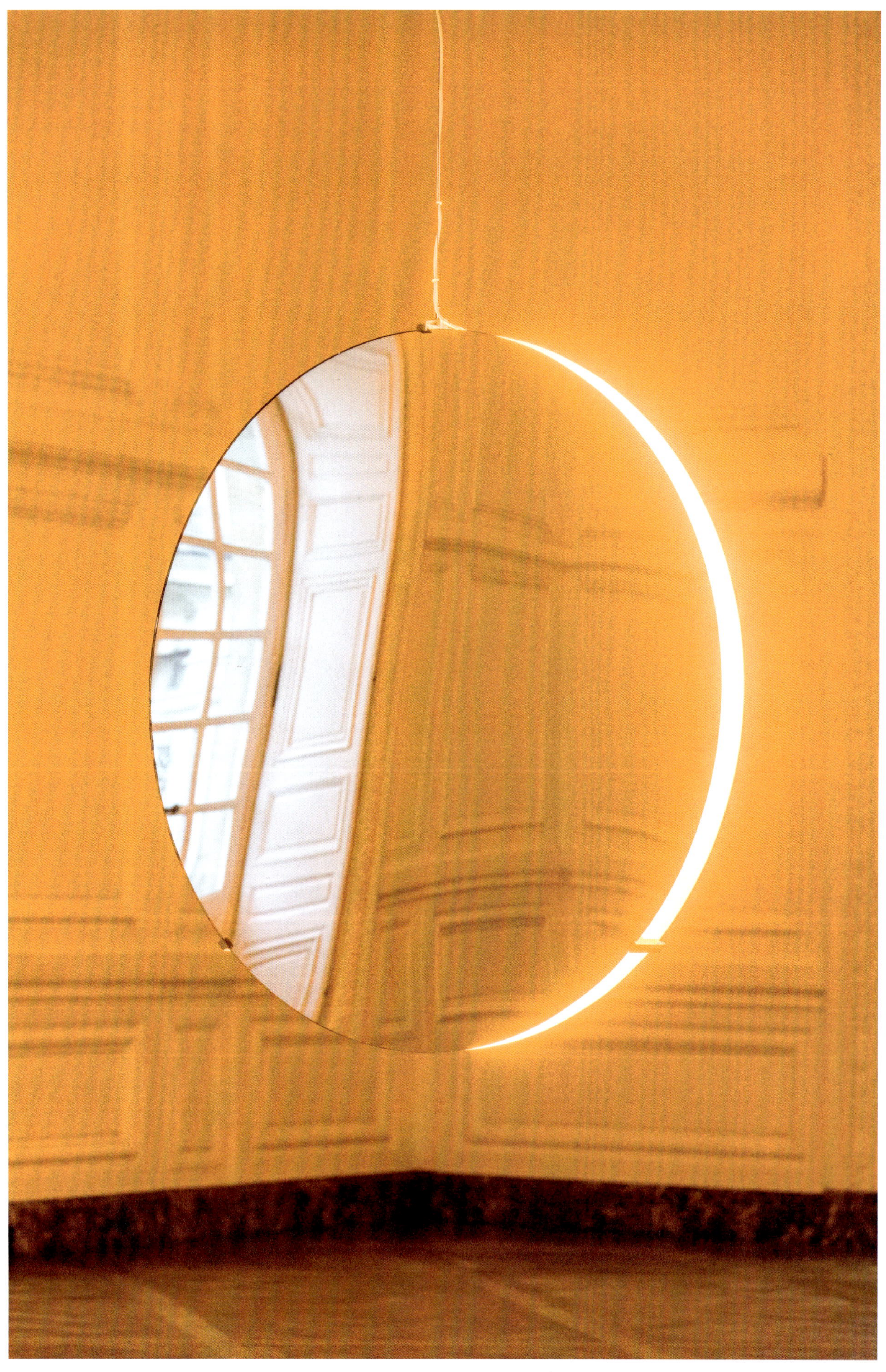

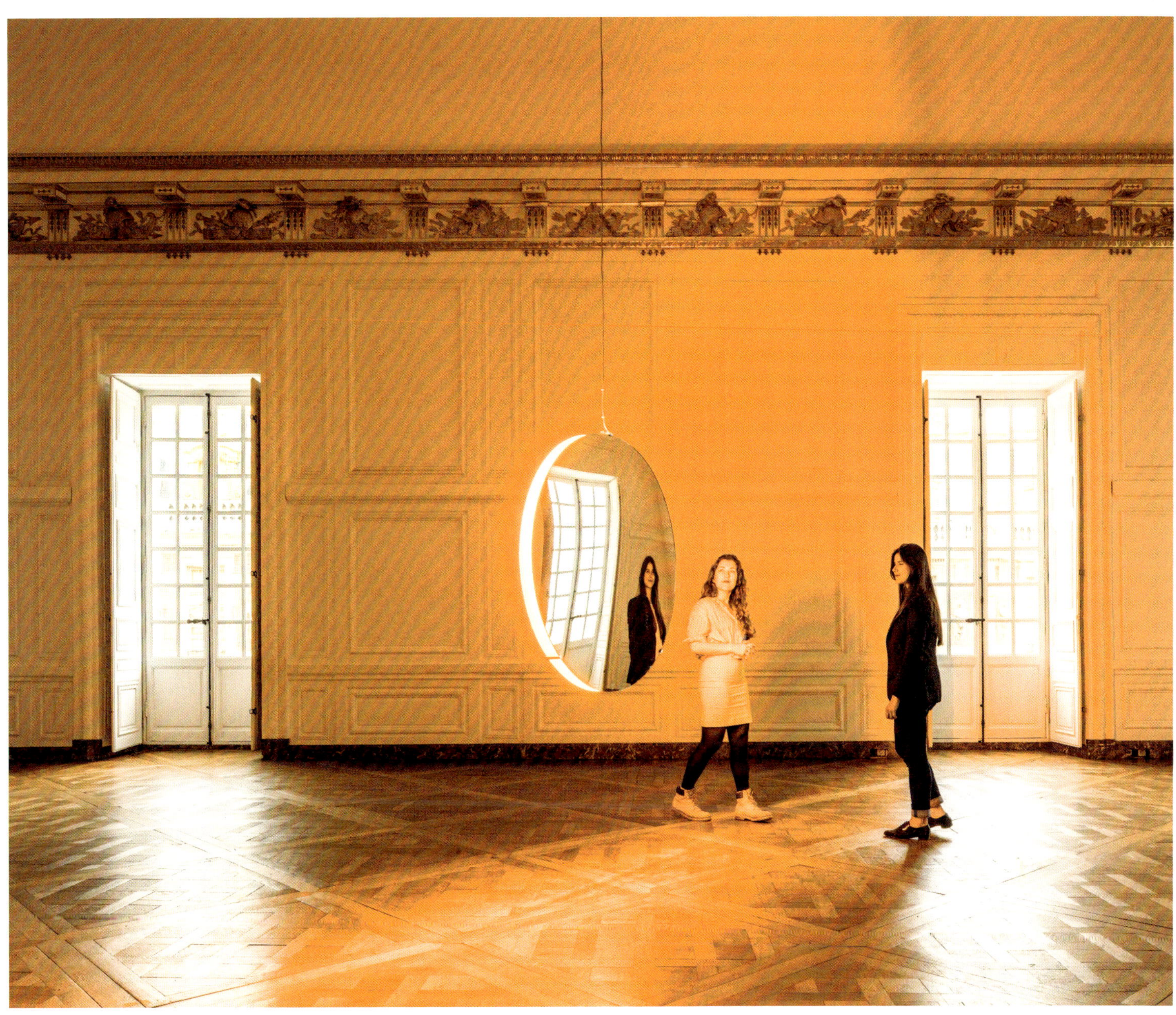

Solar compression, 2016
Palace of Versailles, Paris, France
Convex mirrors, monofrequency light,
stainless steel, paint (white), motor,
control unit
10 cm × diam. 120 cm (4 × diam. 47¼ in)

Icelandic-Danish artist **OLAFUR ELIASSON** (b. 1967) has used mirrors and lenses in his practice for many years, perhaps the most well-known example being *Solar compression*, which was one of many installations he exhibited at the Palace of Versailles, Paris, in 2016. Other, very large-scale, works at that exhibition included *Waterfall*, where a cascade appeared to be literally falling from the sky, and *The curious museum*, which used mirrors to make trompe l'oeils inside the palace. The grand scale of the works referenced the ambitions of Louis XIV, but the artist has said of his Versailles project that 'It invites visitors to take control of the authorship of their experience instead of simply consuming and being dazzled by the grandeur'. In the *Solar compression* room the mirror disc – consisting of two convex mirrors back to back – slowly rotated, beaming a yellow light that caused viewers' colour perception to be reduced to shades of grey and yellow.

American artist **TREVOR PAGLEN** (b. 1974) worked for a decade to create *Orbital Reflector*, an artwork intended to be the first satellite in space not to fulfil a scientific, monetary or military function. He launched the work in 2018 against a background of disapproval from the scientific and commercial community, which saw his project as a slight and a disruption to their own use of space. The spacecraft–sculpture was designed to reflect sunlight back to Earth at dawn and dusk, appearing as a slow-moving artificial star, and disintegrating after a few months. That work and others by Paglen, including *Prototype for a Nonfunctional Satellite (Design 4; Build 4)*, shown here, help build awareness and pose provocative questions about who owns space. Paglen states: 'My intention has been to bring some awareness about how profoundly compromised space has become by the world's militaries and corporations.'

Prototype for a Nonfunctional Satellite (Design 4; Build 4), 2013
Installation test at hangar
Mylar
Dimensions variable

Prototype for a Nonfunctional Satellite (Design 4; Build 4), 2013
Unseen Stars exhibition, OGR Torino, Italy, 2020–21
Mylar
Dimensions variable

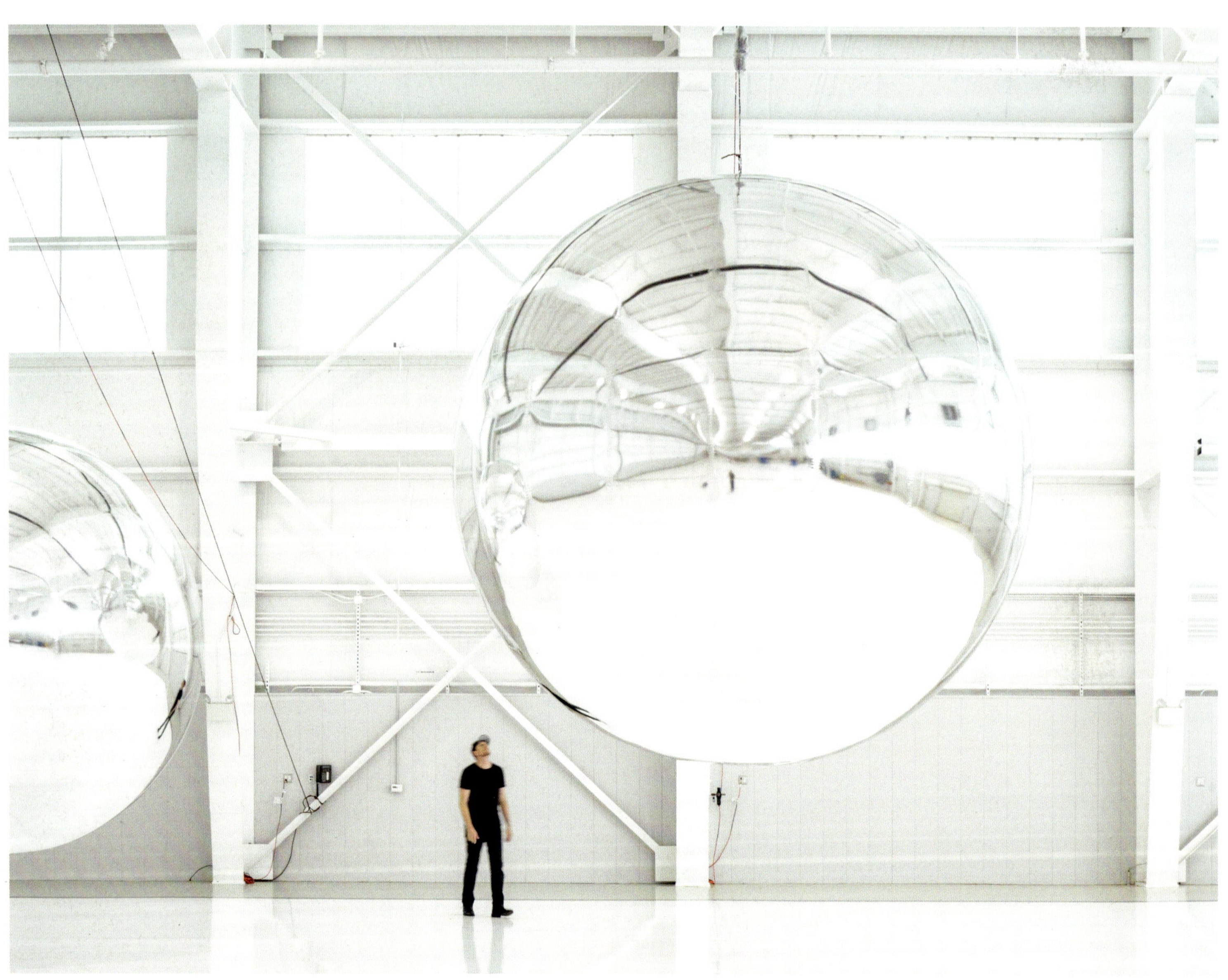

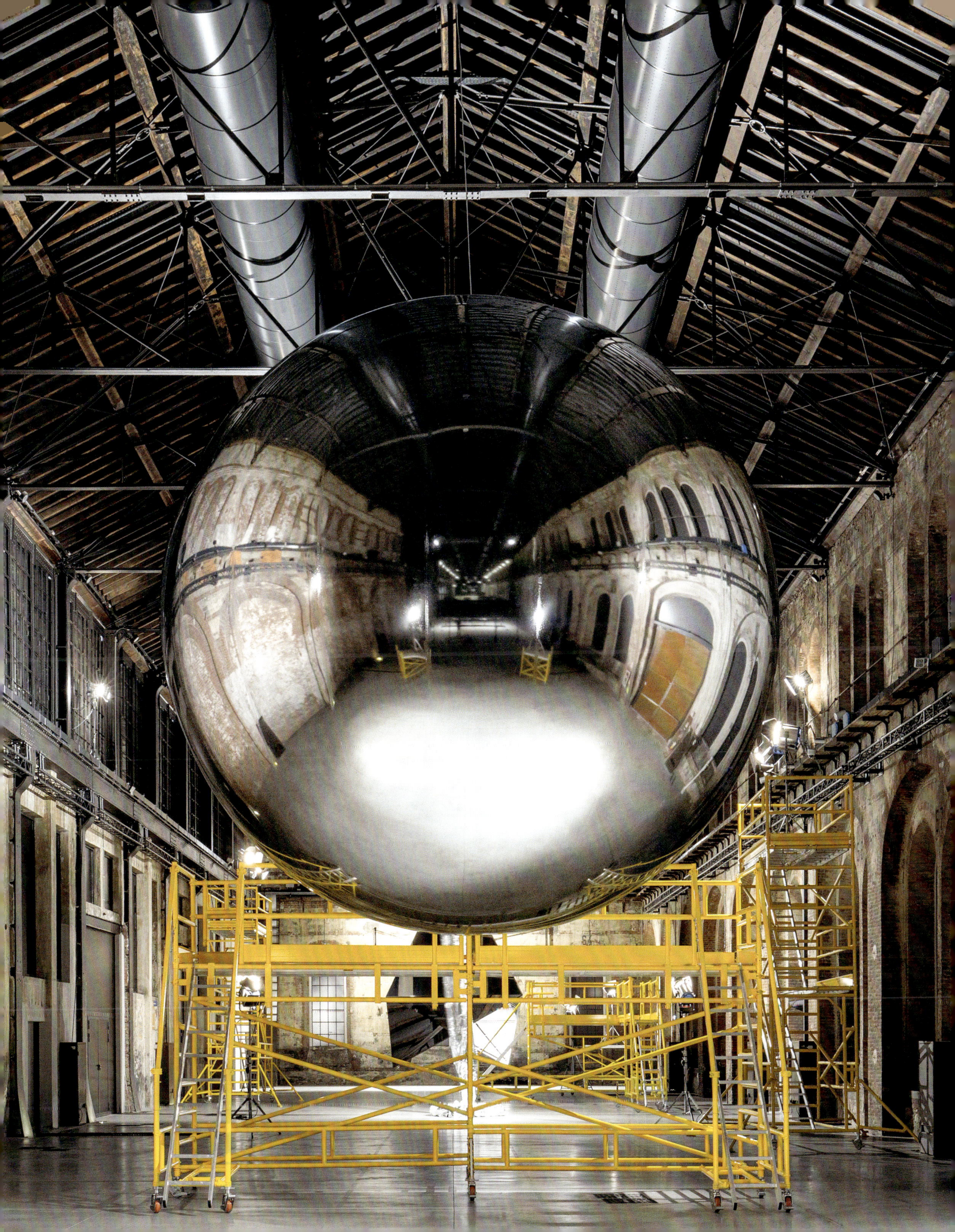

DOUG AITKEN (b. 1968) is an American
artist working across multiple media.
Mirage is a large, completely mirrored
building that reflects the natural setting
of the desert outside Palm Springs,
California. Made for Desert X, a site-
specific art exhibition engaging with the
desert, the structure is in the shape of a
classic American suburban ranch home.
The work is perfectly camouflaged as
the mirrors reflect the desert setting.
The inside of the house is also covered
in reflective surfaces, producing a
proliferation of kaleidoscopic views on
looking out. The house, unlike a real home,
has no windows or doors (but does have
those openings) to keep others either in
or out. The sculpture is clearly not a home
but an artwork that shares the shape of
a house. The work changes continuously
as the light of day fades or brightens
and as the seasons bring greenery, flowers
and rain. It is in a way alive: Aitken says,
'I saw *Mirage* as a human-scale lens that
the viewer would enter into, and in the
process, they would become the work.'
In 2019 (through 2021), *Mirage Gstaad*
was installed in the snow-covered
Swiss Alps.

Mirage, 2017–ongoing
Desert X, Palm Springs, California, USA, 2017
Mirrors, steel, plywood
Exterior dimensions: 5.6 × 13.3 × 5.6 m
(18½ × 43½ × 18⅓ ft)

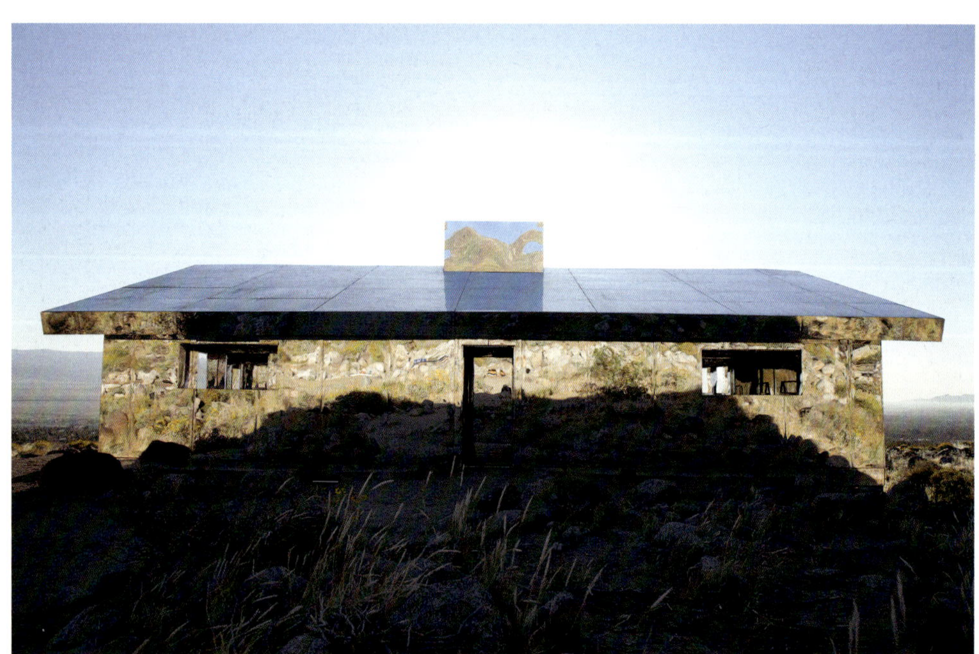

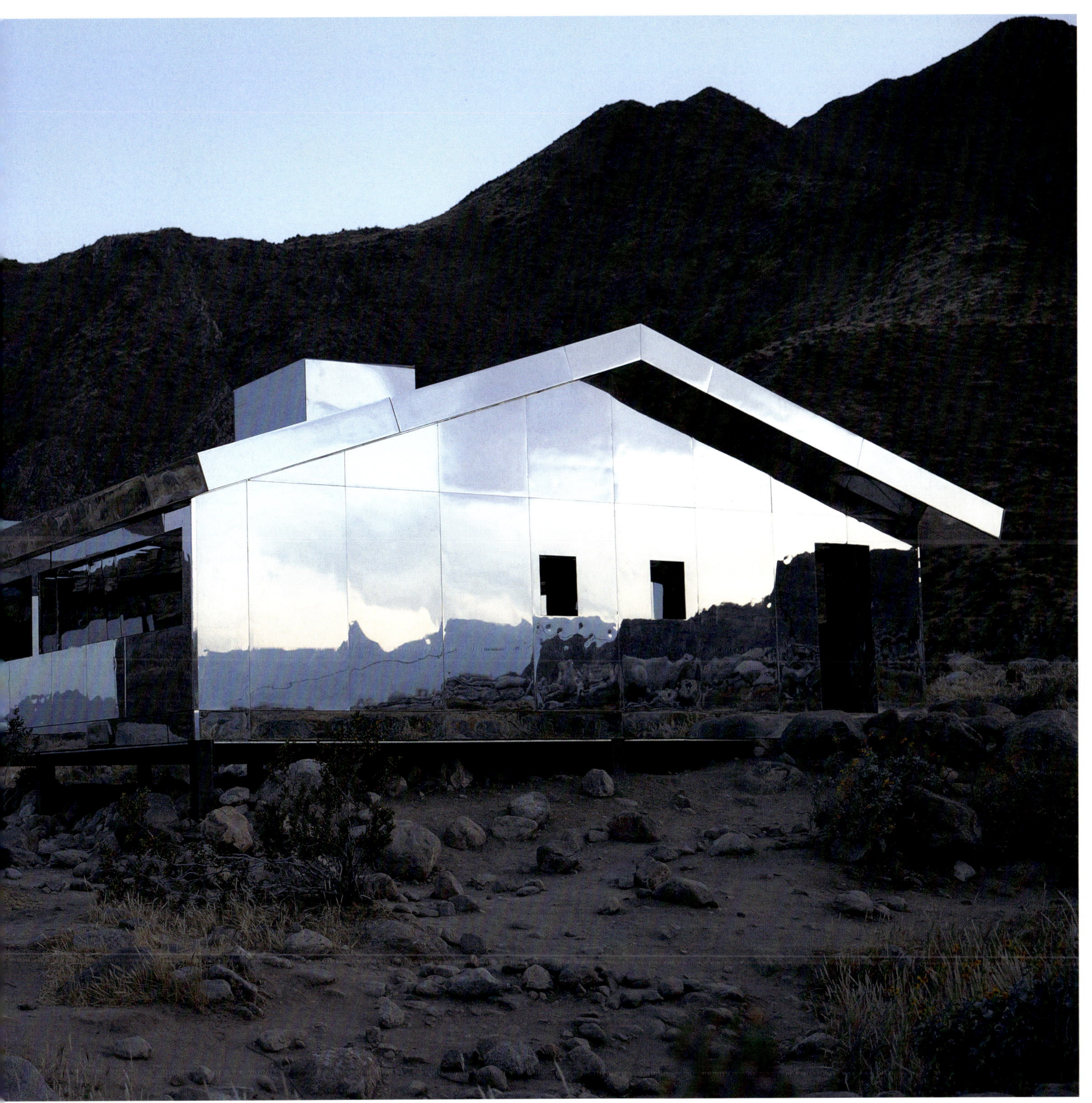

One of the origin myths in the Christian Old Testament and the Hebrew Bible is the tale of 'the city and the tower' – better known as the Tower of Babel – intended to explain the existence of different languages. In the story, humans all spoke the same language, and they worked together to build a tower up to the heavens. God was so angered at their presumption that he made them all speak a world of languages and scattered them across the globe so that humanity would never again challenge God. Similar myths can be found in Sumerian, Greek, Aztec and many other cultural histories. Iranian artist **SHIRIN ABEDINIRAD** (b. 1986) has made an interactive installation (below) where the tower is mirrored to reflect the sky as well as the earth and is made up of sections that move independently via sensors and motors, fracturing the overall image.

Swiss artist **NOT VITAL** (b. 1948) works across many media, sometimes even within a series of works, such as in his *Houses to Watch the Sunset*. The 2015 version shown overleaf was made from polished stainless steel; others have been made in, for example, mud, straw and dung in Aladab, Niger (2005), or concrete at Tarasp, Switzerland (2018). Vital uses the skills of local craftspeople to make the structures, ensuring that the local population benefits from these projects. Each house, with its three platforms accessed by external staircases, has the feeling of an object that has almost miraculously appeared, as if a sun deity has called it into being so that the sun can be properly observed and honoured. Vital has said that the houses are 'an invitation to dream'. Vital's *Parkin* project in Sent, Switzerland, is part of his Foundation, which incorporates several other large-scale projects. He and his brother restored an abandoned park and installed many of his works, including *Bridge* (opposite), which reflects back the natural setting to the park's visitors.

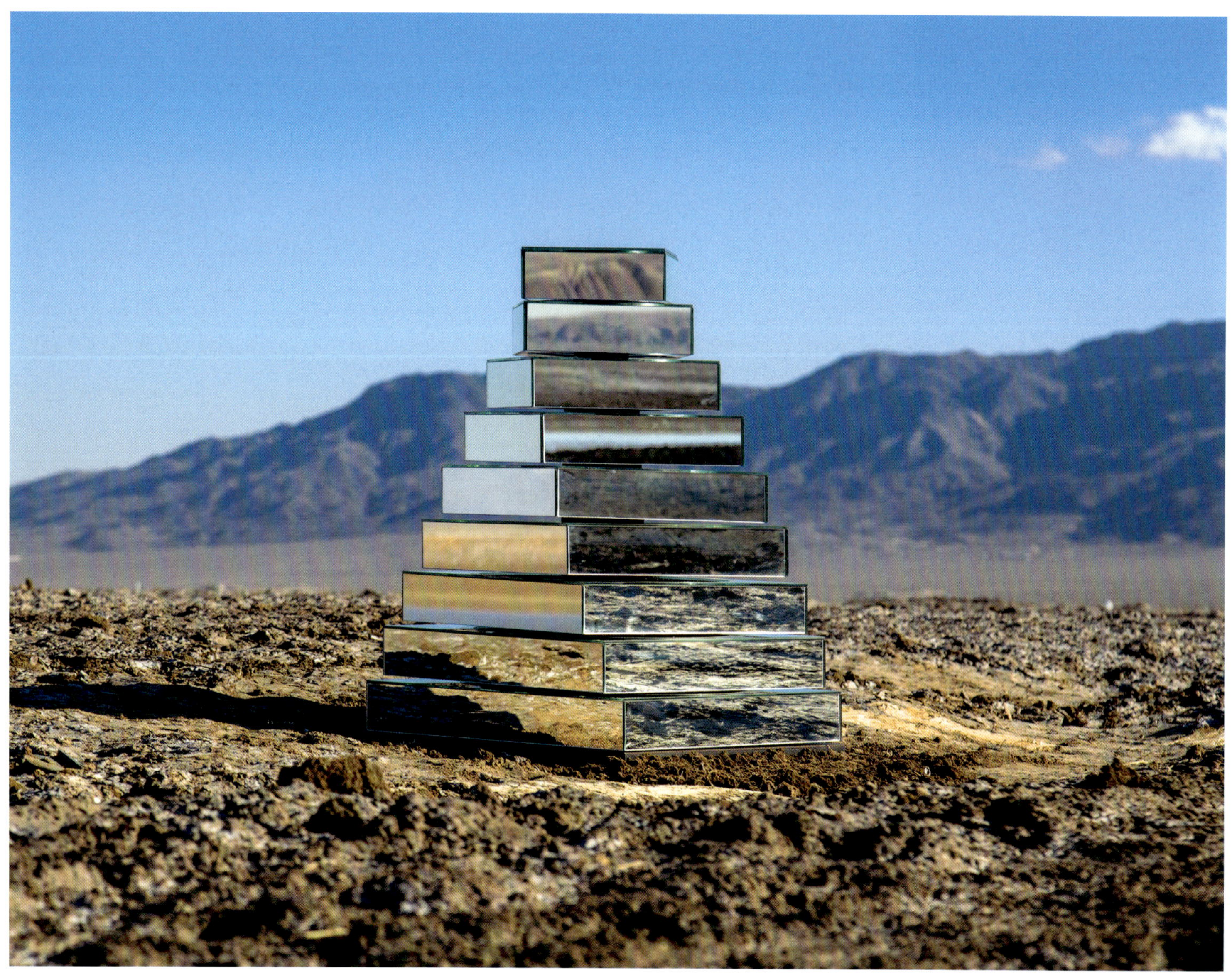

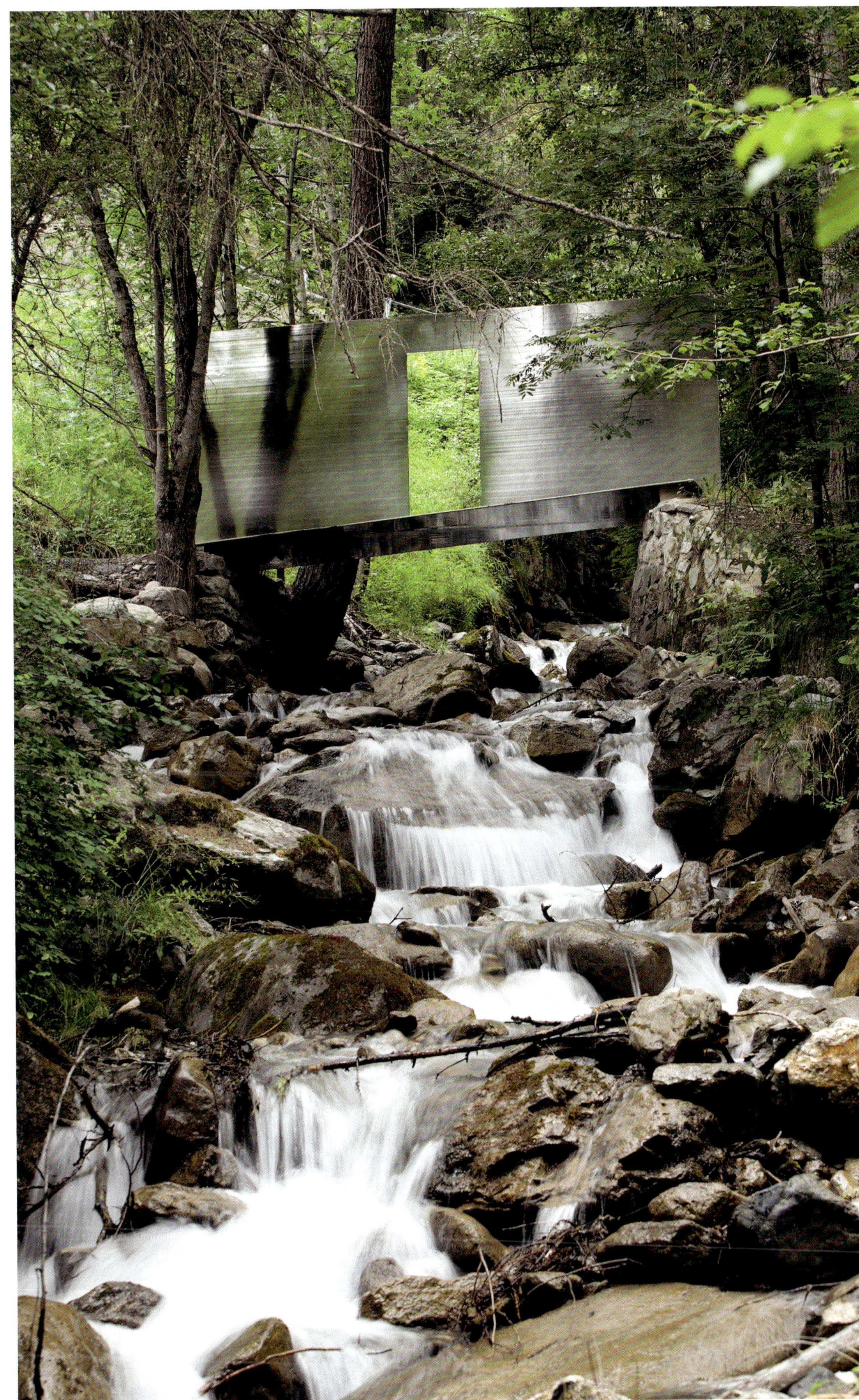

INSTALLATIONS

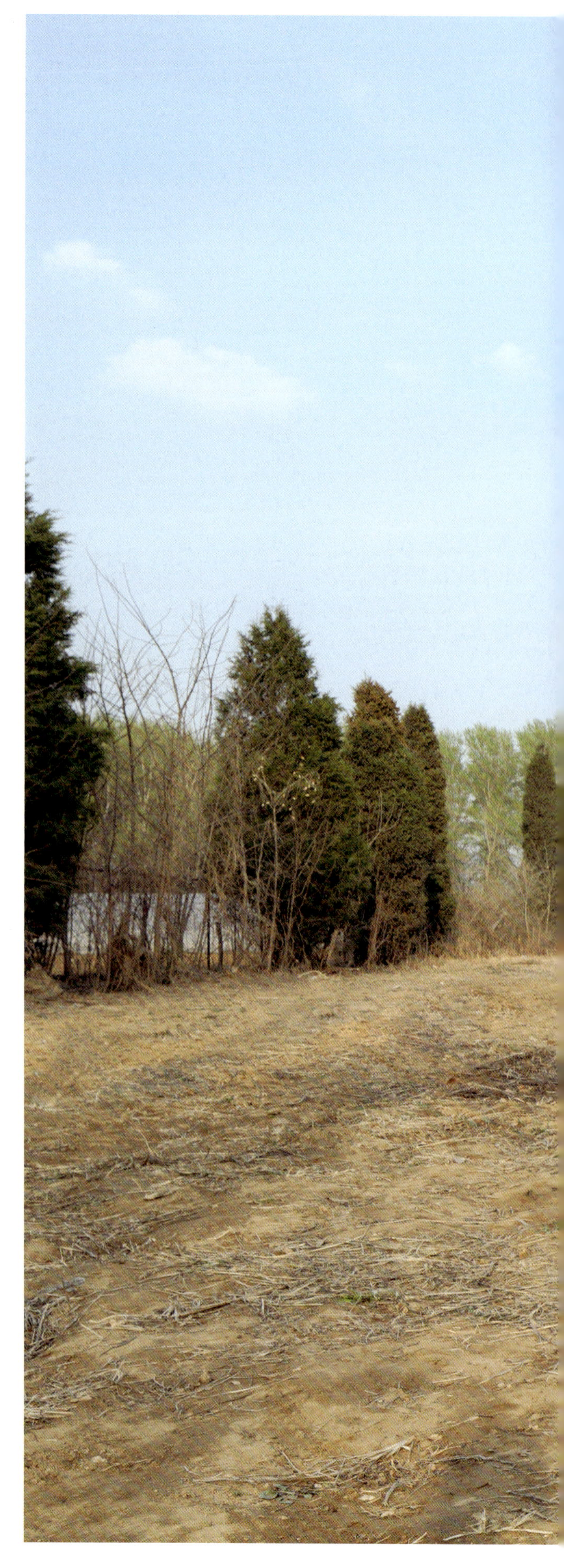

Not Vital, *House to Watch the Sunset*, 2015
Stainless steel
2.6 × 3.3 × 2.15 m (8½ × 10⅘ × 7 ft)

INSTALLATIONS

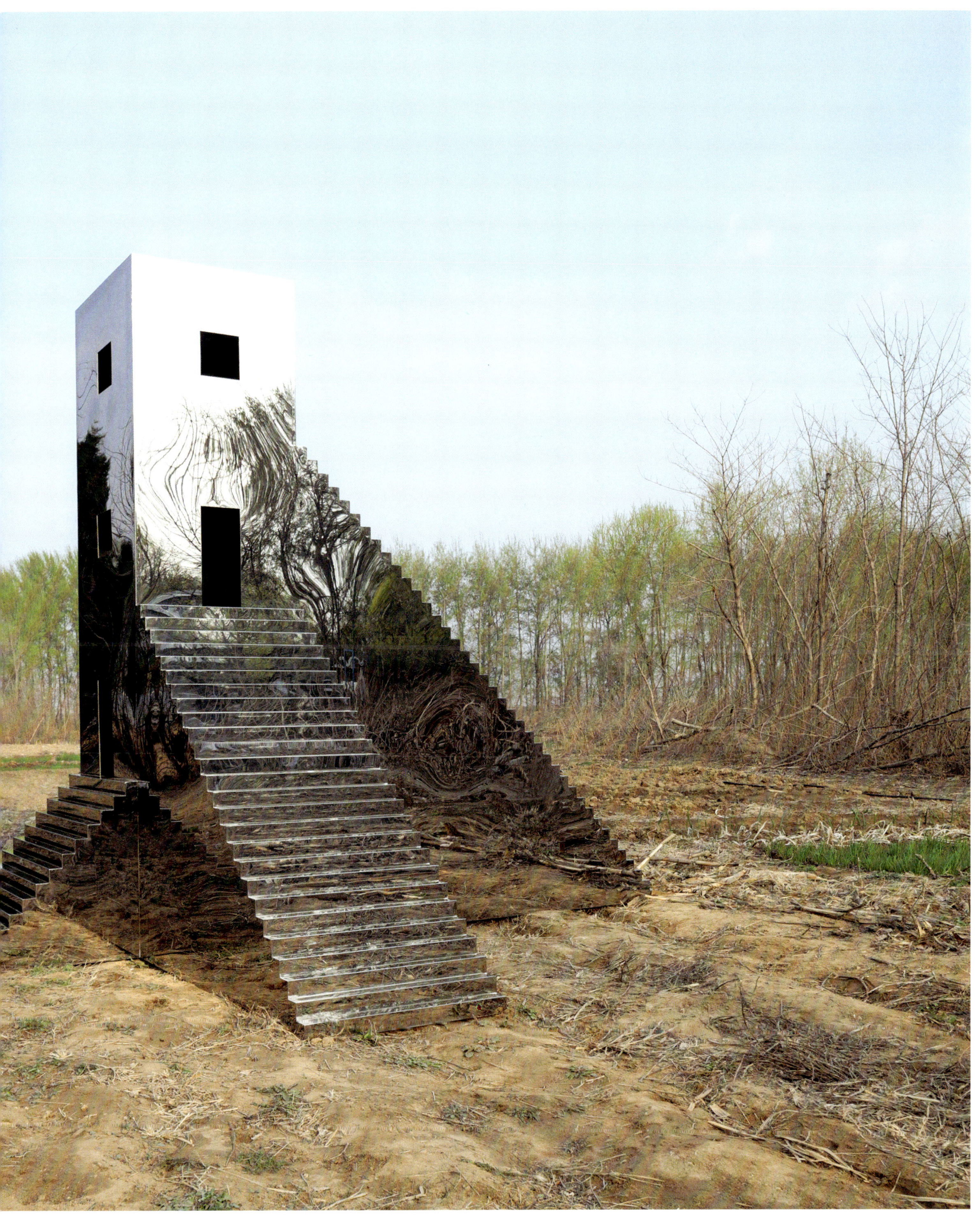

CAROL BOVE (b. 1971) was granted the prestigious Façade Commission by New York's Met Museum in 2021, to make four sculptures for the empty niches on its Fifth Avenue-facing entrance. Bove is known for working in an improvised fashion and had life-sized mock-ups of each niche made in her studio so that she could work directly with the sandblasted stainless-steel tubes and large reflective aluminium discs (at 1.5 metres / 5 feet in diameter, each is the same width as the flanking columns). The in situ works look playful despite their weight and the complexity of their making. They sit on the empty pedestals between each of the Corinthian columns and reflect and disrupt the well-loved frontage. Bove's installation engages with the architecture but by deconstructing the pillars of its foundation also questions its original intention as a collecting body founded in empire.

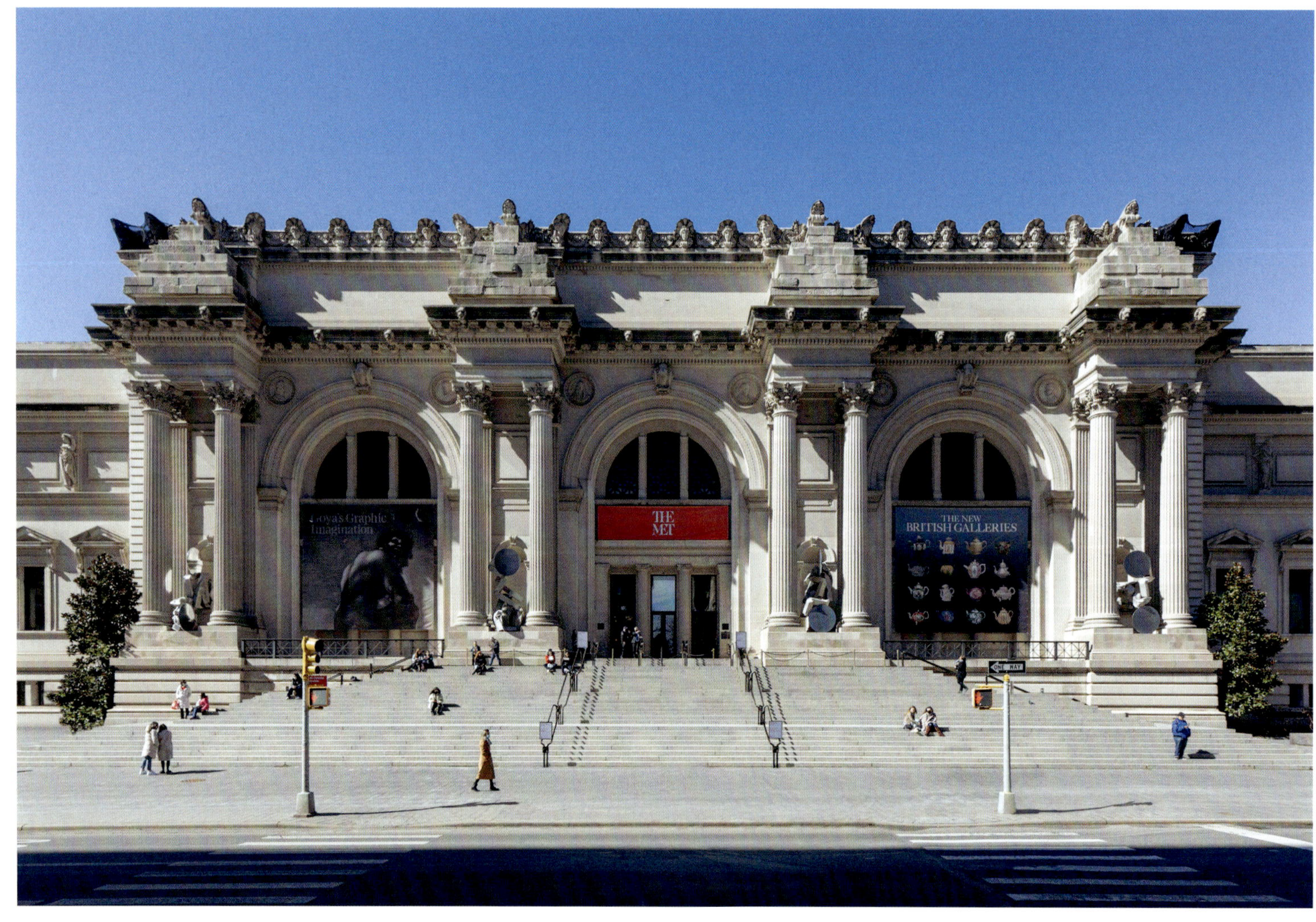

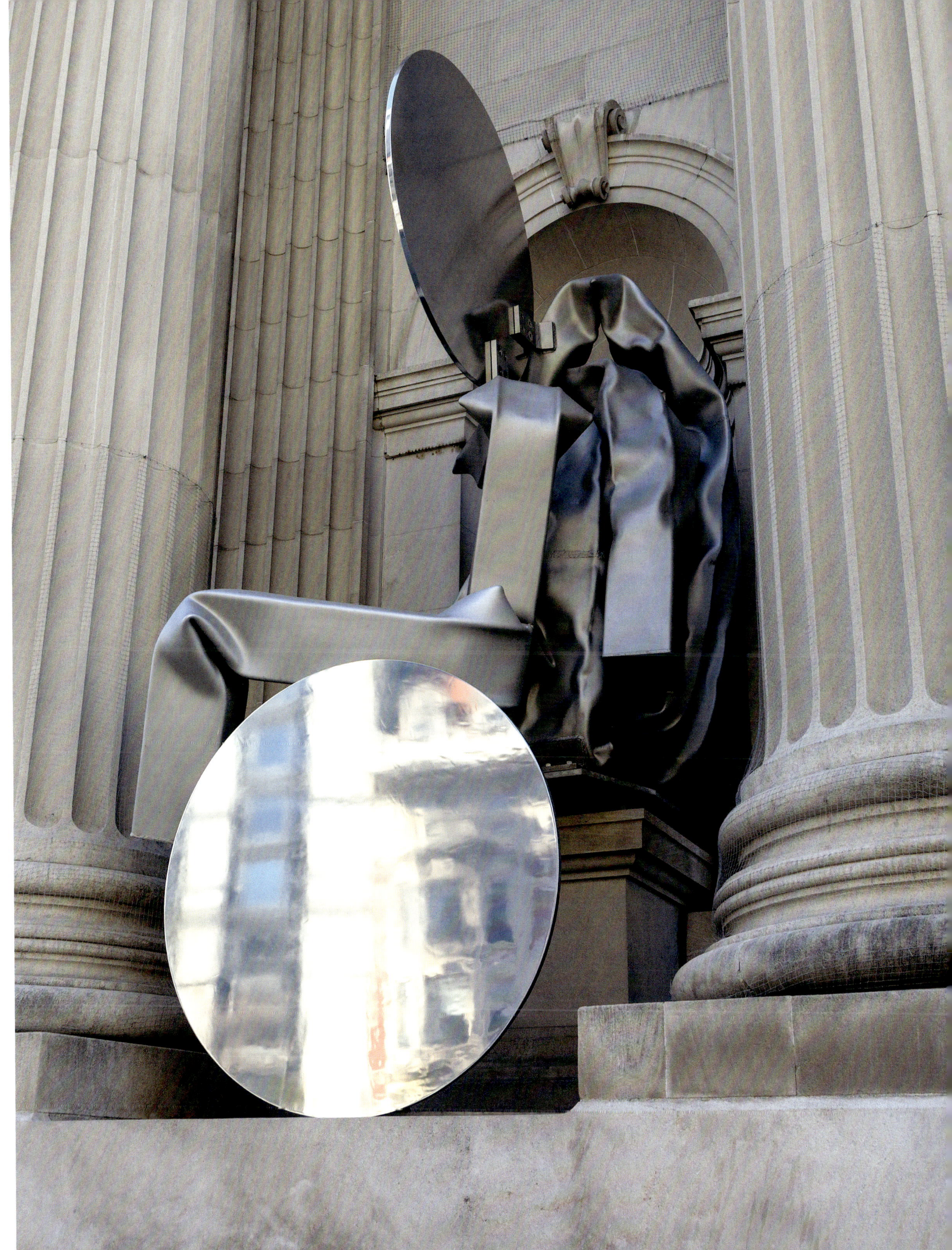

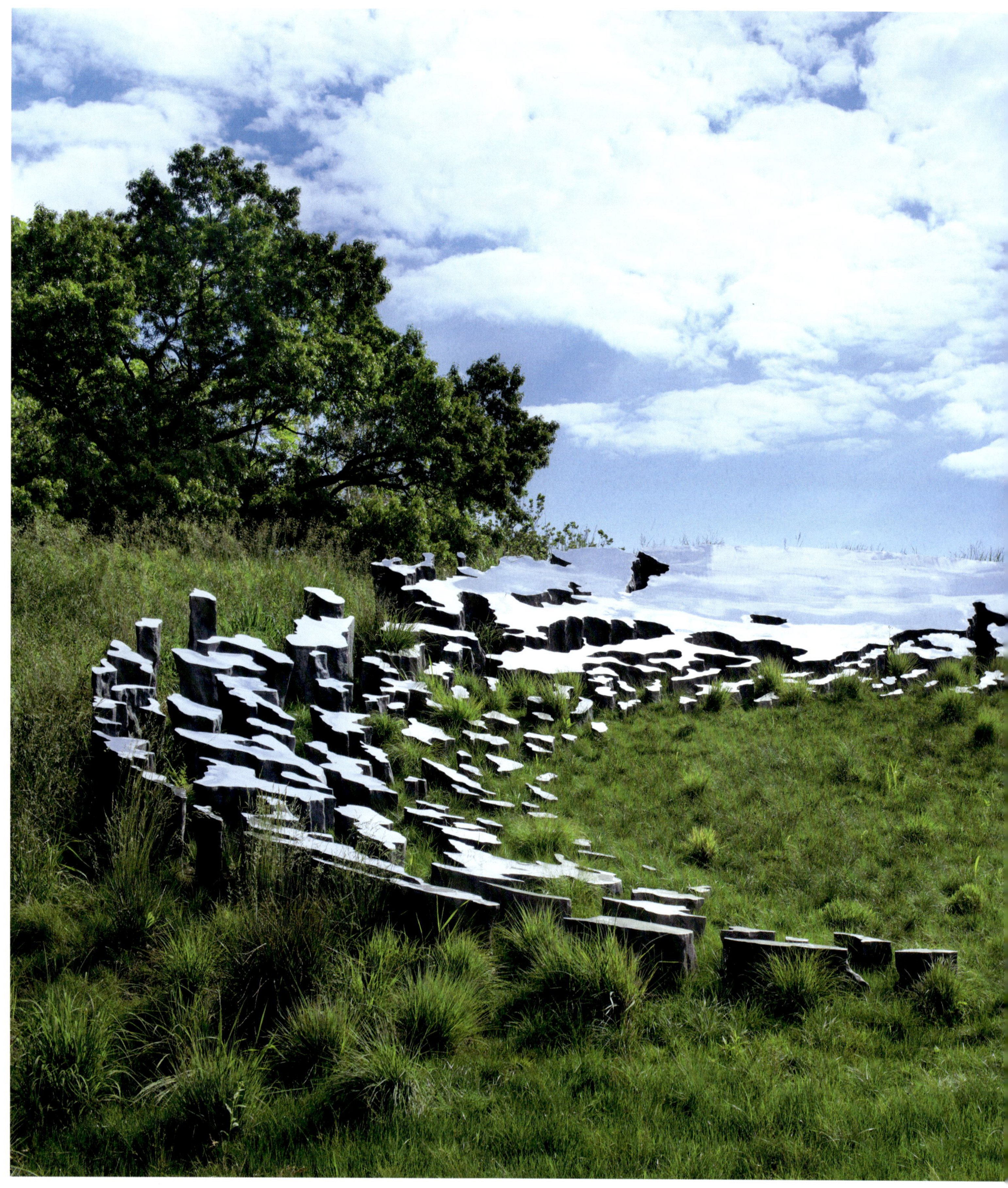

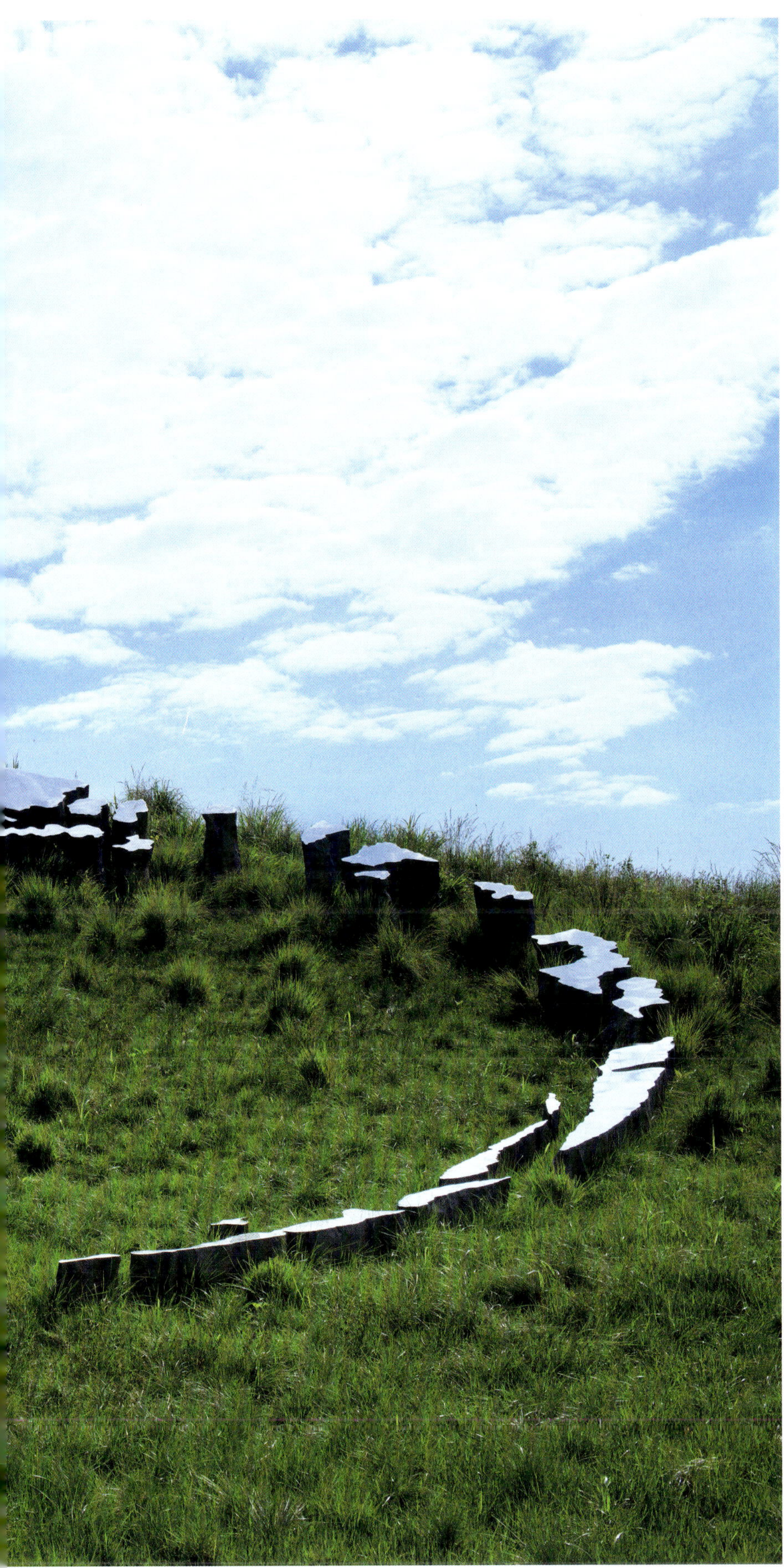

American artist **SARAH SZE**'s (b. 1969) permanent public work *Fallen Sky* sits at the base of Museum Hill at the Storm King Art Center, an open-air sculpture park in New York's Hudson Valley. Measuring 11 metres (36 feet) in diameter, the work comprises 132 pieces, each with a flat mirrored face of polished stainless steel that reflects the shifting sky. Sze describes the work as 'filmic', in that the viewer witnesses a constantly evolving metal face as the clouds and sky alter over the day. One is given the impression that each individual piece has been eroded or worn by time, a feeling that gestures to the fragility of the natural world.

Fallen Sky, 2021
Stainless steel
Storm King Art Center, New Windsor,
New York, USA
11.2 × 1.1 × 1.1 m (36¾ × 43¾ × 43¾ ft)

Over the past fifteen years or so, Scottish sculptor **ROB MULHOLLAND** (b. 1962) has made a series of public sculptural installations around the theme of 'encounter'. For these works he places mirrored stainless-steel silhouettes of men and women in the forest or on the seashore, reflecting the surrounding environment as well as any passing viewers. In *Vestige* (shown here), Mulholland hints that the images have a spectral quality and seem to recall the ghosts of those who might have walked the same paths over the ages. The mirrored figures lurking in the woods ask the viewer to question their own relationship to the natural environment. Versions have been seen at Horatio's Garden, Queen Elizabeth University Hospital, Glasgow (2022), Piazza Santa Maria Novella, Florence (2021), Heysham Head and Birkrigg Common, Cumbria (2018) and Parque Quetzalcoatl, Mexico City (2017).

Vestige, 2009
The Lodge Centre, Trossachs, Scotland
Stainless-steel plate with mirrored Perspex
Each figure approx. H 80 cm (31½ in)

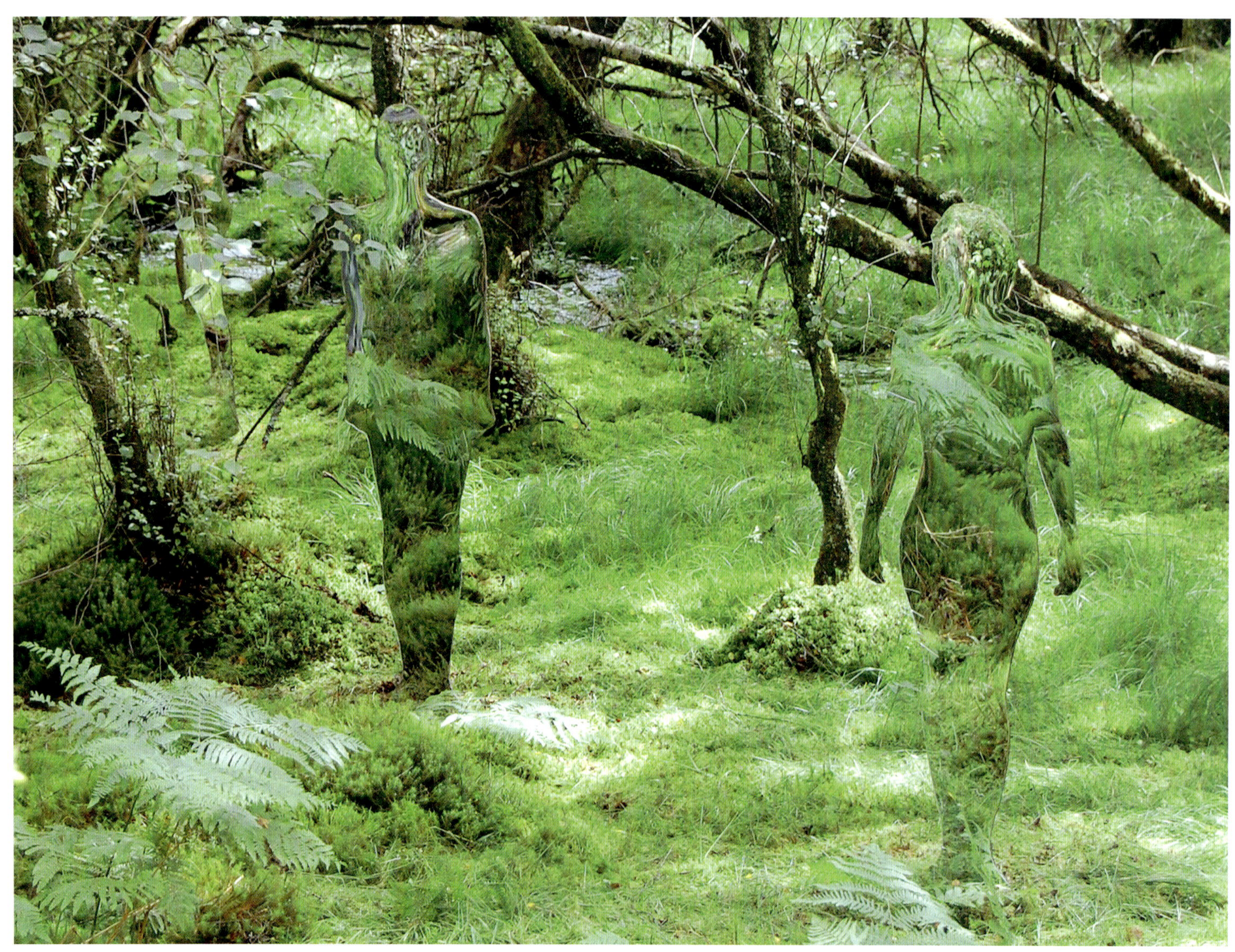

GORAN TOMCIC from Croatia (b. 1964) is interested in the transitory, the ephemeral and the momentary nature of the experience of art, and his installations in holographic vinyl as well as his fabric pompoms look as fragile as petals in the wind. His use of shiny reflective gold or silver vinyl has most often been seen in indoor spaces, but for his *Golden Trees* at the Schlosspark Kaarz, Tomcic wrapped sections of three outdoor trees in the castle grounds. The work was part of the 'Freely Invented' exhibition curated by Ruzica Zajec and Broder Burow at Kaarz Castle Park as part of their ongoing 'GRÜNE ZITAT' (Green Quote) project that has been placing works in the gardens since 2015.

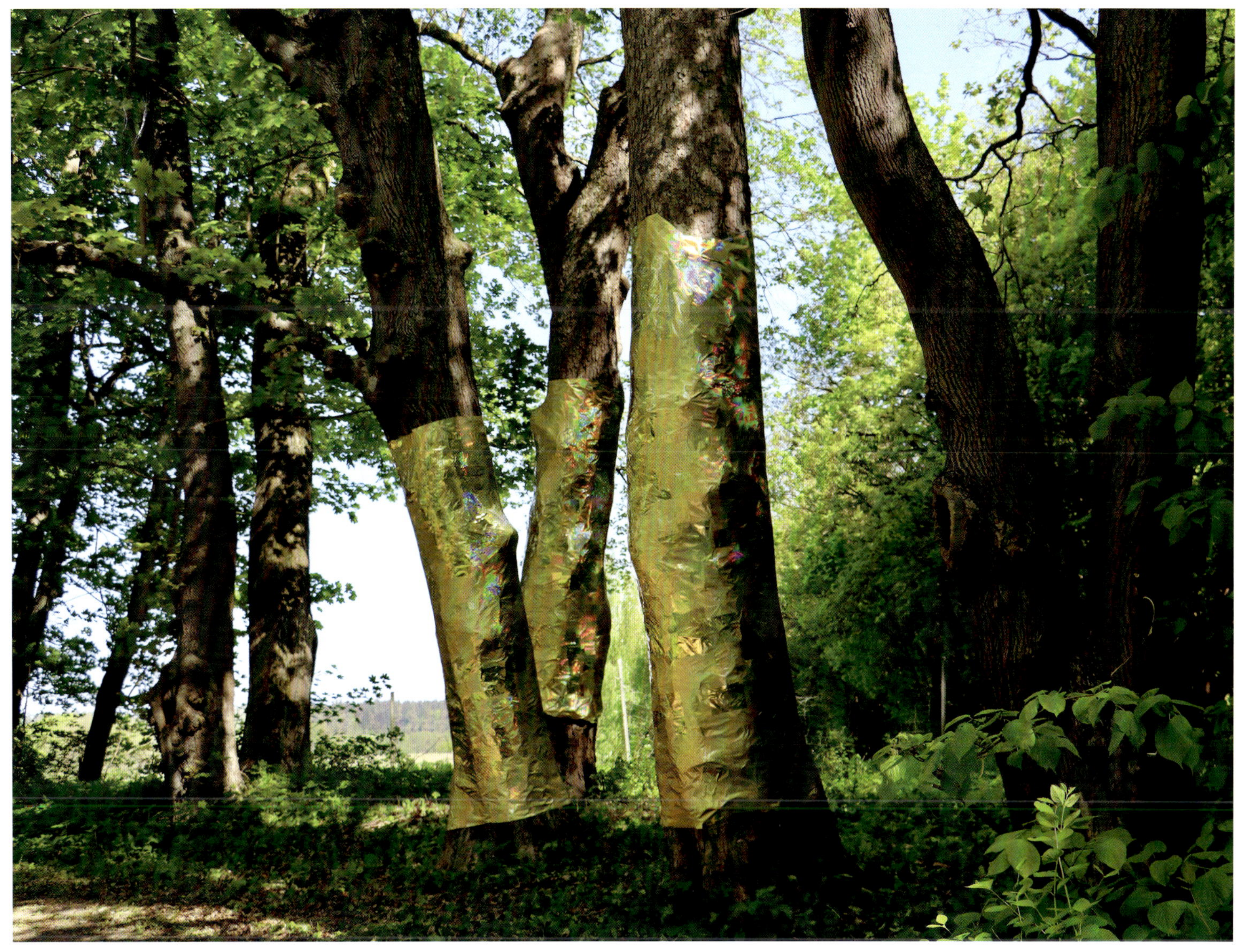

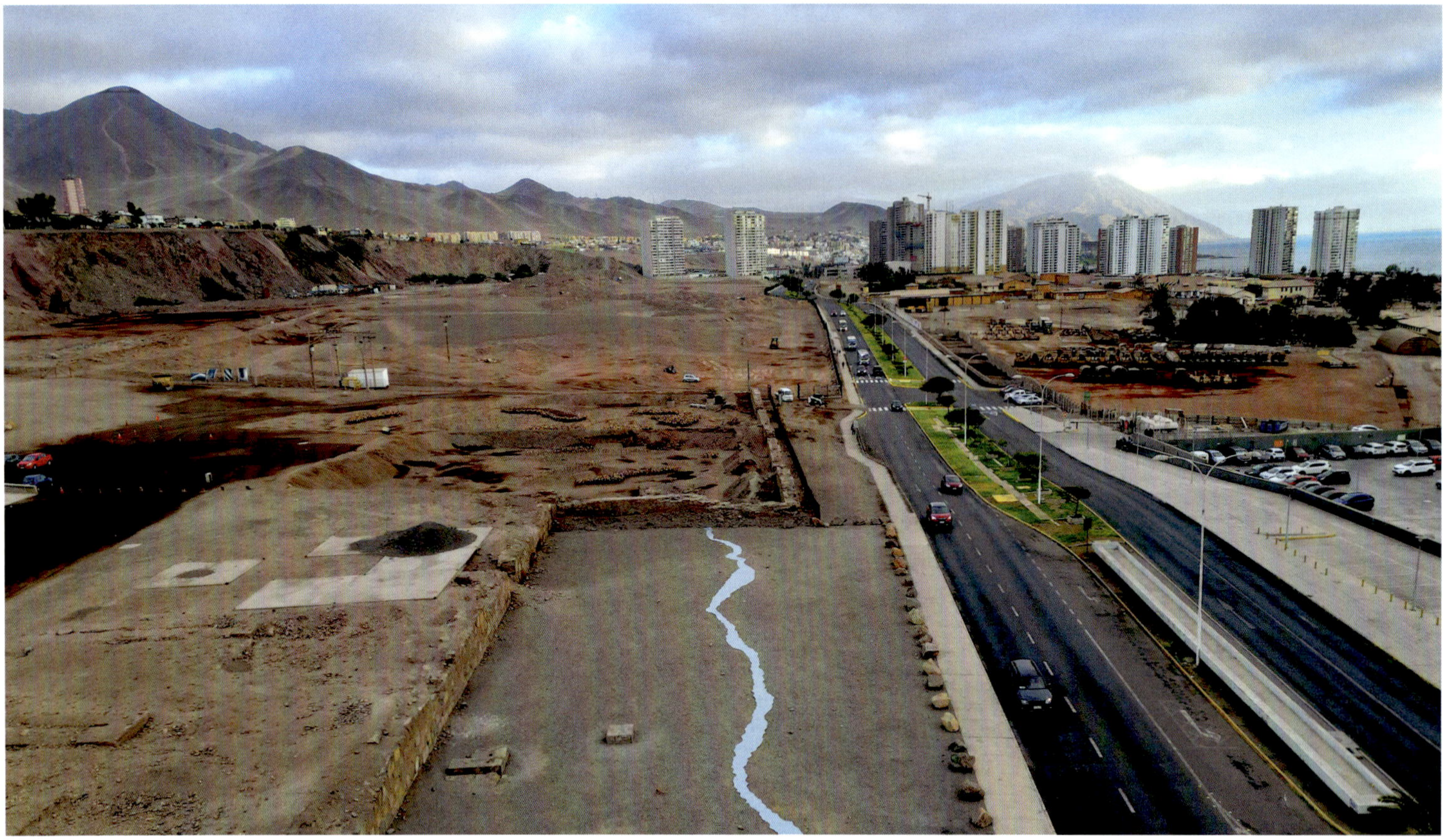

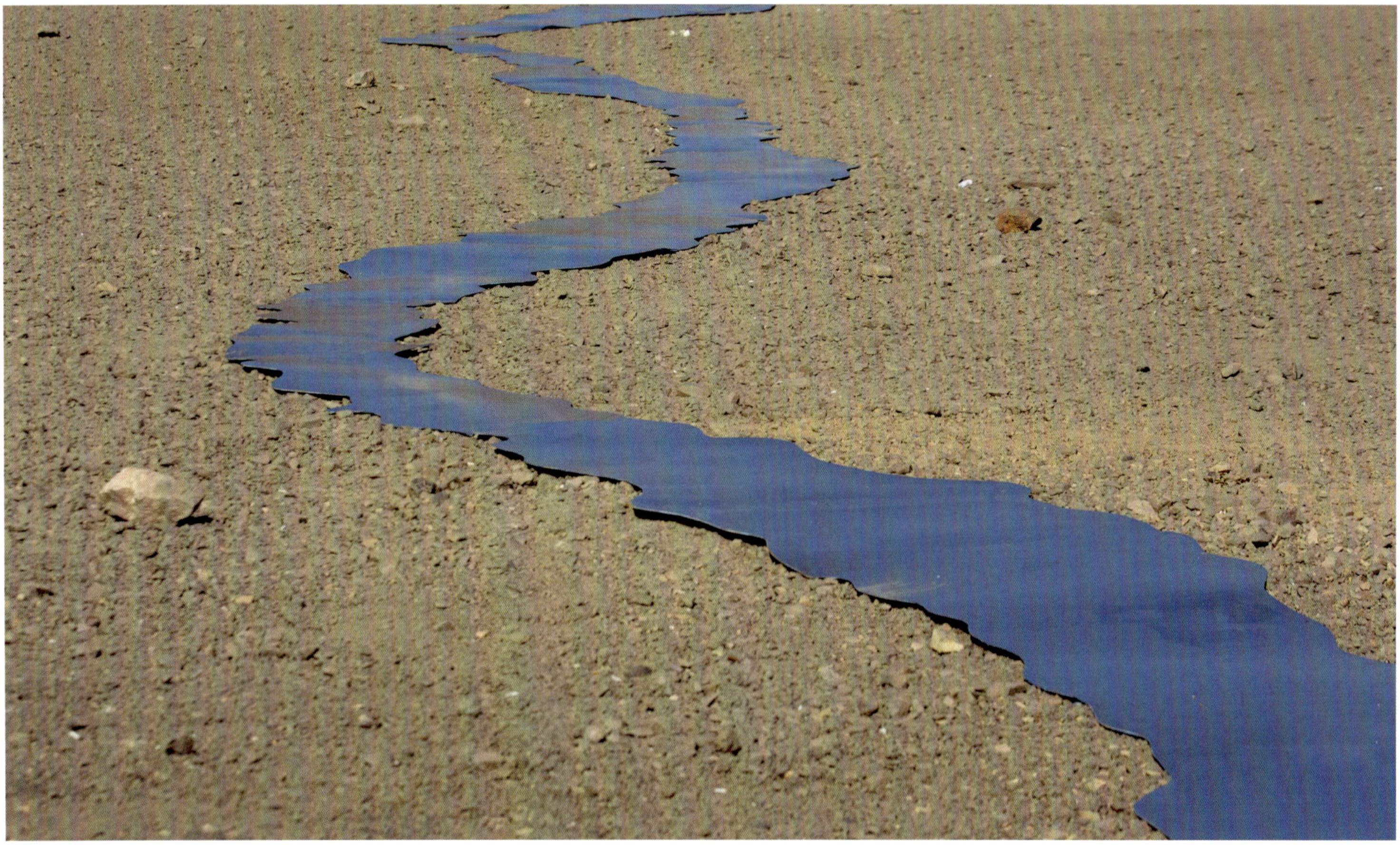

La Memoria del Desierto, 2023
Huanchaca Ruins Cultural Park,
Antofagasta, Chile
Polished sheet metal
87 × 8 m (285½ × 26¼ ft)

SANTIAGO VÉLEZ (b. 1972) is a Colombian artist whose *La Memoria del Desierto* (The Memory of the Desert) was installed at the Huanchaca Ruins Cultural Park as part of the 2023 Bienal SACO, Chile's contemporary art biennial. The ruins are in the Atacama Desert in the north of Chile; now the driest place on Earth, the area was once covered by the sea and later had rivers flowing through it. Between 1892 and 1902 the Huanchaca site was used as a silver foundry, forming what was at the time South America's largest industrial complex. When the silver ran out, the manmade site was left to decay. Vélez installed a temporary metal river that ran through the desert, reflecting the sky, the viewers and seemingly time itself. He first made a life-sized river out of paper, which was then fabricated in metal by the Bienal SACO team and installed on the dry rocky ground. Vélez's reflective river acted as a memory of water, an evocation of the passage of time, and a reminder of the stream of silver that once flowed forth from the foundry.

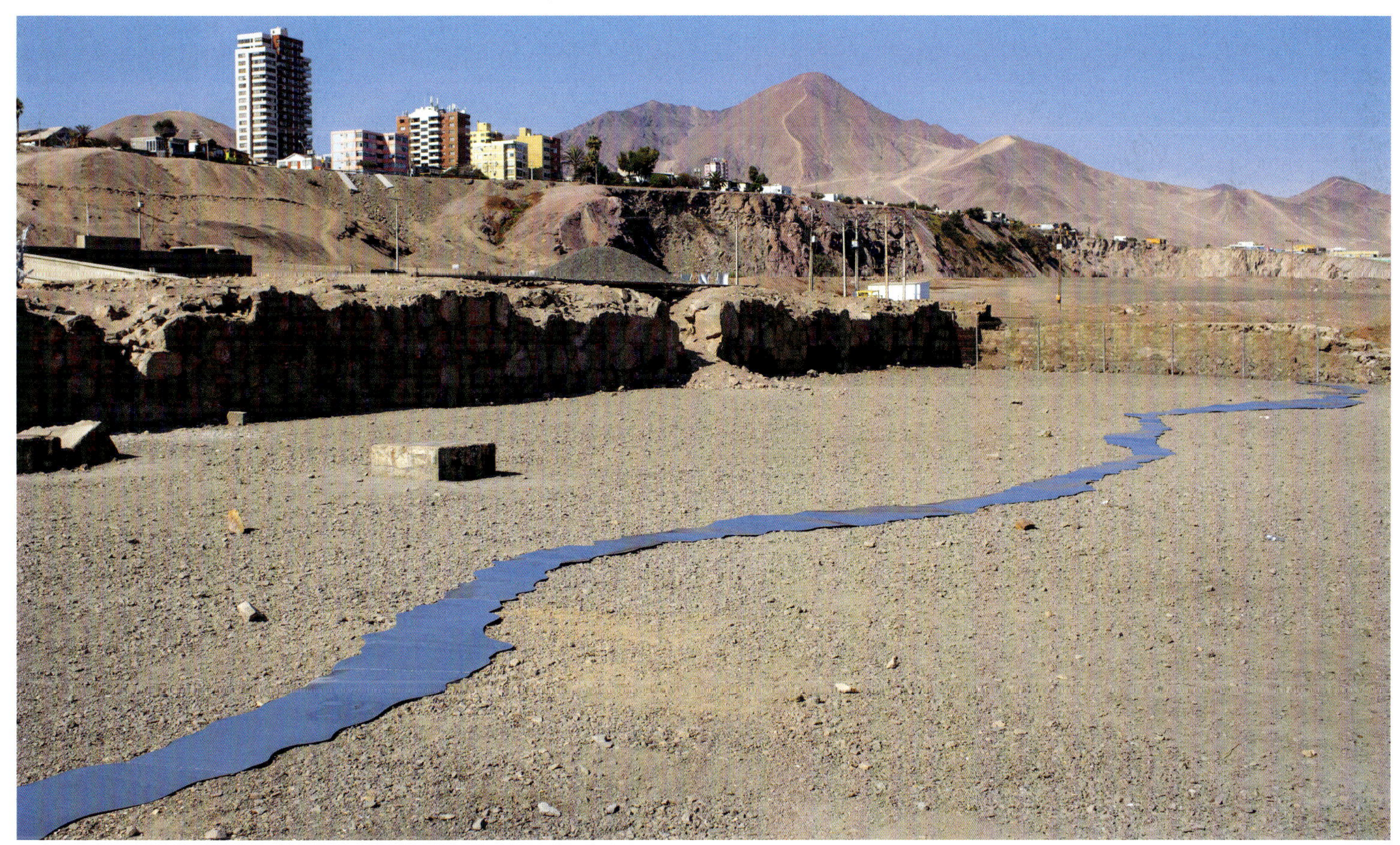

The works of Irish artist **ANDREW KEARNEY** (b. 1961) are most often site-specific interventions that relate to the architecture of the showing space as much as to the social and political context they find themselves in. The works are abstract, but queer all the same. Several works are lit in pink or use pink materials in contrast to their machine-like forms that recall science experiments, science fiction and surveillance. His 'Mechanism' exhibition toured the Centre Culturel Irlandais, Paris (2017), The Dock, Carrick-on-Shannon (2017) and the Crawford Gallery of Art, Cork (2019). Although many of the elements were common to all three spaces, Kearney altered the environment through their careful placement and the introduction of new elements to each site. At The Dock arts centre (right), viewers encountered a circular silver foil curtain before entering a room containing a 4-metre (13-foot) rotating inflatable sphere that reflected their own distorted image back to them. Kearney's *On Arriving* in the grounds of Watts Gallery – Artists' Village in Surrey (overleaf) featured a mirror installed in the trees, again evoking notions of surveillance, otherness and fear of the unknown.

'Mechanism', 2017
The Dock, Carrick-on-Shannon,
Co. Leitrim, Ireland
Mirrored chrome PVC inflatable,
suspended and rotating by a motor
housed within the ceiling of the gallery
Diam. of sphere: 4 m (13 ft)

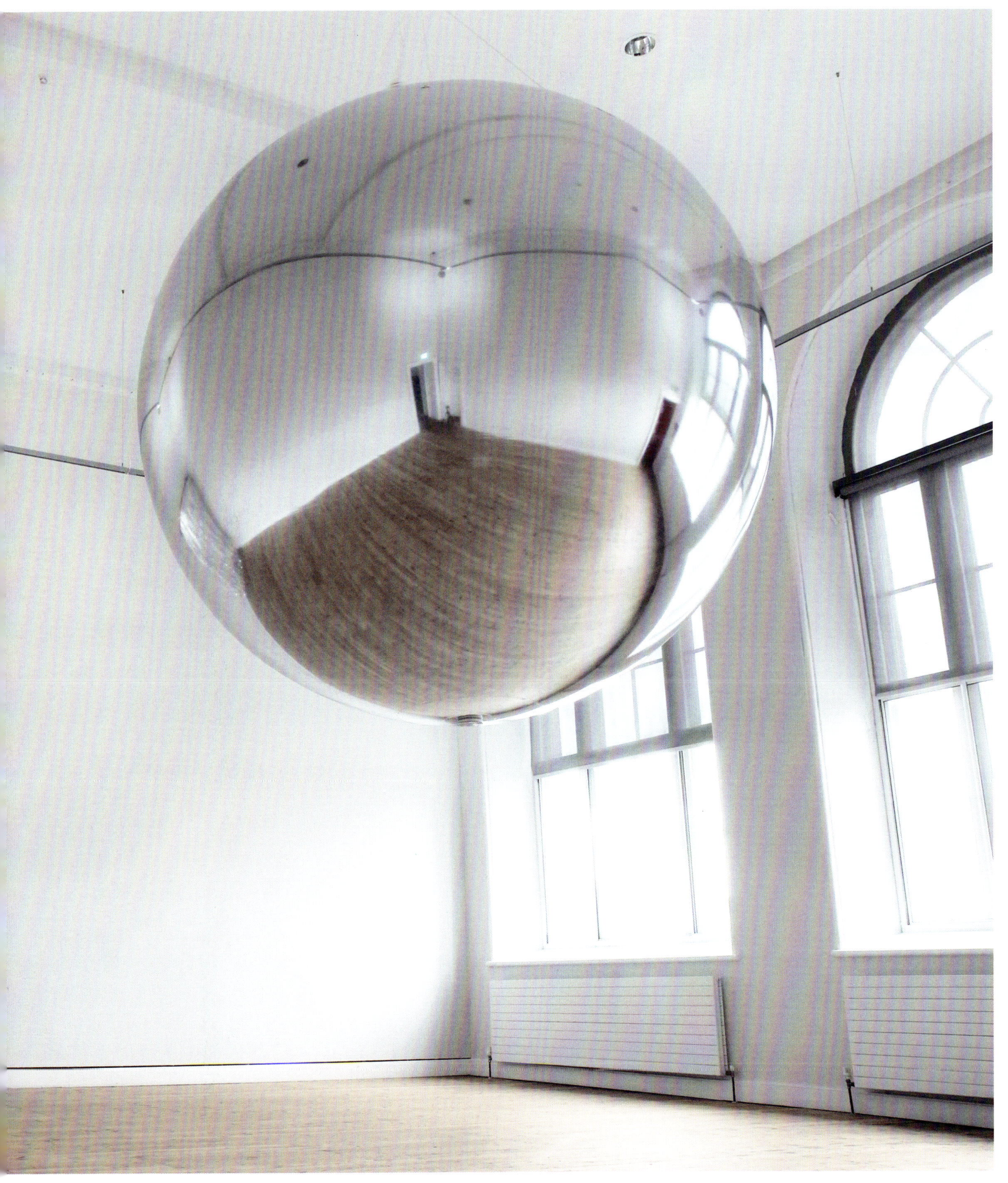

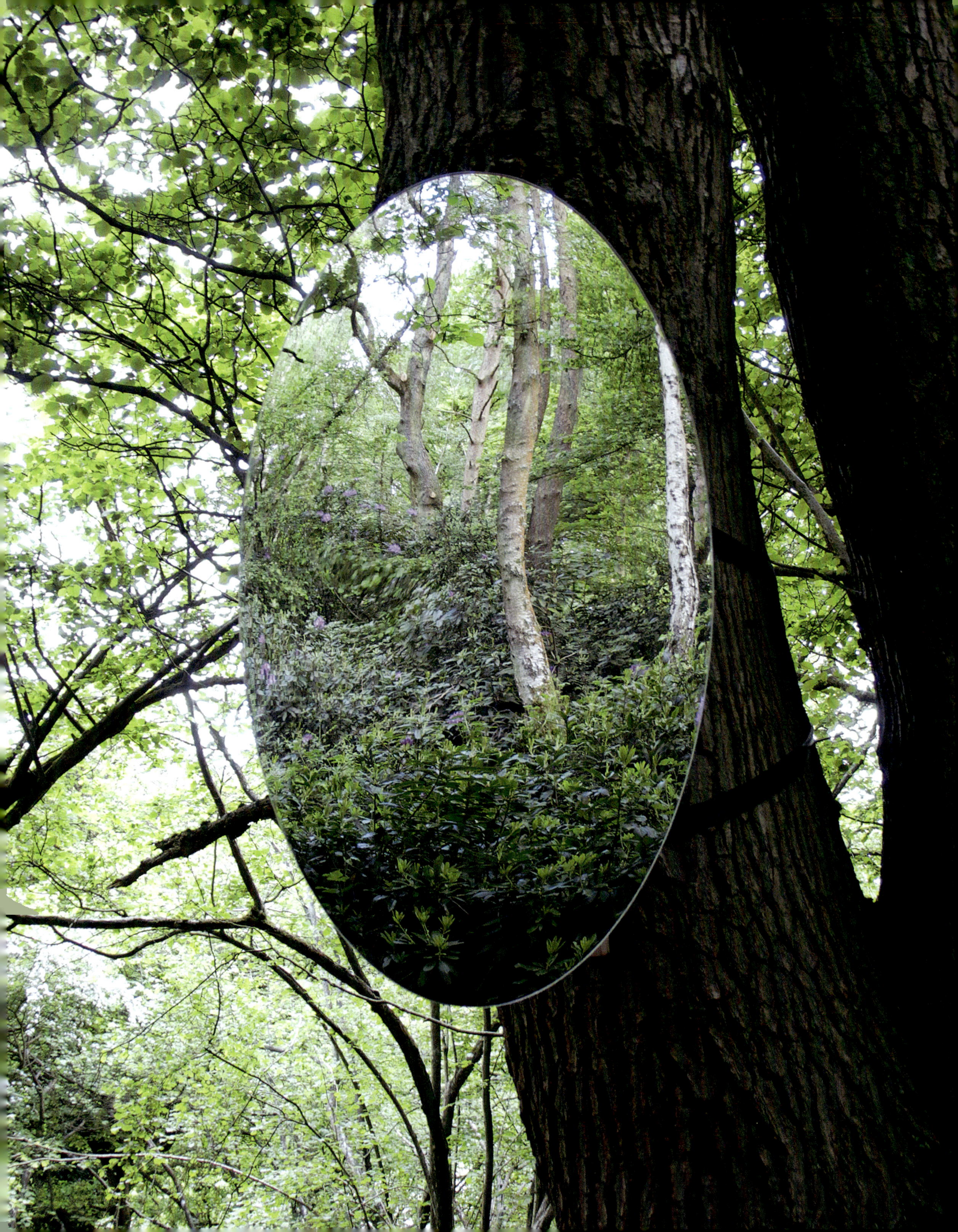

New York-based American artist **TERESITA FERNÁNDEZ** (b. 1968) makes monumental, immersive installations that often reflect their architectonic spaces and the contextual aspects of the site. She was chosen to develop *Paradise Parados*, a new permanent work at BAM Strong on the Robert W. Wilson Sculpture Terrace. In its lattice of mirror-polished stainless steel bands the work reflects BAM's Harvey Theater, emphasizing its dramatic and cinematic nature, and reflecting also visitors to the site, the fluctuating light and the urban landscape. With its organic forms it references the many ivy-covered walls seen in Brooklyn. Framing the entrance to a lounge area inside, the artwork becomes a passage and canopy that suggests the entrance to a stage with its flowing curtains.

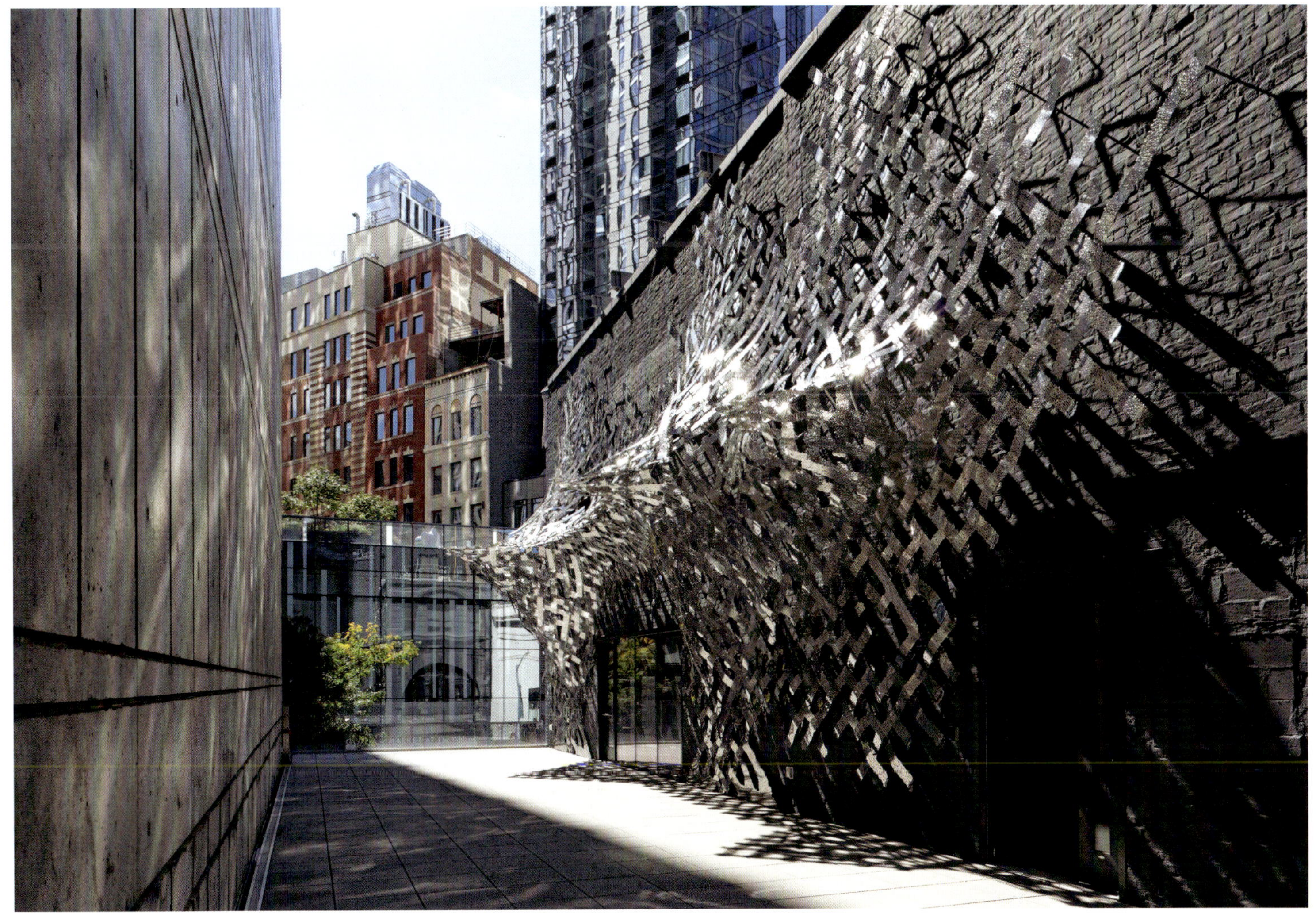

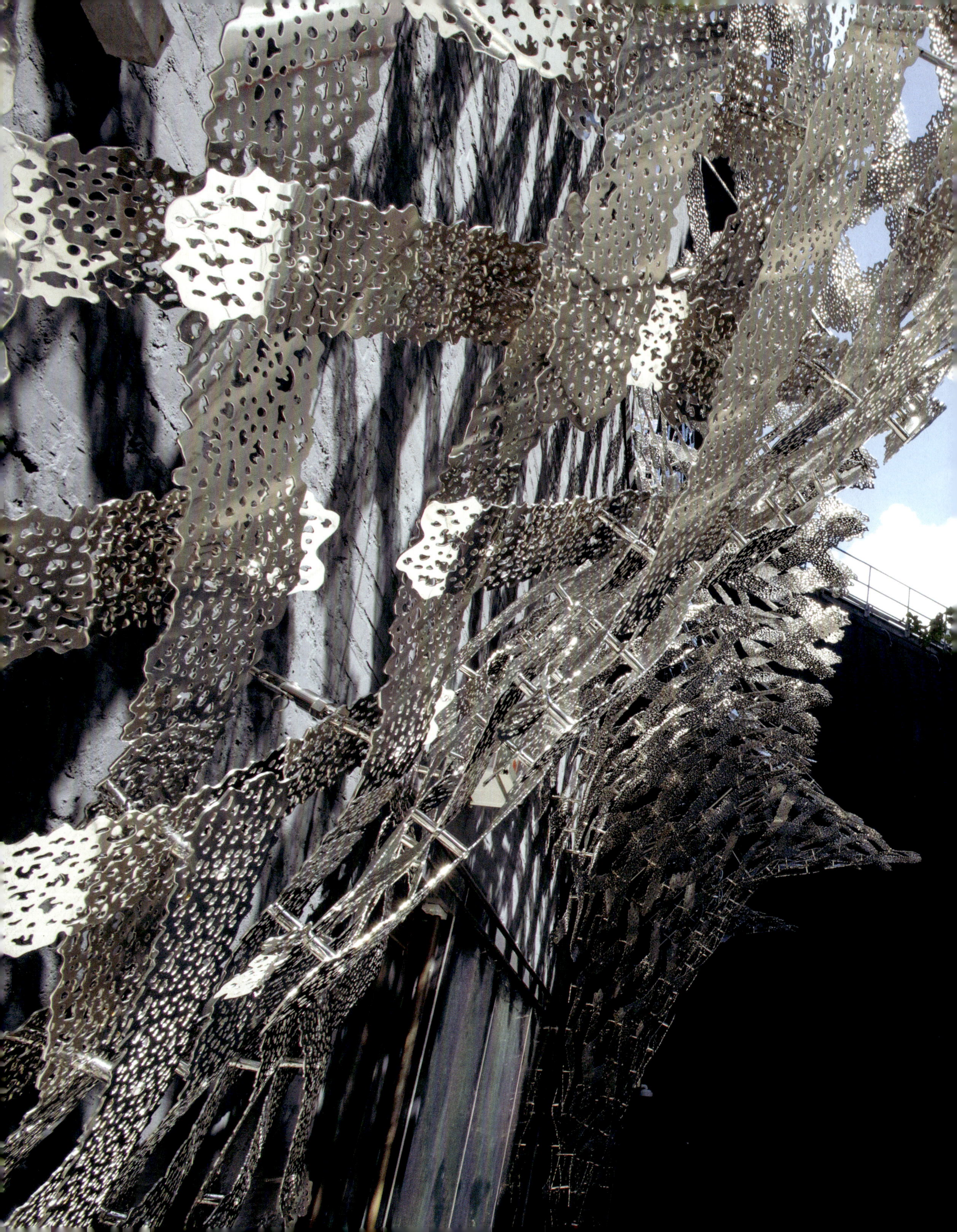

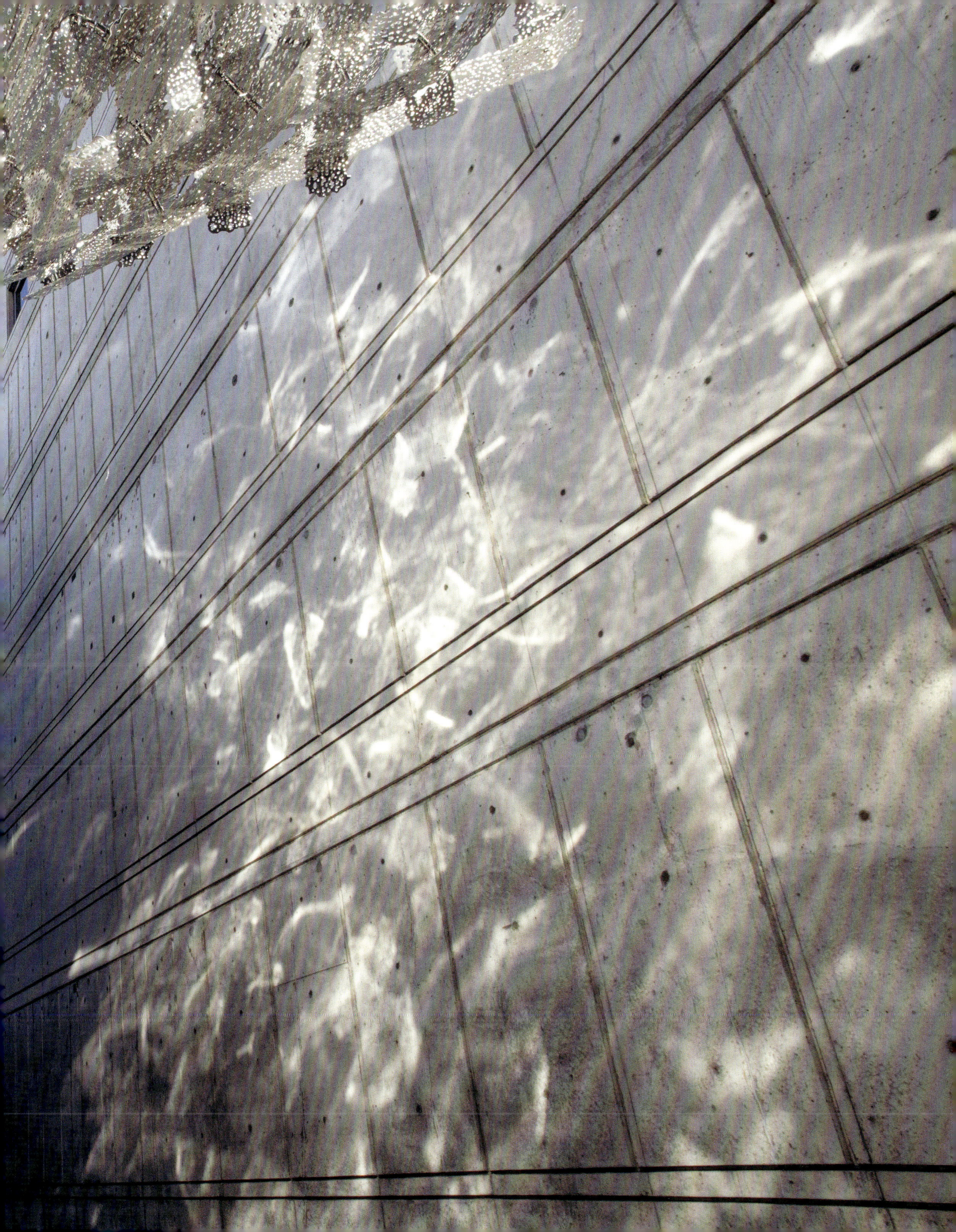

The Swedish duo **BIGERT & BERGSTRÖM**
(Mats Bigert (b. 1965) and Lars Bergström
(b. 1962)) have worked together since
1986 on a large number of conceptual
projects that have included film, installation
and sited sculpture, such as their *Wave
Pillar*. The 8-metre (26-foot) tall sculpture
is located on the Kajpromenaden on the
shore of the coastal city of Helsingborg.
The surface of the work illustrates how the
movement of waves changes in stormy or
windy conditions, increasing in size as the
wind speed goes from 2 to 10 m/s (6½ to
33 ft/s). The structure is made of polished
mirrored steel and the rippled surface
of the manmade waves reflects the actual
sea and the city surroundings, including
lamp posts and another sculpture on the
promenade, as well as passers-by.

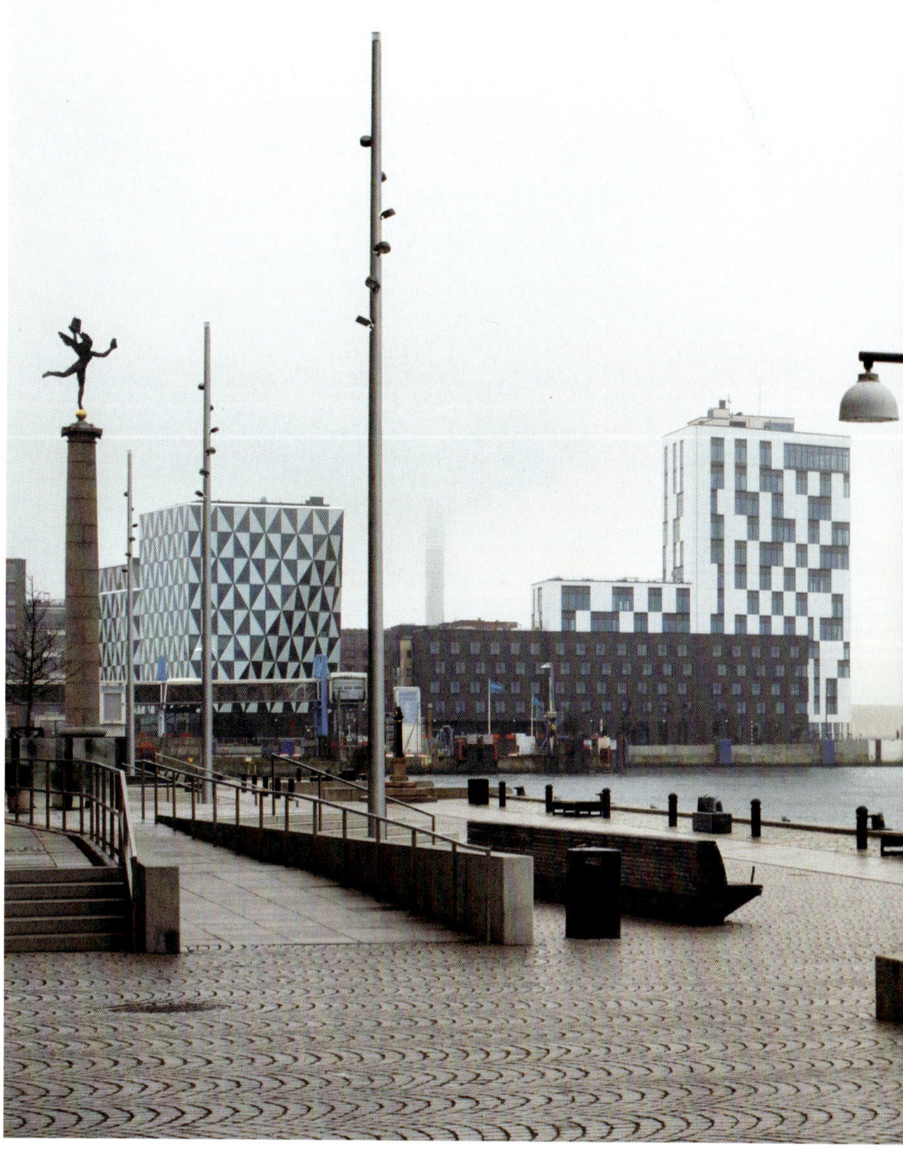

Wave Pillar, 2022
Kajpromenaden, Helsingborg, Sweden
Hammered stainless steel
8 × 1.4 × 0.87 m (26 × 4½ × 2⅘ ft)

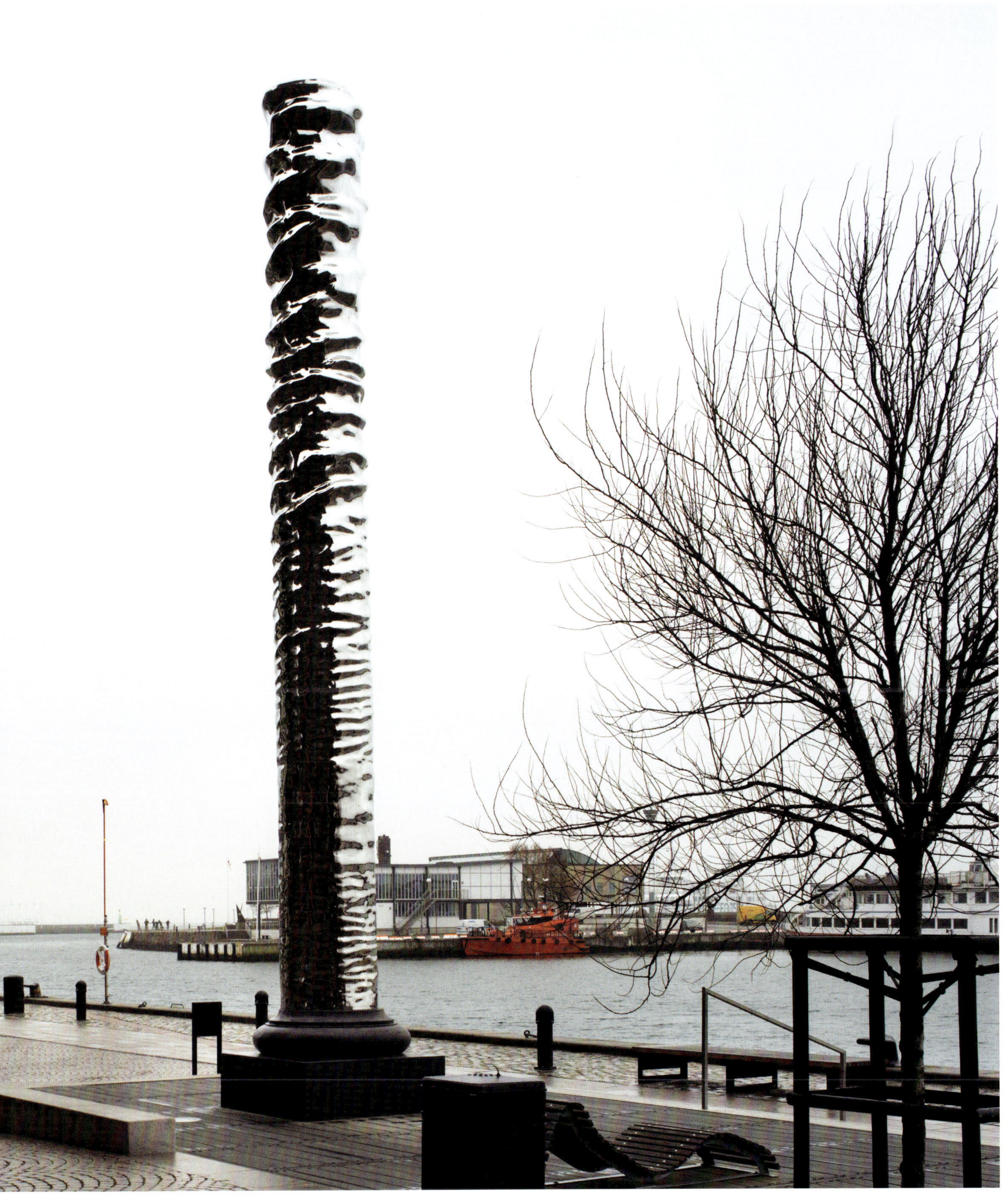

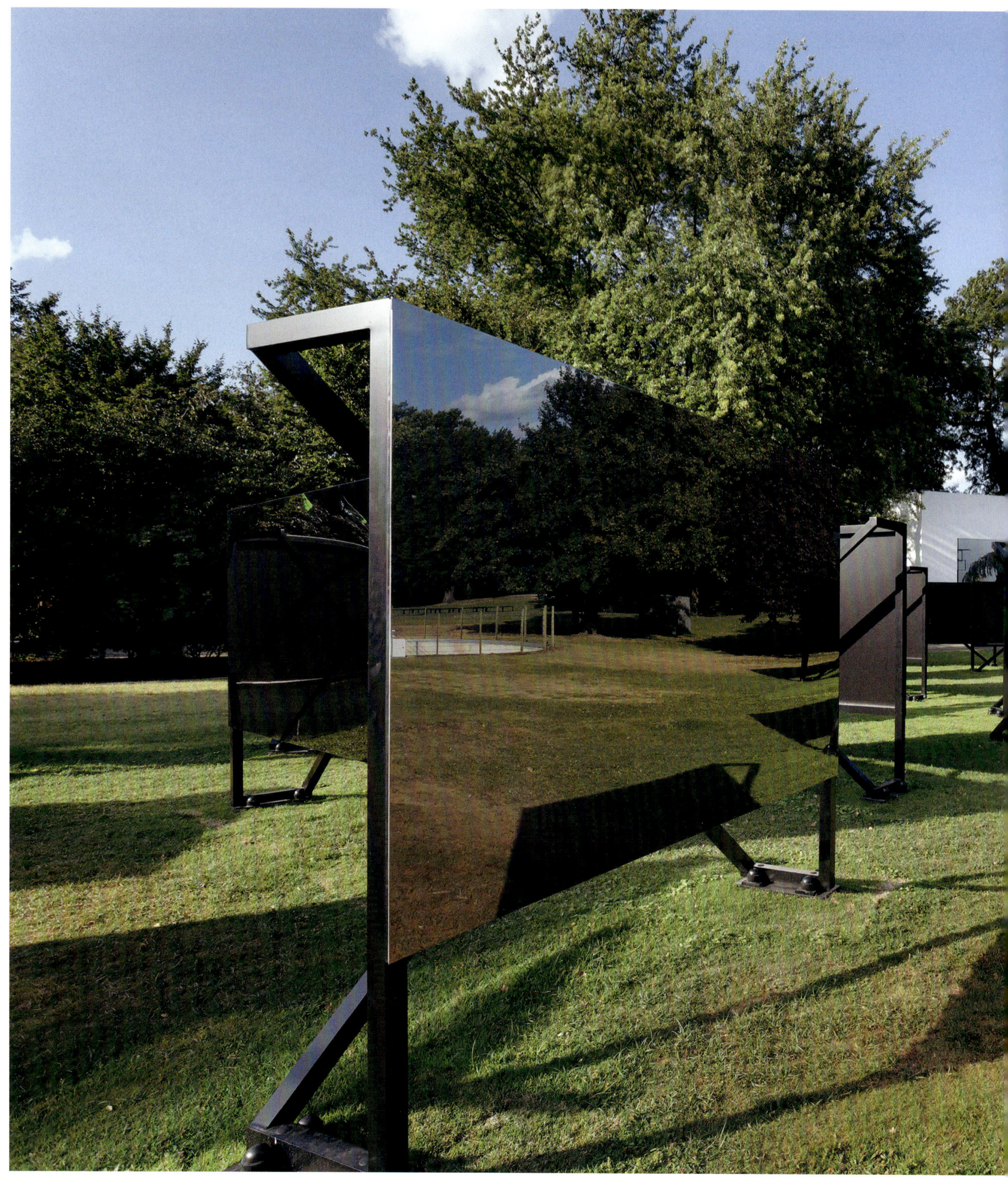

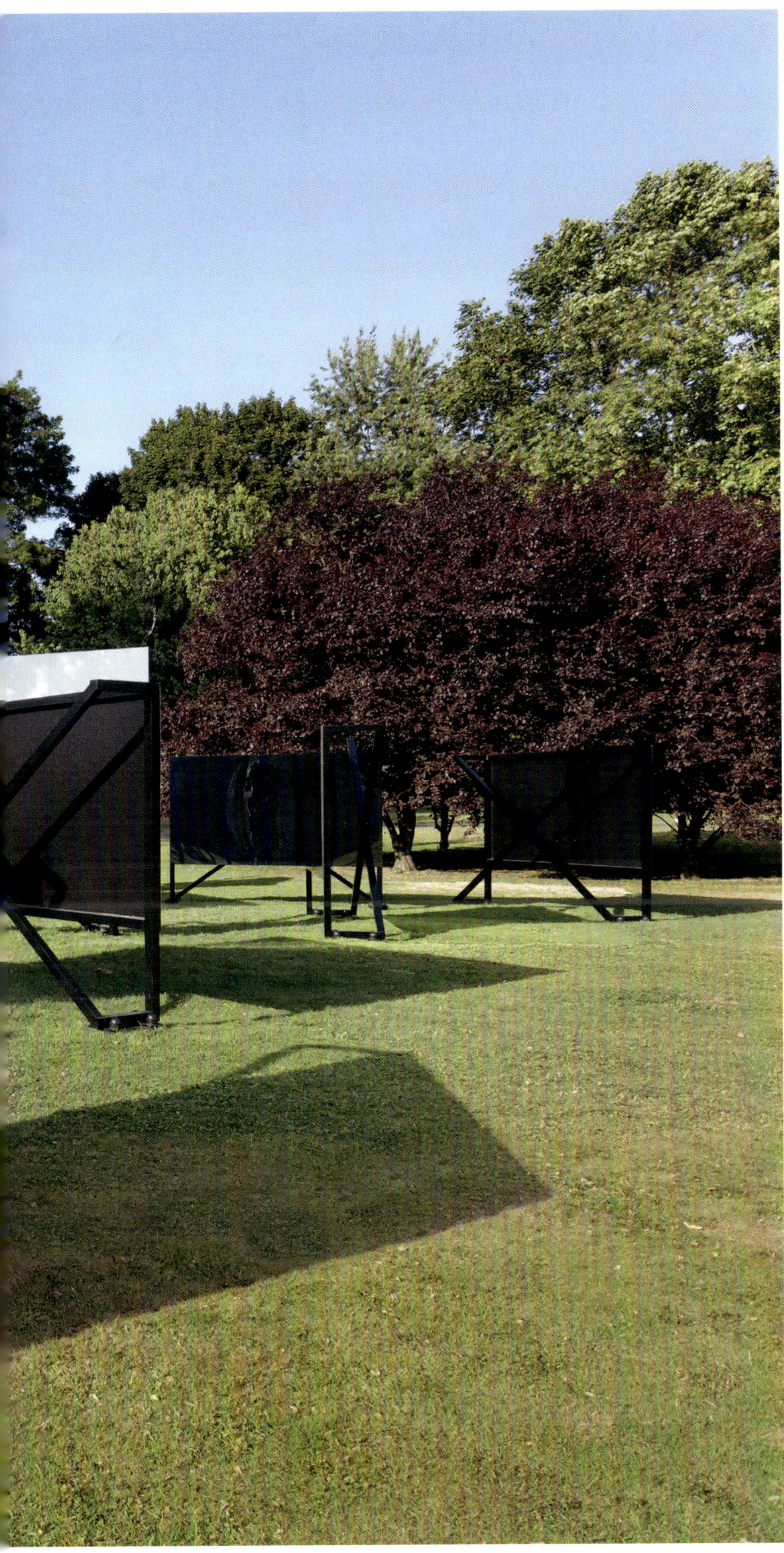

No Access by American artist **TOM BURR** (b. 1963) was first installed at the Skulpturenpark Köln (Cologne Sculpture Park), Germany, in 2015, before moving to the Savannah College of Art and Design's Museum of Art in 2017. The work comprised eighteen large metal X-shaped frames that held a reflective tinted steel mirror face on the opposite side. The faux billboards were located around the museum's gardens and ruins and reflected the buildings, plants and visitors. Seen up close, the reflections were in sharp focus, but when seen from afar they appeared distorted. These mute signage objects are a concern of Burr's, whose work looks at modern technology as something that both gives and withholds information. *No Access* also opened up the space to creative processes of thinking, imagining and introspection as the viewer walked around. The non-topiary maze referenced historical garden structures, often built for private conversations and assignations.

No Access, 2015
Skulpturenpark Köln, Germany
Aluminium frames with a polished, tinted steel face
Each: 200 × 252 × 50 cm
(78¾ × 99¼ × 19¾ in)

Brazilian artist **VALESKA SOARES** (b. 1957) studied architecture, and many of her sculptures and site-specific installations recall the rigour of that discipline. Her work for inSITE2000, *Picturing Paradise* (below), utilized a section of the US–Mexican chain-link border fence between San Diego in the USA and Playas de Tijuana in Mexico. She placed two sections of highly polished steel on each side of the border, so that in a way they became a visual or at least conceptual mirrored entrance from one state into another. The surfaces were inscribed with texts from Italo Calvino's *Invisible Cities*, in which Marco Polo describes fifty-five unique and marvellous fictitious cities to the Mongol emperor Kublai Khan. Soares quotes from the section on Valdrada, a city built over a reflecting lake, in which everything is mirrored, effectively making two cities: 'The two Valdradas live for each other, their eyes interlocked; but there is no love between them.' The text in America is in English with the Spanish translation in reverse and so illegible, while on the Mexican side it is the opposite. Soares's *Fainting Couch* (opposite) is a life-sized chaise that has hidden drawers underneath the drilled surface. The overpowering scent of the Stargazer lilies that fill the drawers almost overcomes the viewer. The border between pleasure and revulsion is as porous as the real-world ones between countries.

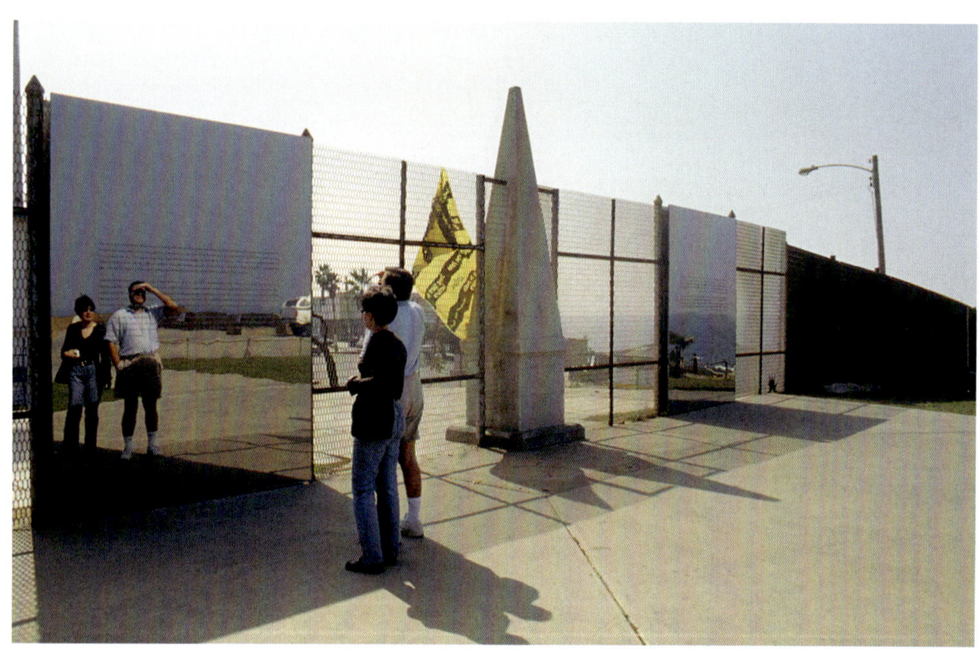

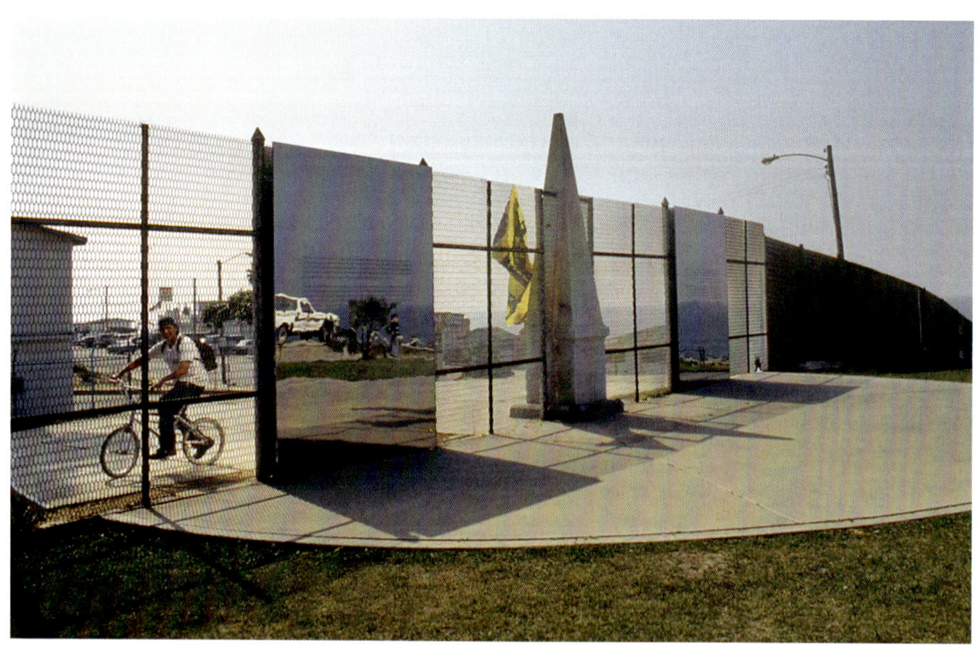

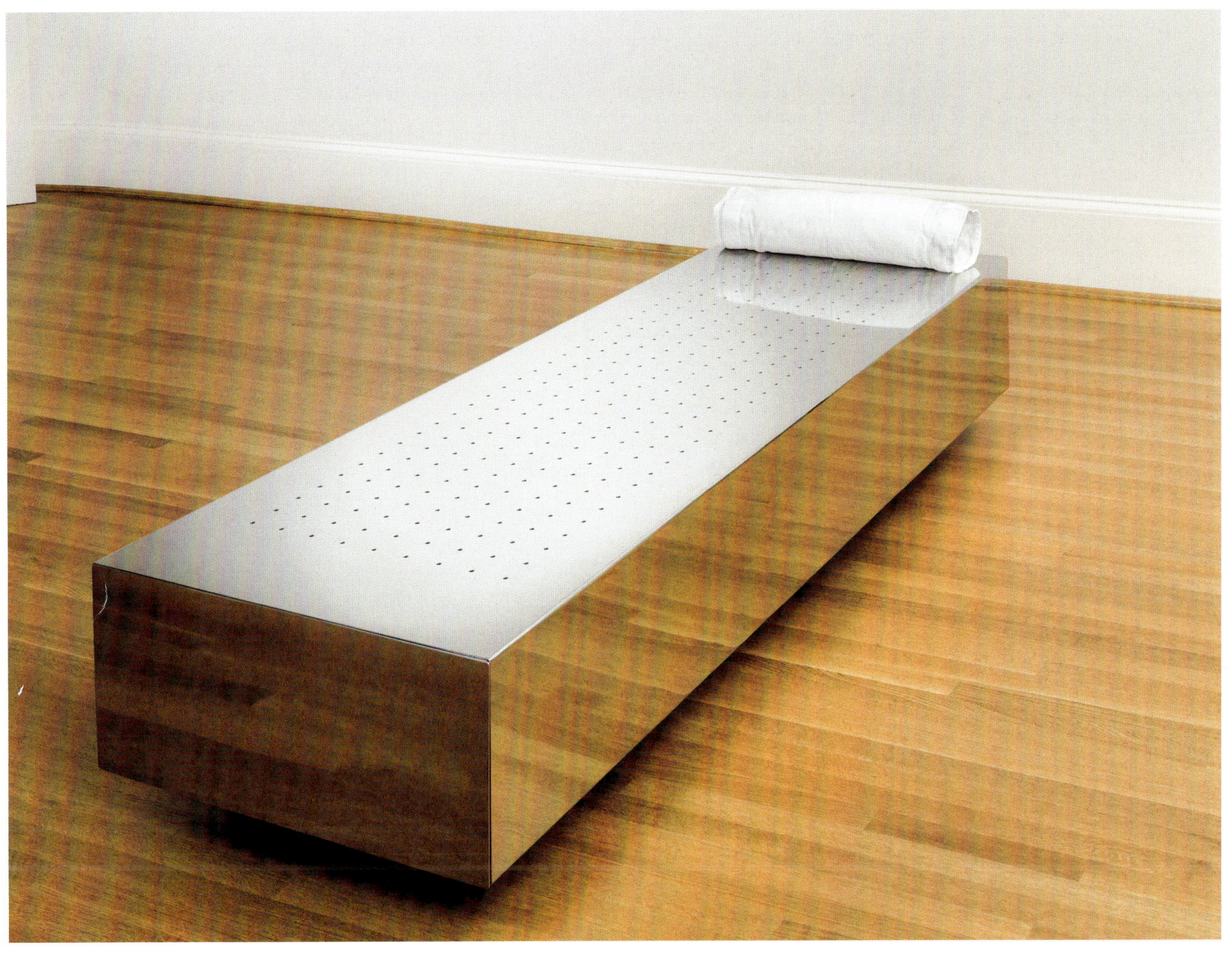

OPPOSITE
Picturing Paradise, 2000
Mirrored stainless-steel panels with
engraved letters
US–Mexico (San Diego–Tijuana) border
Four units, 3.04 × 1.52 m (10 × 5 ft) each

ABOVE
Fainting Couch, 2001
Stainless steel, pillow, pillowcase
and flowers
35 × 200 × 60 cm (13⅞ × 78¾ × 23⅝ in)
Edition of 2 + 1 AP

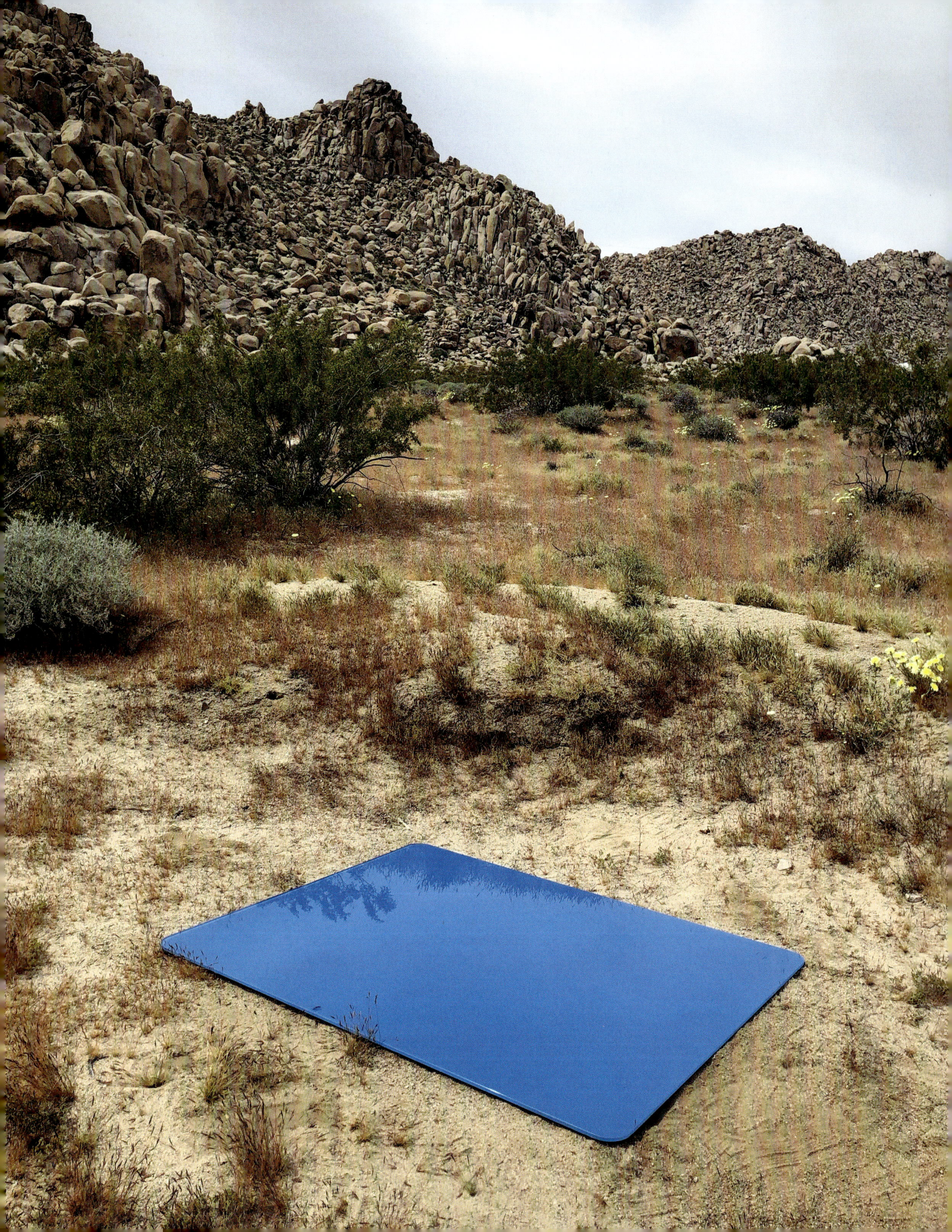

The Pool of Narcissus, 2019
Joshua Treenial, California, USA
Polished blue glass, fabricated
by Glass London
Dimensions variable

The Pool of Narcissus was an installation by **MICHAEL PETRY** (b. 1960) for the 2019 Joshua Treenial in California, for BoxoHOUSE, curated by Kóan Jeff Baysa and Bernard Leibov. Petry's large blue-glass work was placed in a sandy area reflecting the sun, the clouds, the moon and the stars, as well as the viewer. The work recalls the classical myth of Narcissus, a young man of renowned beauty. Yet he had never seen his own reflection. In one version of the story, the nymph Echo saw him while he was out hunting, and fell in love; but she could not answer his replies other than to echo his calls of 'Who's there?' Thinking she was mocking him, he thrust her aside. Brokenhearted, she turned to Nemesis, the goddess of revenge. Nemesis waited until Narcissus went to drink from a pool. She showed him his own face in the water, and he fell in love, not realizing that his reflection was himself. He was so drawn to his own image that he could not be torn away from the pool, and he wasted away.

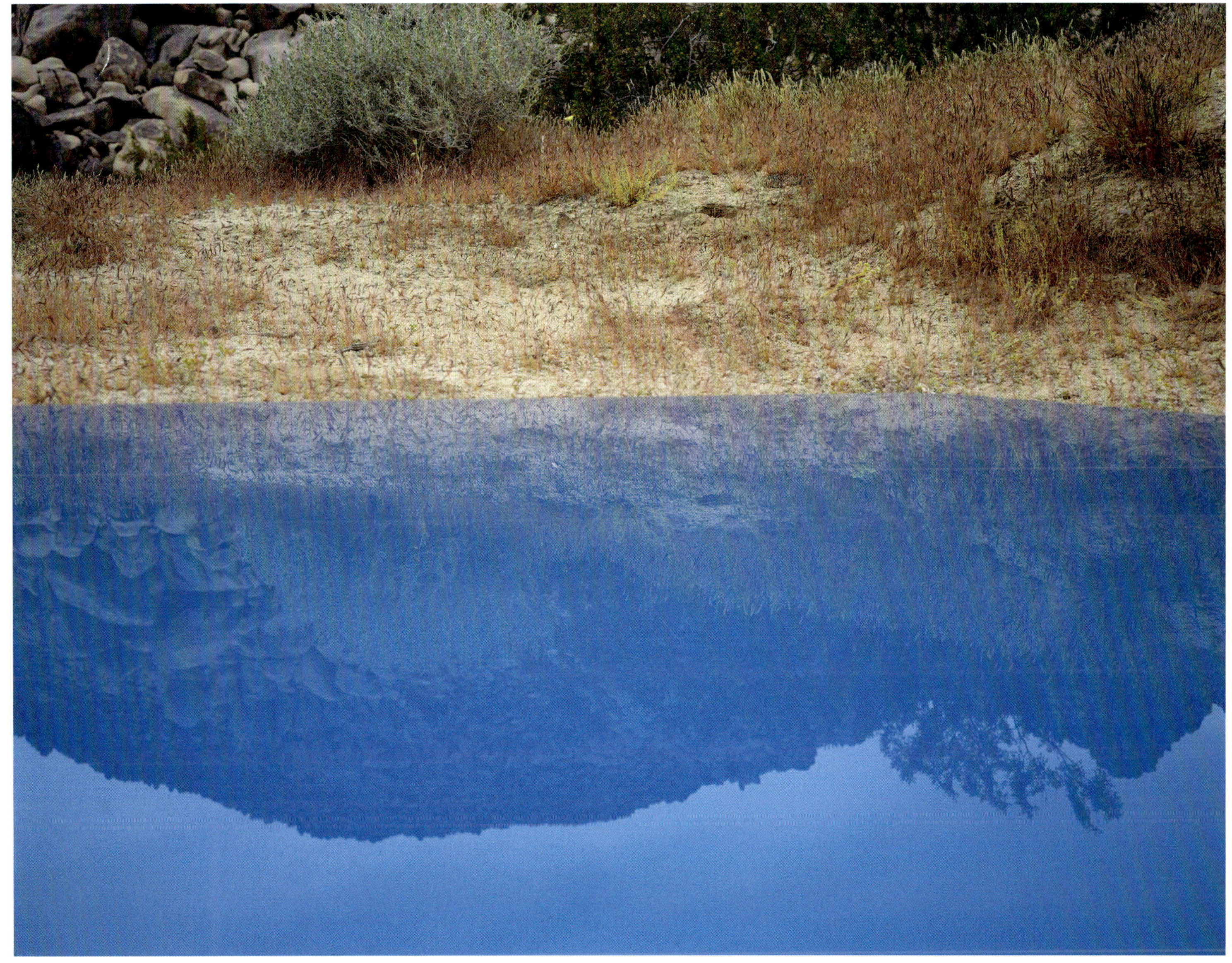

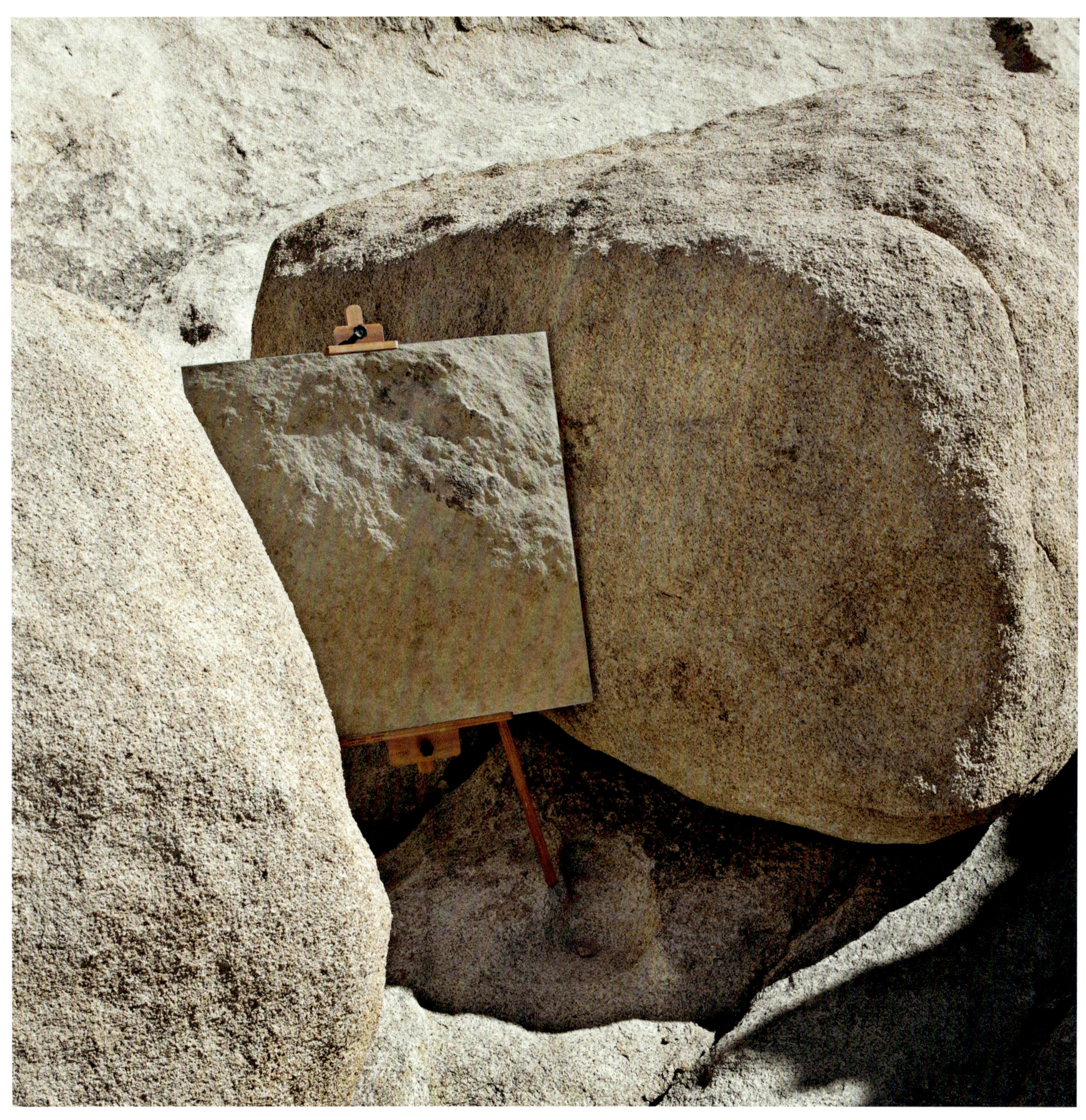

In 2012 American artist **DANIEL KUKLA** (b. 1983) was given a residency at Joshua Tree National Park with the United States National Park Service. Playing on the fact that the park incorporates parts of two deserts, the Sonoran Desert and the high Mojave Desert, he made a series of works called *Edge Effect*, which is a scientific term for 'the border space created by the meeting of distinct ecosystems in juxtaposition'. Kukla placed a large square mirror on an artist's easel in spots of opposing elements, documenting these border zones without reflecting his own image in them. He is absent, as is the viewer, yet it is impossible to be unaware of his presence in the image by its very omission. The landscapes are beautiful but under threat from a warming climate, and the work speaks of the impermanence of the natural world and of humankind (and of its destructive urge).

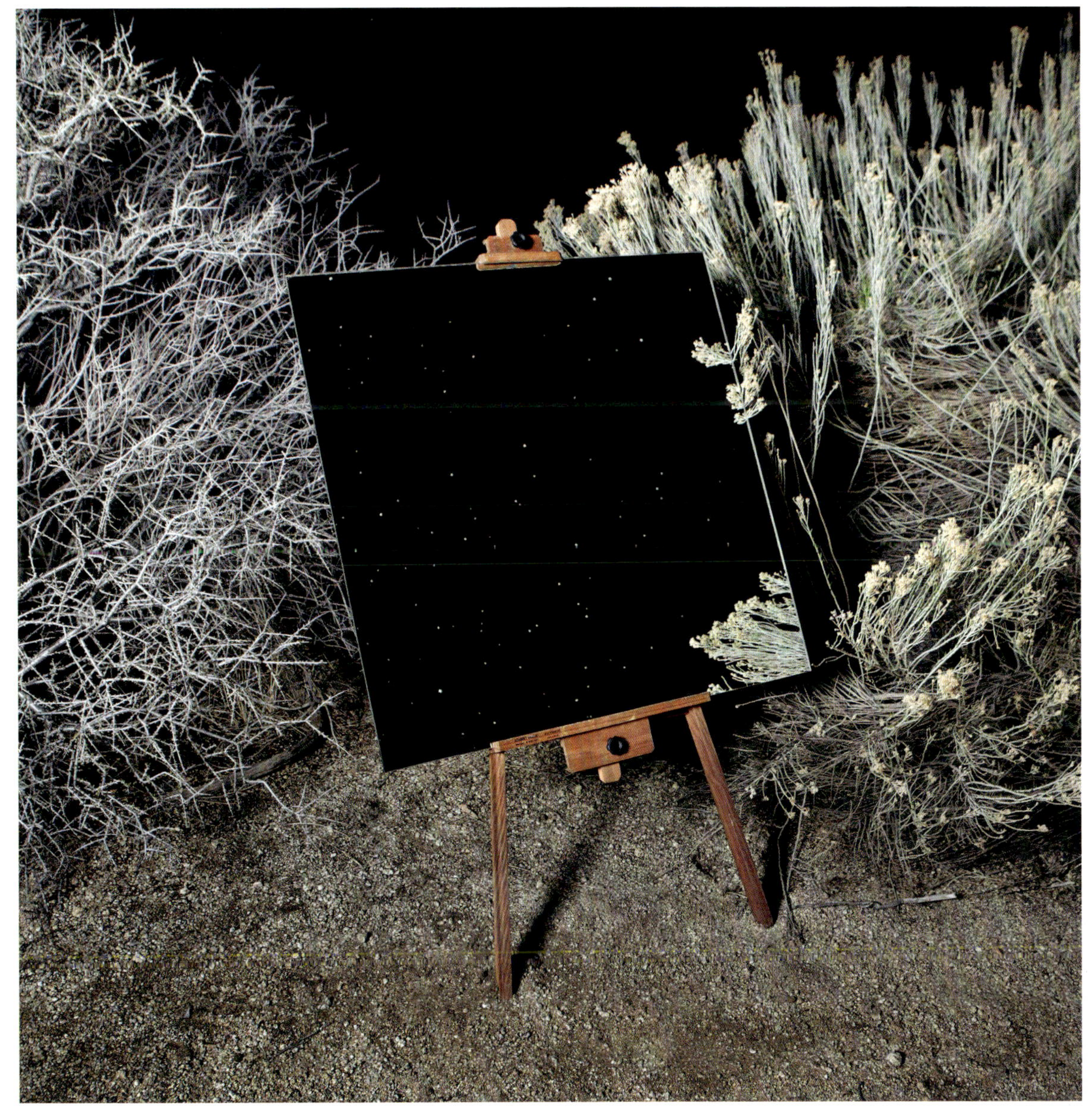

, an American
sculptor based in Los Angeles, wanted
to make a work that was impossible to
look directly into, 'something so highly
reflective (like a windshield at high-noon)
that it would be bright and intense, but
hard to comprehend'. Vanderlip used
two convex oval endcaps from oil tanker
truckheads, welded together, to create her
curved disc. She polished the aluminium
surfaces until they were like a mirror,
and the disc was then installed as part
of the *High Desert Test Sites 3* project.
The piece reflects the sky and desert rocks
that form the distinct landscape of the
Joshua Tree area. Fifteen years later she
was able to expand on the project with
her *Untitled (Double Ellipses)*, placing two
adjacent mirrors (one vertical, the other
horizontal) so that they reflected both
each other and the desert.

Untitled (CA Truckheads), 2003
Joshua Tree National Park, California, USA
Highly polished aluminium endcaps
244 × 152.4 × 53.3 cm (96 × 60 × 21 in)

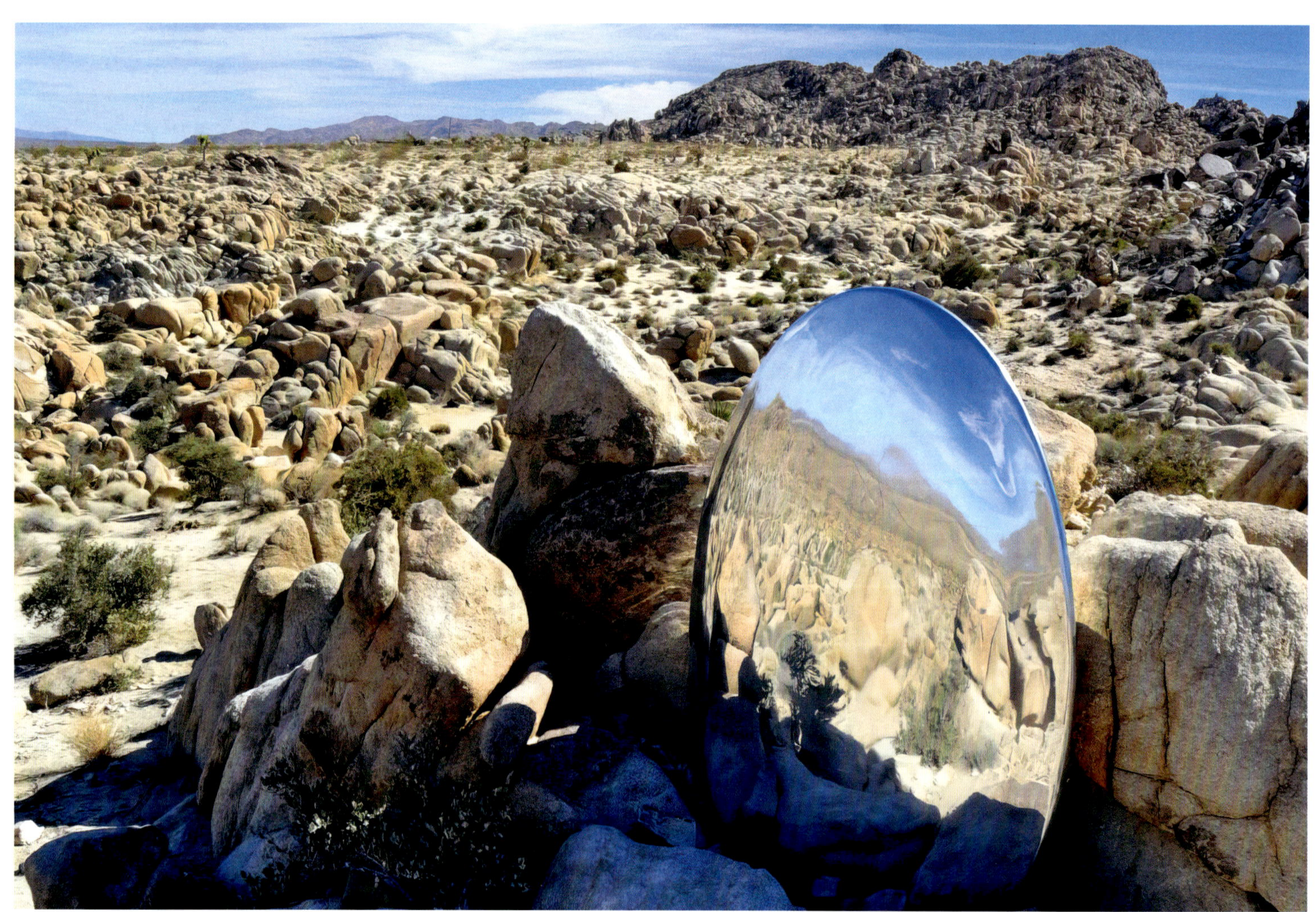

Multidisciplinary German artist **PHILIPP FÜRHOFER** (b. 1982) uses oil on acrylic glass and spy, or two-way, mirrors to paint complex scenes that often reference nineteenth-century Romantic painters but are in a continual state of flux, as internal lights turn on and off to reveal different aspects of the work. Fürhofer is also a successful opera stage designer. His large-scale installations often have a dramatic effect on the viewer. In the Schirn Kunsthalle rotunda, his *[dis]connect* made every viewer a performer in his unique vision of the space. The artist had a mirrored ceiling put in place across the huge expanse so that on the underside, it reflected the cobbled floor and passers-by. Above this false ceiling the intervention became a mirrored floor, which visually extended the glazed structure upwards. Viewers on the upper floor could see down into this reflection but those above never saw those below, and vice versa.

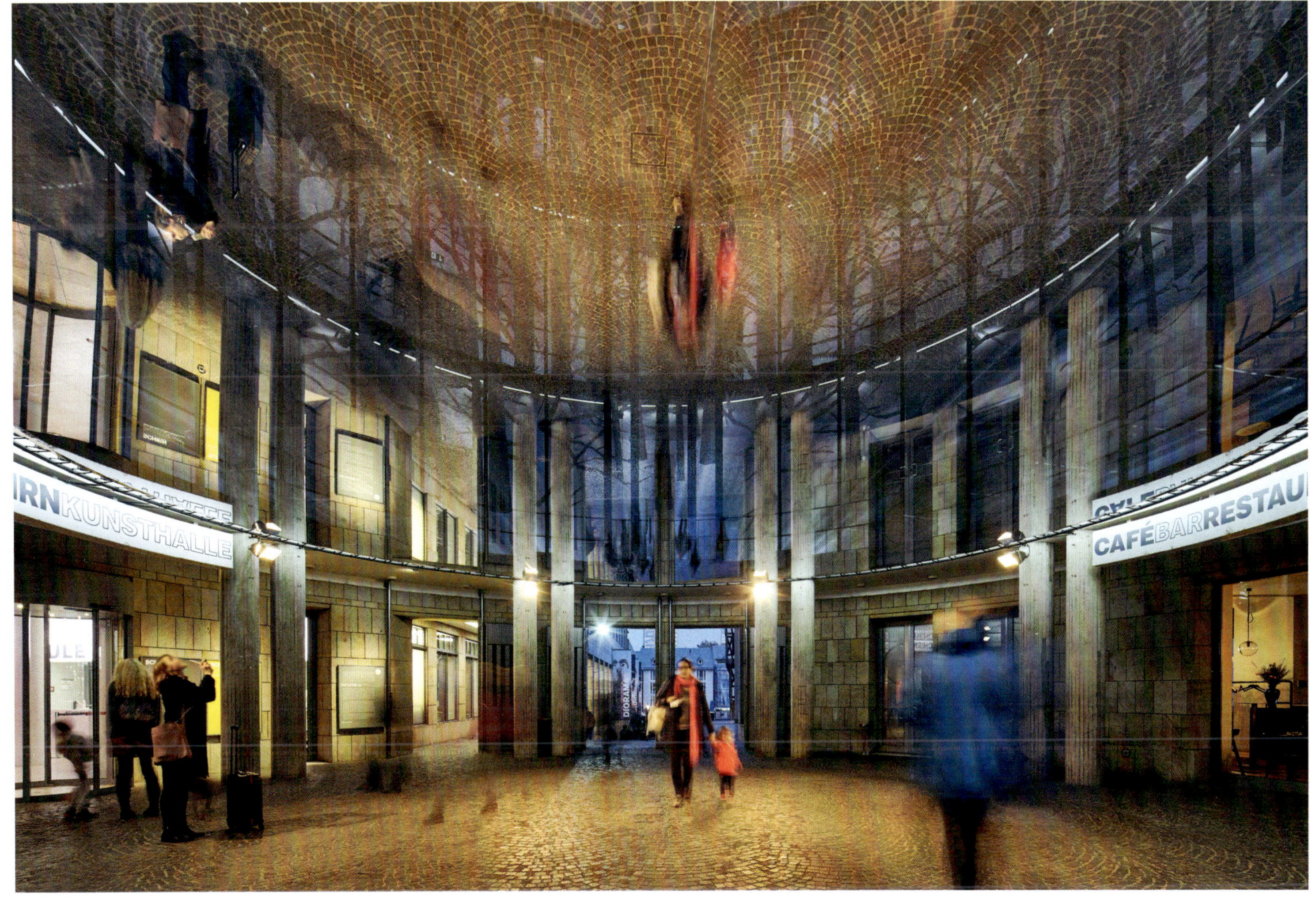

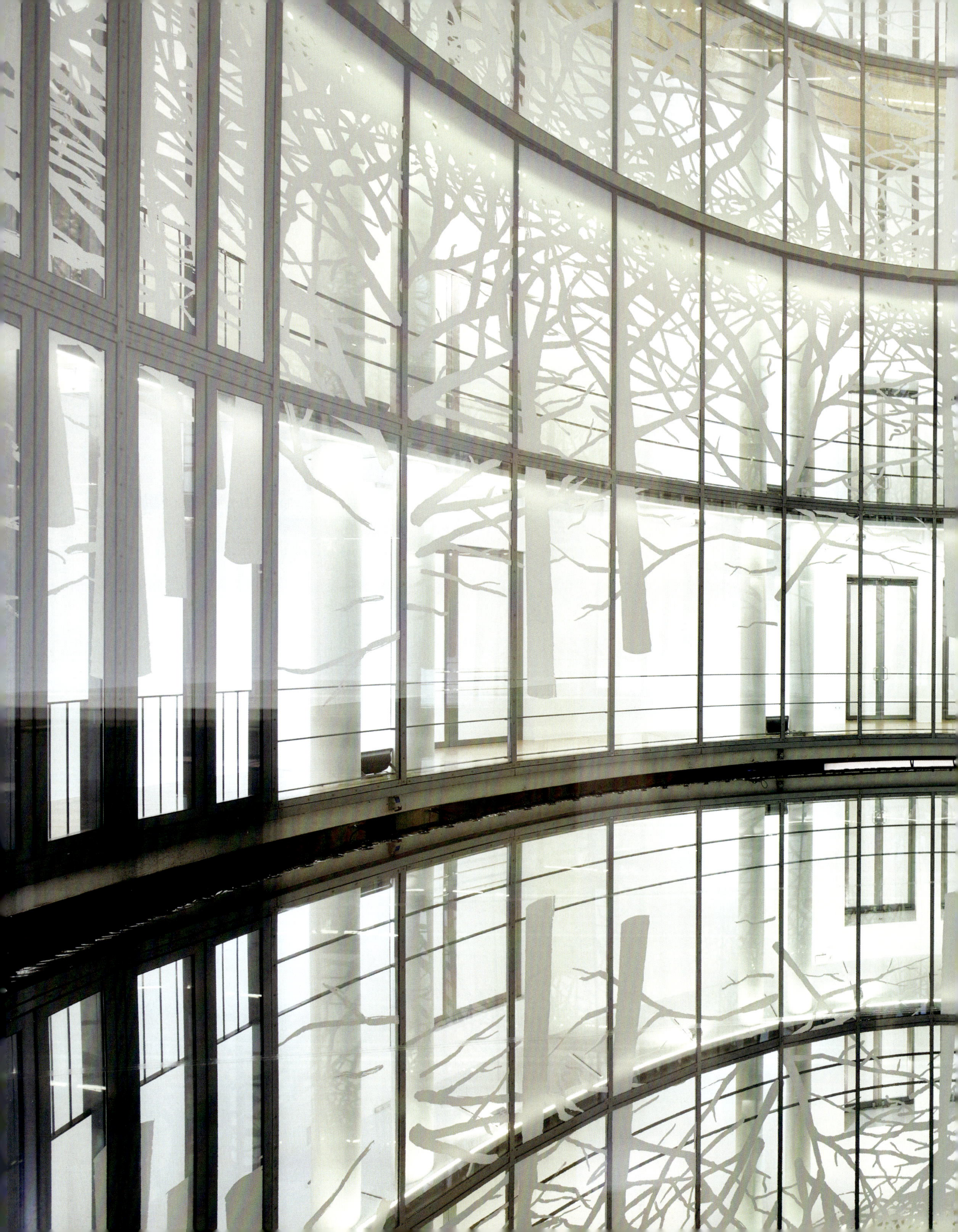

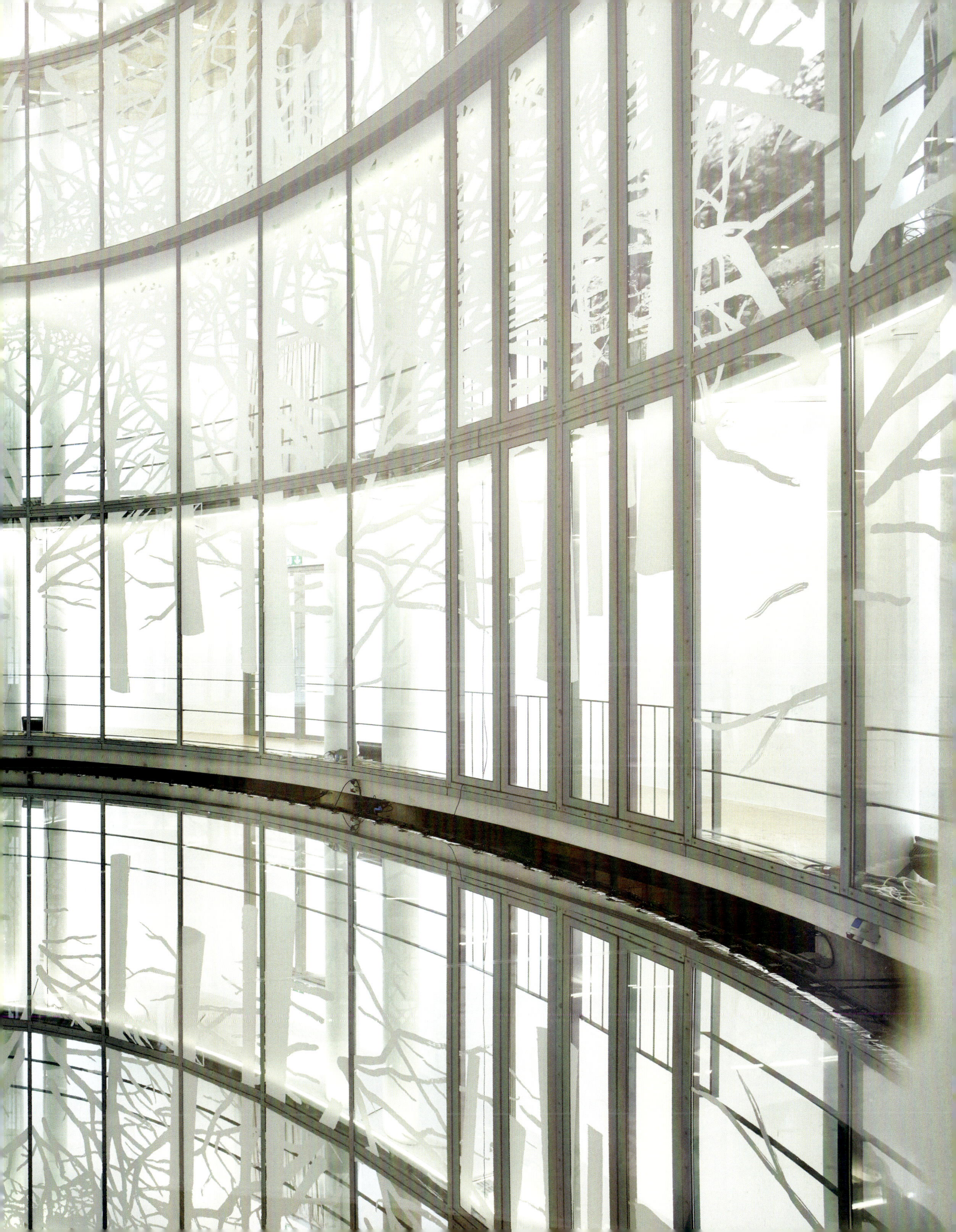

Belgian conceptual artist **MICHEL FRANÇOIS**'s (b. 1956) exhibition 'Panoptique' at the Halle Verrière, a former glass factory, saw him place just a few large-scale works in the vast brick building. In the centre was a work called *Panoptique*, a tower of metal and mirror that was ascended by a spiral staircase. From the vantage point at the top, the interior of the whole building could be surveyed. The work was a dialogue with Michel Foucault's writing on the topic in *Discipline & Punish: The Birth of the Prison* (1975) – a panopticon is a design of prison, usually round, in which all cells are visible from the centre. Two other works were installed in the space, both featuring silver mirrored blown glass. *Souffles dans le verre* (2006) is a large droplet-shaped cluster of glass balloon forms hung on clear nylon, which also reflect the architecture of where they are placed. These and the similar deflated forms that lay on the other side of the central structure reflected the viewer and functioned to keep them under surveillance – the job of all panopticons.

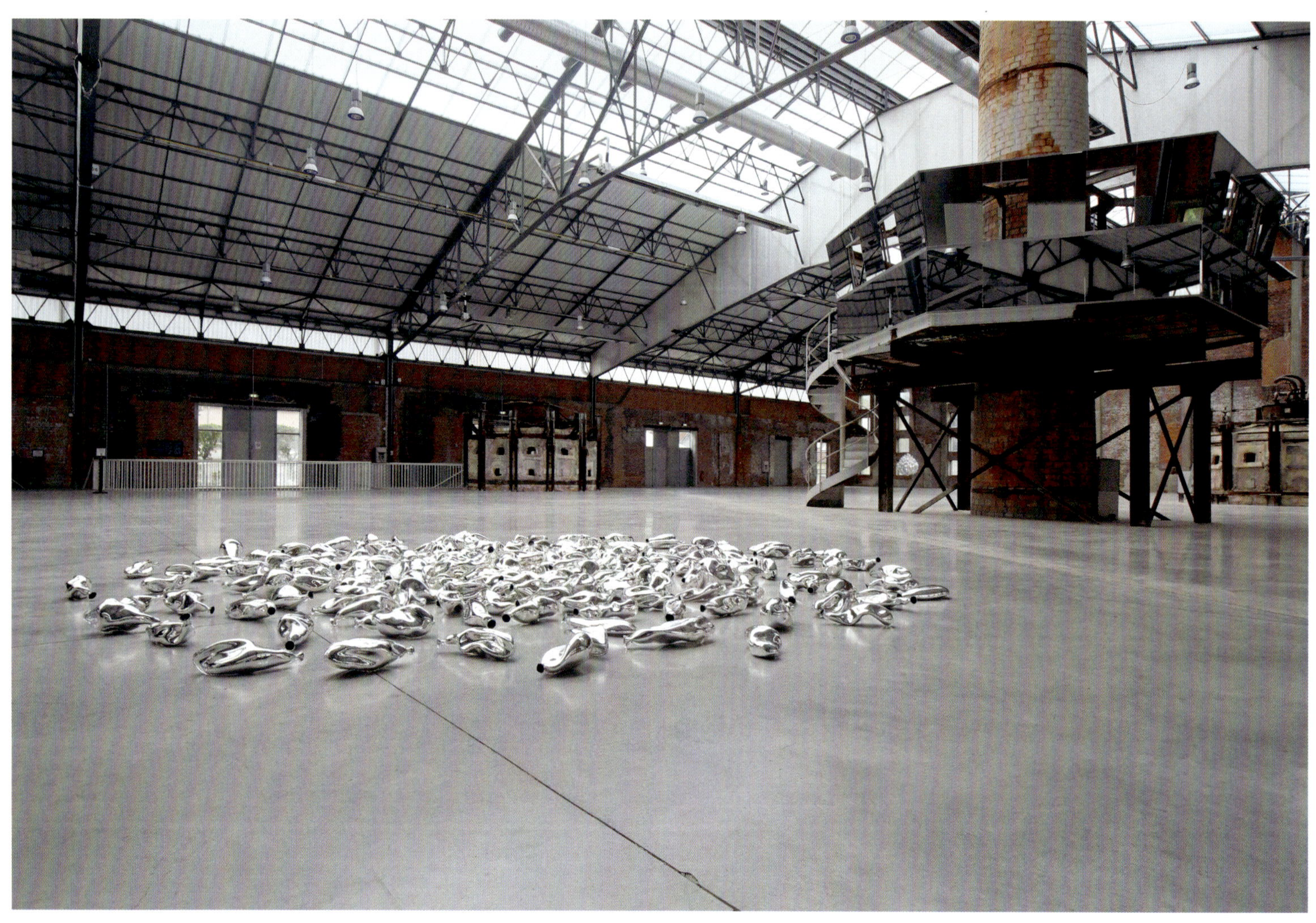

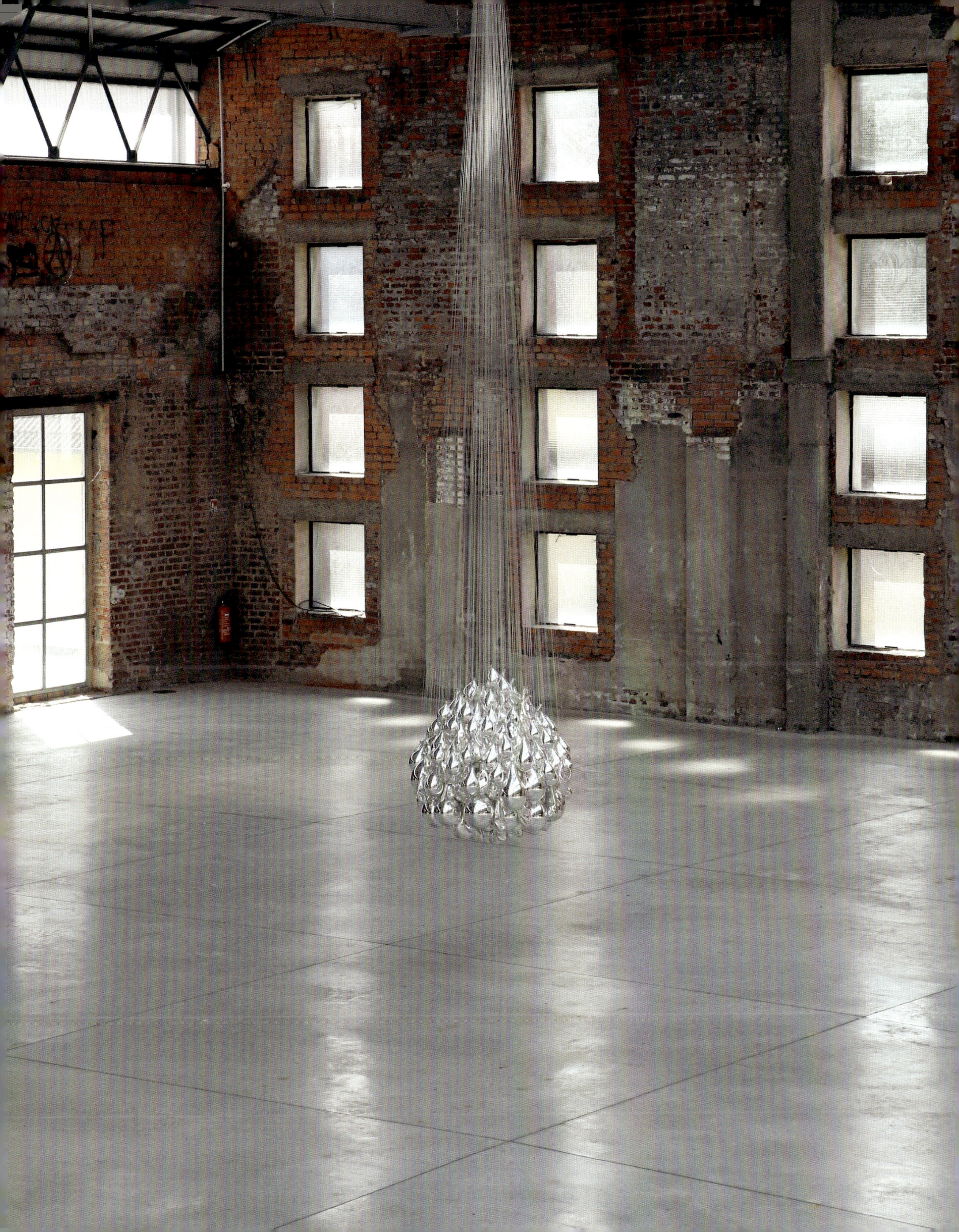

The large golden meteorite by American artist **C. MATTHEW SZÖSZ** (b. 1974) is named after Pieter Bruegel the Elder's 1560 painting *Landscape with the Fall of Icarus* (owned by the Museum of Fine Arts, Brussels). In the painting, no one seems to have noticed the drowning winged lad, Icarus, fallen into the sea after flying too close to the sun owing to his own hubris. Life continues at its usual pace for everyone else, a metaphor for our own times, with climate change and other disasters heading towards us like Szösz's sculpture. At the same time, the work is so dazzling that viewers are captured by its opulence, hardly daring to wonder how such a work functions within a global system of exchange. Szösz wants viewers to see it in context of the asteroid 16 Psyche, believed to hold so much iron, nickel and gold that it would be worth more than 10,000 quadrillion dollars, a concept too large for most people to even begin to imagine. The asteroid contains enough gold to make every person on Earth a billionaire, but that much gold would devalue the metal to the point of worthlessness.

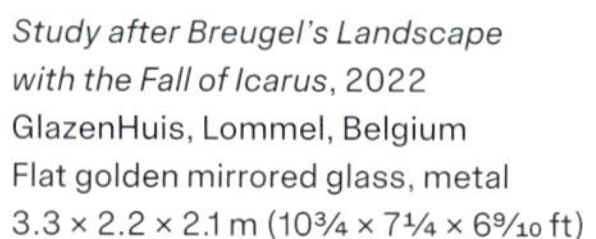

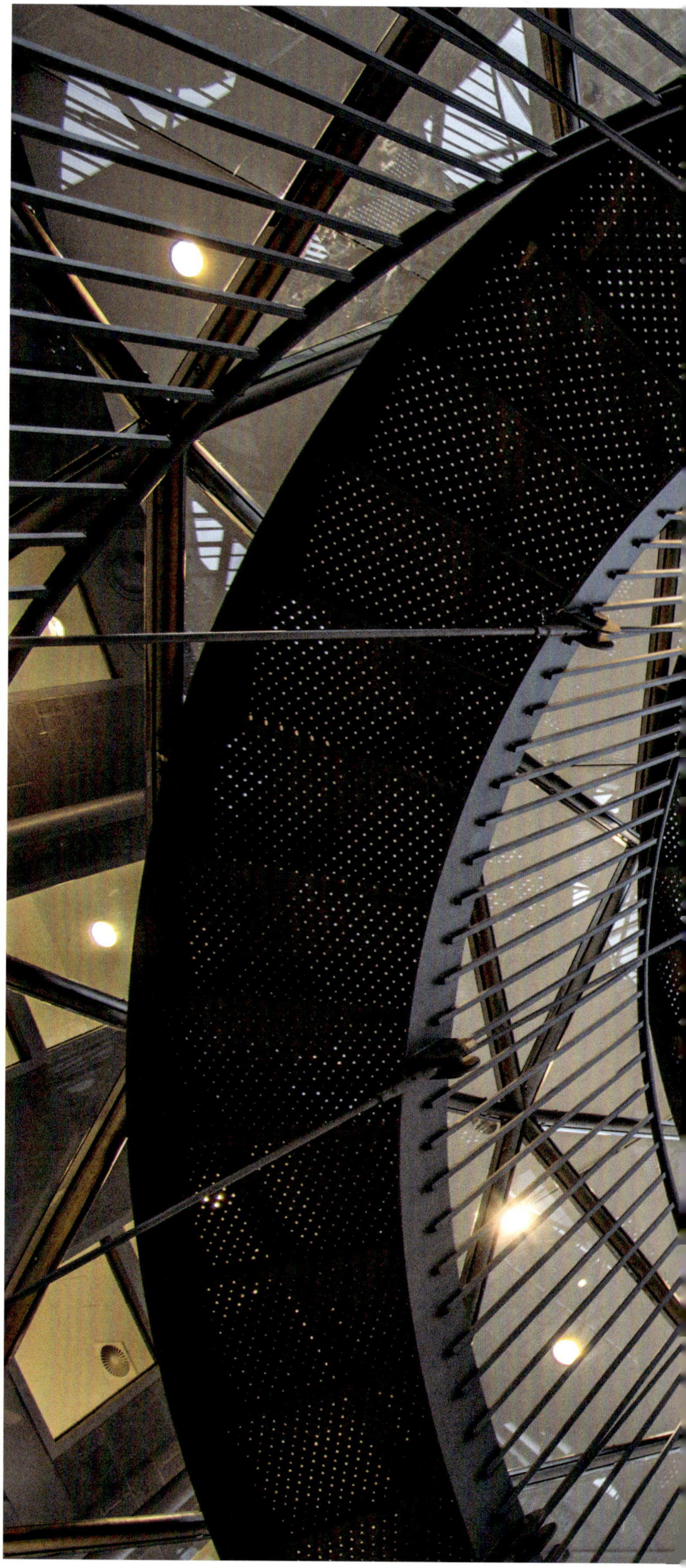

Study after Breugel's Landscape with the Fall of Icarus, 2022
GlazenHuis, Lommel, Belgium
Flat golden mirrored glass, metal
3.3 × 2.2 × 2.1 m (10¾ × 7¼ × 6⁹⁄₁₀ ft)

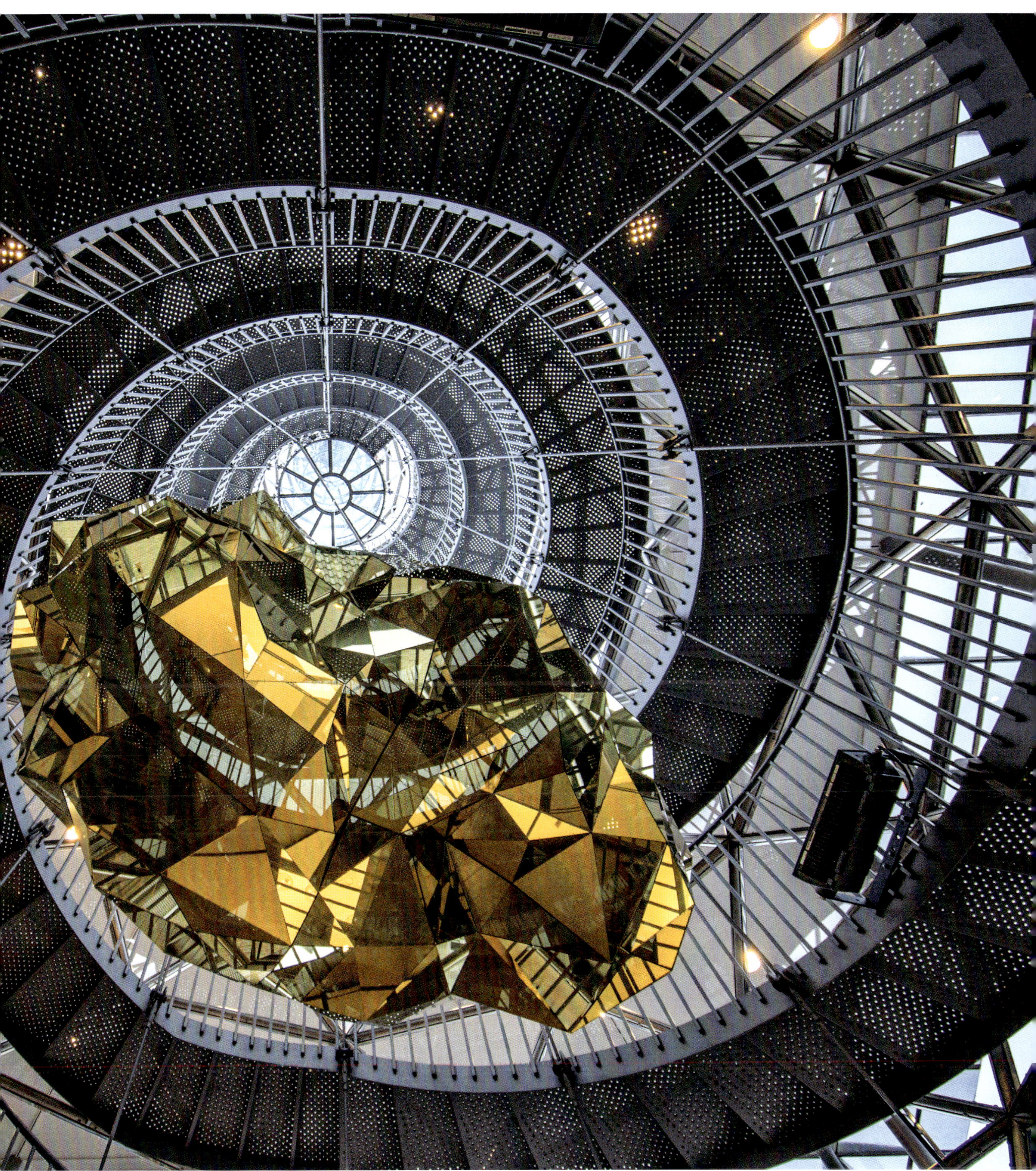

SUPERFLEX is a collective founded in 1993 in Copenhagen, Denmark. The co-founders, Jakob Fenger, Bjørnstjerne Christiansen and Rasmus Rosengren Nielsen, have always been concerned with collaboration, and their projects span many artistic practices including public works, installations and painting, but also performance and the creation of plant nurseries. They were invited to make work for Tate Modern's 2017 Hyundai Commission and two works were sited in the vast hall. *One Two Three Swing!* saw part of the hall and exterior sites installed with a giant swing system, while the Turbine Hall was the site of *And Yet It Moves/Pound Sterling*. The work references Galileo's alleged comment 'And yet it moves' after he was forced to retract his statement that the Earth moved around the sun. SUPERFLEX posit that the current orthodoxy is capitalism and they made a large mirrored silvered pendulum (following the example of Galileo, who explored pendulums in his early work) that swung across a carpet made in the colours of international banknotes. Viewers lay on the carpet gazing up at the swinging pendulum and saw that the orb did indeed move.

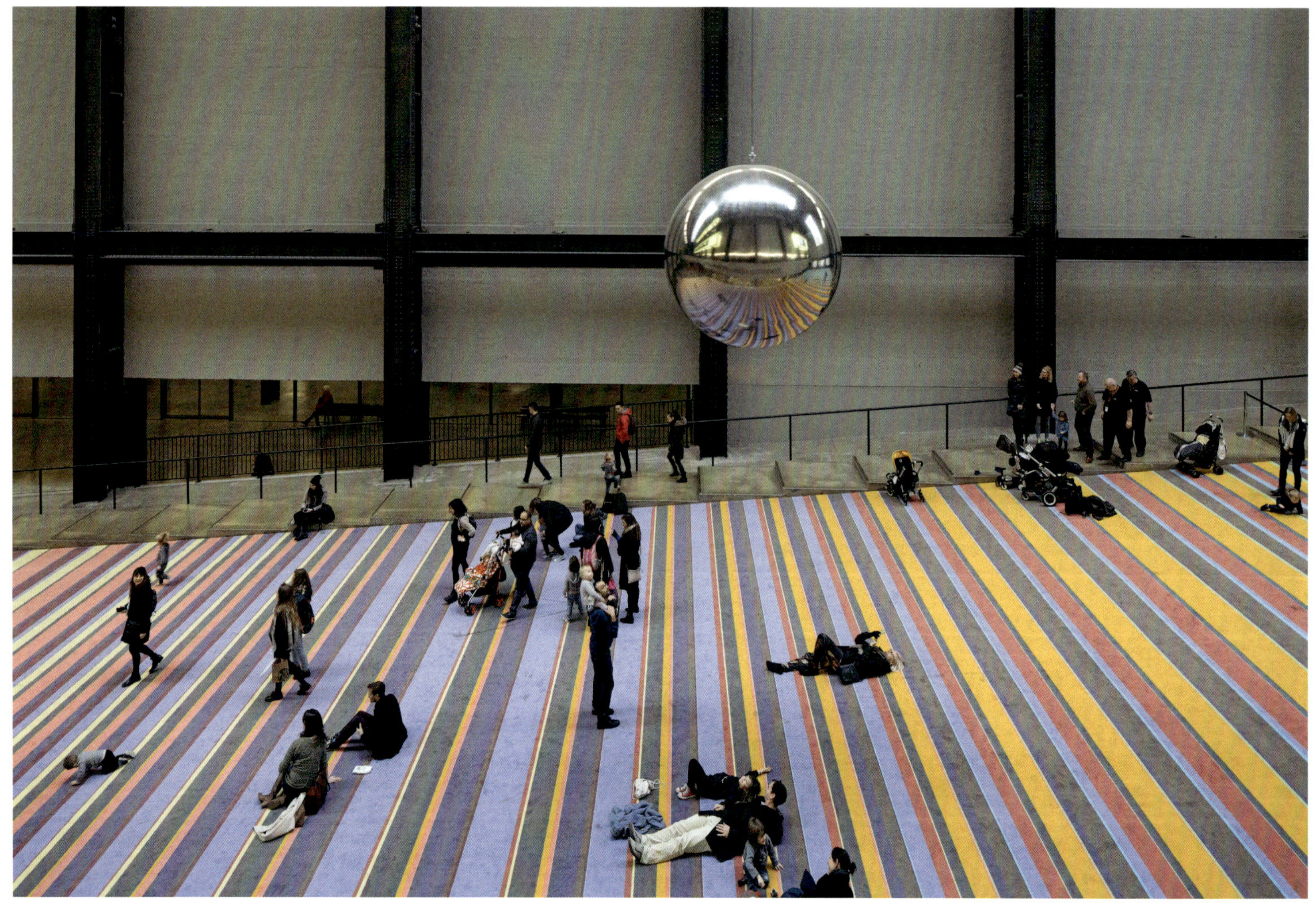

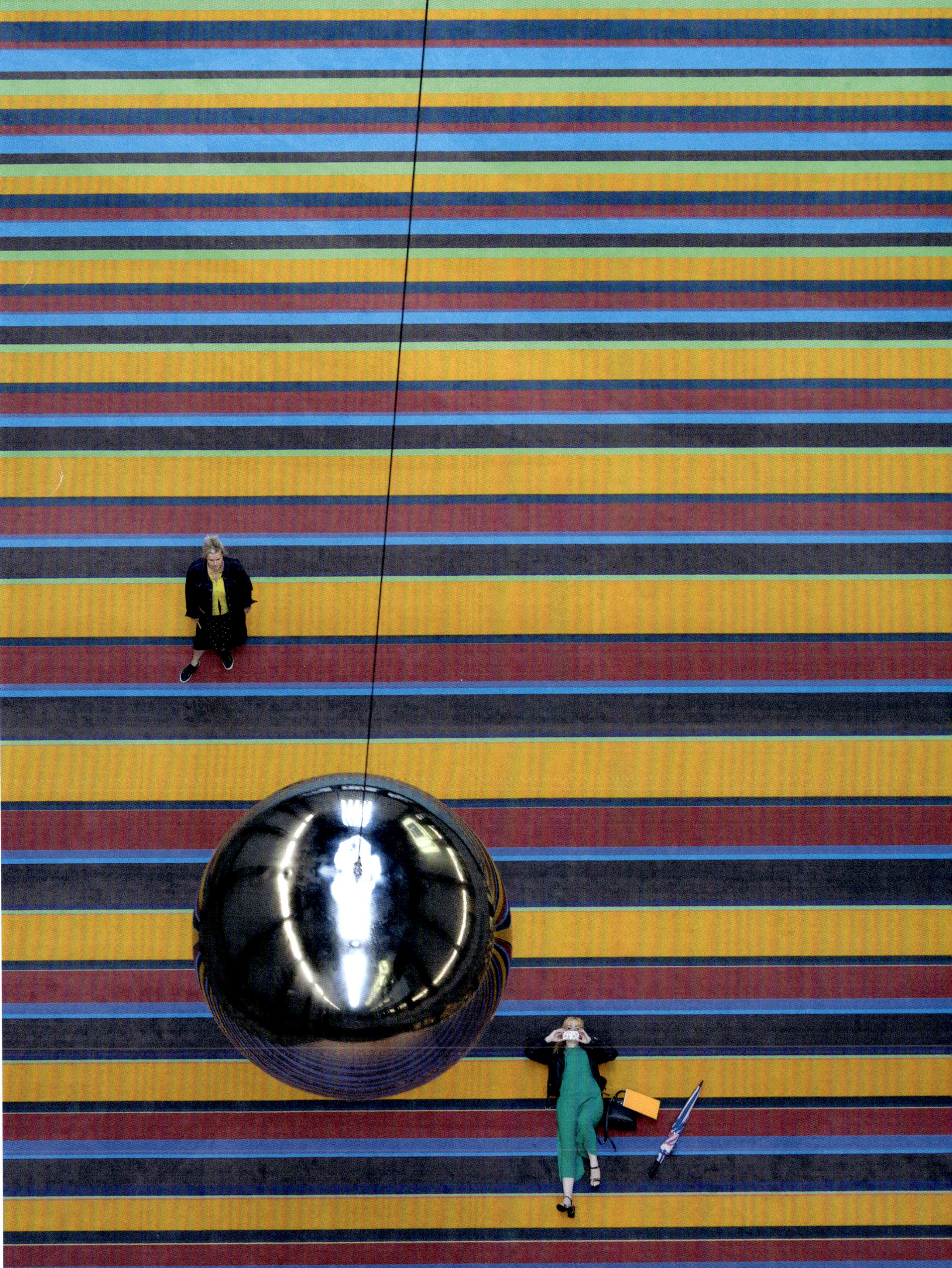

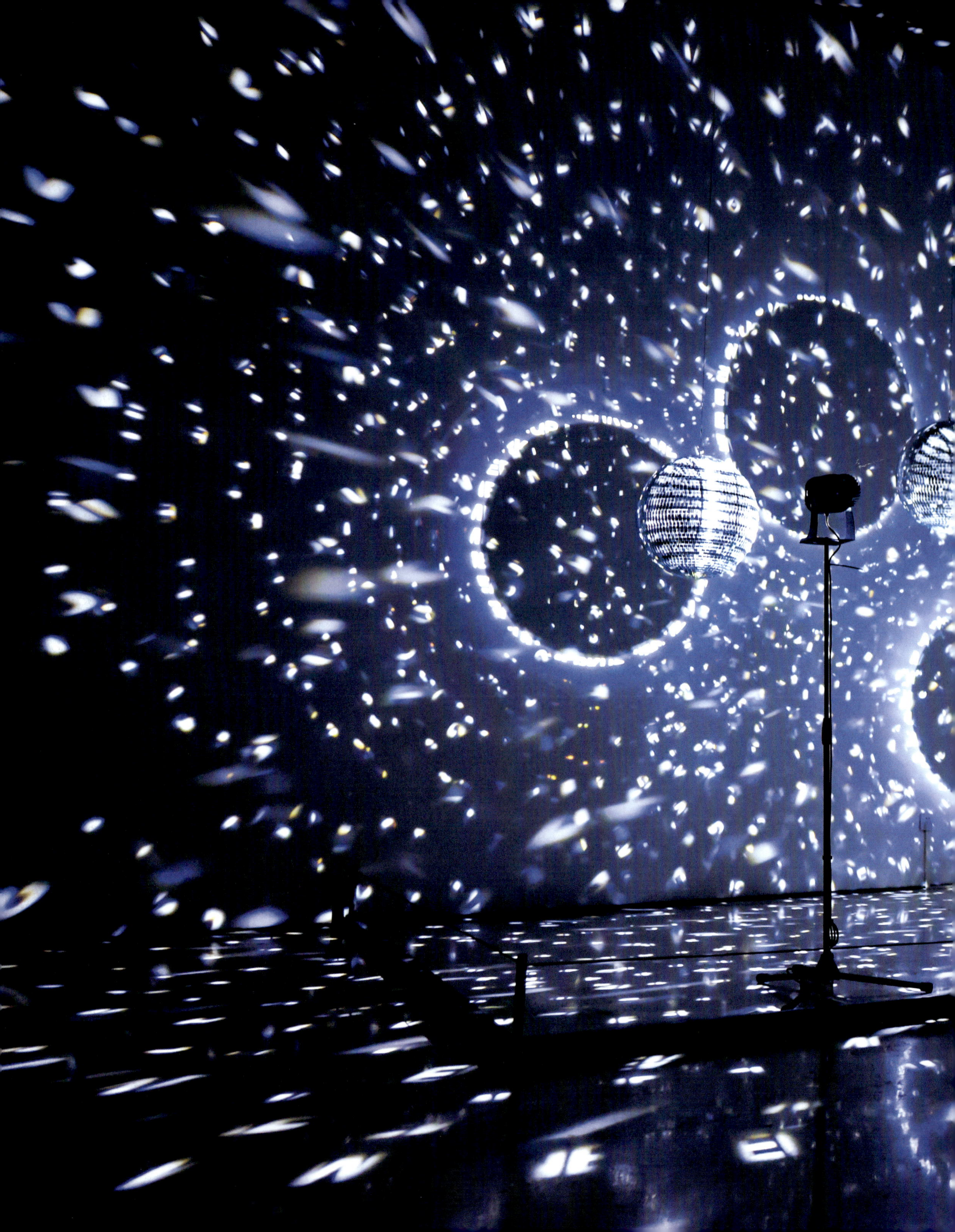

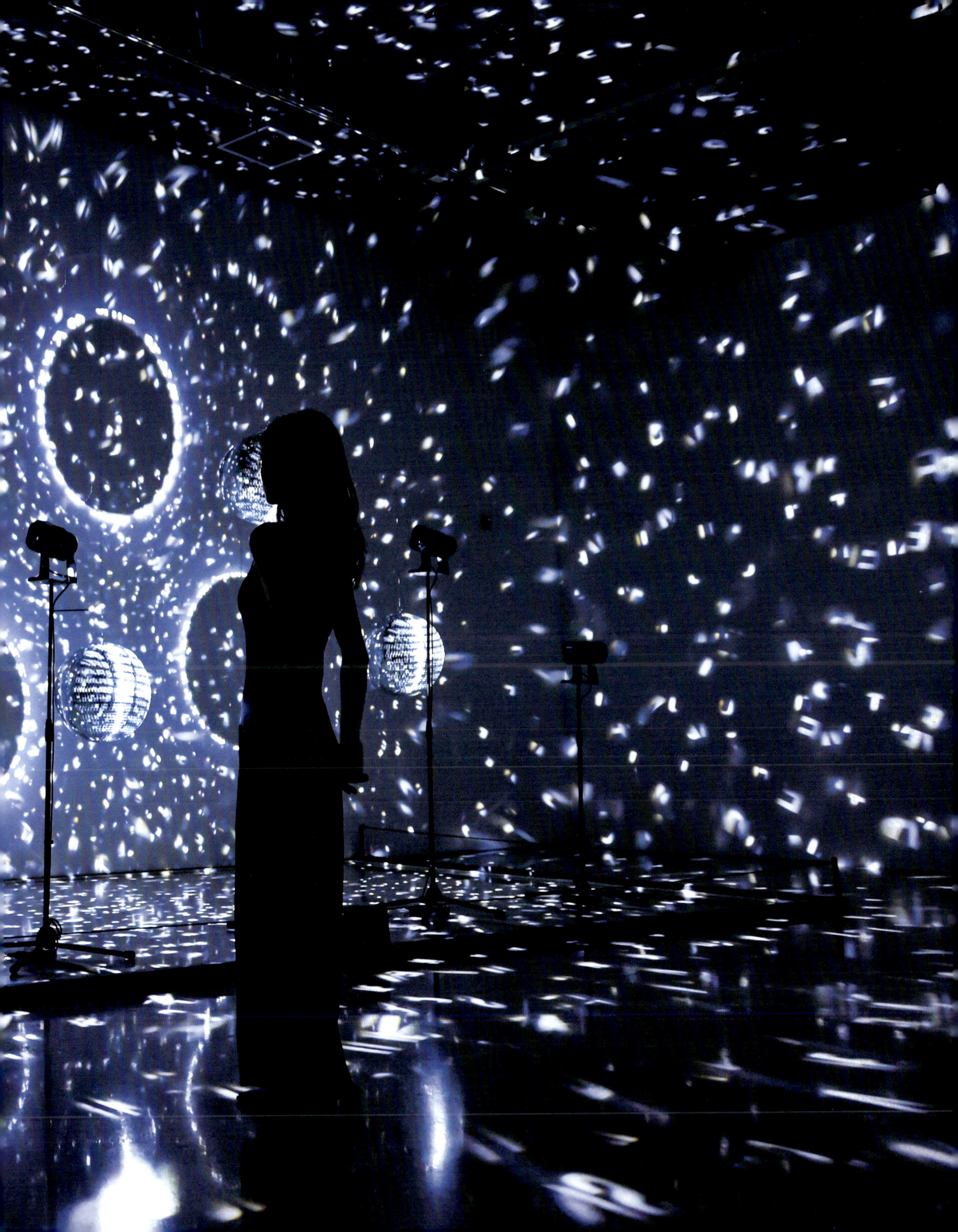

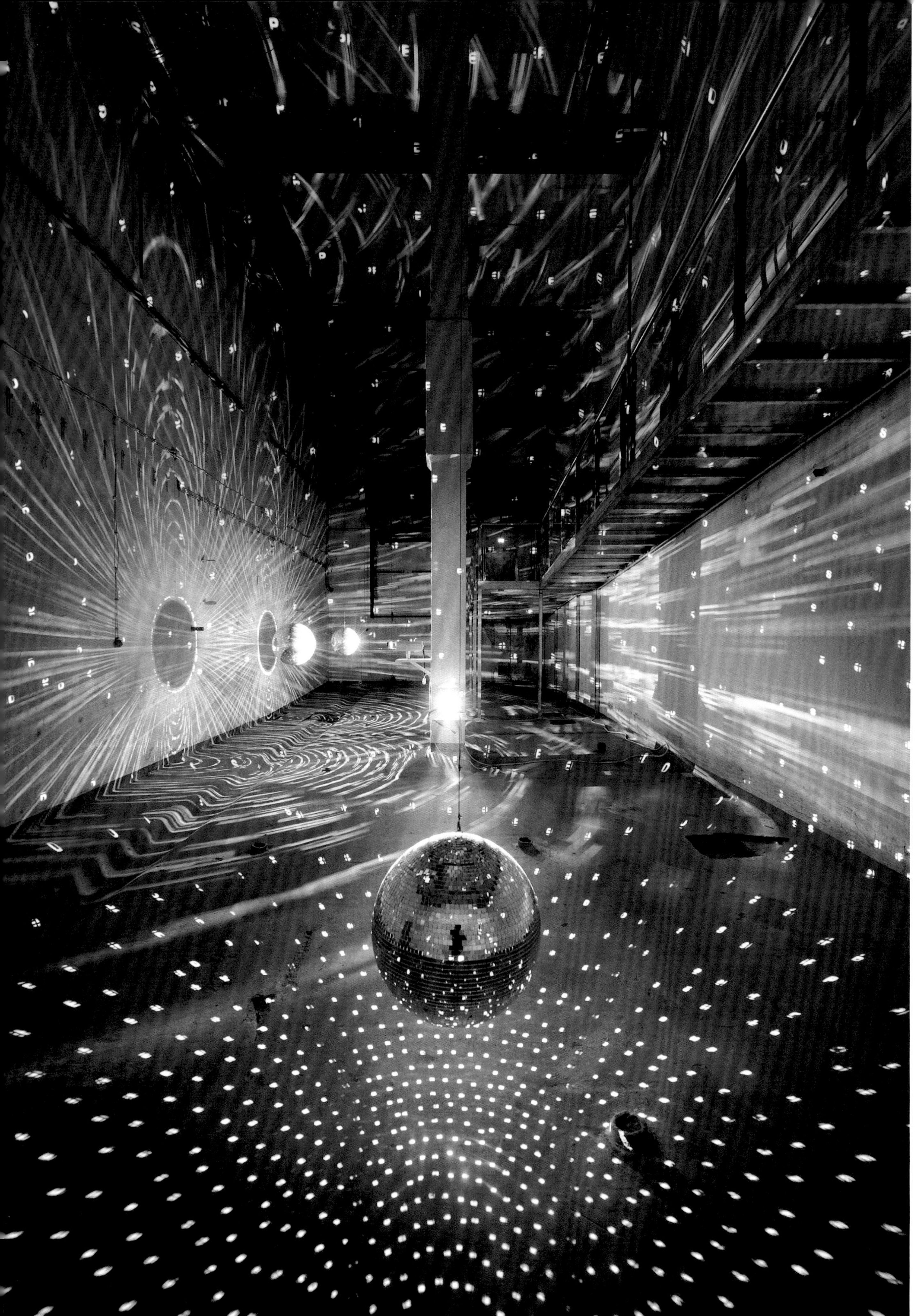

German conceptual artist **MISCHA KUBALL**'s (b. 1959) *space – speech – speed* (below and opposite) was originally made for the Power Plant in Toronto in 1998 and has been shown in many venues across the globe. Completely remade for each site, the work interacted with the architecture of each exhibition room differently. All the installations featured one still and two revolving mirror balls in a dark room. Projected onto them were the words 'space', 'speech' and 'speed', which reflected back around the room, drenching it with letters made of light and creating a visual rhythm that viewers had to work hard to read. Their own bodies and shadows interrupted and interacted with Kuball's conceptual imagery. Similarly, in *five planets* (previous spread), five rotating mirror balls reflected the names of five planets, often inducing feelings of vertigo and disorientation in viewers and evoking a physical sense of the vastness of the cosmos.

Japanese artist **YAYOI KUSAMA** (b. 1929) has been making work for more than eighty years across a wide variety of media. She is perhaps best known for her distinctive use of polka dots and for her 'infinity mirror rooms'. In the Instagram age, images of young and old visitors to these rooms taking a selfie must number in the hundreds of thousands. Any web search will bring up hundreds of such images, so fixed in the cultural imagination have these works become. Since the first *Infinity Mirror Room*, made for the 'Floor Show' (1965) at New York's Castellane Gallery, more than twenty others have been created. These works have been sited across the globe, including in New York, where the work overleaf was shown. Kusama has indicated that these rooms, with their endless, disorientating reflections, are like a form of obliteration of the self and possibly a simulation of death, yet one with the promise of some sort of rebirth.

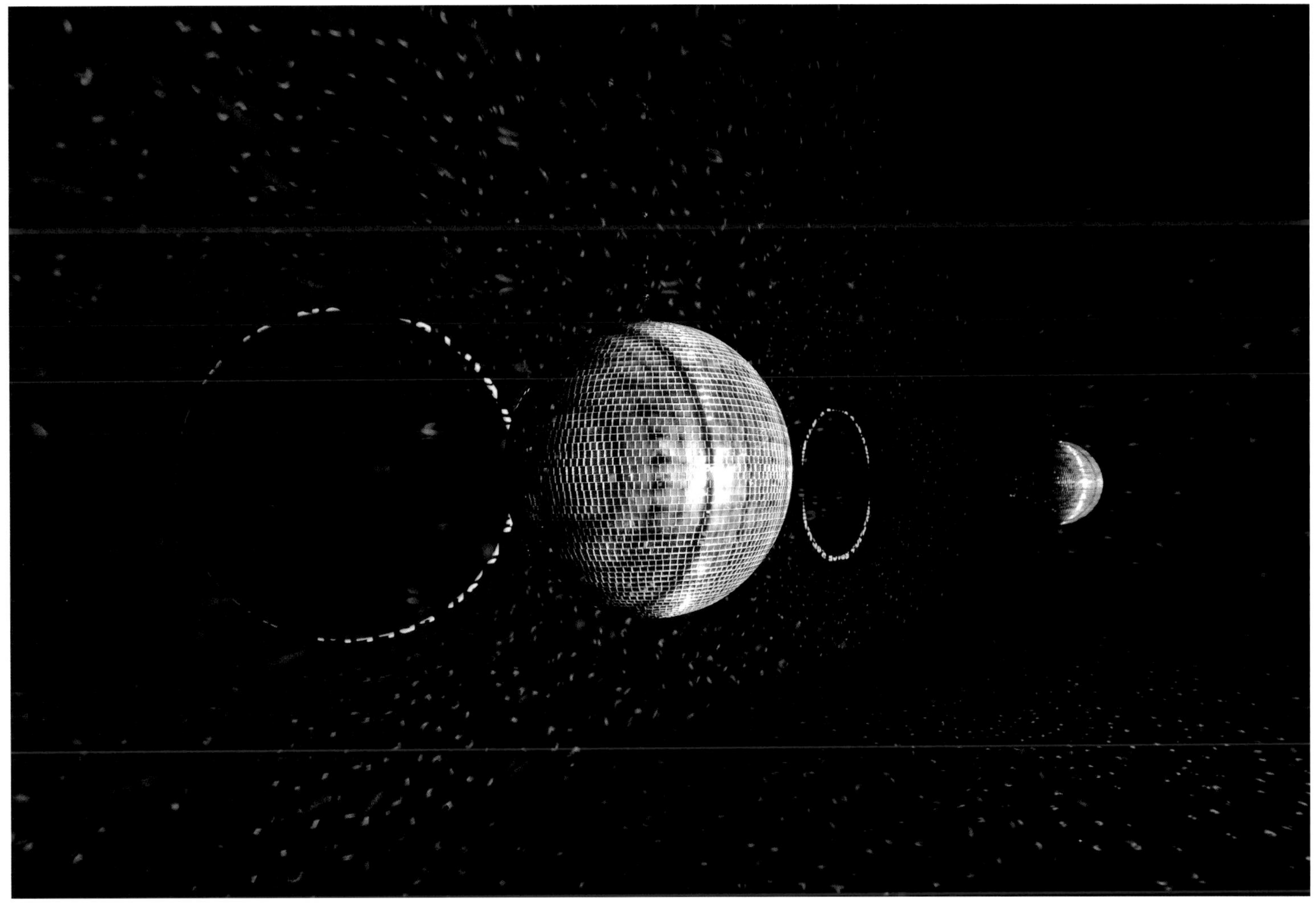

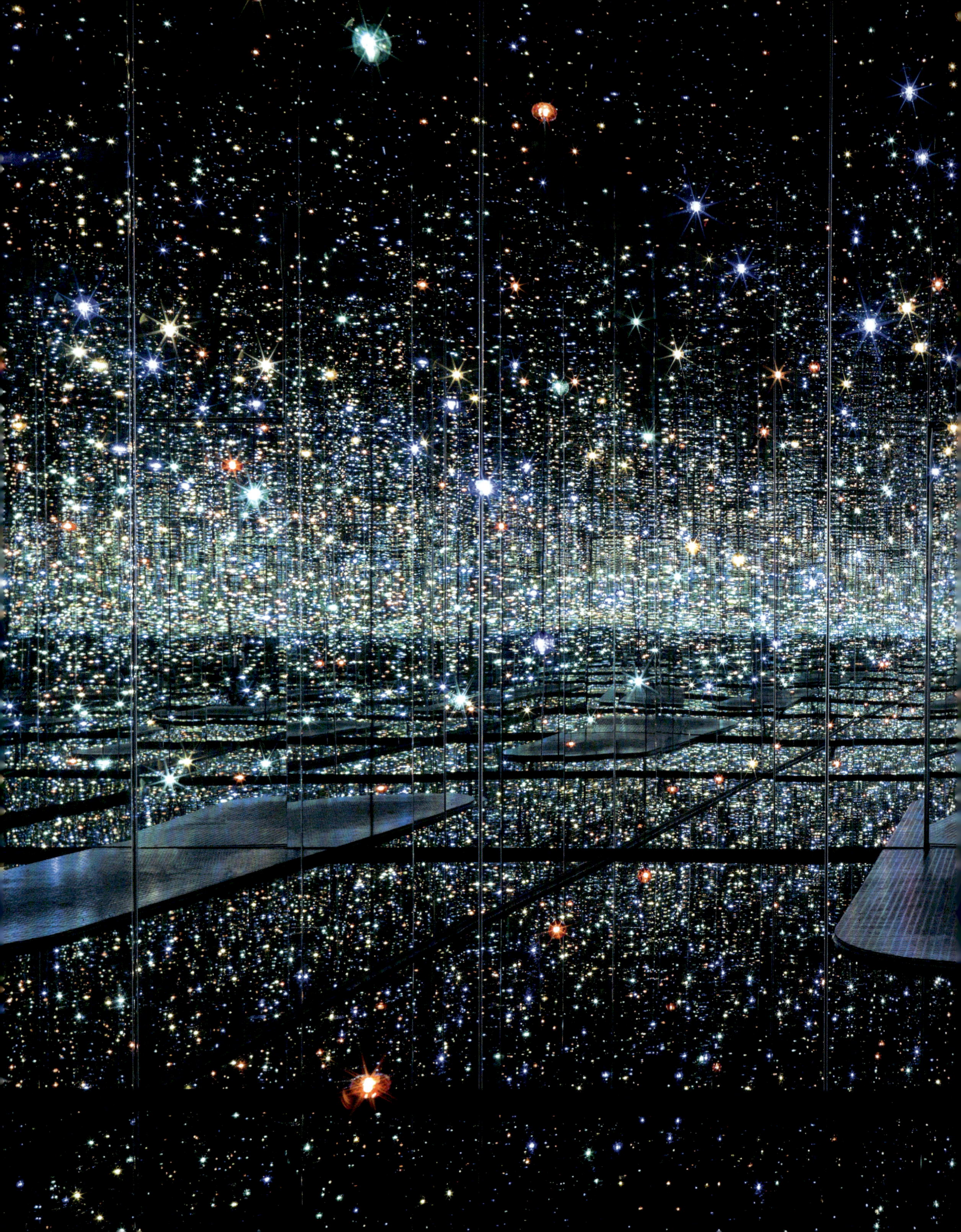

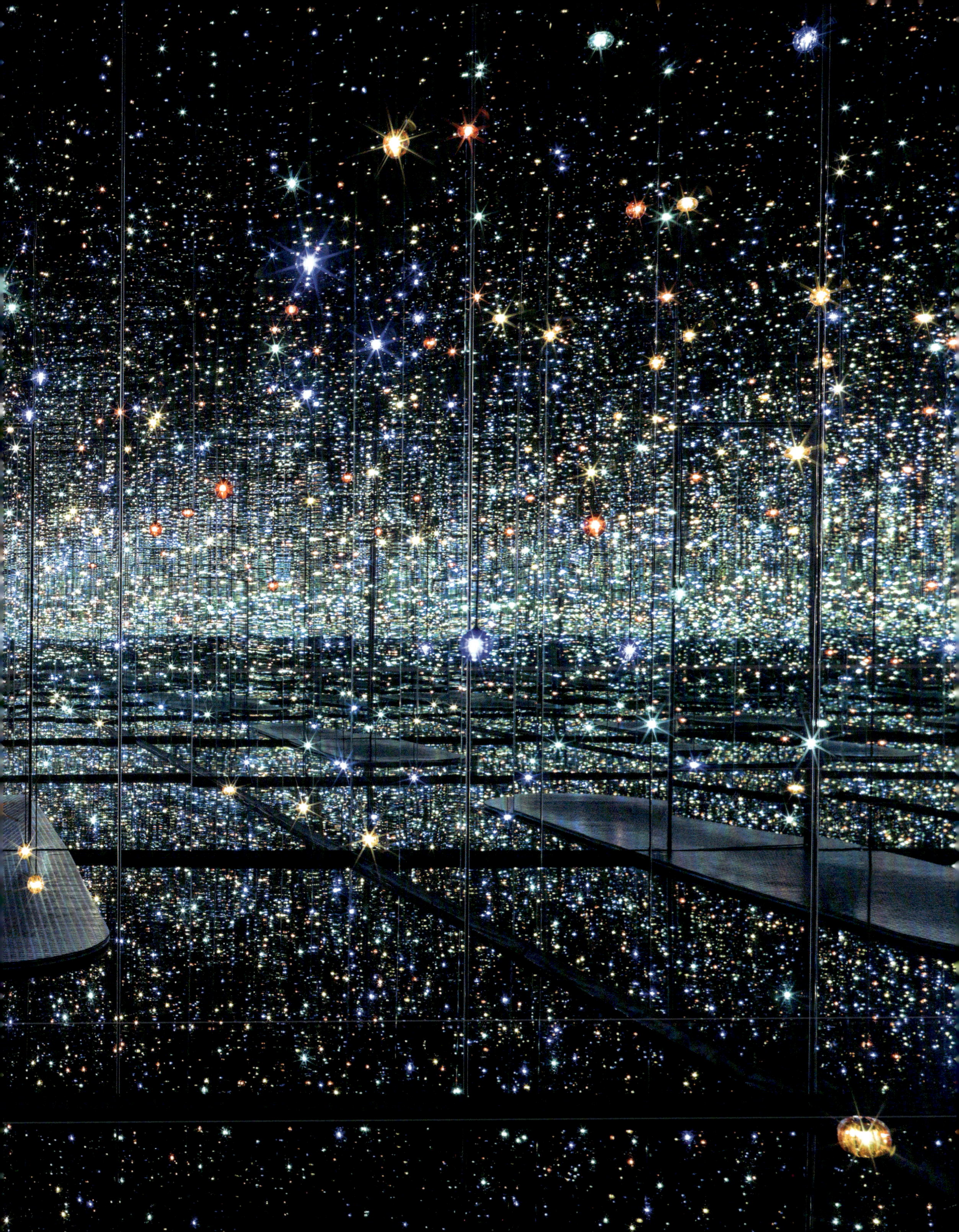

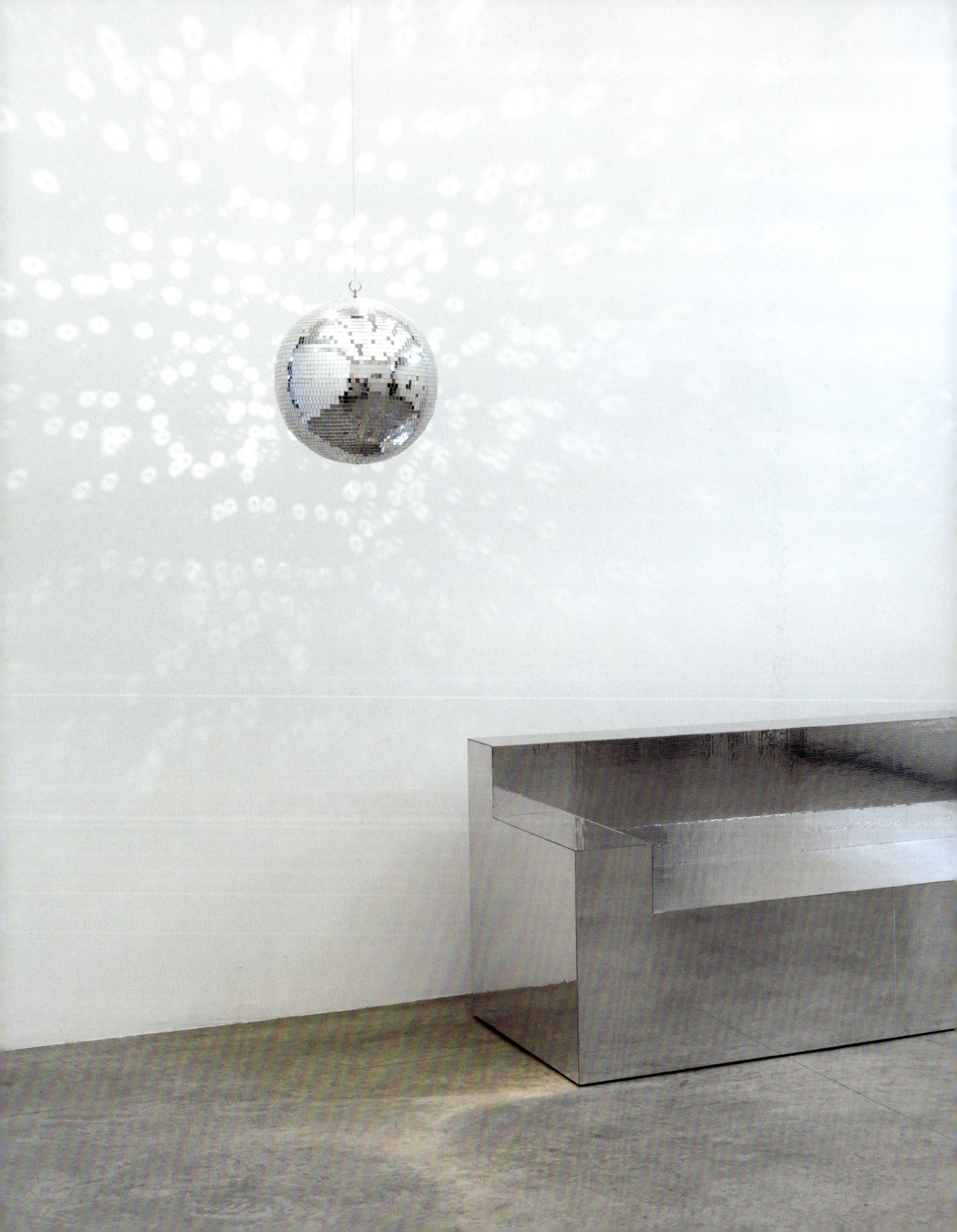

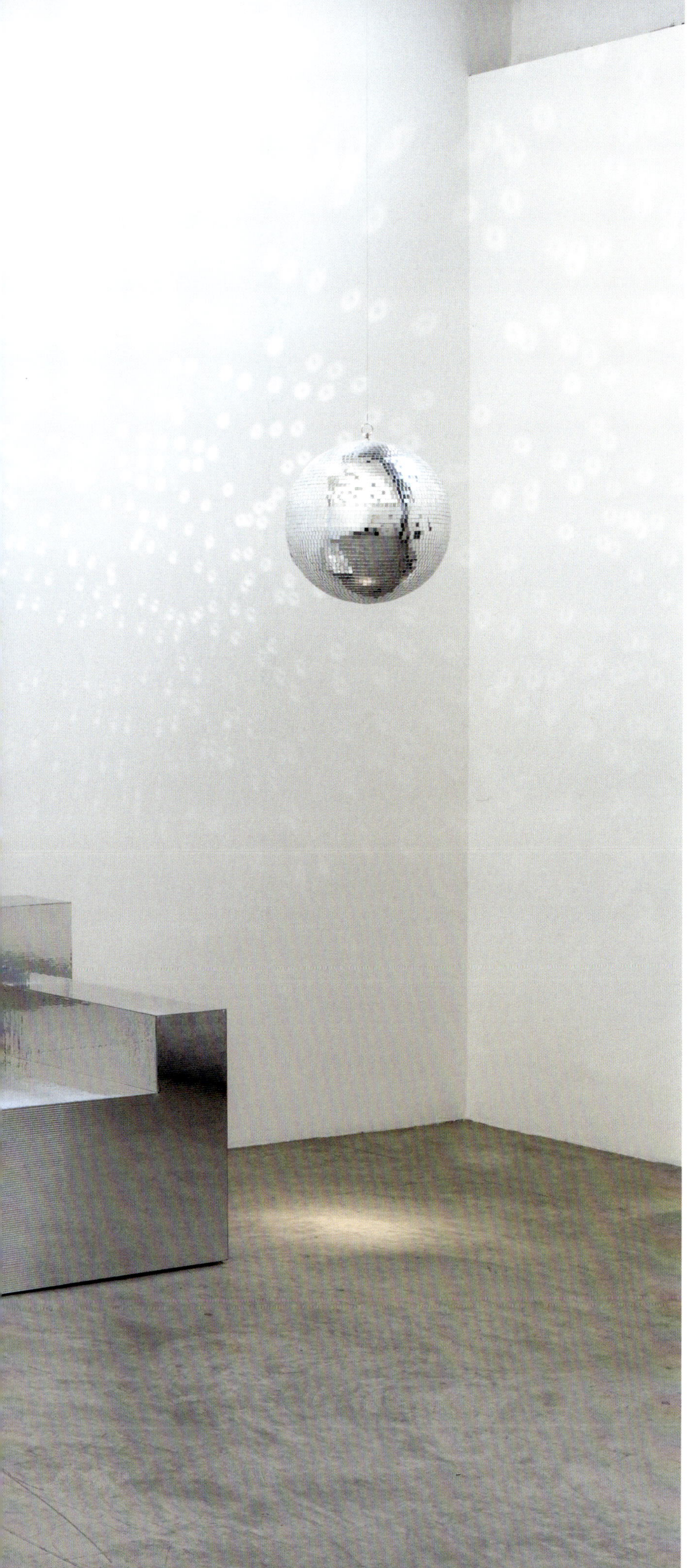

Swiss artist **JOHN ARMLEDER** (b. 1948) has been using mirrored disco balls for some time in his work. *FS 271* from 1992 features two, while his 2019 immersive installation at the Schirin Kunsthalle in Frankfurt saw him place twenty large mirrored disco balls in the main rotunda, with the facing windows covered in reflecting foil so that their number seemed infinite. Armleder says that the work animates the surroundings and 'you are put into it because you have the reflection of you' in each ball. By taking iconic objects such as the disco balls and placing them within his work he aims to disrupt the everyday and has said that all works of art have 'more than one identity' based on the context in which they are seen.

FS 271, 1992
Wood, mirrored plastic laminate,
two mirrored disco balls, spotlights
2.05 × 2.2 × 0.8 m (6¾ × 7¼ × 2²/₅ ft)

Los Angeles-based American artist **SUZY POLING** (b. 1975) works across many media, including video and sound, and she also makes abstract conceptual light and mirror installations such as *Mirror Crystal System*. The work features a floor-based moving mirror sculpture made up of triangular sections sitting on a large reflective Mylar base. The object slowly rotates, reflecting light and the video projection onto the surrounding walls and onto viewers, who can also see themselves in the mirror object. They are not outside of the work, becoming a part of the immersive environment. Poling's *Primary Optic Shift* (2019) uses a similar vocabulary to create a largely pink and purple space, introducing colour into the mix of reflections. These works 'describe a changing abstracted scene in space or light painting that transforms slowly through a process of rotation'.

Mirror Crystal System, 2016
Cult/Aimee Friberg Exhibitions,
San Francisco, California, USA
Mirror, Mylar, video projection
Dimensions variable

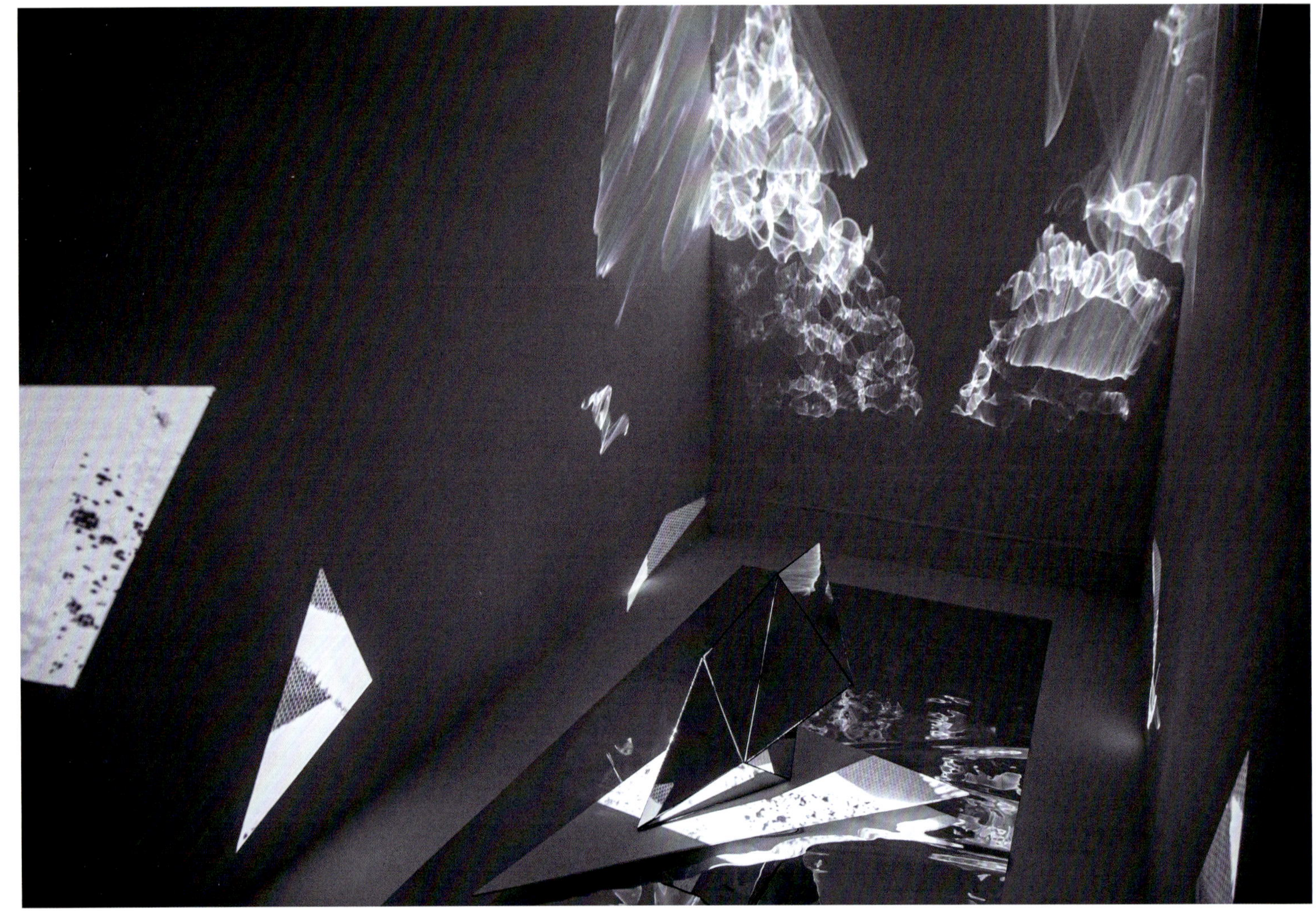

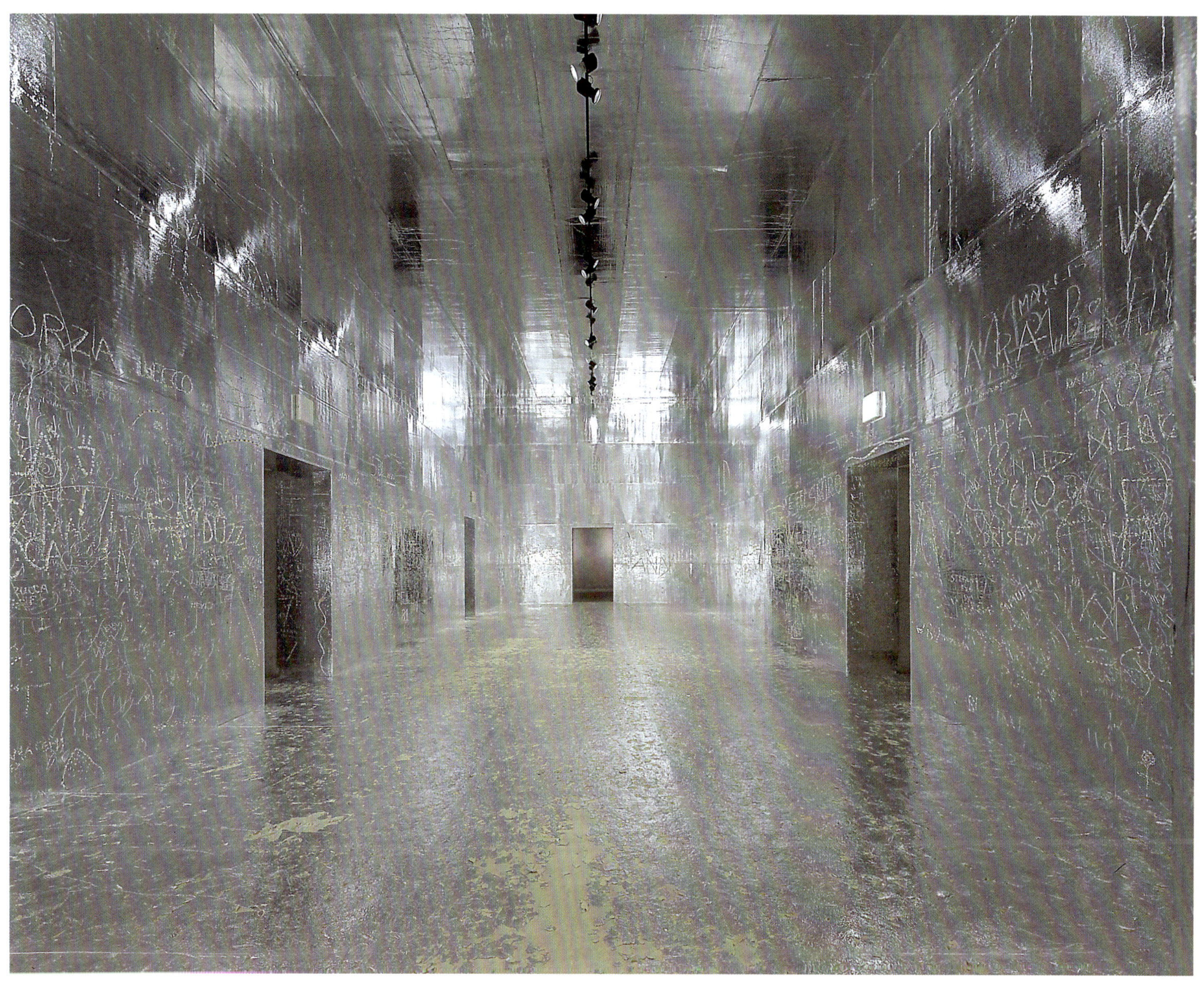

Untitled, 2001
Installation view: *Rudolf Stingel*, Museo
di Arte Moderna e Contemporanea, Palazzo
delle Albere, Trento, Italy, Mar–July 2001
All surfaces of a room covered with
Celotex Tuff-R
Dimensions variable

Italian artist **RUDOLF STINGEL** (b. 1956)
is known for his monumental conceptual
monochrome paintings and installations.
These are in contrast to his extremely
large figurative paintings based on found
imagery. Many of his installations are
all-encompassing (immersive) spaces
that alter the existing architecture via
the application of patterned carpets or
mirrored board. For his *Untitled* work
in Trento he completely lined the space
with Celotex insulation board, which

reflected the viewers as they engaged
with the space. They were allowed to carve
into the board's surface or add to it in any
way they thought appropriate. In other
projects people have added paint, sticky
notes and many other objects. Stingel sees
the space as completed only when the
visitor is in the space, activating it, marking
it or simply observing the relics of other
viewers' actions.

ISAAC JULIEN (b. 1960) is a British installation artist and filmmaker. His *Stones Against Diamonds* reflects the Italian-born Brazilian architect Lina Bo Bardi's book of the same name, which documents her writings and ideas about the use of semi-precious stones as opposed to diamonds. Julien's installation, which exists in a five- and a ten-screen version (see right at York Art Gallery) features a film he made, inspired by one of Bo Bardi's letters in the book and by her famous helicoidal wooden staircase for the Solar do Unhão in Salvador de Bahía, Brazil (a restored historic site that now houses the Museum of Modern Art of Bahía). Julien made a replica of the staircase on-site in the famous ice caves of the Vatnajökull region in southeast Iceland, where he also filmed actress Vanessa Myrie walking in the frozen landscape. The film makes reference to Bo Bardi's glass and concrete easels, used to hold the installation's screens, which are backed by mirrors. As visitors walk in the space they too can lose sight of the real and the reflected. A five-screen version was installed in the Jerusalem Botanical Gardens in 2021, contrasting the heat of the local environment with the cool of the work.

Stones Against Diamonds (Ice Cave), 2015
Strata – Rock – Dust – Stars exhibition,
York Art Gallery, York, England
10 × 70 in LCD monitors in portrait
with HD playback, glass-backed mirrors
5.1 surround sound
Duration 58 minutes 28 seconds
Plinths size 60 × 60 × 60 cm
(23½ × 23½ × 23½ in)

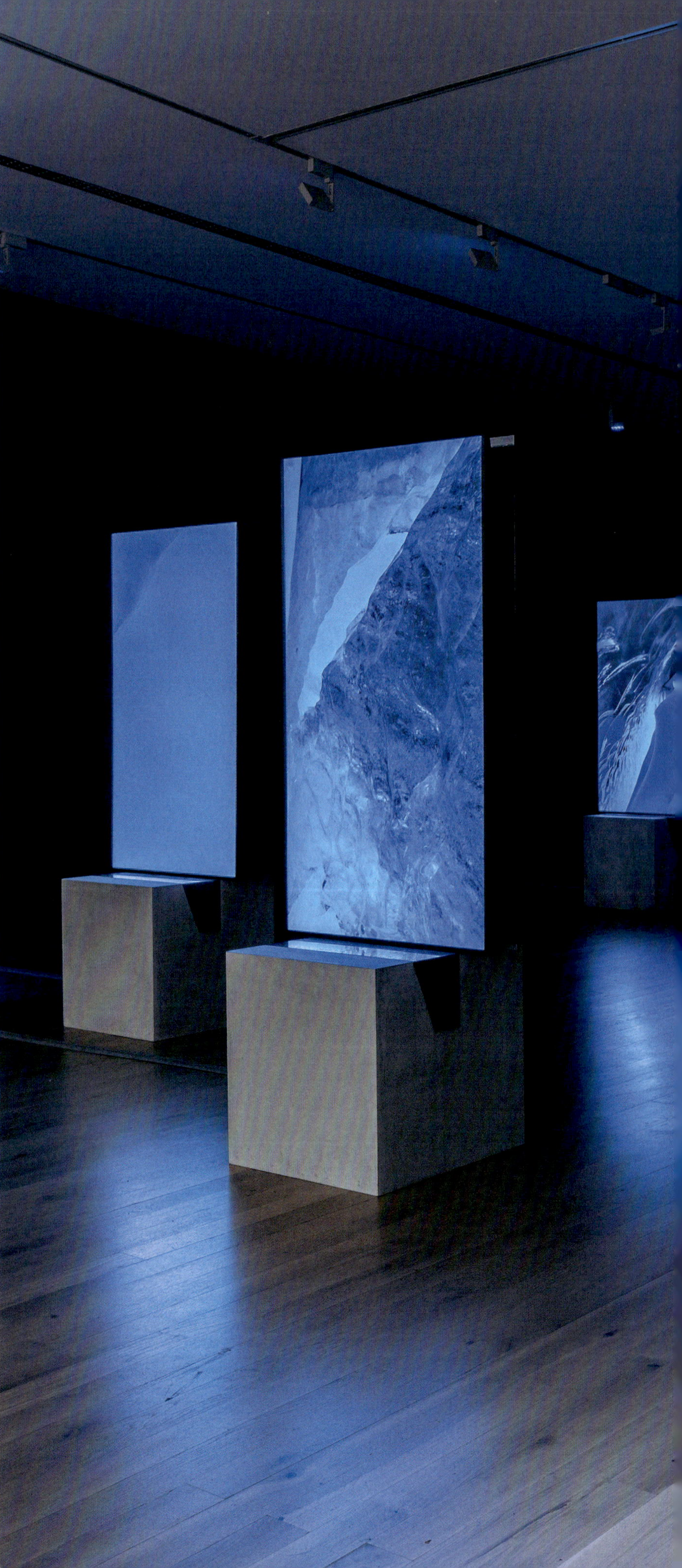

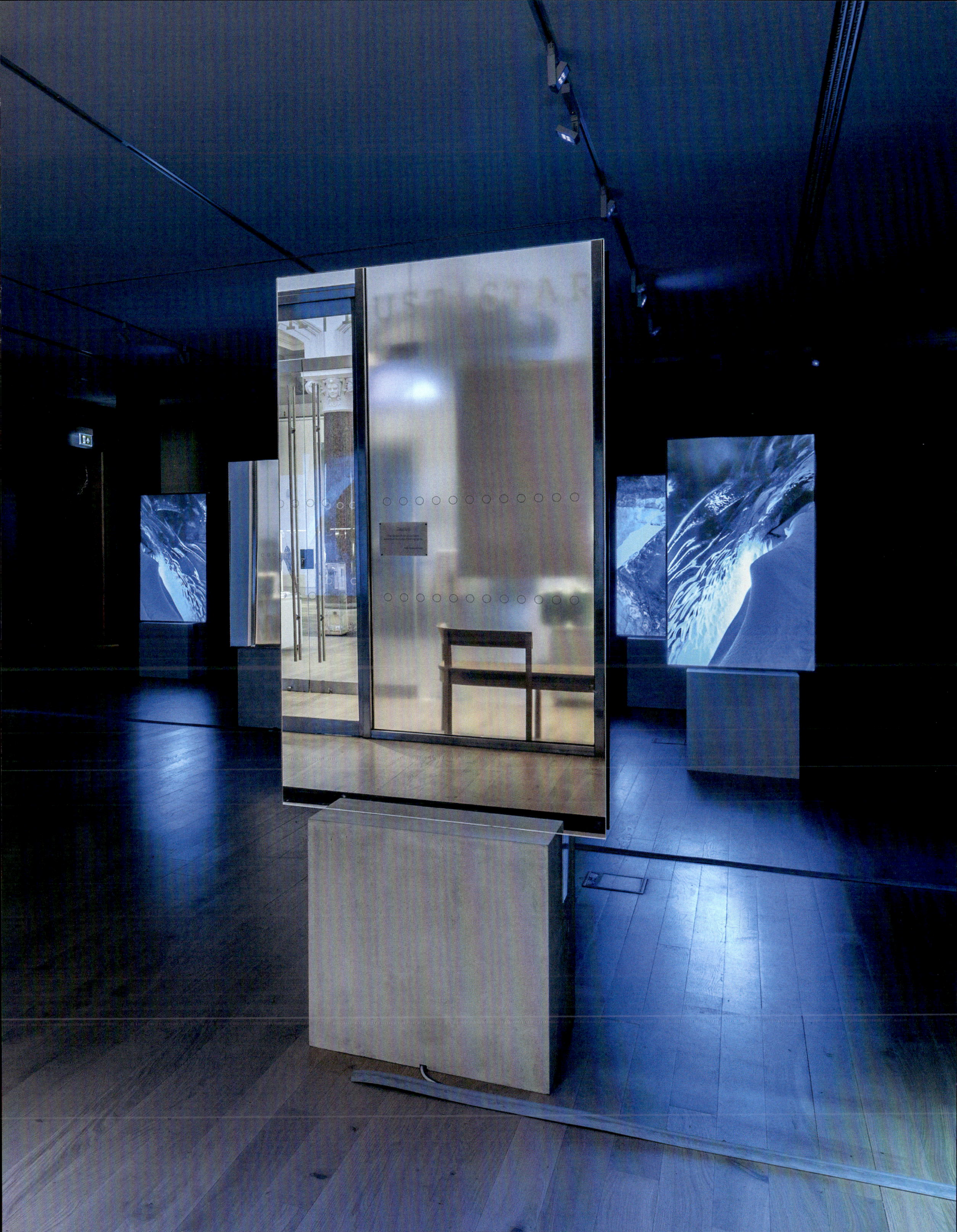

Viewers entered the gallery room where
URS FISCHER's *pond* was installed and
came across an oval-shaped, mirror-calm
surface of water. It reflected the potted
plants that surrounded it, and the viewer
if they peered over it. However, the surface
was not consistently still but had periodic
ripples generated by tiny drops of water
that fell onto the surface, disrupting the
calm image. Fischer (b. 1973), a Swiss
conceptual artist living in the USA who
mainly works with sculpture, often places
disparate objects together so that they
form a new dialogue with themselves
and the viewer.

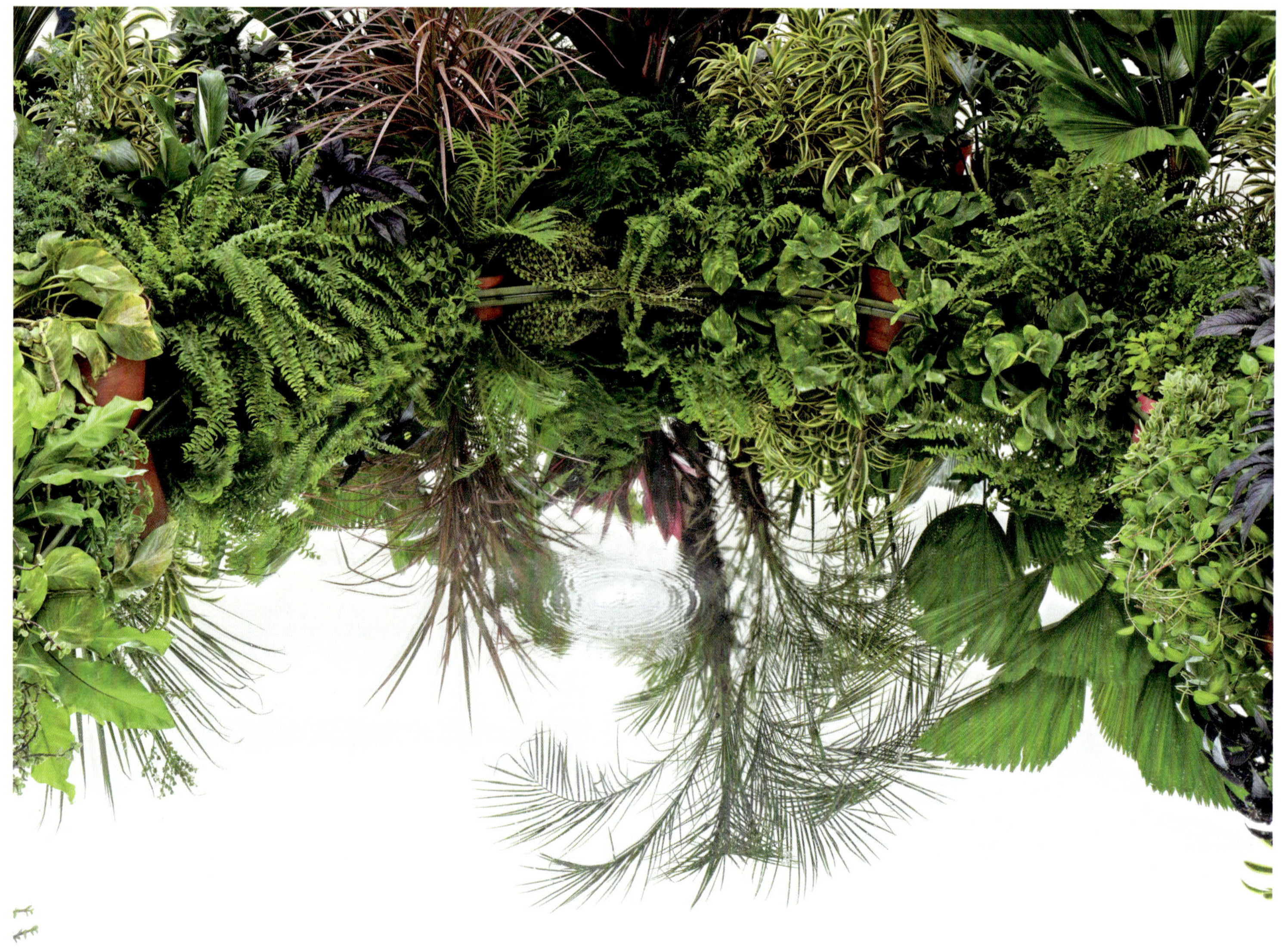

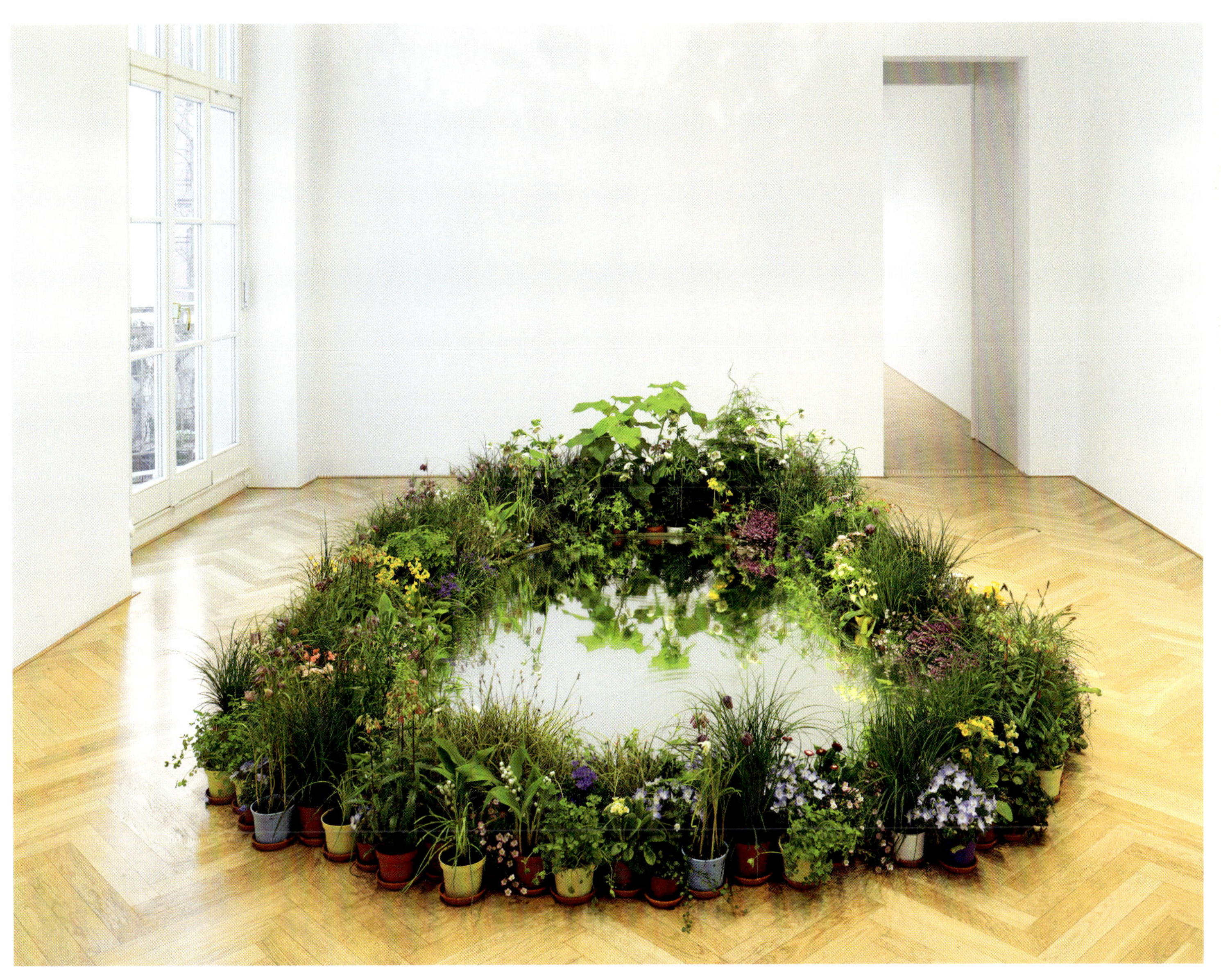

INSTALLATIONS

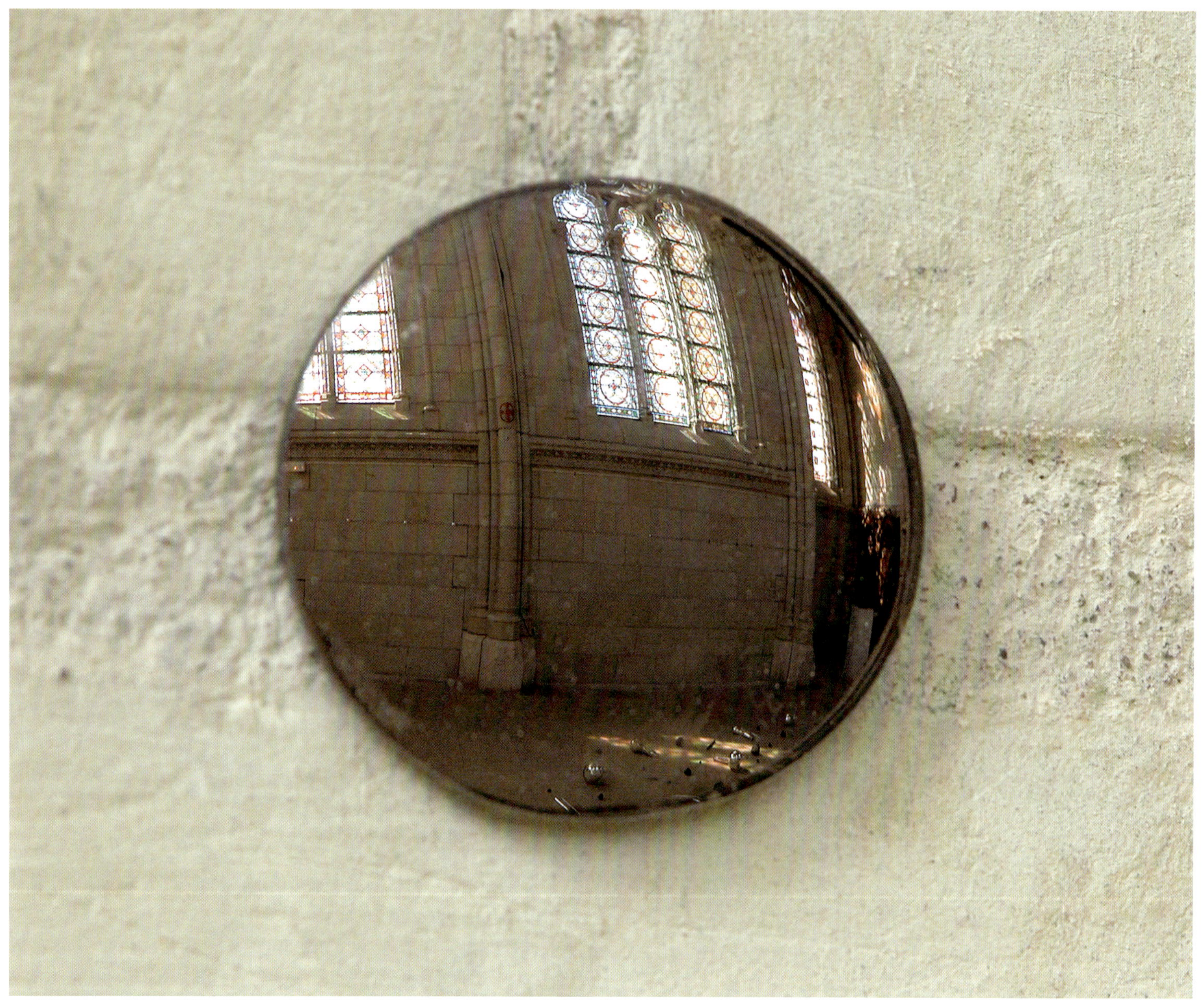

British sculptor **PETER BRIGGS** (b. 1950) lives and works in Tours, France. In 2005 he held a one-man show in the deconsecrated neo-Gothic Joan of Arc chapel in Thouars. Within this building full of history and architectural beauty, Briggs used optics to reflect the space in on itself by mounting a series of tiny curved glass mirrors made from the lenses of second-hand reading glasses, which were fixed directly into the walls at regular intervals. In stopping to examine these one by one, viewers inadvertently replayed the actions performed when attending the Stations of the Cross, a devotional path associated with the contemplation of the Passion of Christ. These mirrors reflected the chancel and the other mirrors placed at eye level, as well as the floor piece. The latter consisted of silvered blown-glass vessels, carved pebble-shaped black stones and drawn glass and stove-enamelled steel rods all scattered irregularly over a large area. All of this was visible in each tiny mirror.

Installation Thouars, 2005
Chapelle Jeanne d'Arc, Thouars, France
Black glass, silvered glass, oval mirrored lenses, polished obsidian, stone, enamelled steel, drawn glass rods
Dimensions variable

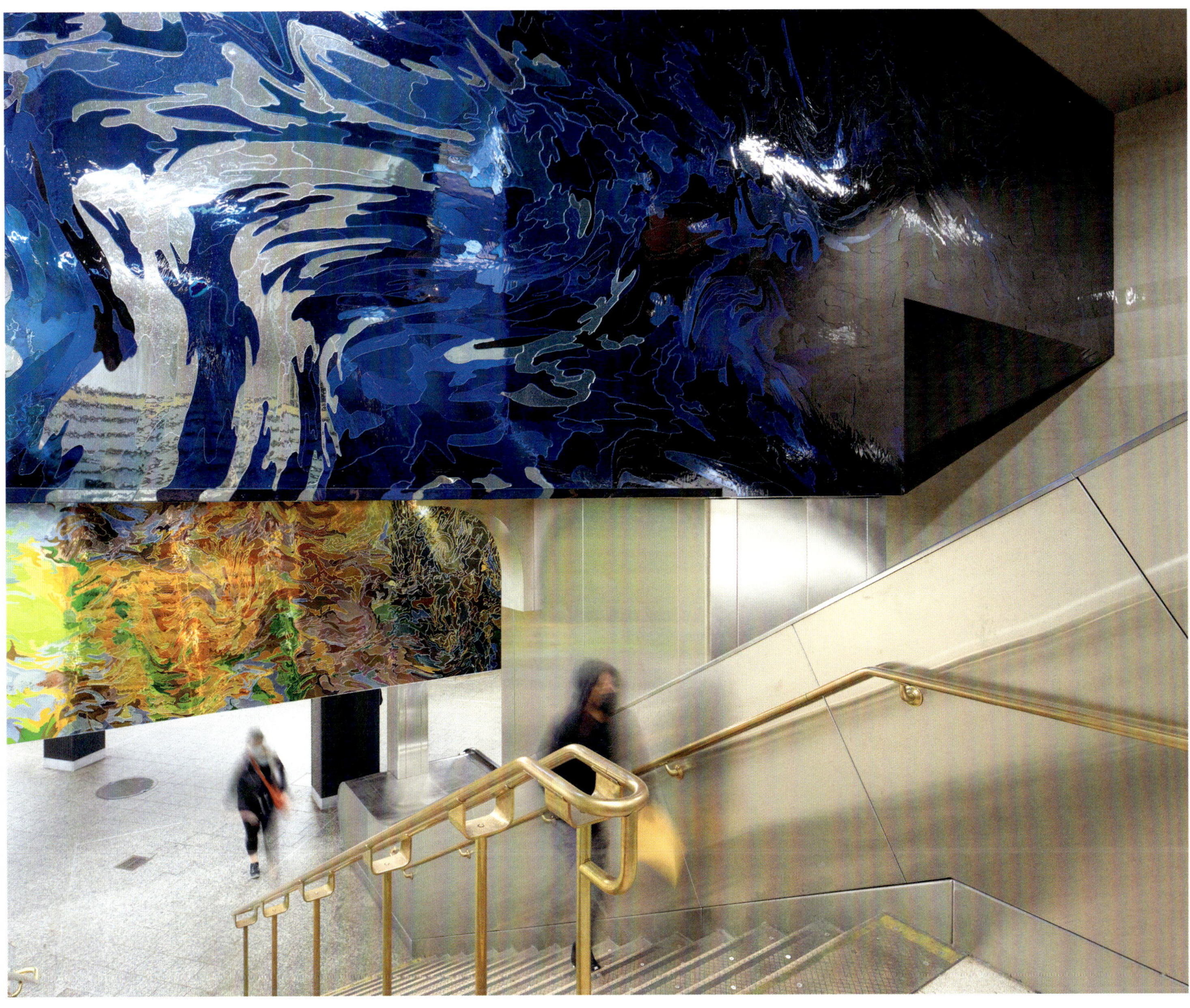

American artist **JIM HODGES**'s (b. 1957) massive mirror work *I dreamed a world and called it Love* was originally made to fit perfectly into New York's Gladstone Gallery (overleaf), reflecting itself, the viewers and the polished concrete floor, which also shimmered with coloured light from the piece. The immersive installation was made up of thousands of interlocking pieces of mirror, giving it the feel of organic camouflage, surrounding the room in 360 degrees of reflection.

Hodges was then commissioned by the MTA (Metropolitan Transportation Authority) to install a permanent version of the work in New York's Grand Central Station in 2021 (above). Sited above the stairs and escalators at the busy 42nd Street subway entrance, the work reflects back the constantly shifting flux of travellers in its dazzling organic mosaic.

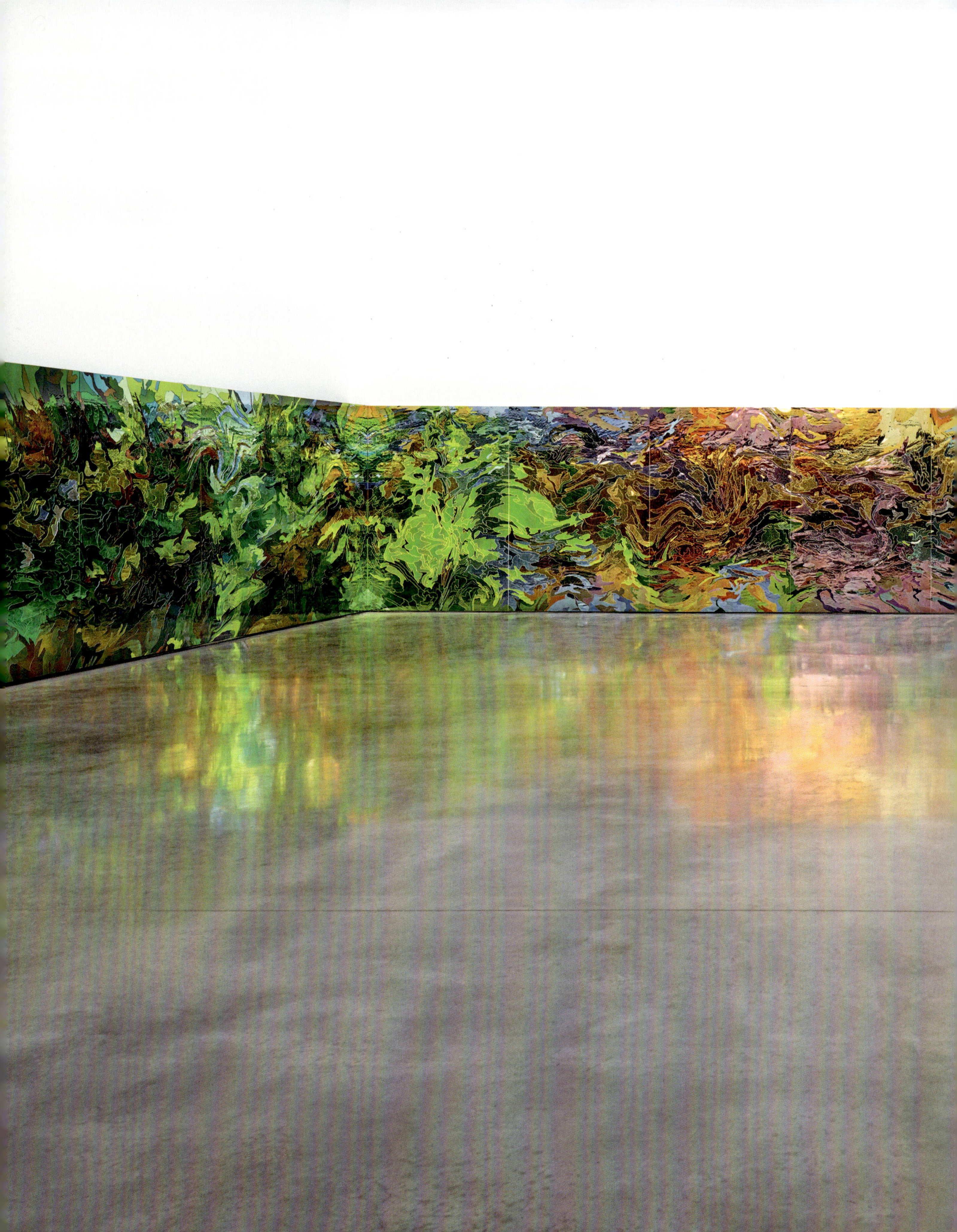

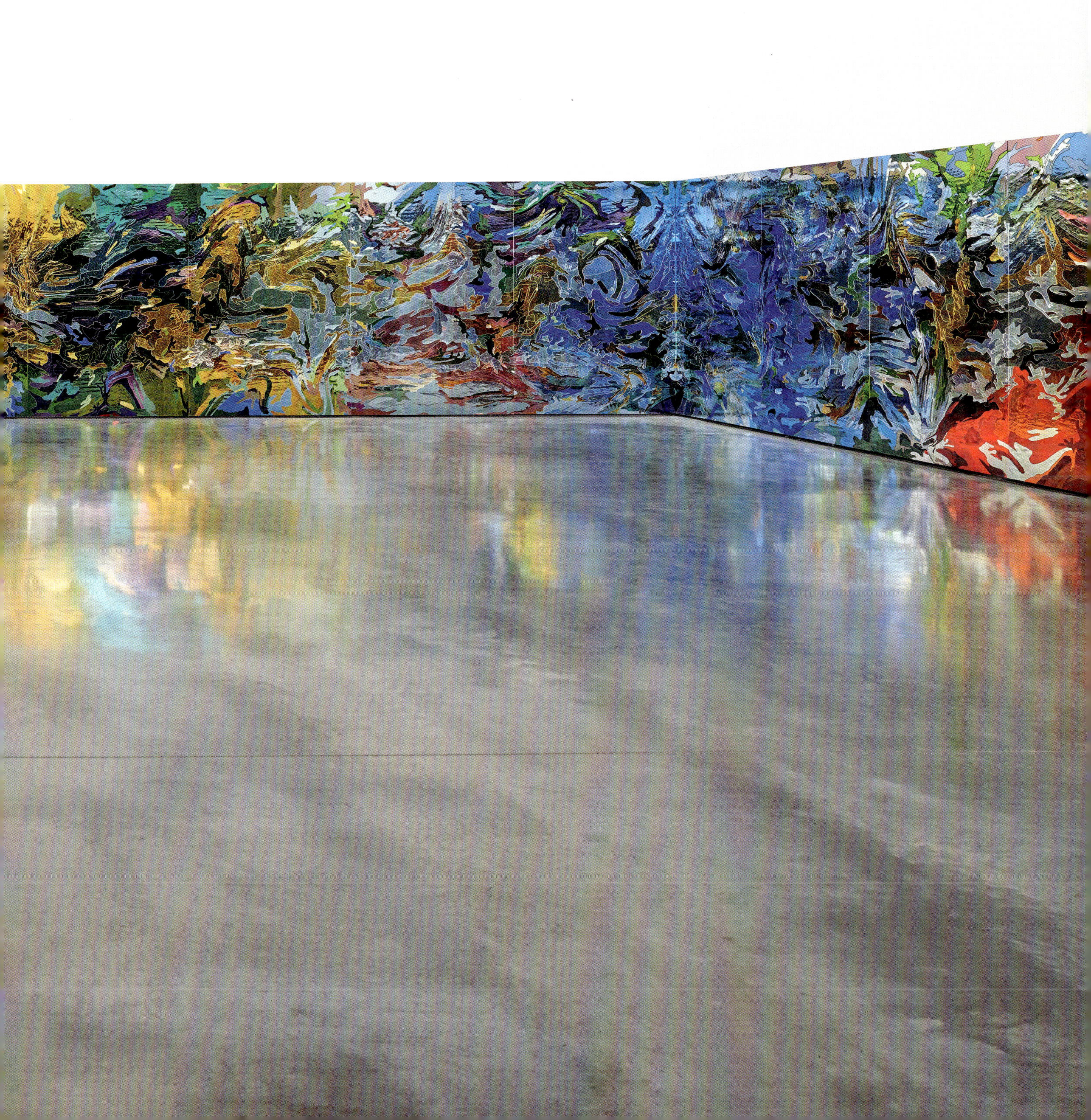

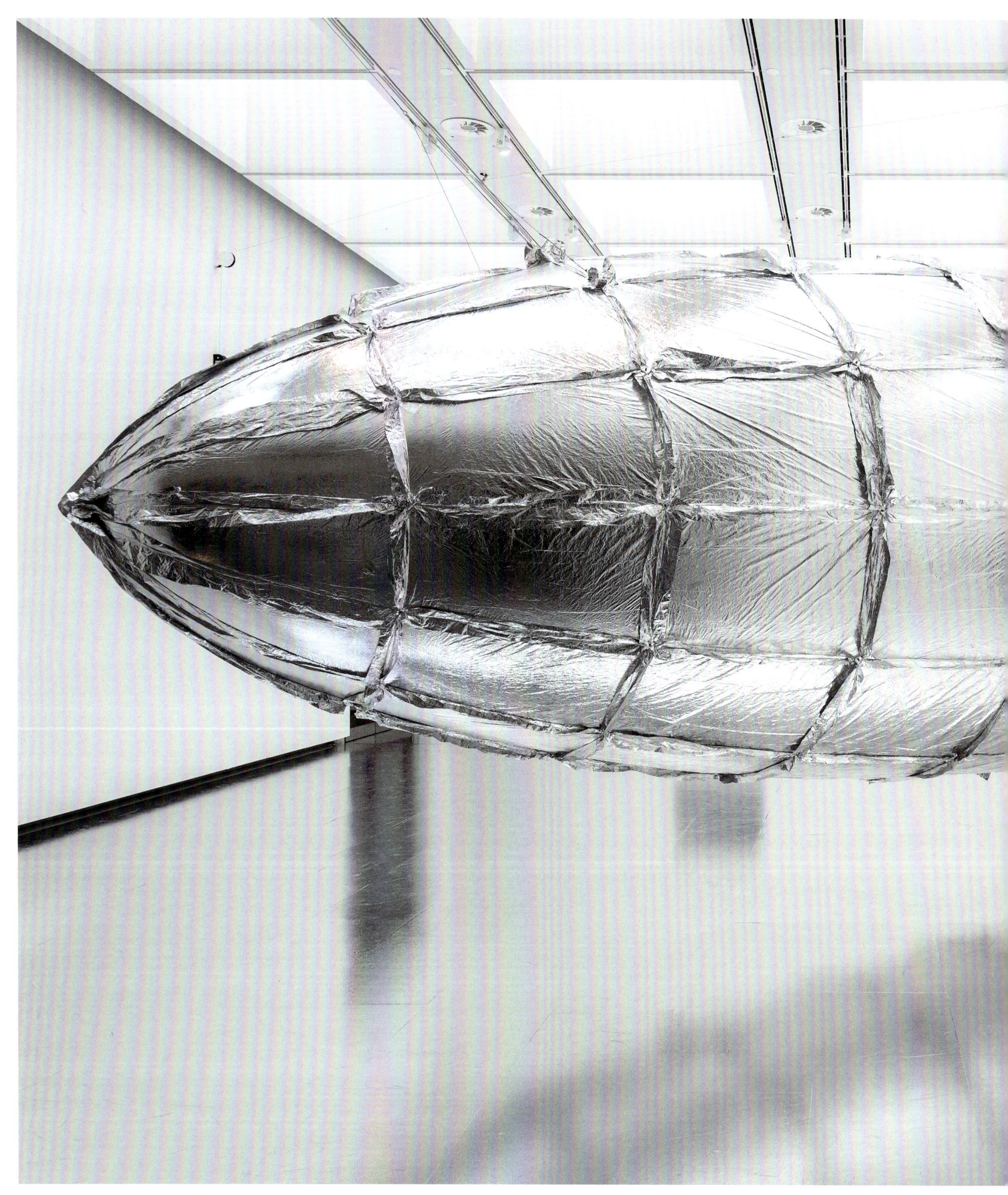

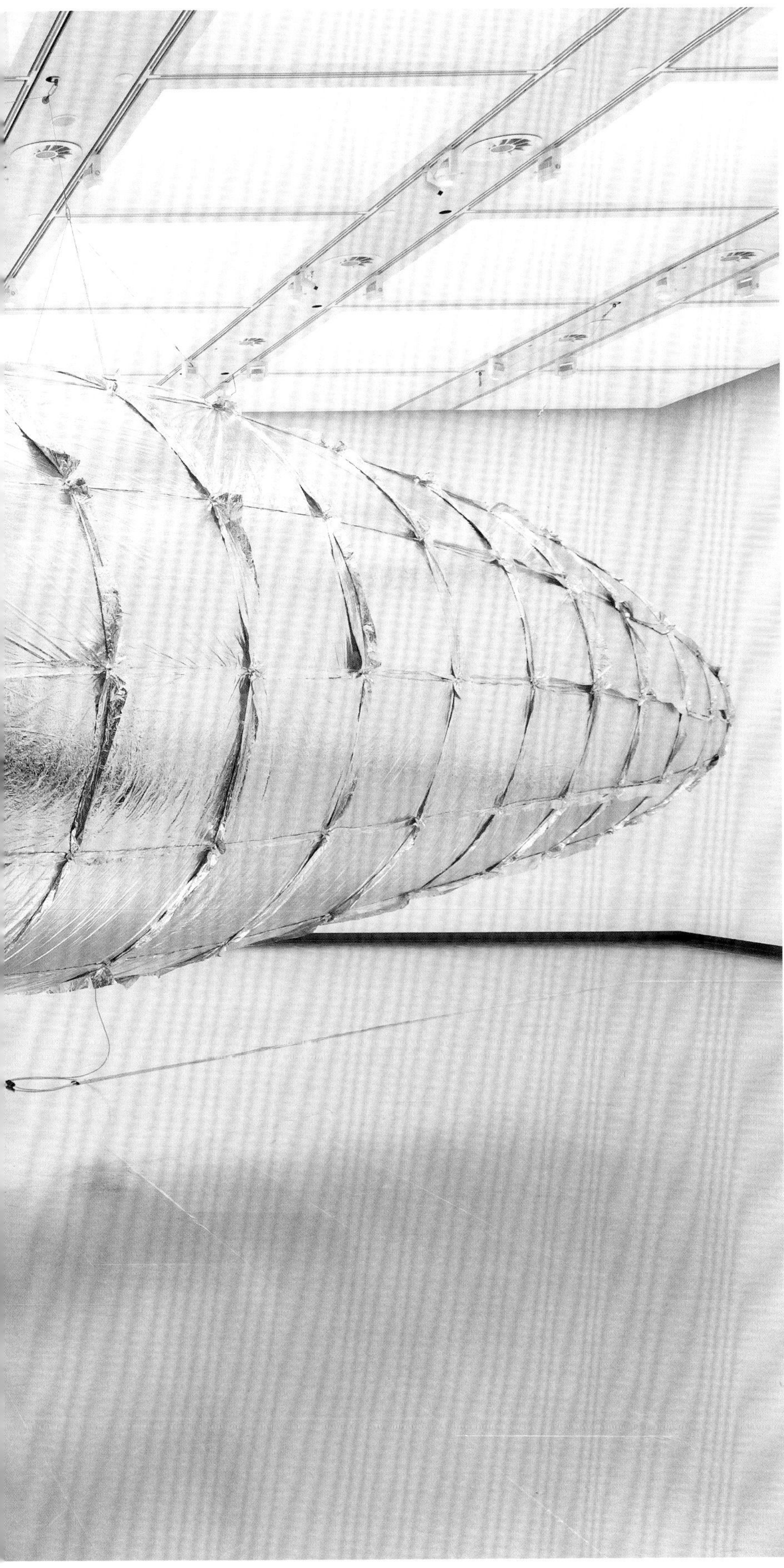

LEE BUL (b. 1964) grew up in South Korea under the dictator President Park Chung Hee, who tortured and killed many of those who sought to oppose him. Lee's early works, often performances, placed her in the sights of the very conservative authorities and society in general. It is no wonder that her work often deals with death and dread, but also intense beauty. She shows both sides of life's possibilities. Her *Willing To Be Vulnerable – Metalized Balloon* is a large inflated zeppelin, which was shown over a silver mirrored floor in her exhibition 'Crashing' at London's Hayward Gallery in 2018. The huge inflatable hung menacingly in the space, inevitably evoking the 1937 *Hindenburg* disaster in which the giant airship was destroyed by fire; and yet, reflected in the floor, its beauty as an object was paramount.

Willing To Be Vulnerable – Metalized Balloon,
2015–16
Hayward Gallery, London, UK, 2018
Metallized film, transparent film, air blower
Approx. 3 × 17 × 3 m (9¾ × 55¾ × 9¾ ft)

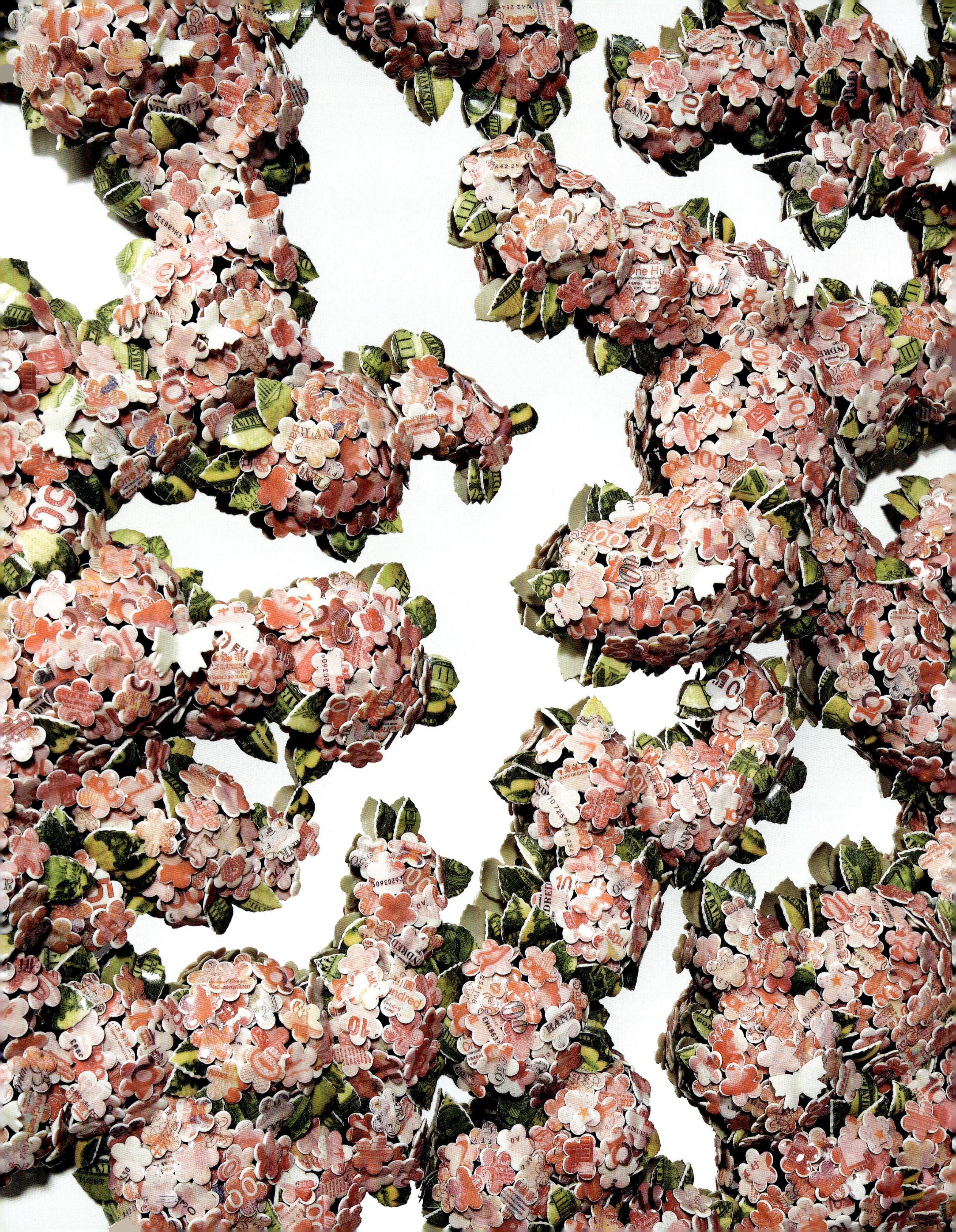

MIRRORS

The use of mirrors to capture a self-portrait in contemporary art has been less frequent than in historical paintings thanks to the relatively recent ability to capture one's own image in a photograph. But several artists of note have made use of this trope, including Lucian Freud (*Interior with Hand Mirror [Self-portrait]*, 1967) and perhaps his artistic opposite, Norman Rockwell, in whose *Triple Self Portrait* (1960) the mirror itself holds the focus. Photographers, of course, have used mirrors to catch their own image, and Helen Chadwick used mirrors in larger works as well. So it is no wonder that today's artists have also turned to the use of mirrors in their sculptures and installations, such as AA Bronson, who uses mirrors to make a large installation; or have turned the mirror into an additional participant, as in Paul Mpagi Sepuya's photographs.

Some artists have used non-traditional materials to create work, including the black obsidian or black glass mirrors of Frida Escobedo, Johannes Wald, Prem Sahib and Peter Briggs. Obsidian, a form of black volcanic glass, has been used as a mirror for centuries, and the name of the Aztec god of obsidian and sorcery, Tezcatlipoca, roughly translates to 'smoking mirror'. These materials have associations with divination and entrances to other worlds; while not necessarily required to evoke such meaning for contemporary artists, such mirrors nonetheless have an added frisson. Other artists have used what most people would recognize as a mirror but alter its context (Kris Martin) or its shape (Barnaby Barford) to make everyday objects into something new and special. People generally understand what a mirror is and how it should be used: when mirrors become something additional, they become objects of curiosity, which when inspected still present the viewer with themselves.

Shirin Hosseinvand, Andrew Logan and Carlos Rolón shatter mirrors, with no regard for potential bad luck, and use the shards to construct completely different forms. They reconstruct an imperfect finish for viewing, like the viewer, who is also always imperfect, and a sum of many parts. How, when and where we look into a mirror alters what we see back, and artists make use of this uncertainty. Mark Woods tries to harness most if not all of the viewer's attention in his work, which, like Yuko Shiraishi's, must be seen through a peephole. The viewer becomes the observed in works like this or in the large mirrors Mungo Thomson presents as documents of history.

Alicja Kwade, Anthony James and Mat Collishaw work hard to disrupt the viewer's sense of stability. Their mirrors shift the ground beneath the viewer's feet and ask them to question what it is they see, not only in the mirror but everywhere outside of that magic and mystical object. Mirrors have long been more than mere objects of vanity: they have held power inside their silvery faces.

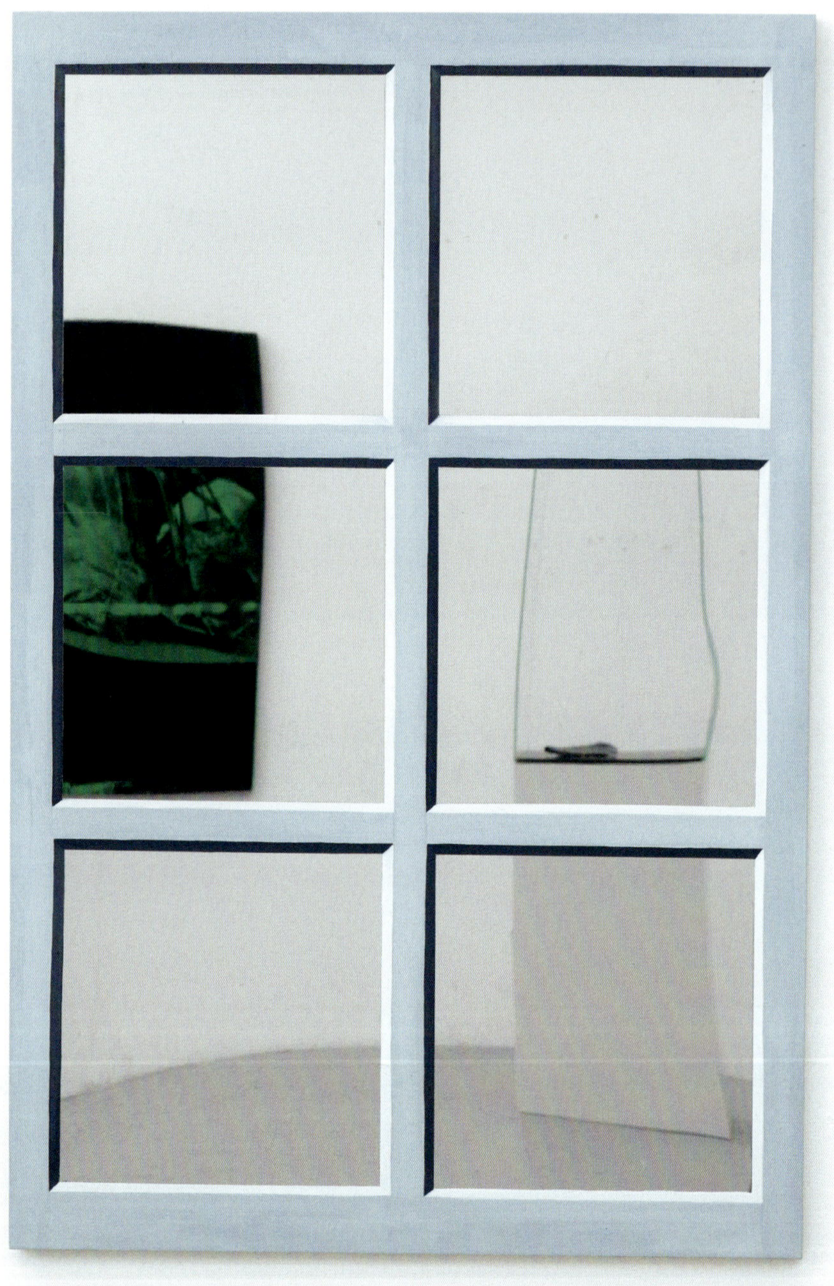

The conceptual works of British artist **GAVIN TURK** (b. 1967) see him inhabit the spirit of other artists, and his body of work has often played on the works of preceding artists, from Marcel Duchamp to Andy Warhol, one example being his *Reflections in a Window*. Here, in both pink and baby-blue versions, Turk presents the viewer with a mirrored example of Duchamp's *Fresh Widow* (1920). Duchamp's work, fabricated for him by a carpenter, was a smaller-scale version of a pair of pale-blue French windows, with each pane of glass covered in black leather. The pun of Duchamp's title ('French window' becoming 'fresh widow') indicated a sly reference to the 'fresh' widows from World War I, who were said to be overly sexually available. Turk reflects all of this underlying meaning in his work back onto the viewers who see themselves in his mirror.

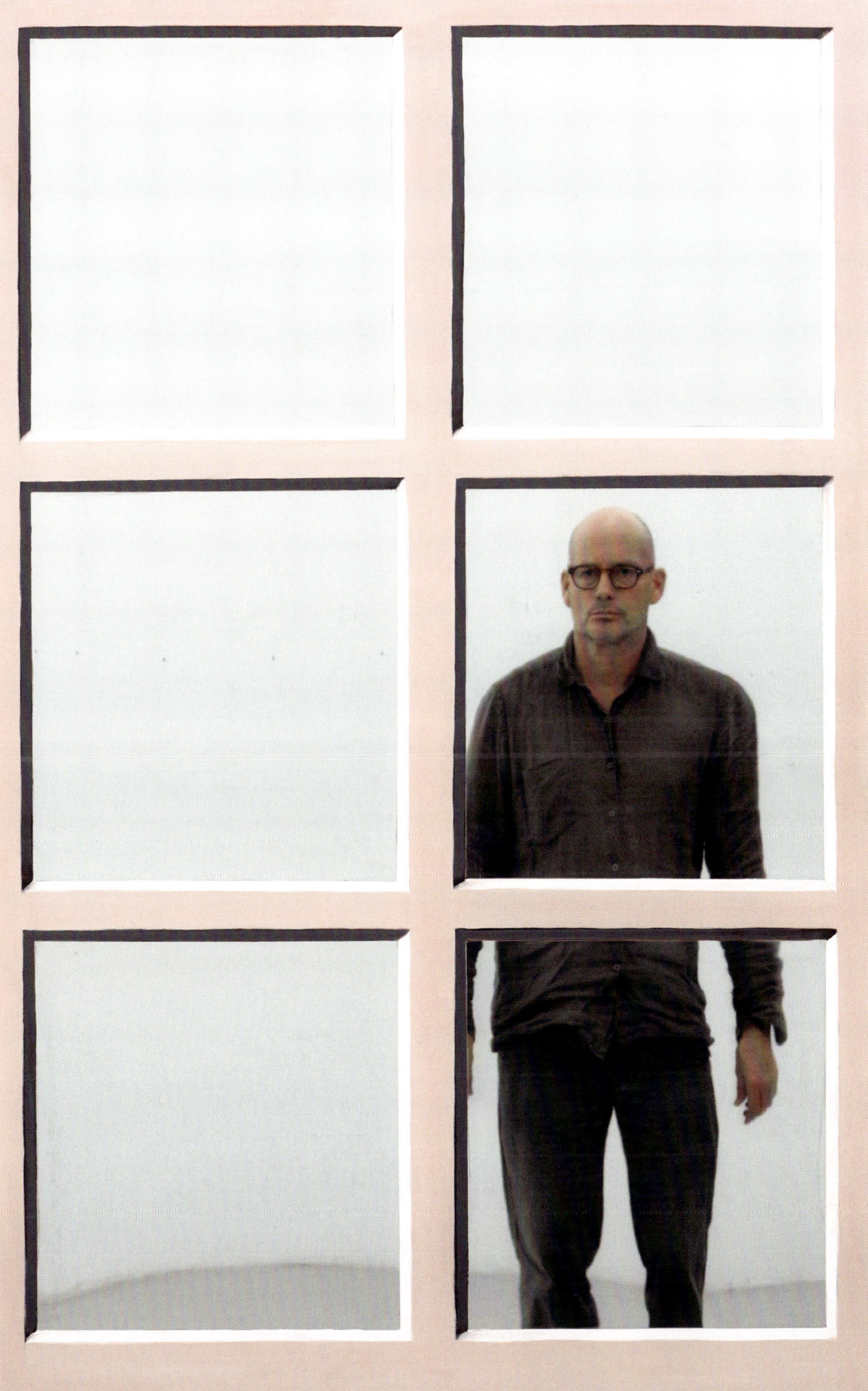

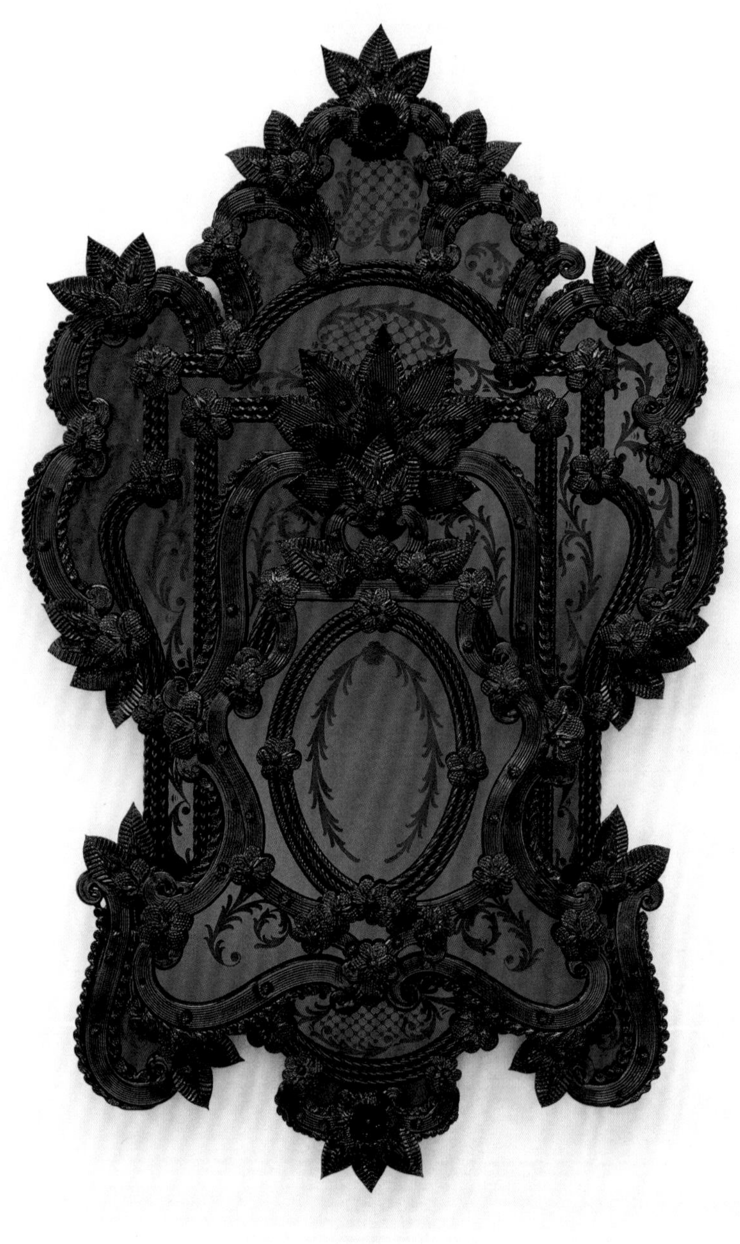

FRED WILSON (b. 1954) represented the United States at the 50th Venice Biennale in 2003. His exhibition incorporated a black Murano glass chandelier titled *Speak of Me as I Am*. It was the first time the Italian makers had used the black glass in this way. Wilson's mirrors are made from many layers of black Murano glass painted out on the reverse, increasing their reflectivity, rendering all viewers in black. He also makes work with American glass blowers. His projects examine the experience of Africans and African Americans historically as well as in the present day. 'My works in black are a mixture of positive affirmation, with a clear-eyed understanding of the racist tropes of the past.'

British artist **BARNABY BARFORD** (b. 1977) made a series of mirrors based on the seven deadly sins: envy, gluttony, lust, pride, sloth, wrath and avarice. Each work has a large central mirror that has been decorated with a variety of porcelain objects that relate to the relevant sin. The small glossy flowers that encircle the *Lust* mirror all have transfer images of the faces (in close-up) of men and women in the throes of orgasm, taken from pornographic magazines, while the *Gluttony* flowers have segments of takeaway menus transferred onto them. The base mirror in his *Avarice* piece, seen opposite, is almost invisible as it is so covered in flowers and leaves. The green porcelain leaves have American 1, 10 and 100 dollar bills transferred onto them, while the pink flowers have euros and Hong Kong dollars on their surfaces. Looking into these mirrors, viewers see (and perhaps recognize) themselves within the setting of these 'sins'.

Fred Wilson, *Mark,* 2009
Murano glass and wood
105.4 cm × 65.4 cm × 15.2 cm
(41½ × 25¾ × 6 in)

OPPOSITE

Barnaby Barford, *Avarice,* 2012
Porcelain, stainless steel, wood,
epoxy putty, enamelled copper wire
225 × 155 × 17 cm (88½ × 61 × 6¾ in)

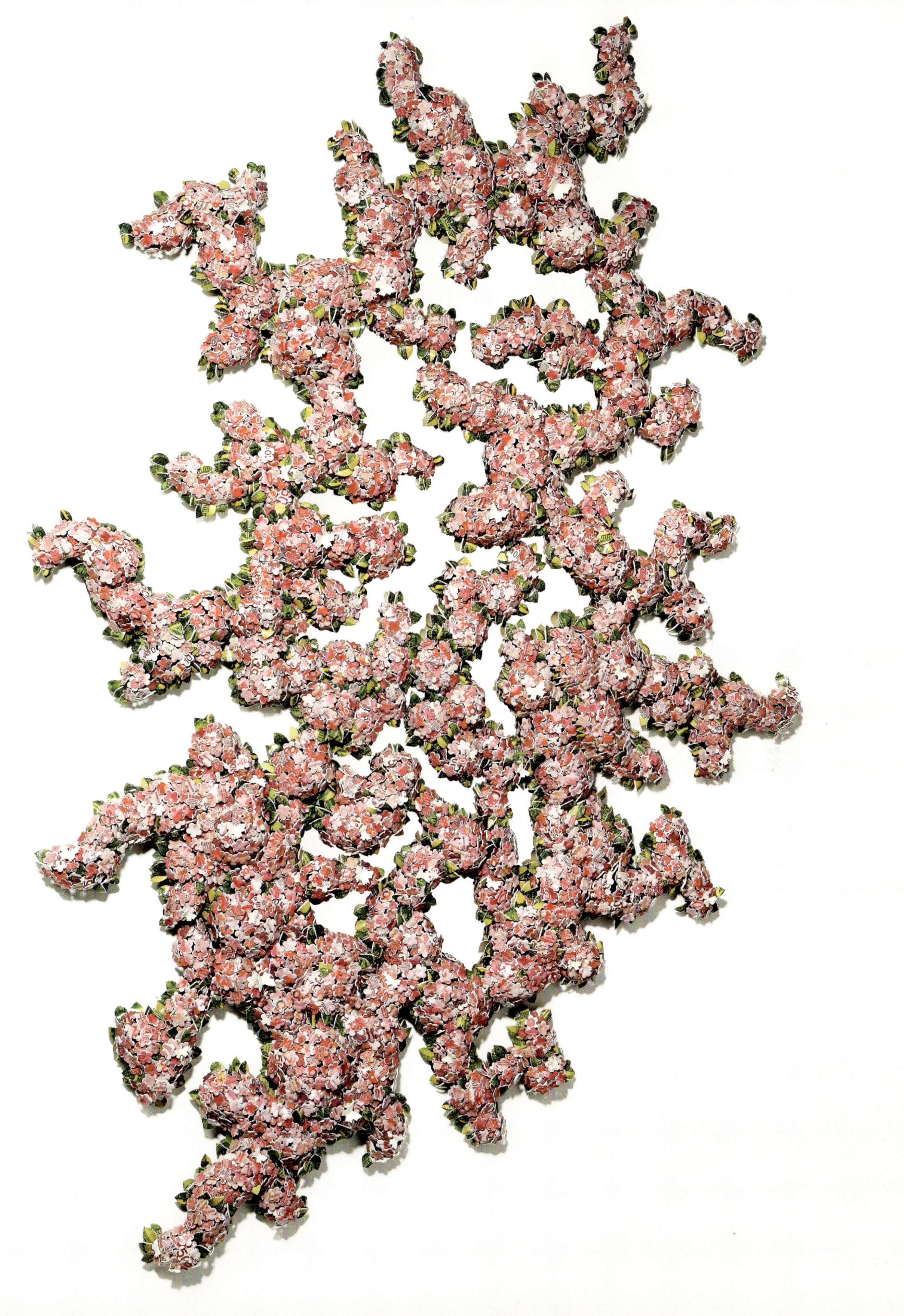

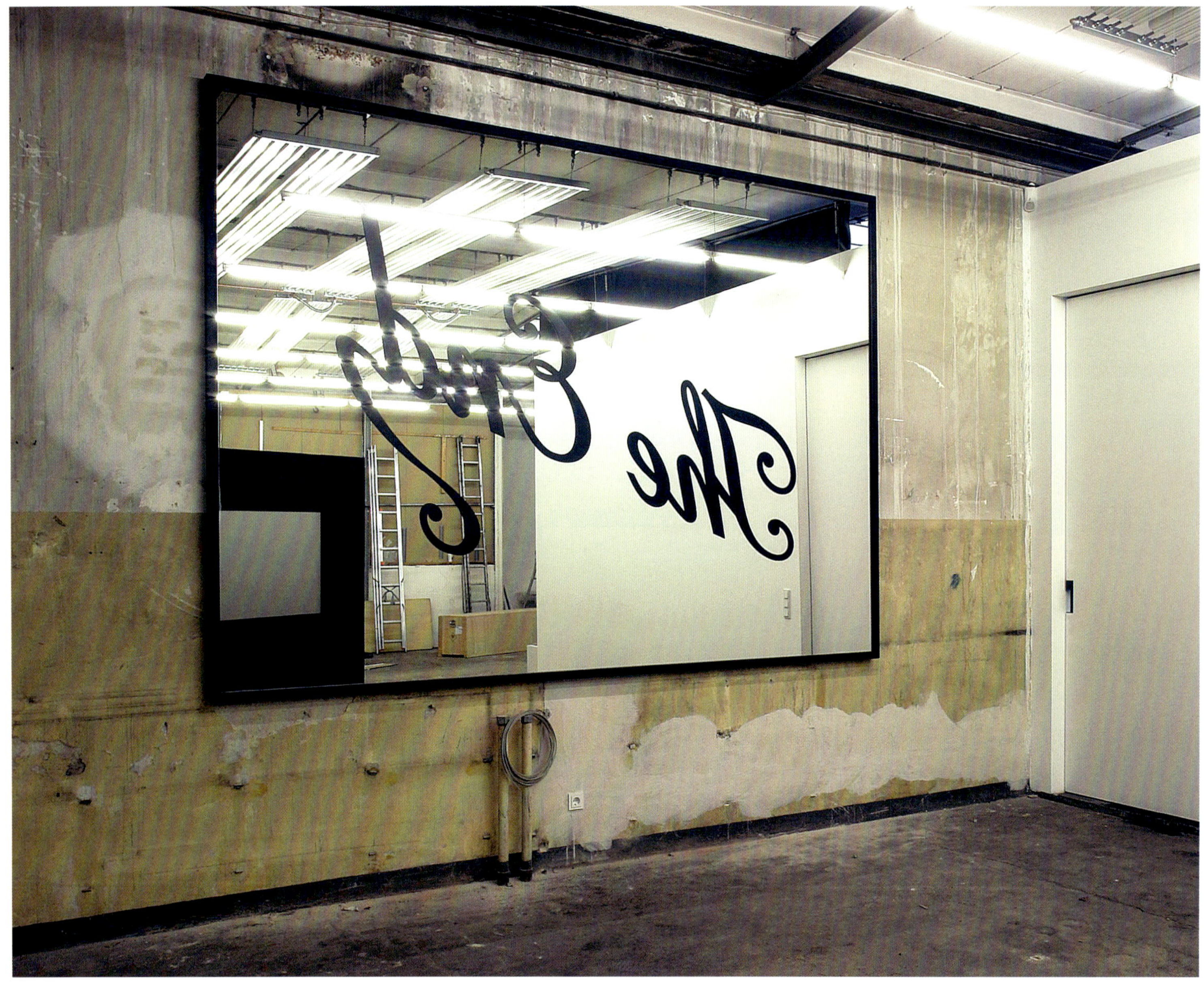

The Belgian artist **KRIS MARTIN** (b. 1972) has made several mirror pieces entitled *The End*. A smaller one painted on a vintage gilt-framed mirror contrasts with a much larger one in a simple black frame for König Galerie in Berlin, which has been shown in many locations, reflecting the environments as well as viewers. The outstanding feature of these works is the cursive script – 'The End' – that is situated in the centre of the mirror but in reverse, as if itself reflected in a mirror.

The only way to 'read' the text on the mirror would be for it to be seen in another mirror. The complex play of languages, visual and verbal, that Martin presents is further disturbed by the message of the text being similar to that of the end of many cinematic experiences – leaving viewers to question whether '*That's all Folks*'.

The End, 2006
Framed mirror
200 × 300 cm (79 × 118 in)

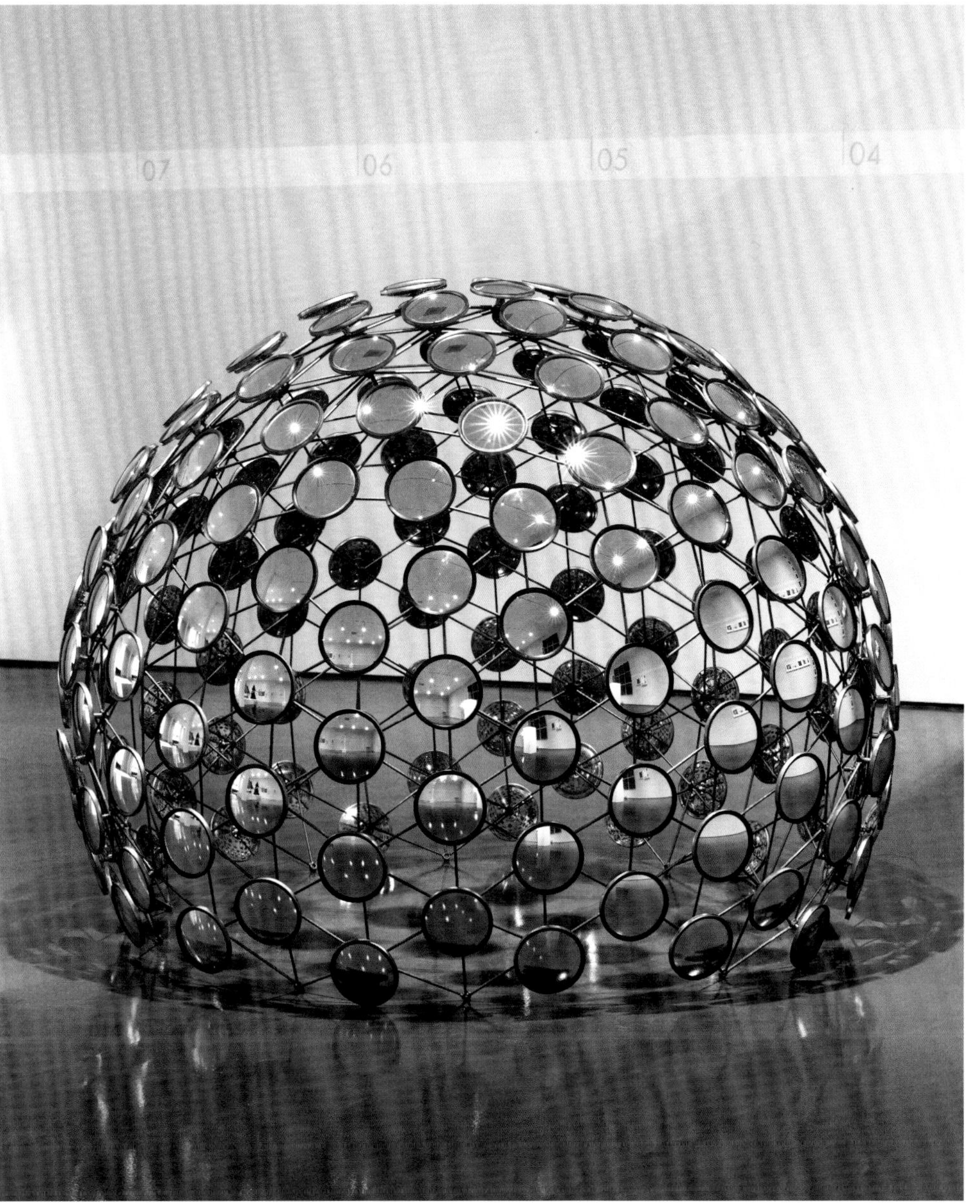

Bubble Machine by Canadian artist **AA BRONSON** (b. 1946) echoes fellow queer-art pioneer David Medalla's 1960s *Cloud Canyon* bubble machines, and is a model of a bubble cluster. The work also mirrors the structure of the HIV virus. As part of the artists' group General Idea (with Felix Partz and Jorge Zontal, who both died from HIV/AIDS-related illnesses) and as a solo artist, Bronson has focused on queer ideas, issues and inclusion in his work.

Arbeit Macht Frie (overleaf) is the title of an 1873 novel by German scholar and author Lorenz Diefenbach that posits that hard work can lead to a virtuous life even for those seen as reprobates. The title was infamously adopted as a motto by the Nazis, who used it over the entrance to many concentration camps, including Auschwitz, where the B was placed upside down by the prisoners who were forced to make it, possibly as an act of defiance. Bronson brings the

phrase with its terrifying echoes into the twenty-first century, a century of surveillance both state and private. Using commercial security mirrors he spelt out the phrase in the gallery, reflecting or surveying the audience who came to see it. The dark colour of the walls recalled that of dried blood.

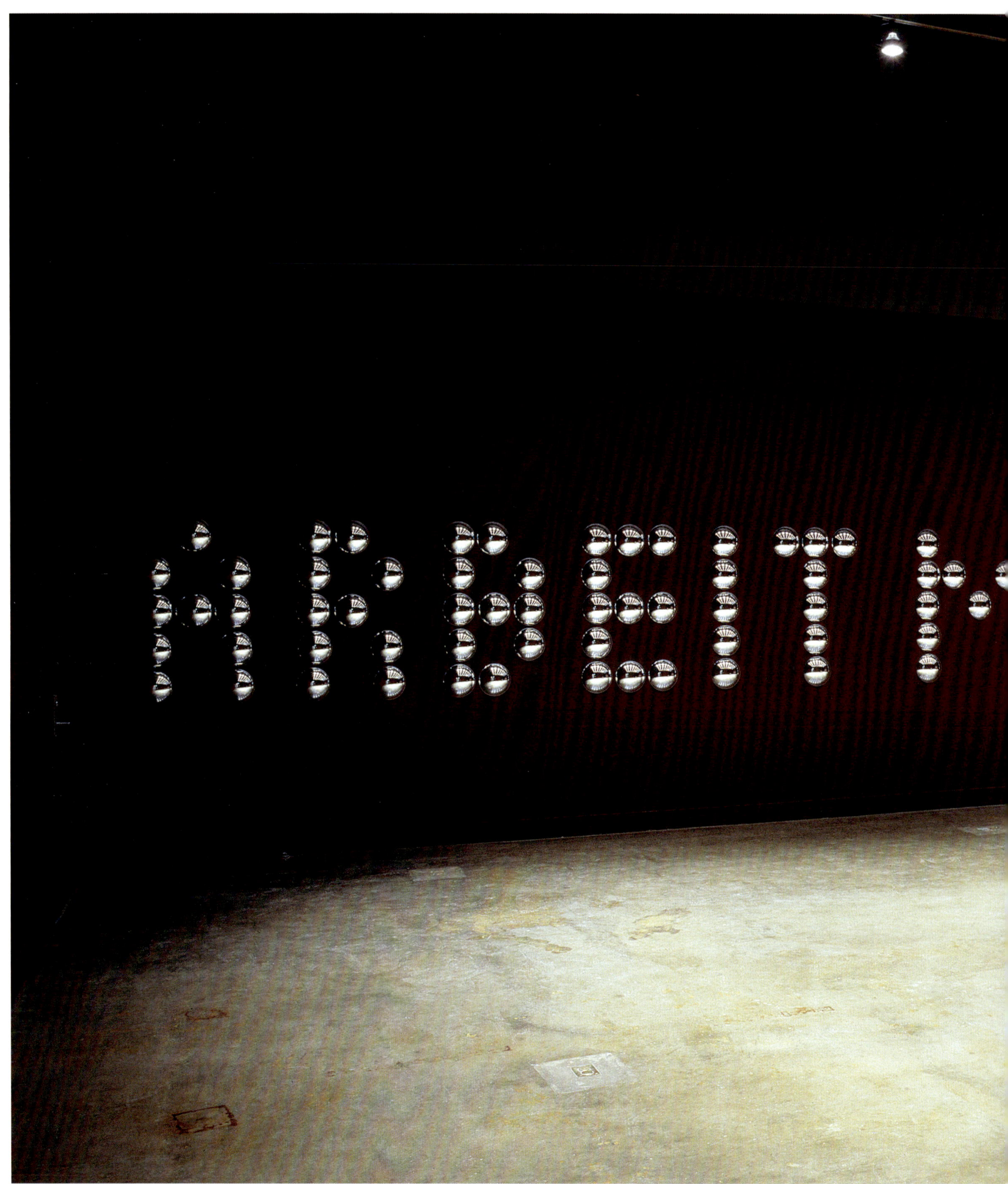

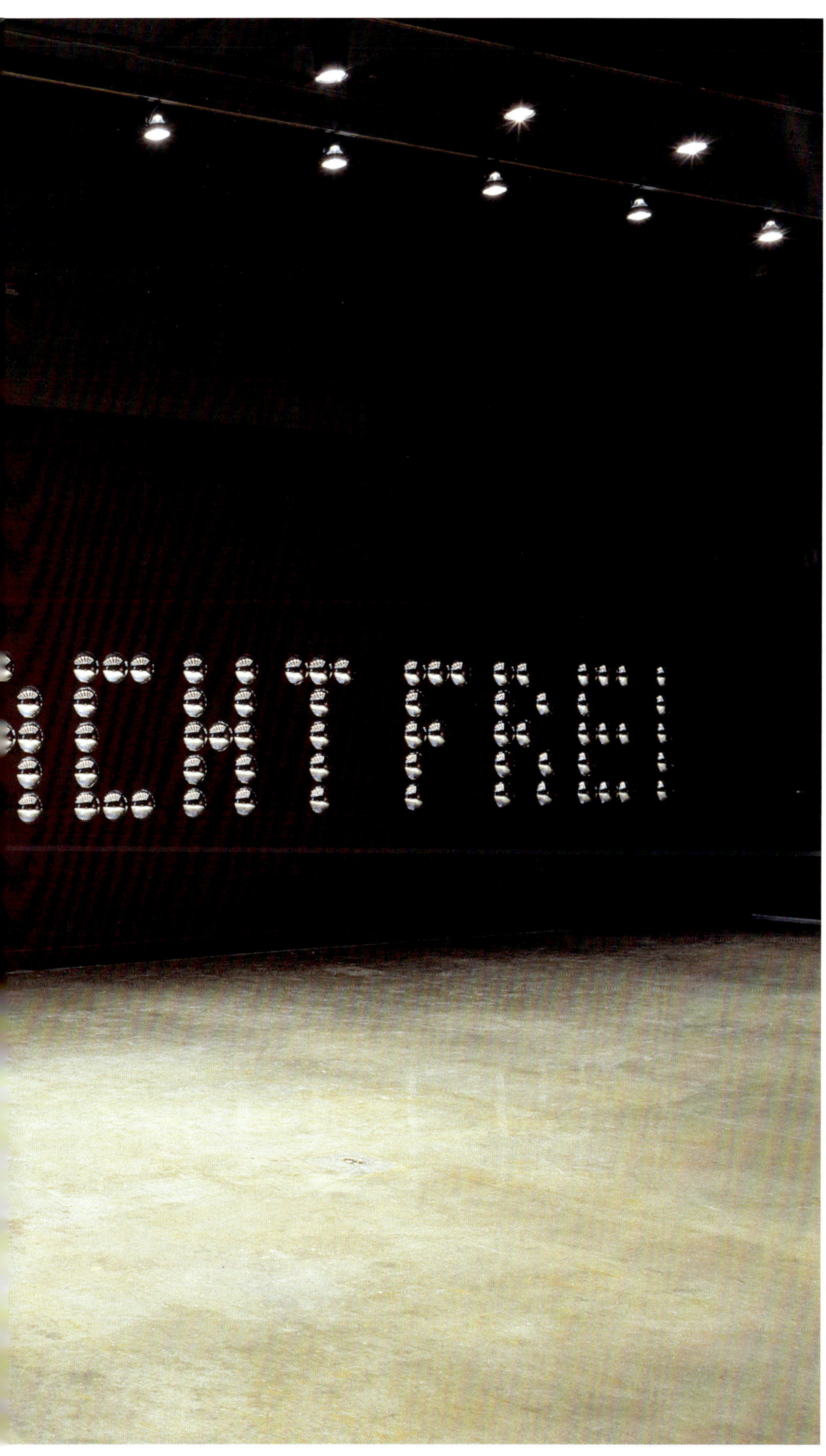

AA Bronson, *Arbeit Macht Frei*, 2001
Installation view: 'AA Bronson: Mirror Mirror',
MIT List Visual Arts Center, Cambridge,
Massachusetts, USA, 2002
133 circular convex commercially
available security mirrors
Dimensions variable

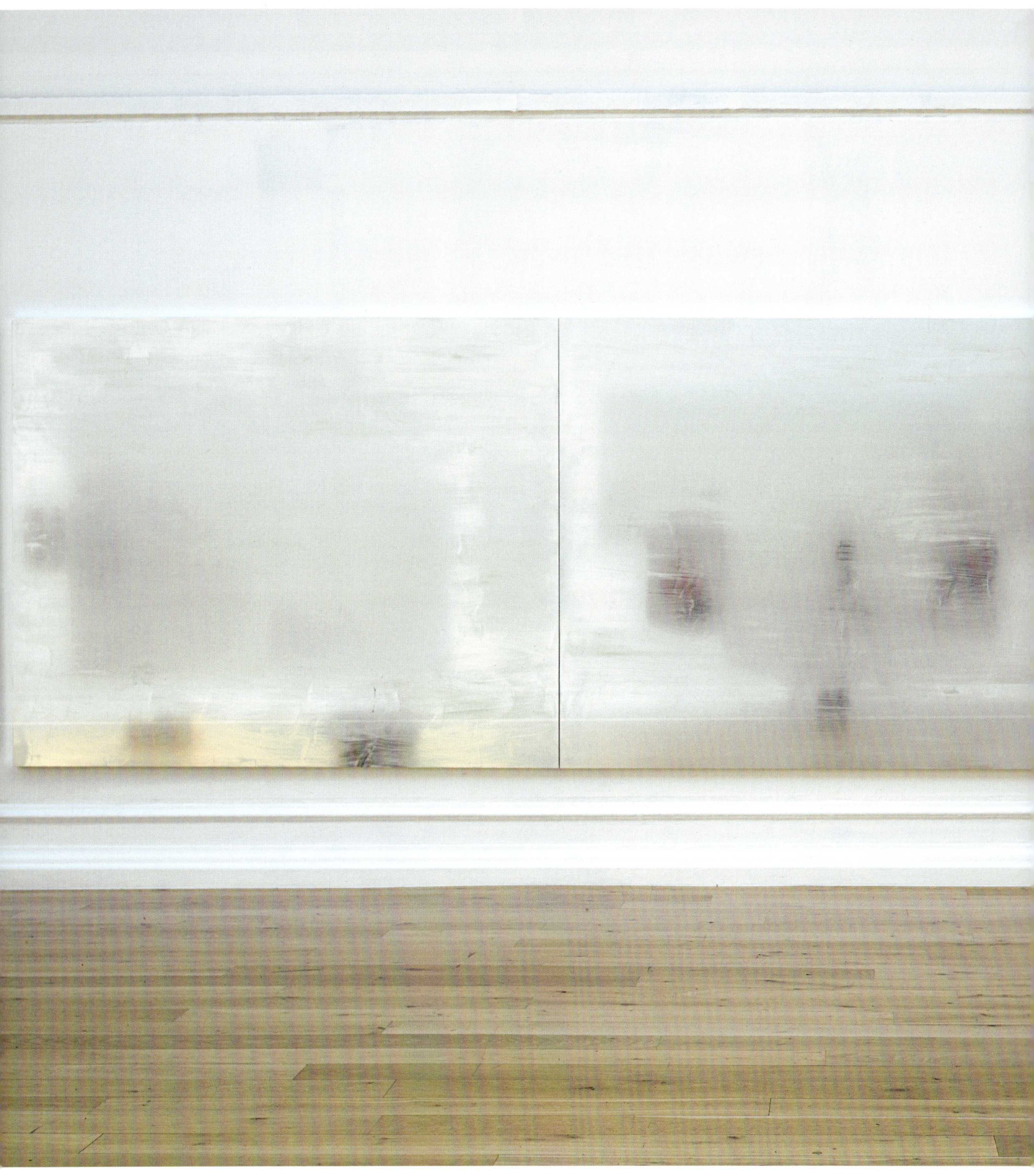

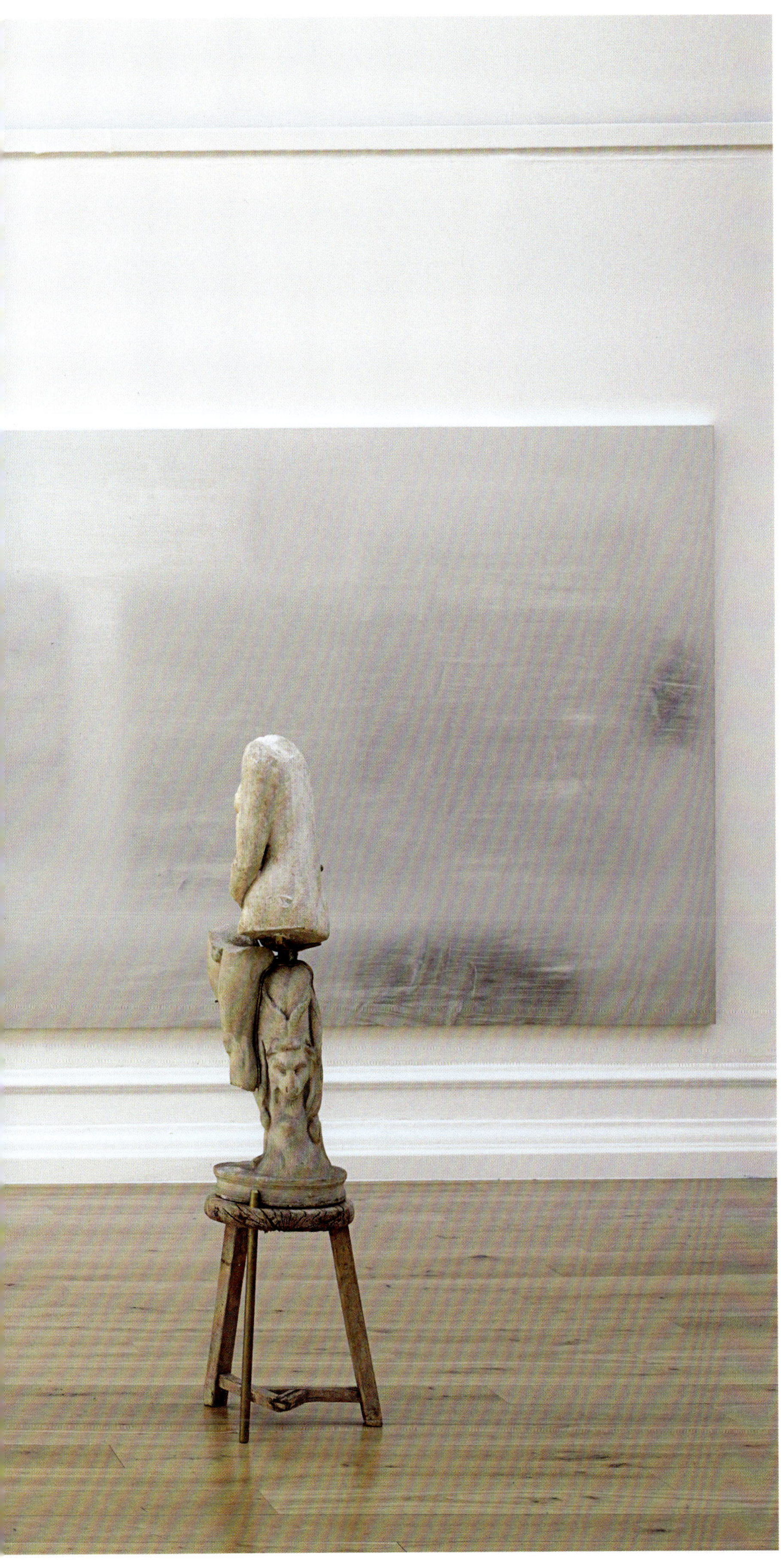

Vietnamese-born Danish artist **DANH VO** (b. 1975) made a series of *Untitled* installations that were a collaboration between his lover (Heinz Peter Knes), his father (Phung Vo) and his former painting teacher (Peter Bonde, who had advised him while at art school to stop painting), which also incorporated other elements that often referred to his Vietnamese heritage. Vo placed Bonde's partially covered reflective paintings throughout the space (as he also did in the 2019 Venice Biennale), so that the works reflected clearly only the legs of the viewer. Knes's photographs of Vo's nephew and muse, Gustav, were accompanied by calligraphic works by the artist's father that are quotes from the movie *The Exorcist* (1973), and by several of Vo's own sculptural works. The last major element was a daybed made from black walnut farmed by Craig McNamara, son of Robert McNamara, a major proponent of the Vietnam War as US Secretary of Defense from 1961 to 1968. The Vo family fled to Denmark when Danh was a child, and the work links all these various aspects of his life.

Untitled, 2019
Installation view: South London Gallery, London, UK, Sept–Nov 2019
Mixed media installation
Dimensions variable

Frisson bleu, frisson rose by the Belgian artist **ANN VERONICA JANSSENS** (b. 1952) comprises two large rectangular pieces, each consisting of a panel of hammered glass laminated on dichroic PVC film on float glass. The effect is to present a shimmering iridescent surface that looks a bit like hammered copper and reflects the viewer in a distorted fashion. The dichroic film between the two sheets of glass makes the individual pieces look different from every angle and the soft pastel colours reflect onto the floor as well as the wall behind the diptych of leaning glass panels. These works are sharp yet liminal and while they are based in the exploration of the optical world, their effect on the viewer is more poetic.

frisson bleu, frisson rose, 2021
Hammered glass laminated on dichroic PVC
film and float glass
Each: 200 × 100 × 1 cm (78¾ × 39⅜ × ½ in)

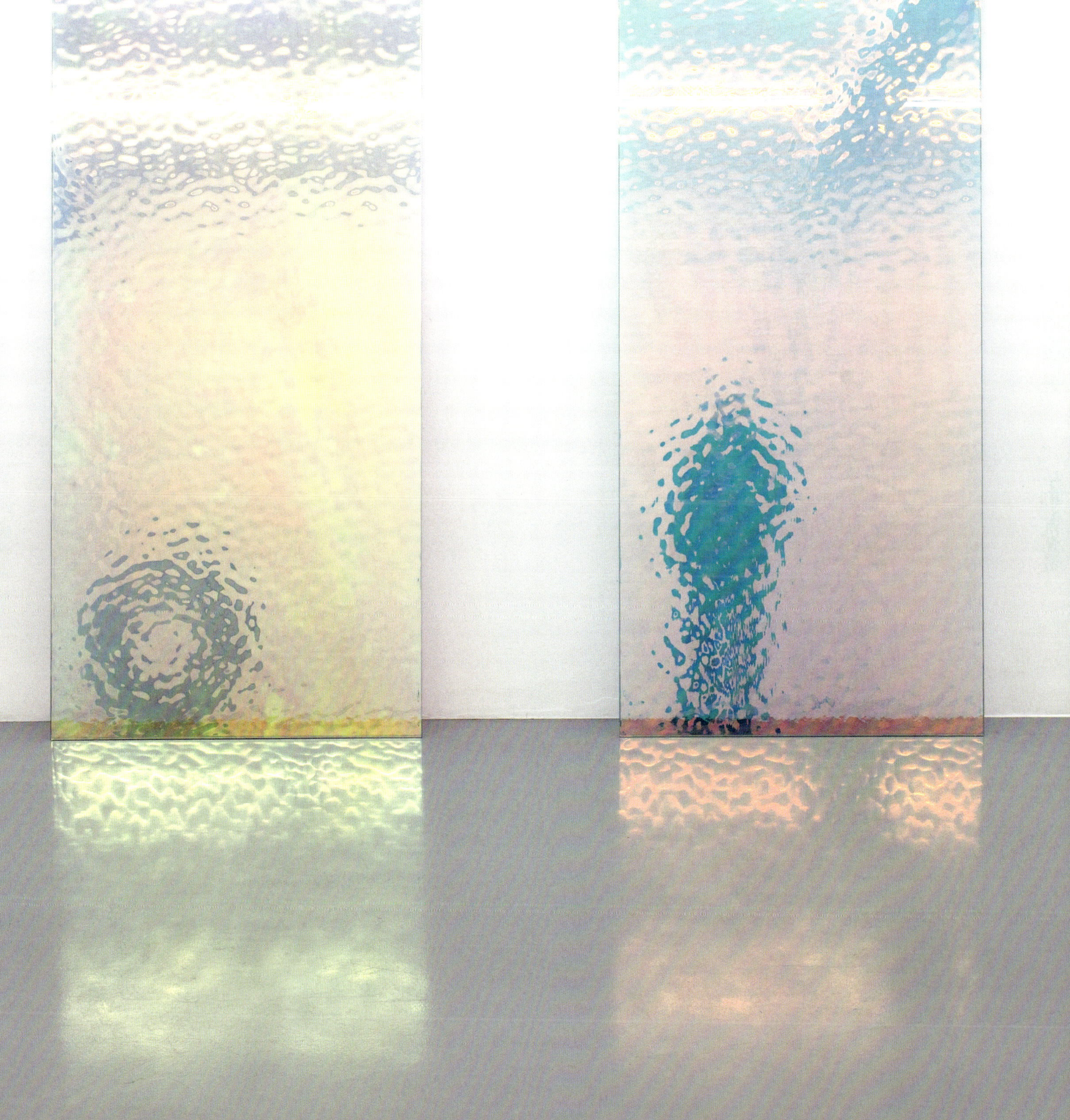

American artist **MUNGO THOMSON** (b. 1969) is drawn to attempt the depiction of time, including by reworking the actual magazine of that name. The company produced small mirrors with the cover's bold typeface and border in the 1970s and Thomson has reproduced the mirrors at full human size. Viewers see themselves on the cover, evoking *Time*'s annual Person of the Year edition, with the original photo image removed. Given modern selfie culture, these works have become very Instagrammable. Mirrors reflect the passing of time, and Thomson says, 'They are vanity but also vanitas. Yes, you are on the cover of TIME, but you are also going to die. The work is both fun and cruel.' Thomson believes art can make the viewer aware of the mundane world around them – a world many have stopped seeing – and the geological and social time it exists in.

BELOW
Installation view: Galerie Frank Elbaz, Paris, France, 2013
Left to right: *March 23, 1987 (The Nature of the Universe)*, 2013
October 13, 1975 (Meditation: The Answer To All Your Problems?), 2013
August 4, 2003 (The Science of Meditation), 2013
Enamel on low-iron mirror, poplar and anodized aluminium
Each: 188 × 142 × 6.5 cm (74 × 56 × 2½ in)

OPPOSITE
November 29, 1976 (Robert Rauschenberg), 2022
Enamel on low-iron mirror, poplar and anodized aluminium
188 × 142 × 6.5 cm (74 × 56 × 2½ in)

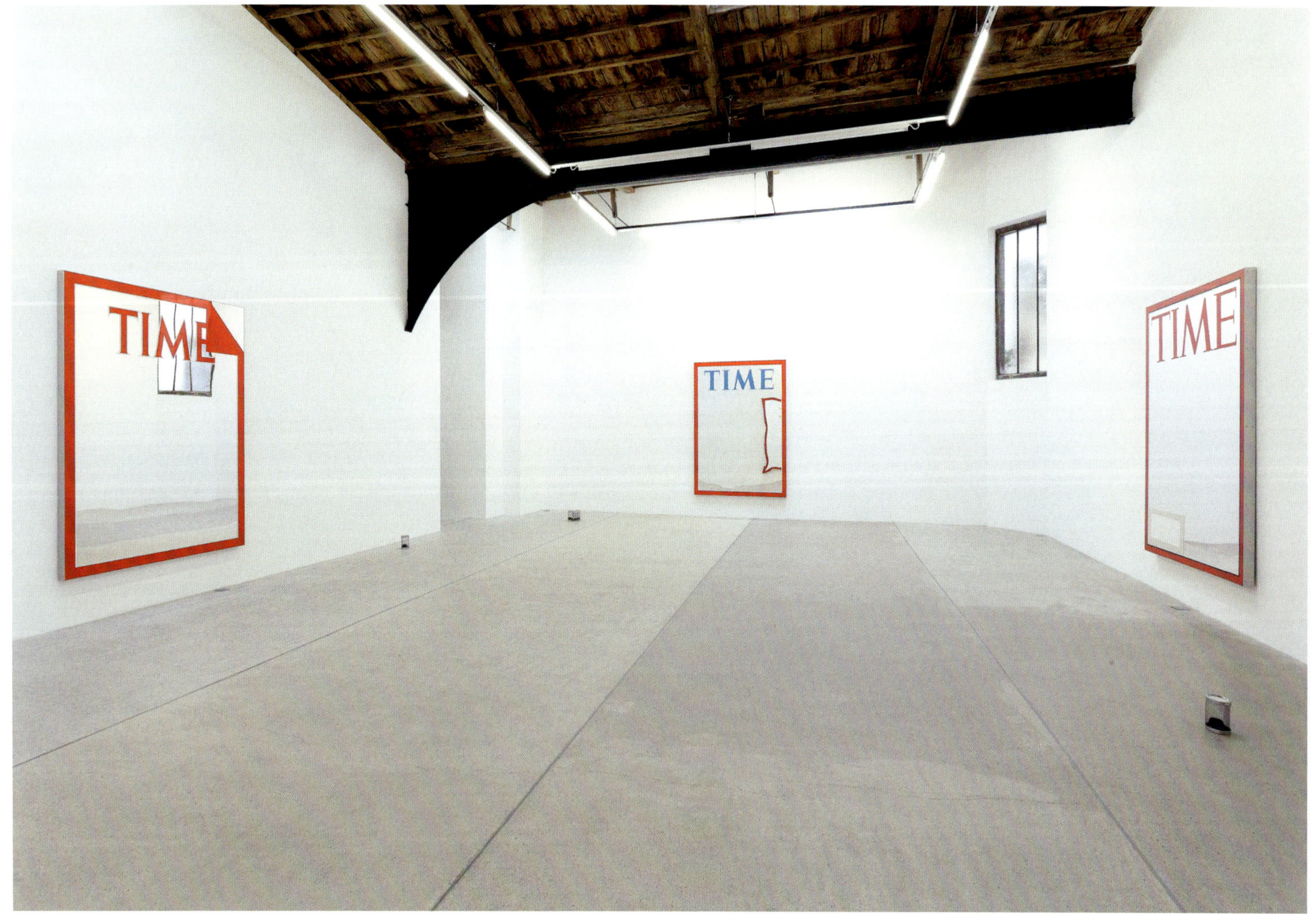

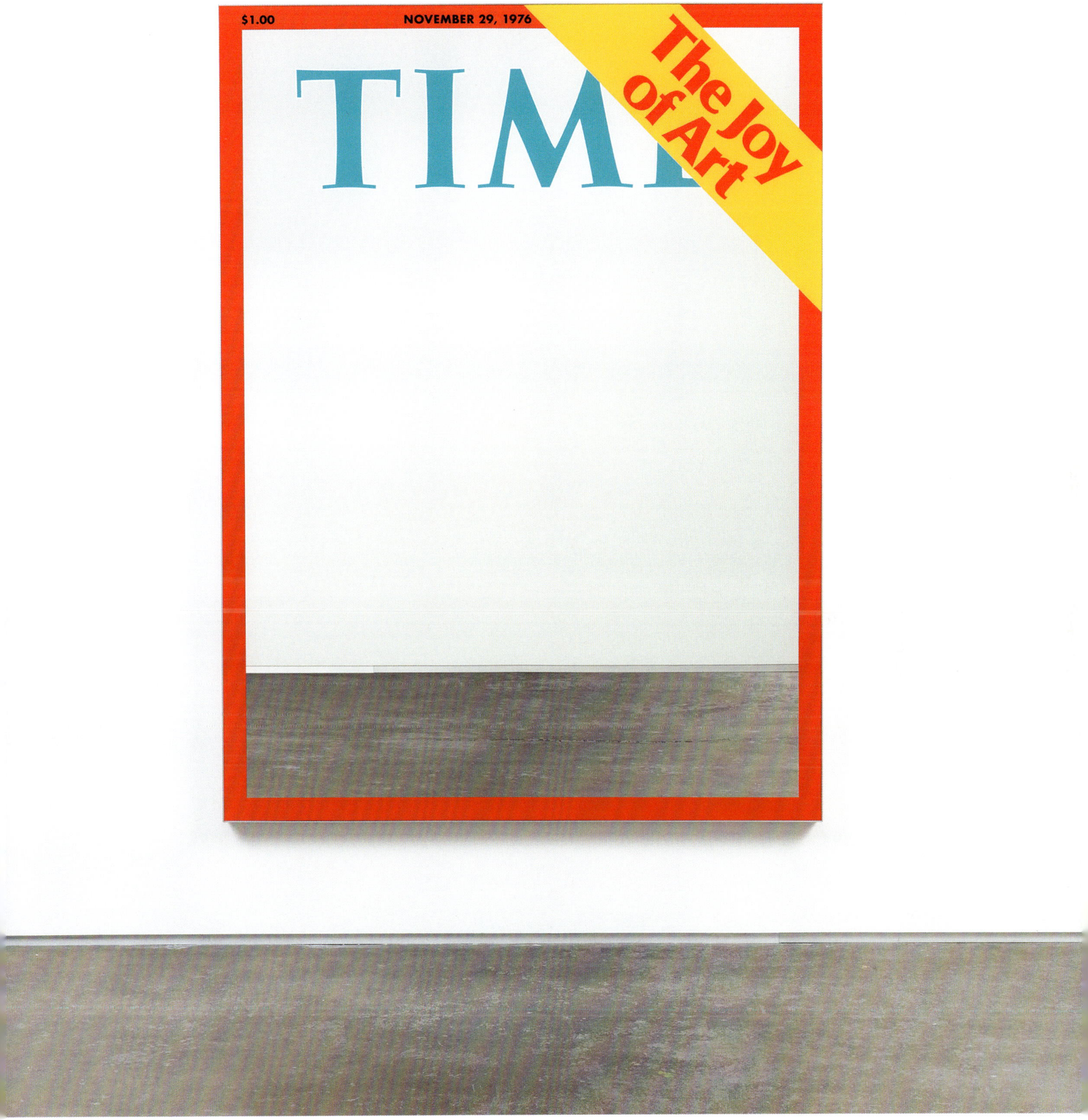

$1.00
NOVEMBER 29, 1976
TIME
The Joy of Art

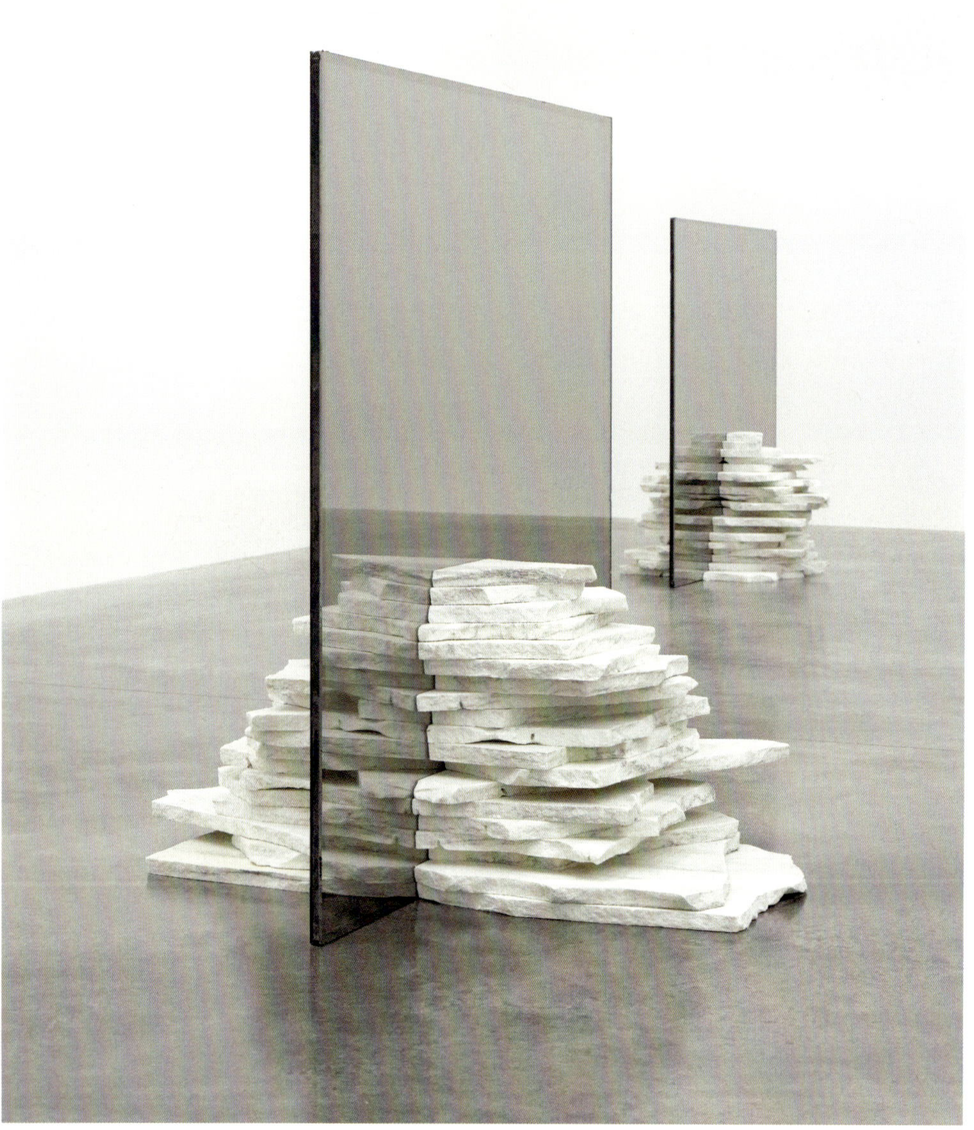

VIRGINIA OVERTON (b. 1971) was born to a farming family in Tennessee, USA, and her sculptures and installations have a make-do-and-mend quality that many frugal farmers would admire. She repurposes found industrial materials, be they timber, stone, mirror or beat-up old trucks. They all find their way into her witty transformation of the objects. In *Untitled* (above), she uses upright mirrors to reflect and duplicate stacks of unevenly shaped white marble slabs, which also function as bookends that hold the mirrors in place. She often reuses the materials of her installations to make new works or different versions to reference notions of labour and hand making. She has said that when she famously placed an old truck on a large mirror on the street in New York, a 'cabbie yelled at me as he drove by. "Hey, lady! You know that mirror is going to break if you drive on top of it!" I thought that was funny that he thought I had no idea what I was doing…maybe he was right.'

Untitled, 2016
Two-way glass mirror and Danby marble
1.5 × 1.4 × 1.38 m (5 × 4½ × 4½ ft)

Berlin-based Polish artist **ALICJA KWADE** (b. 1979) often uses mirrors to prevent the perception of any kind of whole. In pieces such as *Trans-For-Men 8 (Fibonacci)*, the viewer is never allowed to see the entirety of the work. There is no one viewpoint from which to see it all or mentally construct what the work looks like, as each object is reflected and each reflection interacts with the next object to create an impossible and temporary whole. The round black sphere merges with its irregular white neighbour and so on, yet as the viewer's gaze moves along the work these interactions create new forms that exist in the mirrored reflection, itself merged with the real objects. Other artists also use this technique of mirror application or interaction, yet there is a scientific and philosophical basis to Kwade's work that questions the very nature of 'reality'.

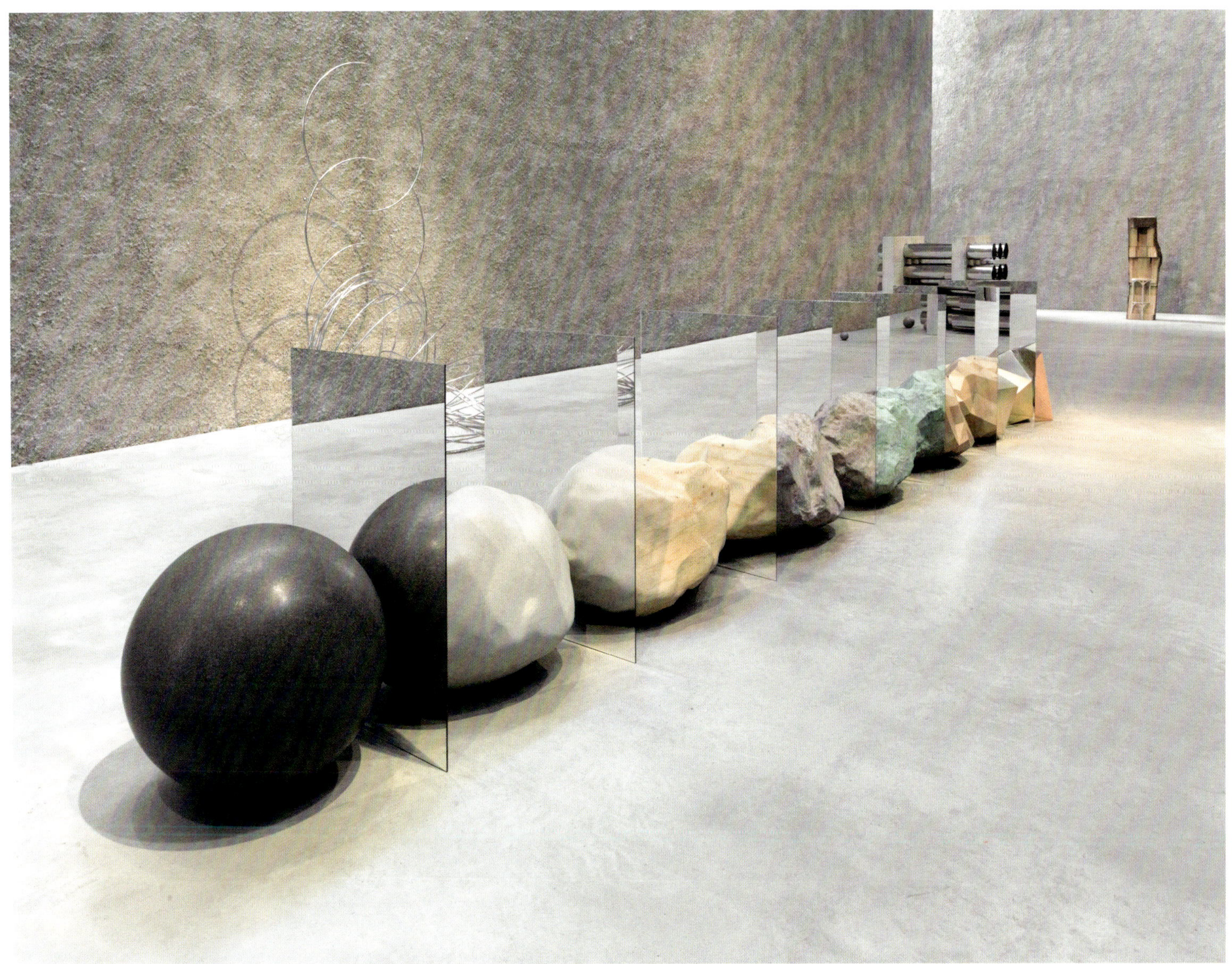

British artist **JAMES HOPKINS** (b. 1976) has made a series of clever works that at first do not appear to be able to exist. *Mirror Image* (2013) is a series of wooden letters on a shelf and their reflection in a mirror. They form the word 'mirror' in wood but also in their reflection, which surely should be impossible. This visual deception is the opposite of another work, *Forwards & Reverse* (2005), where a white wall-mounted clock shows the time correctly only in the mirror next to it. *Bottle and Skull*, shown here, comprises a mirrored bottle next to a strange, curved,

3D-printed white mass; on approaching, the viewer sees that a skull is reflected onto the surface of the bottle. This type of reflection is known as catoptric anamorphosis, in which a distorted image is revealed, undistorted, in a mirror. On a larger and more permanent scale Hopkins made a similar work, *Playful Seating* (2014), for Futurecity's commission for the Berkeley Group in Cambridge, UK. Here the bottle is replaced by a 4-metre (13-foot) polished stainless-steel column that reflects two large, misshapen bronze benches as two normal-sized school chairs.

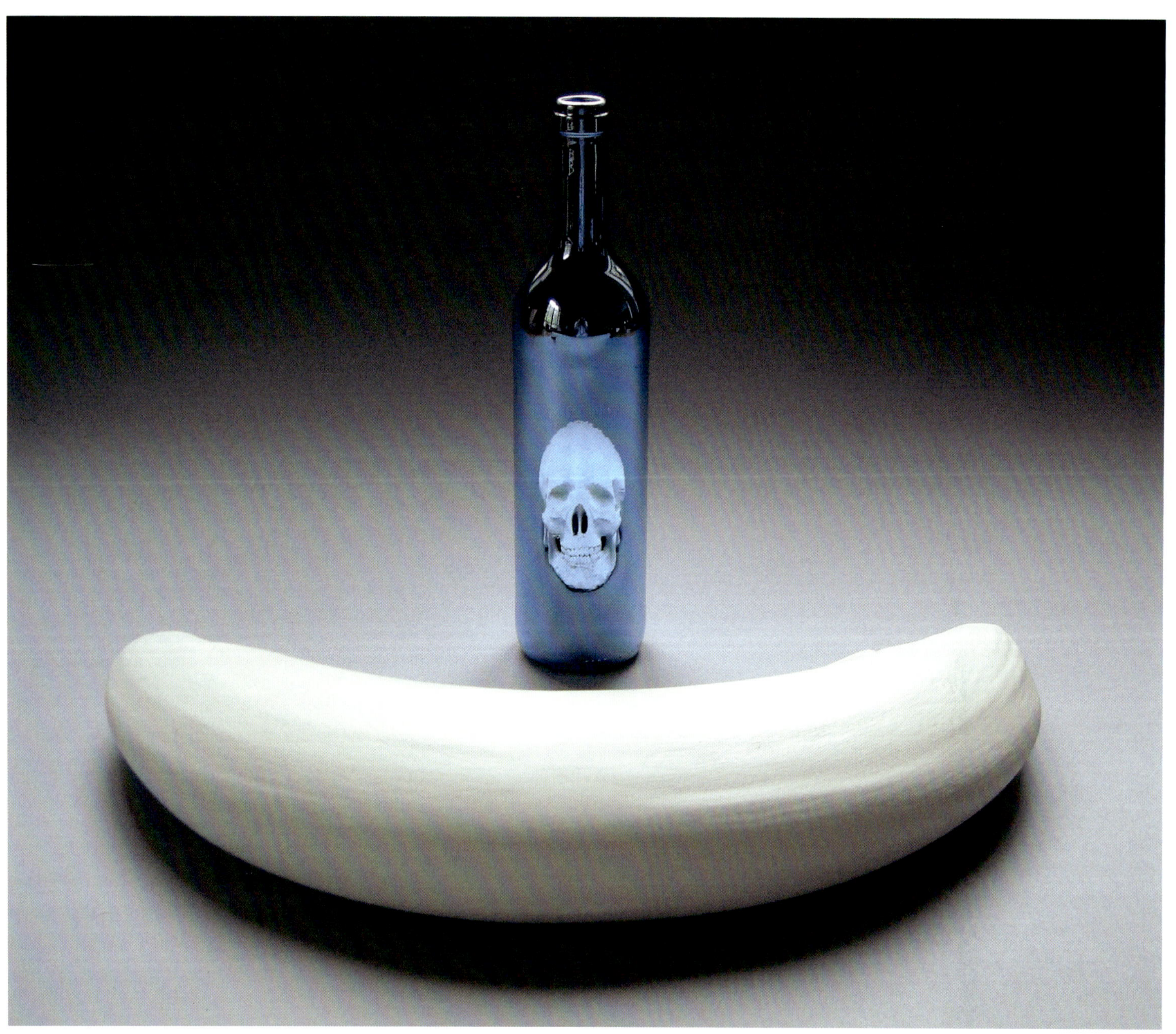

BELOW AND OPPOSITE
Bottle and Skull, 2013
3D print, polychromed bottle
50 × 50 × 28 cm (19¾ × 19¾ × 11⅛ in)

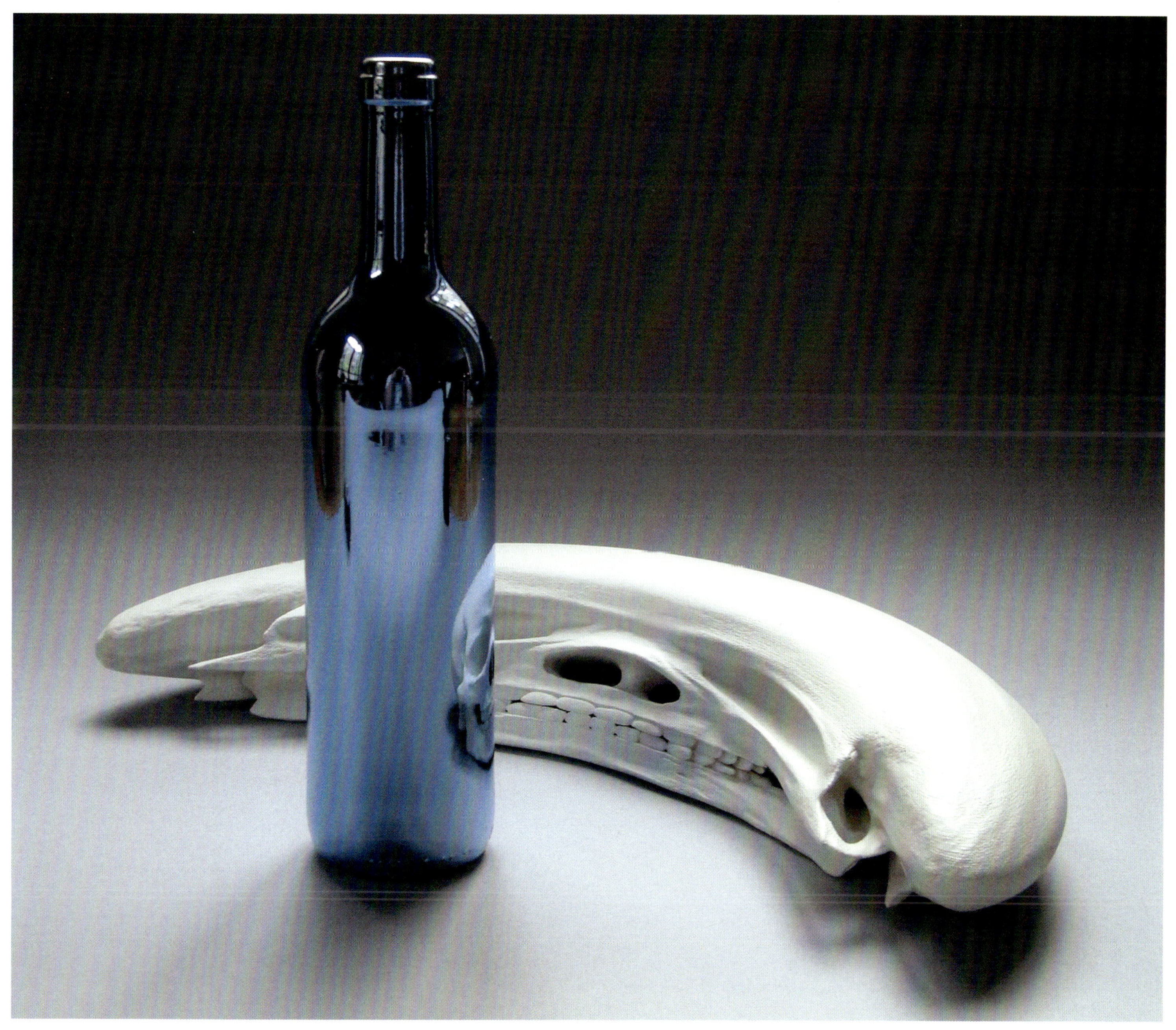

The diverse practice of Algerian-French artist **KADER ATTIA** (b. 1970) incorporates numerous types of objects and forms, many being sited for maximum disruption to traditional ways of seeing. His work questions how Western power in all forms continues to inform and shadow other cultures. His work often focuses on 'injury and repair', but not necessarily on returning an object to its exact former state, as in his series of *Repaired Broken Mirrors* (2012–20), where the metal staples that hold the work together not only are obvious but are the focus of the piece. The mirror returns the viewer's image but it too is no longer wholly what it was before, alluding to the invisible individual scars that everyone bears and the social ones that are not so evenly distributed.

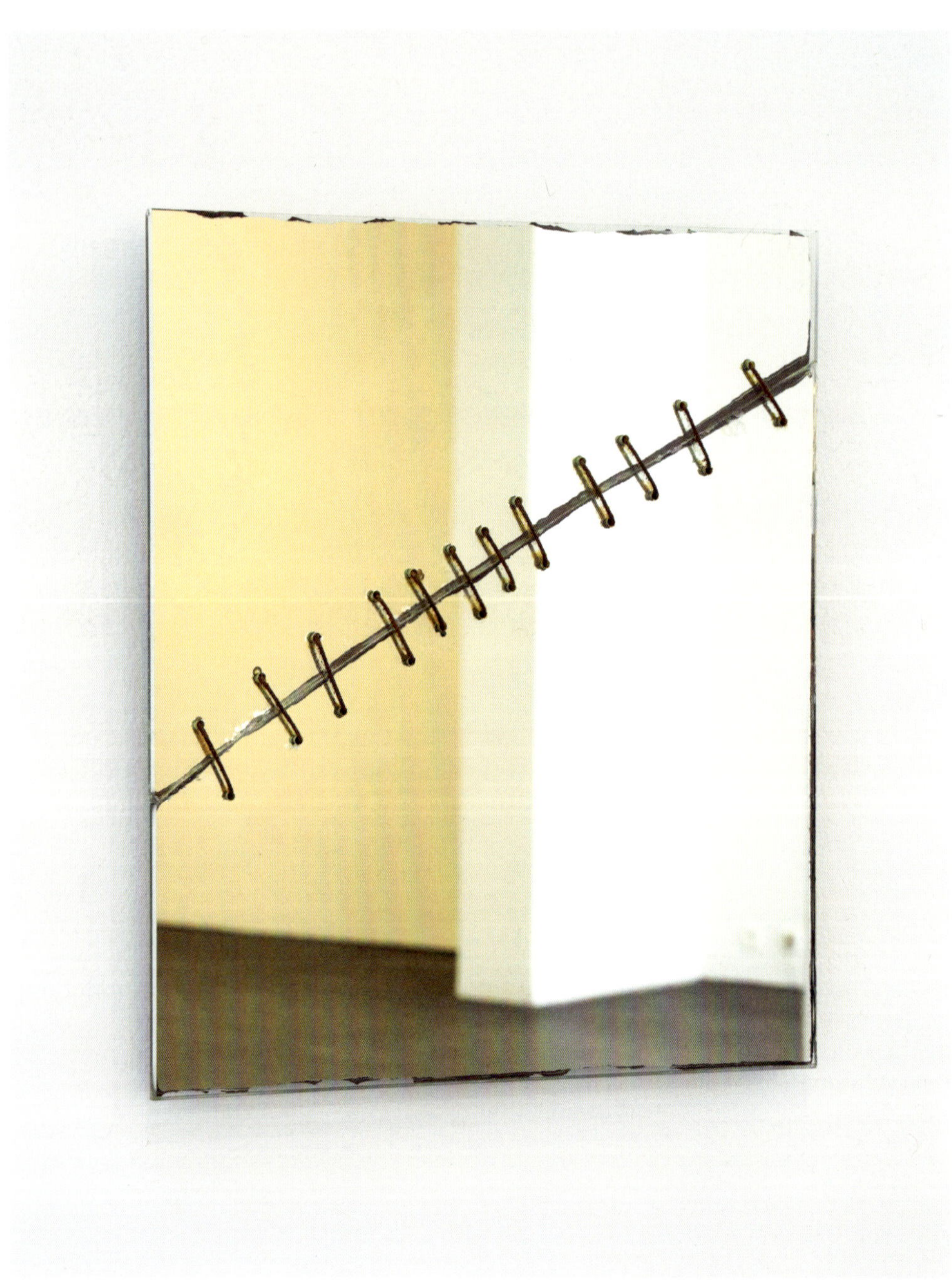

Repaired Broken Mirror, 2013
Mirror, metal staples
30 × 20 cm (11⁷⁄₈ × 7⁷⁄₈ in)

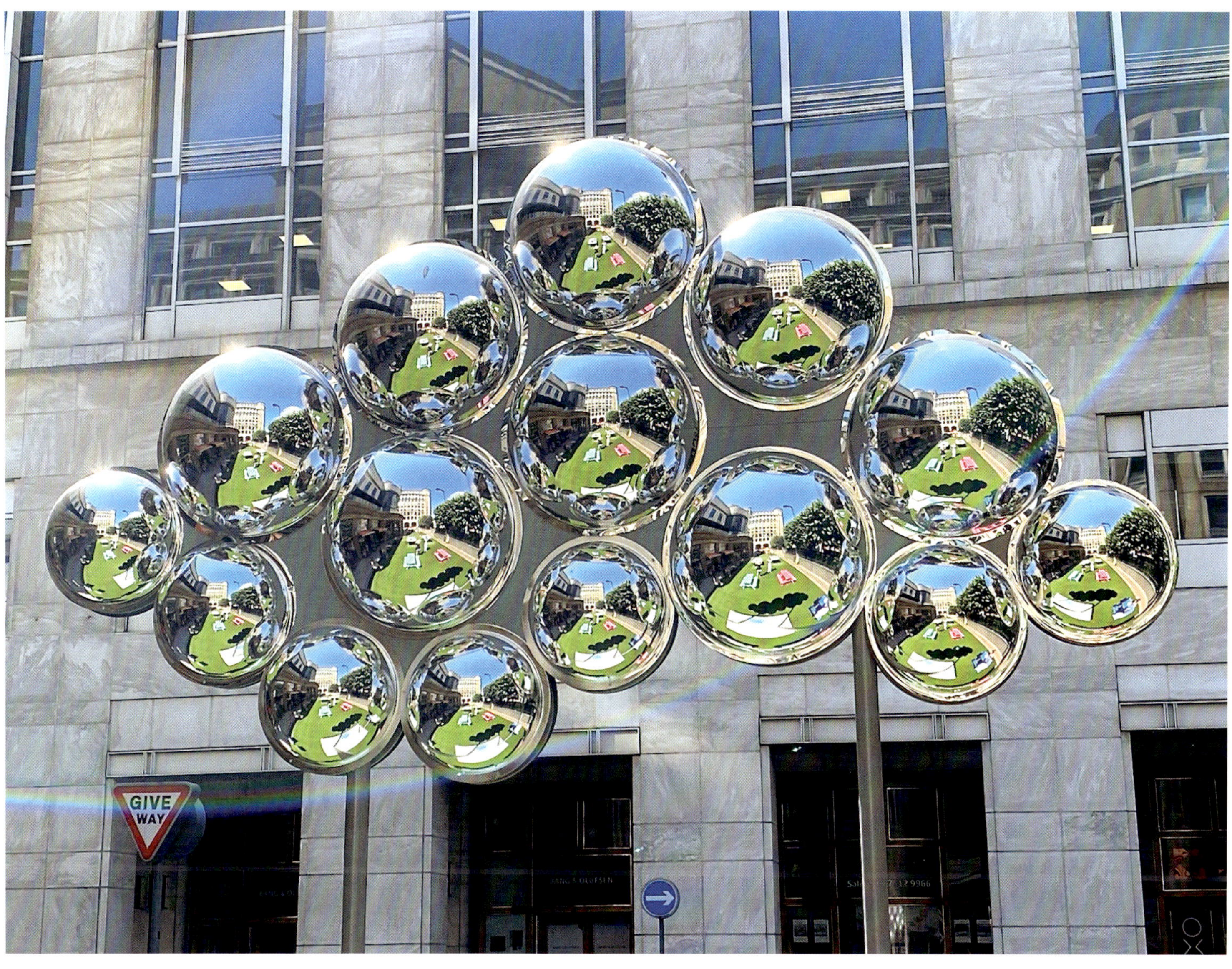

Summer Cloud – We Dream of You, 2021
Polycarbonate mirror
4.2 × 3.8 × 1.9 m (13¾ × 12½ × 6¼ ft)

Danish artist **TINE BECH** has said that 'there is an essential roundness in life's building blocks from electrons to our planet', and in her works the sphere and the disc are recurring images and forms. Her sculptural work *Summer Cloud – We Dream of You*, installed in London's Canary Wharf, sat in an artificial grass square outside a modernist building. The location reflects the dream of town planners, though is possibly not what those who have to work and live there would have come up with. Bech invites the visitor to look into her cloud of multiple curved mirrored hemispheres and dream.

SHIRIN HOSSEINVAND is an Iranian-American artist who started by painting Persian miniatures from the epic poem the *Shahnameh* (*c.* 977–1010 CE) onto Coca-Cola cans, before constructing oversized cans decorated with mirror work that harks back to traditional Persian artistic traditions. The practice of using small fragments of mirror for making decorative geometric patterns on walls and ceilings date backs more than 500 years. Hosseinvand merges American capitalism and global product branding with a focus on hand crafting to make her unique artworks. Her Coke cans replicate the brand's English-language logo and also depict it in Farsi.

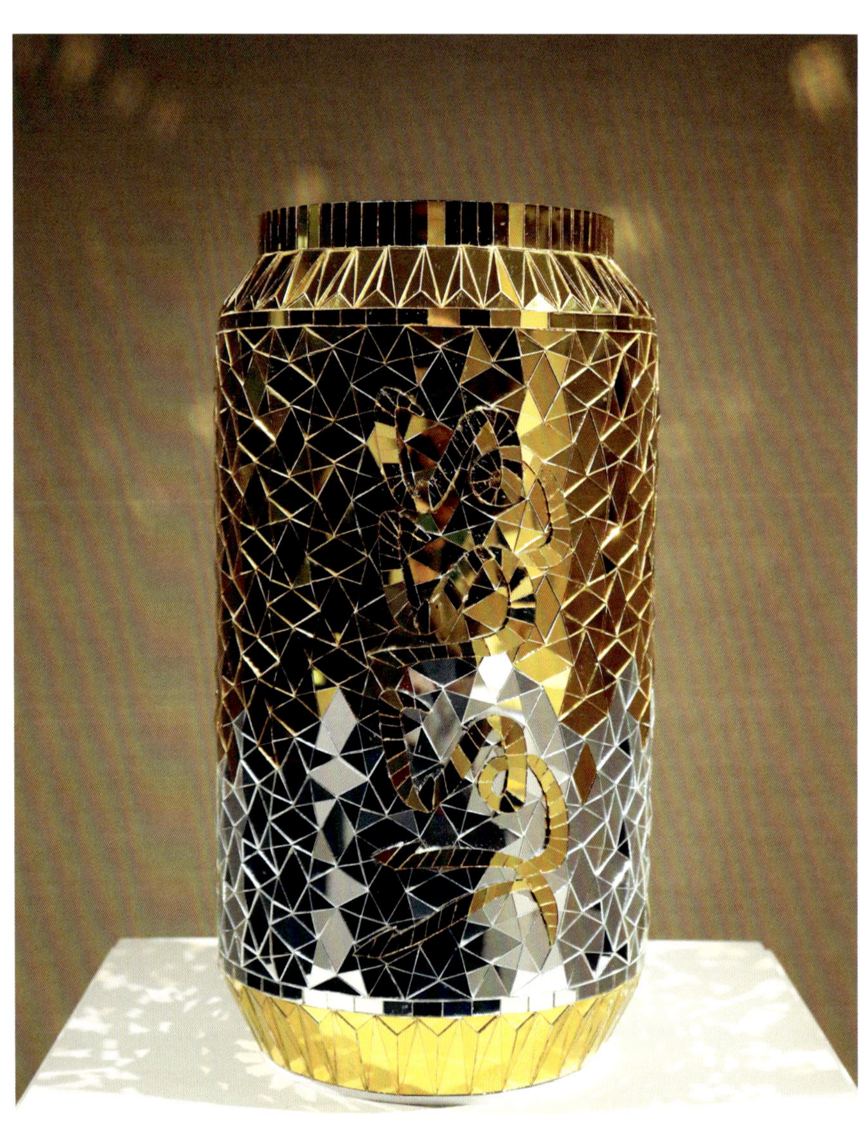

RIGHT
A beam of sunshine (*Coca-Cola* series), 2017
Styrofoam and mirror
H 45.7 × diam. 23 cm (H 18 × diam. 9 in)

OPPOSITE
Star Cluster at Night (*Coca-Cola* series), 2017
Styrofoam and mirror
H 45.7 × diam. 23 cm (H 18 × diam. 9 in)

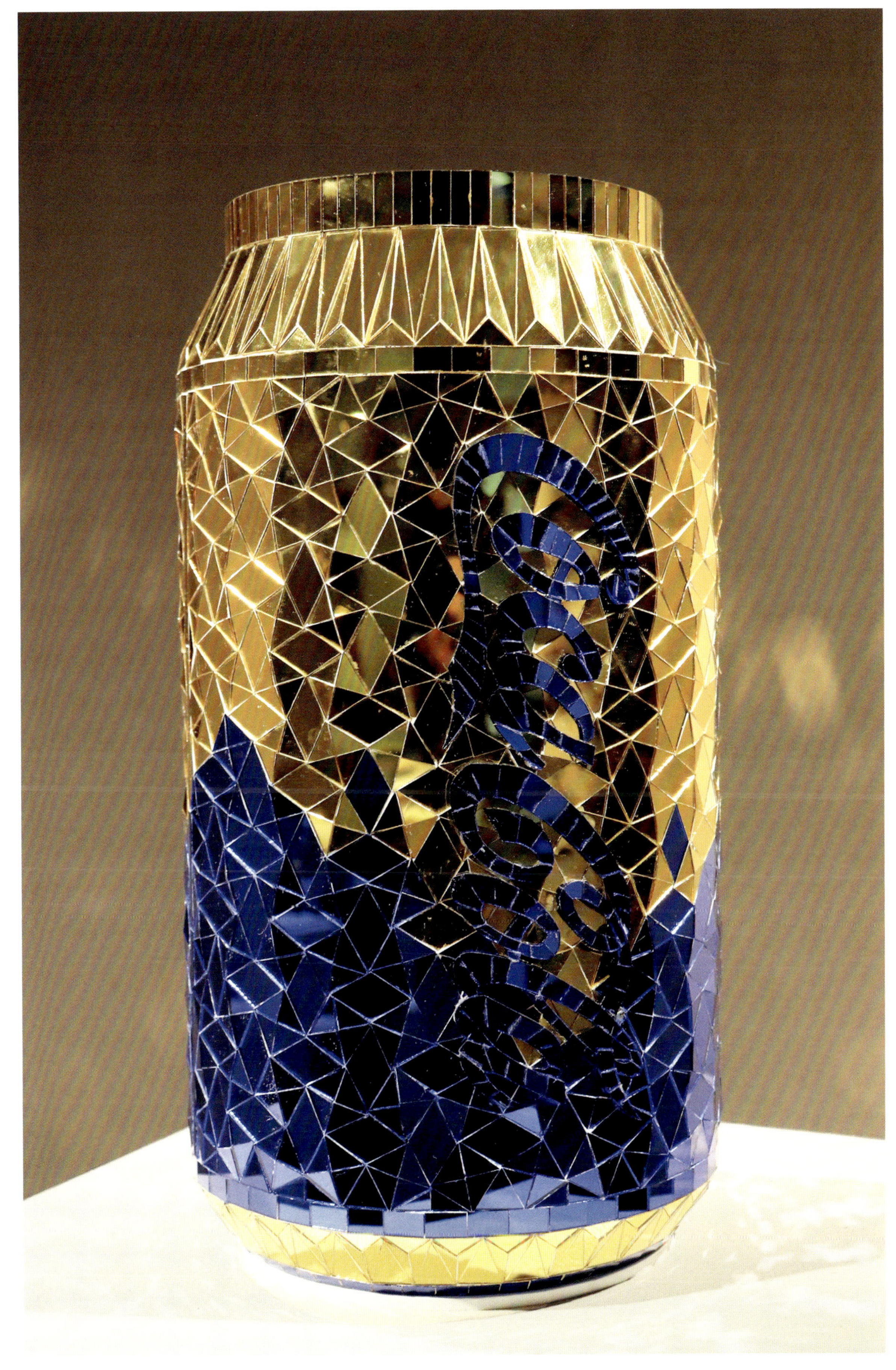

British sculptural artist **ANDREW LOGAN** (b. 1945) is perhaps best known for his performance art event the Alternative Miss World contest, held sporadically since 1972. Many contestants have borrowed from his visual vocabulary of shards of broken mirror, which he uses to make sculpture and jewellery. *Cosmic Egg*, one of his largest sculptures, is a mosaic of the cosmos made from thousands of mirror pieces laid on to a wooden superstructure. His larger works include a life-sized Pegasus with mirrored wings. Since the 1980's Logan has made a series of wall based mirror portraits including *Derek Jarman* (opposite). Drift wood pieces found at Jarman's Prospect Cottage, Dungerness, sit atop sections of mirror that form his face and allow the viewer to see themselves in relation to the work. This is in contrast to the intimacy of Logan's mirrored jewelry, which is meant to be worn on the body and reflect those the wearer encounters as much as the self.

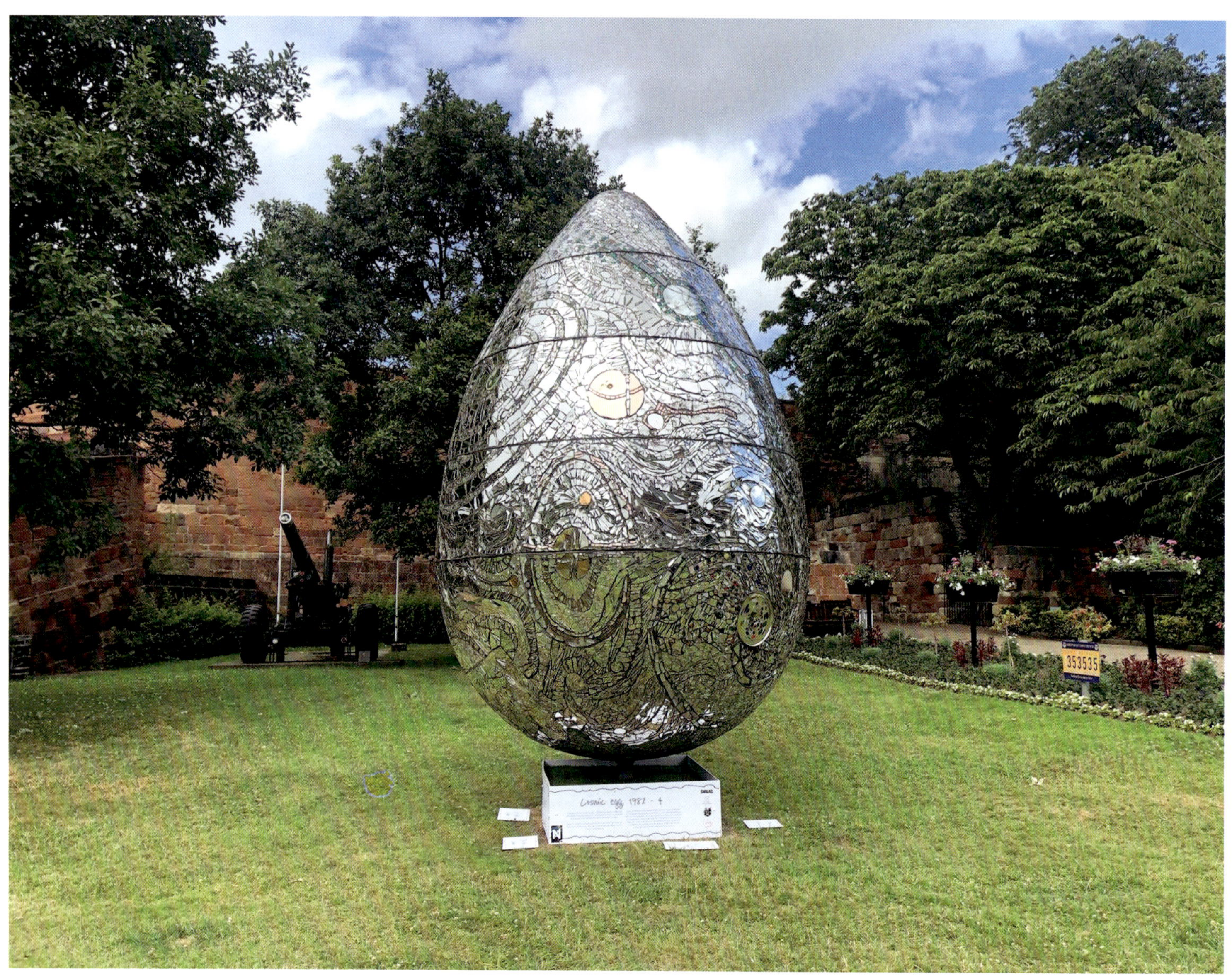

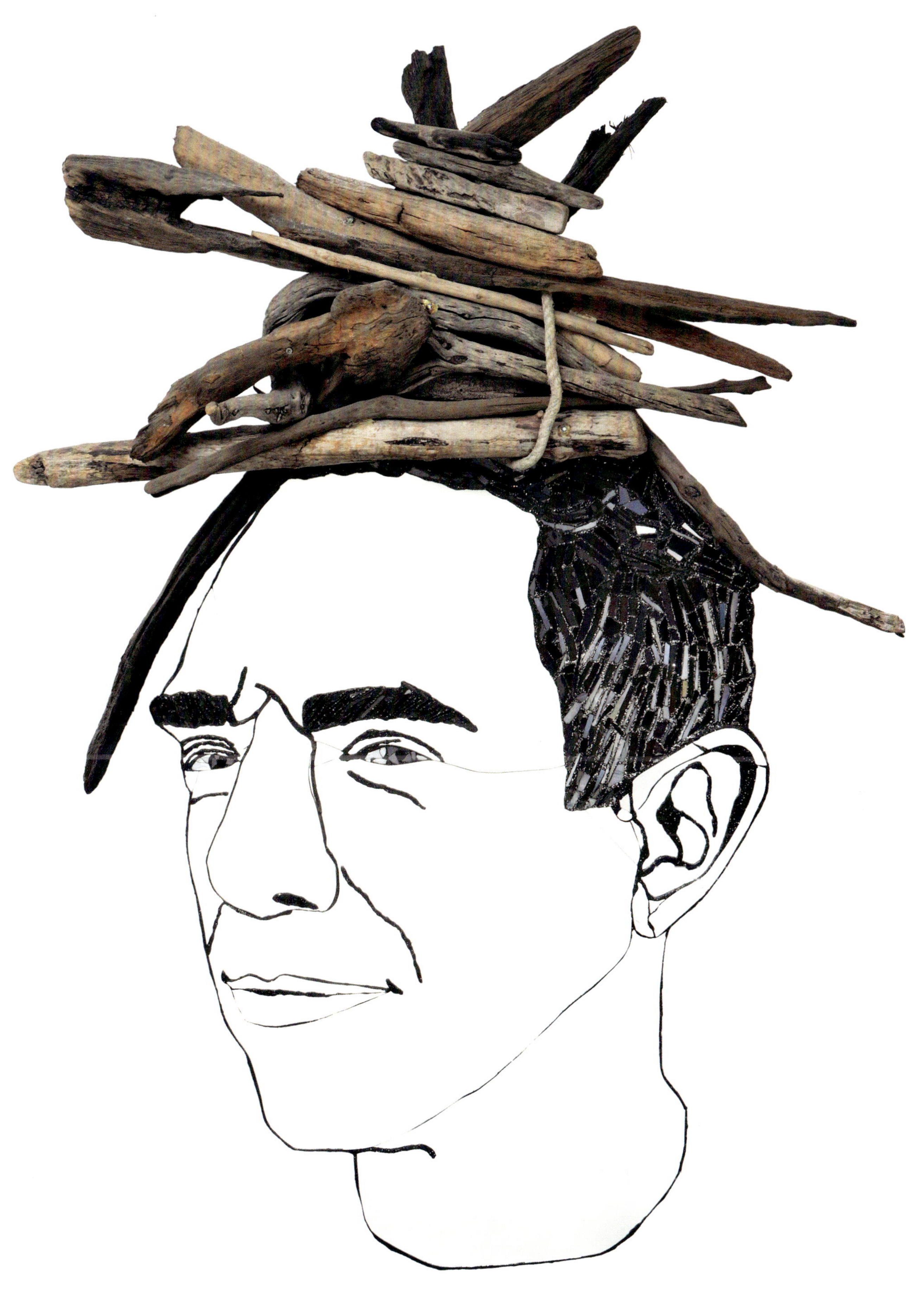

CARLOS ROLÓN (b. 1970) is an American artist of Puerto Rican descent. Rolón's use of mirrors functions to visually collapse the distance between people and institutions by connecting viewers to the artwork, to each other and to the surrounding space. He has created a large body of wall-based mirror works, as well as site-specific pieces such as *Fragments of Utopia* at the New Orleans Museum, Louisiana. On entering the museum, visitors encountered their own reflection scattered amid fragments of historical paintings and snippets of Neoclassical architecture in the mirrored work at the top of the staircase. *Fragments of Utopia* provided a powerful place of recognition for people and perspectives often underrepresented on museum walls, reflecting the diverse histories and people that have formed the rich culture of places such as New Orleans and Puerto Rico. In wall-based works such as *Untitled (Firozi Royal Blue)*, incorporating coloured grout, the hand-cut mirrors create a ruptured cinematic or shattered dreamlike quality. Literally and figuratively, viewers are on both sides of the work, dissolving any sense of clear division or borders.

BELOW
Untitled (Firozi Royal Blue), 2016
Mirror, resin and crystalline
on aluminium panel
1.53 × 1.53 m (5 × 5 ft)

OPPOSITE
Fragments of Utopia, 2018
Installation view: New Orleans
Museum of Art, Louisiana, USA
Mirror, resin and 24ct gold leaf
on aluminium panel
3.35 × 1.47 m (11 × 4¾ ft)

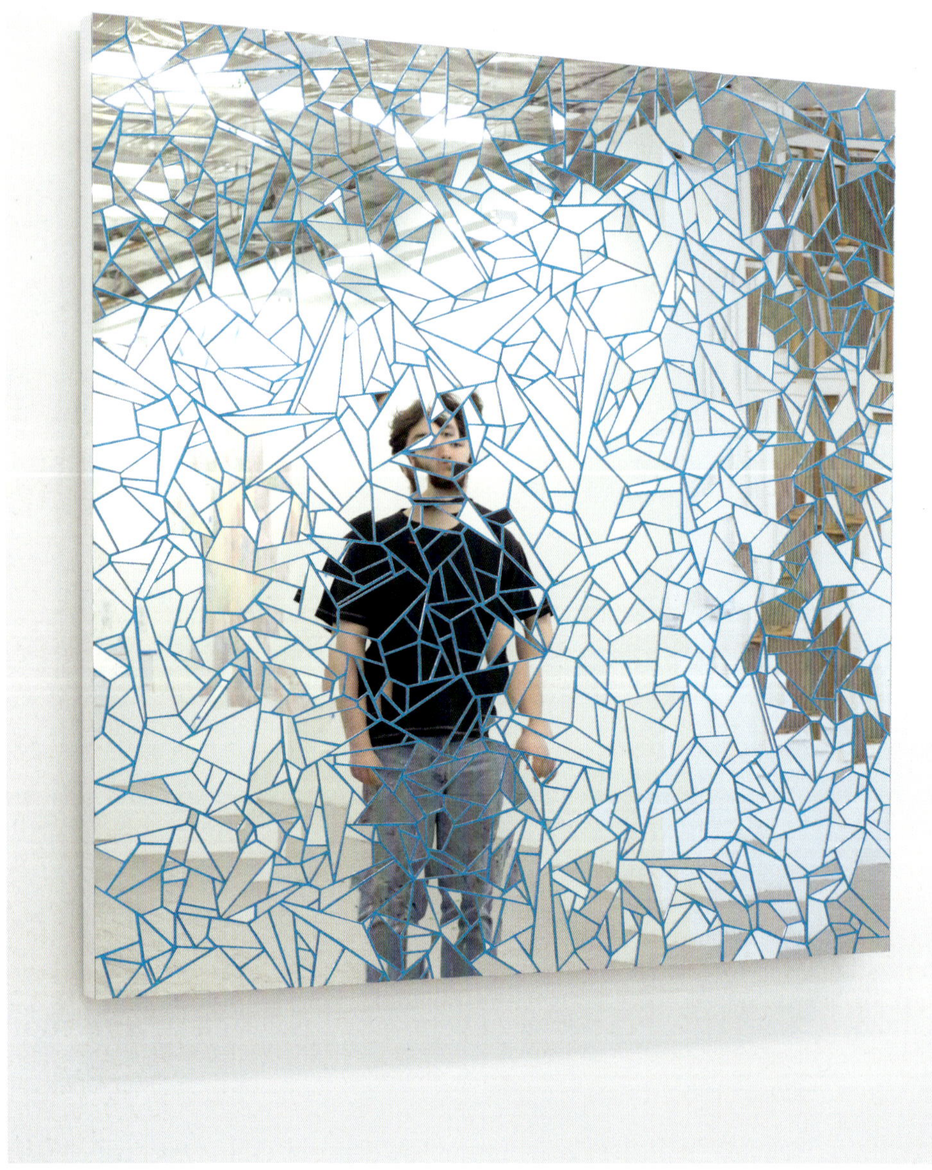

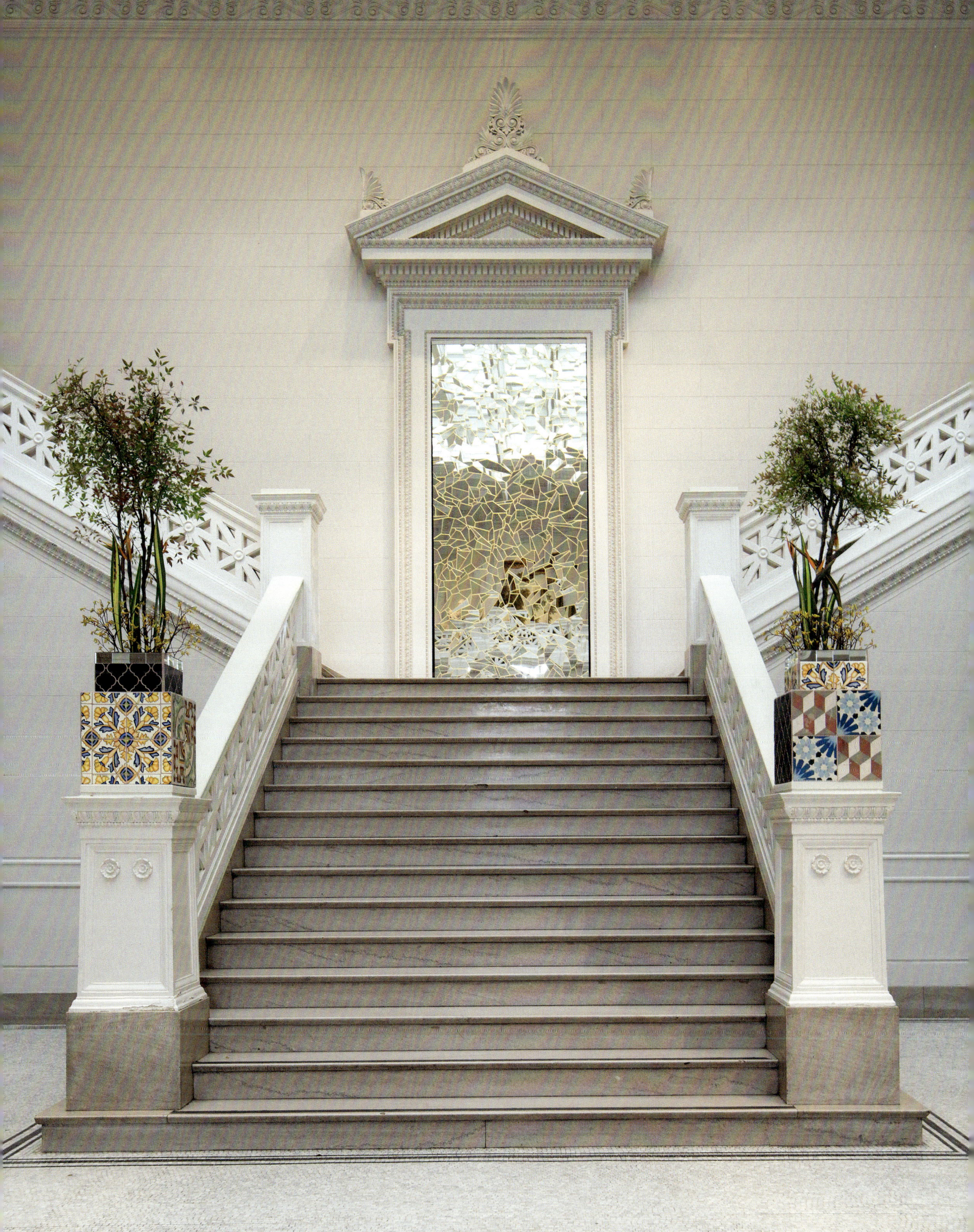

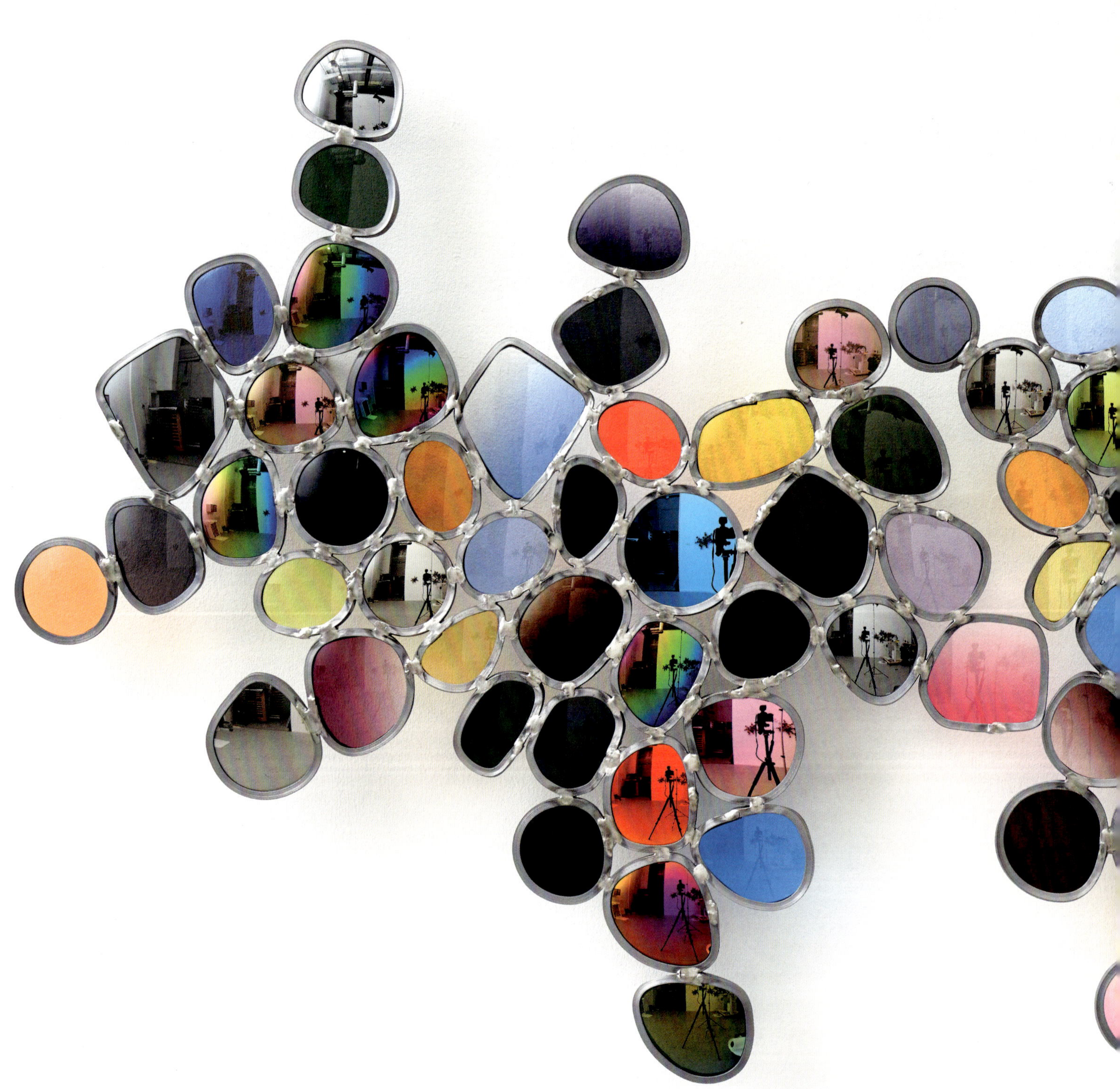

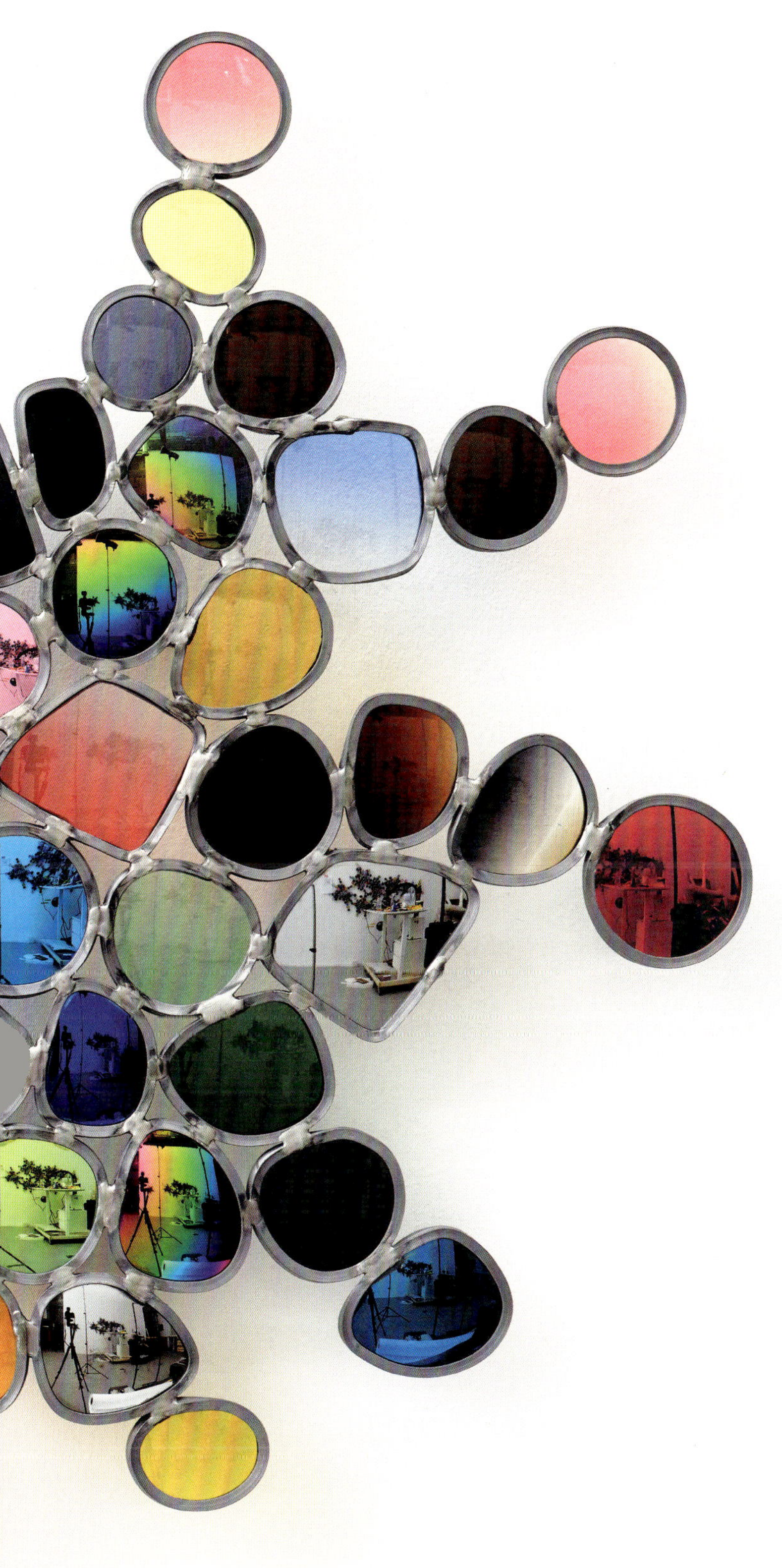

The work of Scottish artist **JIM LAMBIE** (b. 1964) is often both a physical and an emotional response to a given space. His highly popular 1999 installation *Zobop* has been recreated many times in galleries across the world, the practice of applying multicoloured vinyl strips to each floor marking out the physical differences of one space from another and meaning that the installation varies each time. His sunglass lens sculptures, including *Glorious Light*, reframe the everyday objects into something very new, and this is a process that he has explored with many other everyday materials. Lambie's work is also rooted in music and how it too changes a space.

Glorious Light, 2023
Sunglass lenses, lead came
54 × 88 × 4.5 cm (21½ × 34 ¾ × 1¾ in)

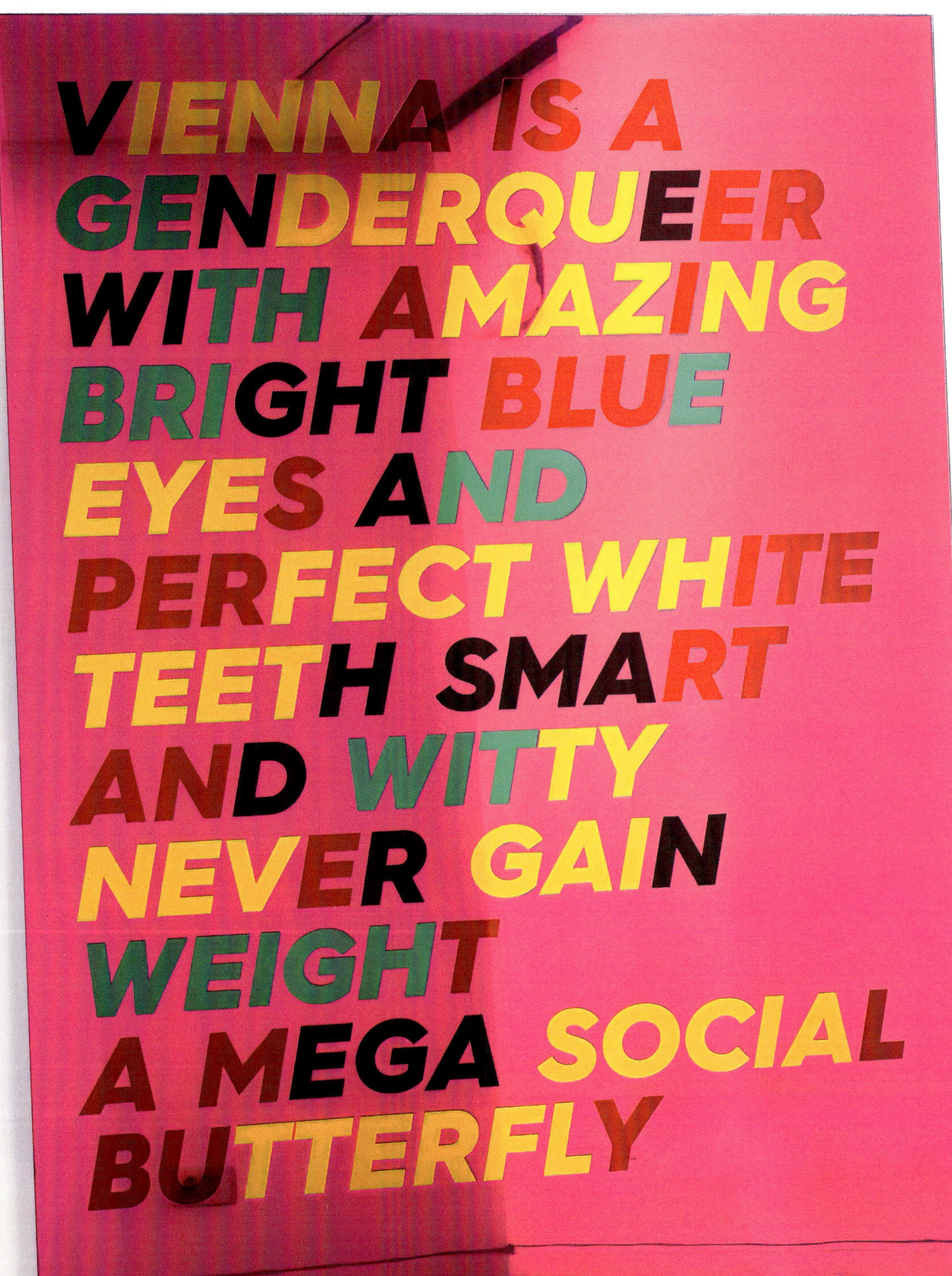

VIENNA IS A
GENDERQUEER
WITH AMAZING
BRIGHT BLUE
EYES AND
PERFECT WHITE
TEETH SMART
AND WITTY
NEVER GAIN
WEIGHT
A MEGA SOCIAL
BUTTERFLY

:MENTALKLINIK are an Istanbul-born, Brussels-based artist duo who have worked together since 1998. Their work often appears luxe as well as disposable, and can take the form of sculpture, installation and video. They play with seduction and the boundaries of truth and fiction. For their series *Profile Vienna Is*, large mirrors had various descriptions of Vienna across their surface. VIENNA IS A SNOWFLAKE A RARE SPECIES NOT A STEREOTYPE NOT FAKE WEIRD WEIRD IS GOOD was set against a yellow solar mirror ground, while neon pink was the backdrop to VIENNA IS A GENDERQUEER WITH AMAZING BRIGHT BLUE EYES AND PERFECT WHITE TEETH SMART AND WITTY NEVER GAIN WEIGHT A MEGA SOCIAL BUTTERFLY. In their *Profile* series of mirrors each solar mirror was given a person's name and offered a description of that person (EMMA: JEZEBEL, ELOPER, TOLERANT, FLORAL, EVANGELIST, BITCHY, SWALLOWER), in a comment on today's ubiquitous social media profiles and identities.

VIENNA IS, 1801, 2018
Tempered glass, micro-layered
polyester solar films
110 × 160 cm (43½ × 63 in)
Unique

American photographer and artist **PAUL MPAGI SEPUYA** (b. 1982) works with complex layers of portraiture, bringing its histories and possibilities to the fore through queer and homoerotic networks of production and collaboration. Sepuya features in many works, along with friends, lovers and collaborators. Viewers see the reflections of the subjects in mirrors positioned in the artist's studio, itself a subject: a place of possibility and staging where the nature of desire and its

construction plays out. Queerness and Blackness are visually represented in Sepuya's images, but are more deeply integrated as the material and conceptual underpinnings that structure his work.

Dark Room Studio Mirror (0X5A5668), 2021
Dye-sublimation print on aluminium
in artist frame
30 × 35.6 cm (11 × 14 in)

Mirror Study (4R2A0857), 2016
Archival pigment print
86.4 × 129.5 cm (34 × 51 in)

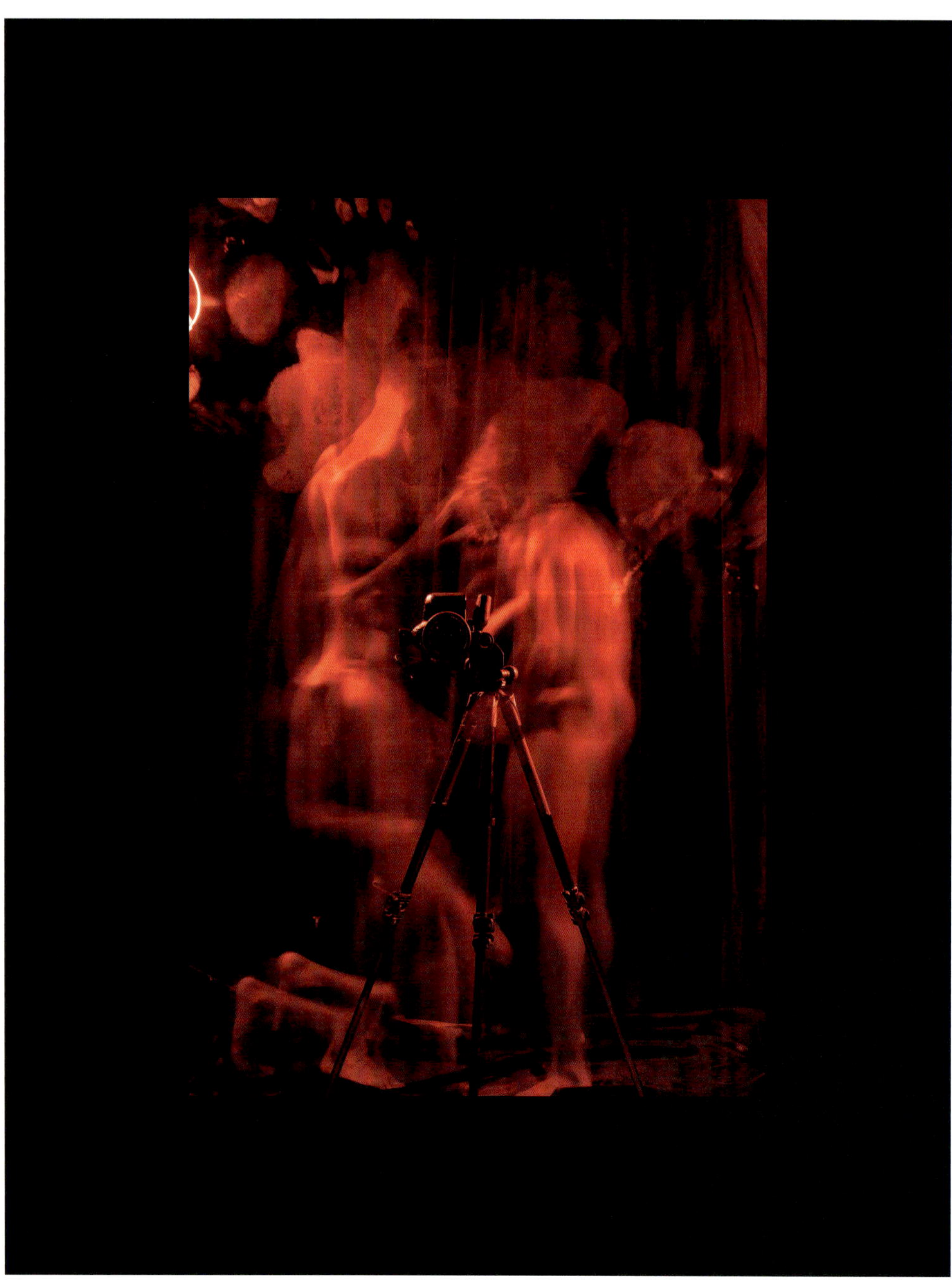

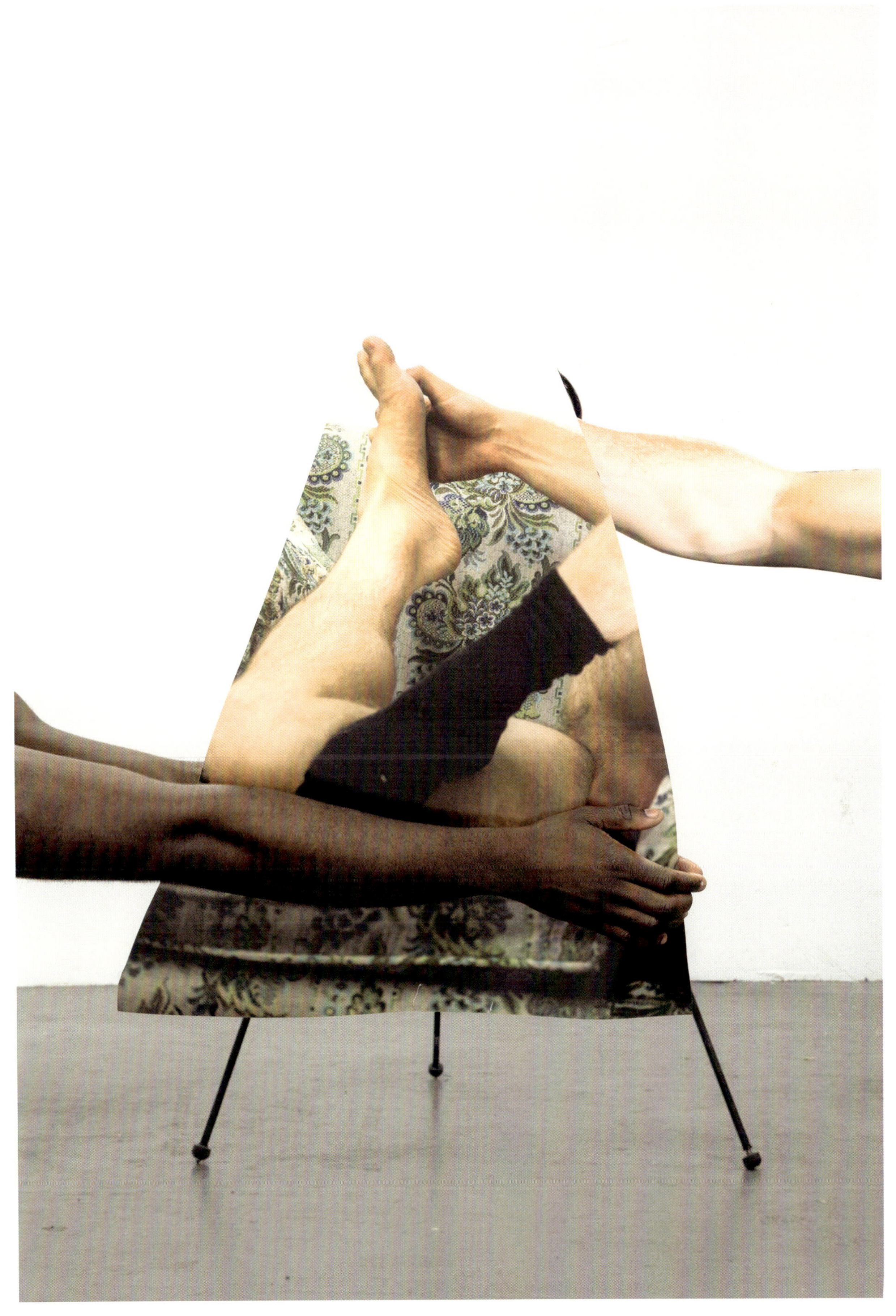

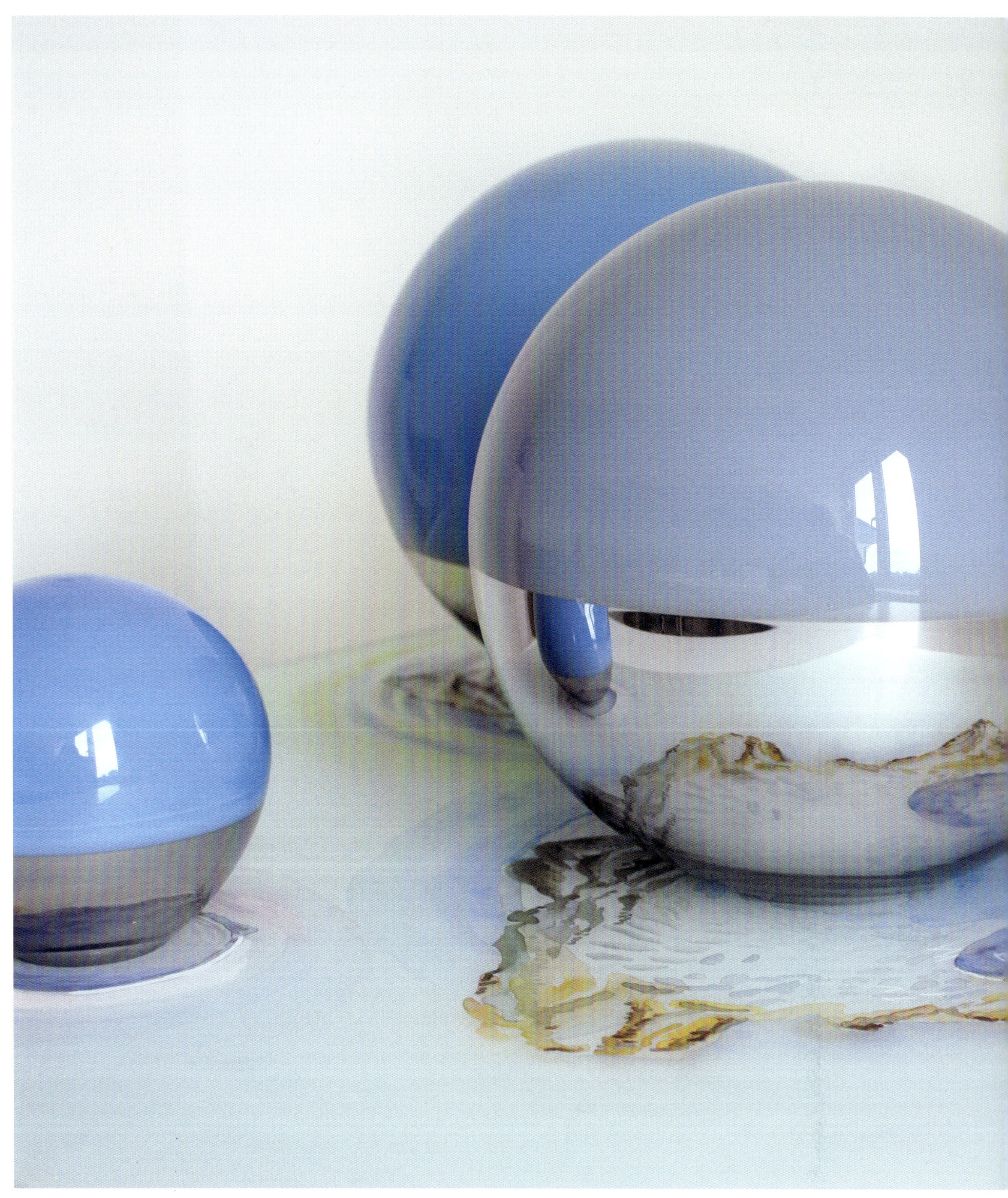

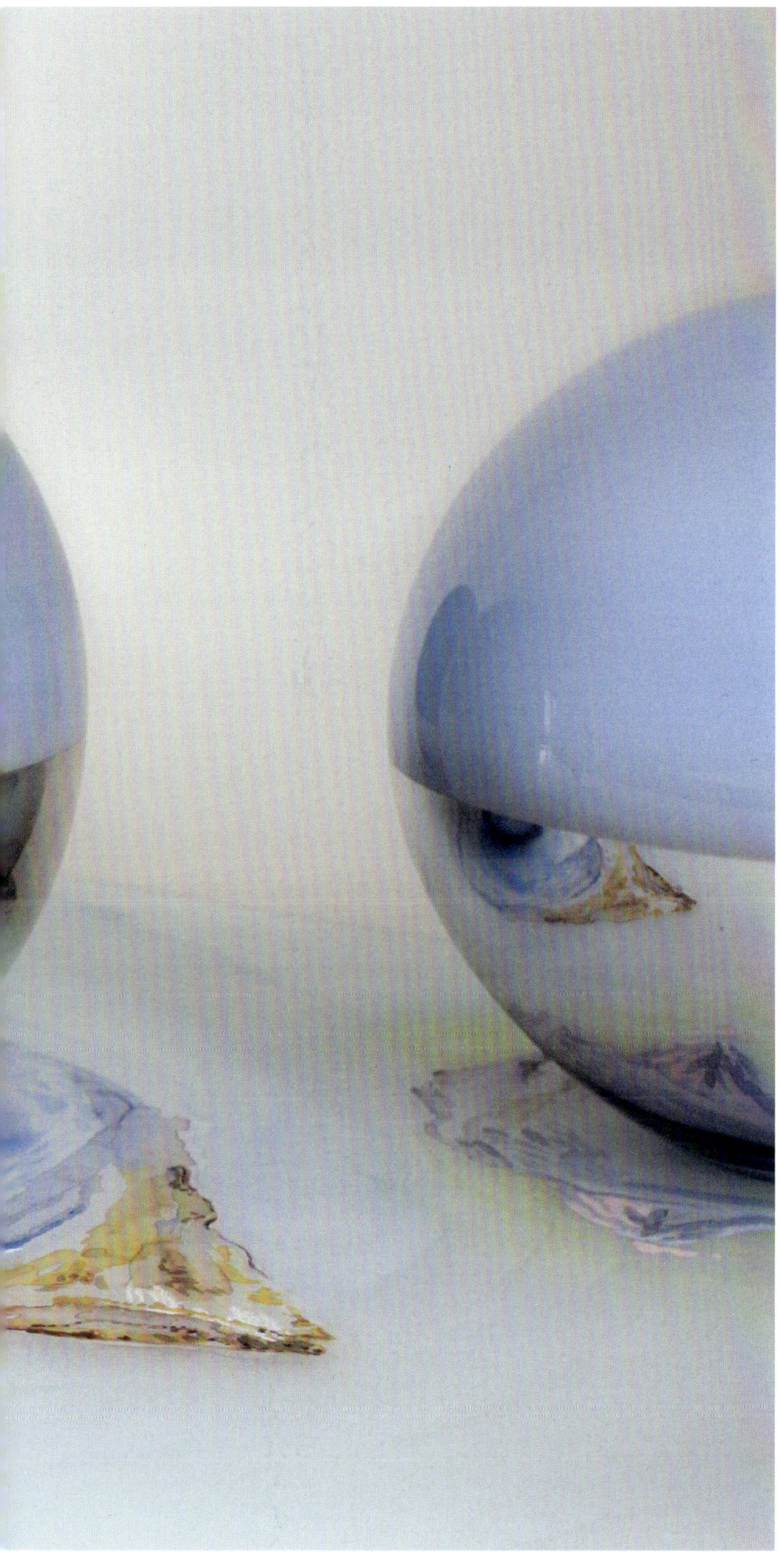

POLLY GOULD is a British artist who works with architecture and anthropology and is also a fellow of the Royal Geographical Society. Aspects of all of these interests come into play in her work *Observation Hill*, inspired by the life and work of the Victorian polar explorer Edward Wilson. Wilson was a self-taught watercolourist and medically trained doctor who brought with him the colonialist attitudes of his class and culture in the 'heroic era of Antarctic exploration' that Gould works to expose. Her project resulted in a book, *Antarctica, Art and Archive* (2020), as well as her sculpture. The work features four blue and mirrored-glass spheres that sit on a sandblasted glass ground. The base has topographical drawings executed in watercolour that reflect up onto the spheres. Gould argues that what is seen, how it is seen and from which background influences or alters what we know, and colours our understanding of science.

Observation Hill, 2012
Hand-blown coloured and mirrored glass,
watercolour on sandblasted glass
72 × 59 cm (28½ × 23¼ in), diam.
from 10 to 22 cm (4–8¾ in)

In British artist **PAUL HAZELTON**'s (b. 1962) *Witness*, the central object is a curved piece of mirrored glass of which he has scratched away the silvering to allow the underlying photograph through. This is in the centre of the image and is the death mask of Abraham Lincoln. The artist's face lies behind it in the reflecting surface, holding a red camera. Hazelton made the work when he came across the historical fact that Joseph Hazelton, a young actor, was witness to Lincoln's assassination in 1865 as a boy. Joseph was born on the 26th of March, Paul on the 27th, and while they share a last name, the artist is not sure if they are related. He does, however, wonder if he is in some way also a witness, if not to the actual act then to the historical memory of it, feeling as he does that 'perhaps mirrors and other reflective surfaces hold memories'.

BELOW
WITNESS without reflection, 2022
Reverse-scored mirror, found image
D 4–6 × diam. 15 cm (D 1½ –2½ × diam. 6 in)

OPPOSITE
WITNESS, 2022
Reverse-scored mirror, found image
D 4–6 × diam. 15 cm (D 1½ –2½ × diam. 6 in)

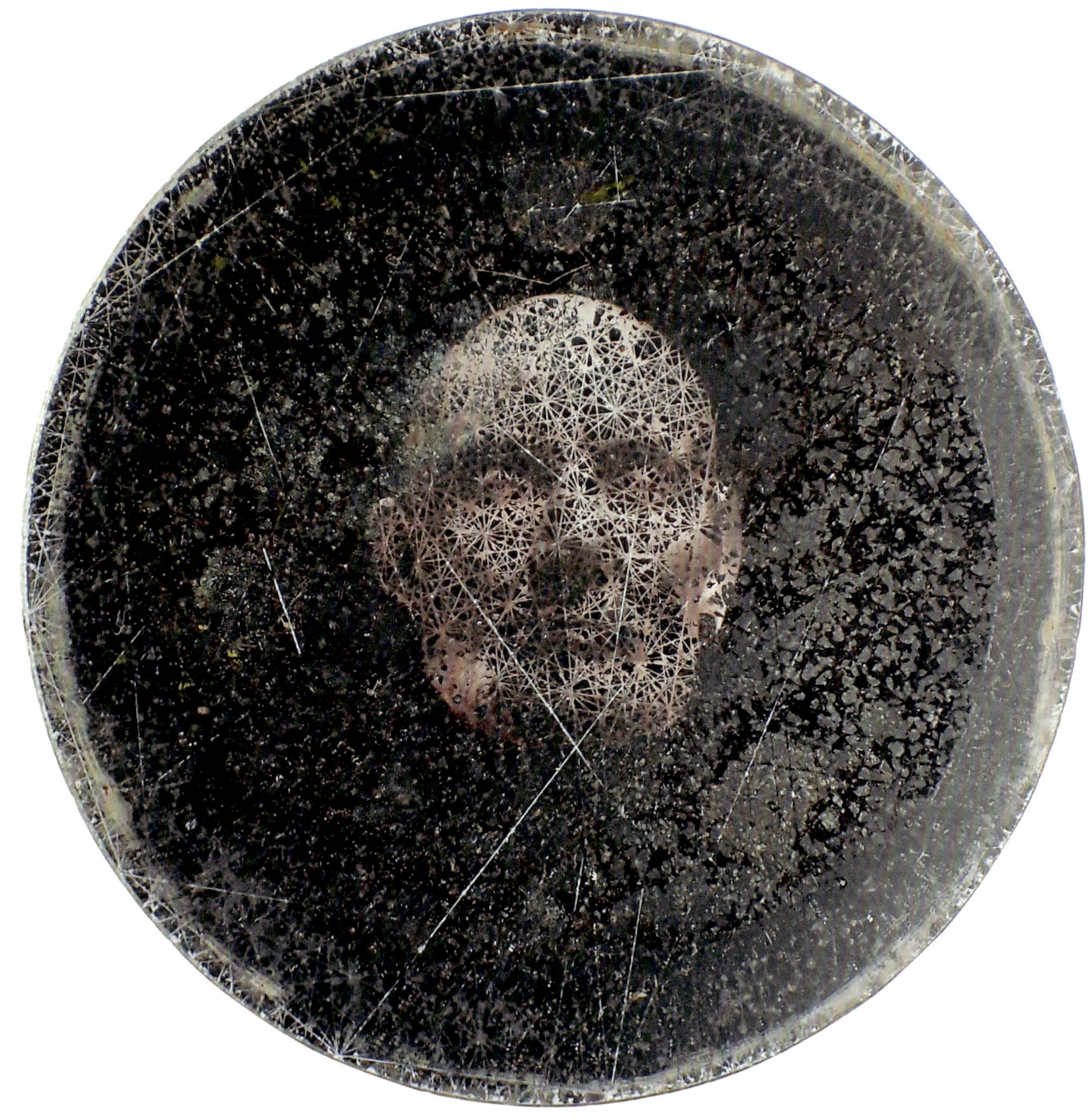

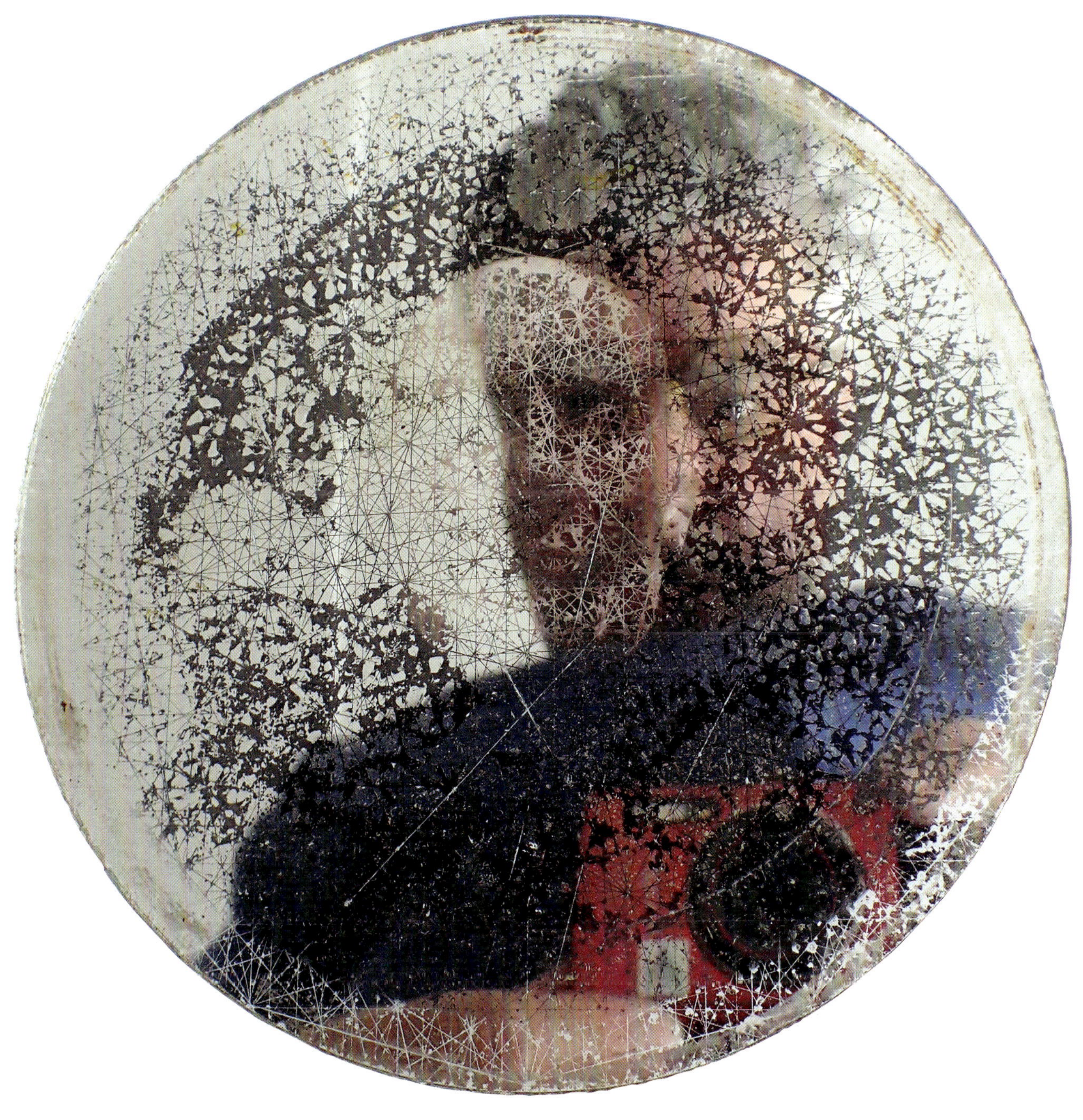

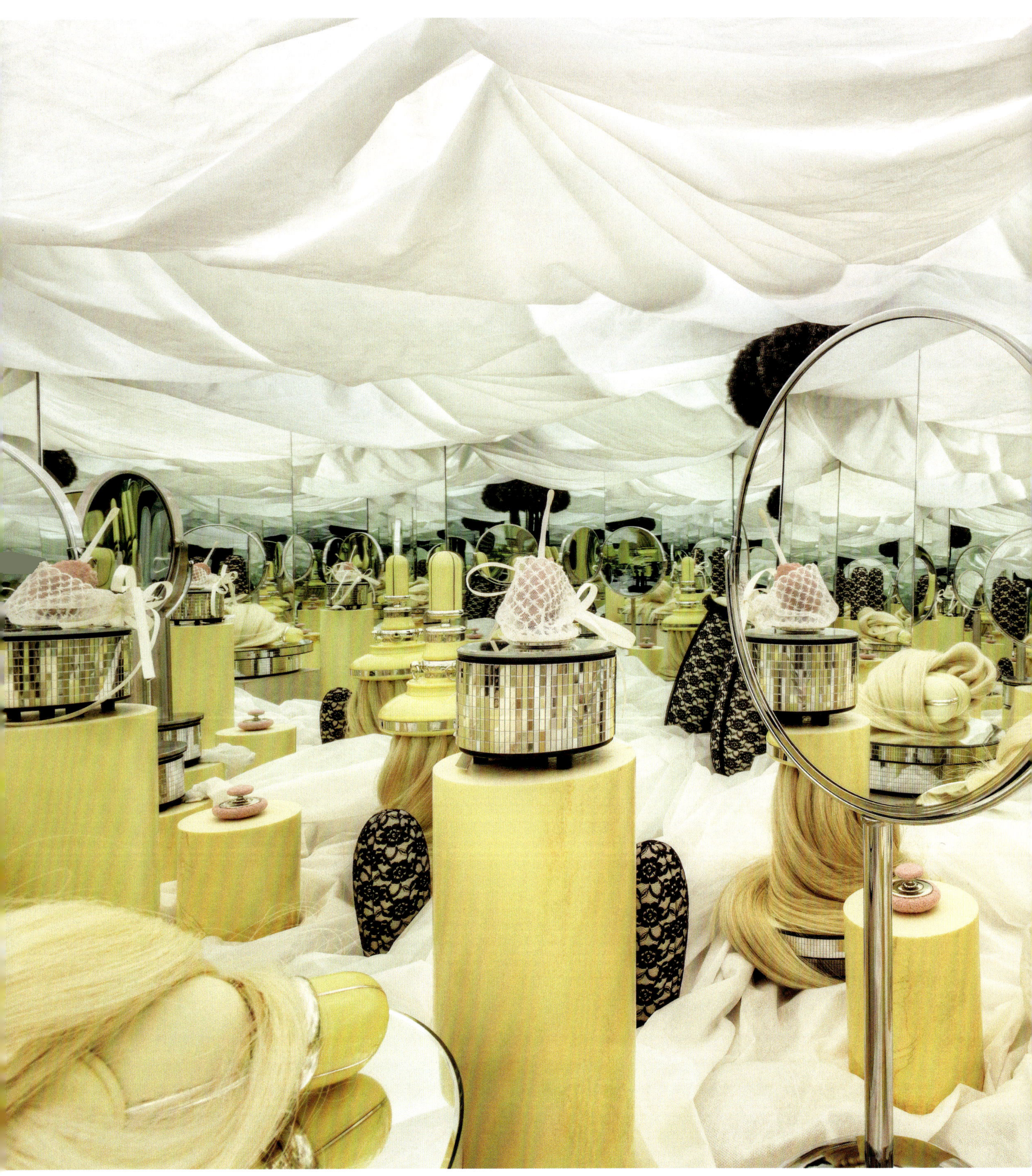

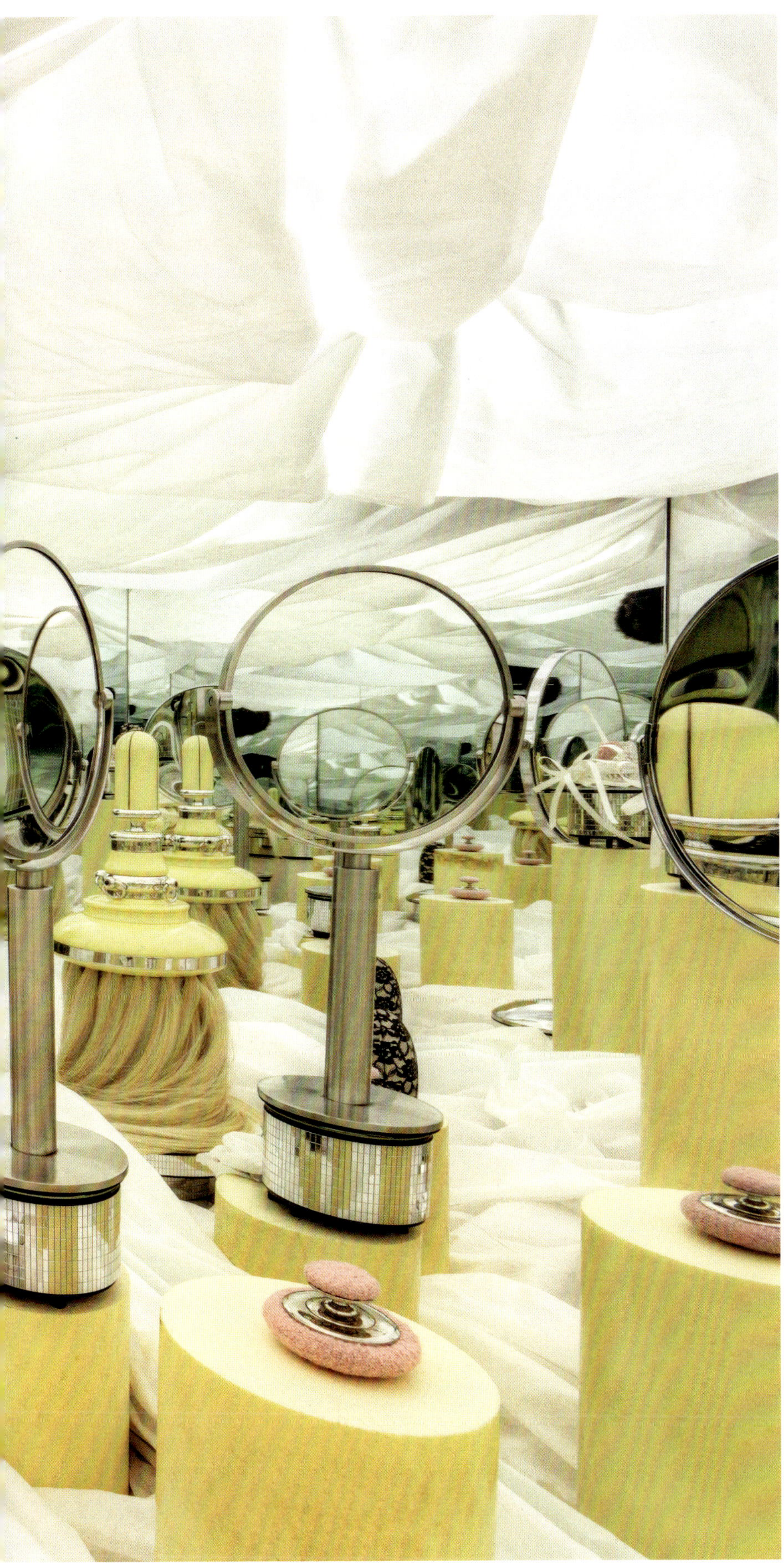

British artist **MARK WOODS**'s (b. 1961) *Unchanging nature of the fetish object* directly references Marcel Duchamp's *Étant donnés* (*Given*), right down to the use of peepholes to view it. In different versions, viewers approached a large structure and peered into it, or, as in its installation at the exhibition 'Nirvana. Strange Forms of Pleasure' (Mudac, Lausanne, Switzerland), they entered an empty room with only the peepholes showing. As in the Duchamp, what viewers saw was a world focused on the erotic. Woods trained as a jeweller, and all the leather, wood, hair and lace objects in the room were meticulously crafted by him. He also constructed the room so that the many mirrors turned on themselves like a child's music box, and the room itself was lined with mirrors, so the objects were replicated endlessly and limitlessly, just like desire.

Unchanging nature of the fetish object, 2013
Installation shot of automata piece, housed in a mirror-lined crate. Viewed through a peephole
91.4 × 120 × 183 cm (36 × 48 × 72 in)

Swiss-born US-based **URS FISCHER**'s (b. 1973) *Pineapple/Melon* featured four large mirror cubes printed on five sides (including the top) with the image of a sponge or an antique claw-footed chair. The viewer was able to walk through the seemingly three-dimensional still life, their own reflection interacting with the original printed objects and their reflection in the other cubes. The complex relations between all the objects, the title and viewers included, were at the core of Fischer's investigation into spatial relationships.

YUKO SHIRAISHI (b. 1956), a London-based Japanese artist, constructs imaginary architectural works such as *Confession Show, Peep Box × Peep Show, Confession Box*, first shown at the Russian Club Gallery, London, in 2010, and then at the Hans Mayer Galerie, Düsseldorf, in 2016. The work is based on two notions of human interaction where 'peeping' is at the core. One is the Roman Catholic tradition of confession in a small architectural structure sited within a church, where the person who wishes to confess kneels inside a private or semi-private space with a grate hiding the priest from full view. The other is the sex peep booth usually found in decaying urban centres where the peeper inserts coins to see (usually) a woman remove her clothes and more. Shiraishi has constructed a grey booth that, when looked into, presents an endless mirrored space with hints of naughtiness. She says: 'I want to explore human fascination with the act of peeping and looking into the hidden and secret world in darkness.'

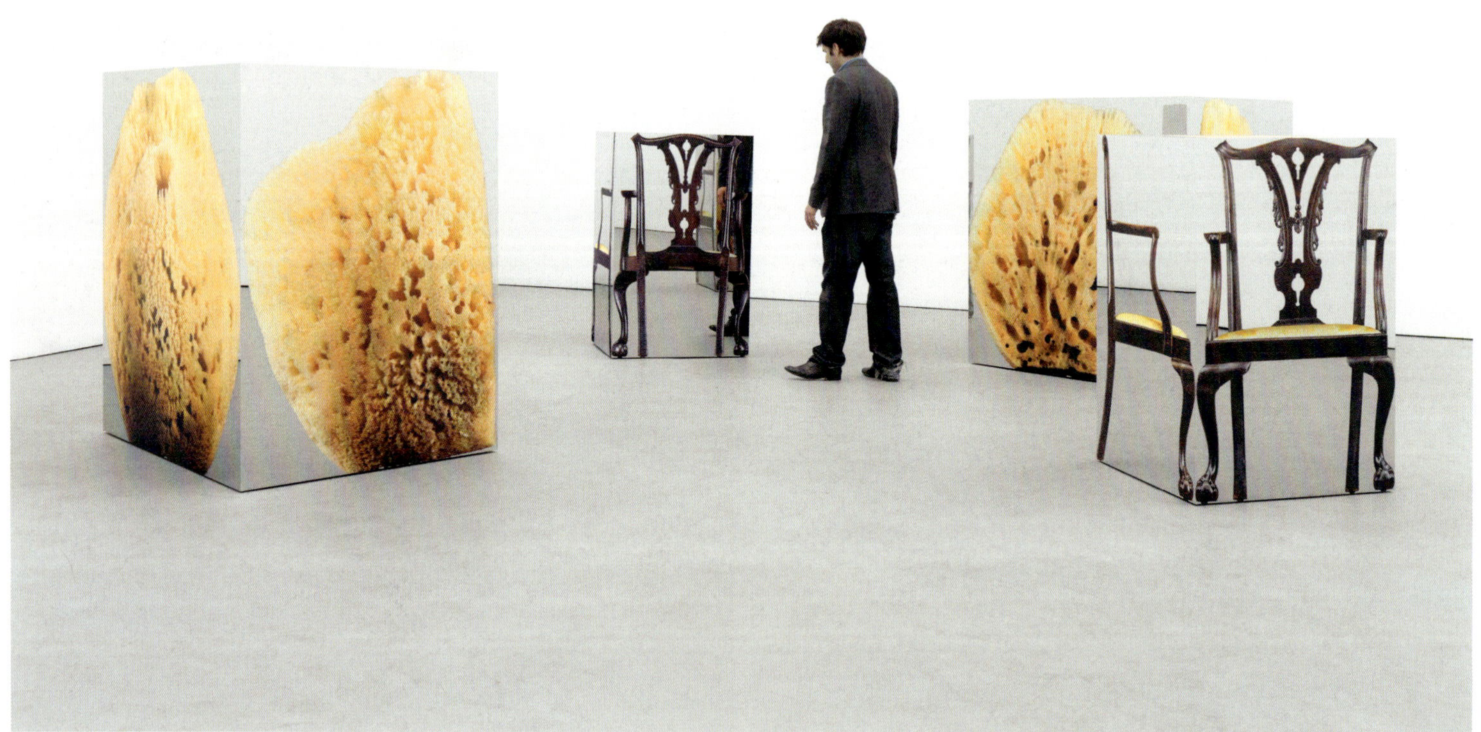

OPPOSITE
Urs Fischer, *Pineapple/Melon*, 2010
Silkscreen print on mirror-polished
stainless-steel sheets, polyurethane foam
sheets, two-component polyurethane
adhesive, stainless-steel beams, aluminium
L sections, screws, in four parts
Sponge, each: 140 × 100.6 × 132 cm
(55⅛ × 39⅝ × 52 in)
Chair, each: 119 × 67 × 132 cm
(46⅞ × 26⅜ × 52 in)
Edition of 2 + 1 AP

RIGHT
Yuko Shiraishi, *Confession Show,
Peep Box x Peep Show, Confession Box*, 2010
Wood, metal, mirror wallpaper and tiles,
fluorescent light, photograph
2.6 × 1.85 × 2.4 m (8½ × 6 × 7⅘ ft)

BELOW
Detail: Yuko Shiraishi, *Confession Show,
Peep Box x Peep Show, Confession Box*, 2010

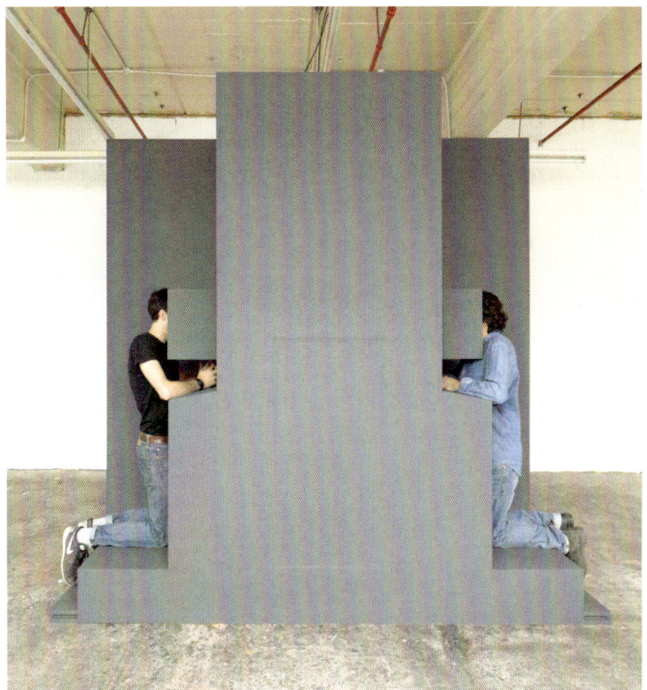

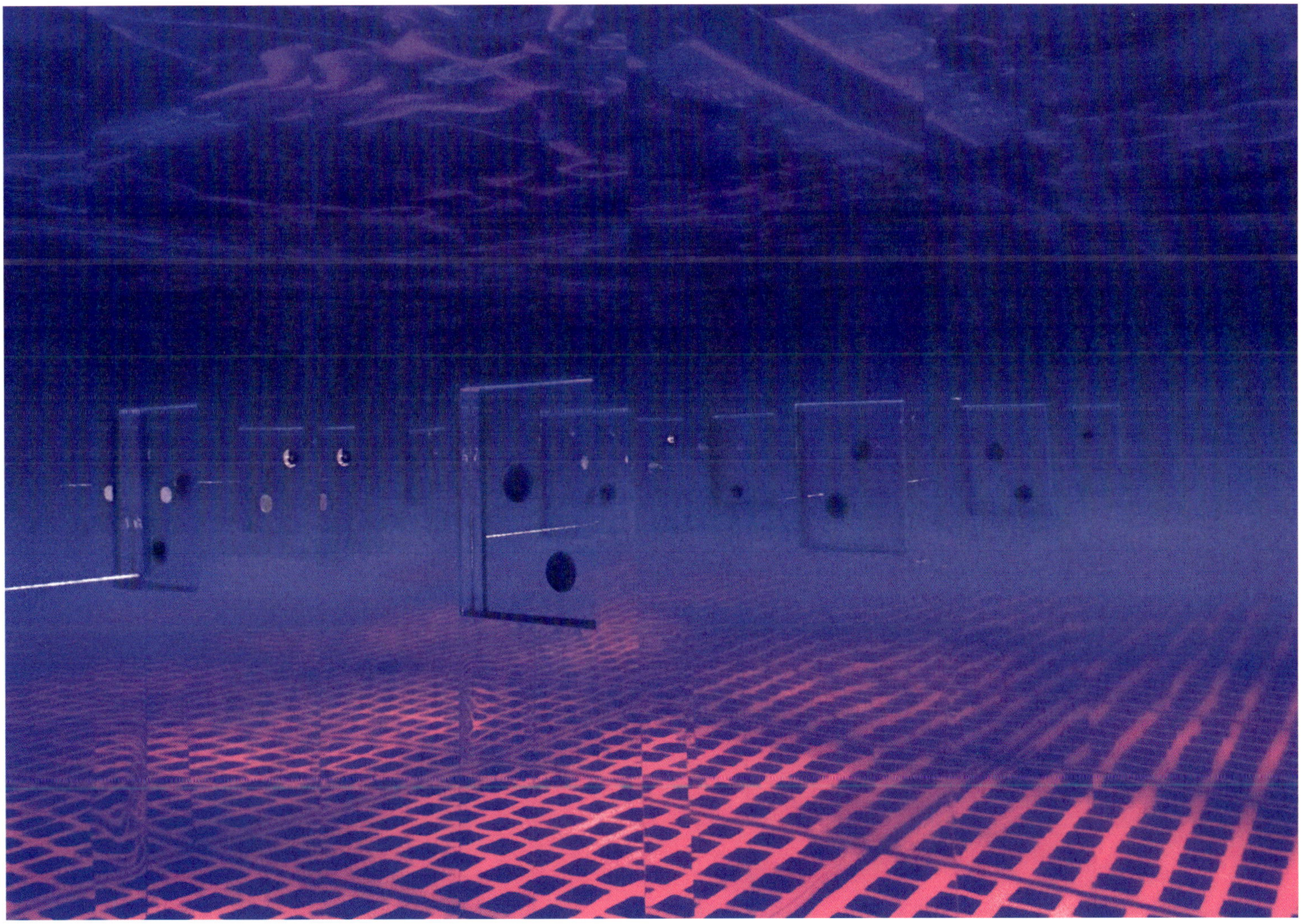

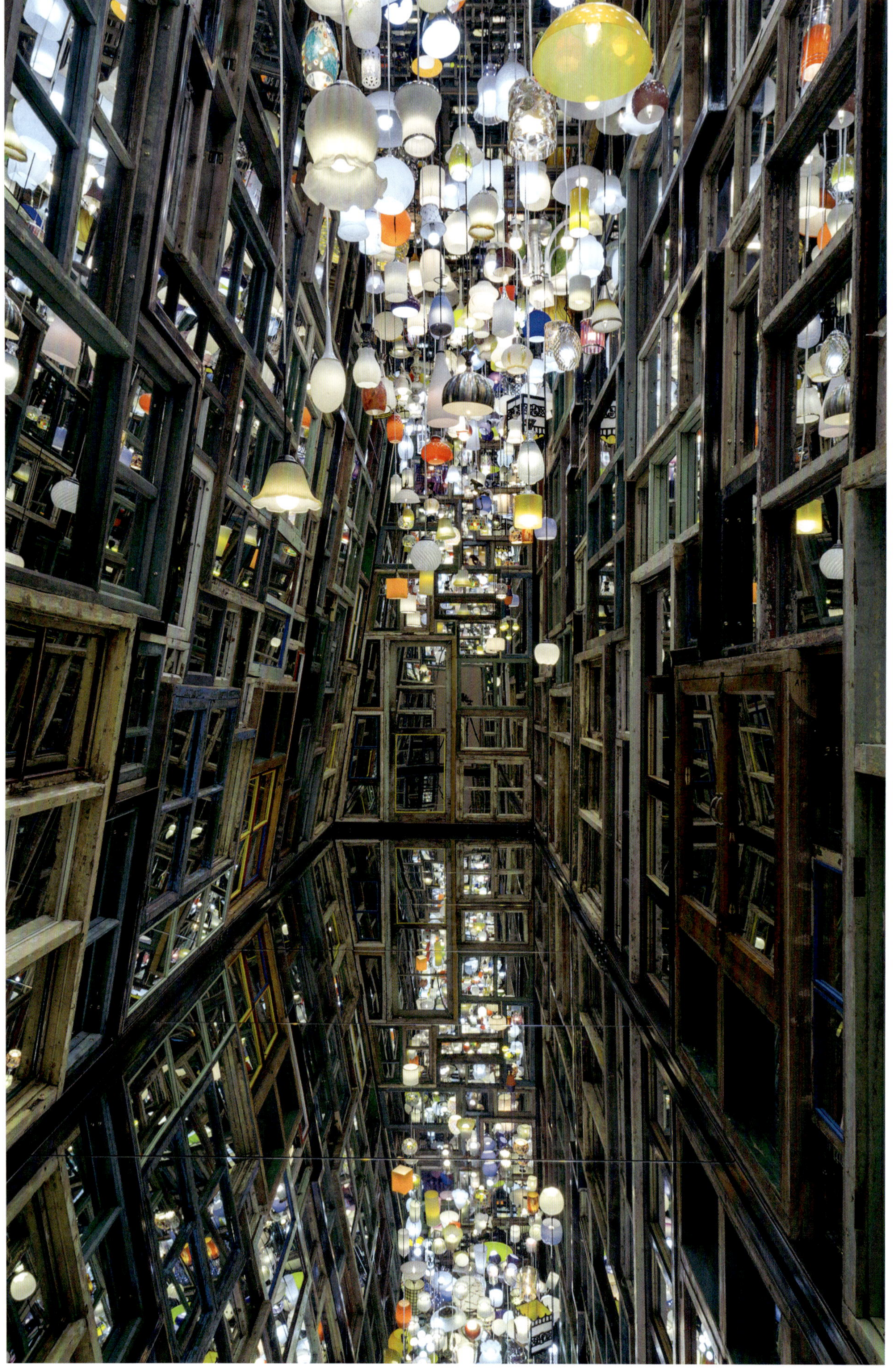

Chinese artist **SONG DONG**'s (b. 1966) *Through the Wall* is made up of recycled discarded objects found in cities across China as it modernizes. Whole parts of old towns are torn down and replaced by modern blocks that house many more people. Song's works question the idea of permanence, memory and history in a country where these notions are not especially prioritized. While these topics are serious, he addresses them in humorous ways, often upending Western ideas about China, old and new. His window sculptures use mirror replacements and reclaimed glass pendant lamps to create sparkling reflective spaces that multiply on themselves.

Marcel Duchamp's *Mirror* (1964) features a mirror framed in light wood and signed on the reverse, the signature scratched into the silvered surface. American artist **SHERRIE LEVINE**'s (b. 1947) *Silver Mirror: 11* clearly references Duchamp's work. Levine has channelled the works of many other artists, including Man Ray and Walker Evans. She has said she wants to 'make art which celebrates doubt and uncertainty'. Levine previously showed 'Mourning Mirrors', a series of twelve black mirrors, at her New York gallery in 2004: these were more funerary and unnerving, and like other black mirrors had an overtone of death about them. Both her silver and her black works mirror the situation she and other female artists face, in which their view is more open to question and their ideas often seen as secondary to or not as solid as those of their male counterparts.

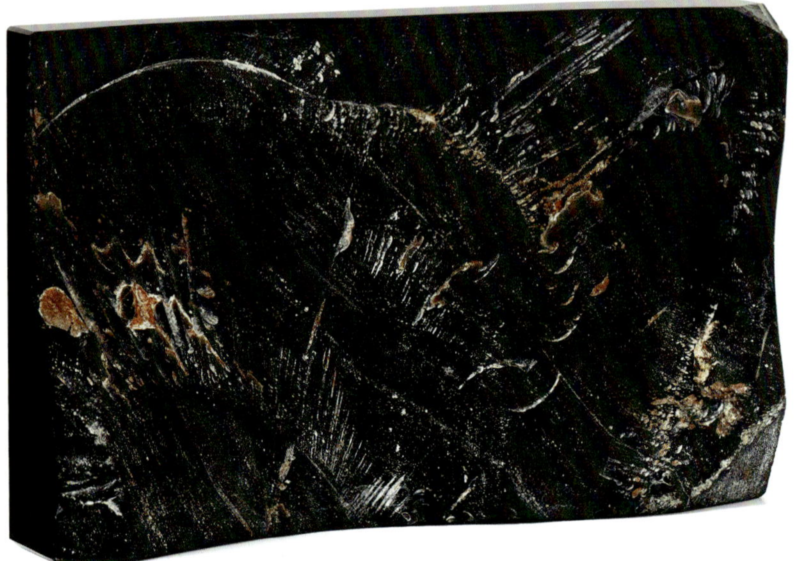

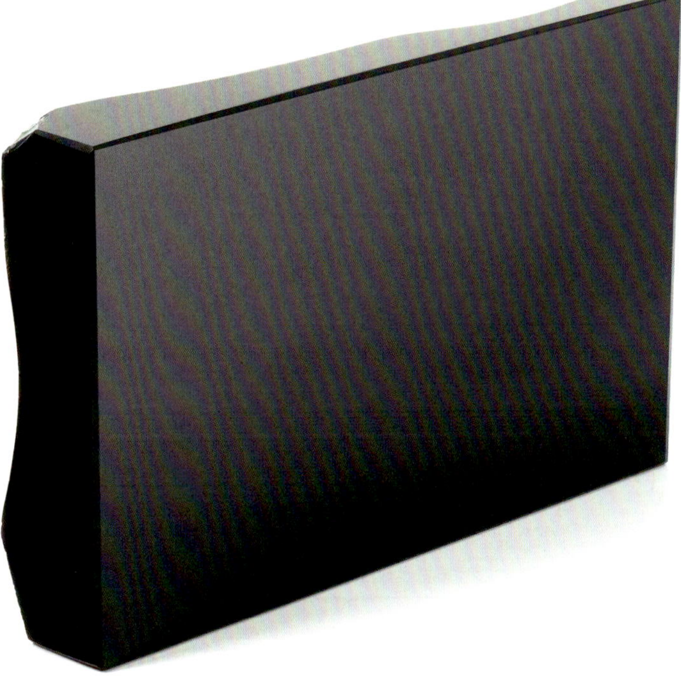

Mexican architect **FRIDA ESCOBEDO** (b. 1979) is well known for having won a number of prestigious architectural commissions, but she also makes installations and limited-edition objects. She was asked to design the 2018 annual summer Serpentine Pavilion in London, and to accompany the structure, she designed a limited edition of black obsidian stone mirrors. Each one is unique but roughly the same size, with one side highly polished and the other left rough. Each is etched on the side with the number that it represents out of the edition of twenty-five. Escobedo's mirror references the 'Claude glass', a darkened mirror popularly used as a drawing aid in the seventeenth century, as well as Aztec mirrors that were designed for the 'black magic' of travelling into the world of the gods. 'Tezcatlipoca', the name of the Aztec god of the night and of obsidian, translates as 'smoking mirror': he was usually depicted wearing or carrying such a mirror, made of obsidian.

Obsidian Mirror, 2018
Obsidian
13 × 20 × 5 cm (5⅛ × 7⅞ × 2 in)
Signed and numbered
Edition of 25 + 5 AP
Produced in Mexico by Punta de Lanza

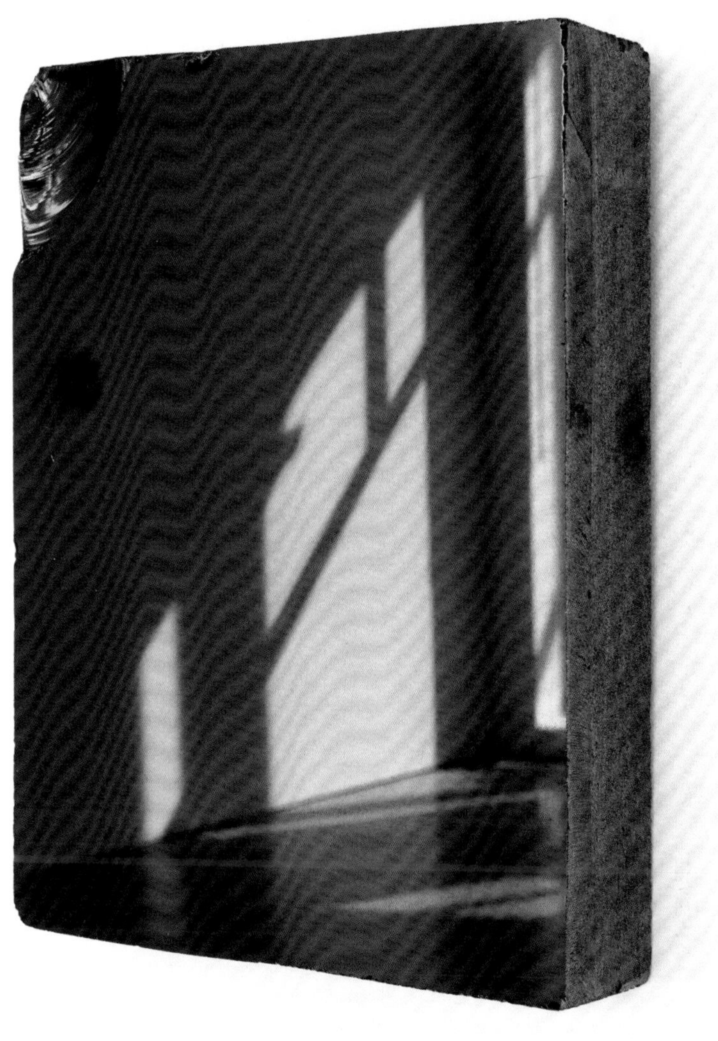

German artist **JOHANNES WALD** (b. 1980) has said that a personal artistic crisis in 2014 led to his ongoing series of handmade mirrors, as he hoped 'to rediscover myself as an artist in the mirror I created in my studio, thus putting an end to my doubts'. He started by hand grinding stainless-steel plates, and then worked with raw obsidian, which he also polished to mirror perfection. He has made reflective surfaces by mirroring old bricks from a demolished studio (using a ceramic process, platinum, and gold). All of these unlikely objects reflect not only the artist, but any viewer who may also be looking to find themselves, even if only in an artwork mirror.

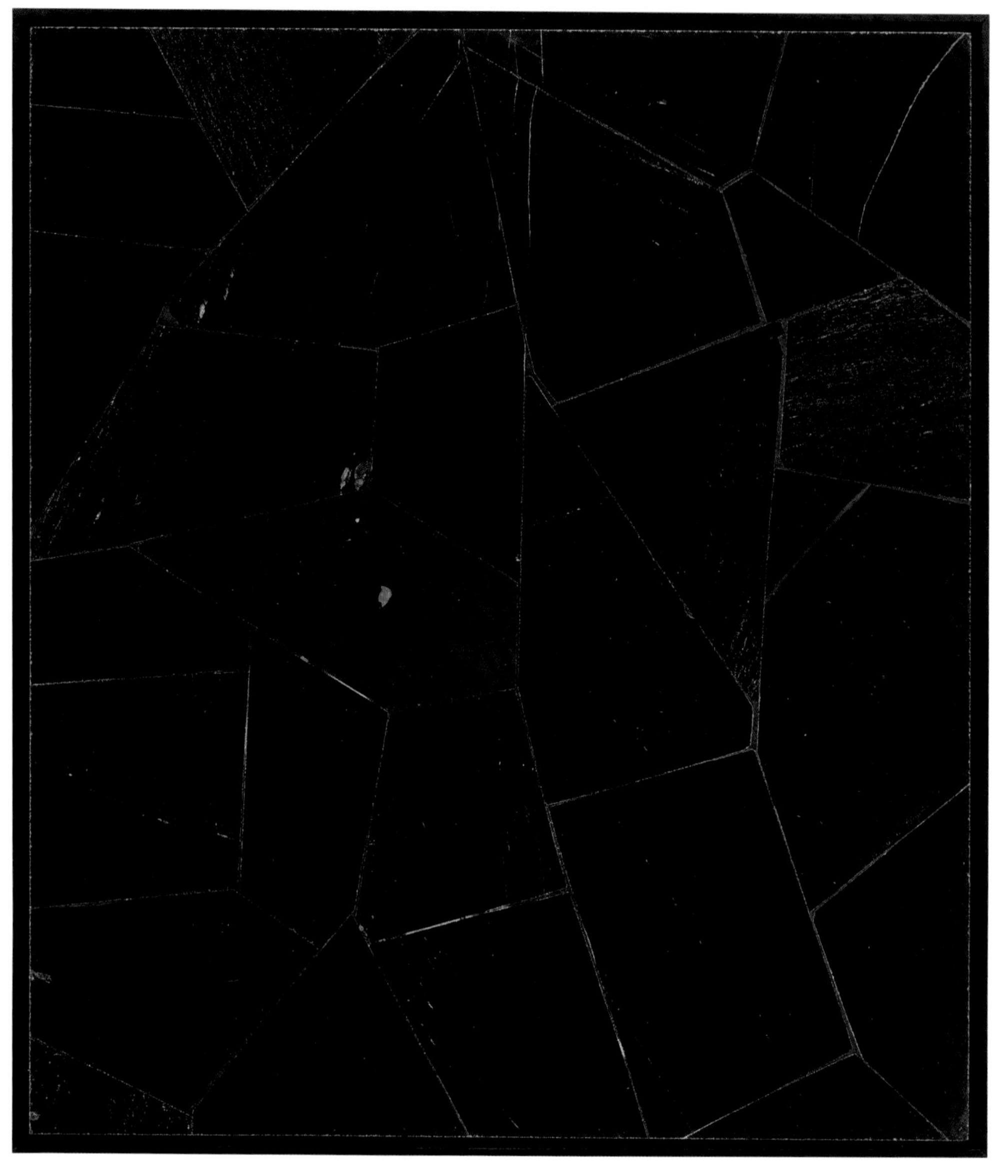

British artist **PREM SAHIB**'s (b. 1982) *Man Dog* resembles a fractured mirror. Each individual piece of obsidian has been polished to a highly reflective surface. The mirror also acts as a sound speaker, through which Sahib plays a racist rant he experienced while in a gay chat room. The individual was highly offensive about any number of topics and most people would deem his words hate speech. The viewer is presented with a distorted tonal experience whereby the words are slowed down and mostly incomprehensible. The soundtrack alters the way in which viewers engage with the mirror and allows many readings, including being seen as the screen the artist would have used to engage this individual. Obsidian has many historical uses, including as a material that can disperse 'negative energy'. In Sahib's *Obsidian Mirror II.VII* (2019), a small shelf holds a burning candle reflected in a surface of mirrored obsidian.

Man Dog, 2020
Obsidian, steel, audio file, amplifier, sound exciter, speaker cable, power pack
41.5 × 36.5 × 4 cm (16⅜ × 14⅜ × 1⅝ in)
Edition of 1 + 1 AP

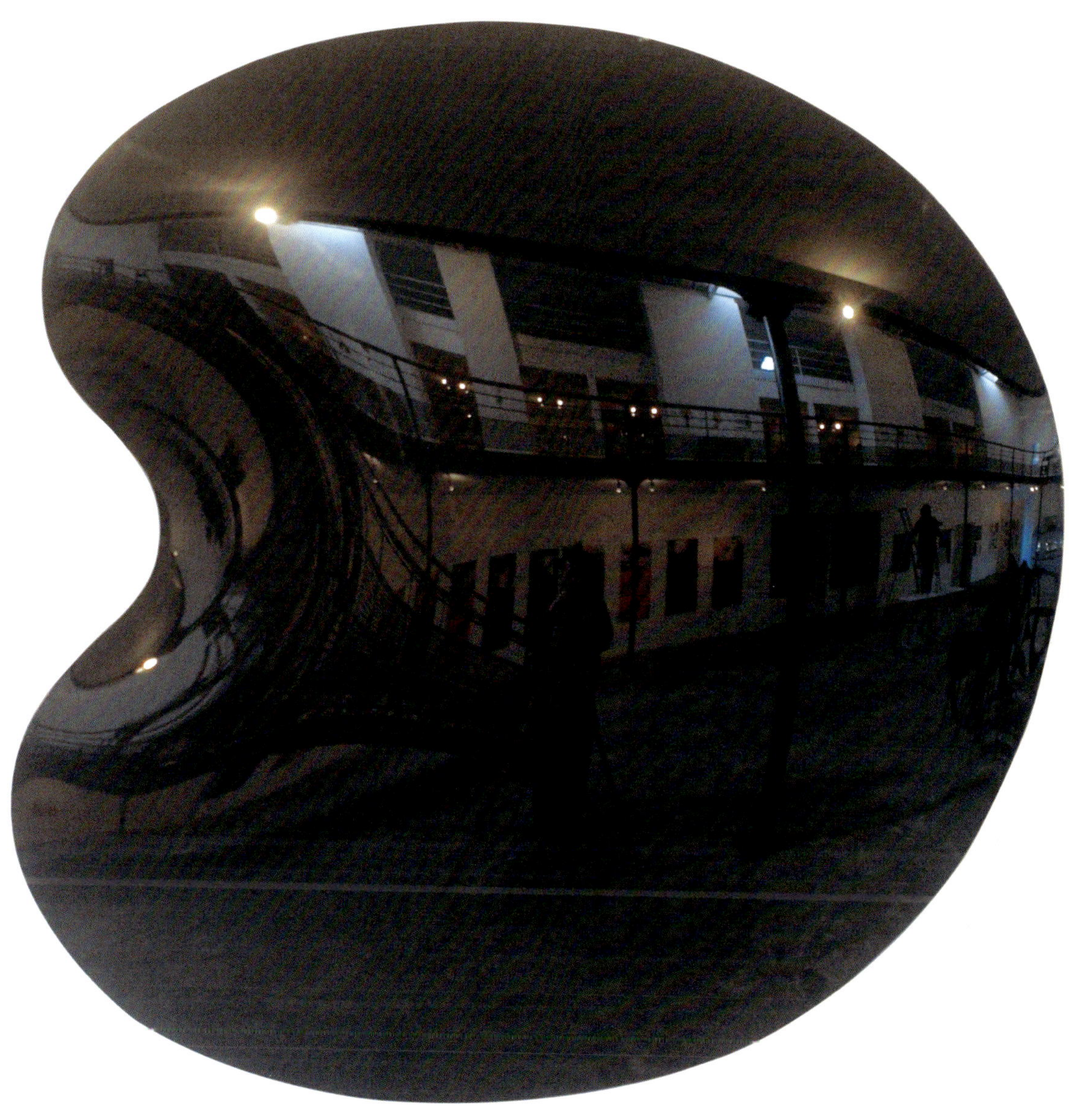

Black Mirror, 2010
Installation view: Chiasma,
La Coopérative, Centre for Art
and Literature, Montolieu, France
Black glass
75 × 75 × 8 cm (29½ × 29½ × 3¼ in)

British artist **PETER BRIGGS** (b. 1950) initially started working with mirrored glass in the mid-1990s, using a water jet to cut out shapes in thick float glass, inspired by heraldry and geography; he then had it slumped into plaster moulds and silvered. This evolved into work using steel ring moulds and the use of black glass and obsidian. These works effectively interact with the architecture they inhabit. Briggs's convex mirrors irregularly reflect the spaces back on themselves, distorting what the viewer perceives, which is modified and twisted in relation to the real volumes. He has said that what interests him 'is the way in which these convex mirrors can model space, modelling is for me the overriding activity'.

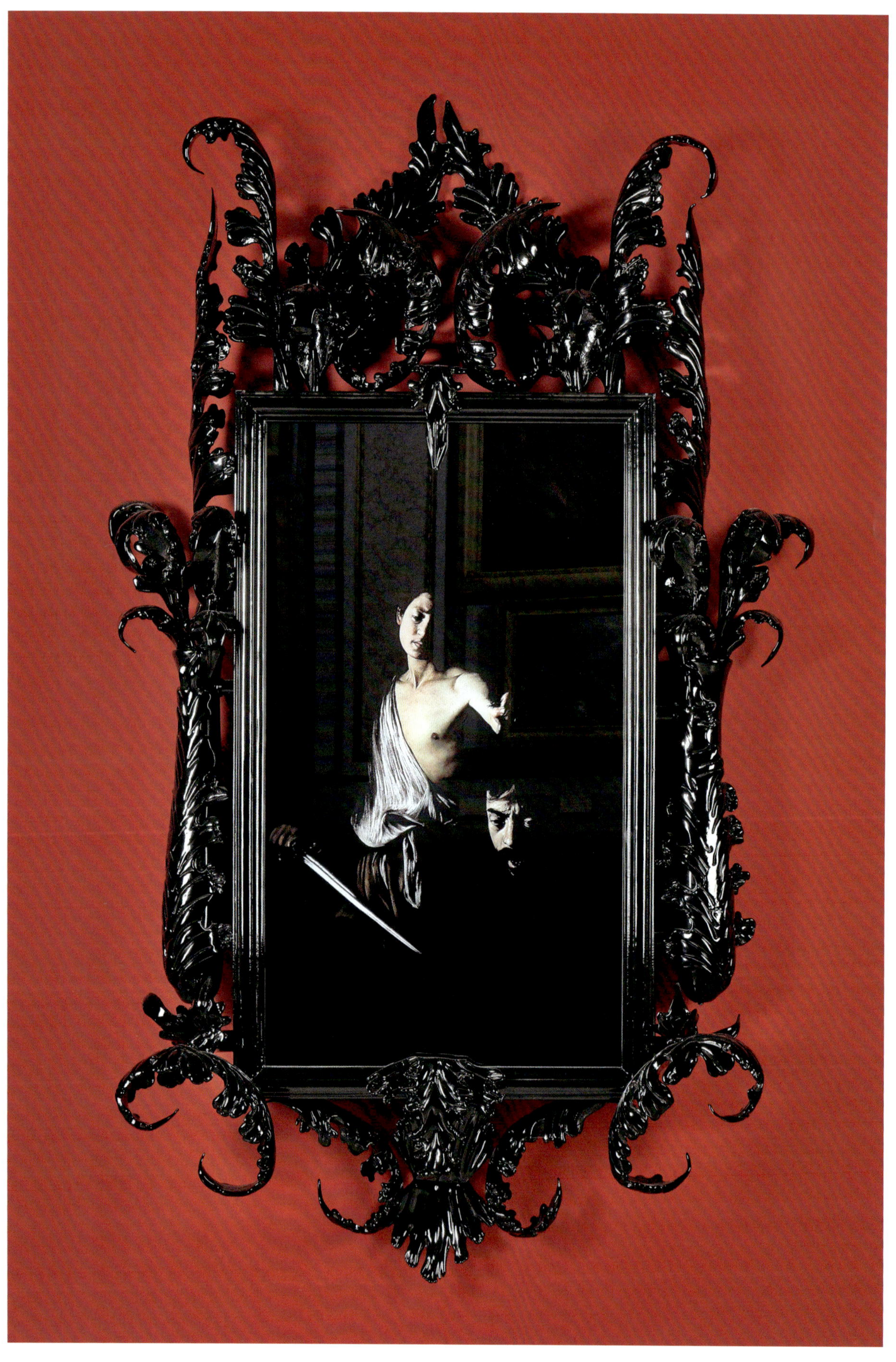

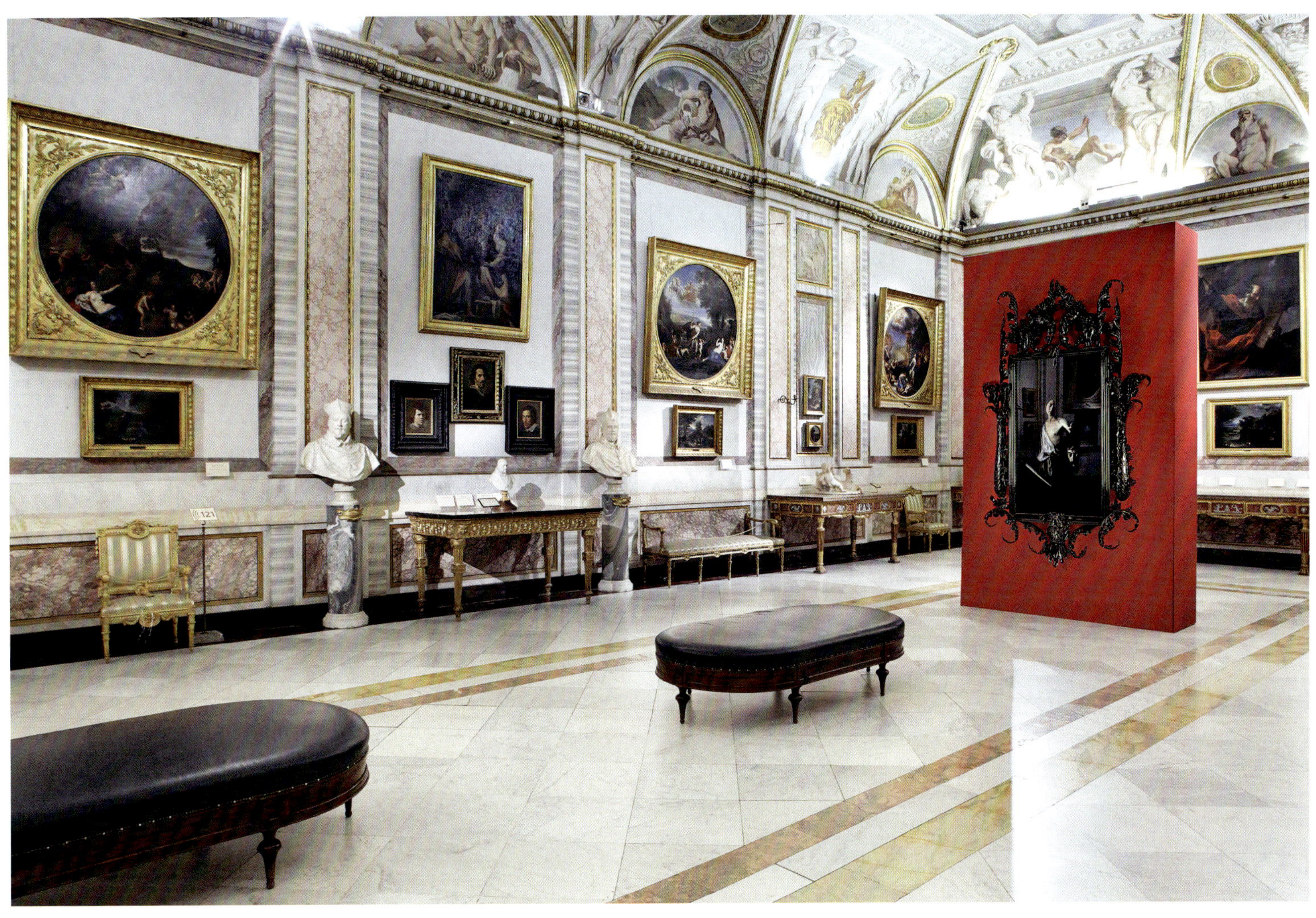

British artist **MAT COLLISHAW**'s
(b. 1966) series of *Black Mirror* works
all feature ornate frames made of black
Murano glass fabricated at the Fondazione
Berengo in Venice. The Baroque glass
fantasies enclose black two-way mirrors
that reflect the viewer and the architectural
space and also present the viewer with
an animated digital ghost of a Caravaggio
painting. In *Hydrus* we see a flickering
David with the Head of Goliath (c. 1605),
where David's hand shakes in holding up
the head of his conquest, which sways
and winks. The original is fairly disturbing
but the new-media version adds another
layer of discomfort to the viewer's
experience. The space between beauty
and horror has long fascinated Collishaw,
who has said that his David holds 'a
slightly jittery pose' and is 'a chimerical
spirit-presence coming back to haunt you
through the mirror'.

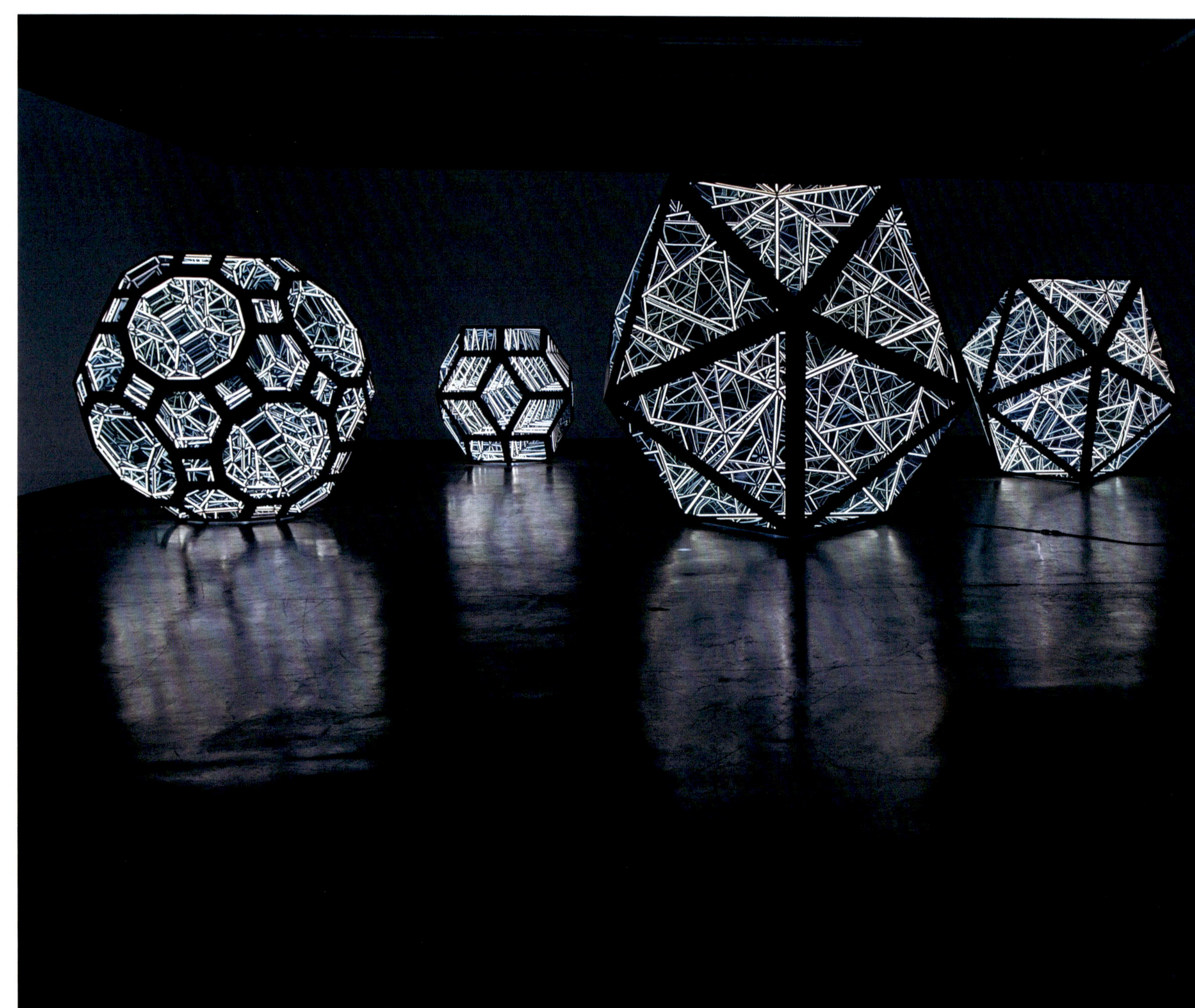

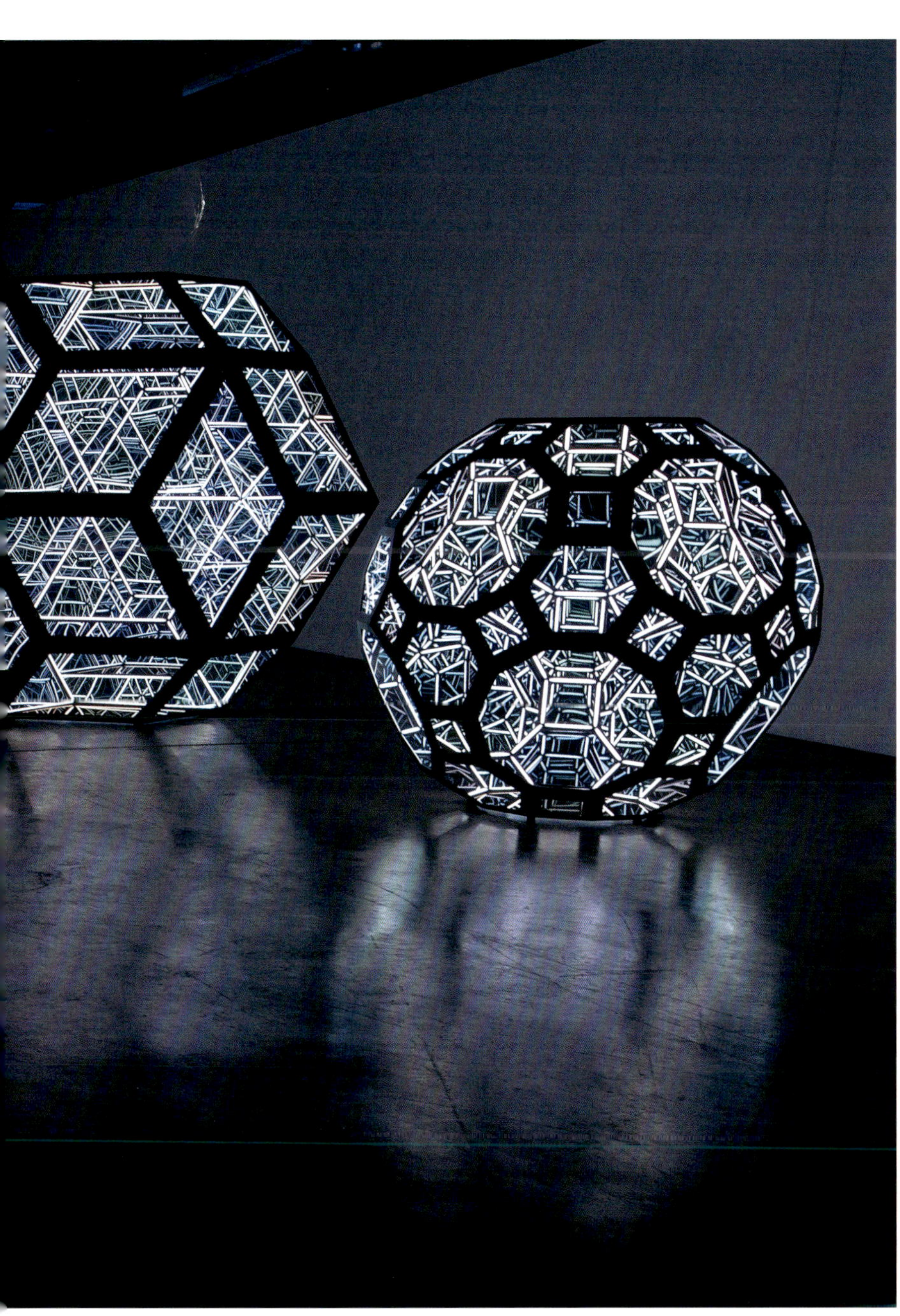

Constellation, 2020
Installation view
Stainless steel, glass, LEDs
Dimensions of largest: 2.54 × 2.54 × 2.54 m
(8⅓ × 8⅓ × 8⅓ ft)

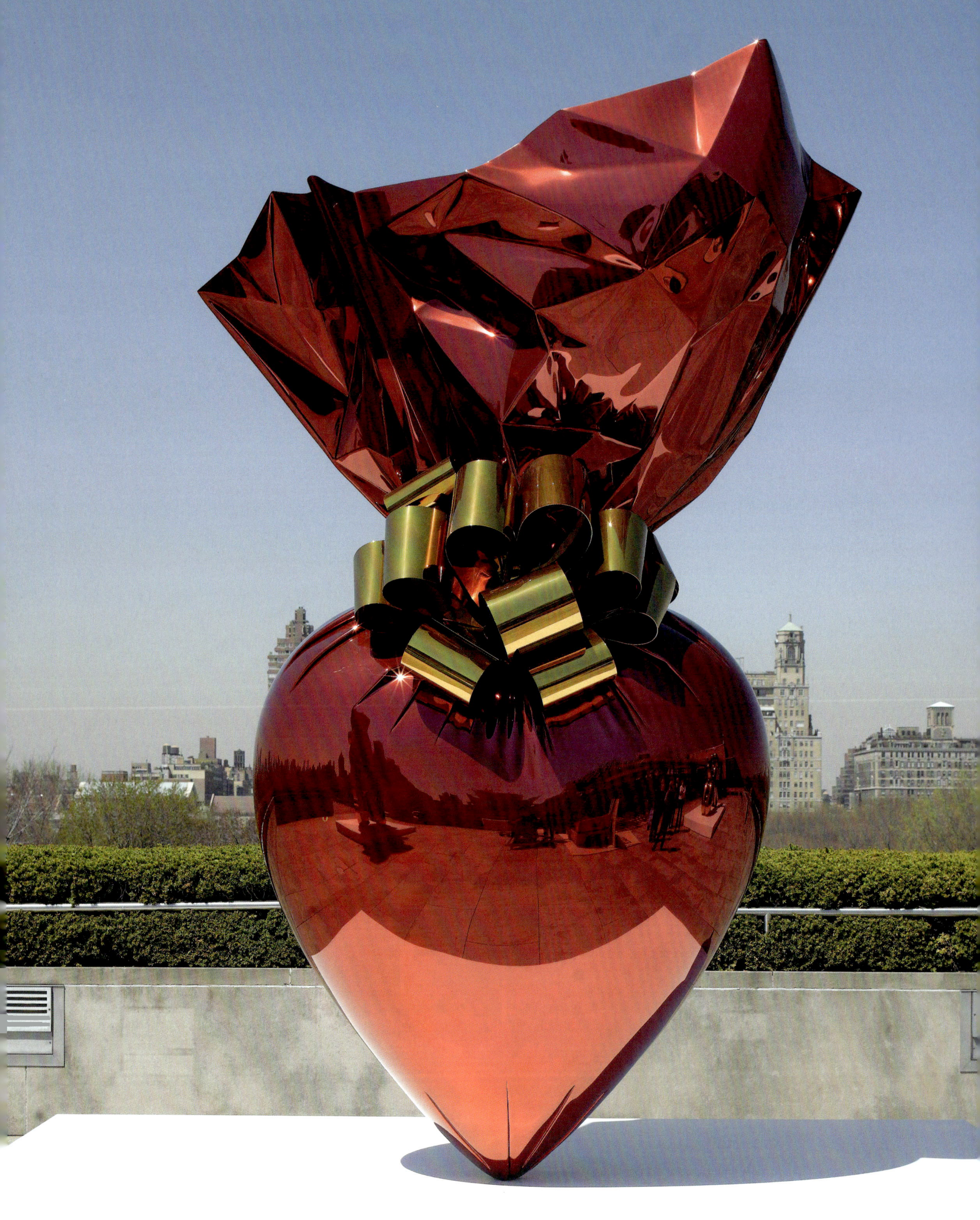

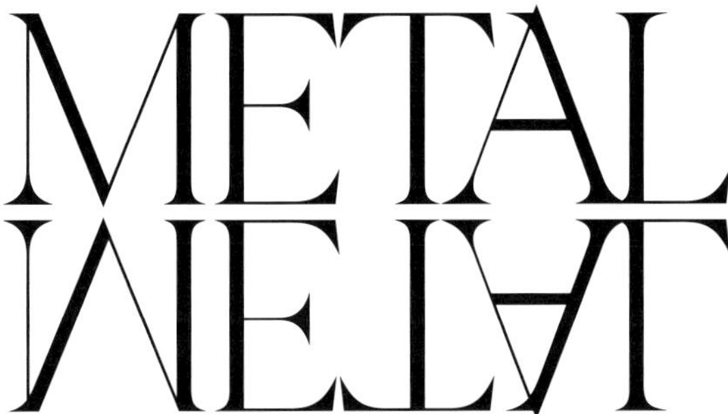

When people think about monumental metal sculpture they often call to mind the bronze works of Henry Moore or Barbara Hepworth patinated a verdigris green as if they had been left outside for centuries so that their exterior skins had turned colour with age. The application of various chemicals allows this visual disruption of time; similarly with hand-polished steel, when a final application of chemicals can remove any oxidized metal. Bronze and other metals can be gradually polished by grinding the surface with ever finer grades of abrasives. The hard physical work needed to achieve the mirror effect is one usually done in a factory or foundry as it is a specialist skill.

A great many of the artists in this chapter have used the skill of fabricators to achieve the artworks they have wanted to make (for example Jeff Koons, Ugo Rondinone, Paul Morrison). In my book *The Art of Not Making*, I explain that this process is not only historical, but one that is used in other collaborative arts such as cinema and music, where the authorship of a work is usually not in question. Jane Campion will not have designed, much less made, the costumes or sets in her films, nor composed the music or (necessarily) written the script, but viewers recognize that the hundreds of names that are cited in the credits do not have 'authorship' of the film. Her films are hers. So when one looks at the massive sculpture by Hubert Phipps, one needs to understand that he may not have physically welded and polished every square metre himself, yet the work is indeed his.

Other artists in this chapter have created their own techniques for fabrication (Tiziana Lorenzelli) or are dedicated to hand production (Paul Derrez). Regardless of the way in which they make their works, they hold in common the desire to create a surface that reflects the light, the surroundings and the viewer. For others, the content of their own artistic narrative is at the core of their practice and their work with reflection is but a part of the way those stories come into being (Dorota Jurczak, Roberto Ekholm). Other artists explored here are using reflection in a very conceptual, if not minimalist, way, as in the floor plates of Poppy Ben Woodeson, or Kader Attia's bullet holes. Sometimes the reflection is as important as the object, and the material almost disappears in looking at it, despite its physical weight. The heaviness of any metal presents itself to the viewer, and the wonder is how these works, reflecting as they do, overcome their physicality.

Jeff Koons, *Sacred Heart (Red/Gold)*, 1994–2007
Mirror-polished stainless steel with transparent colour coating
357 × 218.4 × 121 cm (140½ × 86 × 47⅝ in). 1 of 5 unique versions

Rabbit by American artist **JEFF KOONS** (b. 1955) is probably one of the most recognizable works of art in the twentieth and twenty-first centuries. The silvery reflective metal bunny is at the core of Koons's interest in the reflective surface. *Rabbit* can be seen as a touchstone for his larger *Balloon Dog* series of sculptures, his large brightly coloured *Easyfun* mirrors and his more recent round blue *Gazing Ball* pieces. Koons is known for his impeccably finished works (he destroys work in production that is flawed in even a minor way) that appear almost as if they have had no human hand in their fabrication. Yet all his reflective works draw out the inner child in the viewer – perhaps the naughty child, as a desire to touch the surface is almost overwhelming. But to leave a fingerprint, a human mark, would be catastrophic to their function as unattainable perfect objects. Viewers can see their reflection in the work but are expected to leave no trace of themselves.

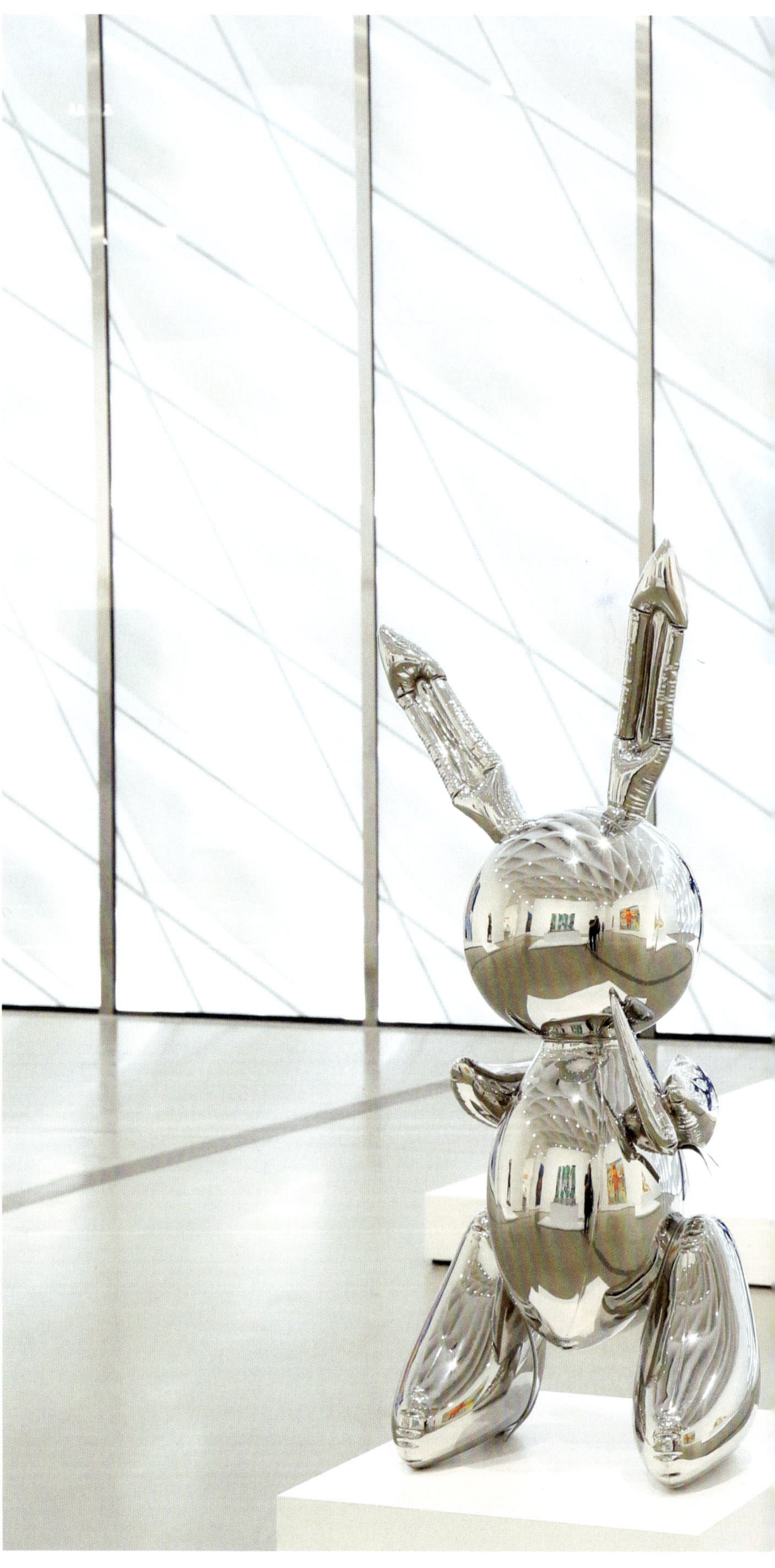

Rabbit, 1986
Stainless steel
104 × 48.3 × 30.5 cm (41 × 19 × 12 in)
Edition of 3 + 1 AP

Balloon Dog (Blue), 1994–2000
Mirror-polished stainless steel with
transparent colour coating
307.3 × 363.2 × 114.3 cm (121 × 143 × 45 in)
1 of 5 unique versions

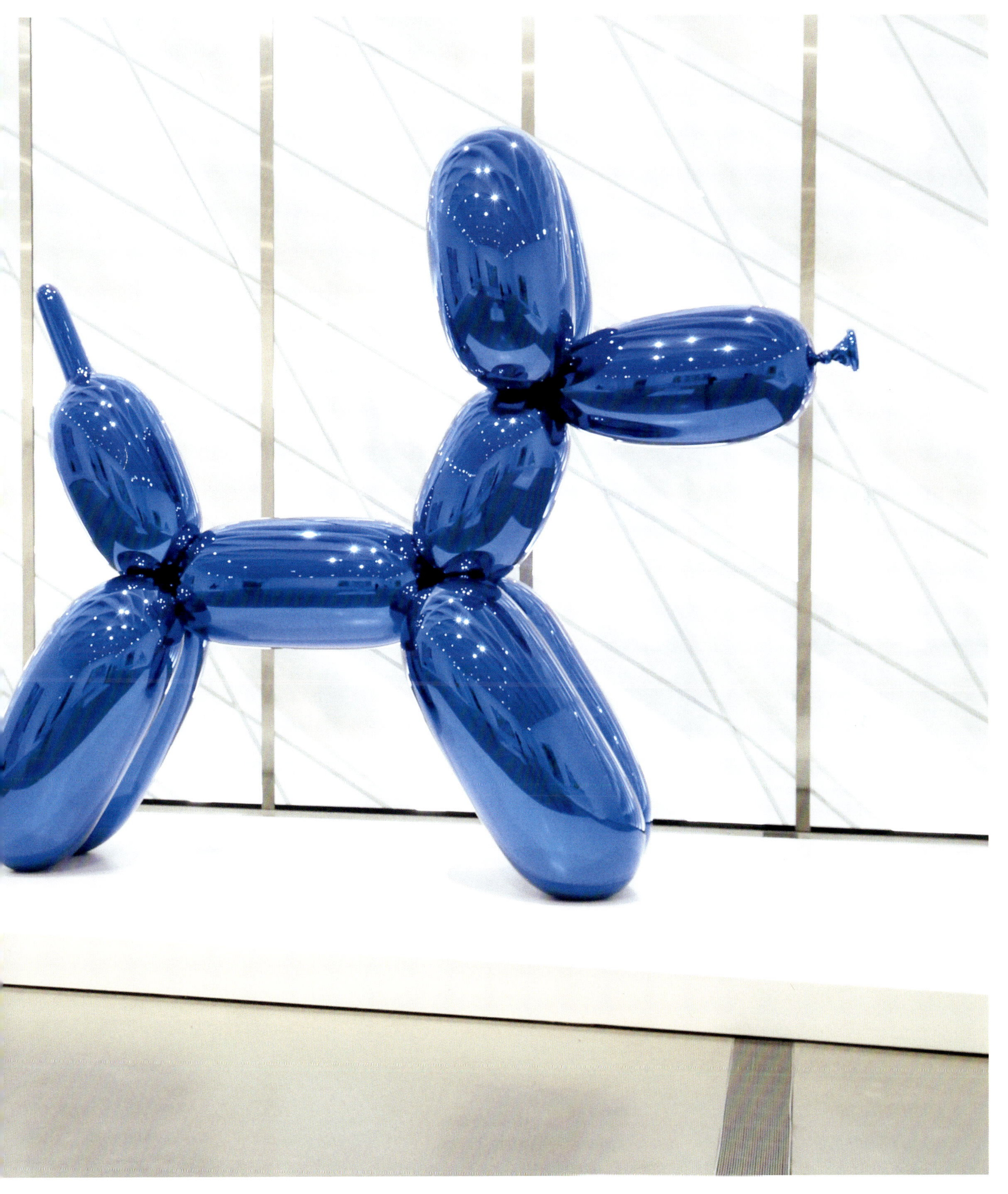

American artist **JIM HODGES** (b. 1957) returned from a trip to India with an idea for this work, which was quickly commissioned by the Walker Art Center, Minneapolis, as an outdoor work, though it was first shown by the artist's gallery in New York before being sited. The huge stones selected by Hodges were each roughly 1.8 metres (6 foot) tall, or the size of an adult man, and weighed more than 8 tons. He and his team cast the exteriors so that when finished, the reflective metal surface would seamlessly flow into the stone as if there were no intervention at all. The dyed metal was then fixed to the stone with epoxy and pins. The altered parts of the stones are highly reflective and create an atmosphere of lightness despite their heavy physicality. Hodges usually names his works but decided that as the boulders were going to be a public sculpture, local people would most likely give them names in any case.

Untitled, 2011
Installation view: Gladstone Gallery, New York City, USA
Granite, stainless steel and lacquer in four parts
1.91 × 6.3 × 7.65 m (6¼ × 20½ × 25 ft)

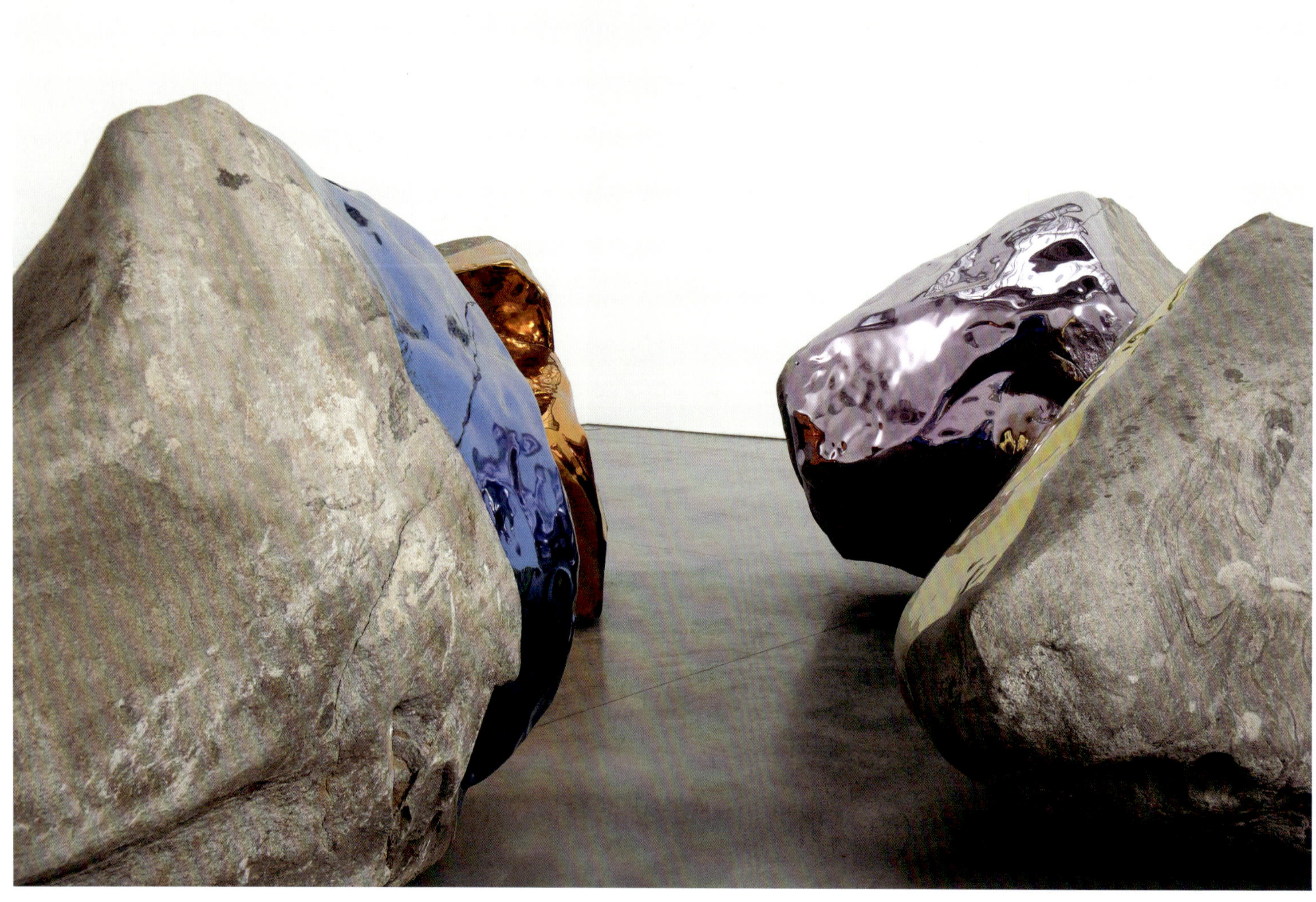

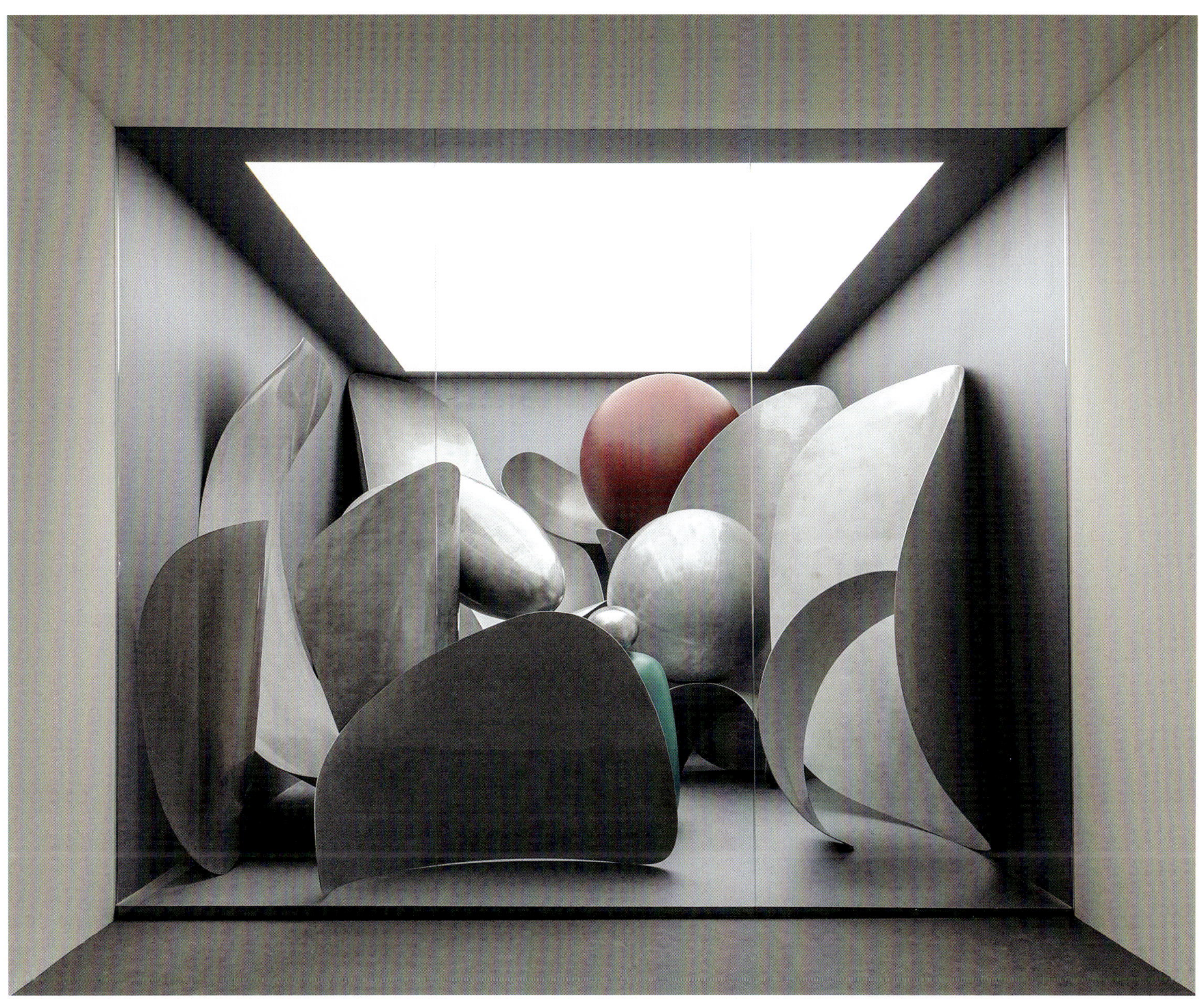

Microworld, 2018
Installation view: Arsenale,
Venice Biennale, Italy, 2019
Aluminium plates
Dimensions variable

Beijing-based Chinese artist **LIU WEI** (b. 1972) presented his *Microworld* installation at the 2019 Venice Biennale. The work was formed of two distinct halves. The first was in the grey raised platform where his highly polished and painted aluminium forms interacted with and reflected each other. The polished shields and geometric volumes are representative of microscopic forms, possibly electrons and other subatomic particles, but on a macro scale. The second half of the installation was the void space that viewers entered as they approached the work, which was placed behind large clear sheets of glass. Like a storefront window, the glass obliged viewers to peer into the space beyond, tantalizingly almost within reach, their own reflection constantly present in the glass.

Germany-based British artist **TONY CRAGG** (b. 1949) is a sculptor known for his unusual and innovative use of materials for large-scale sculpture, including glass, resin, bronze and mirrored stainless steel, as in his series of *Points of View*. These extremely sophisticated forms recall Gian Lorenzo Bernini's spiral stone columns in St Peter's Basilica in the Vatican (1623–34) and Constantin Brancusi's World War I memorial *Endless Column* (1937) but take these shapes forward using a scientific if not futuristic language. Cragg uses simple geometric forms yet makes his work look organic. He has said that 'I want to make a work that has the same intense effect that looking at Nature has on me. In this sense, I was fascinated by how the rational constructions underlying the forms translate into emotional qualities.' His sculpture in Florence (opposite) is part of a larger series of works that have been sited across the globe, reflecting the local environment and architecture, nature and construct merging into one.

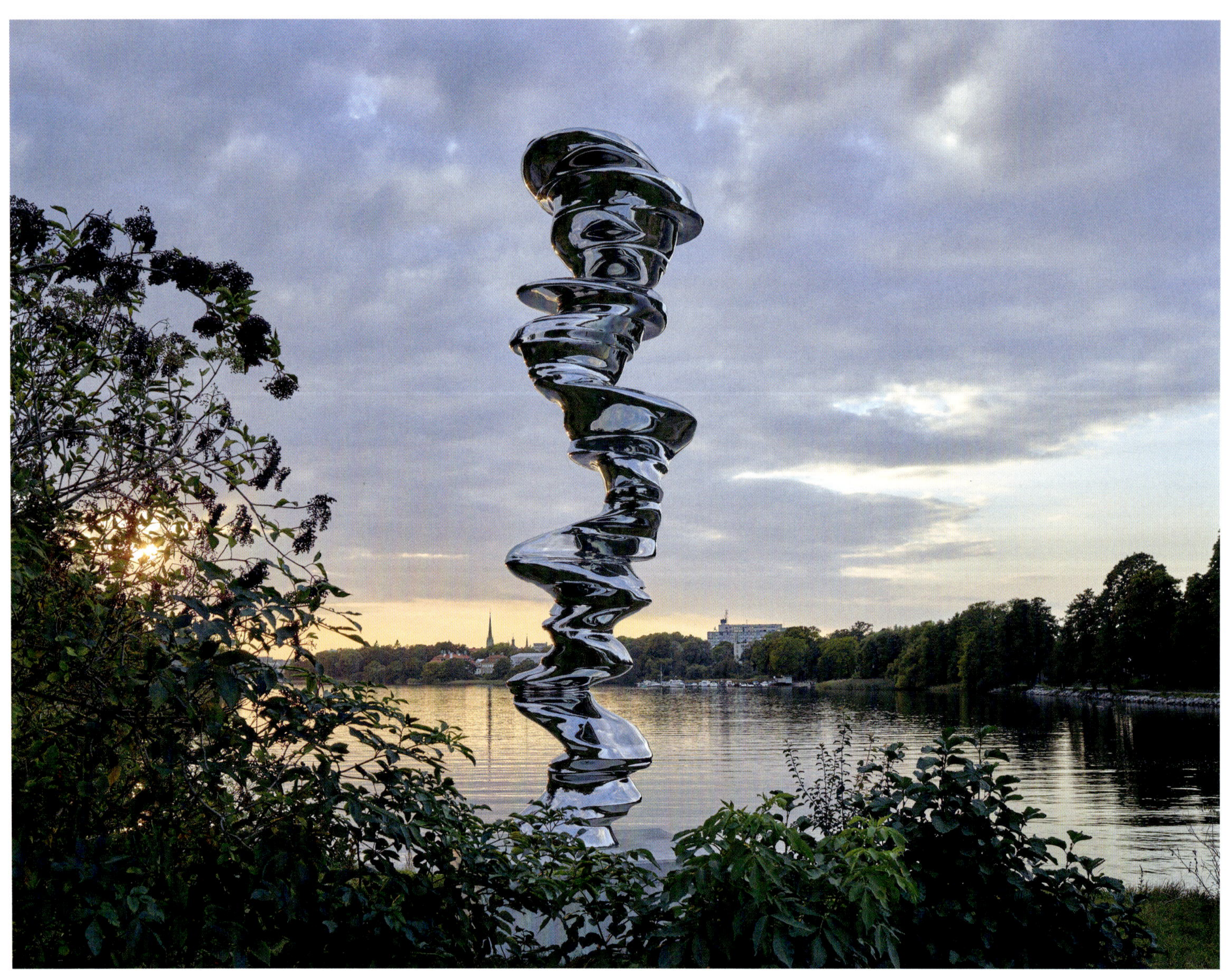

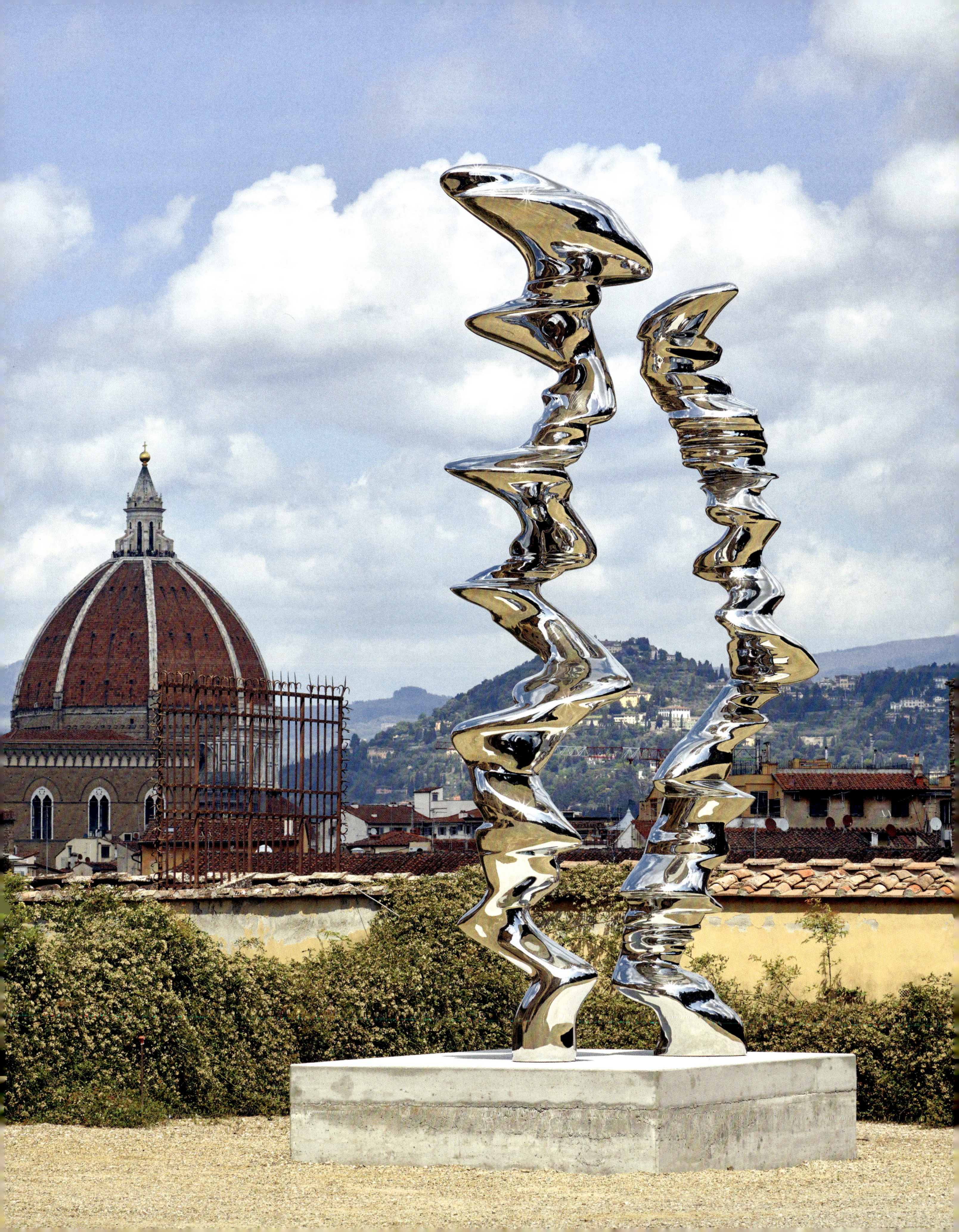

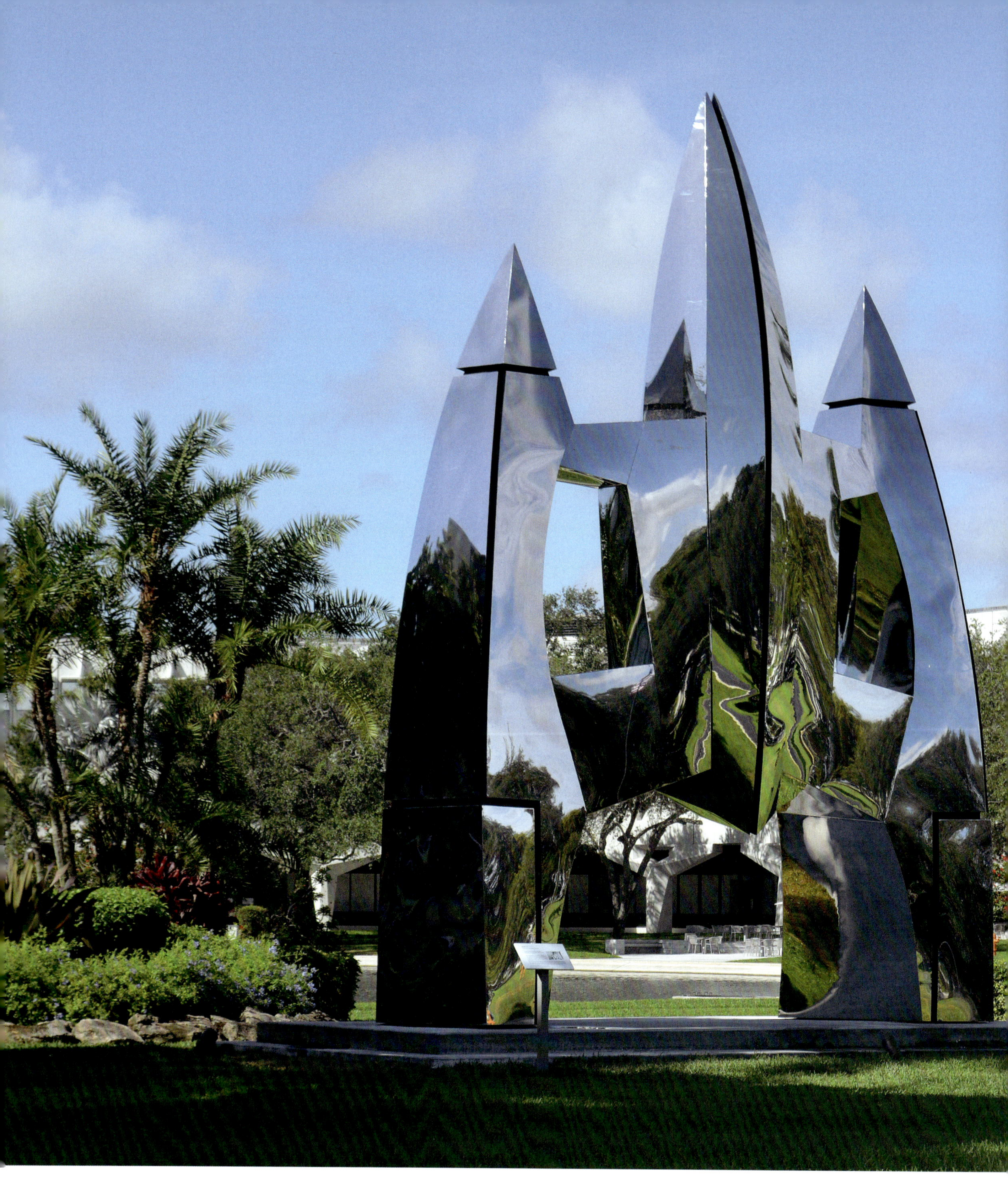

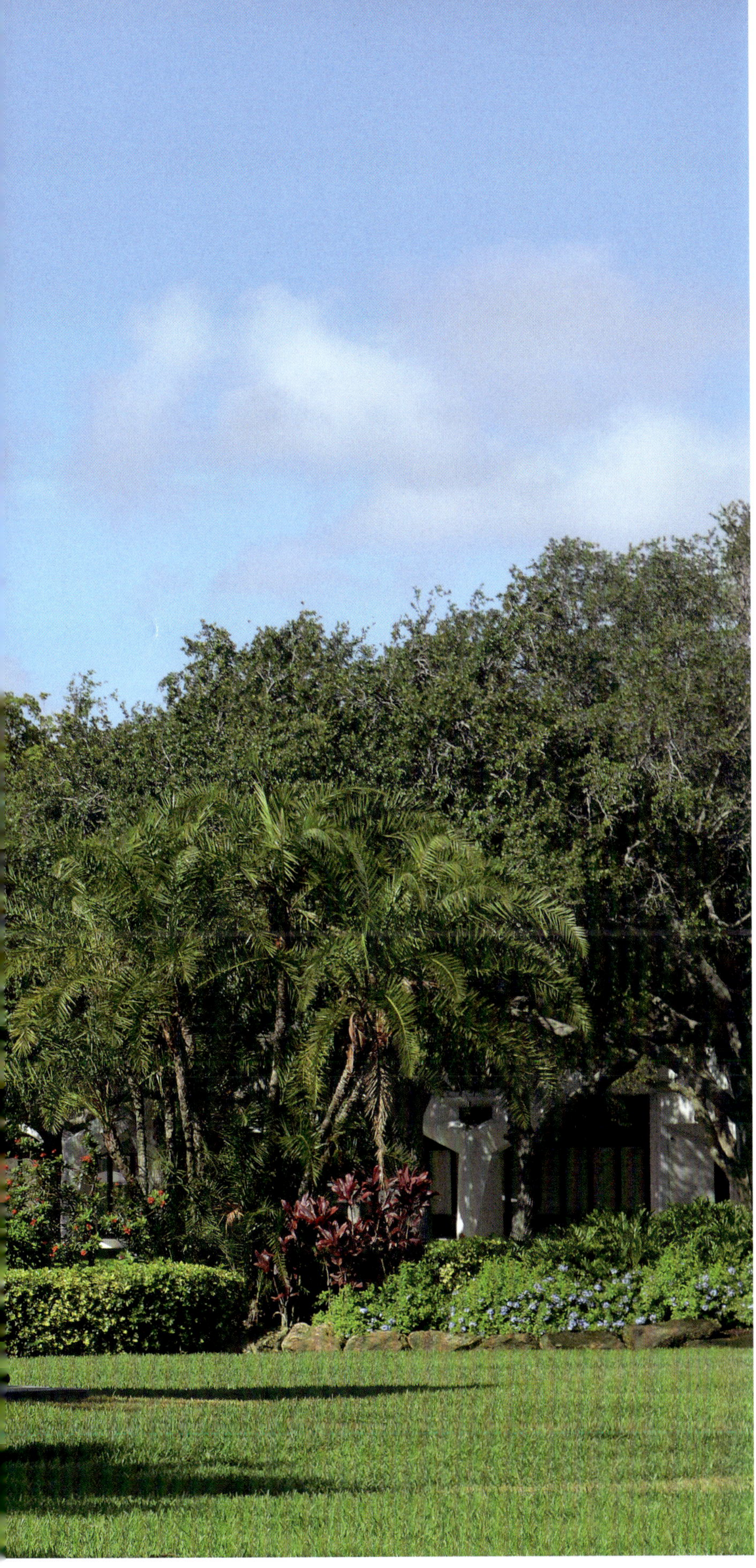

American artist **HUBERT PHIPPS** (1957–2023) said that as a child in Florida he could hear rocket engines being tested at aircraft manufacturer Pratt & Whitney's West Palm Beach facility and it gave him a lifelong interest in space and flight (he was also a pilot). He was commissioned to create a public sculpture for the Boca Raton Innovation Campus (BRiC), where the first IBM Personal Computer was invented. The work would have to stand up to the category 5 hurricanes that can strike the Florida campus, and Phipps used the Maya 3D-modelling software program to refine his design. The monumental 9-metre (30-foot) high *Rocket* sits near the modernist buildings Marcel Breuer designed for the university, reflecting them and the rest of the campus in its polished stainless steel. *Rocket* was fabricated at the Tany Foundry in Hangzhou, China.

Rocket, 2021
Stainless steel
9.1 × 7.5 × 2.8 m (30 × 24¾ × 9½ ft)

ARIK LEVY (b. 1963) is a Paris-based Israeli sculptor and designer who works across many media including glass, steel and bronze. He is best known for his *Rock* sculptures, whether they are in Corten or stainless steel. They usually take the form of a collection of geometric rocks that form a single work, like the growth of crystal structures. The reflective woven carbon-fibre or stainless-steel works, usually sited in a natural setting, also reflect the passing of time, be it summer or winter, altering their visual form as the weather changes. For example, in the snow *Rock Growth 170* looks predominantly white, but in warmer weather it mirrors the summer sky and green grass. *RockGate 203*, seen here, features two monumental freestanding mirrored-steel stones that reflect each other, their surroundings and any viewer that passes between them.

RockGate 203, 2023
Installation view: Blickachsen 13,
Outdoor Sculpture Biennial, Bad Homburg,
Germany, 2023
Mirror-polished marine-grade stainless steel
203 × 78 × 48 cm (80 × 30¾ × 19 in)
No. 1 from an edition of 3

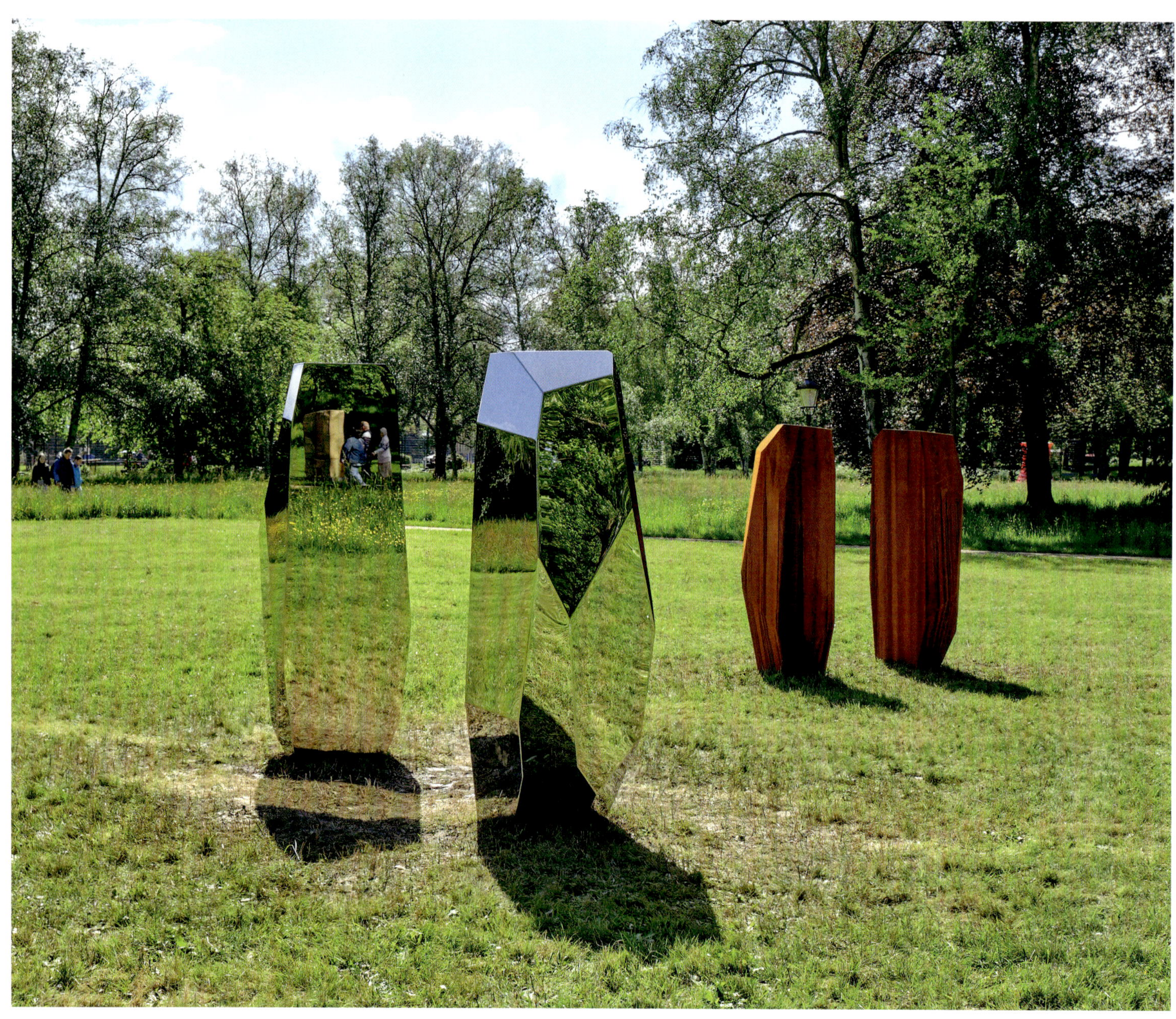

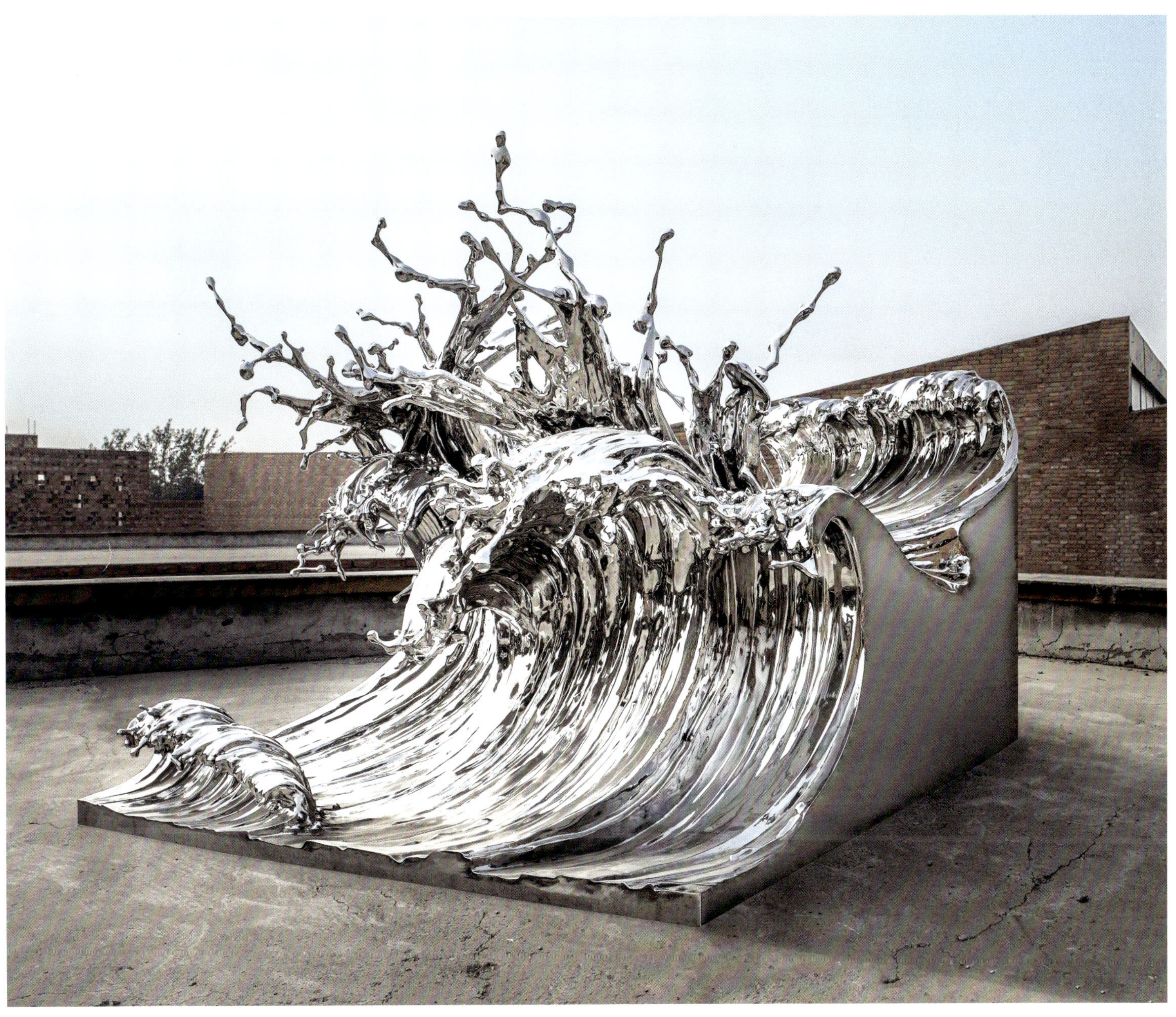

Shiosai, 2017
Stainless steel
2 × 2 × 2.2 m (6½ × 6½ × 7¼ ft)

Chinese artist **ZHENG LU** (b. 1978) makes metal sculptures that look like water crashing onto a shore or as if a massive stone has been dropped into a lake. Some of his mirror-polished stainless-steel sculptures are more than 5 metres (16½ feet) long (*Water Dripping – Longli*, 2016) or the height of a small building (*Water Dripping – Splashing*, 2014). They sparkle in the light, reflecting the sunshine and distorting their surroundings in their bright surfaces. Set in a remote coastal community, *Shiosai* (*The Sound of Waves*) is a 1954 novel by Japanese author Yukio Mishima, about the beauty of first love and the need to respect nature and act in harmony with its forces. Zheng captures the visual quality of a wave in his sculpture *Shiosai* and the viewer can almost hear the roar of the sea when encountering it.

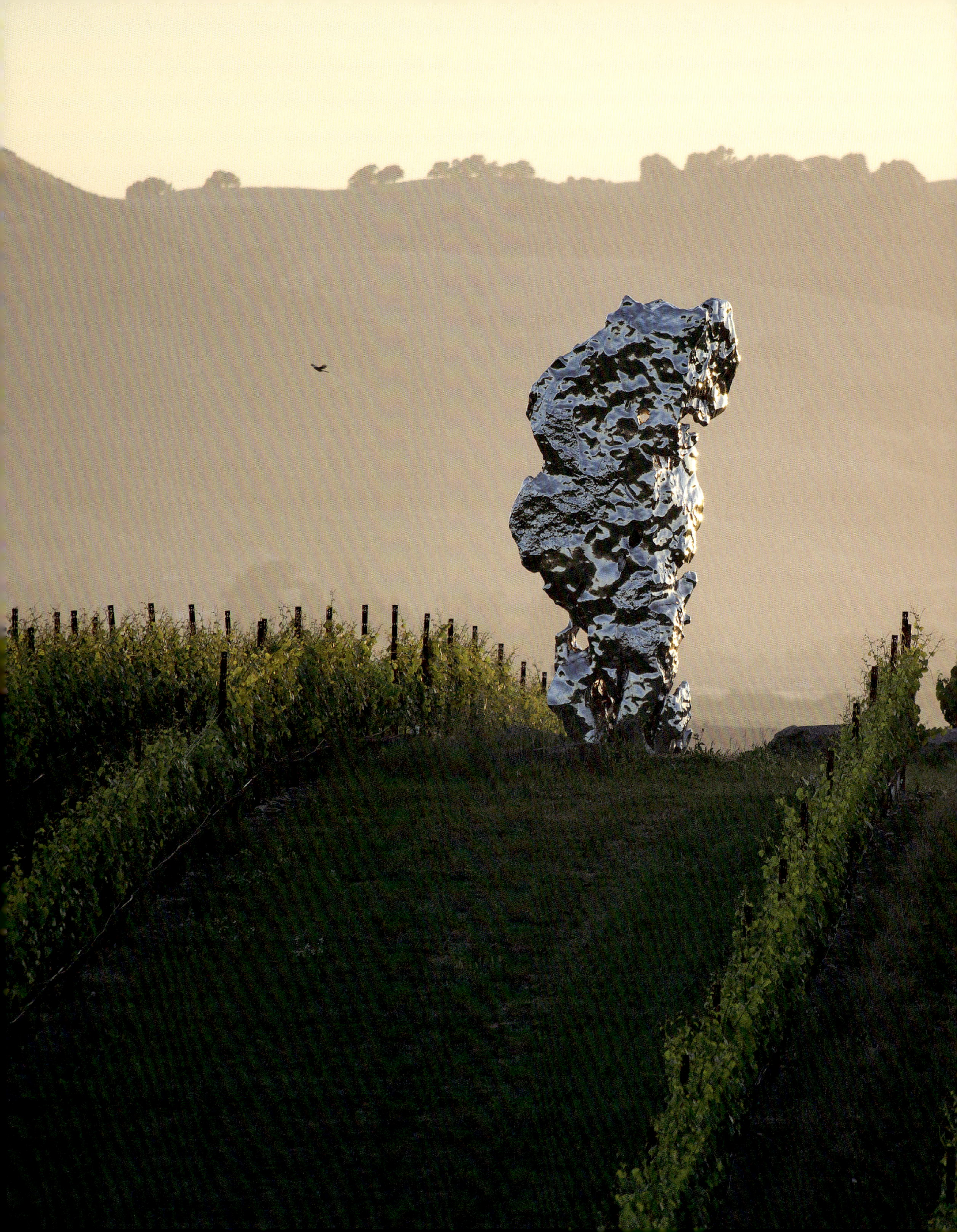

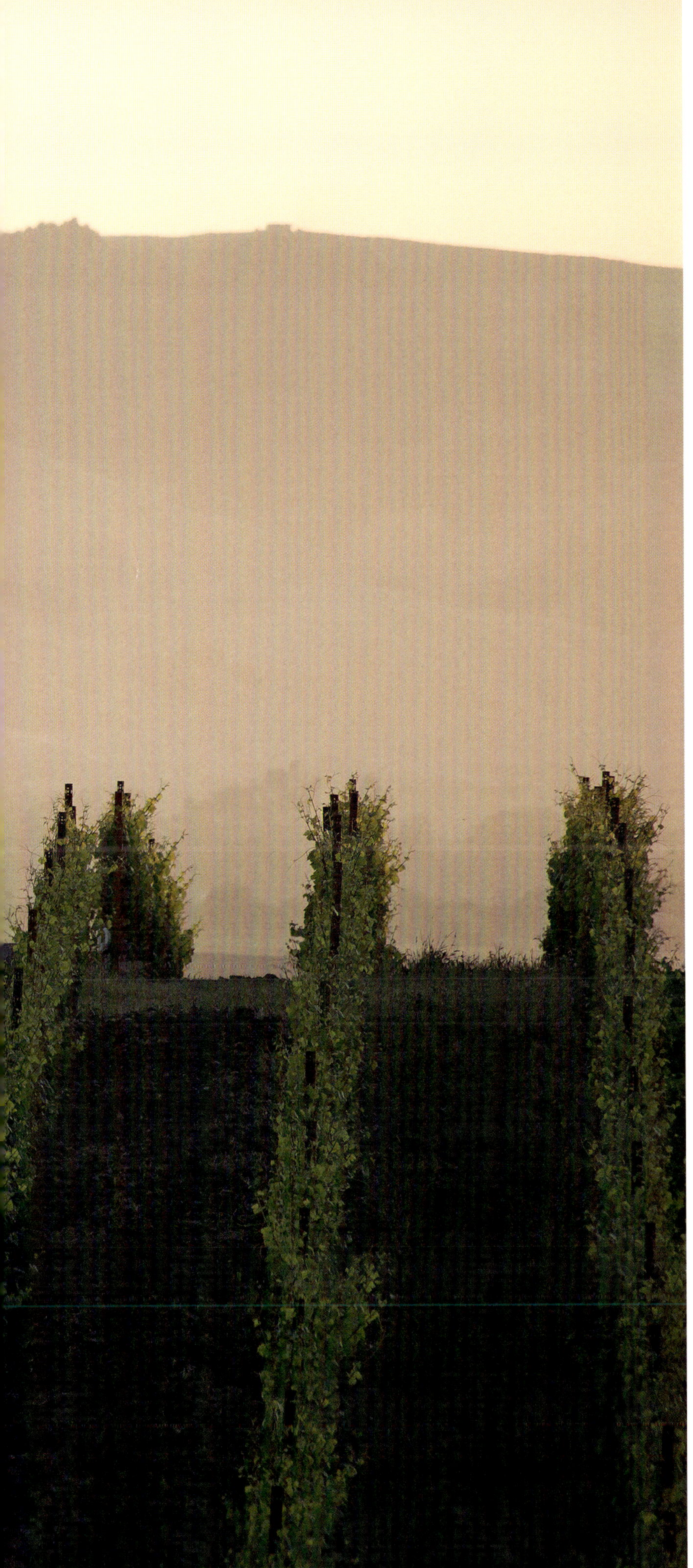

Chinese sculptor **ZHAN WANG** (b. 1962) started to make huge reflective metal 'scholar stones' in 1995 in an attempt to connect to ancient Chinese traditional art, bringing it into the modern world. Historically scholars would collect and study stones that had unusual shapes, often those that resembled mountains. These studies were 'based in Taoism and the pursuit of nature' and for Zhan Wang 'the stones can present the very essence of such a philosophy'. His sculptures require a high degree of technical prowess as he and his team first carefully wrap actual stones with steel sheets. These are hammered into shape to resemble the stones as closely as possible, and then the separate pieces are removed, welded together and polished into the final metal stone.

Artificial Rock No. 126, 2007
Installation view: Donum Estate,
California, USA, 2007–13
Stainless steel
5.15 x 2.15 x 1.55 m (16⅞ x 7 x 5 ft)

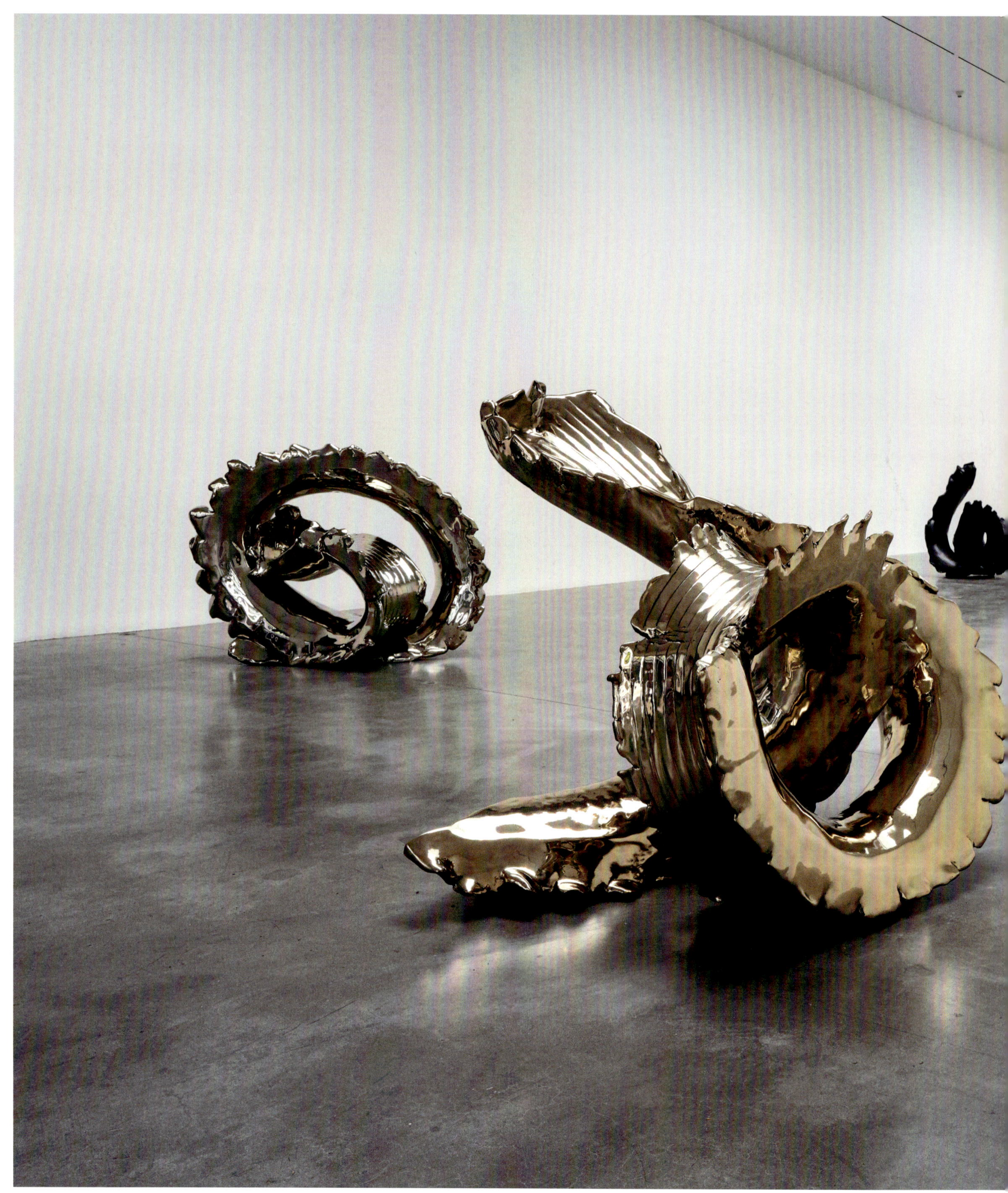

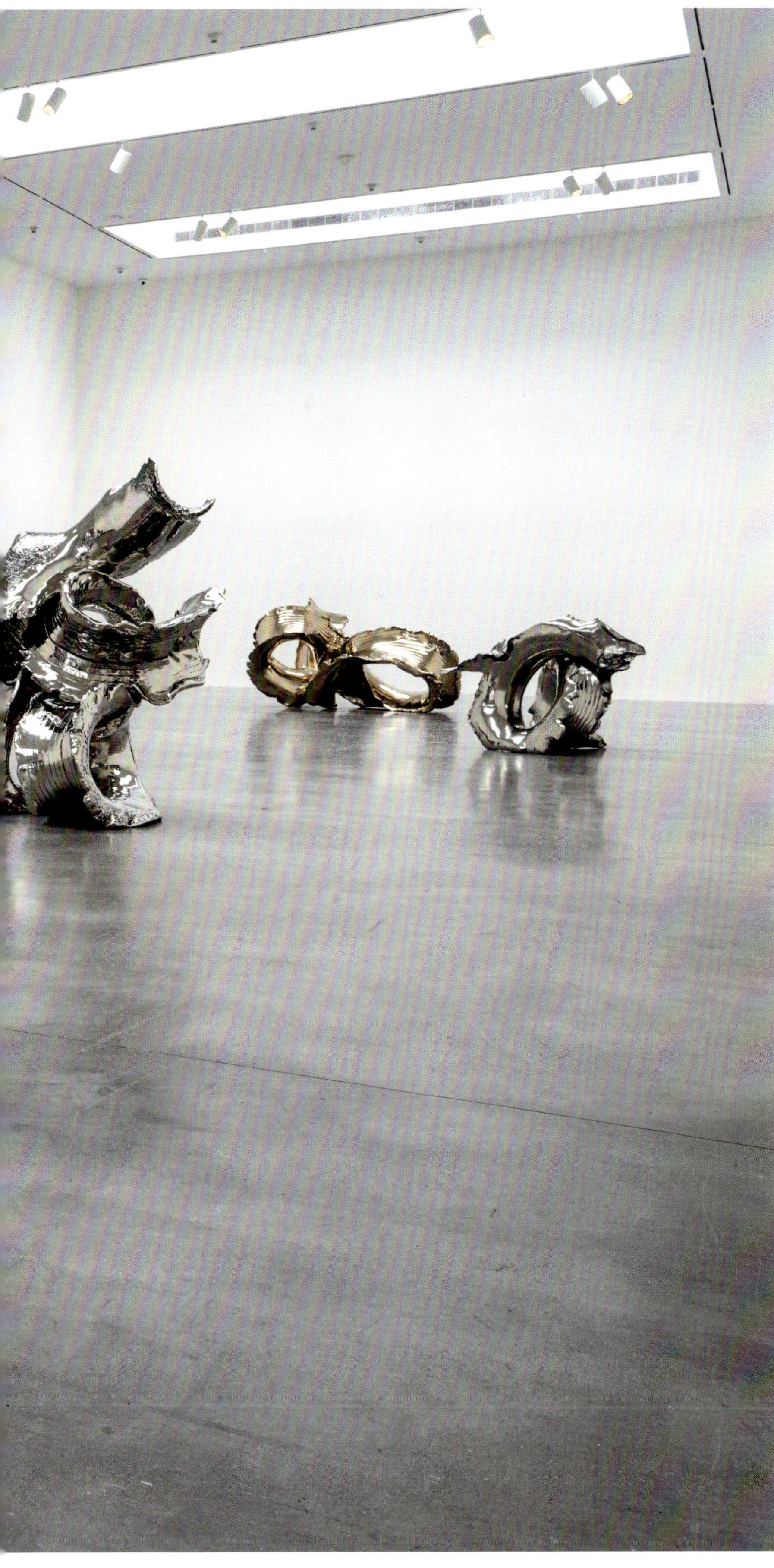

American sculptor and visual artist **LYNDA BENGLIS** (b. 1942) has been making knotted forms for more than forty years in a wide variety of materials, shapes and sizes. Her exhibition 'Lynda Benglis: An Alphabet of Forms' (2021) saw her place six massive sparkling, knotted metal forms in the gallery. The works looked liquid and flexible, as if they could be re-formed by the viewer should they lay hands on the perfect surfaces. Benglis starts by making small clay forms, which are then expanded in scale to the large bronzes, linking the intimate with the imposing. Her knot forms refer back to the many cultures, across many continents, that have used knots as a form of language or code. These include the Incas and their *quipu*s, sets of knotted strings that were used to collect and record various types of information, including census data, taxes, royal bloodlines, astronomy and calendars. Benglis's reflective forms allow the viewer to see themselves and to construct their own meaning within her formal language.

'Lynda Benglis: An Alphabet of Forms', 2021
Installation view: Pace Gallery, New York City,
USA, May–June 2021
Bronze
Dimensions variable

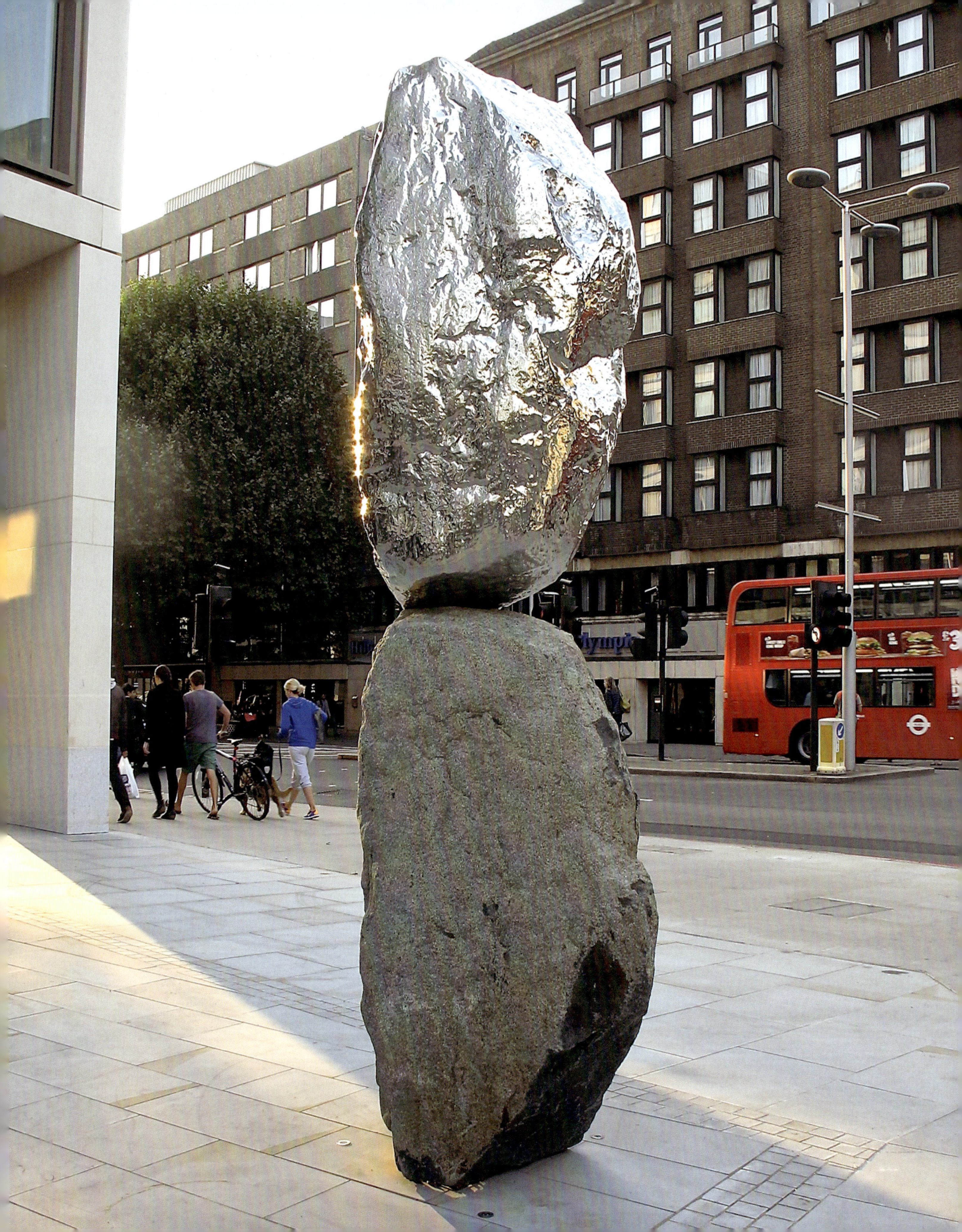

Glorious Beauty (opposite) by British artist **SIMON HITCHENS** (b. 1967) aims to bring the natural world and the human-made into direct conversation. Hitchens selected a huge glacial boulder and had it digitally scanned in order for it to be replicated in mirrored stainless steel. The making process was extremely complex, with six specialist companies being needed to fabricate the different stages of the work. Hitchens made the mirror image of the stone, and balanced it upon the original boulder installed in an urban setting. The reflective surface of the work shows the rock its own face, and allows passers-by to see the delicate balance needed when humans intervene in the environment. Hitchens says of his work *The Other I* (below) that 'Mirrors are often seen to reflect the soul, to offer a different point of view: this work suggests there can be a variety of different "wholes" sitting within one parent body – a meditation on the nature of being'.

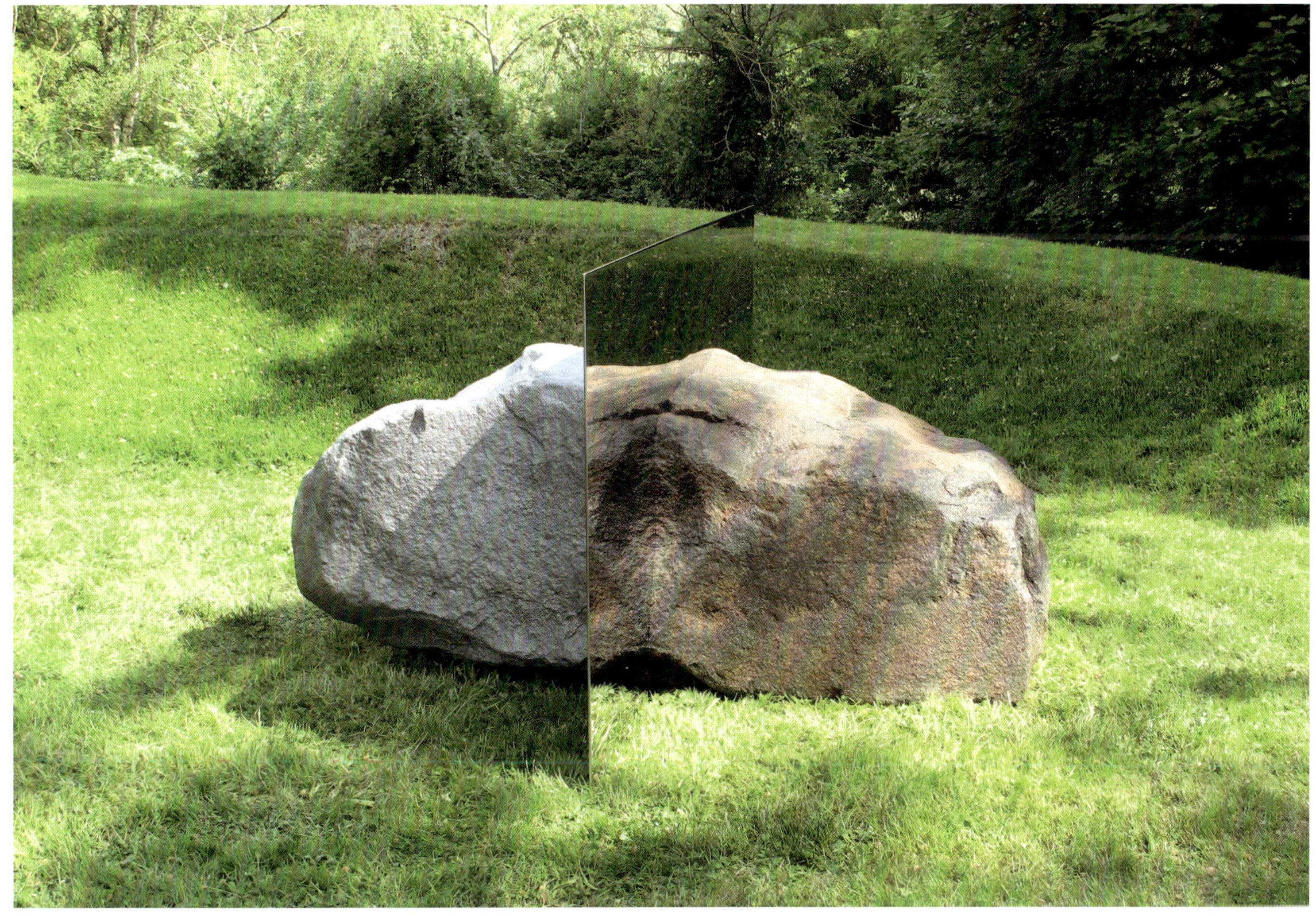

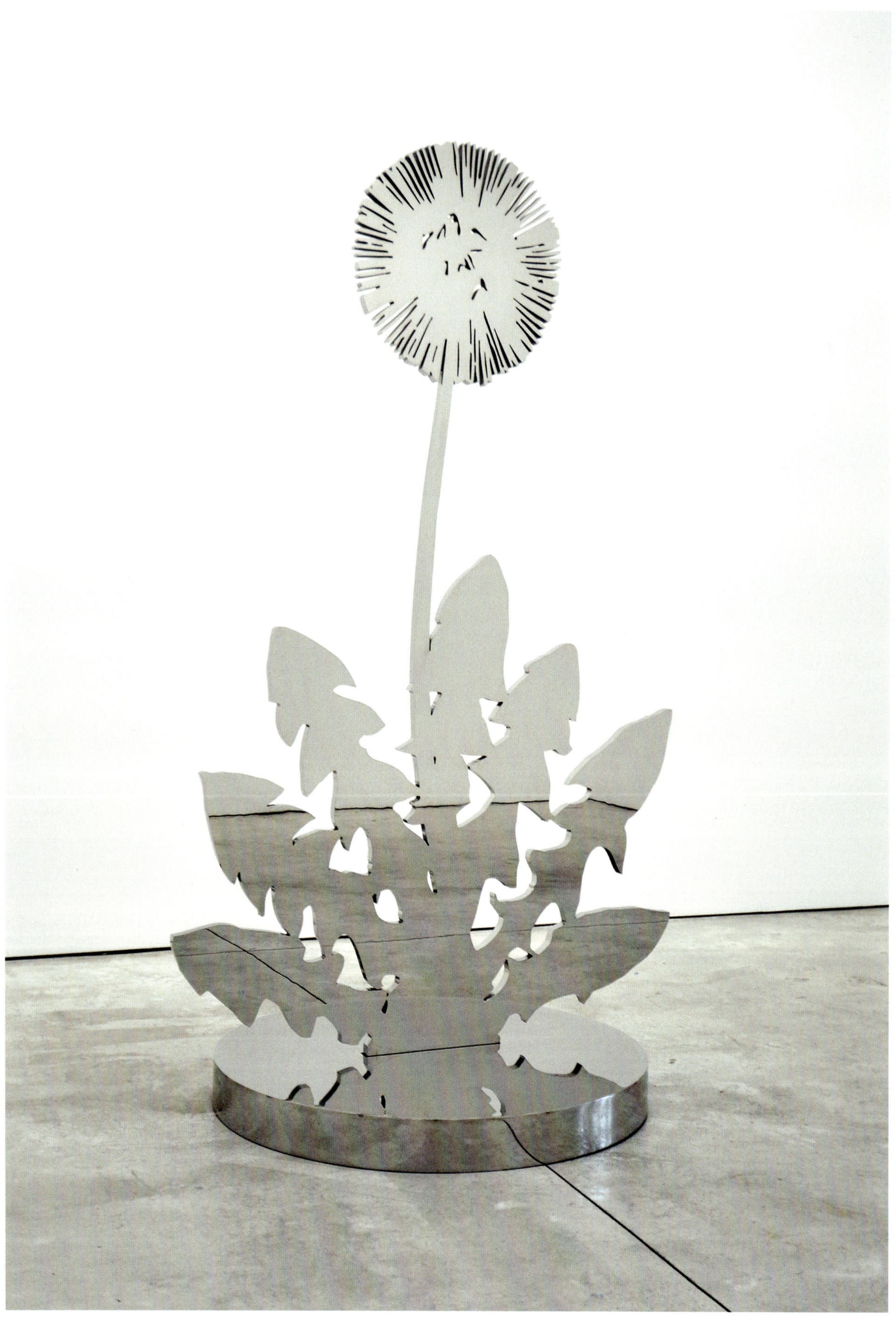

When British artist **PAUL MORRISON** (b. 1966) started painting in the 1990s he kept his palette to black and white and deployed a variety of motifs that allowed him to explore what landscape painting might be at the end of the millennium. Large, simplified plant forms often blocked any view of distance or scale, and it allowed him to open up an area of work long thought to be old-fashioned. His scale grew larger as he started to do murals and permanent works on the surfaces of buildings, adding in 24-carat gold leaf as an additional colour. He has also made a series of large sculptures that again are monochrome black or white; for *Phylum (mirror)*, the stainless steel has been polished to a mirror-like surface so that the huge dandelion reflects the landscape it inhabits, whether that be a gallery, a hillside or an urban landscape where such plants are usually seen as weeds.

British artist **ANGELA PALMER** (b. 1957) works at the borders of art and science, from her use of MRI and CT scans to make self-portraits of her brain, to her exploration of the effects of humans on the planet over the past 3,000 years. She made a 'spine' comprised of sixteen rocks from across Britain, representing all the geological eras starting from three billion years ago; the final element in the work is a sculpture titled *Anthropocene*, a mirror-polished stainless-steel rocklike shape, in which viewers can see themselves. The Anthropocene, from the ancient Greek *ánthropos* ('human') and *cene* ('new'), is the name of the proposed new geological era to succeed the current Holocene, reflecting the fact that humans have changed the planet in unprecedented ways, generally to the Earth's detriment. Palmer's mirrored rock represents the new era, and reminds viewers that they too have an impact on the environment and a duty to respect it.

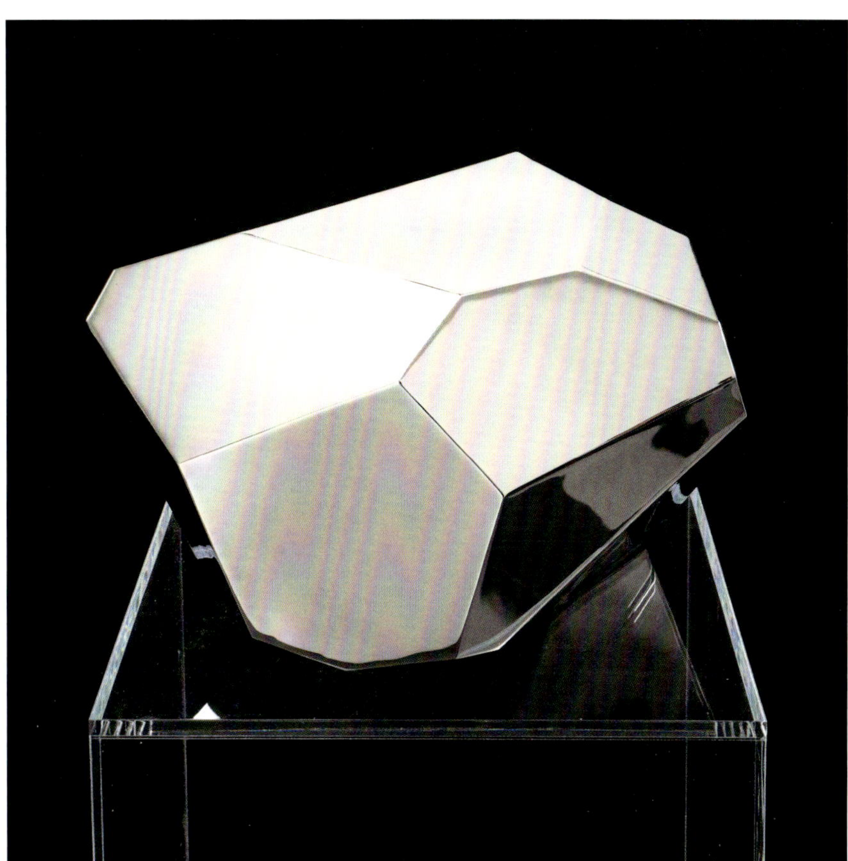

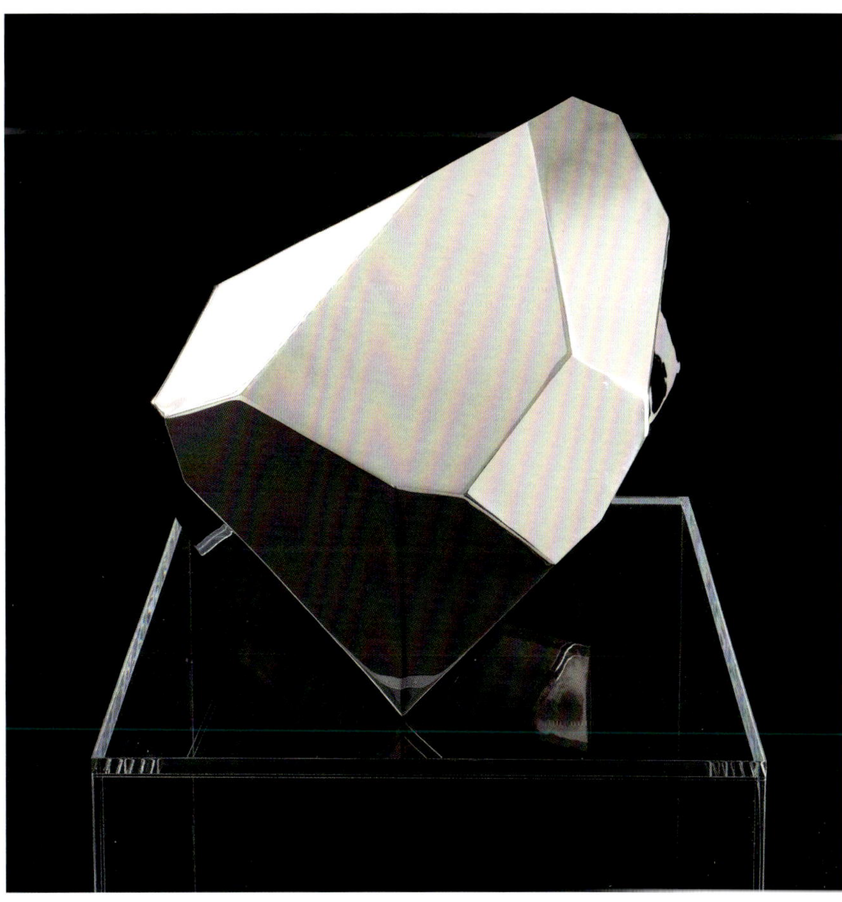

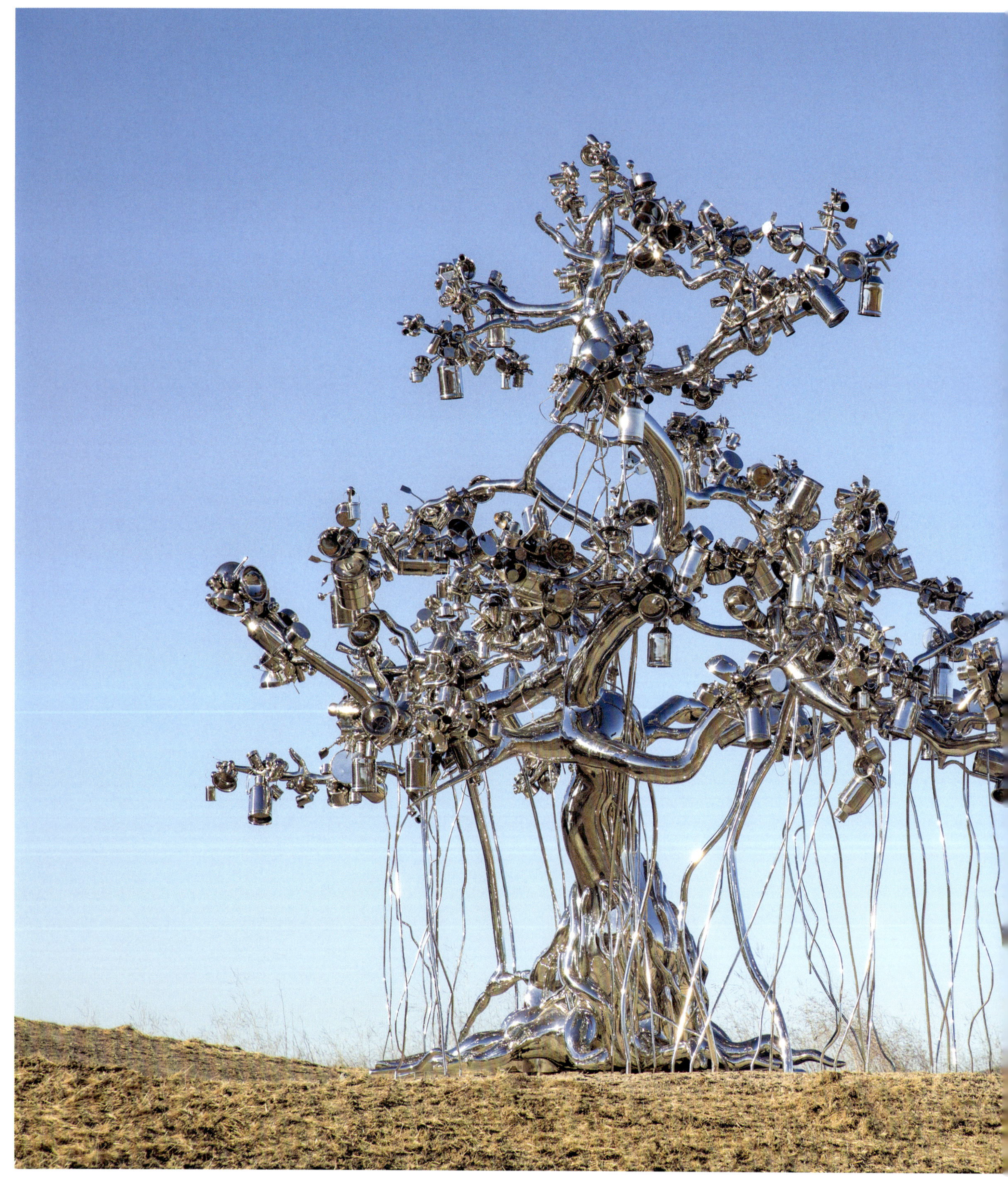

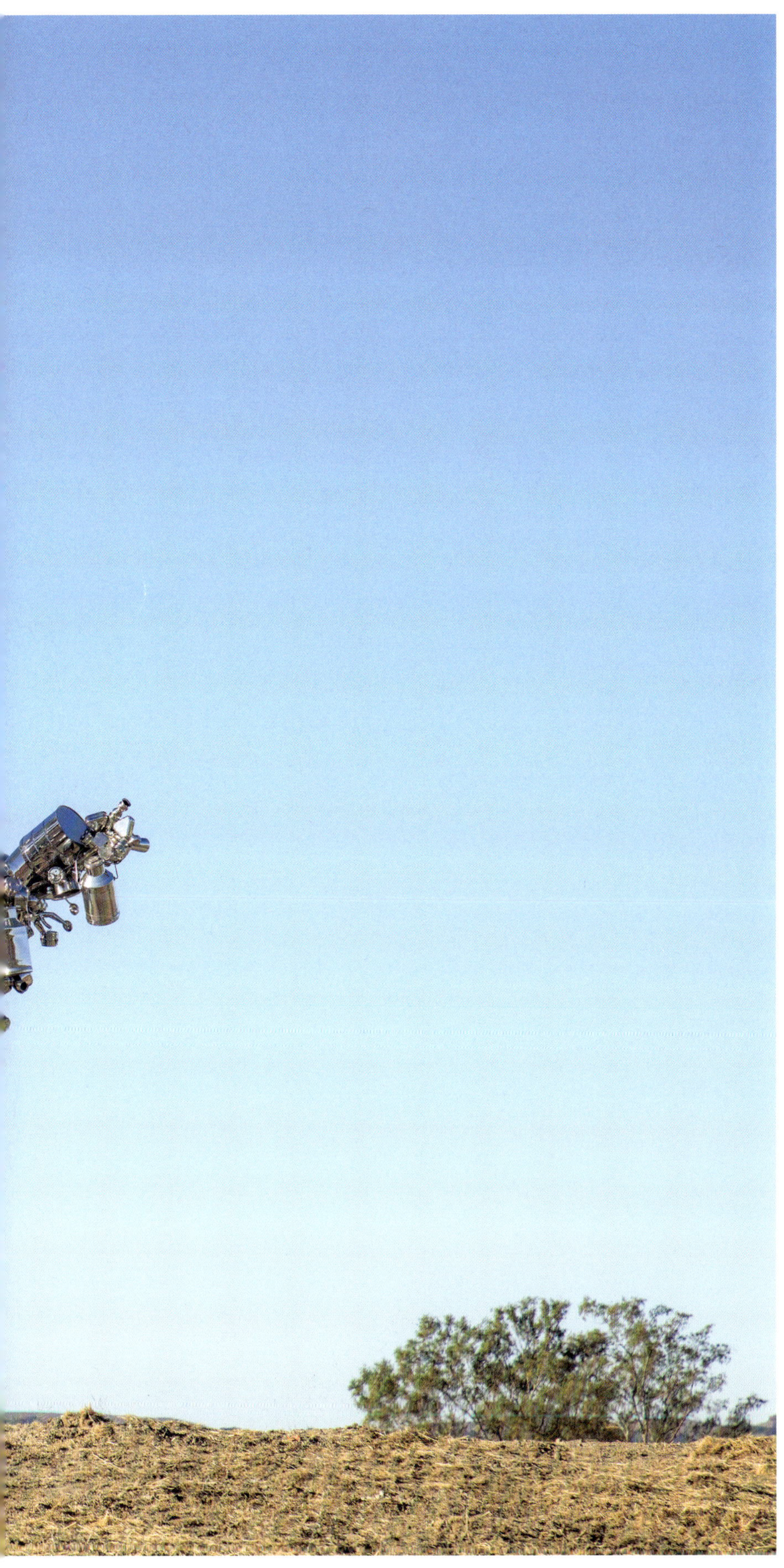

People Tree by Indian artist **SUBODH GUPTA** (b. 1964) is sited at the Donum Estate in California's Sonoma Valley, where more than fifty monumental sculptural works are open to public view. *People Tree* is in the shape of a life-sized banyan, India's national tree, which is sacred in Hinduism and, according to Gupta, epitomizes a 'rooted' existence. The pun is obviously rendered effective when seen in congruence with its physical manifestation – the robust primary trunk, the aerial roots that lend a particular peculiarity to this tree that starts out as an epiphyte (growing on another plant). With its use of mundane stainless-steel kitchen pots and utensils polished to a high shine, Gupta transforms the everyday into something spectacular and surreal.

People Tree, 2017
Stainless steel
H 7.6 m (25 ft)

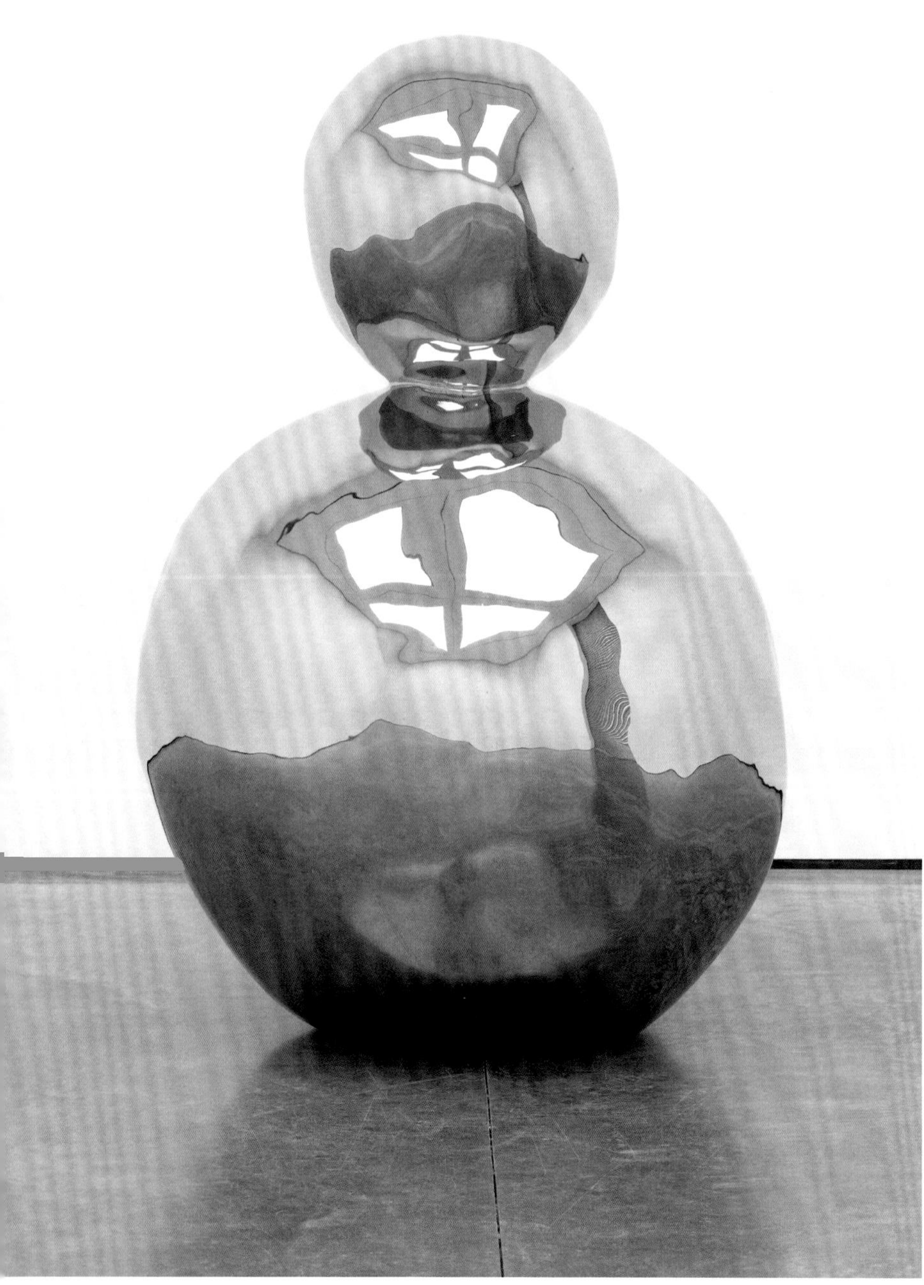

British artist **GARY HUME** (b. 1962) is best known for his highly stylized paintings of everyday objects, often in flat, bold colours, where the surface of the paint is as important as the images. Hume's paintings eschew details of rendering and traditional perspective, and it is easy to see his hand in his series of large metal snowman sculptures. These human-sized works are mirrored stainless steel, as in *Neptune* (left), or they have a coloured lacquer applied. Hume's *Back of Snowman* (2016) is a bright neon blue, while *Back of a Snowman (Black)* (2000) is dense black-painted bronze. The works reflect their surroundings and many are permanently installed outside. When exhibited inside (as seen here) they show a distorted view of the room, and it is clear the shapes of the snowmen are not perfect spheres. They appear handmade, like compacted snow, and embody a sense of fun and a reminder of childhood.

SIMON PERITON (b. 1964) is a British artist well known for his large, intricately cut-out works on paper; in recent years he has moved to incorporate reflective materials in his works, as in *Addi* (2006, gold Perspex) or *Rotten Amethyst* (2006, coloured paper and Mylar), and copper- or nickel-plated steel, such as *The Lookout* (opposite). Periton is interested in the decorative and has taken that to extremes in the creation of large architectural screens, but he returns to the idea that the content and the form should jar. Earlier paper and glass pieces were in the shape of cut-out barbed wire, and he takes an ongoing interest in the craft/art debate. He has said that 'There probably isn't really a thing that's actually "beautiful" – you simply get caught up in it or you don't'.

LEFT
Gary Hume, *Neptune,* 2012
Stainless steel
152.4 × diam. 124.5 × diam. 44.5 cm
(60 × diam. 49 × diam. 17½ in)
Edition of 3

OPPOSITE
Simon Periton, *The Lookout,* 2015
Nickel-plated steel
101 × 54 × 6.3 cm (39¾ × 21¼ × 2½ in)

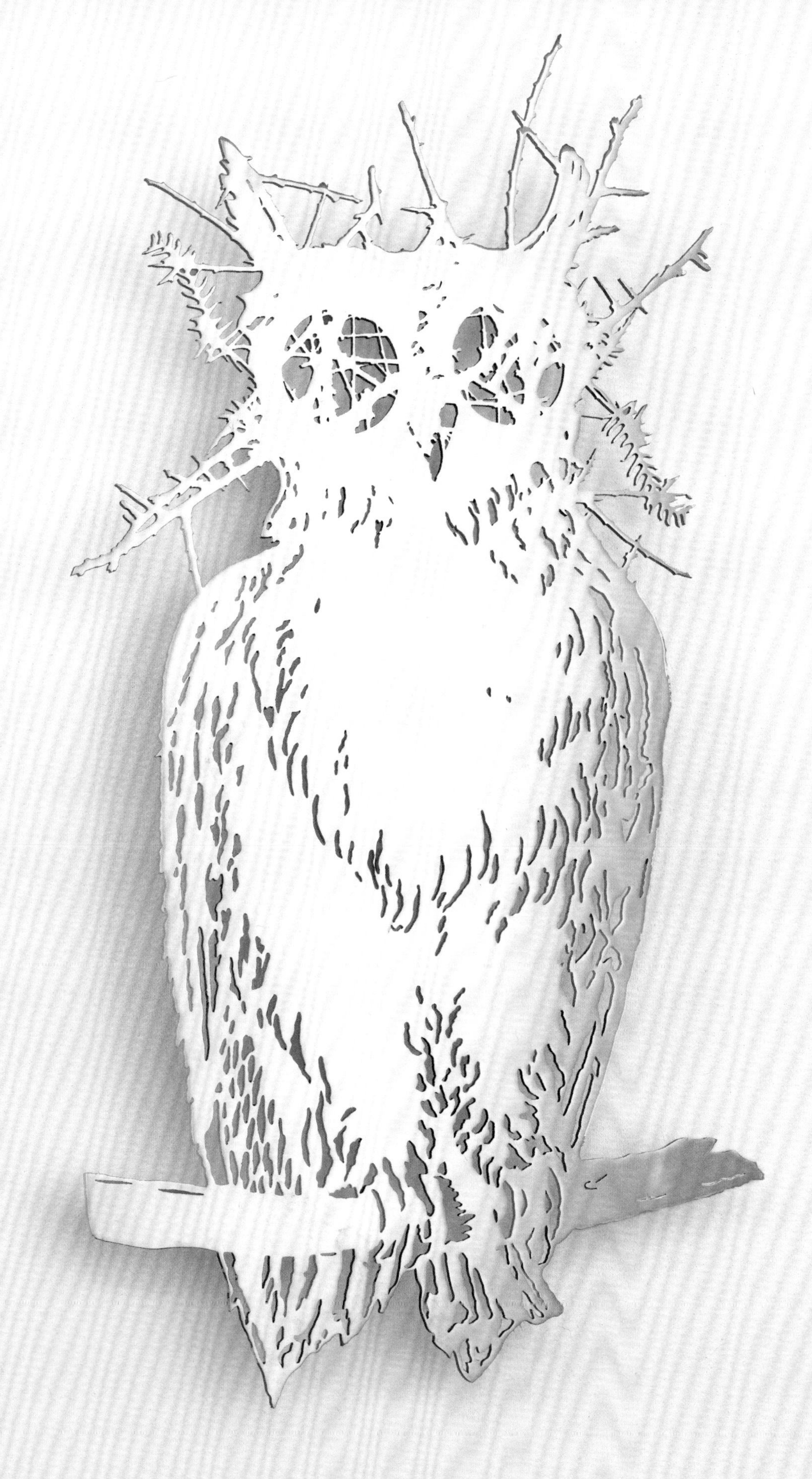

German sculptor **KATHARINA FRITSCH** (b. 1956) is well known for her uncanny use of body parts (hands, skulls, brains), religious objects (the Madonna, Saint Katharina) and animals. One of her best-known works is the monumental blue *Hahn/Cock* that sat on the fourth plinth in London's Trafalgar Square in 2013. Her works, made from a wide variety of materials (stainless steel, copper, bronze, plaster), are sculpted (life-sized or larger) and then painted in a variety of bold, flat colours, which she says 'evens it out, makes it abstract – like a visual sign, an icon'. Her series of metallic and reflective *Betende Hände (Praying Hands)* references spirituality, religion and myth, but also the loss of those things.

Betende Hände (Praying Hands), 2002/2004
Plastic, aluminium
20 × 15 × 13 cm (7⅞ × 6 × 5⅛ in)

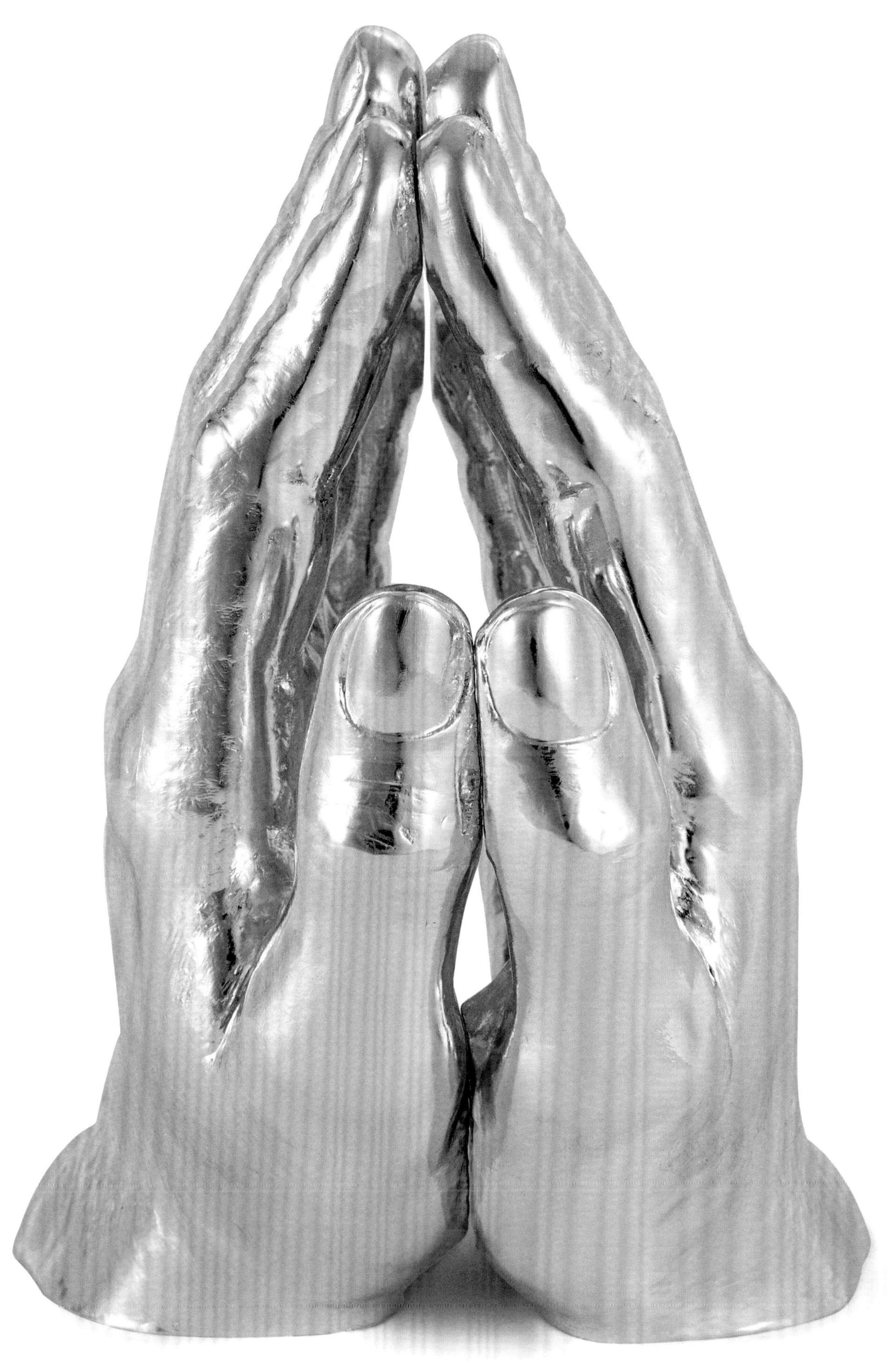

Welsh artist **CERITH WYN EVANS** (b. 1958) collaborated with the industrial music pioneers Throbbing Gristle to make the work *A=P=P=A=R=I=T=I=O=N*. The sculpture, whose name comes from the title of a poem by the nineteenth-century French symbolist poet Stéphane Mallarmé, combines with Throbbing Gristle's unique form of sound production to 'reconfigure the elegiac and the romantic'. It consists of three moving mobiles using sixteen audio spotlight panels that are highly mirror-polished on one side, and emit the recording on the other. The multi-channel soundtrack was composed by Chris Carter, Peter Christopherson and Cosey Fanni Tutti of Throbbing Gristle. Visitors moved through the space created by the glistening mirrors and speakers, which used a hypersonic sound system to generate audible sound from ultrasonic signals. The work was shown at the 2008 Yokohama Triennial, then at Glasgow's Tramway (2009), before becoming part of the permanent collection of the Centre Pompidou, Paris.

Now based in Paris, **TARIK KISWANSON** was born in Sweden in 1986 to a Palestinian family. Always operating at the intersection of different cultural contexts, via his abstract works he examines subjects related to memory, heritage, birth, loss and belonging. His various modes of production include sculpture, drawing, writing, video and performance. His mobile sculptures titled *Vestibules* and *Father Form* are made from steel strips and were first presented in his exhibition at the College des Bernardins, Paris. Kiswanson hand polished the metal strips so that they would reflect the visitors, who could see themselves in the strands of the work. The shape was Kiswanson's response to the site's history (a former sacristy), vaulted ceilings and social context.

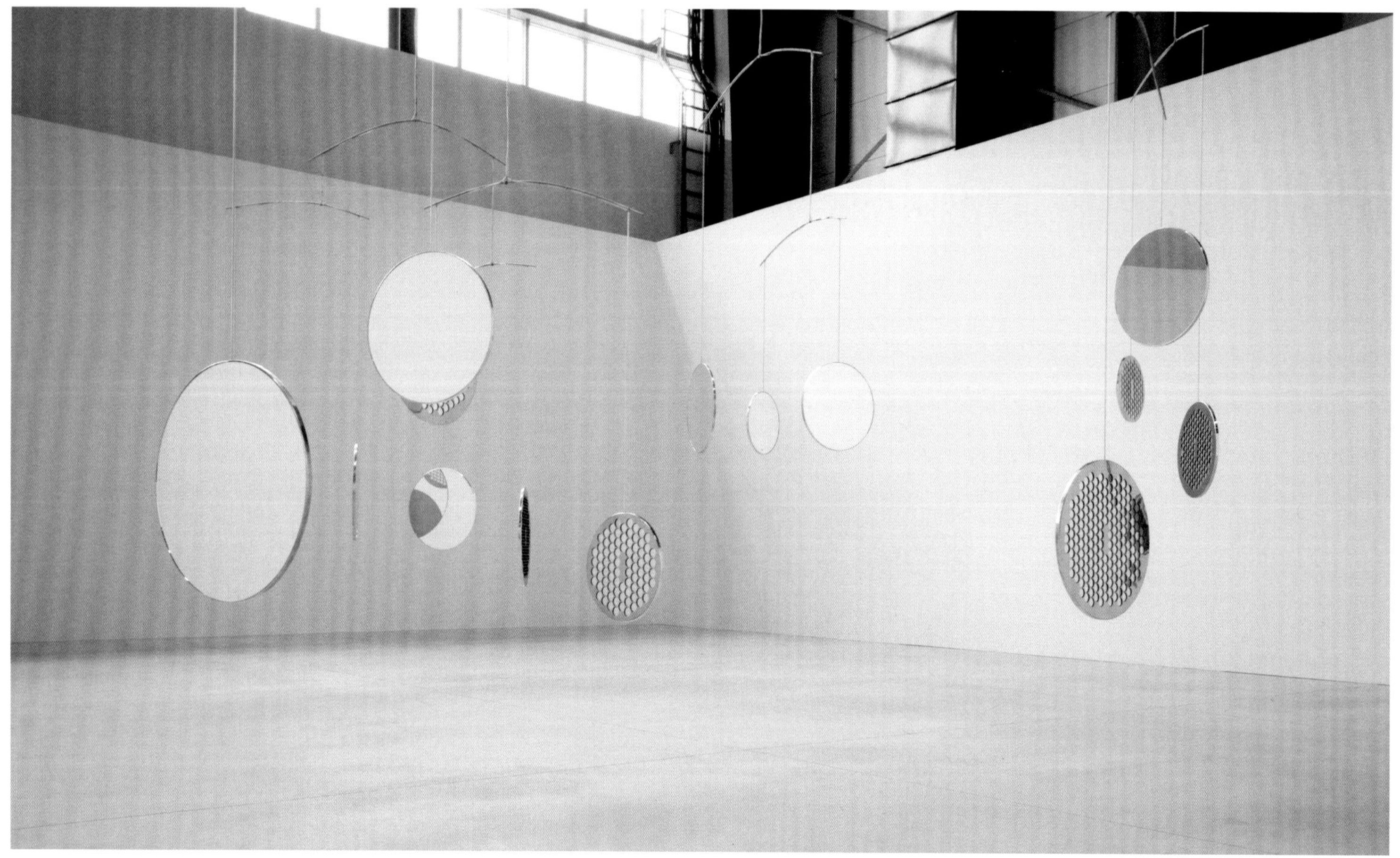

OPPOSITE
Cerith Wyn Evans,
A=P=P=A=R=I=T=I=O=N, 2008
Mixed media collaboration
with Throbbing Gristle
Sound system (Holosonic speakers),
computer, electronics
Dimensions variable

RIGHT
Tarik Kiswanson, *Father Form,* 2017
Sculpture activated during Tarik
Kiswanson's performance *The Ear
That Hears Me*, carlier | gebauer,
Berlin, Germany, 2017
Steel
4.48 × 0.92 m (14½ × 3 ft)

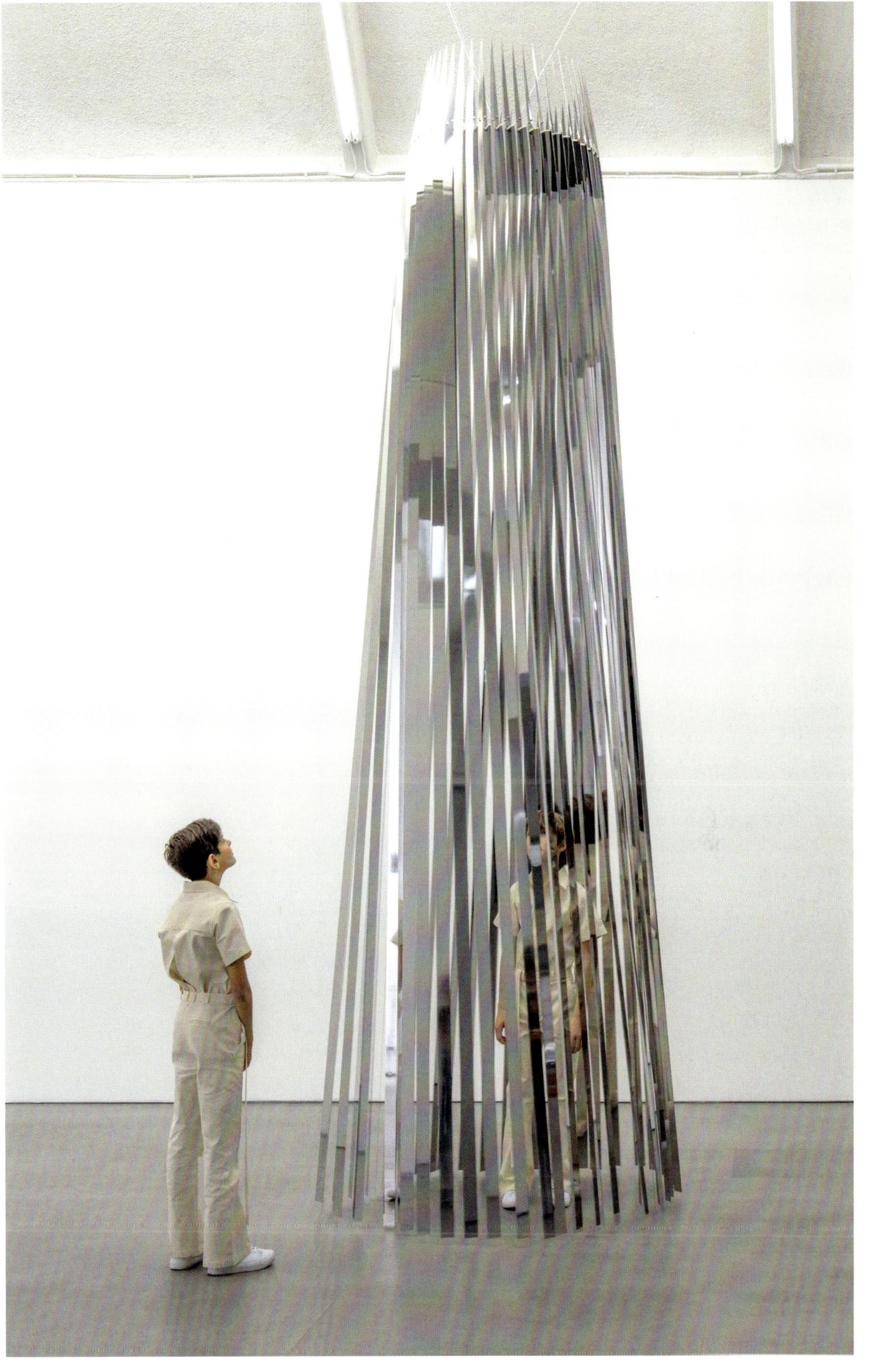

American artist **KATHRYN ANDREWS** (b. 1973) works with mirrored surfaces to explore and disrupt patriarchal views of making. She uses the mirror as a 'standin… shifting the presence of the artist's hand away from the traditional painted gesture and towards something more industrial, ubiquitous, and implicative of everything beyond the self'. Most of her sculptures feature mirrored stainless steel (some are aluminium), including *Stormtrooper*, where a replica of a *Star Wars* movie costume hangs on a steel cylinder. The empty shell of a warrior (a bad guy in the film series) is raised from the ground, as if by Darth Vader, and is forced to forever hover impotently, looking at its own masculine image. In her 2019 work *Tarzan (J.W.)* Andrews presents a certified film prop of Tarzan actor Johnny Weissmuller's skimpy leather loincloth perched between two mirrored columns and a metal Olympic torch.

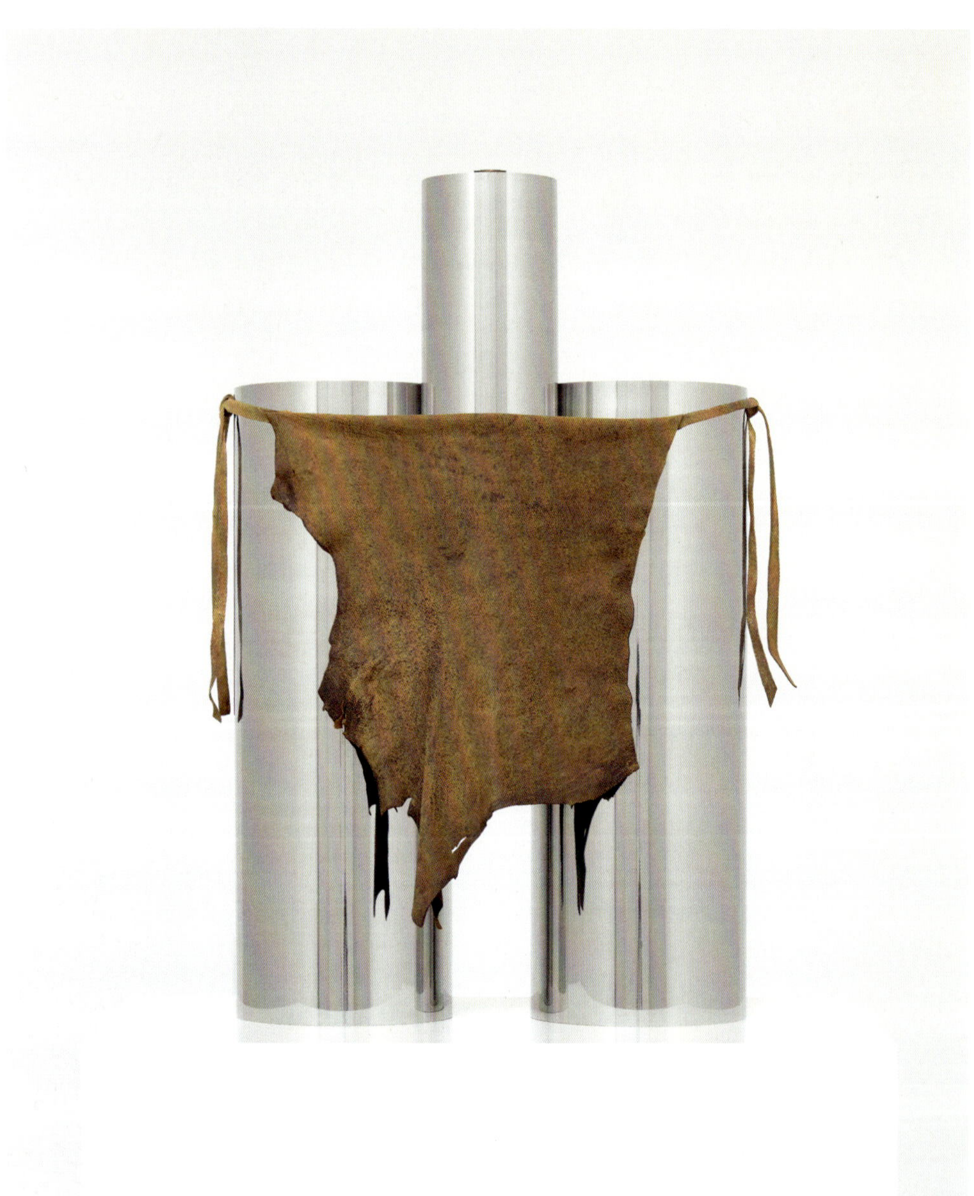

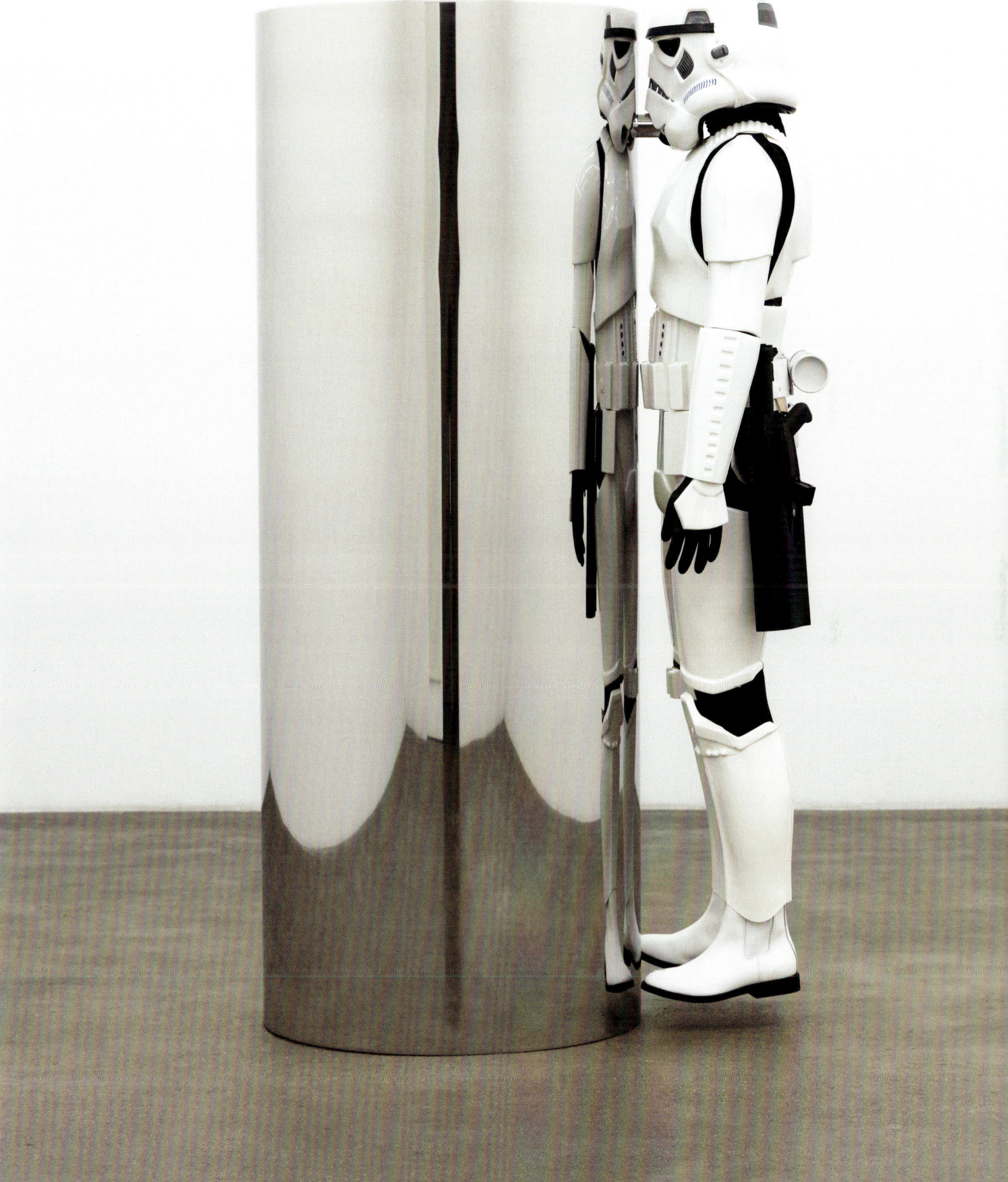

Handle (Dirty Knob) by London-based Swedish-Spanish artist **ROBERTO EKHOLM** (b. 1976) is a doorknob fixed to a wall and opens to nothing physical, but perhaps to imaginary worlds. The viewer can see a dirty smudge on its surface, and on closer inspection, the sealed fingerprint of the artist is visible. The raised ridges are like those in a dusted crime scene. Ekholm has long investigated illness and state responses to it, and the work addresses their attitudes to such diseases as AIDS (in the 1980s hospitals would remove handles) and then Covid (when automatic doors were frequently installed). Fear is at play, and while *knob* is a somewhat comic term in the UK for a penis, within queer online culture *dirty* refers to those who are HIV positive, while those people who are *clean* are negative.

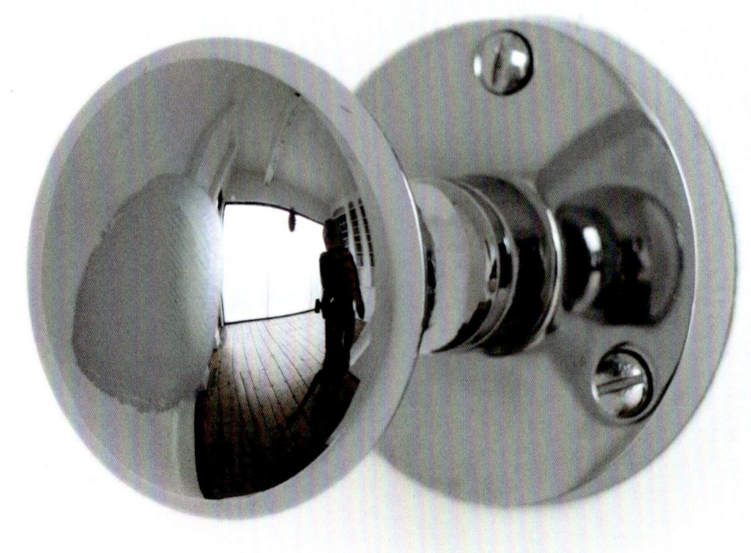

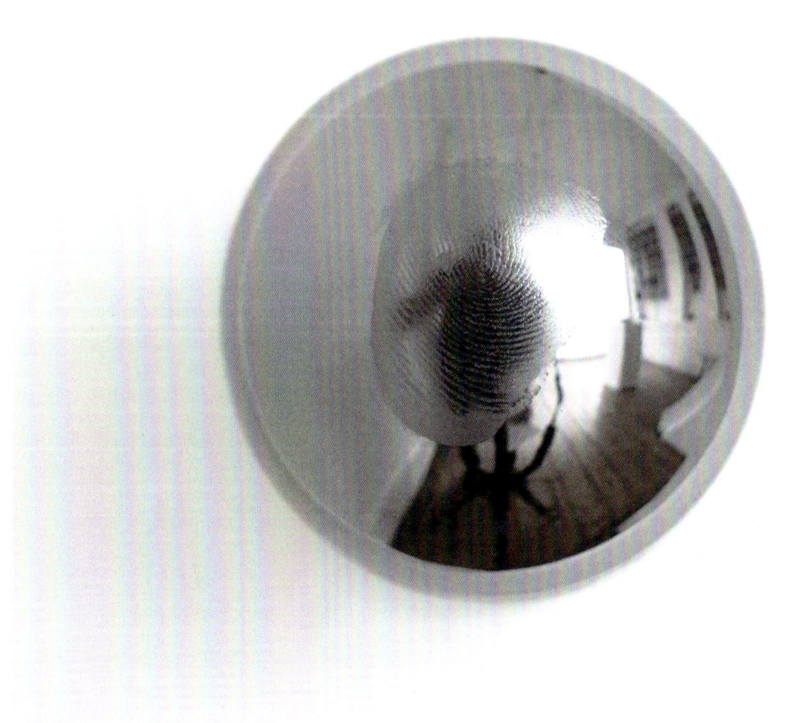

Handle (Dirty Knob), 2023
Victorian mortice door knob, polished
chrome, sealer, screws
H 8 × diam. 6 cm (H 3¼ × diam. 2⅜ in)
Unique edition

PAUL DERREZ (b. 1950) is one of the Netherlands' best-known conceptual jewelry makers, renowned for the extreme polish and finish of his works. For *In Gods Name*, he presents the viewer with a mirror-polished three-sided dagger engraved on each side with the symbol of one of the three major monotheistic religions – Christianity, Islam and Judaism. The blade extends towards the viewer, but thanks to the mirror quality of the hand shield, which reflects the blade, visually, at least, it attacks the one who might wield it. The work cleverly keeps the idea of multiple gods at play and at the same time suggests that violence in the name of any god is a terrible thing.

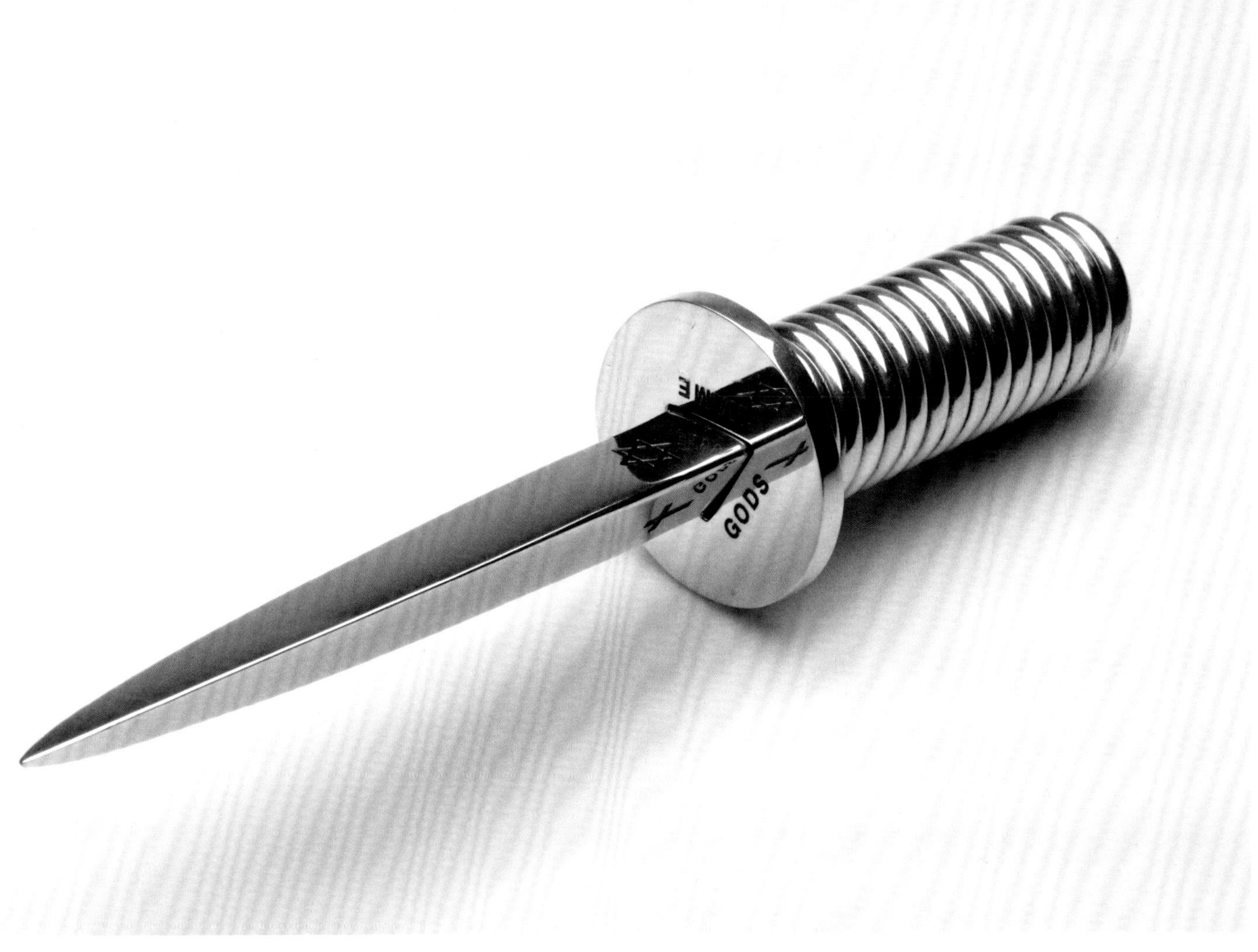

British artist **DAVID MUSGRAVE**'s
(b. 1973) understated works can often
be missed in the loud arena of current art.
He aims to disrupt the idea that figurative
and abstract works are true to themselves
or any objects they relate to. That is,
figuration, even a close resemblance, is
always a distortion and never objective;
and abstract works are never free from
reference or without their own context.
He comments, 'Even traditionally
"correct" drawing is a total falsification
and transformation of the subject matter.'

Musgrave has used tromp l'oeil techniques
to depict everyday things such as crumpled
paper or masking tape, and he has made
a series of sculptures of painted aluminium
(including *Paper golem*, 2003) that look
like torn paper just hinting at a figure. His
gleaming titanium *Damaged head*, which
hangs from the ceiling like a plumb line,
is a pliable-seeming, crushed and battered
form fixed in one of the most intractable
materials. It is a hybrid of the peripheral
and the stridently present, capturing room
and viewer within its ambiguous presence.

Damaged head , 2018
Titanium, nylon cord, steel fixings
12.6 × 24.3 × 9.8 cm (5 × 9⅝ × 3⅞ in)

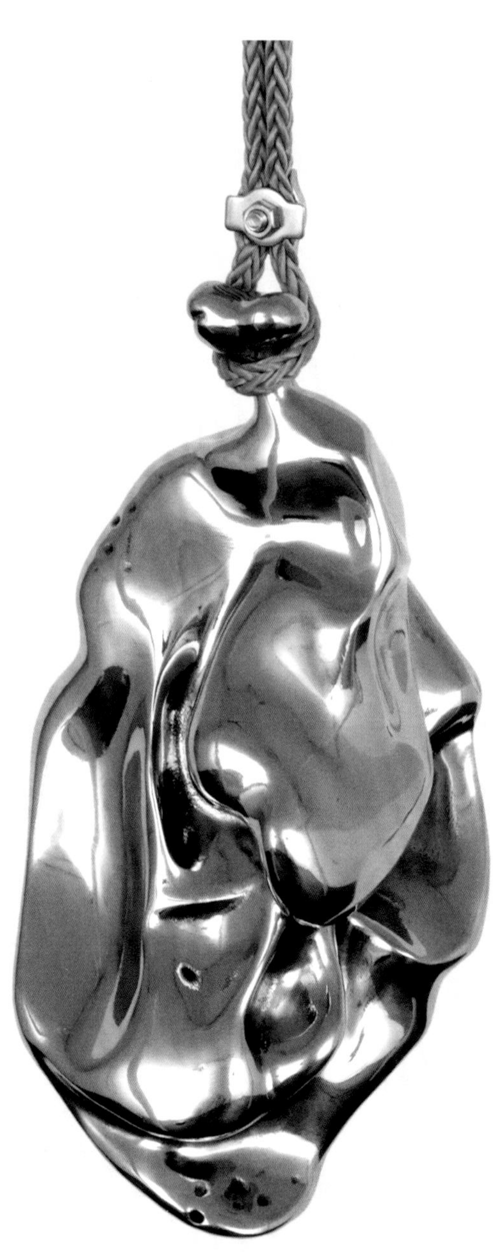

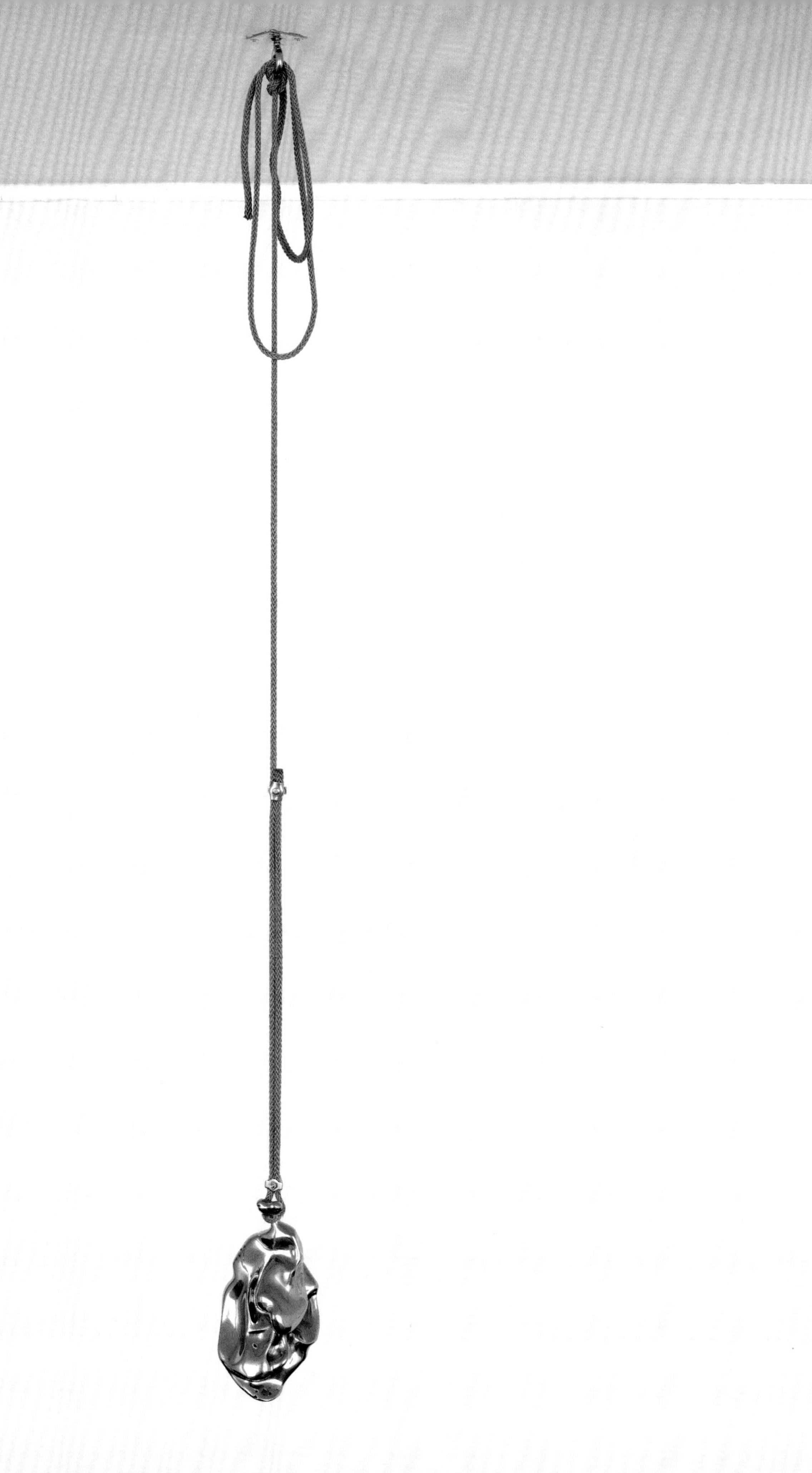

Four mirror-polished stainless-steel panels are the basis of **KADER ATTIA**'s *Untitled* work, which from a distance looks like a large minimalist wall sculpture or a designer mirror with a few black holes drilled into its surface. But on closer inspection it is clear that the surface has been violently abused: the metal has been torn, and its sharp edges protrude towards the viewer. Attia has had the work shot with real bullets and the holes remember the trauma. Raised in France and Algeria, Attia (b. 1970) has long worked with colonial violence as a theme, reflecting the difficulties of growing up in the Paris *banlieues*. Observing the mirror, the viewer is confronted with their own reflection riddled with bullet holes, forcing them to confront their own mortality.

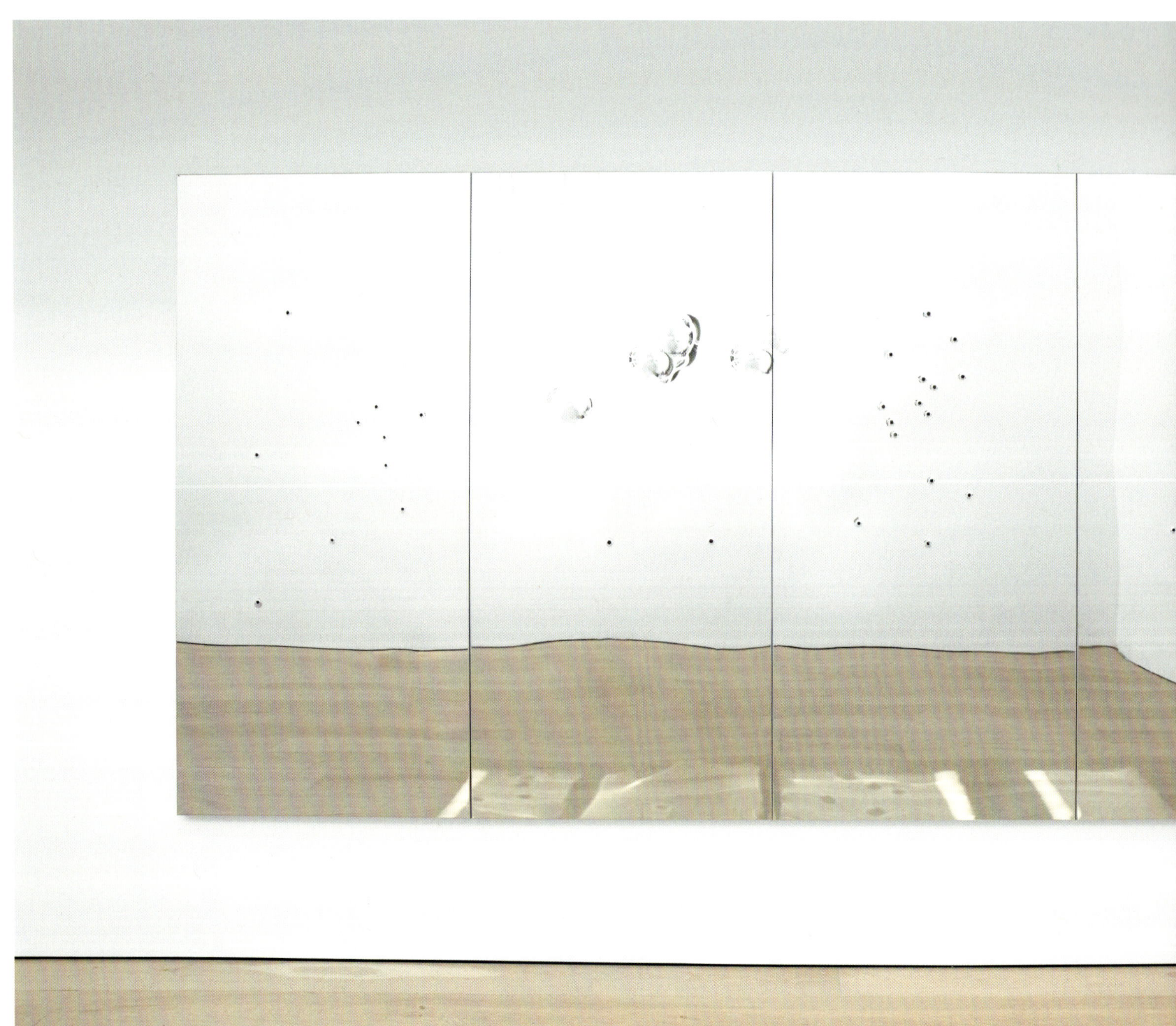

Untitled, 2019
Mirror-polished stainless steel, bullet holes
191.8 × 368.3 × 3.2 cm (75½ × 145 × 1¼ in)

In **ANTHONY JAMES**'s (b. 1974) first
work with an actual car, *KO* (*Kalos
Thanatos*, 2008), the British artist
'sacrificed' his Ferrari 355 Spider by
setting fire to the car and then entombing
it inside a mirror vitrine. Its beautiful
death led to his working with renowned
Los Angeles fabricator Peter Carlson
to create a series of car-shaped artworks
called 'Repose'. James says it 'means
stillness. These were built for speed, but
now they're static…a warrior laid to rest.'
Each car was hand hammered into the
body shape of a high-performance car,
the first in aluminium, then one in
bronze and another in copper. The shiny
metallic bodies look like the skeletons
of cars stripped of their skins of paint.
They resemble *nature morte* artefacts
that remind the viewer of their mortality
each time they go for a ride.

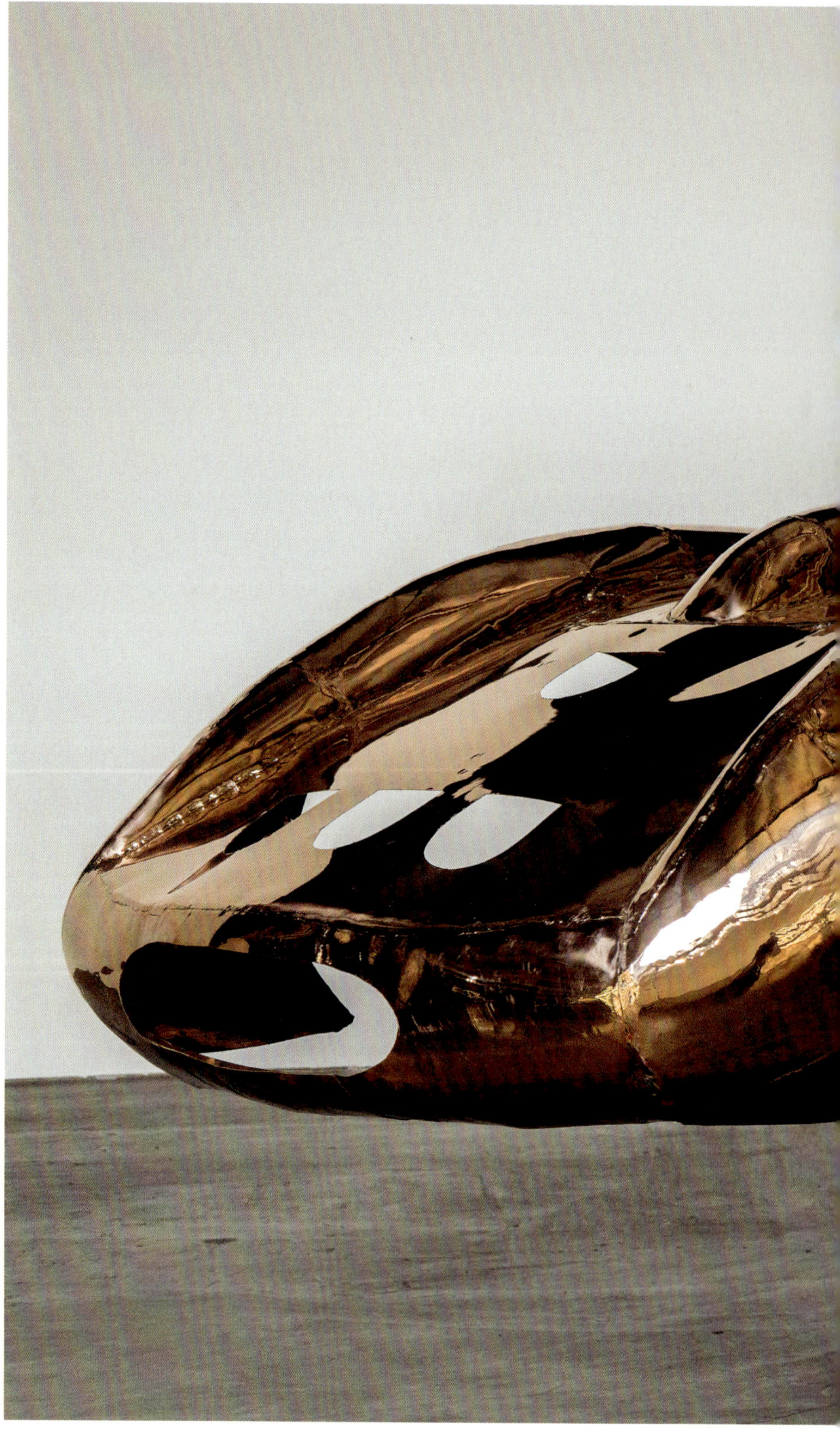

1957 Ferrari 250 Testa Rossa, 2020
Hand-formed bronze
1.5 × 4 × 0.8 m (5 × 13 × 2⅔ ft)

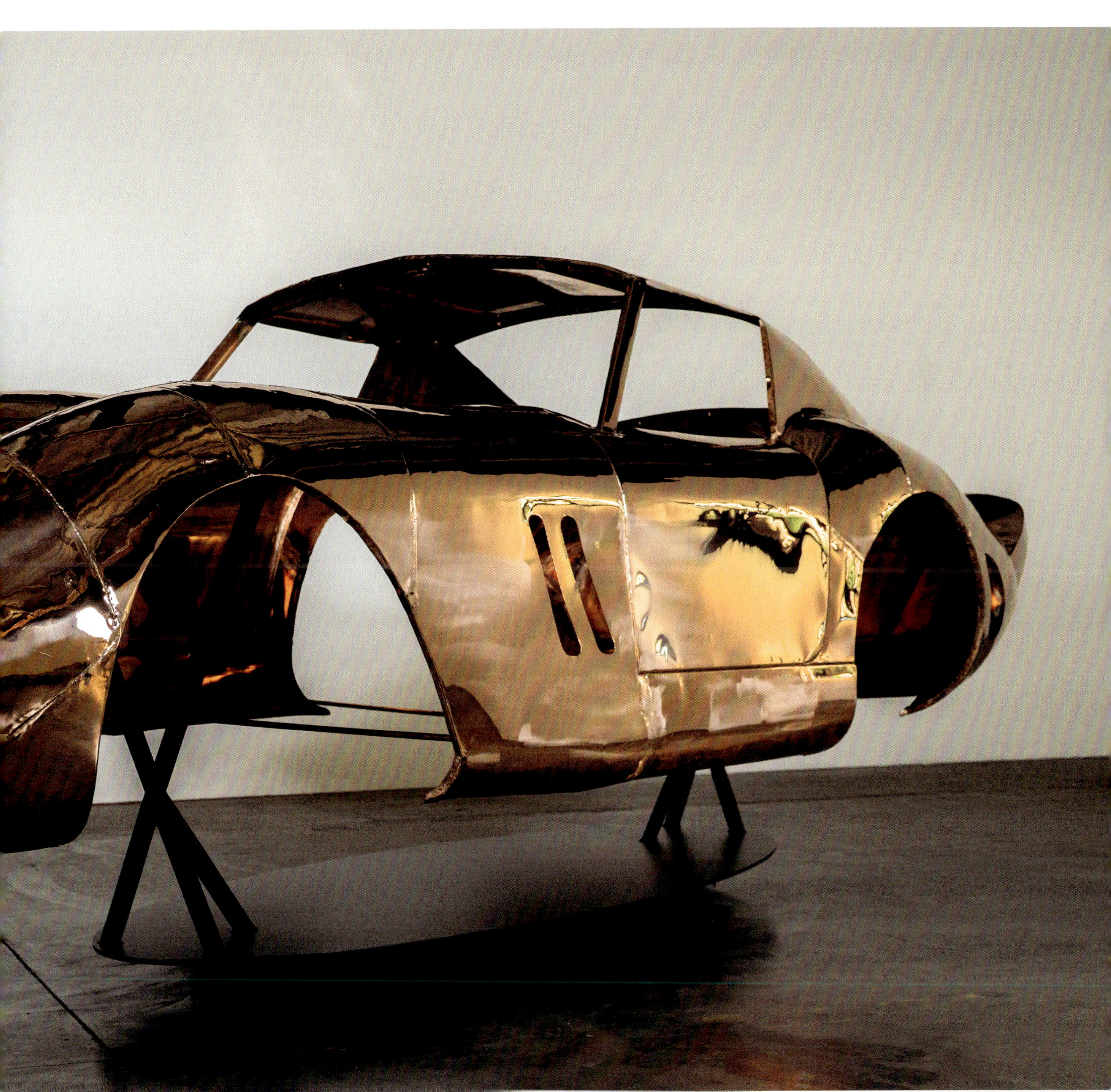

EMMA PEURA AND SAIJA KIVIKANGAS
(b. 1988 and 1984 respectively) are individual Finnish artists who worked together to make a kinetic sculpture for the exhibition 'The Immaterial Quality of Distance' in Helsinki. The metal revolved as 'two projectors work(ed) as two different light sources depicting time, repetition, continuation and loops'. One projector sent a 'live video stream from the street outside the gallery…during the exhibition'. The second projected video documentation of the making of the piece onto itself, and in every future showing footage is added of its last iteration. They say that 'the resulting reflection the sculpture makes is actually a reflection of the reflection from the past. History repeats itself in this endless loop of light and movement.'

Project(ion), 2018
Copper, DC motor, video projection
Dimensions variable
(copper 1 × 1.8 m / 3⅓ × 6 ft)

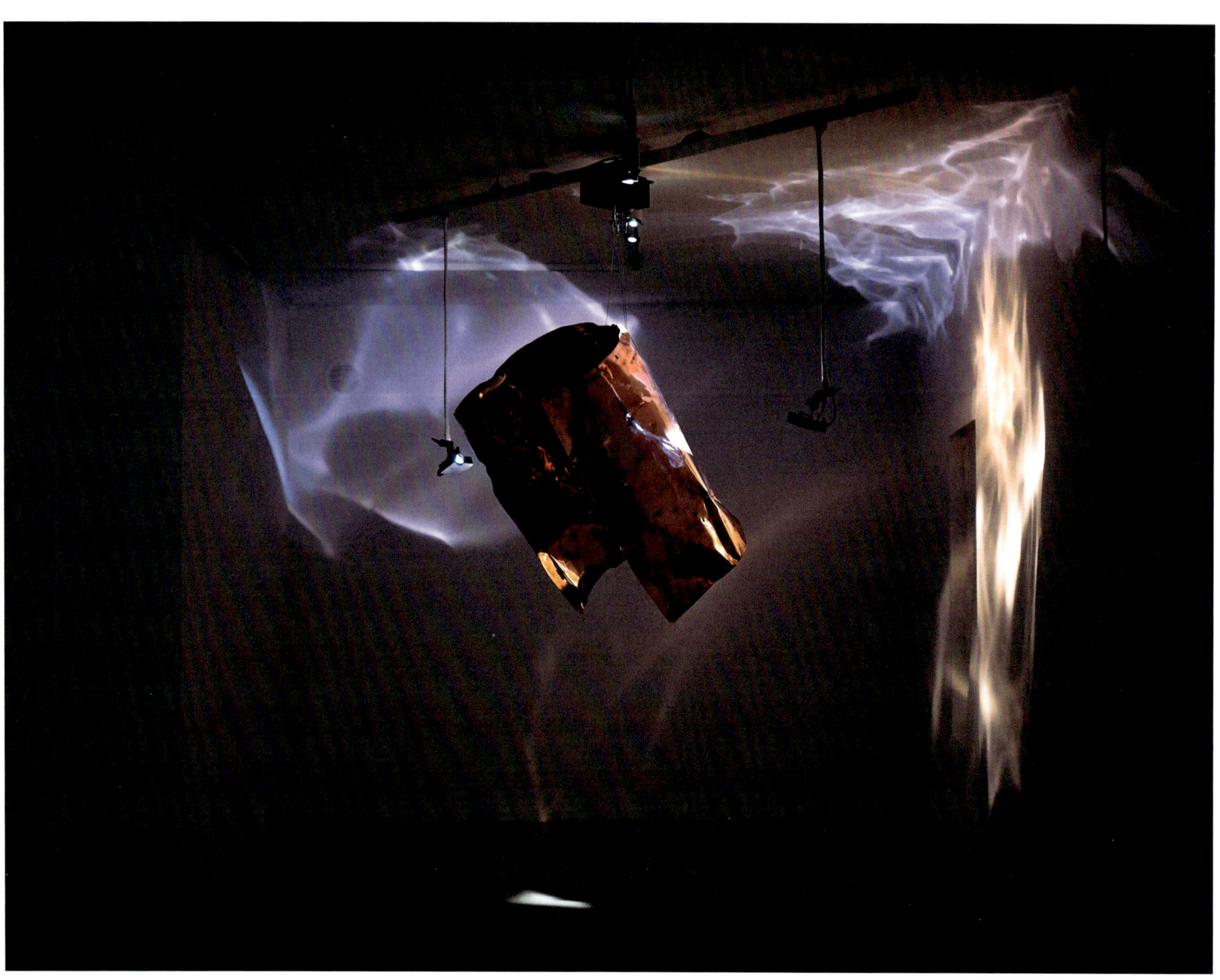

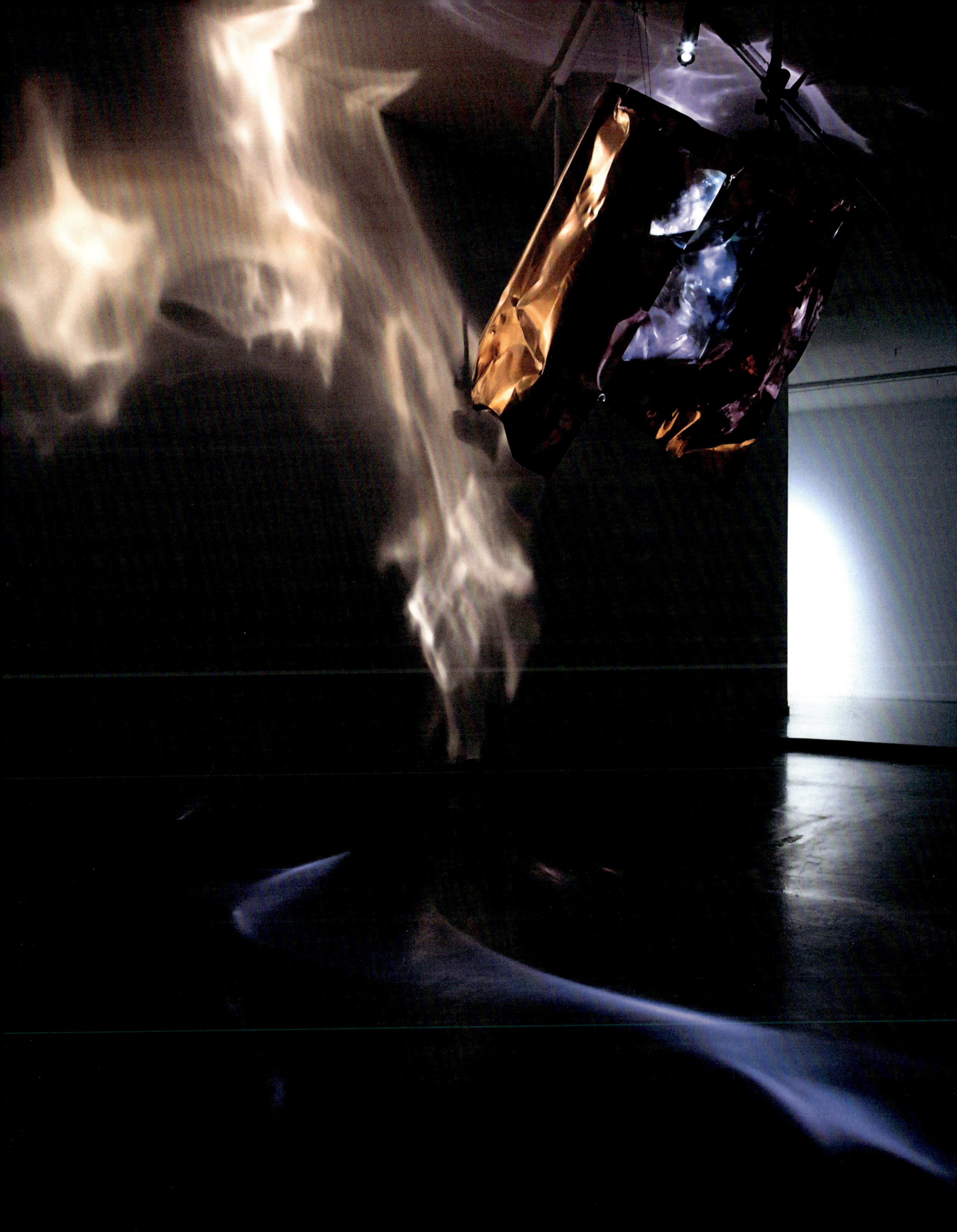

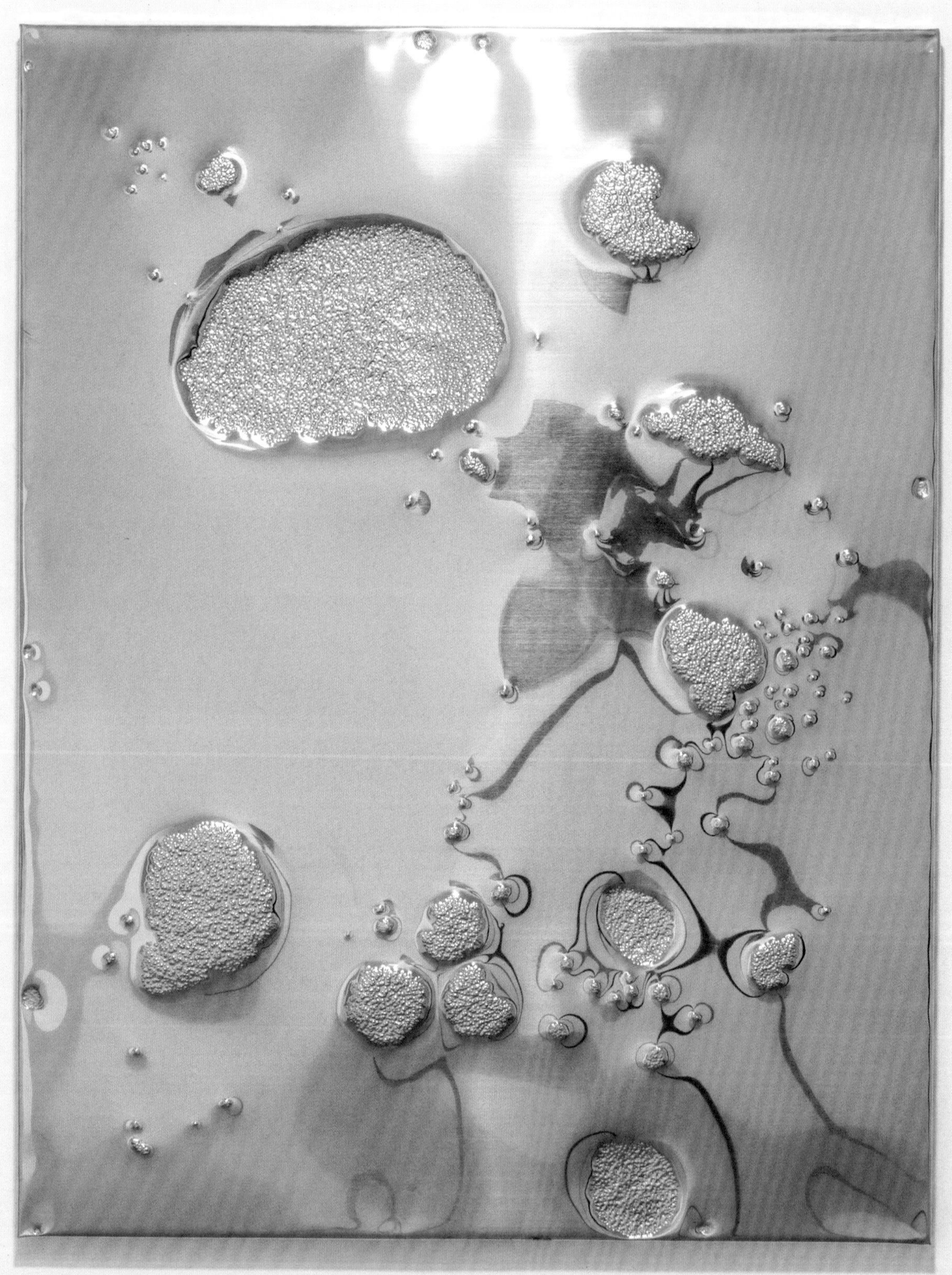

Danish artist **JESPER SKOV MADSEN**
(b. 1982) works with a variety of metal
materials, which he often attacks with
all manner of tools, both hand and electric
powered. Some of his wall-based sculptures
read more as paintings, in the way he
interacts with the canvas so as to obscure
the shiny reflective surface of the mirrored
metal. In *Mirror mirror on the wall* the
copper is punched out in oval blobs that
appear organic, as if the viewer is looking
through a microscope or the surface is
alive. His highly crafted works reference
minimalism and conceptual work, yet are
painterly in the way he marks the surface
and disrupts the viewer's reflection.

British artist **JANE BUSTIN**'s (b. 1964)
Nijinsky Project looks at the famed
Russian dancer Vaslav Nijinsky (1890–
1950), whose lover was the director of
the Ballets Russes, Sergei Diaghilev.
Diaghilev commissioned many works to
showcase Nijinsky's talents. Nijinsky was
bisexual and when he married a ballerina,
Romola de Pulszky, in 1913, Diaghilev
fired him from the company. Nijinsky
started his own, unsuccessful company
and soon slipped into mental illness,
from which he never recovered. Bustin's
project looks at three elements of dance:
rehearsal, programme and performance.
Each part uses a variety of materials
to bring forth the emotive and sensual
qualities of dance and of Nijinsky's tragic
story. She comments that her material
choice reflects weakness and fragility
(the cloth) as well as strength and rigidity
(the copper).

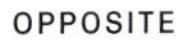

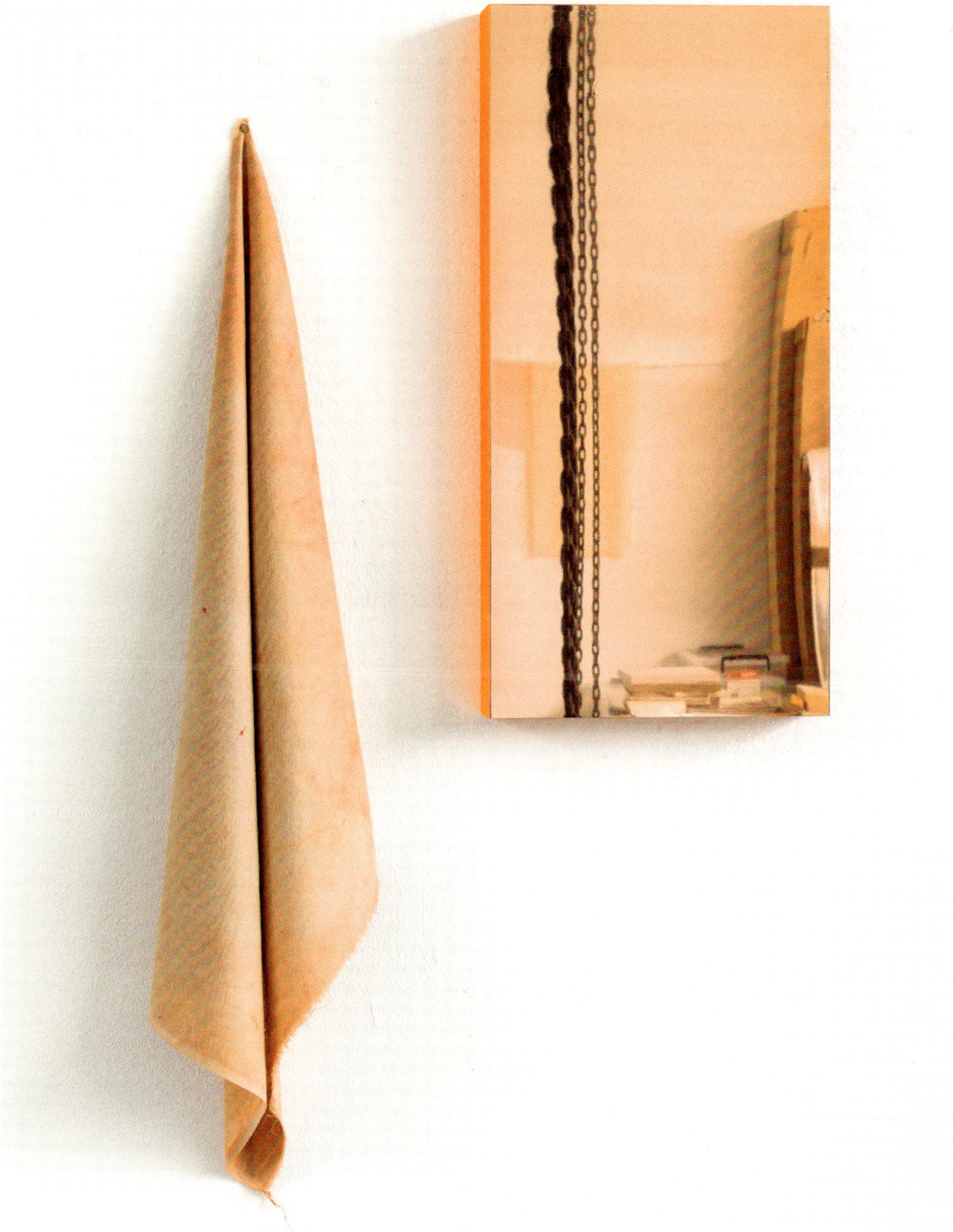

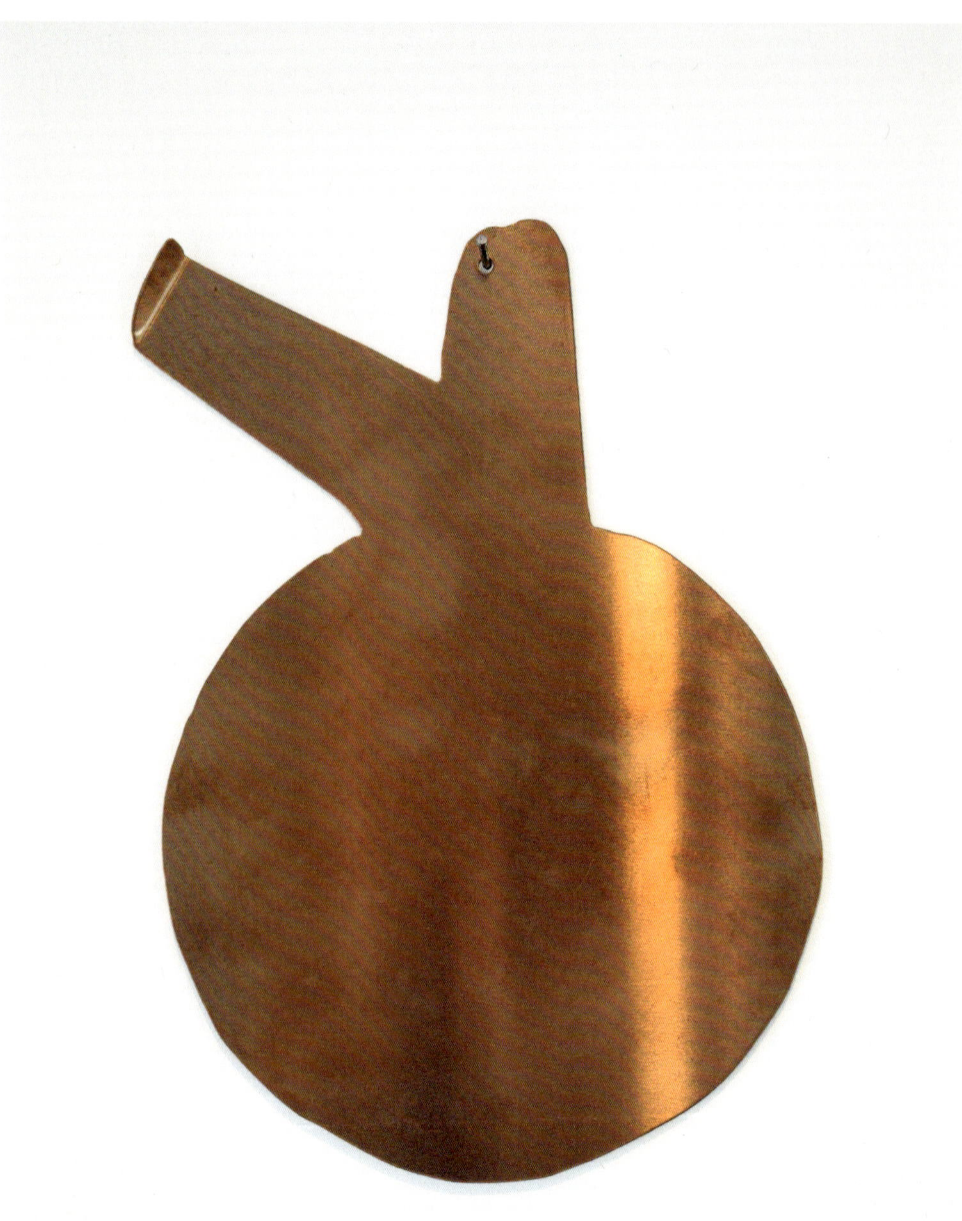

A found object (made of sheet iron) was German artist **IMI KNOEBEL**'s (b. 1940) first iteration of the *Hase* (Rabbit). He placed the offcut on his studio wall for a trial of his installation *Eigentum Himmelreich* (The Property of the Kingdom of Heaven). The work was officially shown publicly at Galerie Schoof in Frankfurt (1983) and then again at Le Consortium, Dijon (1984), Musée Municipal, La-Roche-sur-Yon (1985) and the Bonnefantenmuseum, Maastricht (1992), which purchased the installation. Each time, the rabbit was placed in a different location in relation to the other objects that formed the complete work, and in relation to the architecture of the various rooms. The shiny copper version works to softly reflect the rooms that the 1,000 rabbits will eventually inhabit.

1000 Hasen, 2021
Copper sheet (1 mm), water jet cutting technique
26 × 18 × 0.8 cm (7⅞ × 7⅛ × ⅜ in)
Signed on the back

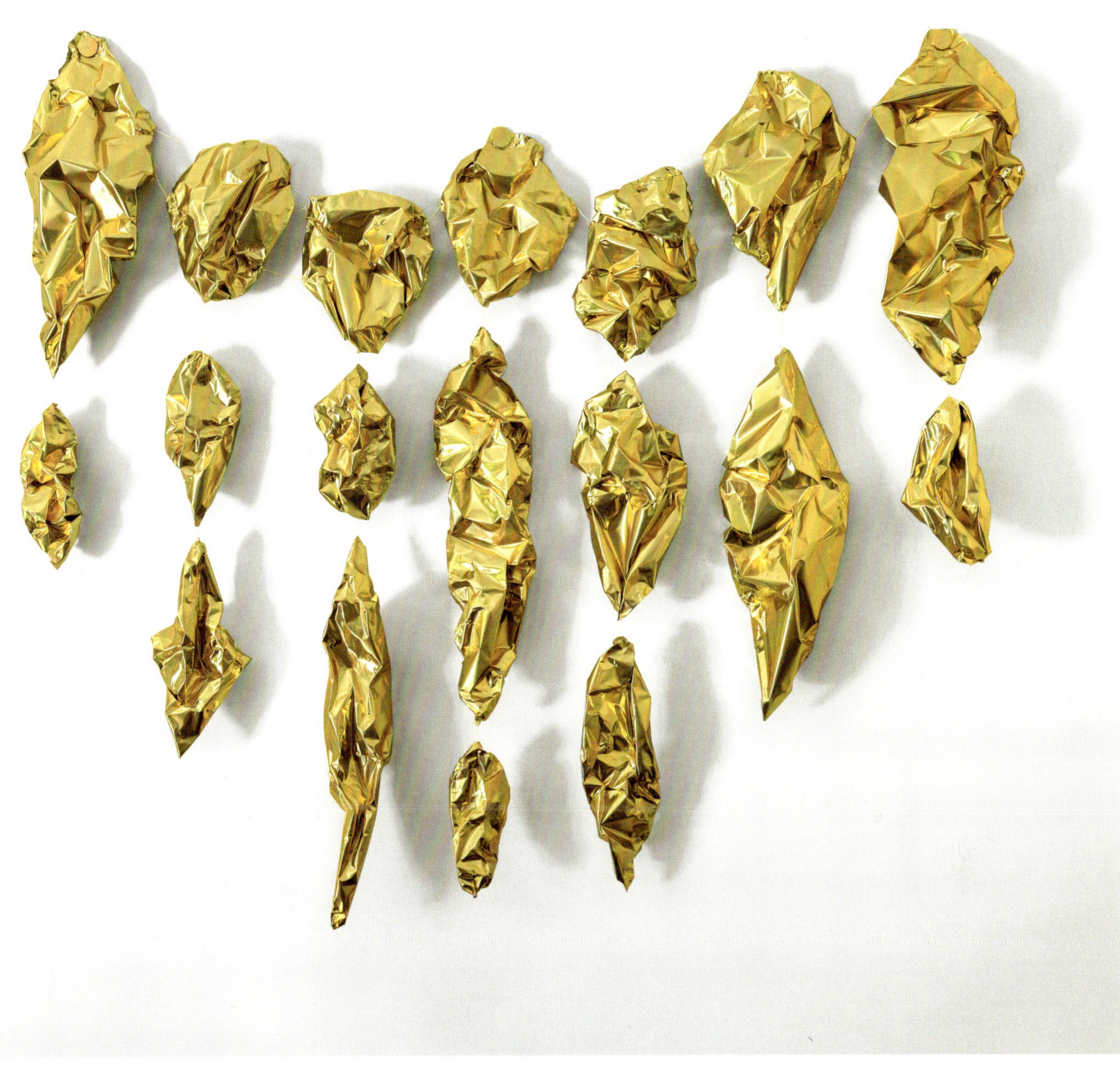

Gold Fractalis Extended, 2021
ALUFLEXIA® (registered trademark by
Tiziana Lorenzelli. Bronze Medal Sustainable
Design IDA Los Angeles 2011), golden thread,
gold magnets for suspension
240 × 200 × 25 cm (95 × 79 × 10 in)

Italian artist **TIZIANA LORENZELLI**
(b. 1961) has used a recyclable material
that she designed and patented, called
Aluflexia, to create a series of sculptures
including *Gold Fractalis Extended*. The
material, an aluminium and polyethylene
sandwich, is very lightweight, almost as
thin as a sheet of paper, but its metallic
structure allows her to make three-
dimensional forms from it, which retain
their shape and have a reflective surface.
She refers to the suspended pieces as
'nuggets', likening them to meteorites; like
the element gold (Au) that they ape, they
do not oxidize or corrupt, giving them a
mystical feel and referencing mythological
as well as scientific aspects.

Over a period of ten years, British artist **POPPY WOODESON** (formerly Ben Woodeson), made a number of dangerous but appealing installations for a series called 'Health and Safety Violations'. *I love you, I want you, I need you…(Hot for Carl)* was the last of these, and it bisected the Berloni Gallery in a solo London show. The large flat brass panels on the floor had an electric current running through them. While they were enticing, and their mirrored surface called out to be touched (and to leave a finger print on that polished surface), if viewers did so, they received a 'hefty electric shock'. The artist has said that no animals or people were ever harmed in her works.

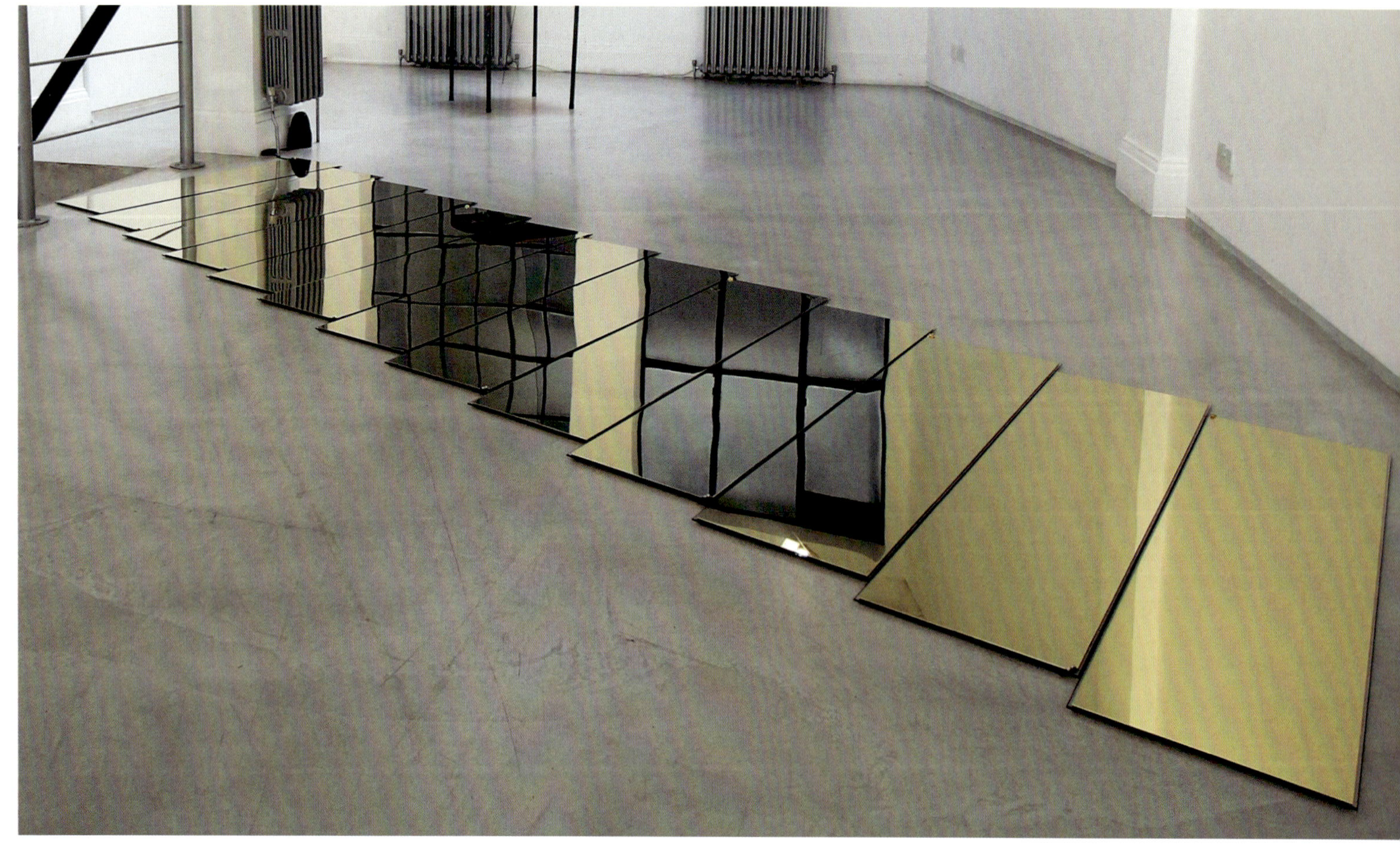

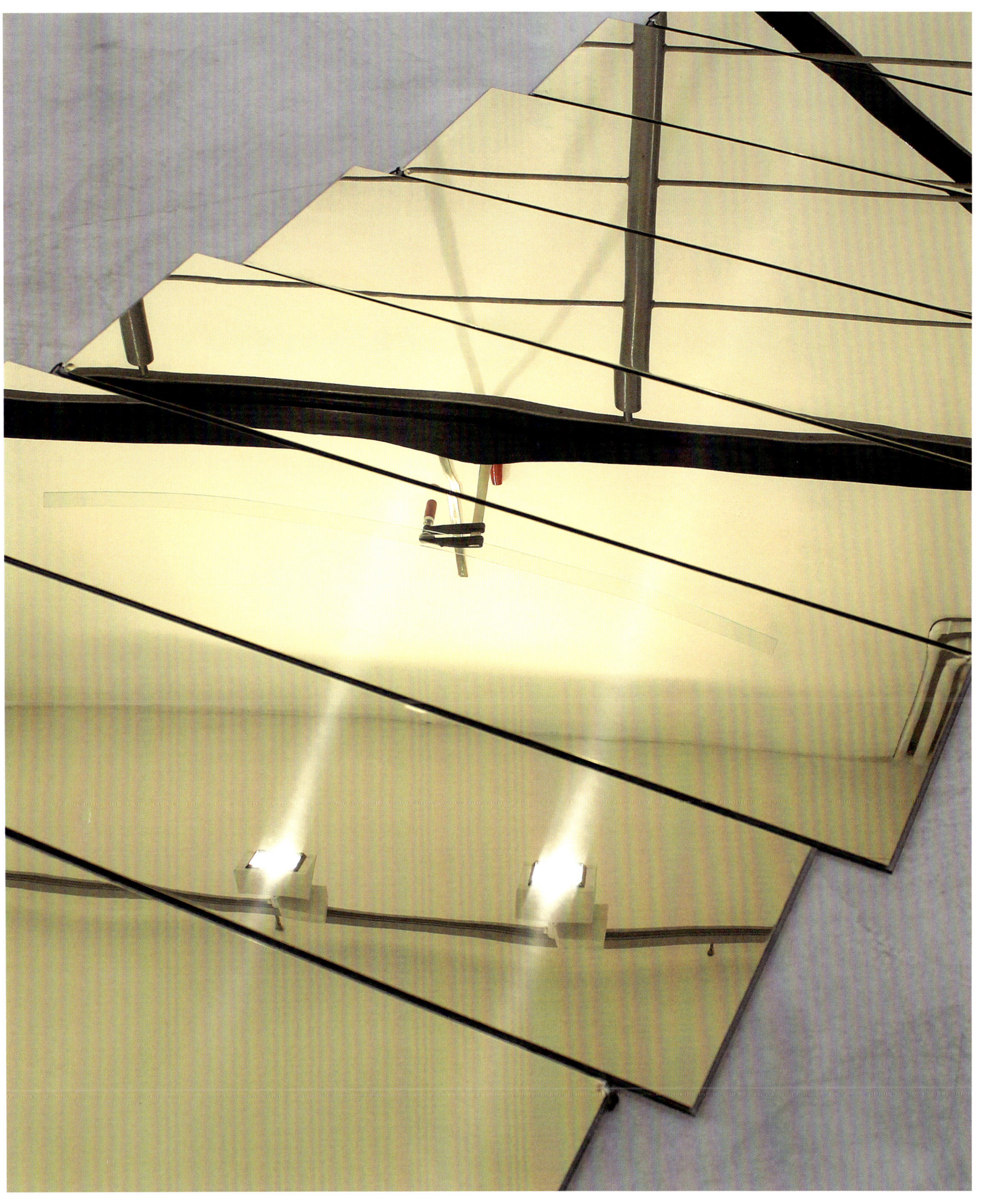

Norwegian artist **FREDRIK RADDUM** (b. 1973) makes large and humorous sculptures, many of which use polished metal as a focus. His *Veiled Animal Alpha* (2020) sees a glossy bronze veil thrown over what appears to be a life-sized dog, complete with wagging tail; *Campfire, Black* (2018) is a highly reflective glazed ceramic life-sized fire. In *La Belle Époque* (below), a small bird is spewing out a massive mountain of fluid. The bronze bird is patinated so that it looks as lifelike as possible, while the brass is mirror polished, reflecting the bird, the space and the viewer. The works are funny in a low-key way, out of kilter and a bit loopy, and always disturbing as if in a bad dream. Raddum notes that the Norwegians have a term, *bortenfor*, which translates as 'intangible' or 'that which is beyond' and his work reflects this concept.

Polish artist **DOROTA JURCZAK** (b. 1978) works across several traditional materials and techniques, including bronze, ceramic and printmaking, all of them infused with a quality of false naivety, as much of her work appears to embrace folklore, or at least its visual traditions. She has created a world of her own mythological characters, many of which are birds or human hybrids; and there hangs over them a sense of dread, melancholy and the uncanny. Her reflective heads *głowy (I + II)* have an ominous quality about them as they stare into each other and, while reflecting their environment, seem to totally ignore it. Her work hints at hidden or partially revealed narratives, ones that certainly exist in the artist's studio, but dissipate when outsiders gaze upon them.

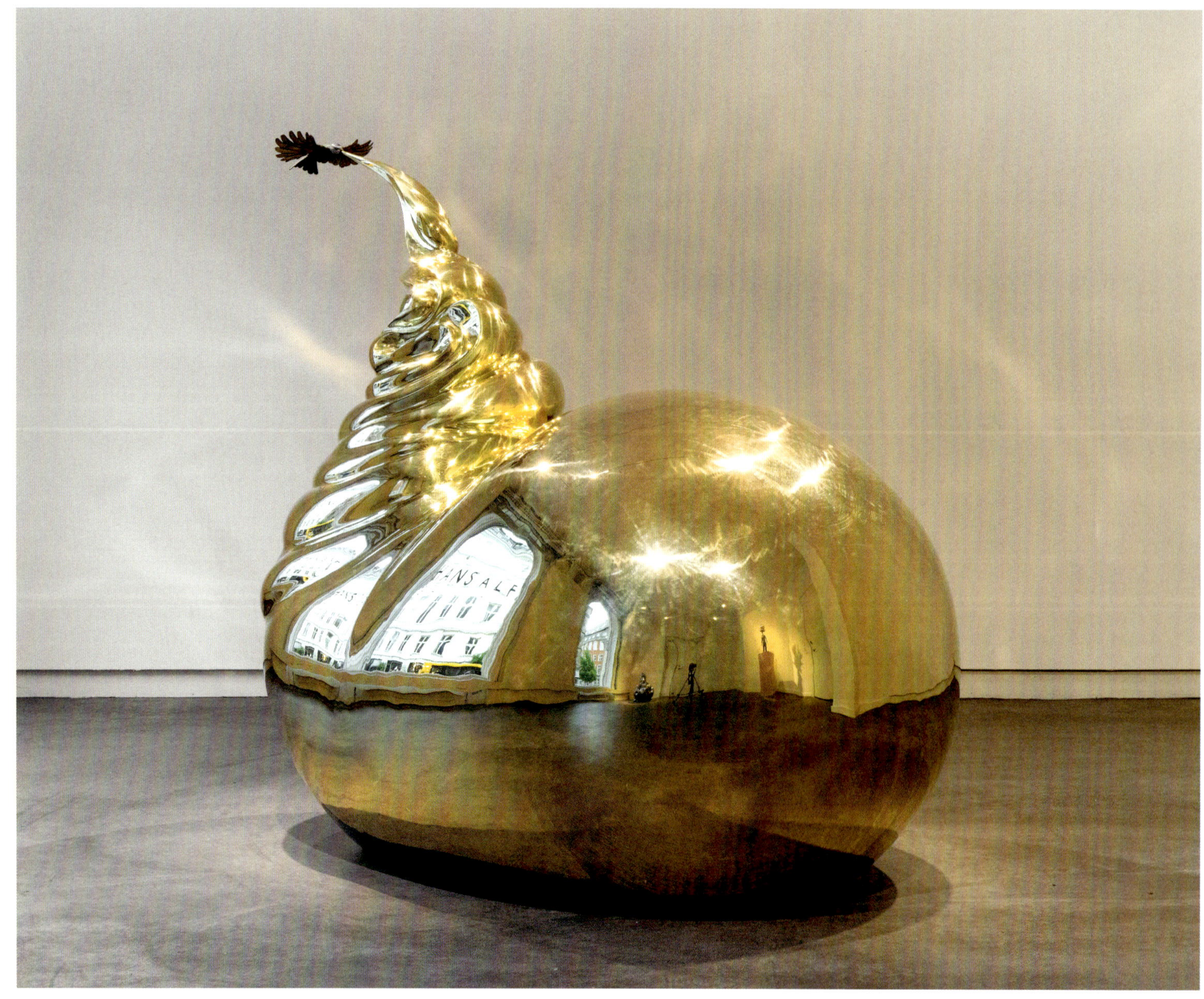

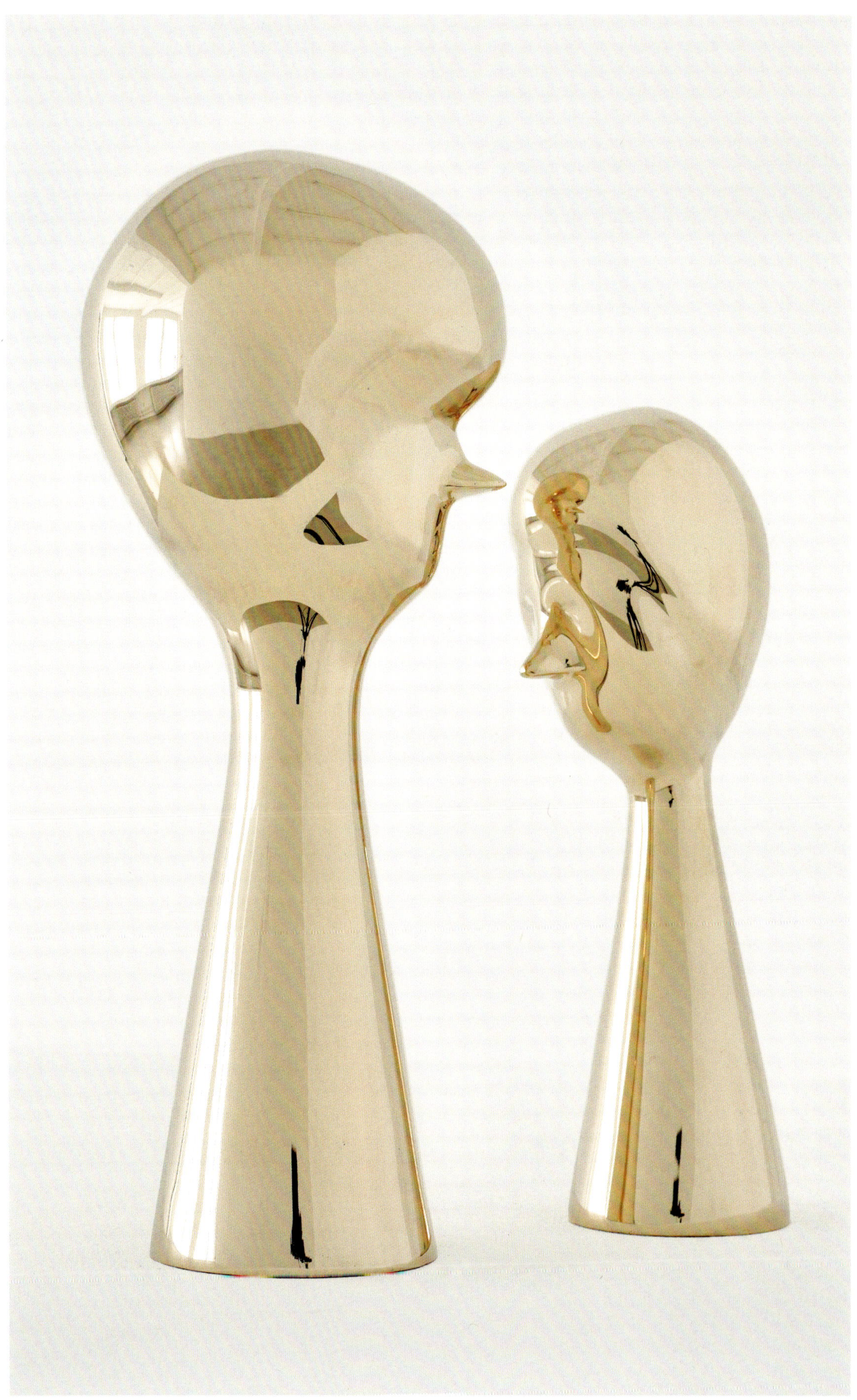

OPPOSITE
Fredrik Raddum, *La Belle Époque*, 2018
Brass and bronze
140 × 100 × 145 cm (55 × 39⅜ × 57 in)
Edition of 3

RIGHT
Dorota Jurczak, *głowy (I + II)*, 2019
Bronze
głowy (I) 48 × 11 × 20 cm (19 × 4⅜ × 7⅞ in)
głowy (II) 37 × 9 × 13 cm (14⅝ × 3⅝ × 5⅛ in)

American artist **SHERRIE LEVINE**
(b. 1947) has long appropriated the art
of other artists, usually core male ones in
the canon of contemporary art, to question
concepts of authenticity and value. It is
still the case that works by even the most
highly renowned women artists are sold
at much lower prices than those of men.
Levine borrows their imagery to make her
own interpretations of their work, from her
1996 *Fountain (Buddha)* – a bronze version
of Duchamp's 1917 *Fountain* urinal – to her
cast-bronze *Beach Ball after Lichtenstein*.
Her shiny three-dimensional ball is much
more detailed than Roy Lichtenstein's
flattened image of one in the painting *Girl
with Ball* (1961), having actual seams and
a nipple to blow it up. Like Jeff Koons's
metal balloon works, hers is obviously
heavy and not for play, and while linking
to her Pop art predecessor she undermines
and destabilizes the image's uniqueness.

Beach Ball after Lichtenstein, 2015
Cast bronze
39.4 × 40.6 × 38.1 cm (15½ × 16 × 15 in)

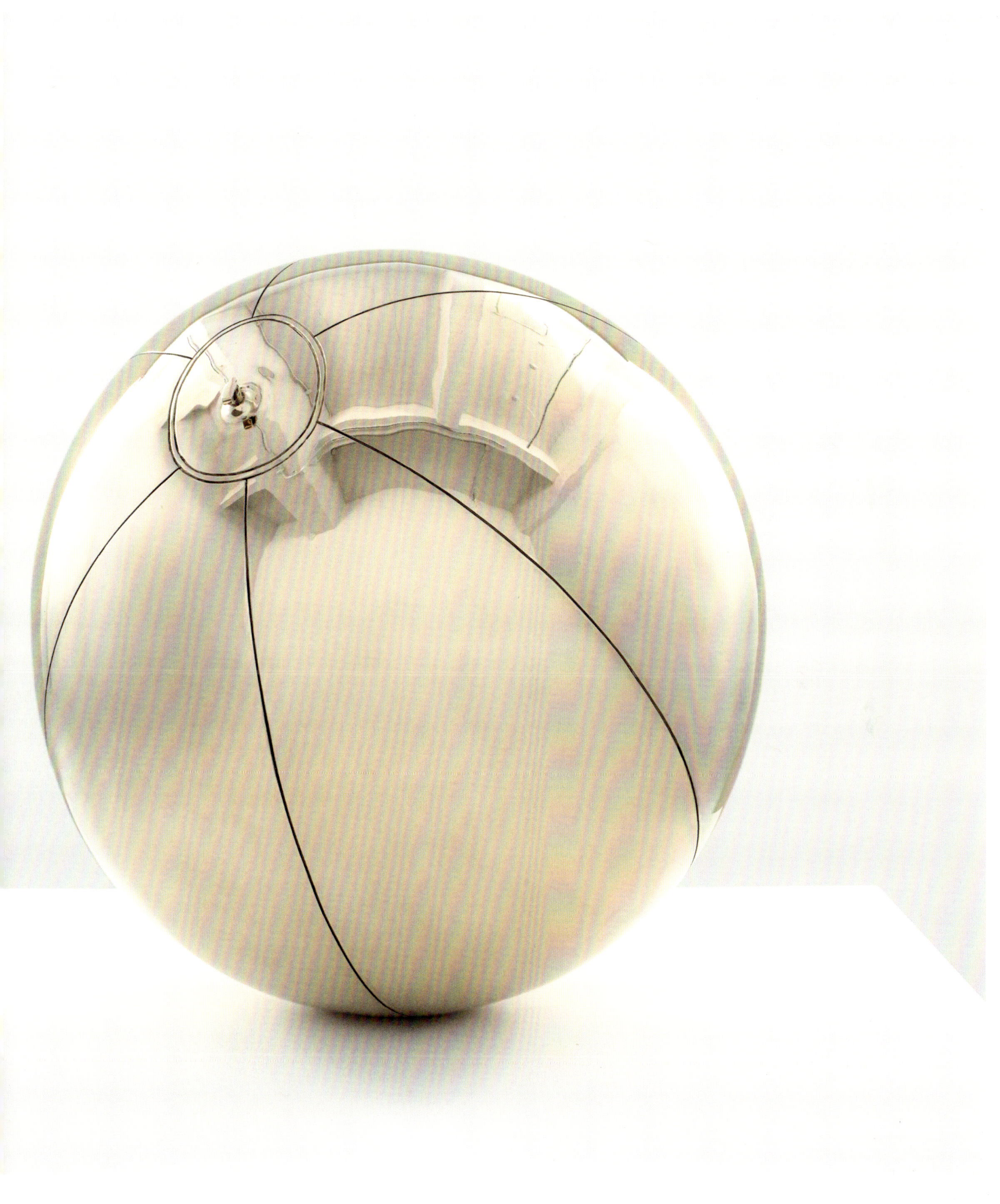

MICHAEL PETRY's (b. 1960) *Apollo's Mirror* was installed in the Wesley Chapel as part of his exhibition 'In League with Devils' at the Dadian Gallery, Henry Luce III Center for the Arts & Religion (Washington, DC, 2023), for which he placed this and other bronze works around the site. The antique-looking mirror stood directly in front of the massive minimal wooden crucifix above the altar, flanked by stained-glass windows on either side. On its reverse face, the mirror took in light from the windows and reflected it back onto the wall and the crucifix. Both deities – the Christian God and the Greek Apollo – are linked to light. Apollo was the god of enlightenment and the arts and daily carried the sun god, Helios, across the sky; to Christians, Jesus was the light of the world. The installation was a dialogue between differing belief systems, and the core of Petry's many mirror works in bronze.

Apollo's Mirror, 2020
Patinated and mirror-polished bronze
D 1 × diam. 41 cm (D ½ × diam. 16¼ in)
Fabrication: Arch Bronze, London, and
Rupert Burdett (white wooden stand)

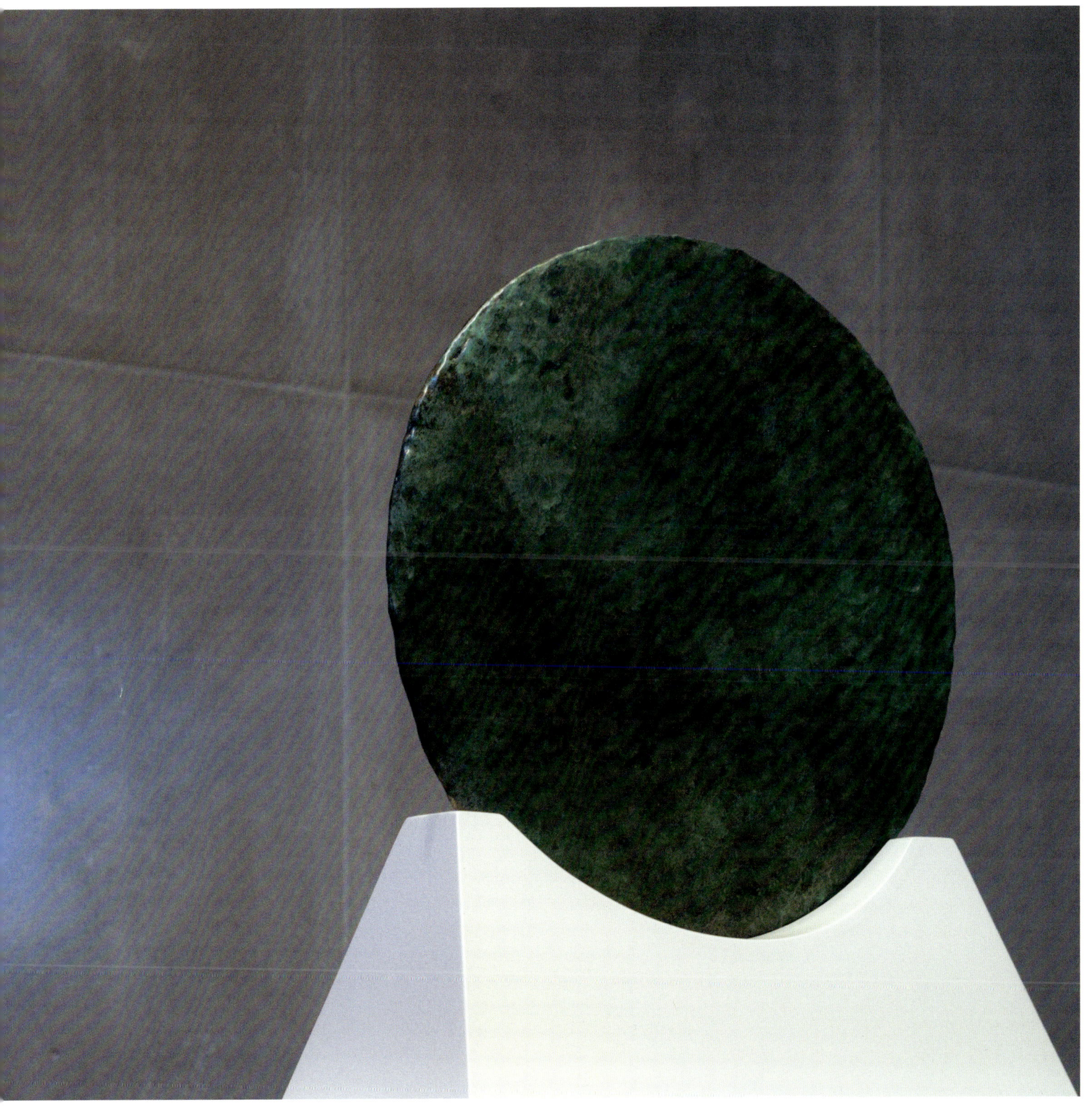

American artist **MEG WEBSTER** (b. 1944) is well known for her sculpture and installations that use natural materials, such as *Sand Bed* (1982/2012), *Stick Structure* (2016) and *Mother Mound Salt* (2016). Her *Volume for Lying Flat* (2016) is a large rectangular bed of packed dark-brown earth topped with soft green moss, and while very inviting, no visitor is likely to rest on it. Her series of polished copper and stainless-steel sculptures, on the other hand, invites viewers to interact with them, allowing them to see not only themselves but also the environment around them, including other works of art. These geometric and symbolic-shaped works aim to help the viewer understand their place in the Earth's order of things. *Polished Stainless Steel for Reflecting Outstretched Arms* is just that, and has no intentional religious connotations. She says, 'I am a sculptor who makes minimal art with natural materials to be directly perceived by the body.'

BELOW
Copper Disk for Facing Hands, 2012
Copper
2.5 × diam. 19.1 cm (1 × diam. 7½ in)

OPPOSITE
Polished Stainless Steel for Reflecting Outstretched Arms, 2012
Mirror-polished stainless steel
1.83 × 1.35 m (6 × 4⅖ ft)

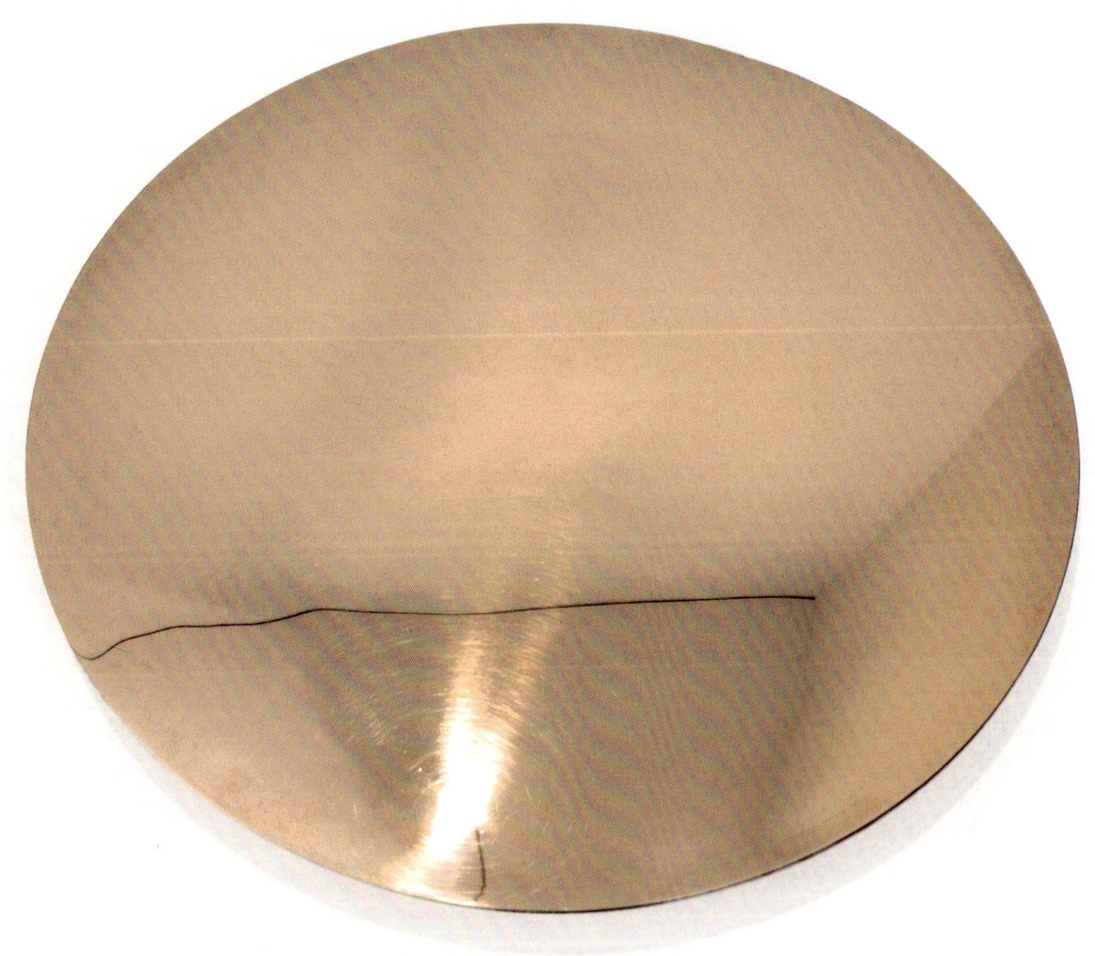

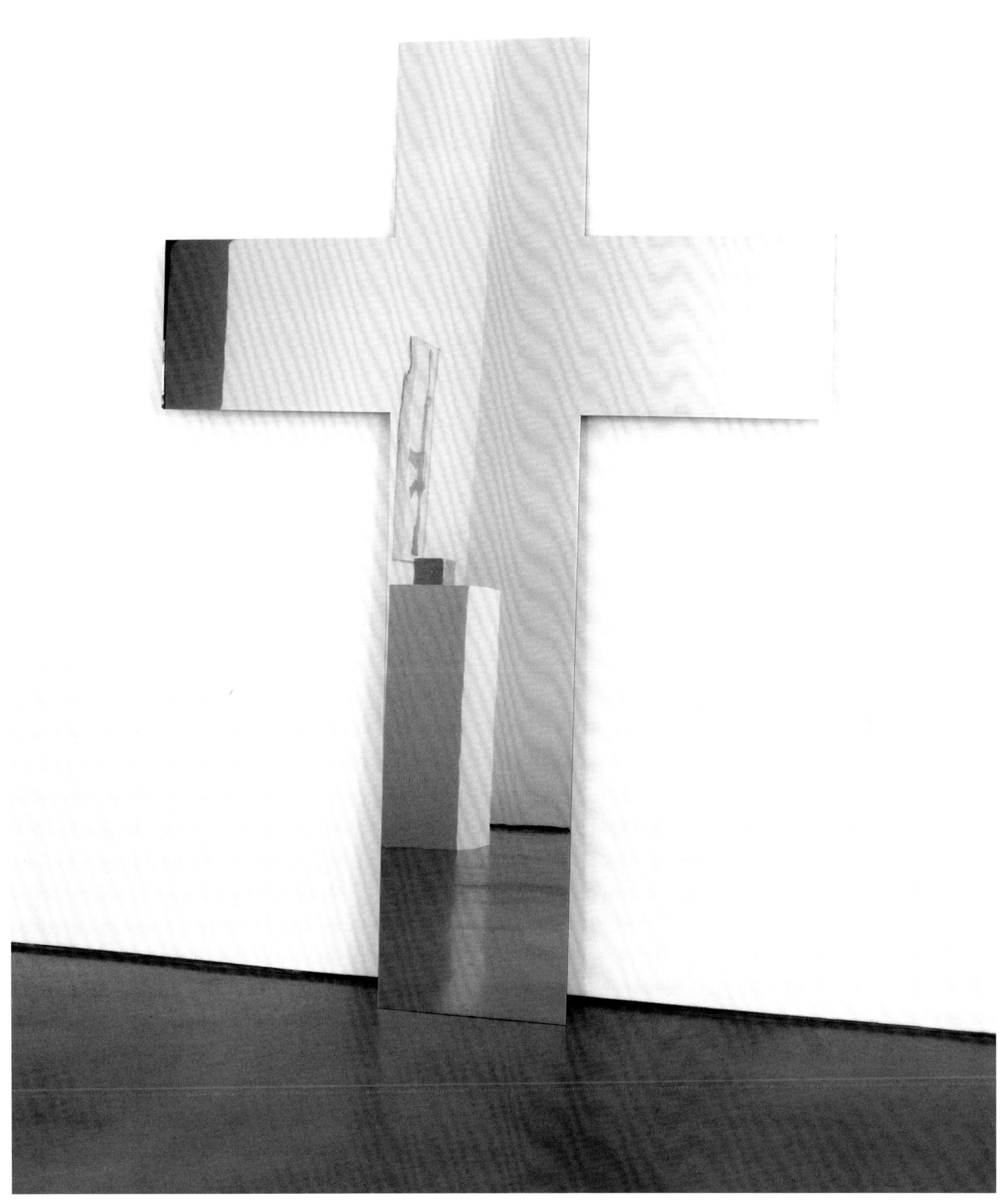

Swiss-born artist **UGO RONDINONE** (b. 1964) has long been interested in water, air, earth and fire as elemental sources in his work, which harks back to the German Romantics and Caspar David Friedrich, who also stood at the edge of the void and aimed for the sublime. Rondinone's *sun* works have been widely exhibited (at the Storm King Art Center, New York; the Musée d'Art et d'Histoire, Geneva; and the 59th Venice Biennale). His original sun pieces, from 2016, were made from real branches cast in aluminium and then gold-plated, while *The sun II*, seen here, was cast in much heavier bronze. The gilding in all the works allows them to reflect the light and shine like the sun in the sky.

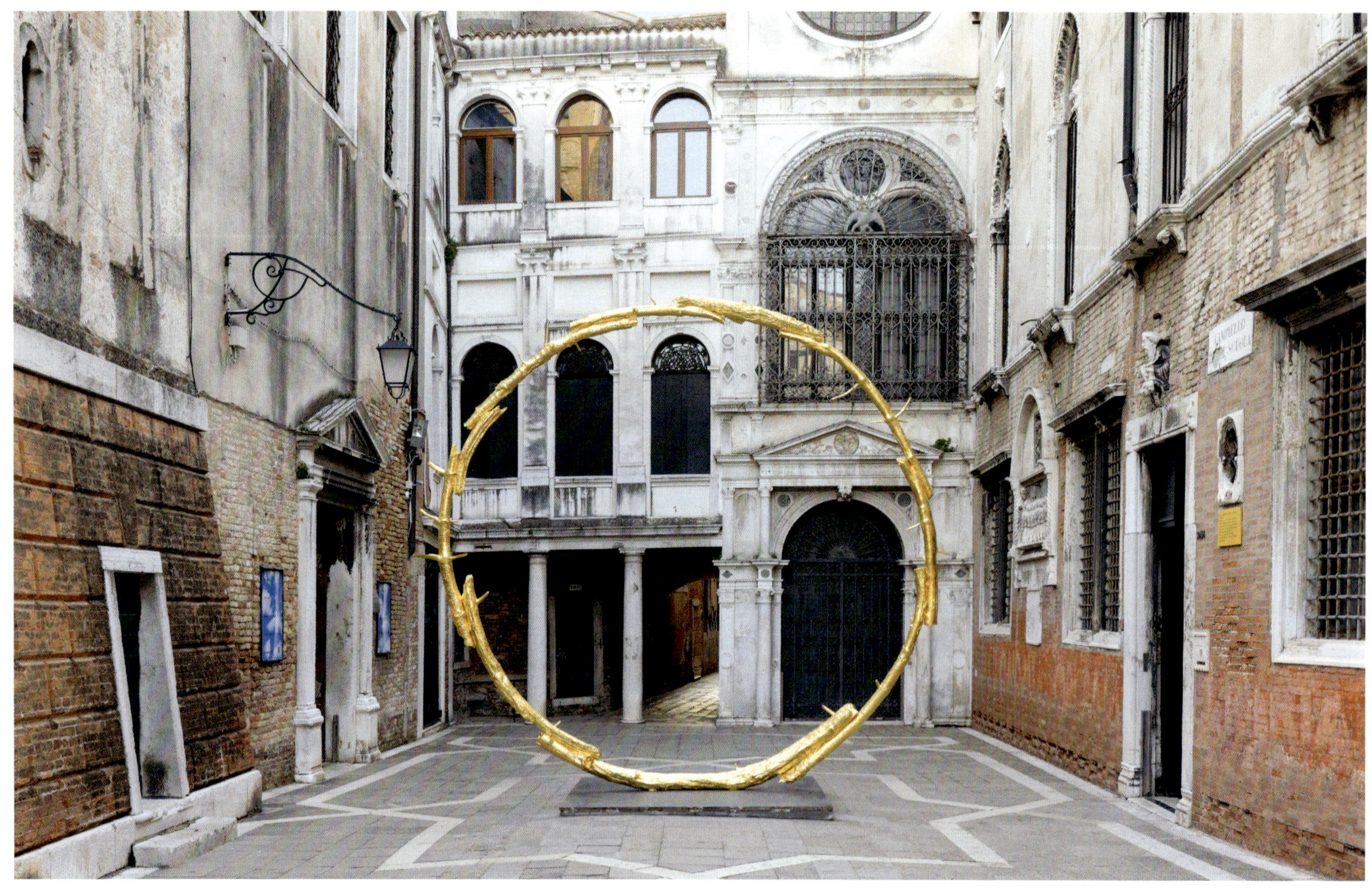

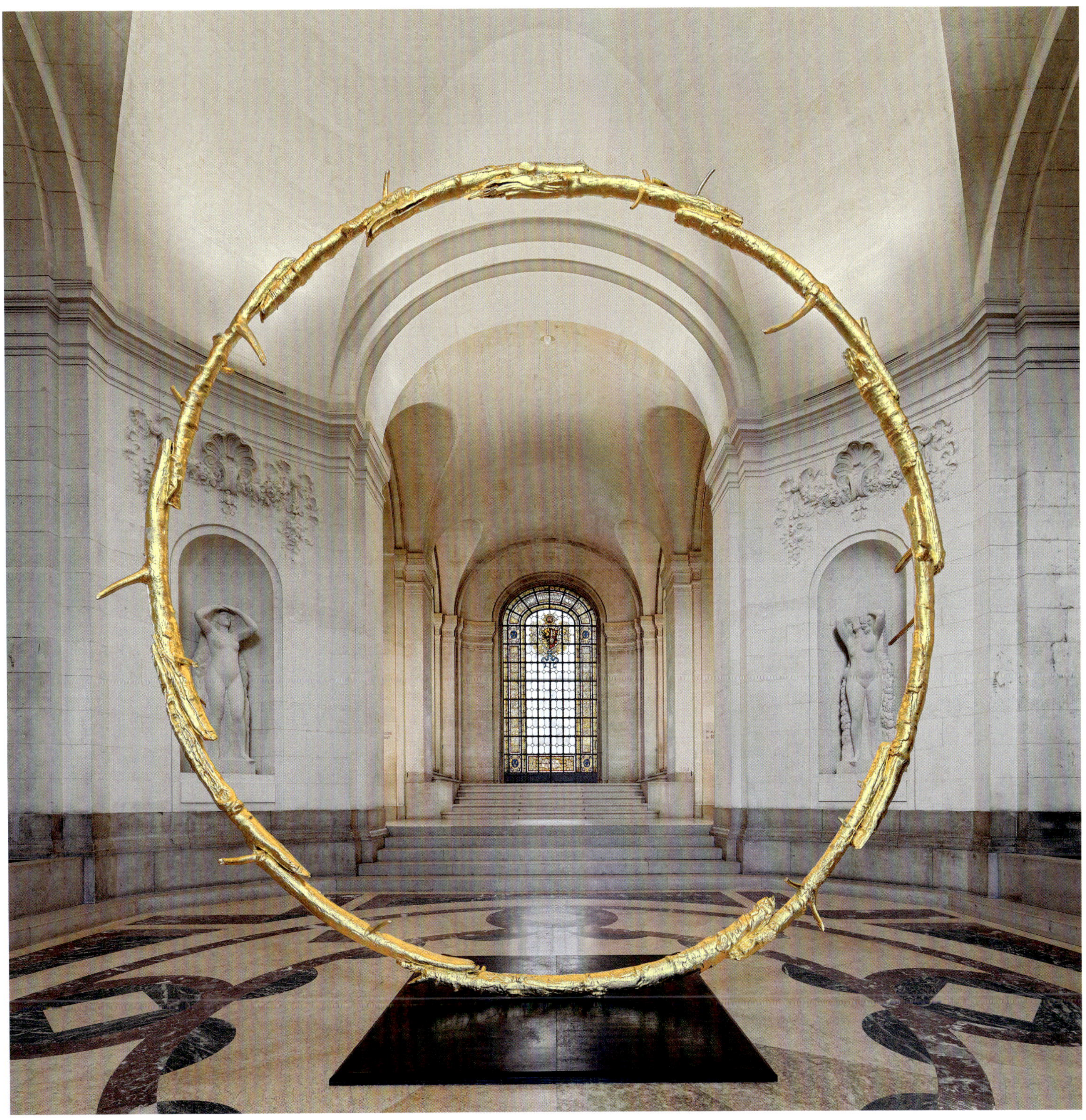

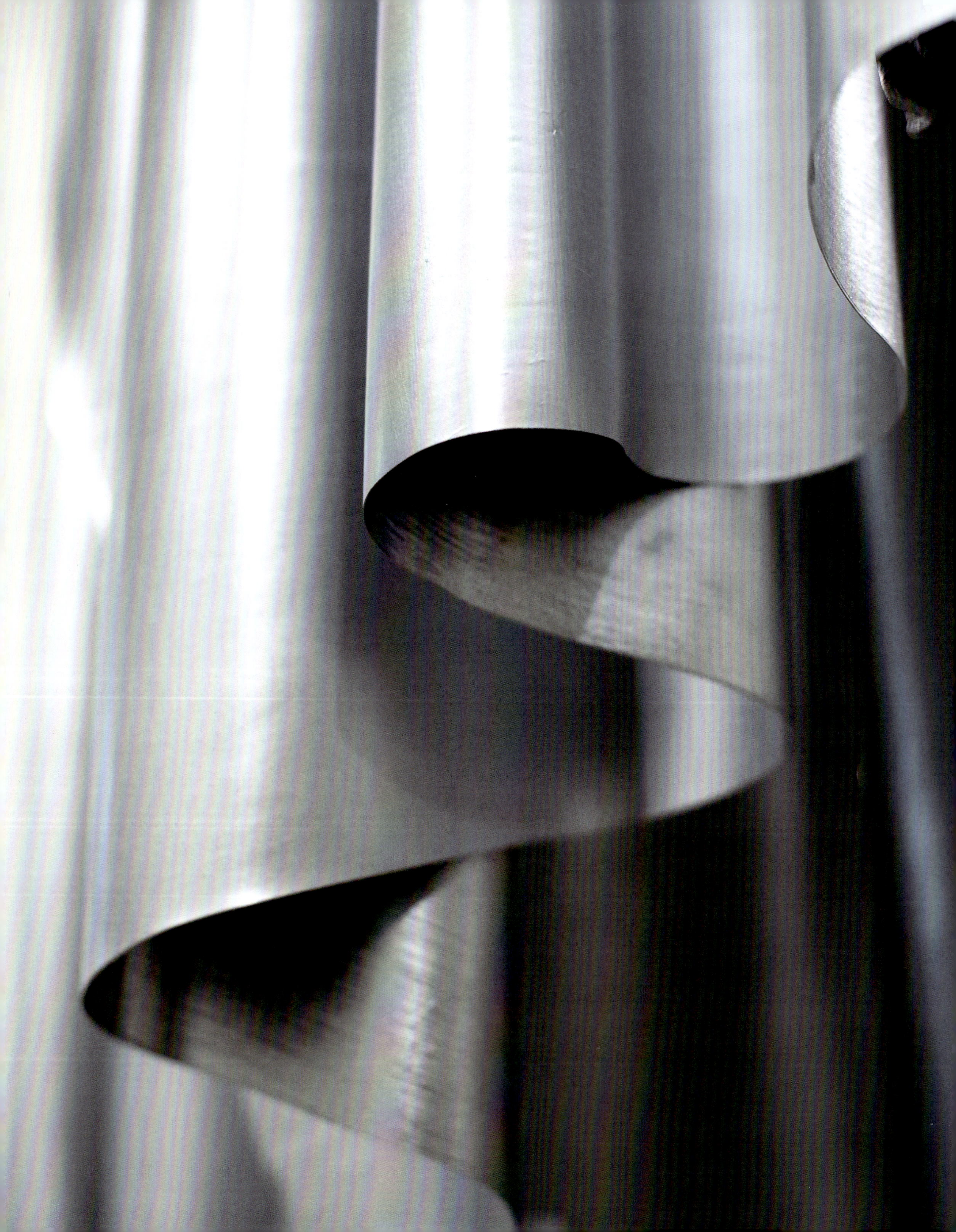

MATERIALS

A great number of materials, natural and human-made, can add lustre to an object or make a surface reflective, and artists have always been keen to use them. The application of 24-carat gold leaf to sculptures goes back to the Egyptians and the Greeks (who covered ivory with it for famous sculptures of Zeus and Athena), and gold leaf became widely used in medieval calligraphy and later religious painting. Carl Hopgood has covered a life-sized marble version of himself in gold, while Alicia Paz has covered 3D computer-printed resin to make her works, and both sparkle and reflect light. The application of silver as a foil, or to form a reflective surface like a mirror, has a long history, and Johannes Wald has explored this concept across different works, including melting a Roman silver coin down to use as the basis for a mirror.

Anne Peabody uses silver leaf to make large-scale reflecting mirrored works, while Amélie Esterházy uses the silver foil from champagne bottles to construct her highly reflective works that send light bouncing off them in all directions like a broken bottle of bubbly. Jeppe Hein, Chandrika Metivier and Theis Wendt all use different types of silver foil or Mylar to construct spaces that the viewer is allowed to enter physically or visually. The reflective quality of the material is the core visual element of those works, but that the material drapes and has the quality of fabric is also key. Deb Covell drapes her sheetlike silver materials to create space and to alter the existing space, but the unique quality of her material is that it is 100 per cent paint: she builds up the paint layer upon layer, until it is possible for it to be used in a sculptural way. Stuart Mayes also drapes his materials so that they reflect the light and the viewer, but he uses hundreds of metres of old gay pornographic video tapes as his source fabric. The black tape is matt on one side and shiny on the other once it has been removed from its protective cassette. Younger readers or visitors may have no cultural reference for this medium.

Dillon Marsh, on the other hand, uses cutting-edge digital technology to create visual representations of the volumes of precious materials removed from the earth. Quite a few artists use earth as a fundamental element of their ceramic practice, which they then coat with reflecting glazes (Yuta Segawa, Frans Franciscus). Equally, the raw material of glass is sand, and artists use the natural reflective quality of glass or have it silvered to increase its lustre, shine and ability to show the viewer their own gaze. Whether human-made or naturally occurring, so many different materials have been used to capture the observer's passing eye that once their curiosity is aroused, these works deliver a perhaps unexpected reward.

Deb Covell, *Silver Drape* (detail), 2016. Installation view: 'The Fold' exhibition,
Blyth Gallery, London, UK. Chrome lacquer on acrylic paint sheet
5.2 × 2 × 0.3 m (17 × 6½ × 1 ft)

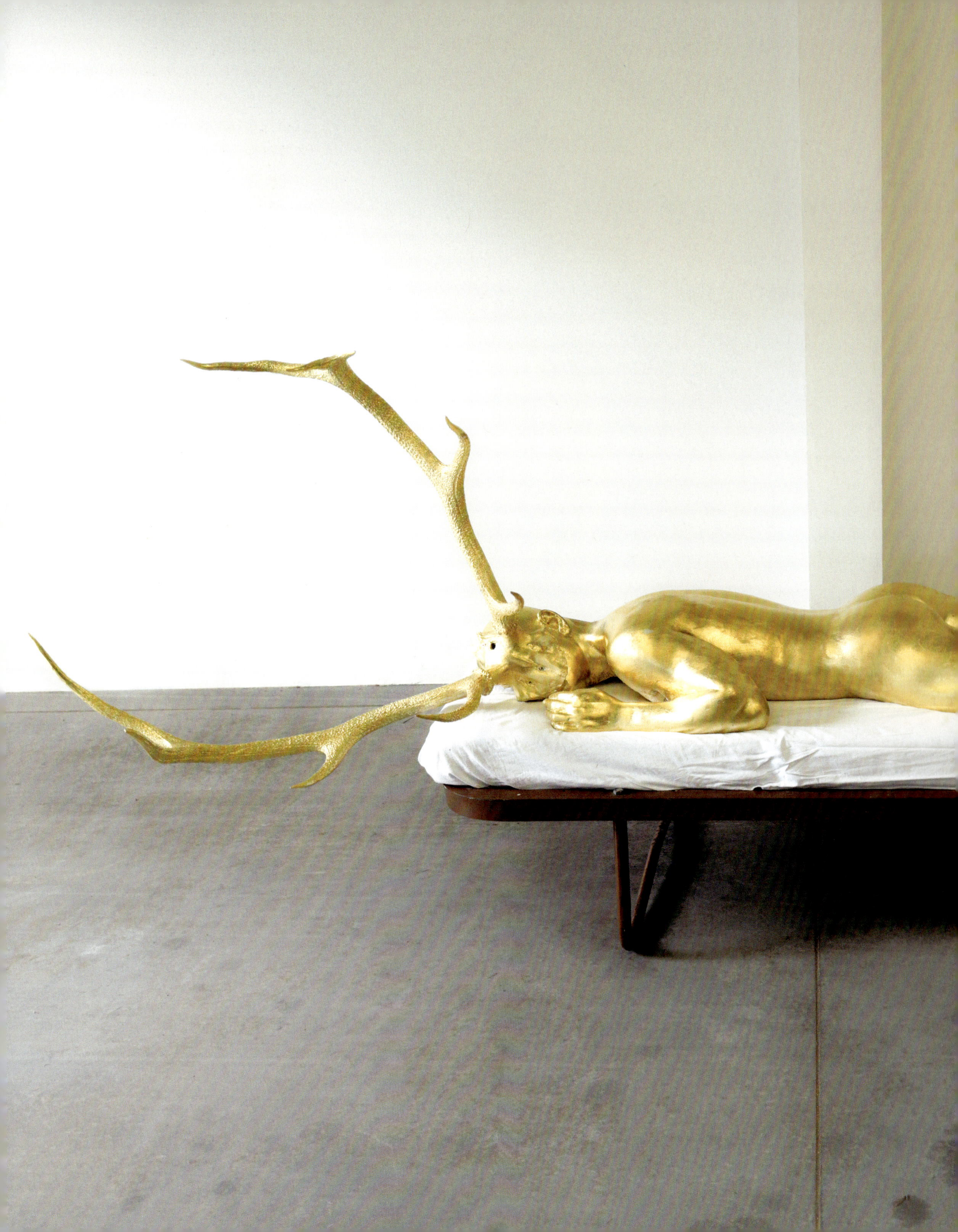

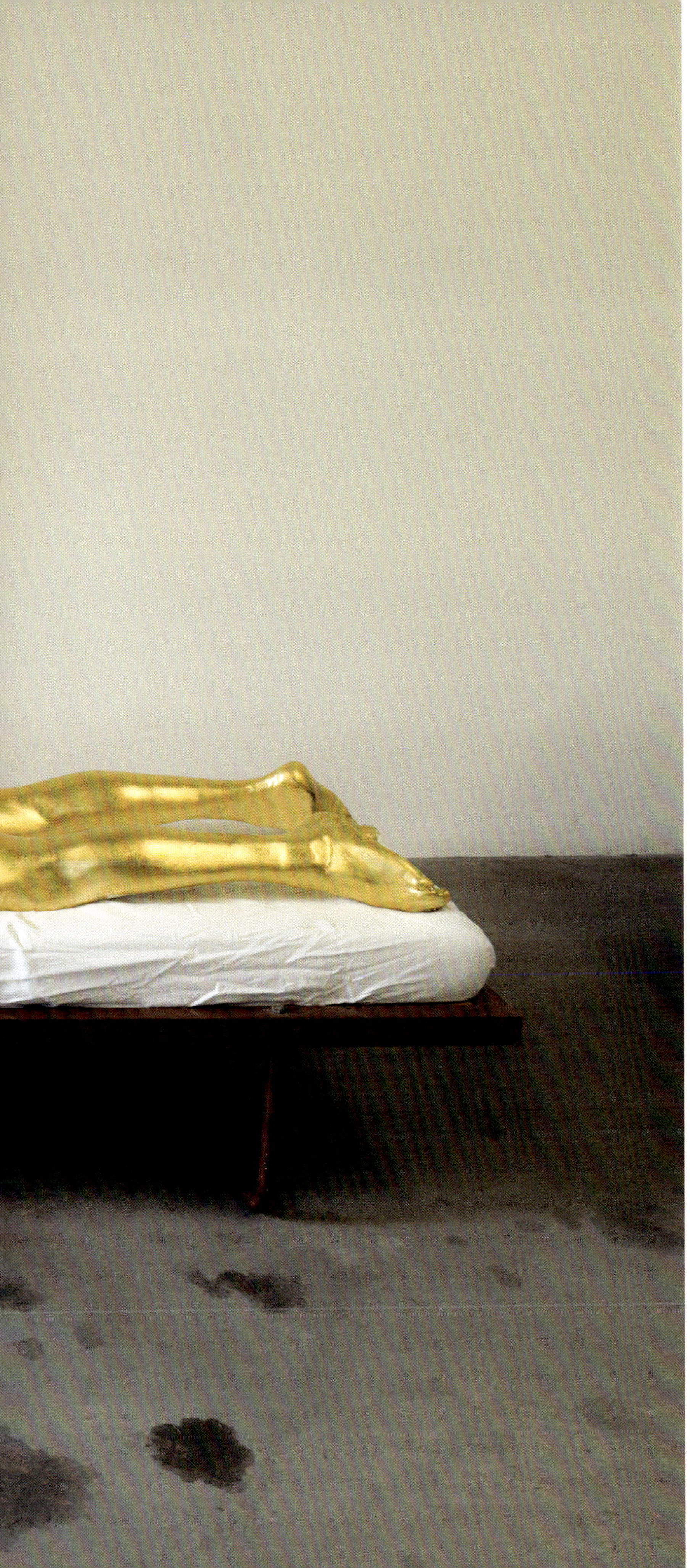

British artist **CARL HOPGOOD** was
born in Wales in 1972; of Greek heritage,
he has called on ancient Greek myths,
including that of the Minotaur, for his
series of *Stag* sculptures. To make *Golden
Sleeping Stag* (and *Reclining Golden Stag*)
he had his own body cast as the basis
for the work. The mould was then filled
with marble plaster, and the cast finally
gilded. The sleeping stag lies on a white-
sheeted mattress and looks as though
the lightest touch would wake him.
Unlike the Sleeping Beauty of fairy tale,
the stag appears dangerous as well as
gentle. Hopgood wants these queer
works to 'reflect the battle of a hedonistic
past and the battle between love and lust,
the conscious and the unconscious…'.

Golden Sleeping Stag, 2013
Marble plaster cast, stag horns, gold leaf,
single bed and mattress
Life size

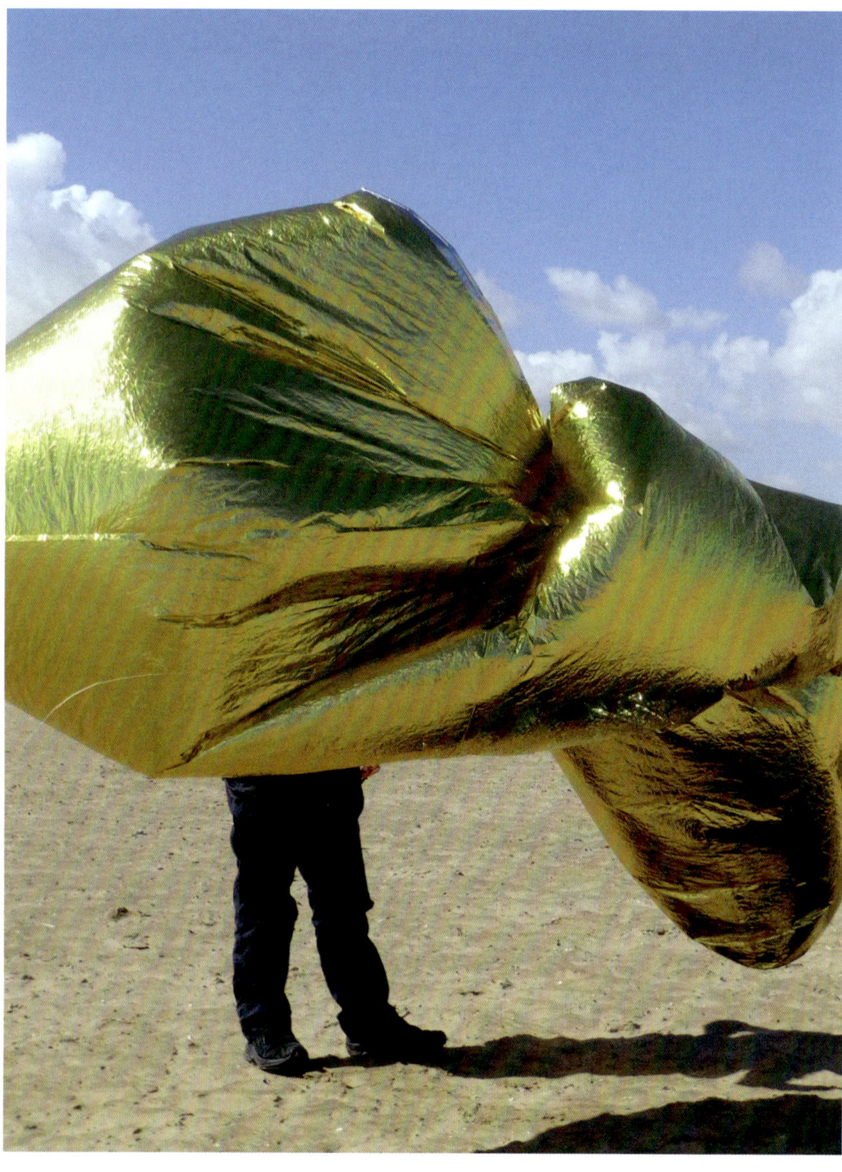

British artist **TRACEY PAYNE** made a large three-lobed gold inflatable cloudlike structure from shiny reflective foil for her *Look at Me* series of performances. Payne, who says she is a 'shy extrovert', used the inflatable to reflect the focus away from herself and onto the object, which was instantly attention-drawing. Payne has said she is interested in 'slapstick, silliness, accidents, surprises', and the mini-dirigible offered viewers the opportunity to become participants in such activities; they were allowed to touch the material, seeing themselves reflected in its surface. Payne was nominally in control of the object, which was easily blown around by the wind and in each iteration took on a life of its own. Payne assumed the role of the handler, like a lion tamer: not the focus, but necessary for the performance of the stronger member of the duo.

A Mexican artist based in London, **ALICIA PAZ** (b. 1967) undertook an artist's residency at Chatsworth House, Derbyshire, seat of the dukes of Devonshire, in 2022. Traditionally, the women of the house have usually been reflected only in relation to the men – as wives, daughters or mistresses. Paz wanted to look at the women themselves, and worked to find ways to disrupt traditional methods of their representation. She used photographic imagery and printing processes on different materials (fabric, paper, 3D-printed resin). *Crystal Slipper* is based on a slipper Paz found in a local charity shop, which she scanned and digitally paired with crystals; she then 3D printed the result in resin. Georgiana Cavendish, Duchess of Devonshire (née Spencer; 1757–1806), had collected crystals, creating the Devonshire Mineral Collection. Interested in both science and fashion, she was a famed beauty, gambler and femme fatale. As a Spencer, she was Princess Diana's great-great-great-great aunt, and like her, was seen as a woman troublesome to the Establishment. Paz's golden slipper nods to Cinderella, and hints at the reality behind such fairy tales.

Tracey Payne, *Look at Me*, 2013
Performances in London and Cleethorpes

OPPOSITE
Alicia Paz, *Crystal Slipper*, 2023
Formlabs V4 grey resin, 3D print gilded
with 22ct gold leaf
16 × 8 × 13 cm (6⅜ × 3¼ × 5⅛ in)
Edition of 10, published by CFPR UWE Bristol

MATERIALS

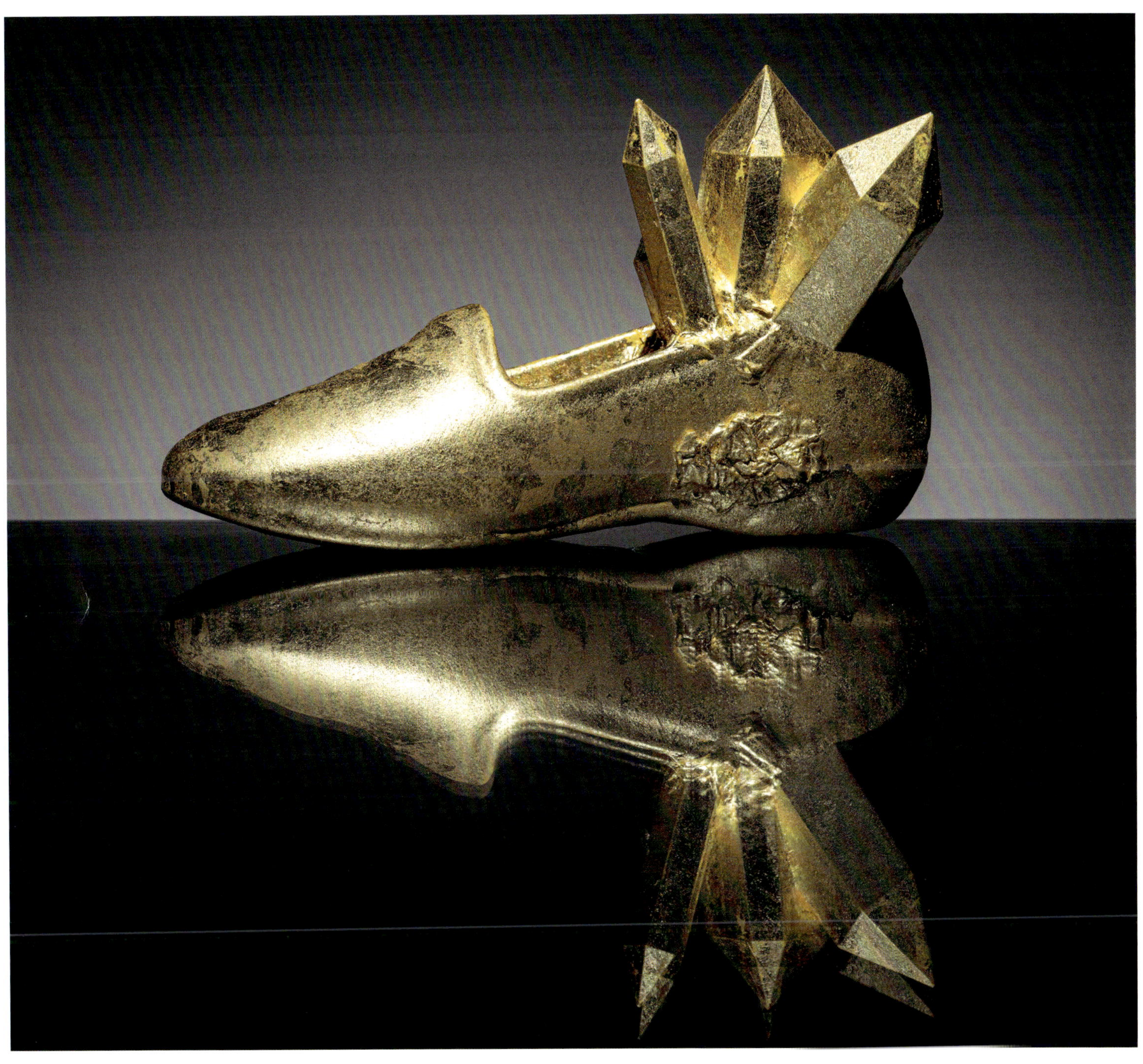

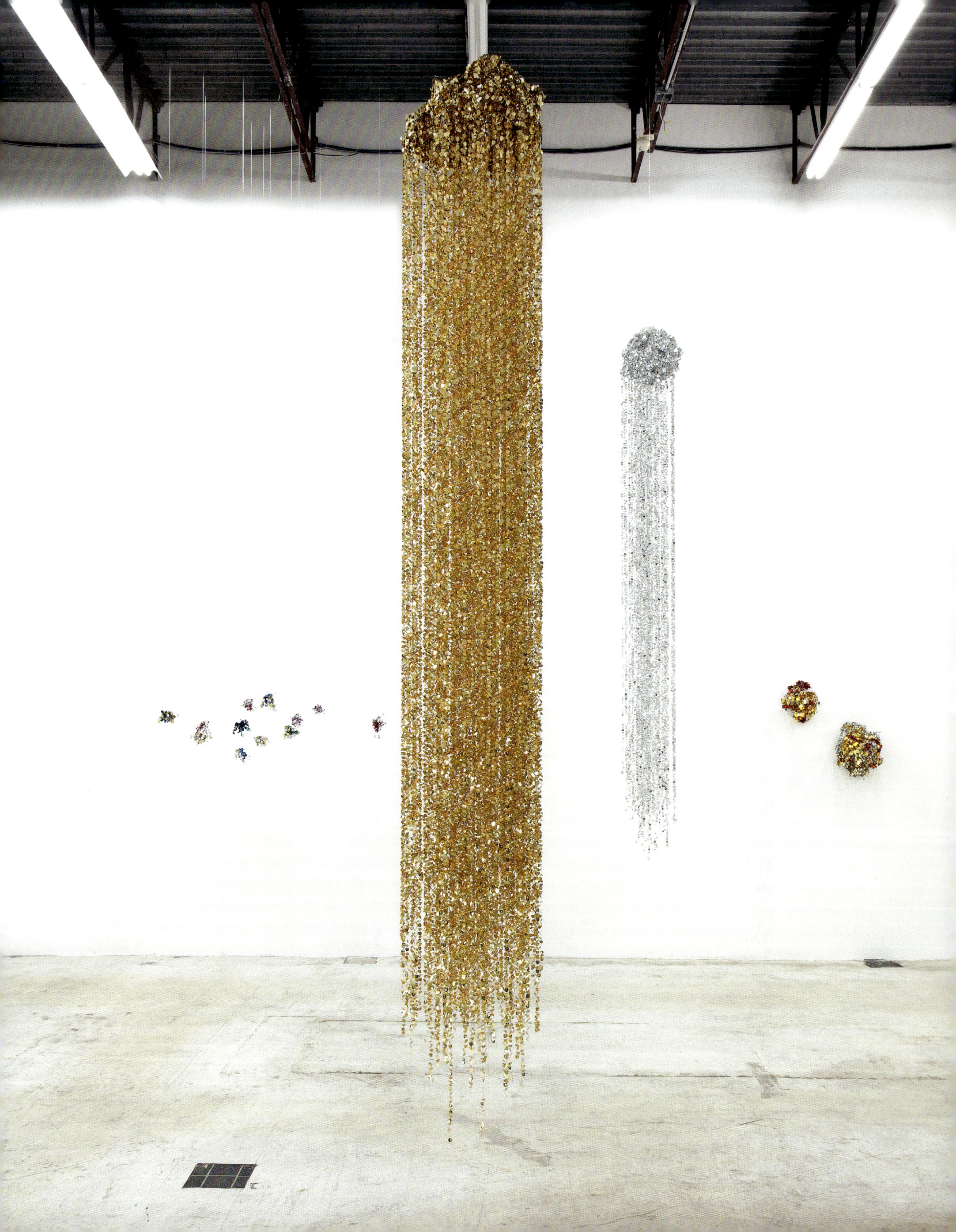

Heart Strings (Gold), 2014
Gold heart-shaped sequins, fishing line,
hanger wire
H 3.6 × diam. 0.6 m (H 12 × diam. 2 ft)

Currently based in Berlin, Croatian artist **GORAN TOMCIC** (b. 1964) has made a series of works that feature shiny reflective plastic sequins. His *Heart Strings* sculptures are all made by sewing thousands of heart-shaped sequins onto fishing line to make either cascading lines of sparkling faux chandeliers or abstract multicoloured clumps. These are very queer objects that are as odd as they are beautiful. They reflect light and shimmer in it, and remind the viewer of nightclubbing and party spirits. There seems to be something naive in their construction and emotional impact, yet Tomcic is clearly in charge of focusing the viewer on emotions and memories.

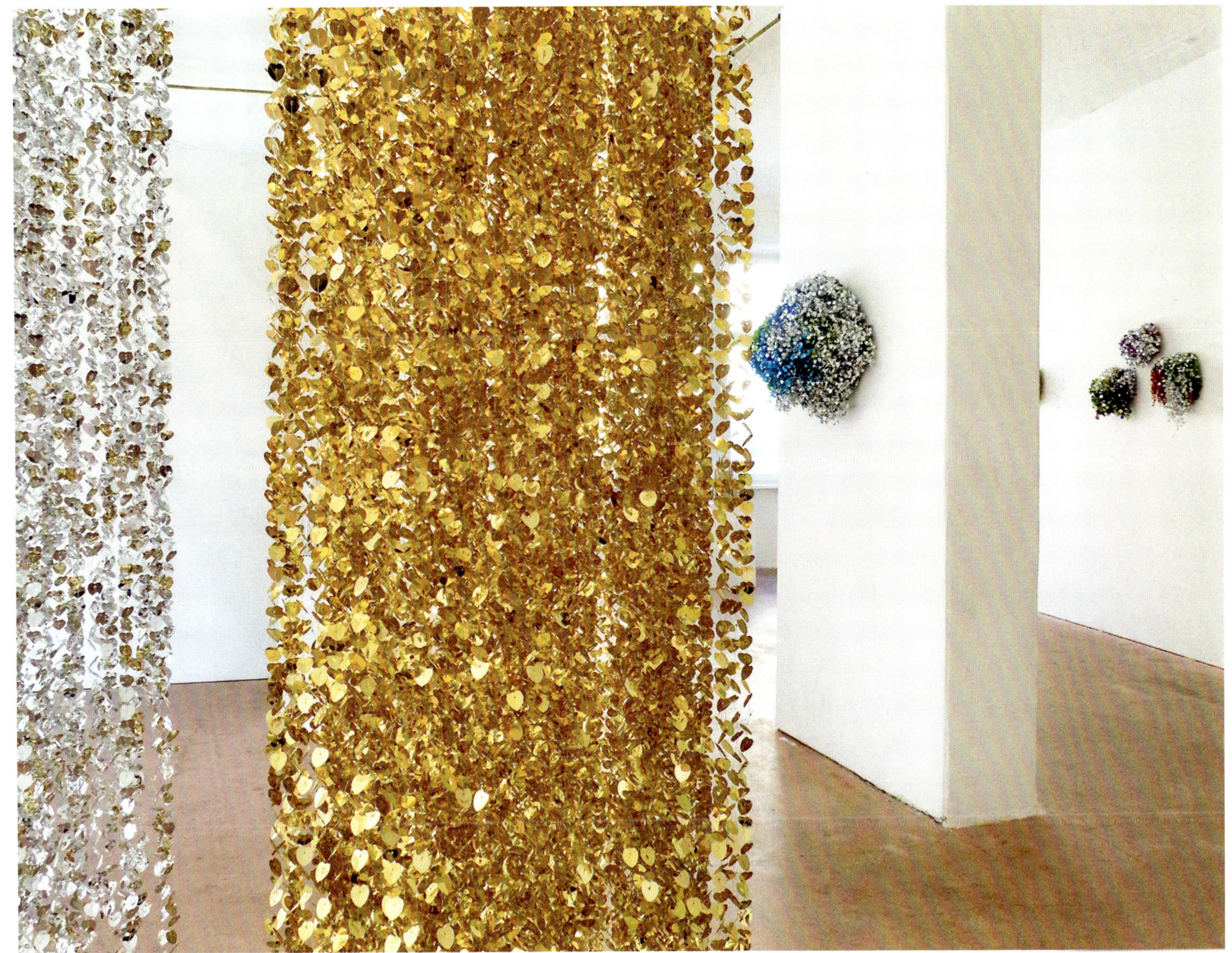

JONNY NIESCHE (b. 1972) is an Australian artist whose work *Mutual Vibration* (opposite) is a suspended and rotating golden acrylic mirror. As it moves on its axis it reflects the room onto itself and the viewers in the space (including the artist – seen in the image). The work is larger than the average person, so their full body is in view when gazing into the mirror. Niesche has developed this theme in other installed works such as *Biting into the corner* (below), where a set of four curved steps reflects the gallery space and the viewers who approach it. In other exhibitions he has used silver mirror to reflect his soft pastel-coloured wall paintings and sculpture to create a dense reflective visual space.

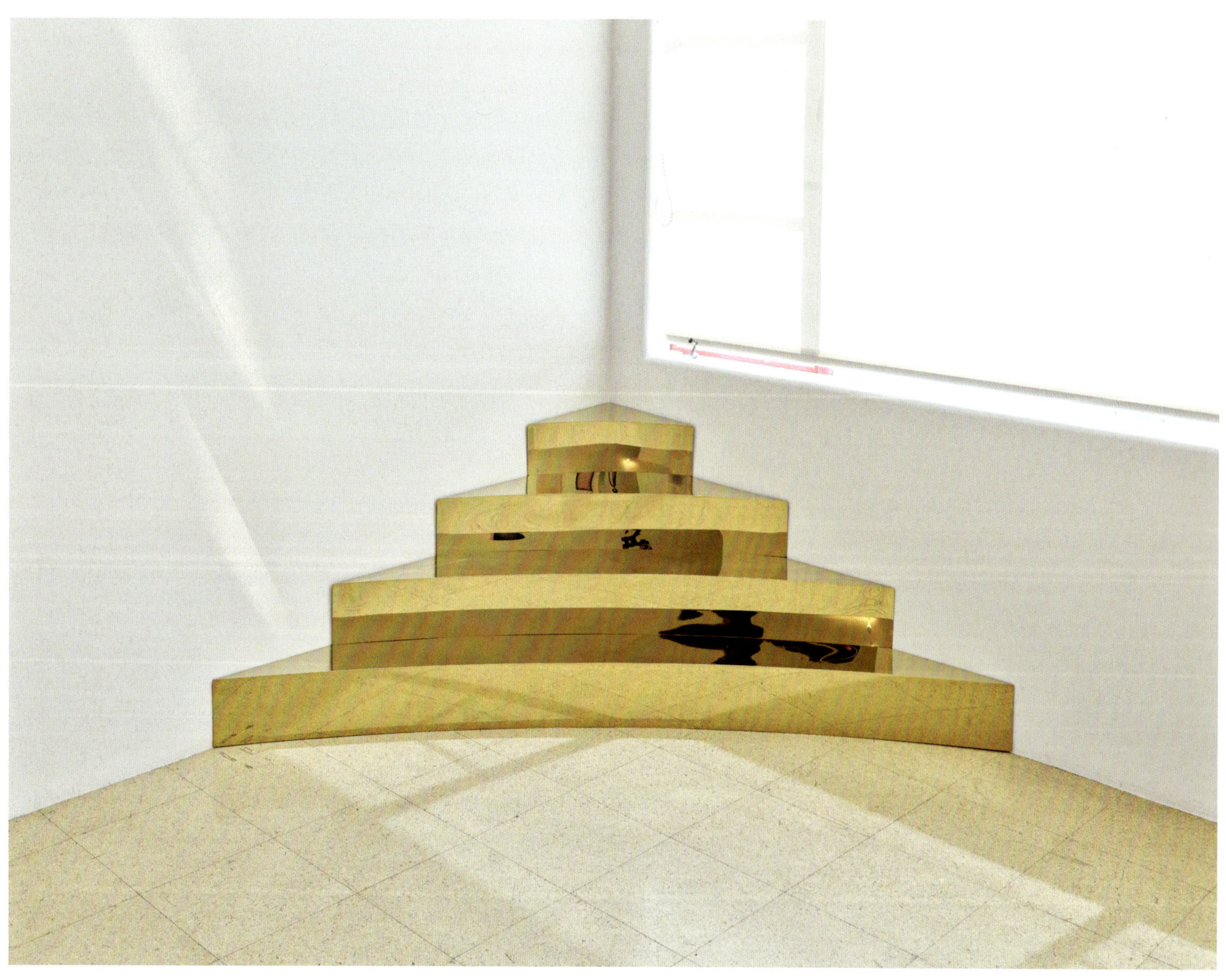

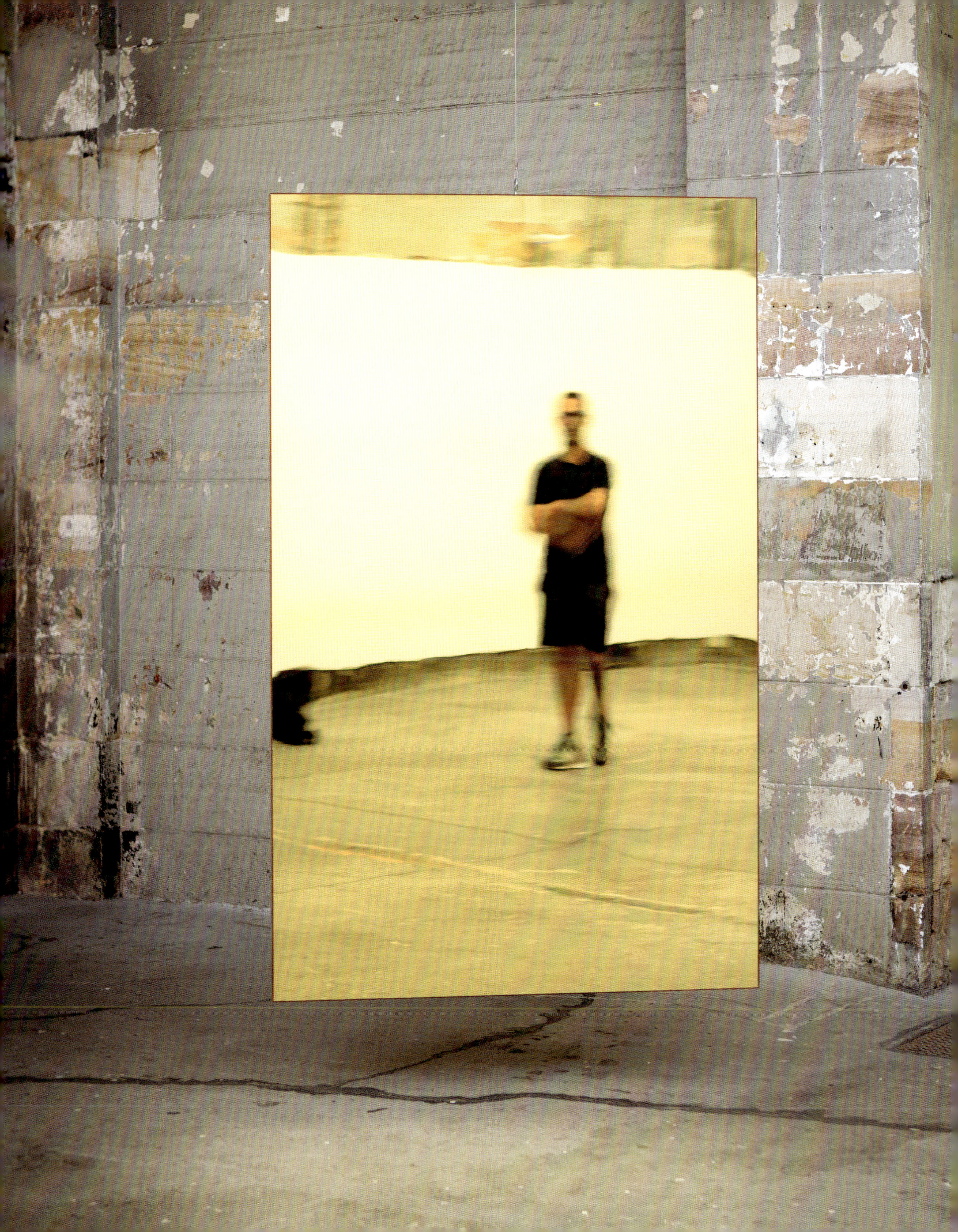

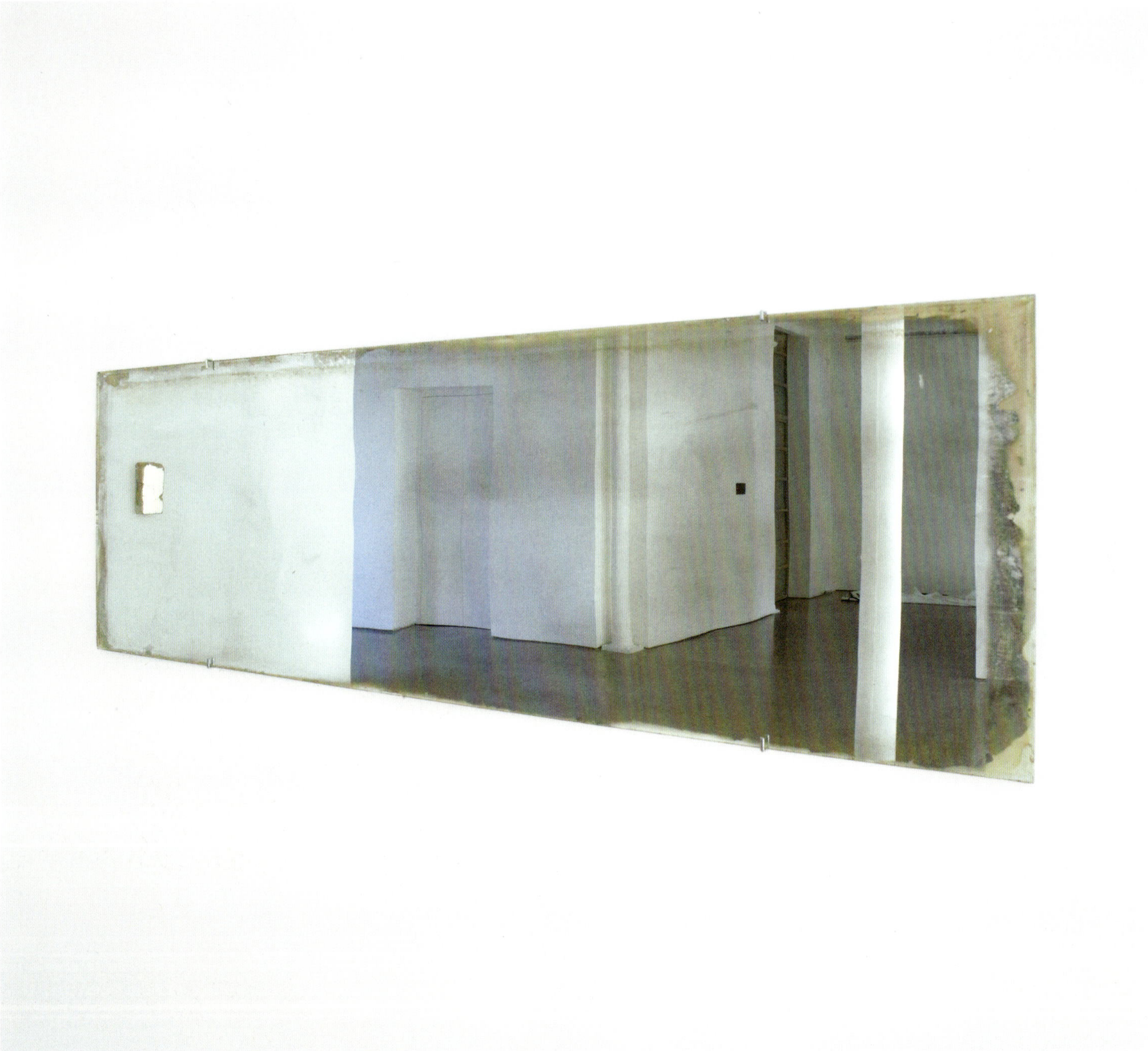

German artist **JOHANNES WALD** (b. 1980) removed a glass pane from his studio window and turned it into a mirror using a traditional method of applying silver dissolved in nitric acid to the reverse and then sealing it. What makes the mirror unique is that Wald used a Roman silver coin instead of a lump of raw silver. Once sealed, the mirror is likely to remain reflective for up to a hundred years, though it might oxidize at some point and turn black. 'I find the concept intriguing: just as I, the person who first saw my own image reflected on [its] surfaces, will eventually pass away, [the mirror's] capacity for reflection will also cease to exist. Nevertheless, [its] poetic essence will persist, perhaps even more intensely.'

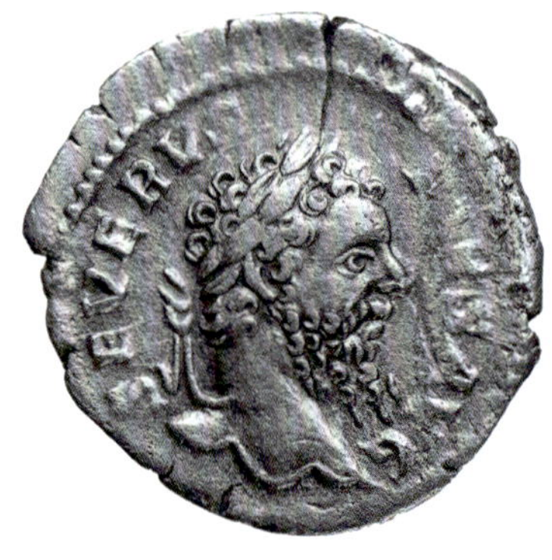

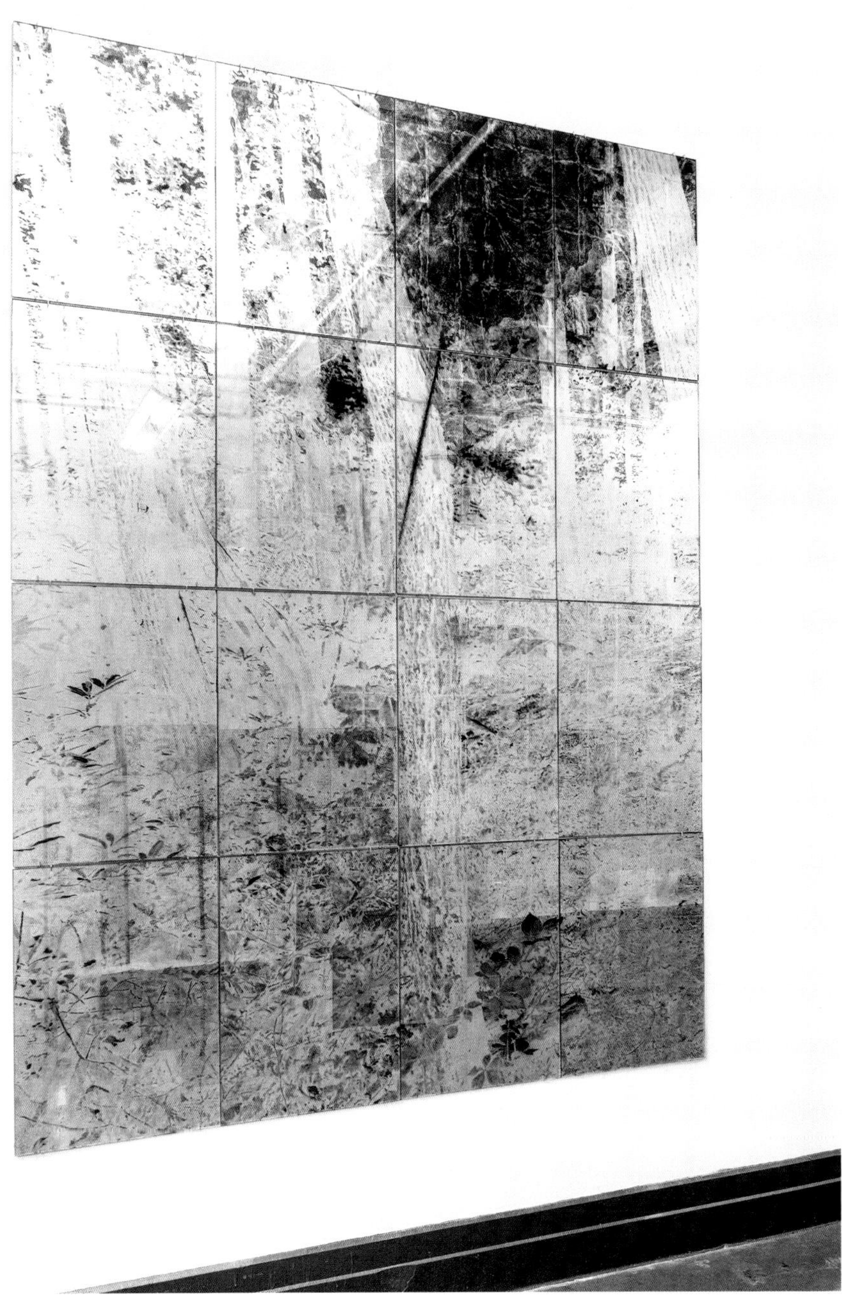

ANNE PEABODY (b. 1967), an American multidisciplinary artist, makes work that resists the photographic impulse yet comes from her own body of photographic images. In such works as *Sunspike* (above), *Black Waterfall* and *Tennessee Woods* she used as a basis photographs taken on hikes in the Smoky Mountains a few months before the area was destroyed by arson, killing fourteen people. Her works are not commemorations, but do hint at rebirth. In other works, equally delicate environments are featured, such as the city of Venice in *Alluvion Myth* (2011). The images are made from her application of metallic paints, silver leaf and other materials that oxidize when she touches them, leaving behind her own skin oils. The results are ghostly, otherworldly, and appear very different from each angle the viewer or the camera sees them from.

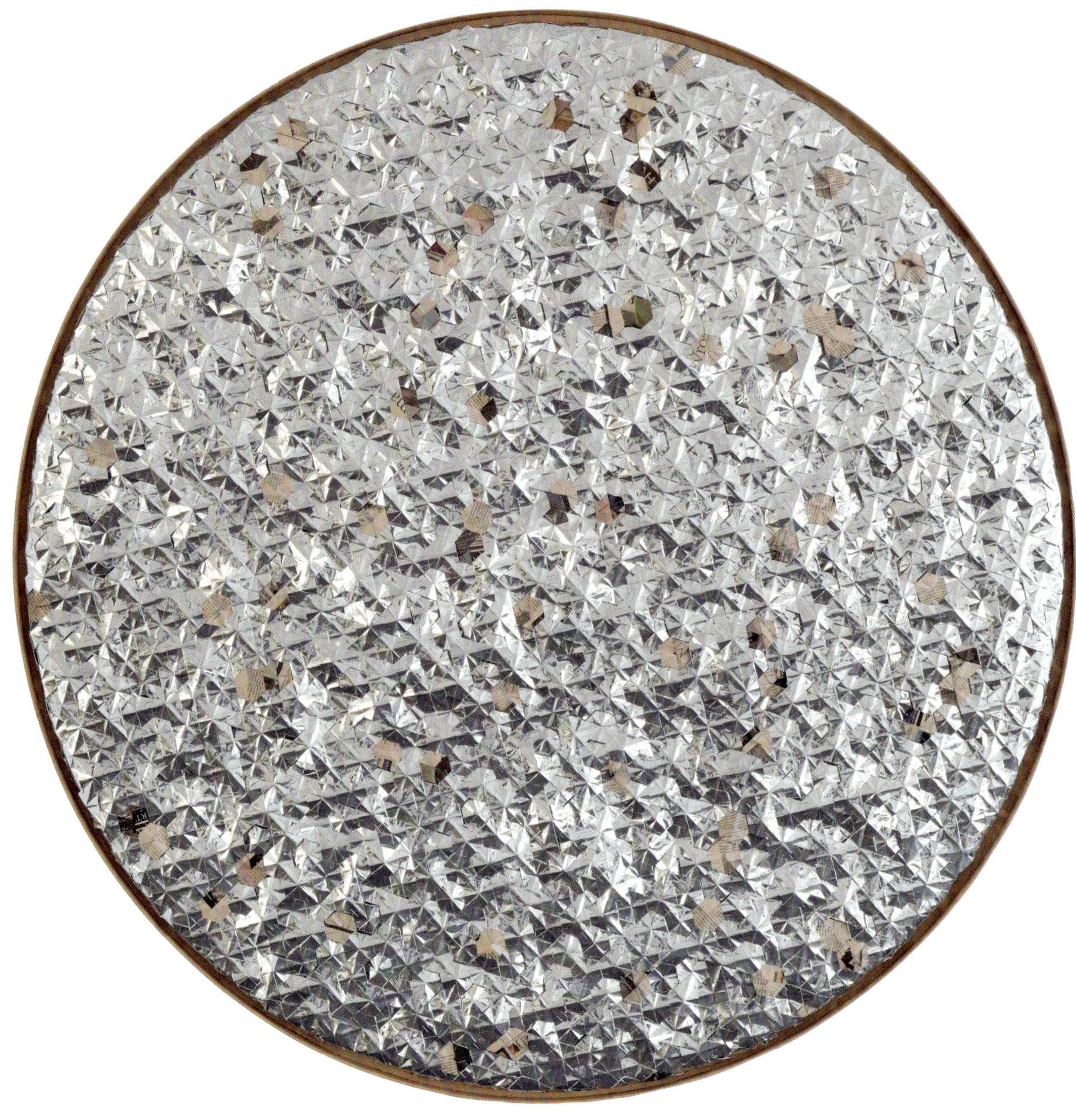

German artist **AMÉLIE ESTERHÁZY**'s (b. 1982) series *Speculum* forensically examines what is possible when one looks for a reflection in another surface. Her works reflect light but disrupt any image thanks to the complex structure of their making. She takes champagne foil and folds it into hexagons, which are stapled to each other to build up a far from perfect, much less flat surface. Added to this are what she terms 'blind spots' of found newspaper or pages from glossy magazines.

These random pieces disrupt the overall structure and any resemblance to a perfect mirror. The folds and staples visually interact with each other over and over again, calling into question the possibility of any surface being able to present a true likeness. A speculum is a medical tool inserted into parts of the body to open them up for inspection; Esterházy's aim is to open up the conceptual space of the reflection.

Speculum no 19, 2017
Champagne labelling paper
and newspaper on canvas
Diam. 134 cm (53 in)

The installation *On-Tilted* by Danish artist **THEIS WENDT** (b. 1981) was part of the Dutch exhibition 'Wintermute' at the Grimm Gallery in Amsterdam in 2015. The works merged the digital and the analogue, similar to the artificial intelligence in William Gibson's novel *Neuromancer* (1984) from which the exhibition took its name. Wendt presented MDF panels digitally printed to look like receding wooden frames, with piles of pulverized MDF on the floor emitting a distinct smell. Central to the work was a large piece of Mylar foil draped on an open wooden frame, which reflected the rest of the pieces in the work, increasing their illusion of being mirrors. What was real, digital or the space in between continually blurred as viewers moved around the installation.

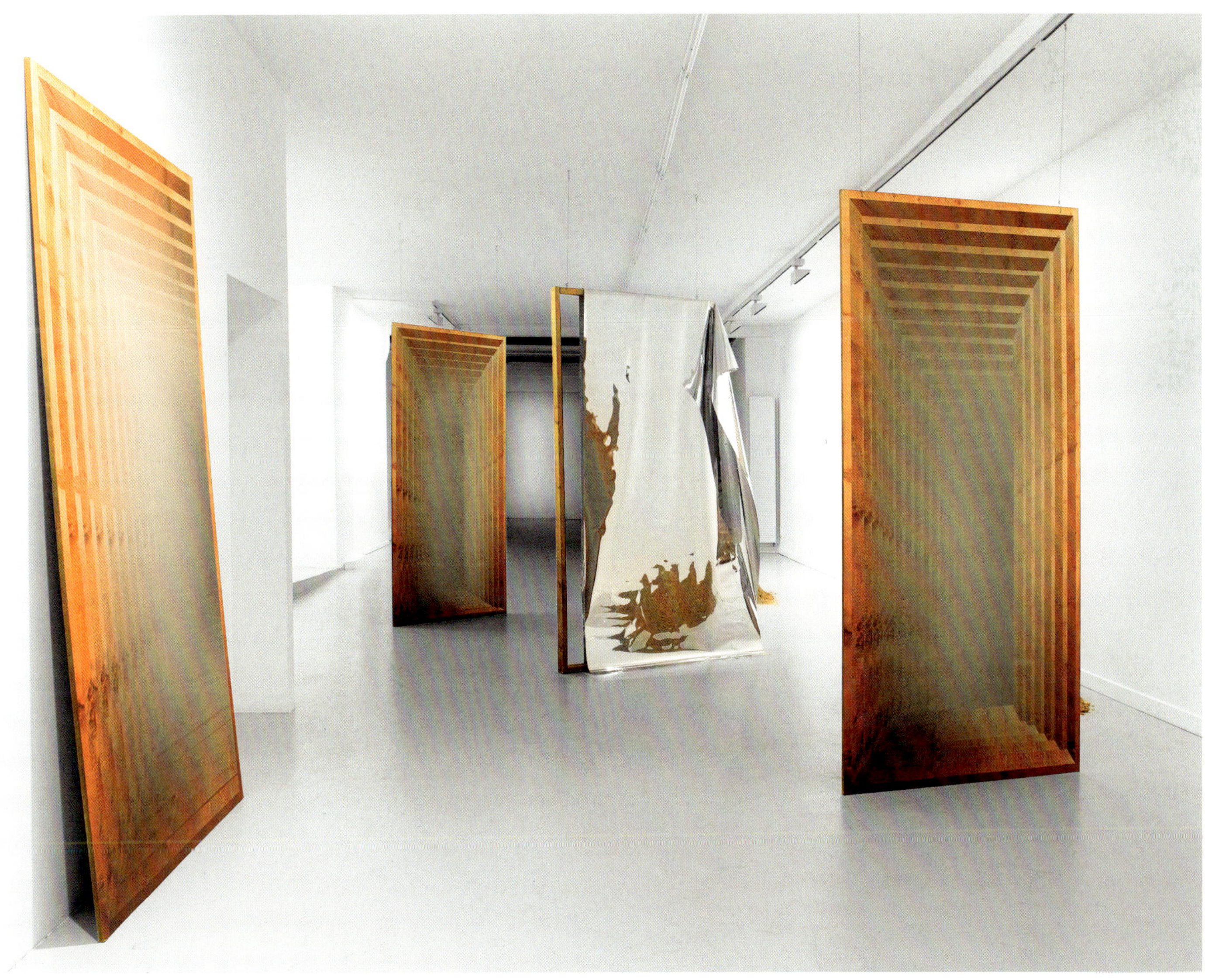

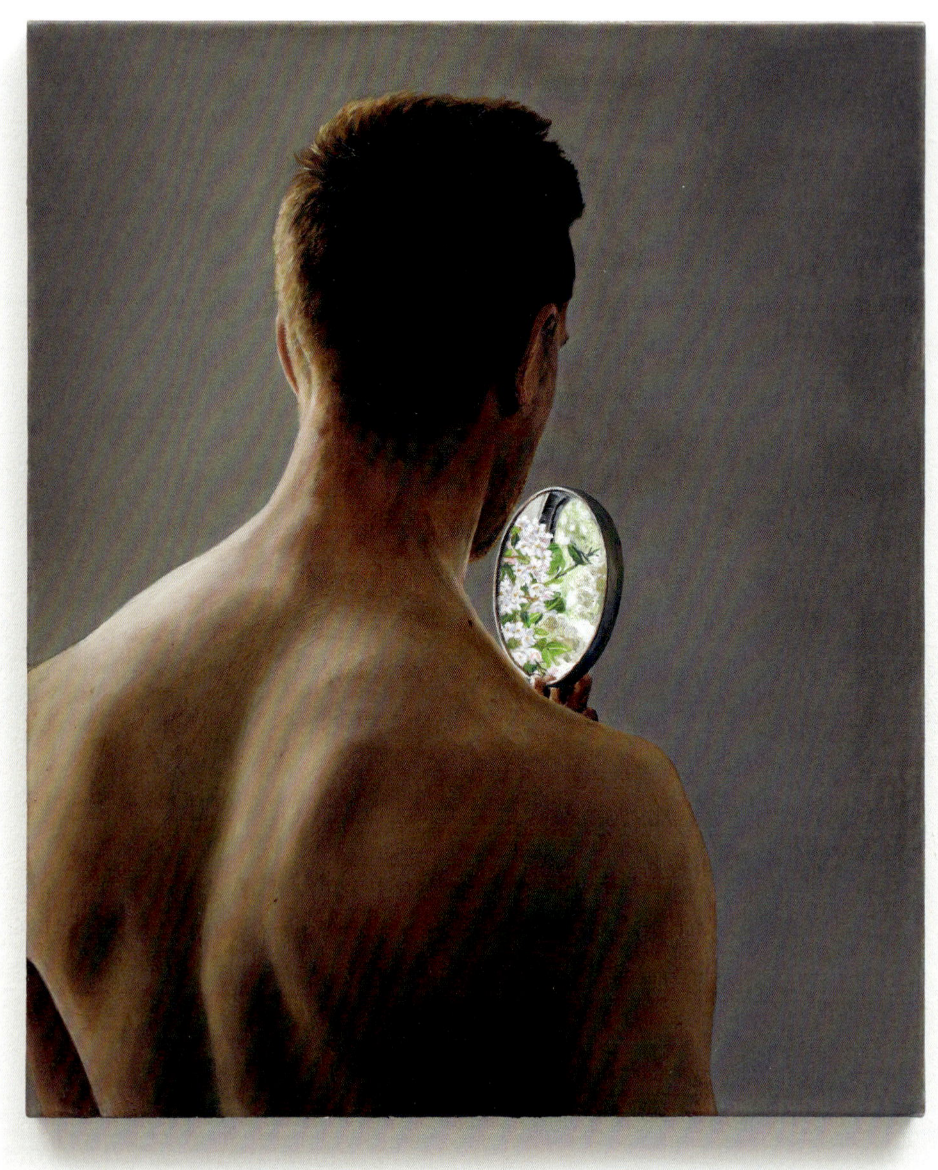

Belgian artist **FABRICE SAMYN** (b. 1981) is a painter who also makes sculpture and performance art, and his *Untitled*, from the series *Only in Space You May Find Your True Face*, looks at first sight as if it is a photograph. A young man holds up a mirror, but instead of his face we see a flowering plant, which appears as if it is outside a window. The image is complex, where the internal and external spaces fold into each other. In *The Moon Is My Host* from the same series, another young man looks into a round mirror at night and again does not see his face; here the mirror is filled with light and looks like the moon, which itself is visible in the sky beyond. These and other paintings ask what is the face in the mirror and who does it belong to. In an age of selfies this fundamental question returns with each new posting.

Untitled, From the series *Only in Space You May Find Your True Face*, 2022
Egg tempera and oil on canvas
65 × 55 cm (25⅝ × 21¾ in)

BELOW
My Mirror #13, 2020
Mirror foil on aluminium frame
30 × 30 cm (11⅞ in × 11⅞ in)

OVERLEAF
All Your Wishes, 2020
PVD-coated stainless steel (balloons);
powder-coated aluminium (benches)
70 mirror balloons, each 43 × 28 × 28 cm
(17 × 11⅛ × 11⅛ in) (10 red, 10 pink, 10 dark blue,
10 light blue, 10 green, 10 gold, 10 silver);
3 modified social benches:
1) 74 × 245 × 57 cm (29¼ × 96½ × 22½ in);
2) 167 × 539 × 162 cm (65¾ × 212 × 64 in);
3) 84 × 168 × 40 cm (33 × 66 × 14¾ in)
Commissioned by LaGuardia Gateway
Partners in partnership with Public Art Fund
for LaGuardia Airport's Terminal B

Danish artist **JEPPE HEIN** (b. 1974) has used mirrors and reflective surfaces in a wide variety of ways in his work. Many pieces unexpectedly play with text, where neon tubes illuminate behind mirrored surfaces. Visual legibility is at play in *My Mirror #13* (below) where the artist has applied a mirror foil to a square structure and then slashed it. When viewers look into the rectified mirror they see themselves but in highly altered fashion. Hein's horizontal cut recalls the vertical slashes of the paintings of Lucio Fontana (1899–1968) and, like those, creates three-dimensional space on the two-dimensional picture face. His *All Your Wishes* (overleaf) at LaGuardia airport in New York features seventy brightly coloured balloons that look as though they have floated up to the ceiling, but are in fact reflective-coated mirrored steel. The work also features three red benches for travellers to sit on. The work as a whole is intended to '…open the viewer to new experiences, and create the conditions that foster moments of empathy and fellowship amidst the hustle of a busy transit hub'.

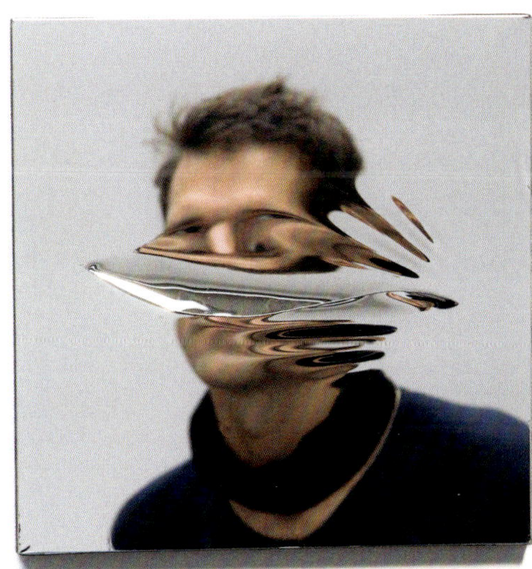

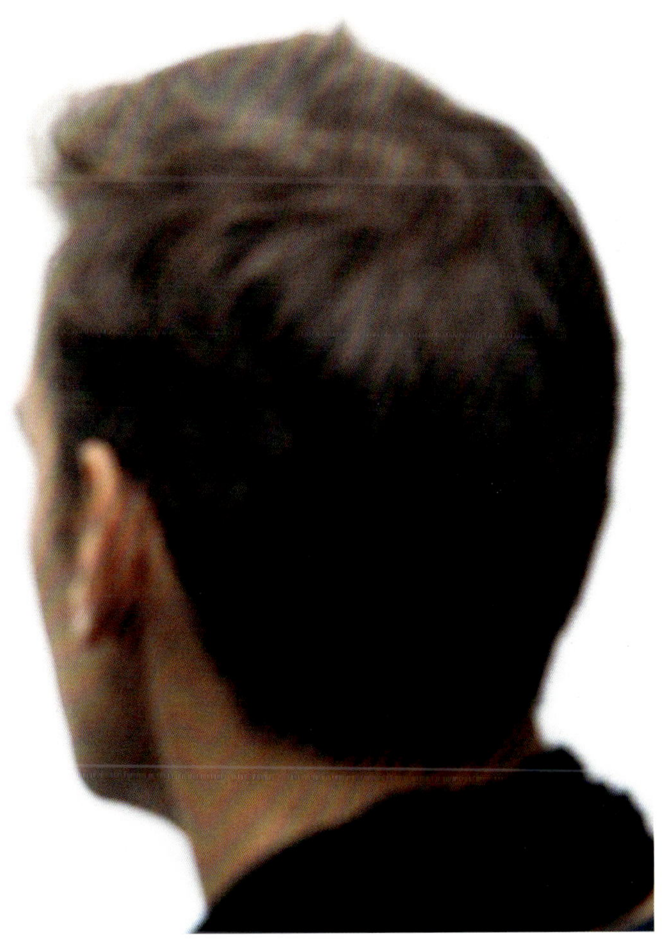

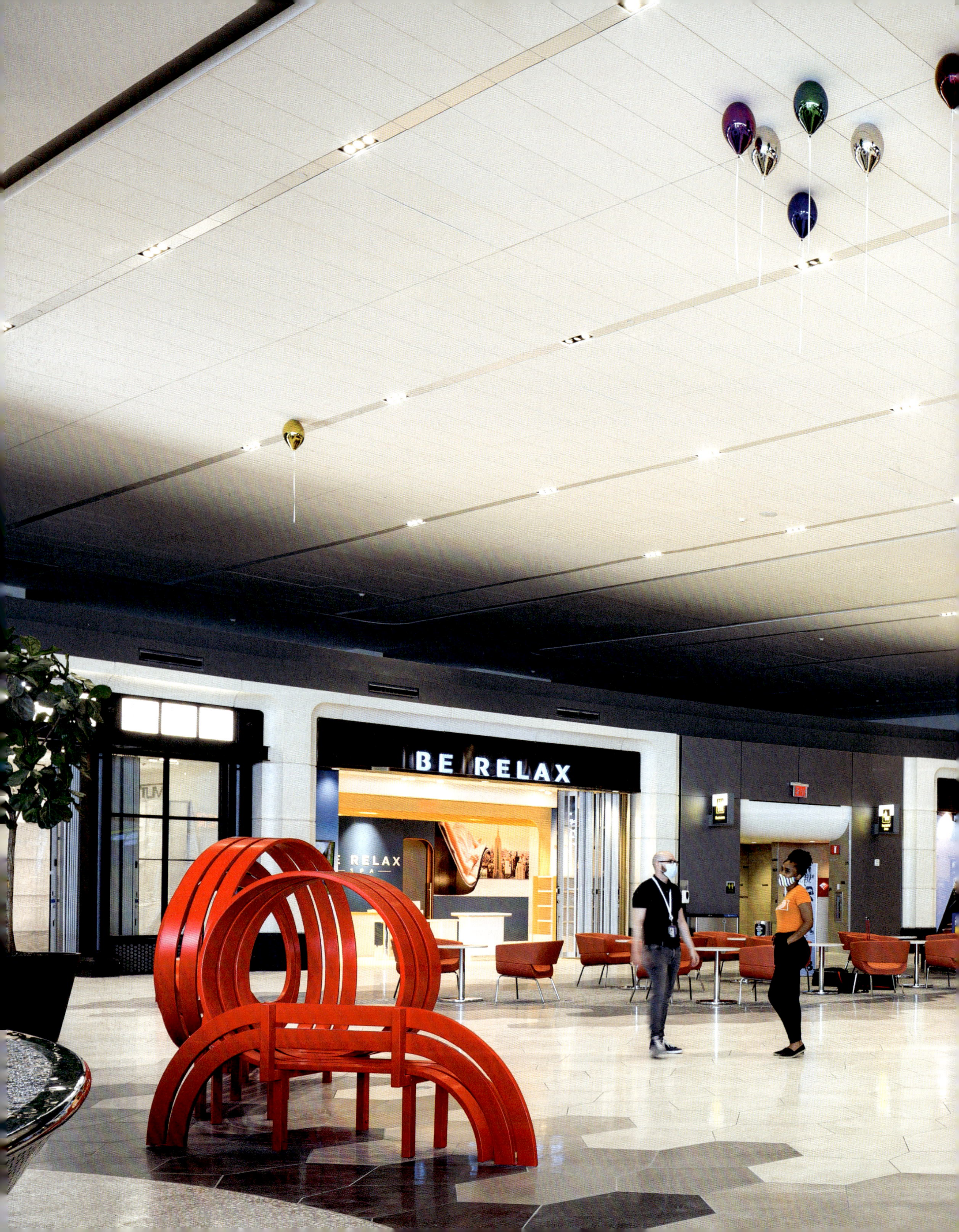
BE RELAX

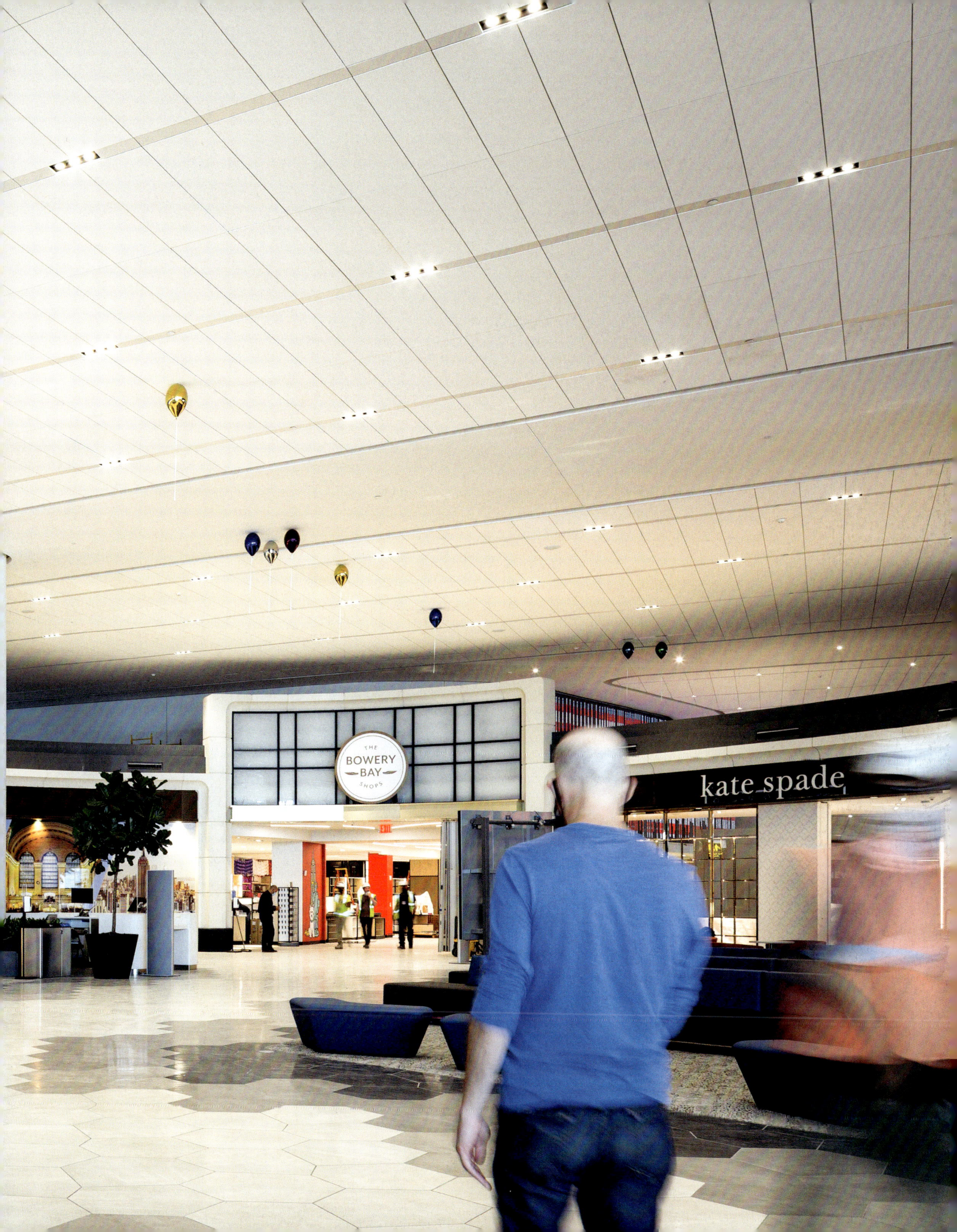
THE
BOWERY
BAY
SHOPS
EXIT
kate spade

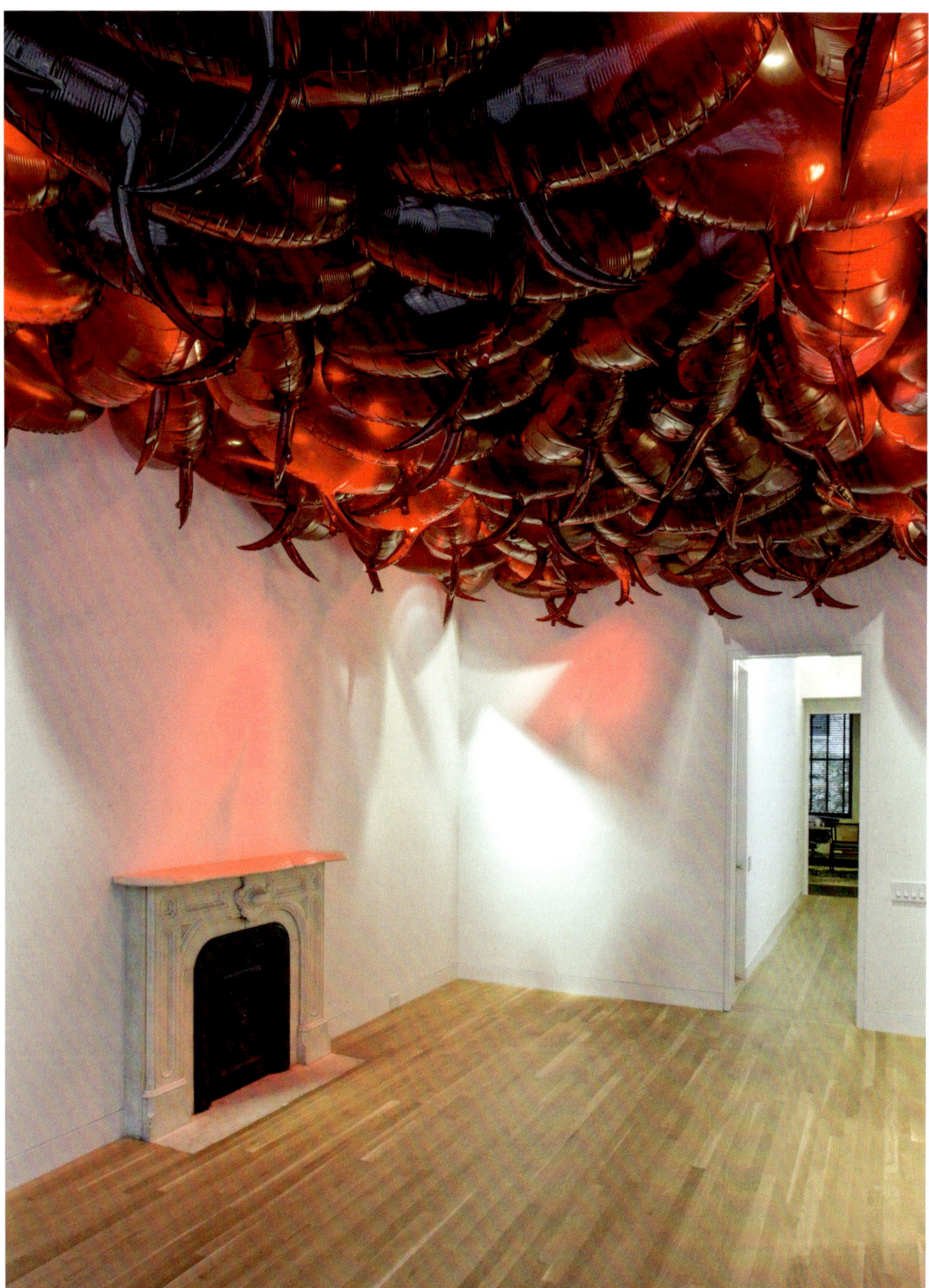

French artist **PHILIPPE PARRENO** (b. 1964) makes very *sited* works, in that he never travels a show; each new presentation is a new exhibition even if it includes previous works. He sees exhibitions as a form of art making in themselves and they often include film, sound, the work of other artists, and his signature speech balloon bubbles. These works float above the heads of visitors and have been made in a wide variety of colours including, gold, silver, red, purple, blue and black. The gallery lighting often reflects these colours onto walls and viewers, as well as altering the physical space. On close inspection it is clear they are not simple round balloons but have a hooked tail, like a comic-book speech bubble. These works demand narrative, asking what are the missing words that should fill the balloons along with the helium that keeps them afloat. Parreno creates spaces where the viewer is left to complete the work, to fill in those empty bubbles.

Speech Bubbles (Transparent Red), 2017
1,500 Mylar balloons, helium
and mould of balloons
68 × 109 × 25 cm (26⅜ × 43 × 9⅞ in)

Speech Bubbles (Transparent Fuchsia), 2017
1,500 Mylar balloons, helium
and mould of balloons
68 × 109 × 25 cm (26⅜ × 43 × 9⅞ in)

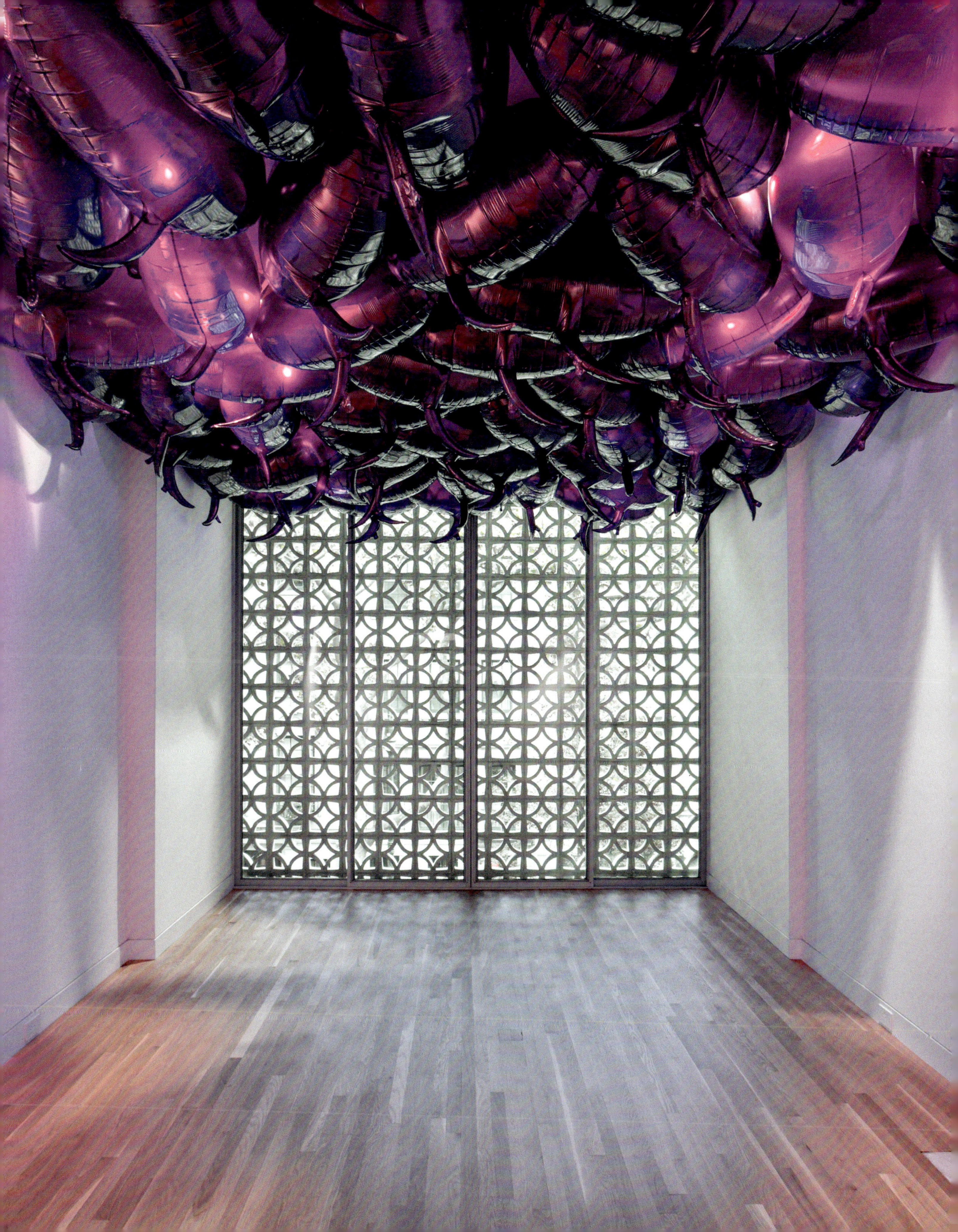

Colombian artist **ANDRÉS MORENO HOFFMANN** (b. 1977) made *Akashá* for Grey Cube Projects' exhibition 'Multiverse' in Bogotá. The curator, John Ángel Rodríguez, presented work inspired by the scientific idea that our universe is only one of an infinite number of such universes, each possibly similar, or vastly different, but co-existing in the now. Moreno Hoffmann presented a series of floating mirror cubes, attached to weights, that reflected each other into infinity. Moreno Hoffmann says that the Sanskrit term *Akashá* refers to the 'matrix of all matter and force in the universe'. The balloons, like those of other artists using this material, hark back to Andy Warhol's seminal *Silver Clouds* (1966) which also reflected each other and the viewers, who were allowed to play with them. Moreno Hoffmann's cubes, on the other hand, were very carefully placed and visitors were actively encouraged not to touch them.

Akashá, 2017
Chromed balloons filled with helium,
nylon and bronze weights
Dimensions variable

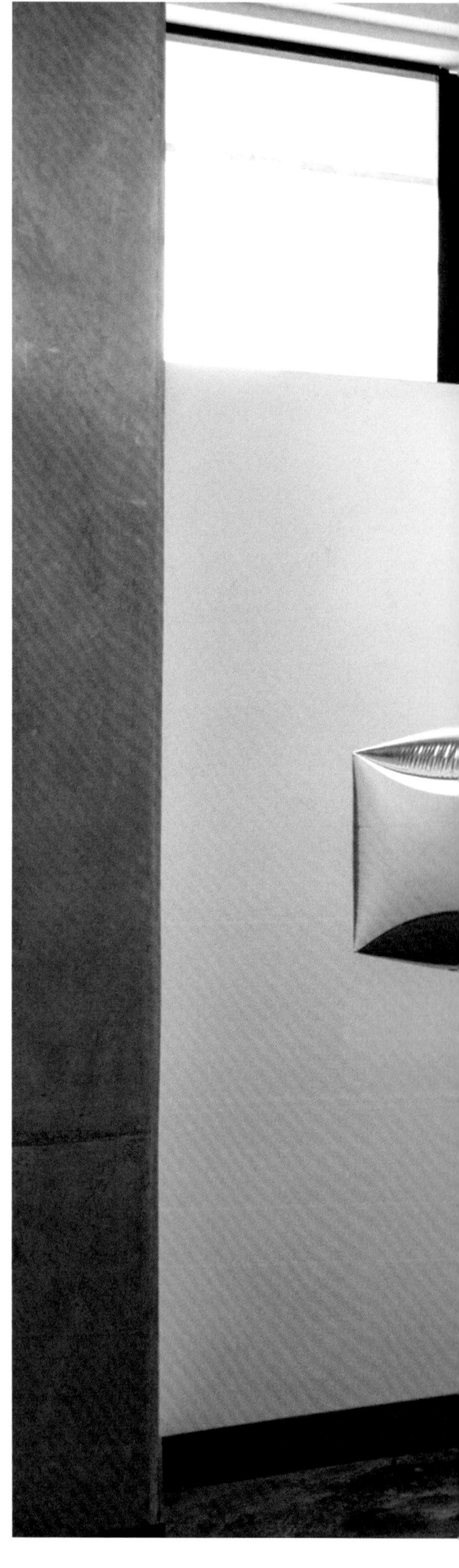

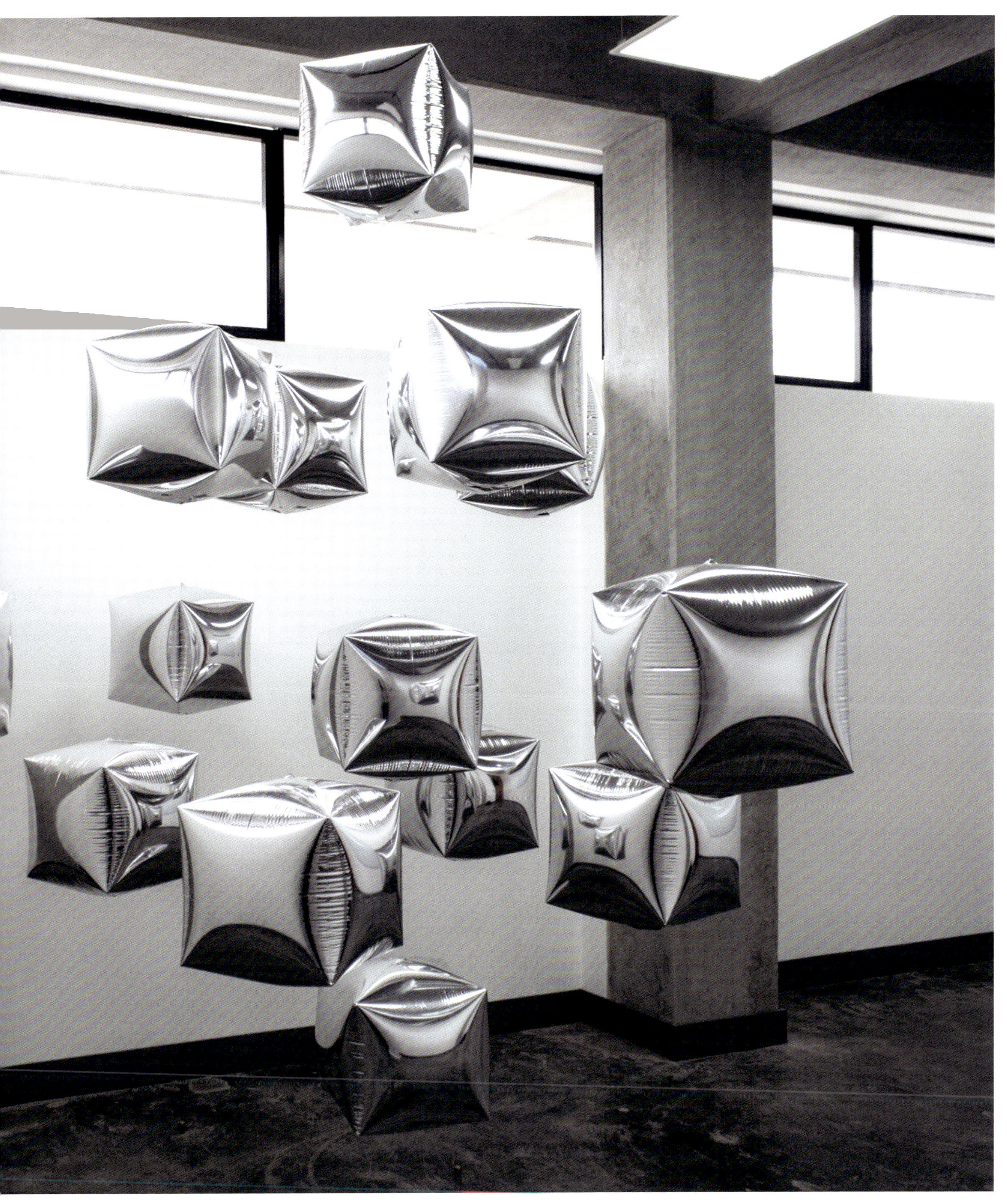

MATERIALS

British artist **DEB COVELL** (b. 1966) makes paint into three-dimensional objects. Her works are still paintings, but they inhabit the world of sculpture. She starts by building up layer upon layer of acrylic paint on top of clear plastic sheets. She eventually peels the plastic backing off, leaving only the paint, usually in a square or rectangular shape and often quite large, as in *Silver Drape* (opposite). Here the unfolded skin of paint is more than 5 metres (16⅓ feet) long and is draped in a different way at each location it is shown, so that the installed dimensions are always variable. Covell allows gravity to have its say over the form the works take after she has cut and folded them into shapes that she considers ready to employ. She has a real dialogue with the physicality of the paint and there is a distinct installed quality to her paintings, which often shimmer in the light regardless of their base colour, as she uses a high-gloss finish.

BELOW
The Bridge, 2018
Installation view: 'Crossings – Art and Christianity Now' exhibition, Southwell Minster, Nottinghamshire, England
Acrylic paint skin
1.55 × 1.55 m (5¹⁄₁₀ × 5¹⁄₁₀ ft)

OPPOSITE
Silver Drape, 2016
Installation view: 'The Fold' exhibition, Blyth Gallery, London, UK
Chrome lacquer on acrylic paint sheet
5.2 × 2 × 0.3 m (17 × 6½ × 1 ft)

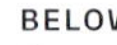

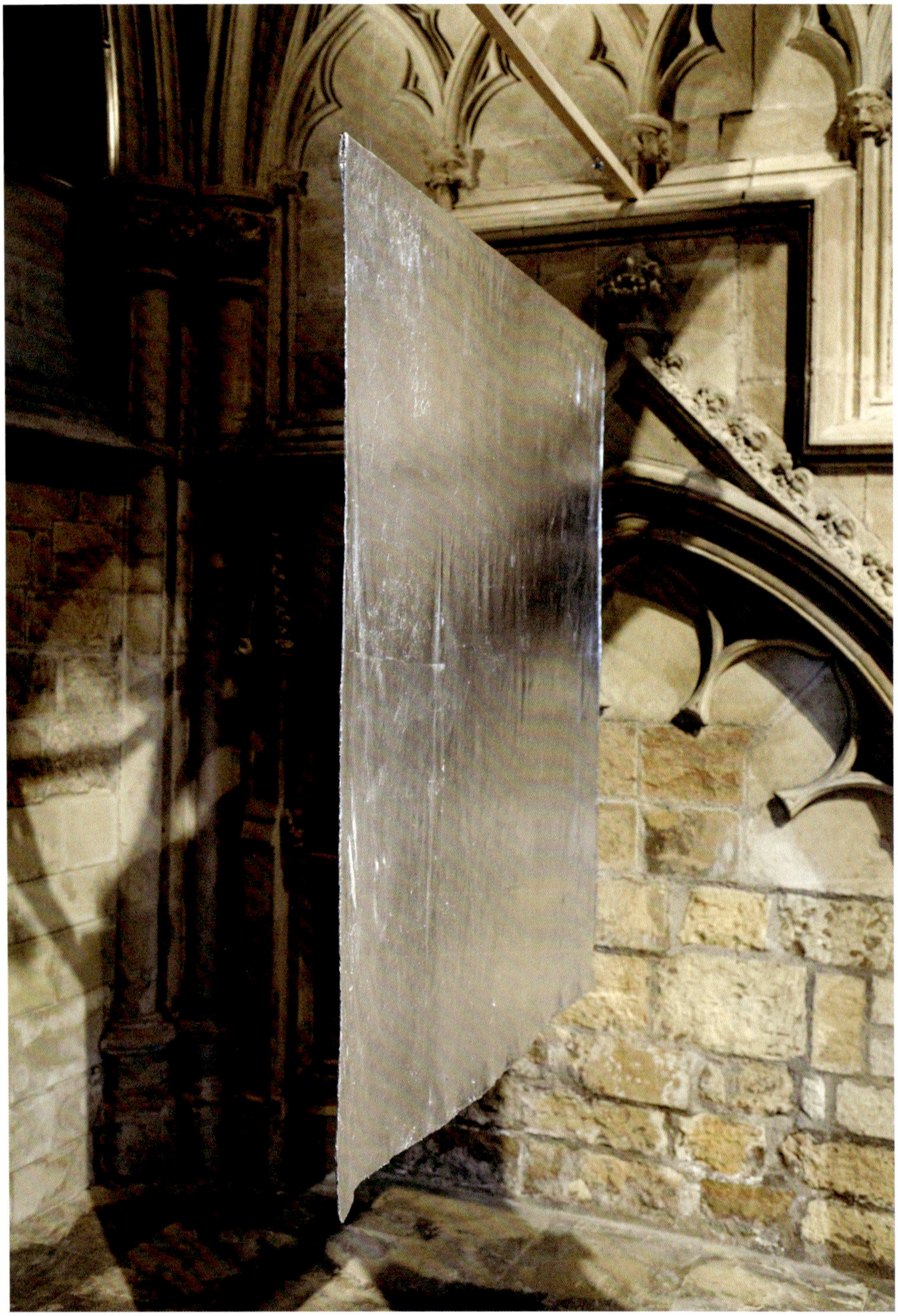

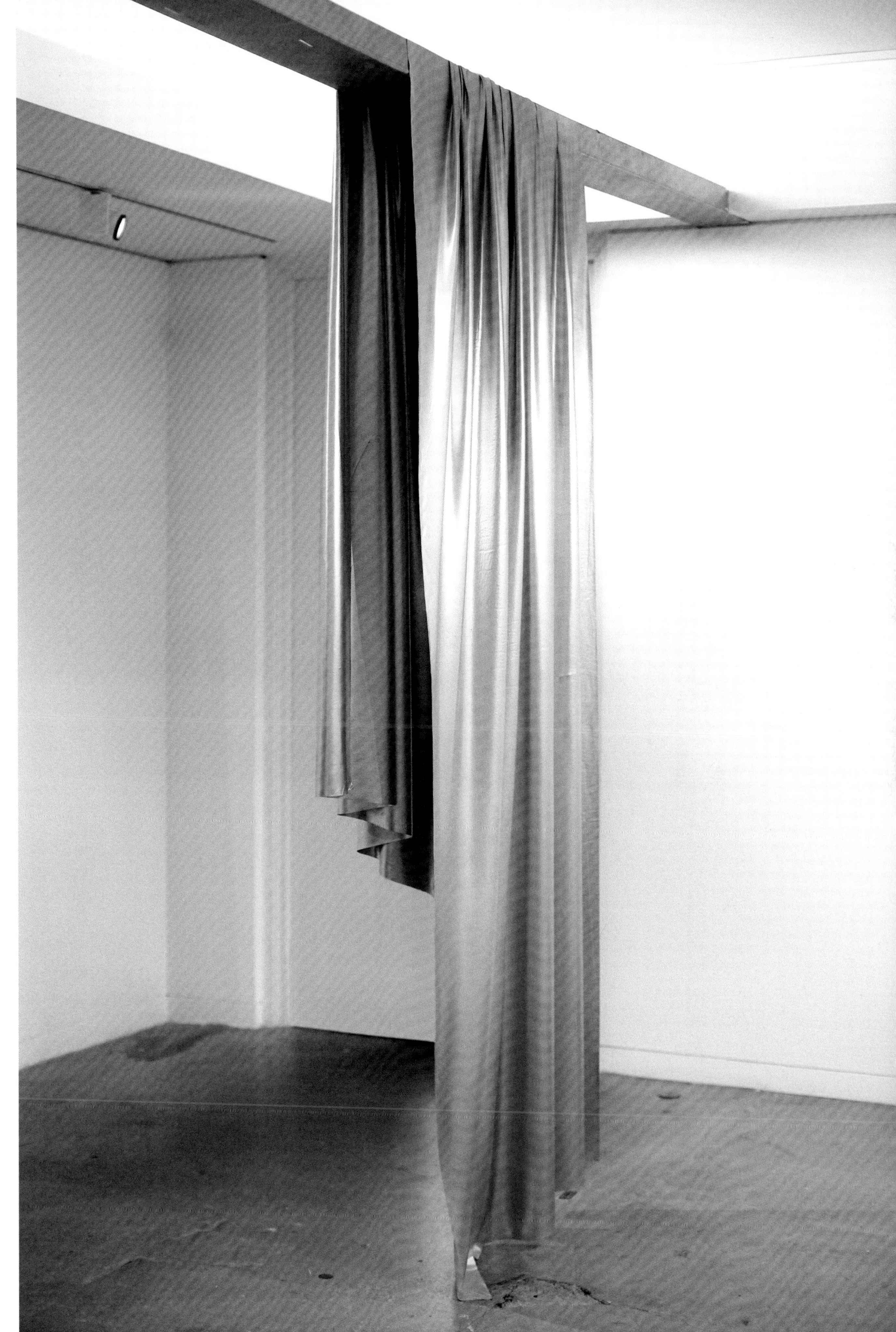

American artist **CHANDRIKA METIVIER** (b. 1995) uses Mylar in most of their work, creating large shiny reflective immersive spaces. *The Fortress* was in a way a collaboration with an 'unhoused' man, James Parker, who had built a temporary cardboard and wood structure on Skid Row in Los Angeles as a makeshift dwelling. Metivier proposed that they wrap the structure in the reflective Mylar for which they are known and Parker agreed. The resultant edifice was thus a temporary site-specific installation as well as a temporary home. Whether artwork or shelter, the police eventually removed the structure.

Mylar is a very durable material and one that Metivier uses to comment on the long-lived problems in contemporary America, including homelessness, human rights and police interaction with non-white citizens.

PLAY by Sweden-based British artist **STUART MAYES** (b. 1968) was an interactive 'video' installation composed of used gay pornographic VHS videotape. The cassettes were anonymously donated to the artist after his online and analogue requests. Mayes made a large, minimal wall bisecting the room. Viewers had to penetrate the black tape curtain to enter the gallery, only to find it empty apart from others already in the space, who watched them enter. Mayes made everyone a porn star, the way that selfies (nude or otherwise) soon would. The hanging tape was similar to the vinyl strips at the entrances to London sex shops, but for younger viewers it was completely alien, and they often held the tape to the light to try to see the imagery. The work referenced earlier film types (zoetropes), and as viewers moved their heads from side to side, the tape flickered and reflected the light, allowing glimpses of the bookcase behind or others about to enter.

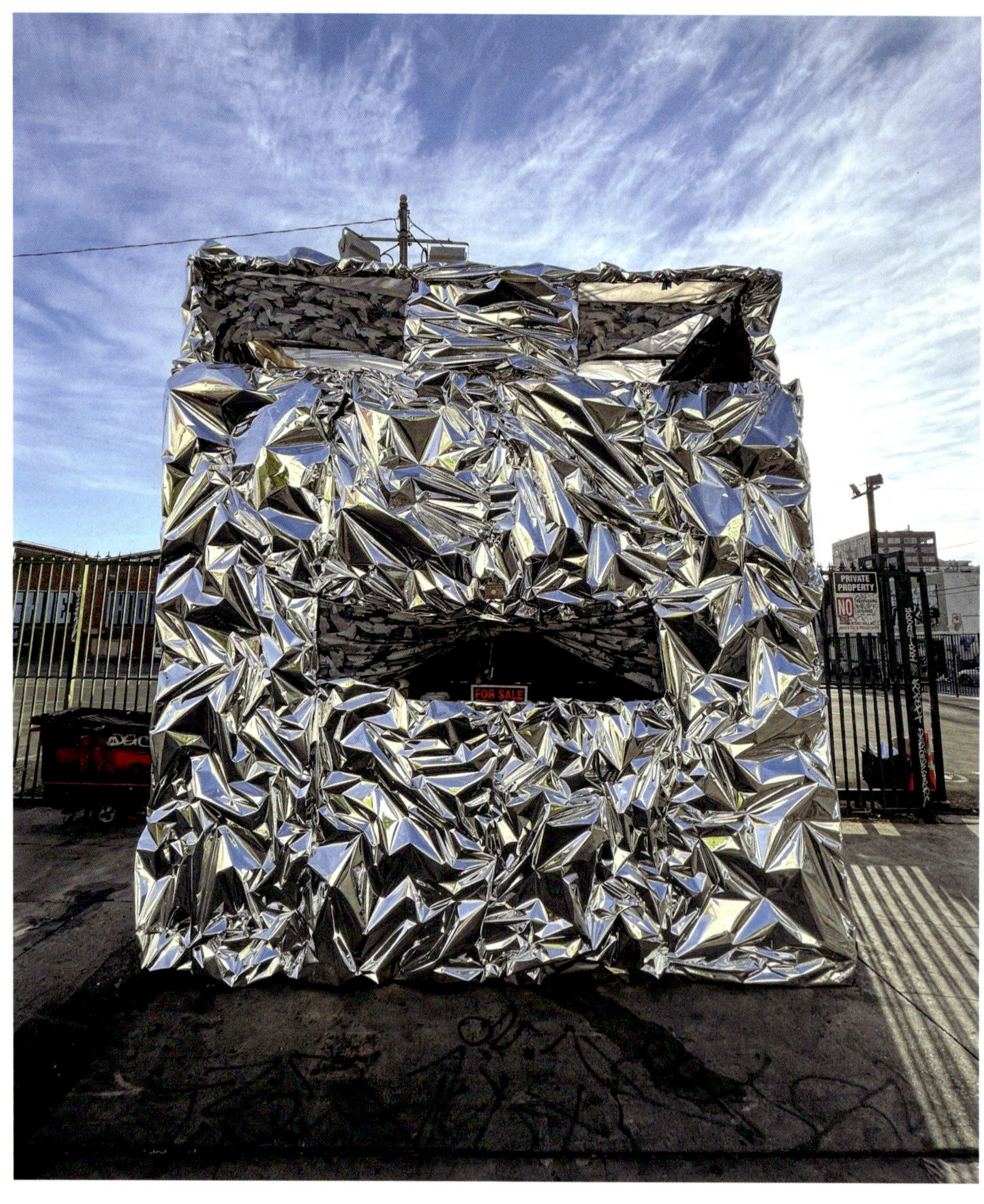

OPPOSITE
Chandrika Metivier, *The Fortress*, 2022
Mylar, wood scraps
4 × 2.7 × 4 m (13 × 9 × 13 ft)

RIGHT
Stuart Mayes, *PLAY*, 2010
Used videotape
Dimensions variable

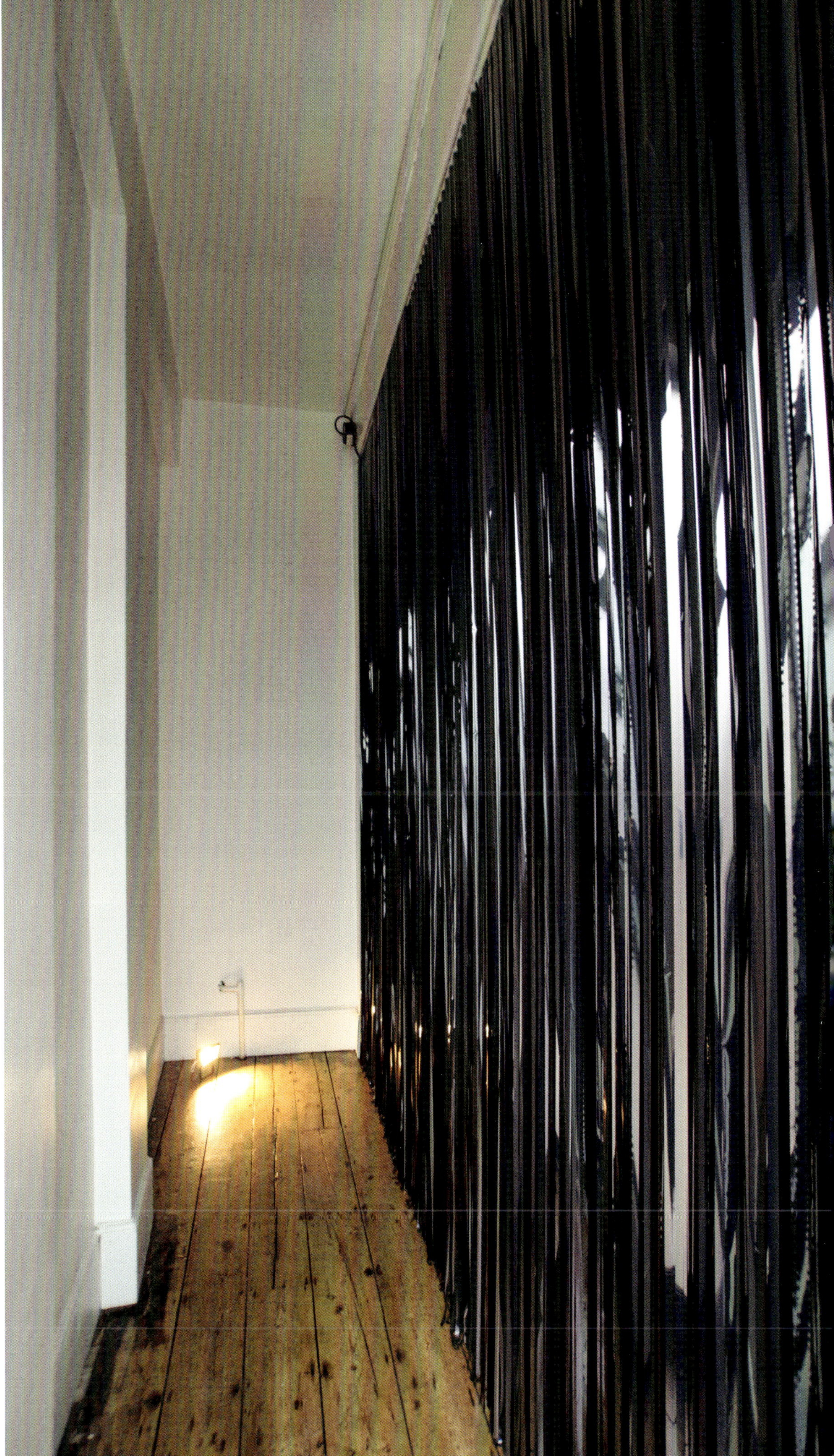

Based in London, **YUTA SEGAWA** (b. 1988) is a Japanese ceramic artist who mainly works on a miniature scale. His hand-thrown pots are all usually less than 9 centimetres (3⅝ inches) tall, with few exceptions; some are only 1 centimetre (½ inch) in height. He uses traditional shapes and glazes to upend the viewer's understanding of what a pot might be, as the tiny vessels look as though they have been reduced in size like Alice in Wonderland. Many of his series have used traditional green, earthenware and simple one-colour glazes. In recent years his glazes have become more complex, and he has also made a series in mirror-reflective gold and silver glazes on white porcelain.

During the London Covid lockdowns, British artist **PREM SAHIB** (b. 1982) took a number of photographs from his flat, looking out of the window on what was then seen as a very unsafe world. Sahib had previously made another series of works on tiles called *Your Disco Needs You*, where the images refer to moments caught in reflections on the tiled walls of public urinals. In the new series, *Middleton Green*, Sahib's works show moments of state surveillance and social control that have been extended beyond monitoring queer sexual practices and spaces, and have moved into the realm of the everyday and the general public. The series documents the various uses of a public space, from people loitering and playing sports to those engaged in prayer at a time when access to spaces of worship was limited, owing to Covid restrictions. In *Middleton Green 18:22*, the presence of the police who patrol the park is recorded, marking their increased surveillance of the area.

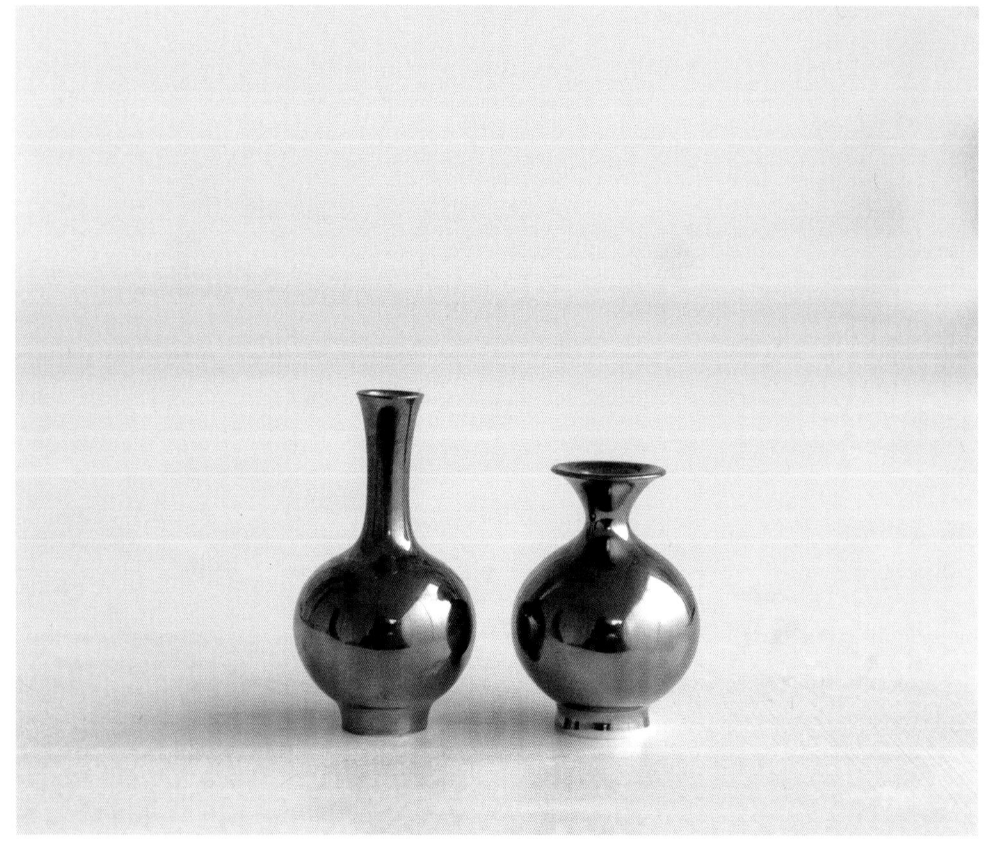

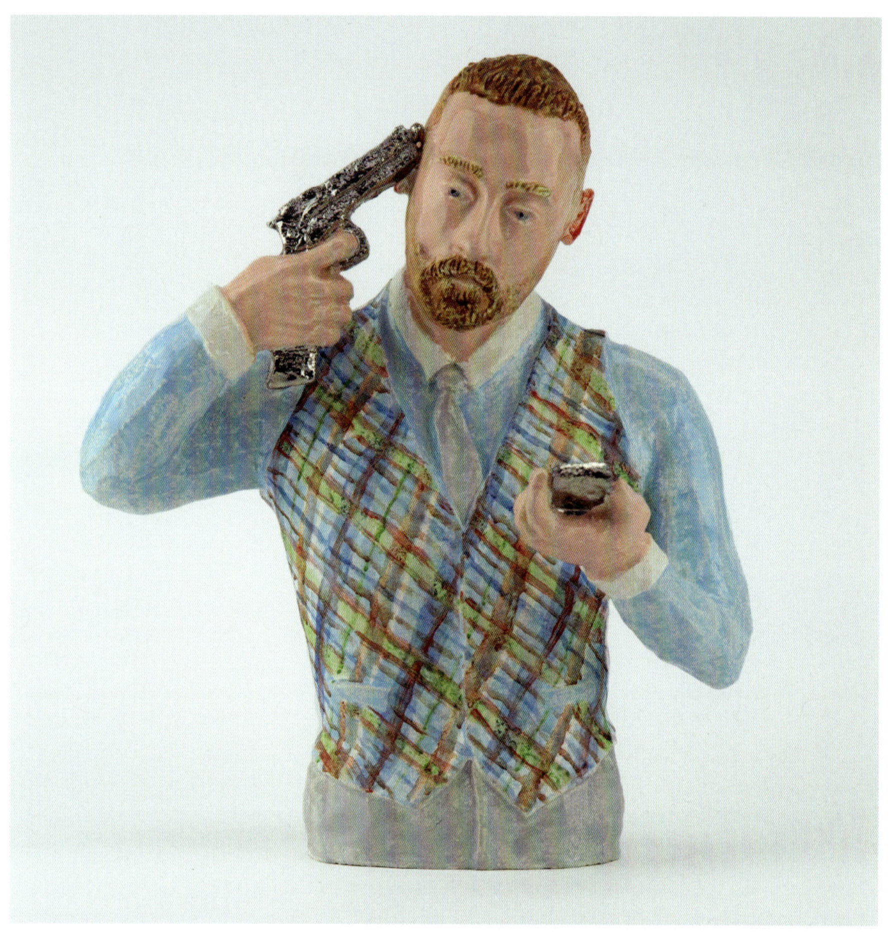

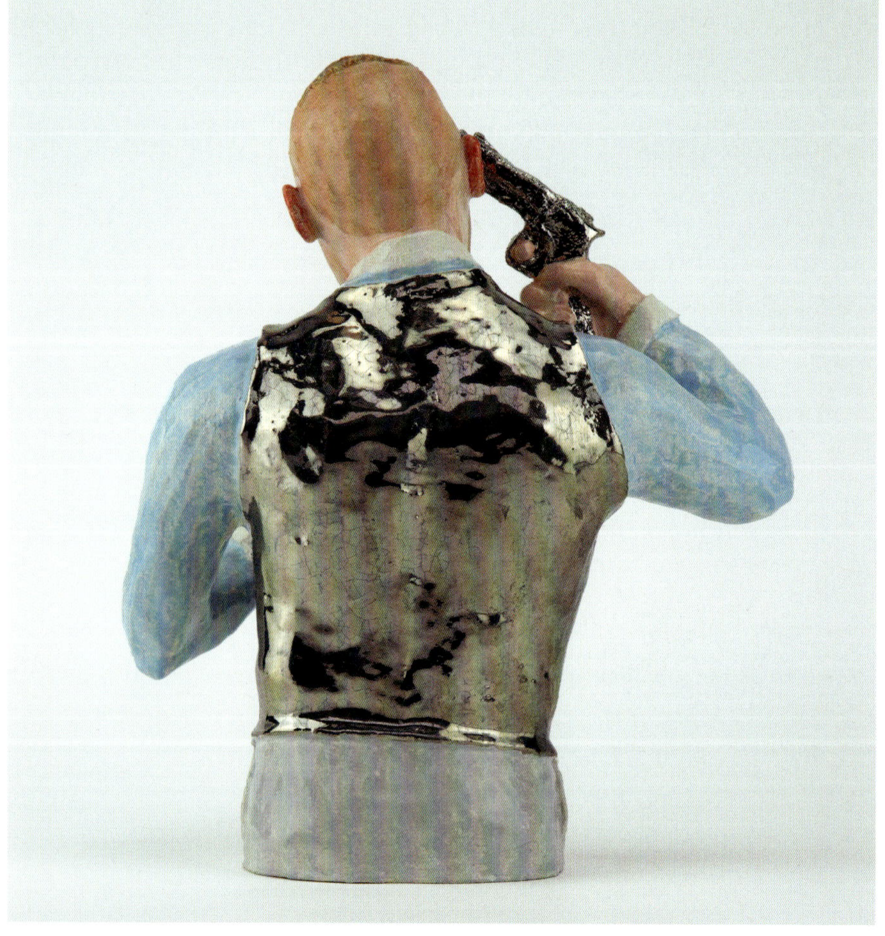

Dutch artist **FRANS FRANCISCUS** (b. 1959) takes Renaissance paintings as the inspiration for many of his ceramic works, but interprets them in a modern vernacular. He likes the way biblical themes can be reworked into a humorous and often dark story. His *Dumped* series of men gaze into their phones thinking about the ultimate revenge selfie. *Dumped Dandy*'s phone, his gun and the back of his waistcoat are glazed in a bright reflective silver. In *Dumped by WeChat* the man holds only his finger to his head, cocked like a gun, and the phone and waistcoat are gold. Franciscus portrays a host of characters, some of whom have their whole faces glazed in gold (*Golden Cheese Head*, 2022) like modern-day saints' haloes.

American **ROB WYNNE** (b. 1948) is a conceptual artist with firm roots in Fluxus (Ray Johnson was his mentor) and the wordplay traditions of Marcel Duchamp. He often takes overheard bits of conversation, cut-ups from existing texts or words and phrases from television and film as the basis for work. He has made a series of witty, word-based pieces that are manufactured from poured and mirrored glass. They can be 'read' as snatches of sentences (*The Vanished World*, 2015), phrases from scientific journals (*Equilibrium*, 2015) or simple matters of fact, as in *Mirror Mirror on the Wall* (opposite), where the mysterious, now frozen glass reflects its title as if a self-portrait in a mirror. Alternatively, as in *Daybreak Vortex* (overleaf), they can resemble observable forms (here, the Milky Way).

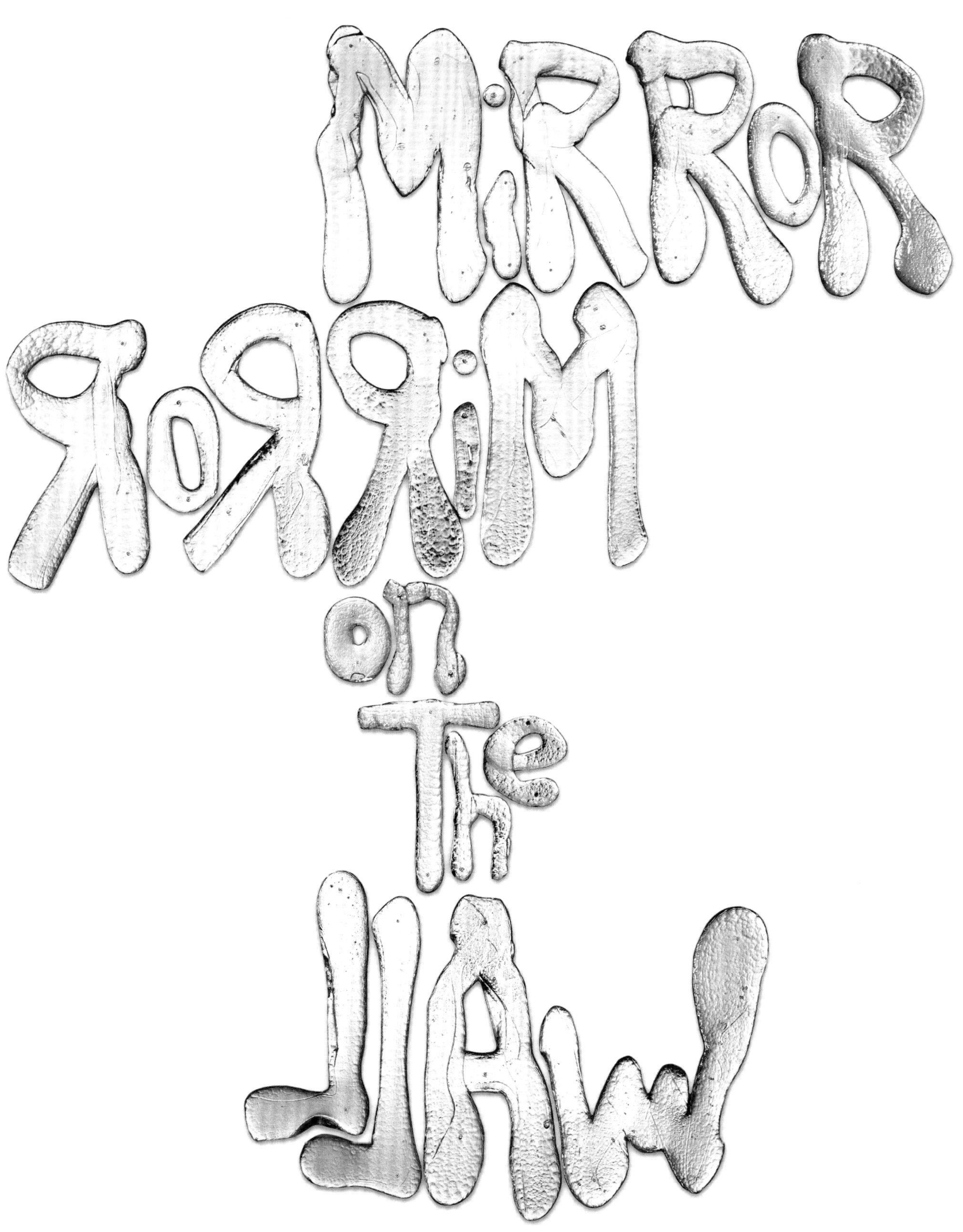

MIRROR
MIRROR
on
The
WALL

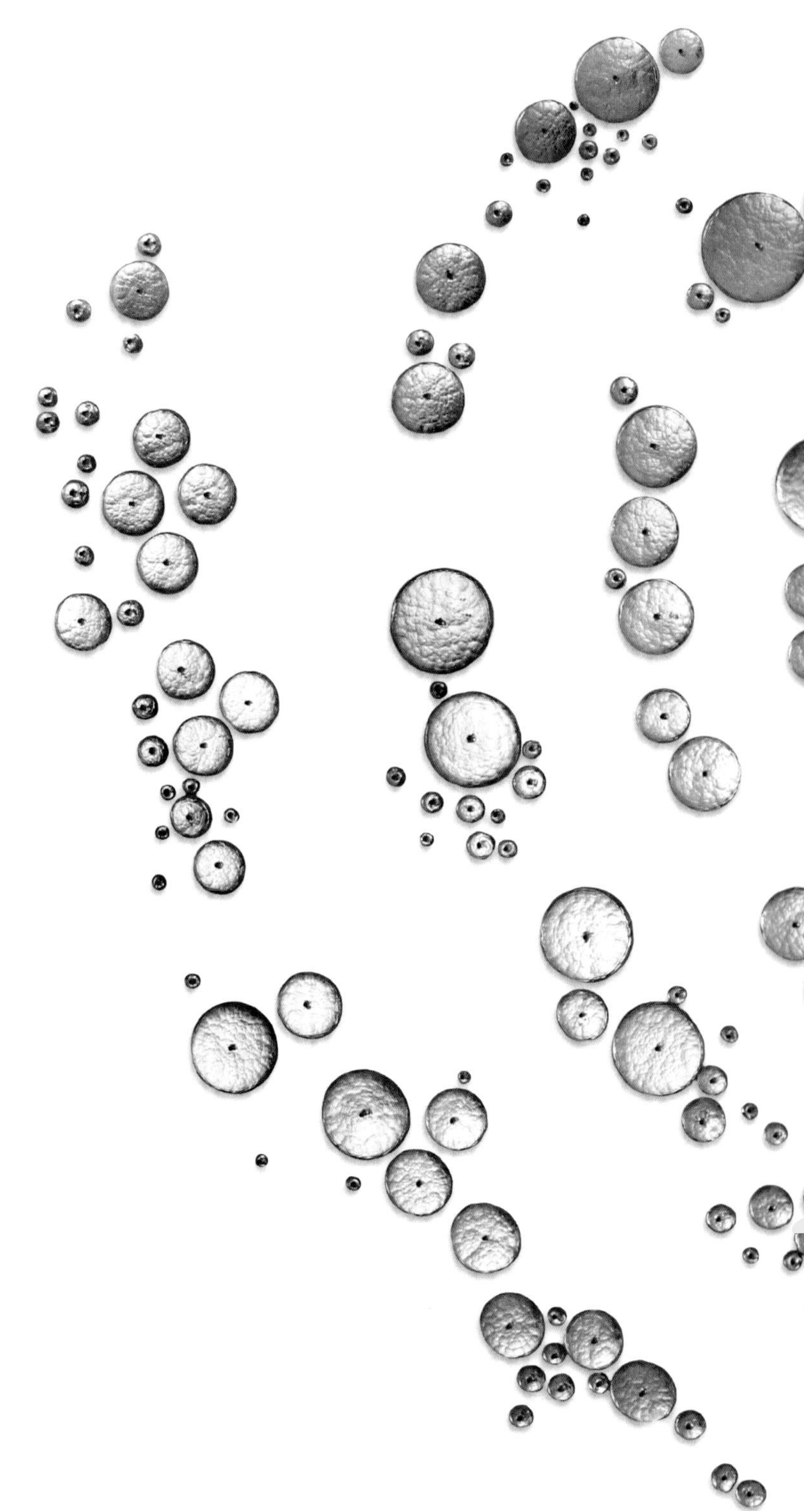

Rob Wynne, *Daybreak Vortex*, 2019
Unique poured and mirrored glass
2.13 × 3.2 m (7 × 10½ ft)

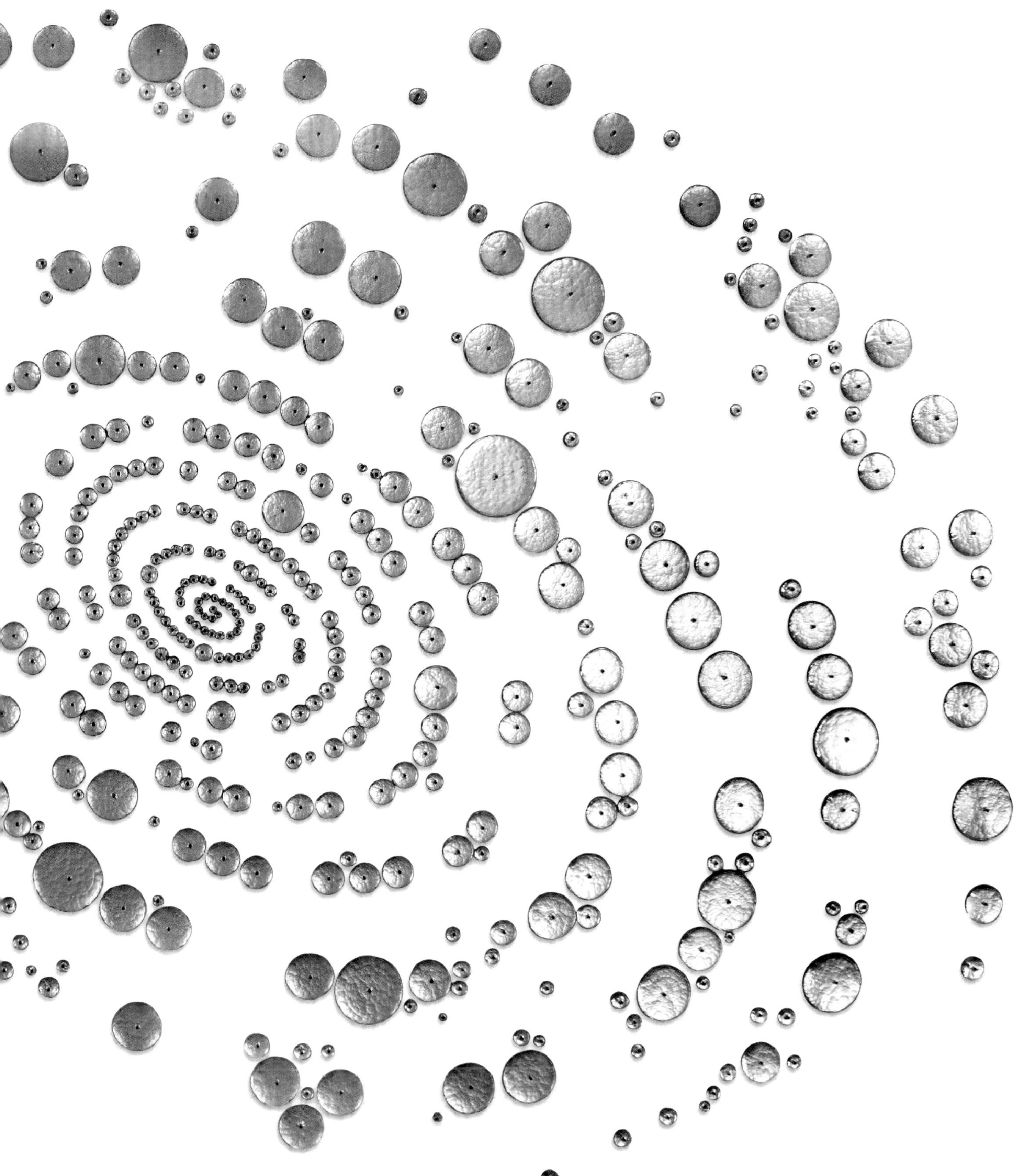

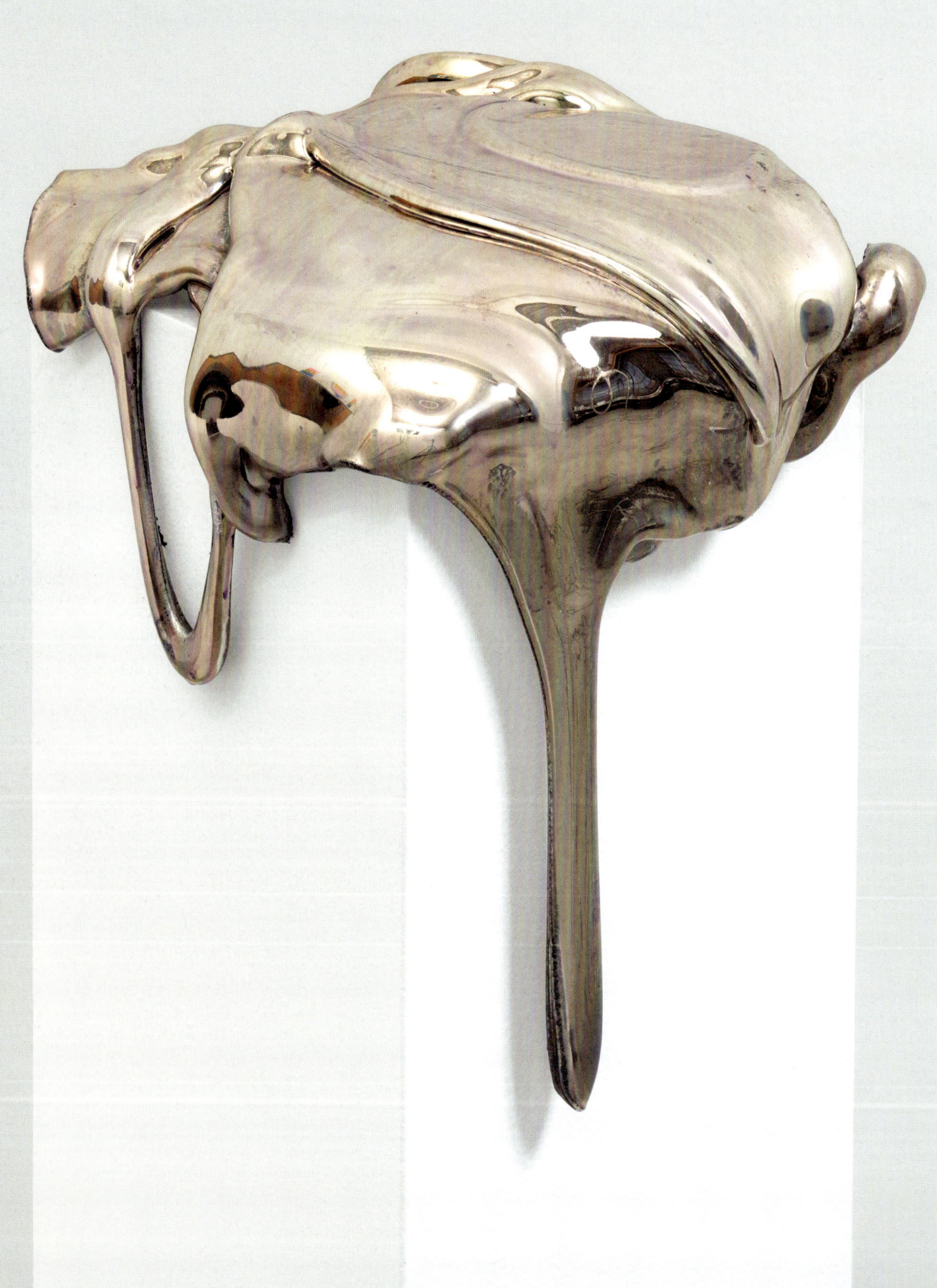

American artist **KATHERINE VETNE**
(b. 1987) has taken a feminist look at the
production of commercially available glass
objects often seen as luxe or tasteful and
has melted them into new works. For
Trophy Wife (2022) she took a cut-glass
wedding gift and melted the lead-crystal
vase so that it looks almost computer
generated, while *Her Inheritance (Sugar
Bowl, Askew)* (2020) is a slump of purple
glass. She has used a wide variety of
lead-crystal pitchers to make works such
as *Selling the Dream*, seen here. She fires
the pieces in a kiln and slumps, or melts,
them into new forms, and then mirrors
their surfaces with silver nitrate. These
objects that in a previous life had a
function and a value (monetary and social)
have been transformed into new, self-
questioning artefacts that upend those
traditional value systems.

Lithuanian artist **REMIGIJUS KRIUKAS**
(b. 1961) set up his own glass studio,
GLASREMIS, in Panevėžys in 2000 in order
to make his own work and bring his designs
to a greater audience. Kriukas uses glass-
blowing and free-forming techniques in
the production of works such as *Misty Blue*
(right) and a series of other works including
Misty Gold and *Pink Sun Sack*. Once the
form is complete the interior is silvered,
allowing the work to be reflective and have
a mirrored effect. While this is a traditional
method of making, Kriukas takes the
technique further with his completely
contemporary designs.

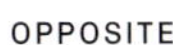

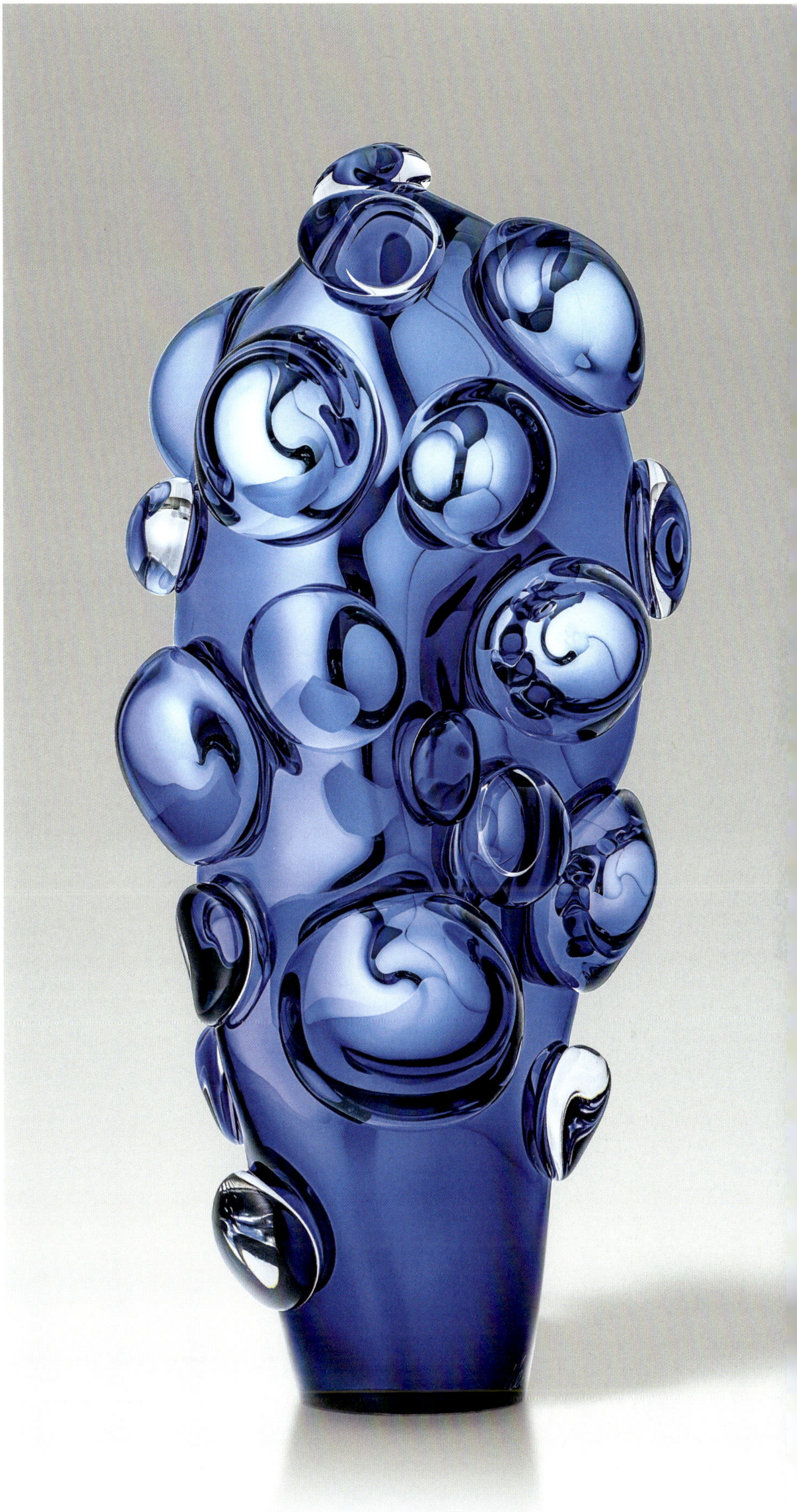

OPPOSITE
Katherine Vetne, *Selling the Dream*, 2017
Three Avon lead-crystal pitchers,
melted and mirrored (silver nitrate)
114.3 × 28 × 27.3 cm (45 × 11 × 10¾ in)
(with pedestal)

RIGHT
Remigijus Kriukas, *Misty Blue*, 2022
Glass blowing, free forming, silvering
62 × 24 × 33 cm (24½ × 9½ × 13 in)

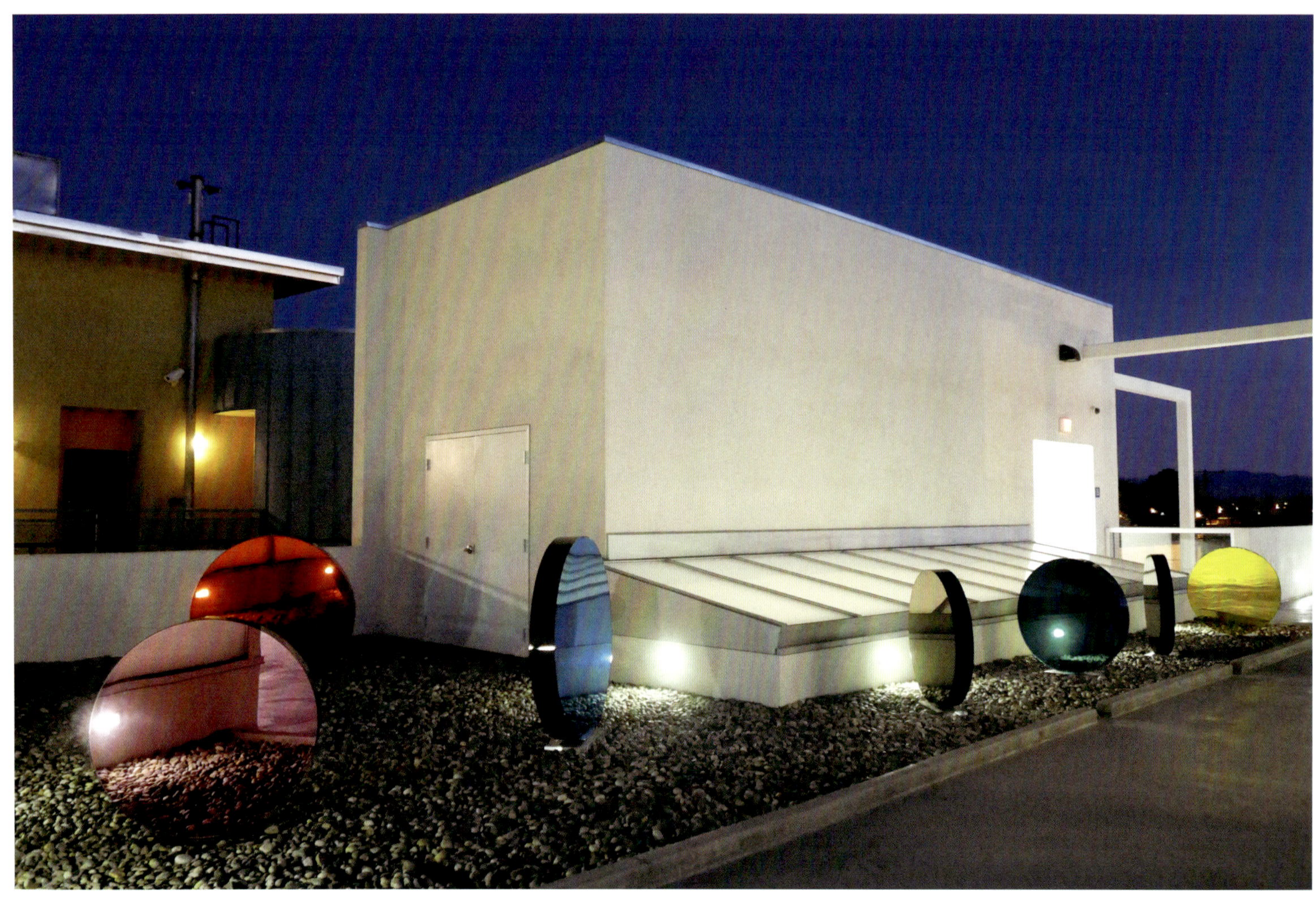

American artist **SHANA MABARI** (b. 1969) has used reflective surfaces for the majority of her production, and her *Diametros Petals* was shown at the Museum of Art and History in Lancaster, California, in 2015. The strong natural light and the reflective quality of the brightly coloured acrylic mirrors made for a complex, multilayered installation. Each disc reflected a variety of the other eleven placed on the outdoor roof sculpture terrace. The interplay of the 90- and 100-centimetre (3- and 4-foot) discs at different angles to each other made it possible for Mabari to choreograph the colours produced in the reflective surfaces. The yellow disc seen opposite reflects a purple one, producing a magenta colour that only ever exists in the reflection. The discs also threw coloured light onto the white museum building as the sun moved across their surfaces.

Diametros Petals, 2015
Installation view: Museum of Art and History, Lancaster, California, USA
Acrylic, mirror
Two sizes: 91.4 × 91.4 × 12.7 cm (36 × 36 × 5 in)
122 × 122 × 15.2 cm (48 × 48 × 6 in)

OPPOSITE

Diametros Petals, 2015
Acrylic, mirror
91.4 × 91.4 × 12.7 cm (36 × 36 × 5 in)

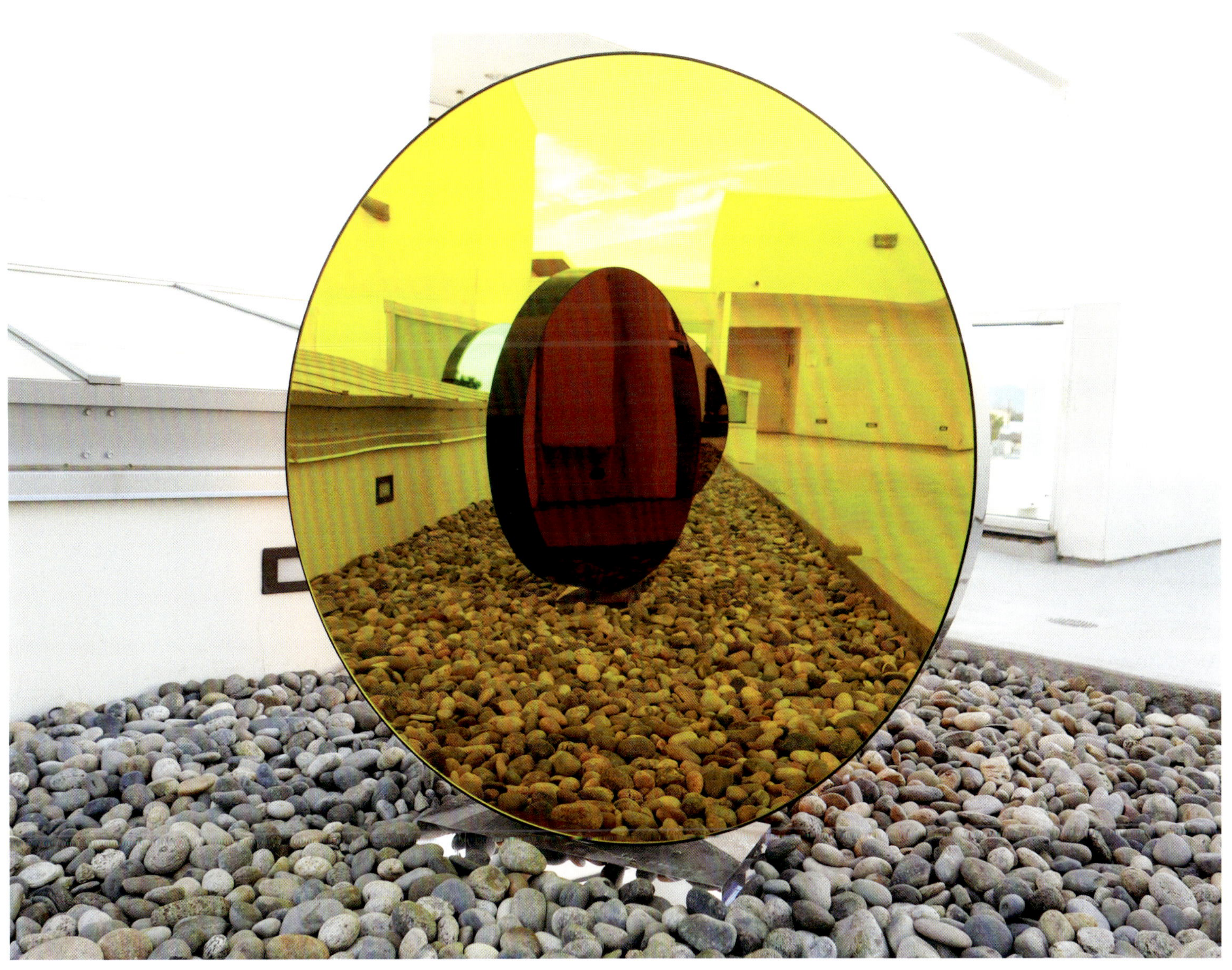

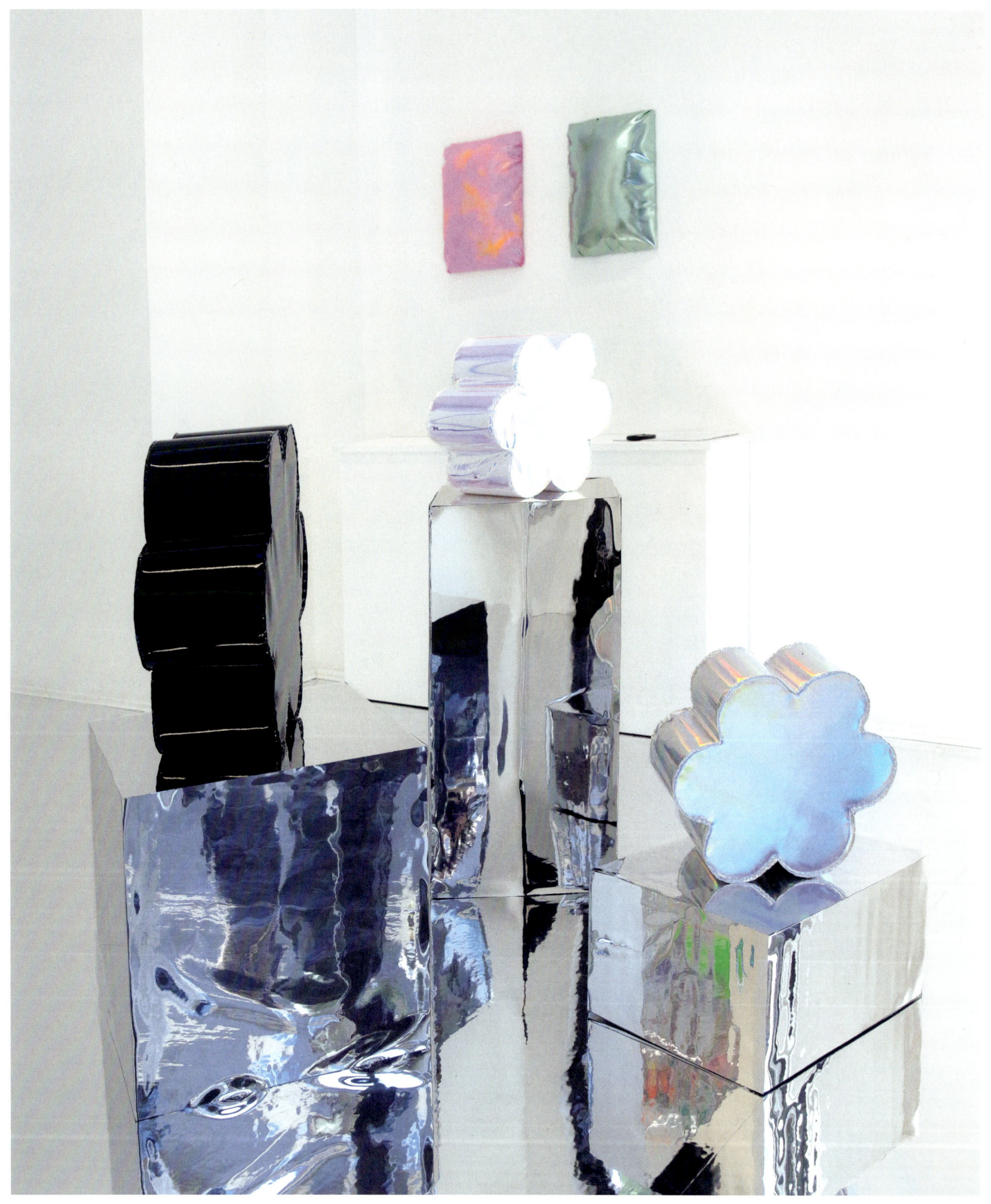

Italian artist **MATTIA SUGAMIELE**'s (b. 1984) installation *Artemis* saw him cover the floor and plinths in mirrored foil so that the discrete sculptures were reflected in the space along with the visitors, who were asked to wear shoe coverings to protect the mirrored floor. Artemis was the Greek goddess of the hunt and later of the moon, and it is also the name of NASA's new lunar programme to create the first human settlements on the moon in the next decade. Sugamiele created his own unsettling environment in a retro 1960s pop culture take on his own computer-designed sculptures. His work starts in the machine and then becomes three-dimensional. Basic flowers and rectangular forms are made from mirror or coloured reflective fabrics and stuffed with wadding or polystyrene so that they become soft forms of the original hard-edged digital originals.

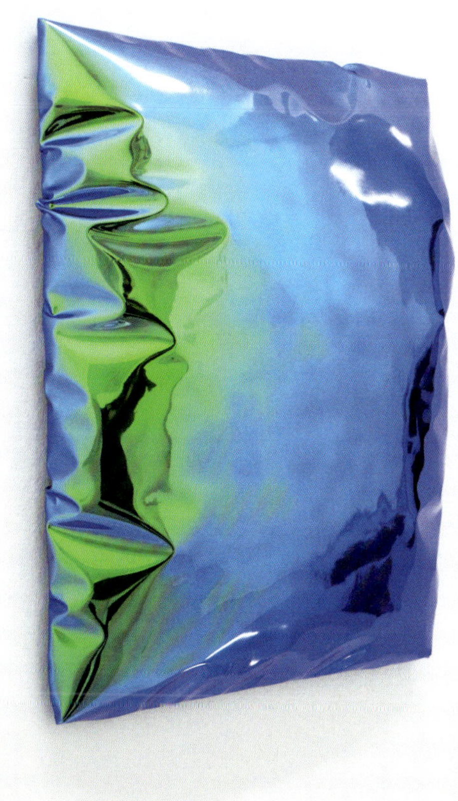

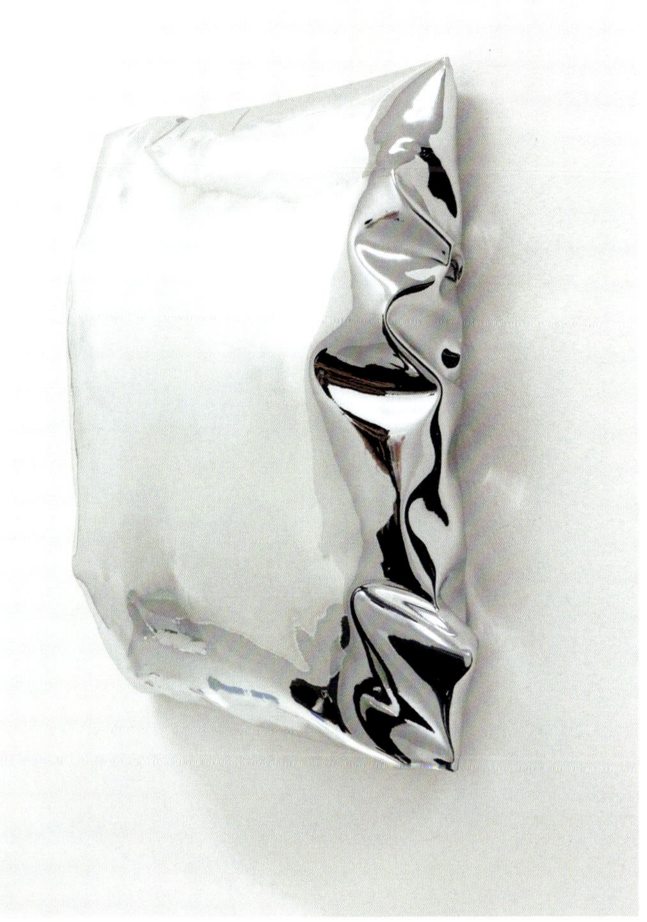

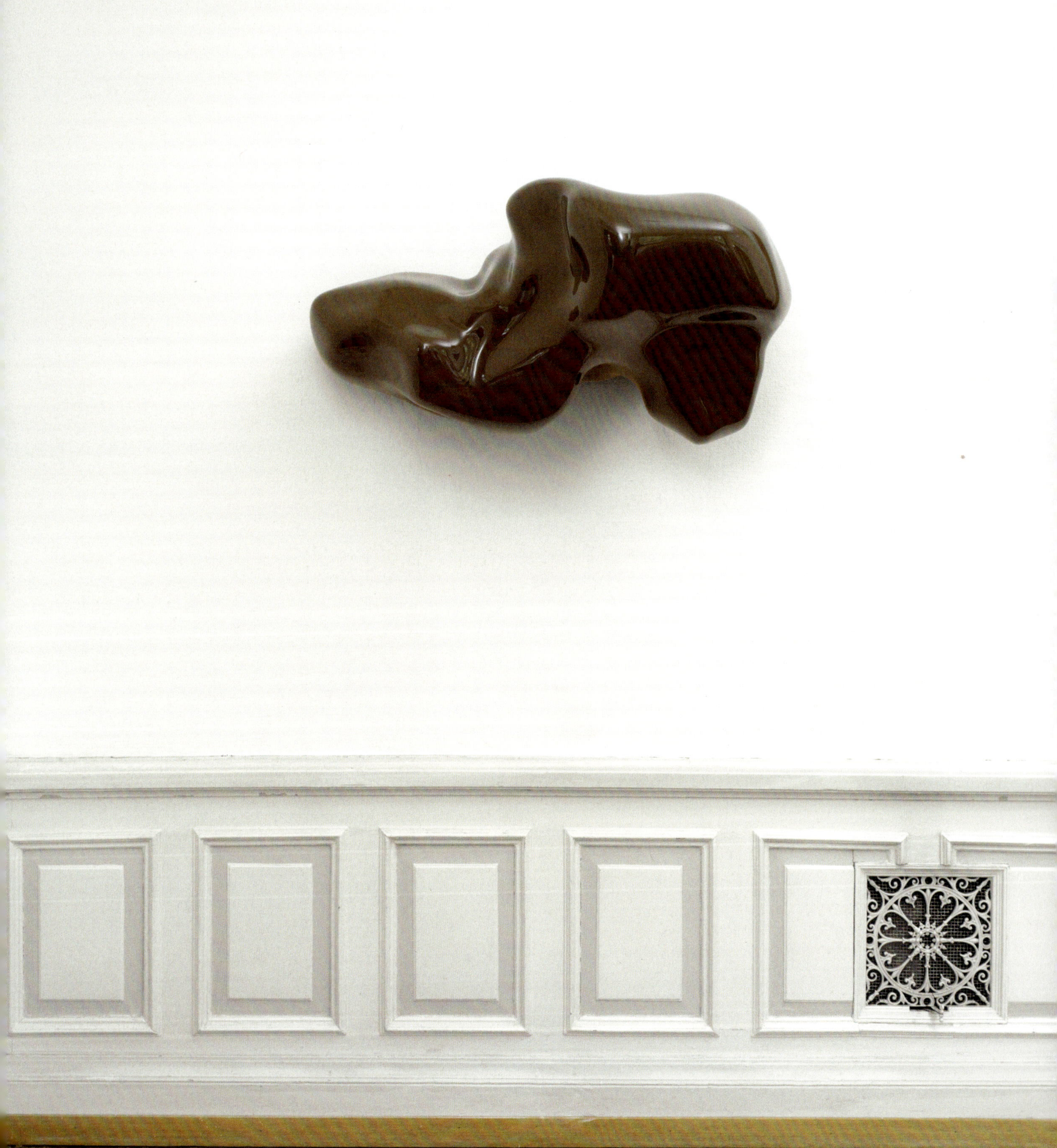

In the 1990s German artist **THOMAS RENTMEISTER** (b. 1964) was making minimalist sculptures of highly polished polyester resin in tones of brown and cream. These biomorphic forms were a bit at odds with his other, more expressive works. But, as with his *untitled* from 2001 (opposite) installed at the Villa Merkel in Esslingen, Germany, there is an understated humour to them. This work was a large brown polyester form that seemed to have extruded itself from the gallery wall or the electric plug. Its skin reflected the ornate room and the whole sculpture appeared as if at any moment it might scurry away. His floor sculptures (below) also reflect their environment, and appear as if large liquid droplets have seeped into the gallery.

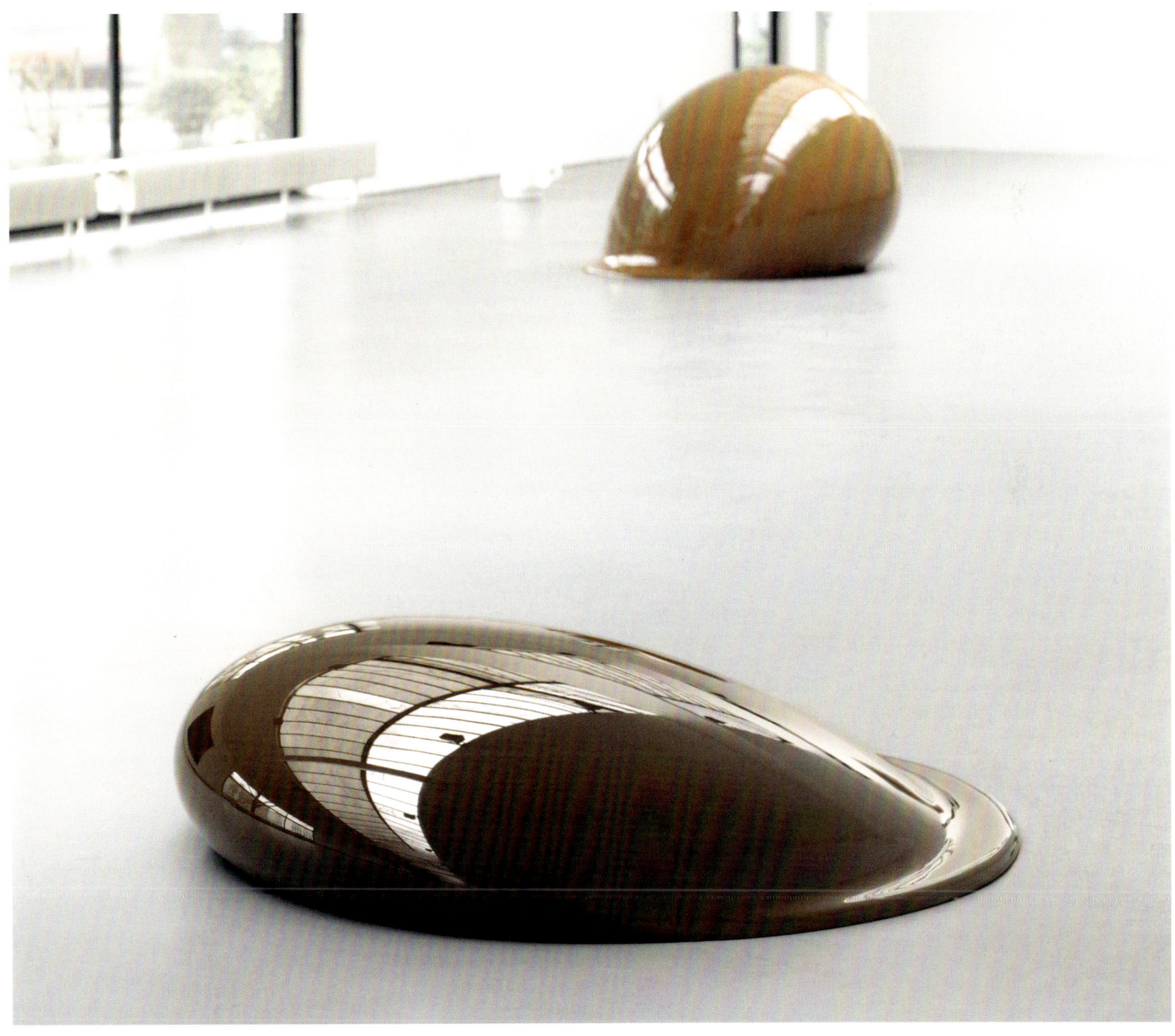

The work of Japanese artist **KENJI TOKI** (b. 1969) is a quiet and sophisticated rebuke to wasteful consumer consumption. His *Forms that are too fine to waste – Sainsbury's Organic Mango x4 – Lid* is just that: a protective lid from a supermarket. He has not covered the original polystyrene in lacquer but has copied the form by taking a plaster cast and then used a traditional Japanese method called *kanshitsu*, which involves layers of hemp strengthened by *urushi* (lacquer). The result is an object that is exactly the shape of the original disposable lid, but which has been transformed into a highly polished, reflective and desirable object. Reminiscent of traditional Japanese trays, it is made of completely natural materials, unlike the manmade lid, which is daily thrown away as rubbish.

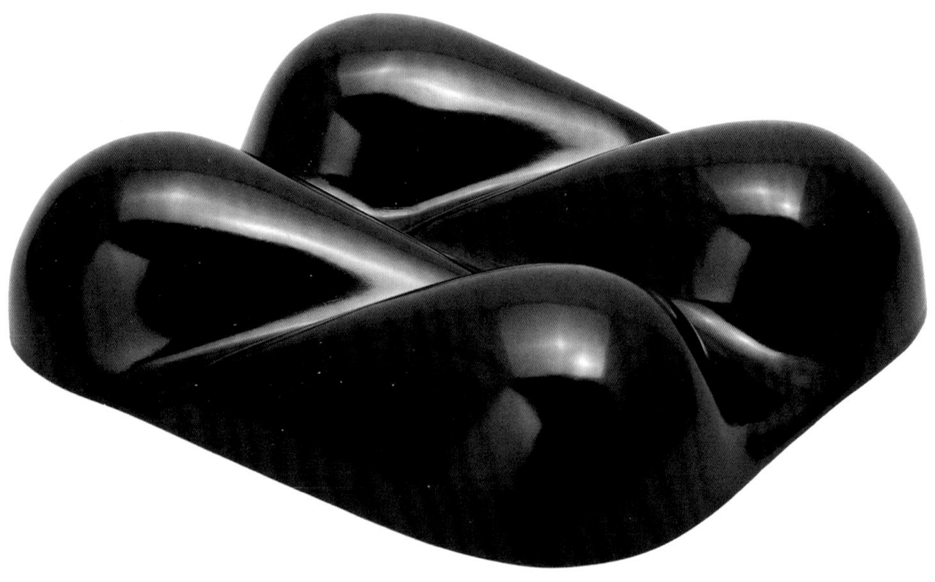

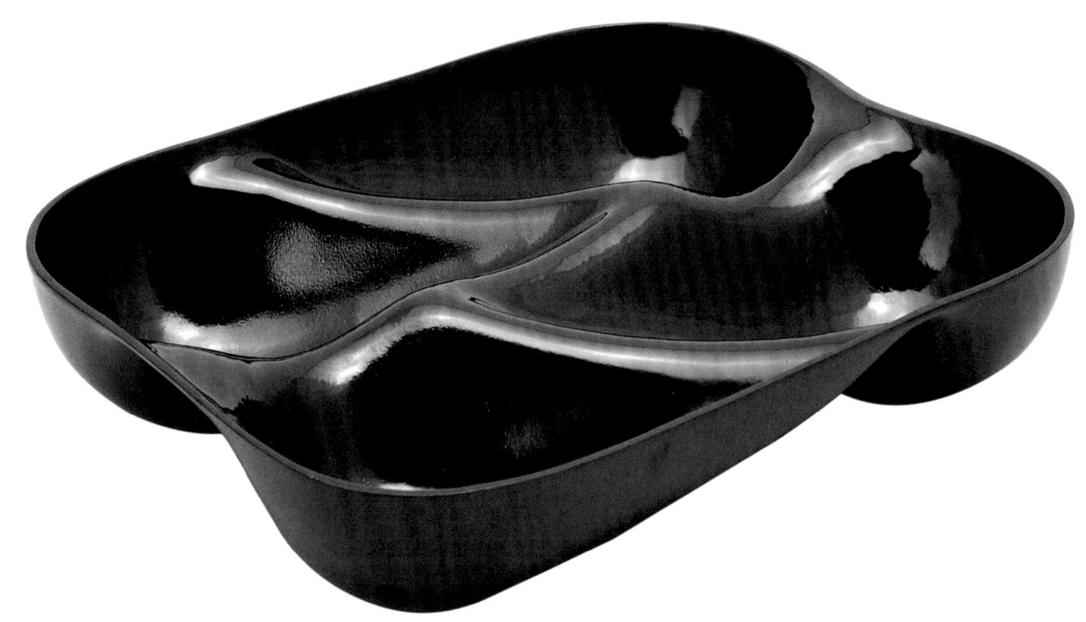

SARAH PUCILL is a British filmmaker and photographer. *Narcissus* is from her black-and-white feature film *Magic Mirror* (2013), based on the work of the French Surrealist writer and artist Claude Cahun. Born Lucy Schwob in 1894, she took the name Cahun in 1914, and was gender fluid in her imagery and life. Her androgynous look and challenging works have been made into 'living tableaux' by Pucill, whose film and photographs focus on Cahun's anti-autobiographical book, *Aveux non avenus* (1930; *Confessions Denied*), which includes the lines: 'Our mirrors are almost perfect. We still suffer from their vertical position.' In Pucill's film, three actresses continually dress up and apply makeup, so that it is difficult to tell their gender or identity, paralleling the fluidity of Cahun's own life and work. Cahun and her artistic collaborator, Marcel Moore, were sentenced to death by the Nazis for acts of resistance in Jersey, but the island was liberated before the sentence could be carried out.

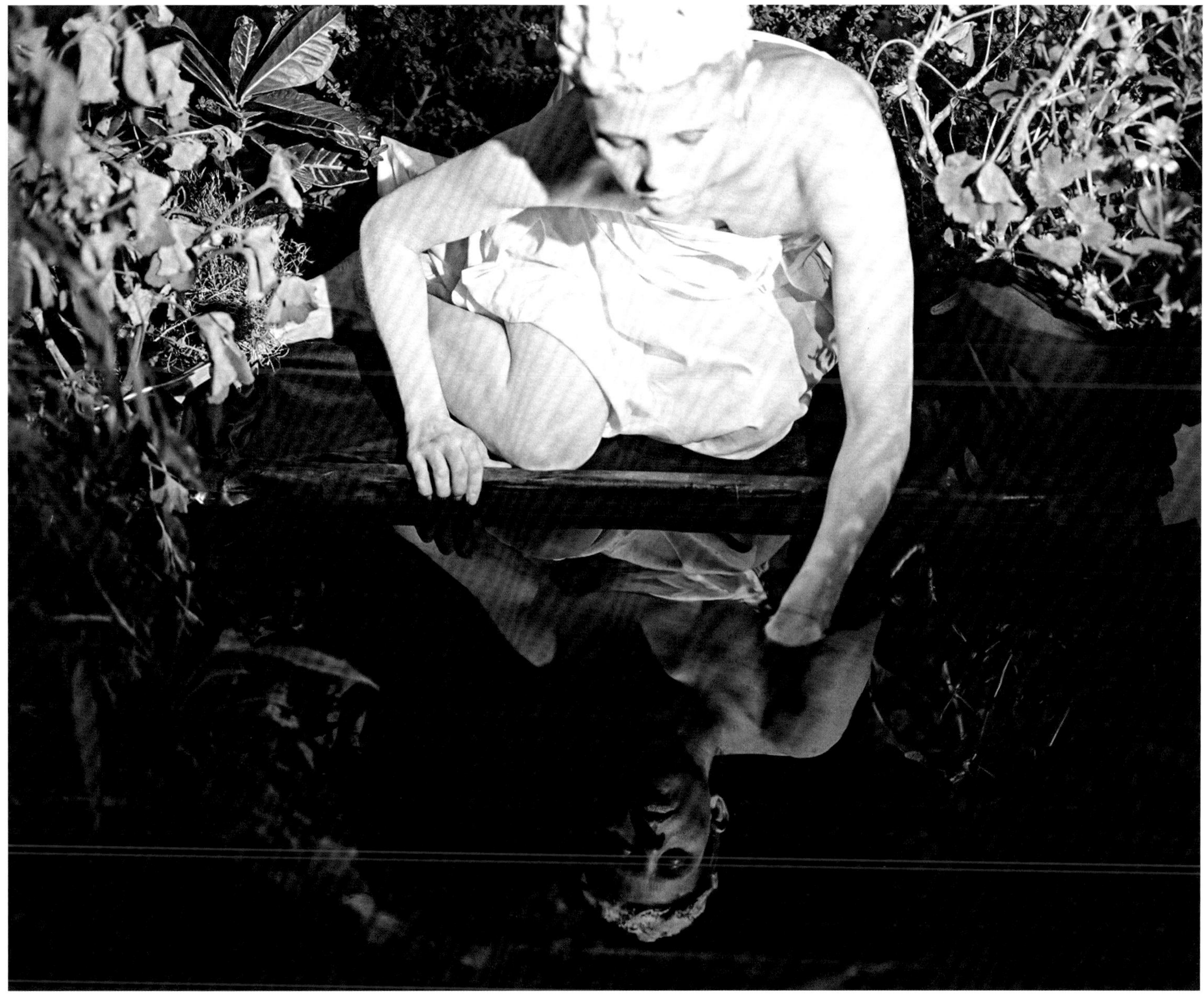

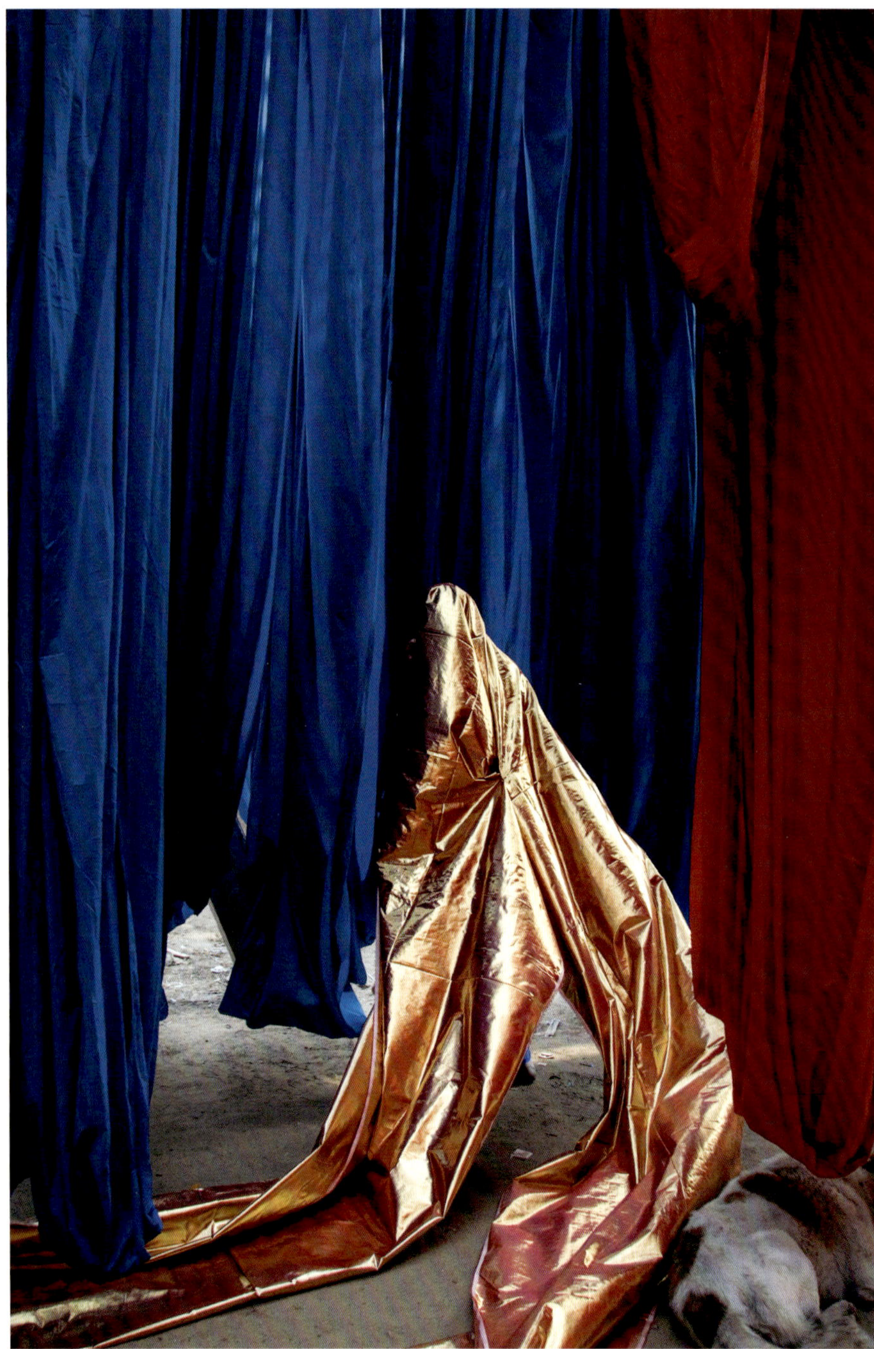

London-based Turkish artist **GÜLER ATES** (b. 1977) makes 'site responsive performances' in historic spaces. She documents women whom she has covered in long flowing shrouds of a single vibrant colour that reflect or contrast their architectural setting. Ates's extensive research into each space informs the movements and costumes. Her work allows the viewer to span time and, in looking at the past in the present, to question the future. Ates is from rural Turkey and during her childhood, books were rare; she now often works in libraries, places not always open to women. These images question who has access to knowledge and learning. In *She and the Dog* (above), the woman wears a bright copper-coloured drape, made in India, where the fabric was woven. In the *Blanket* series (2018), women wear reflective gold metallic heat blankets of the type given to survivors of disasters. In *Golden* (opposite) sensual gold fabric drapes over the body like liquid metal.

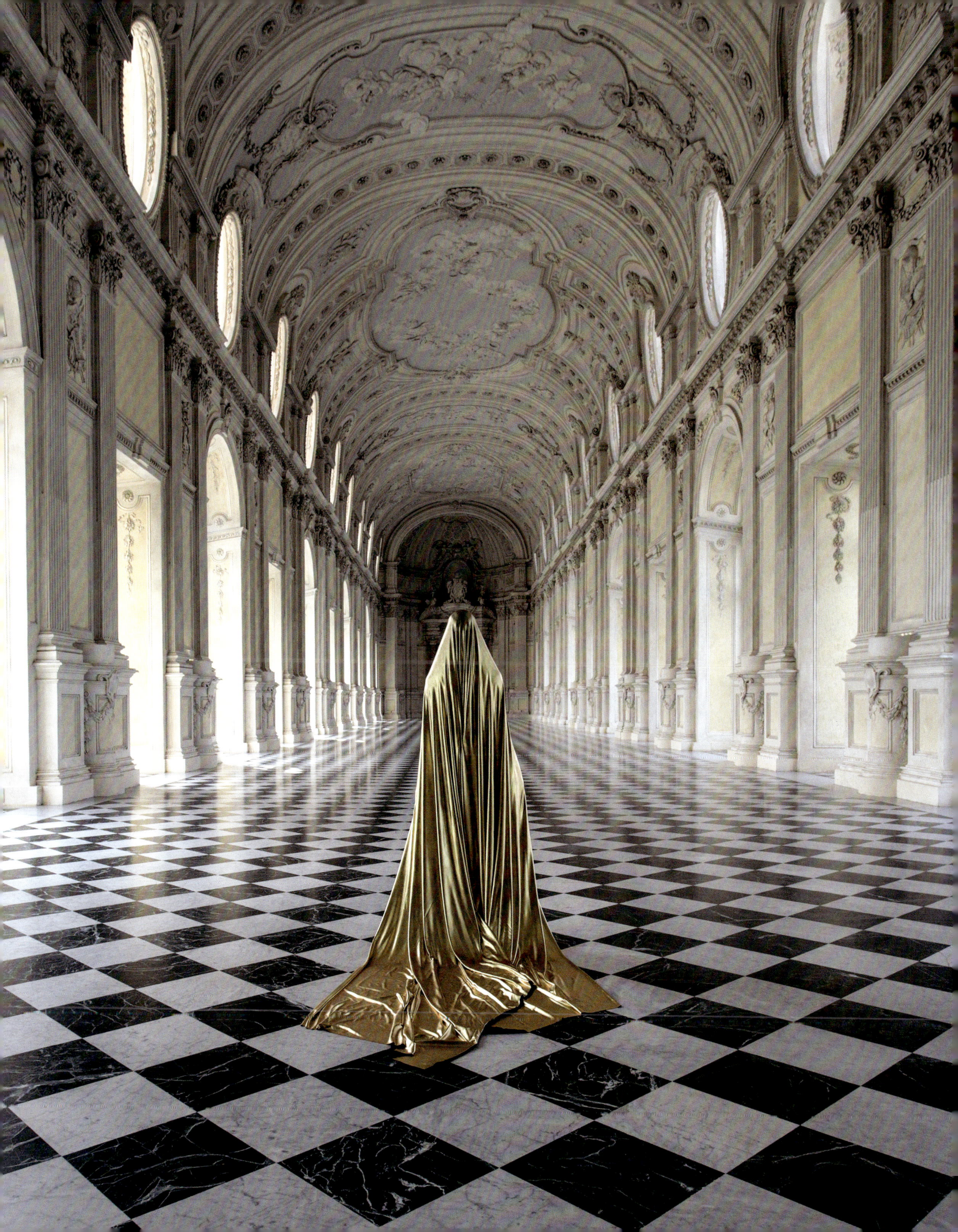

DILLON MARSH (b. 1981) is a South African artist who has used computer-assisted photography to explore the effects of the vast amount of mining the country has experienced for more than 100 years. In his series *For What It's Worth* he has documented the terrible price the landscape has paid for the extraction of copper, gold, platinum and diamonds, with vast mines stripping and scarring the ground where the deposits were found. Combining photography and CGI, Marsh has placed spheres of each of those materials into these barren landscapes in proportion to the amount of material removed. The country's first commercial copper mine was opened in Springbok in 1852, but like most is now disused. Marsh's imagery is haunting and all the more frightening for the emptiness of the landscapes, free of the people and their suffering in bringing those metals to the surface and the market.

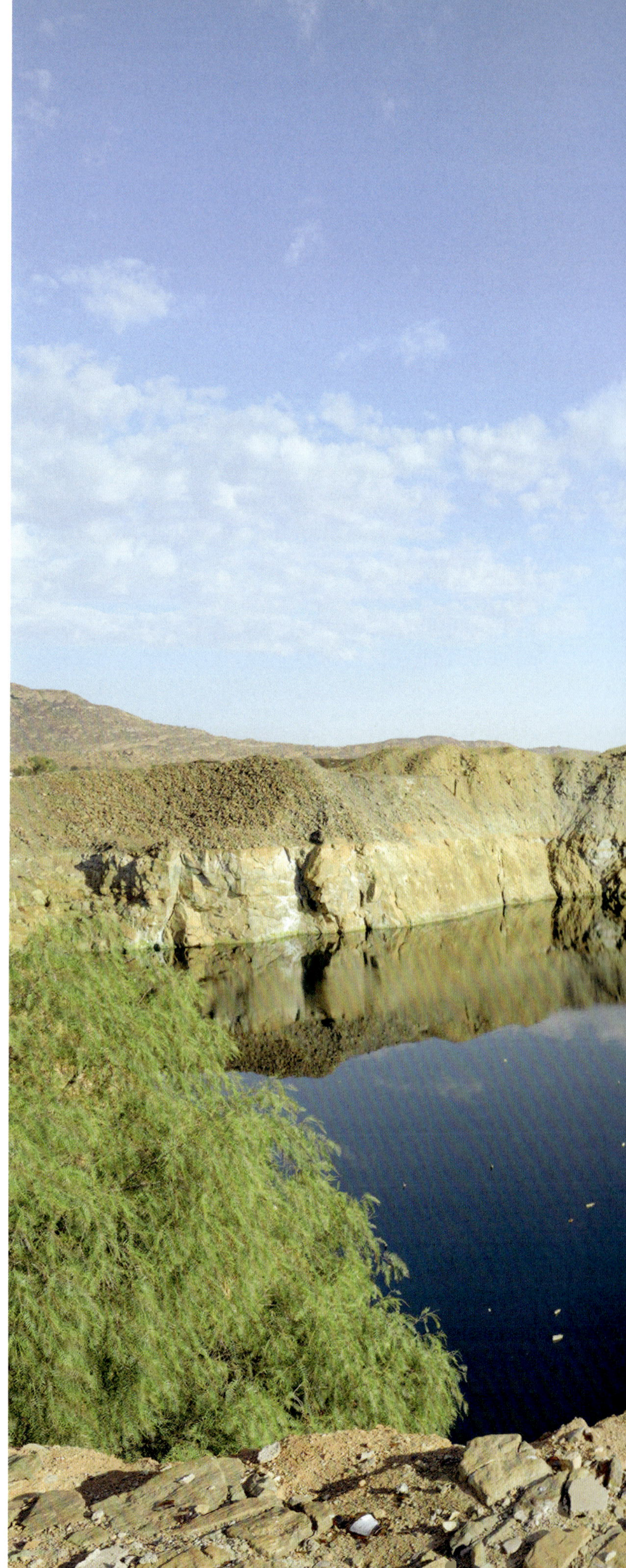

O'okiep Mine – 284,000 tonnes of copper, 2014
Digital inkjet print
100 × 125 cm (39⅜ × 49¼ in)

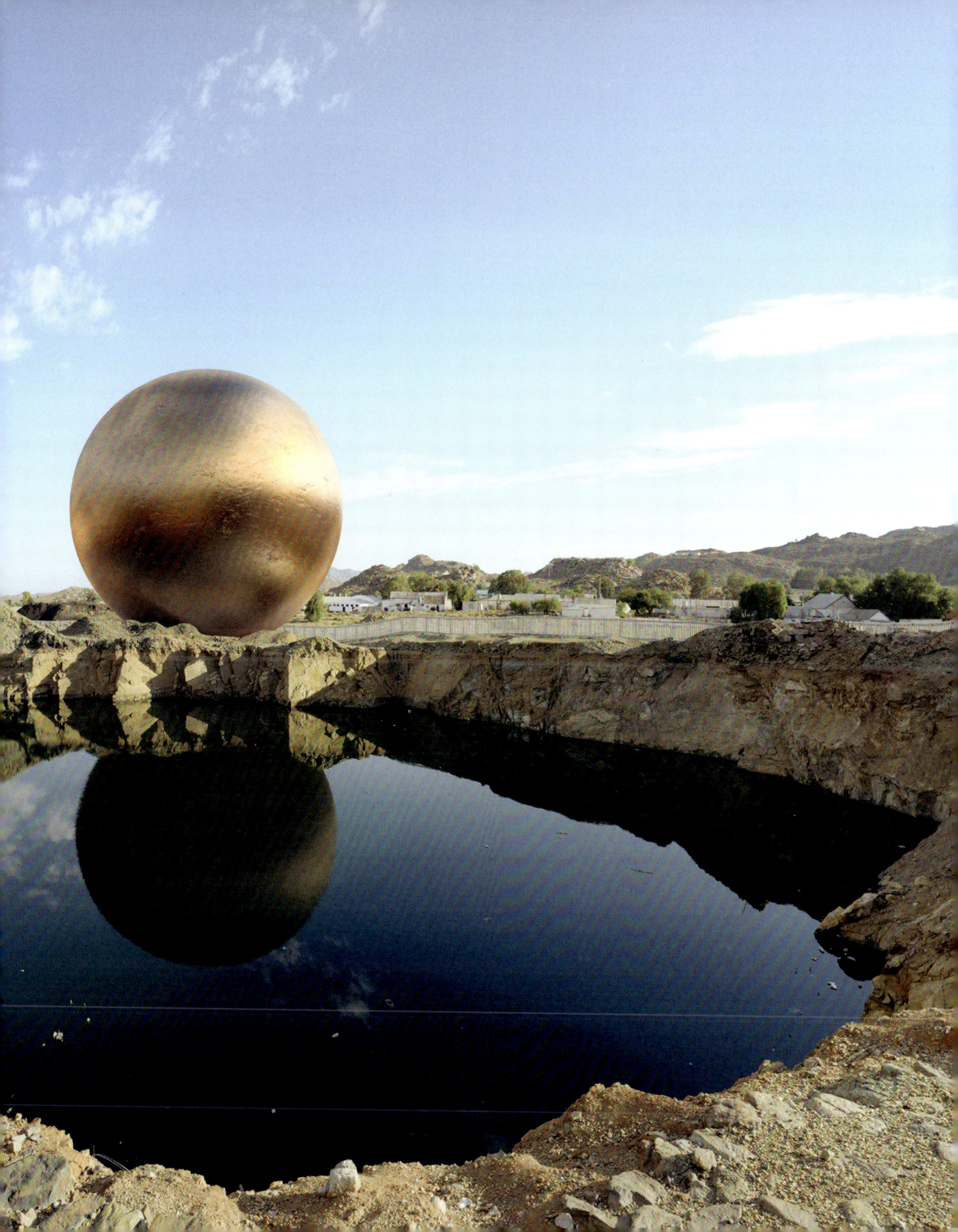

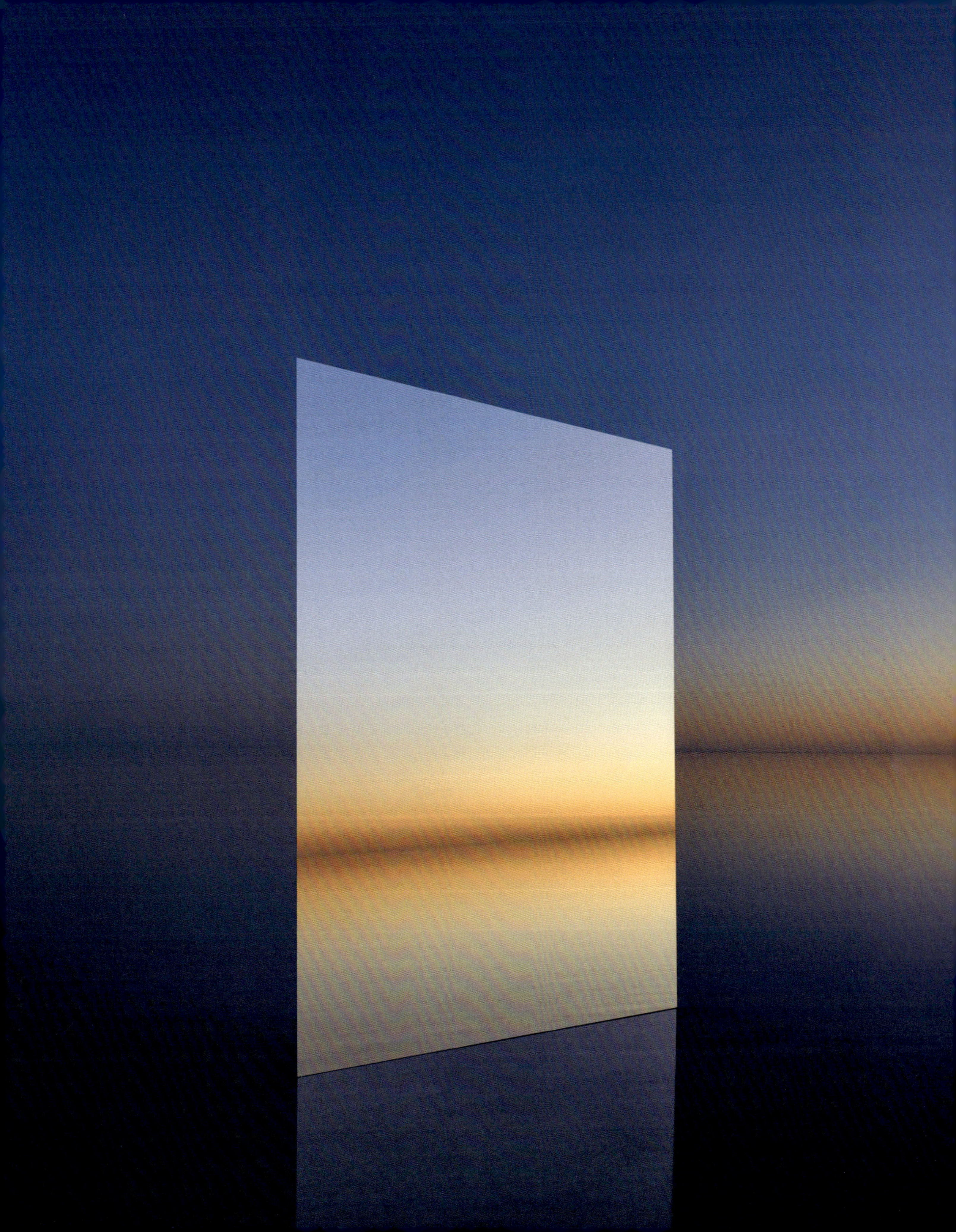

Lake Eyre (Kathi Thanda) is a salt lake and extensive salt pan in the central desert of Australia. For his *Vanity* series of images, Australian photographer **MURRAY FREDERICKS** (b. 1970) carried a large mirror out to the desolate, haunting and beautiful site and placed it in the water before documenting the almost alien landscape. Other images show cloud formations duplicated or the streaks of stars across the night sky. He mainly took images at dawn or dusk and the poetic colours and atmosphere of the site seem almost computer generated. He has said: 'The mirror can be seen as emblematic of our obsession with ourselves, individually, and collectively… [R]ather than reflecting our own "surface" image, the mirror is positioned to draw our gaze out and away from ourselves, into the environment, driving towards an emotional engagement with light, colour and space.'

Mirror #8, 2017
Digital pigment print on cotton rag
120 × 160 cm (47¼ × 63 in)

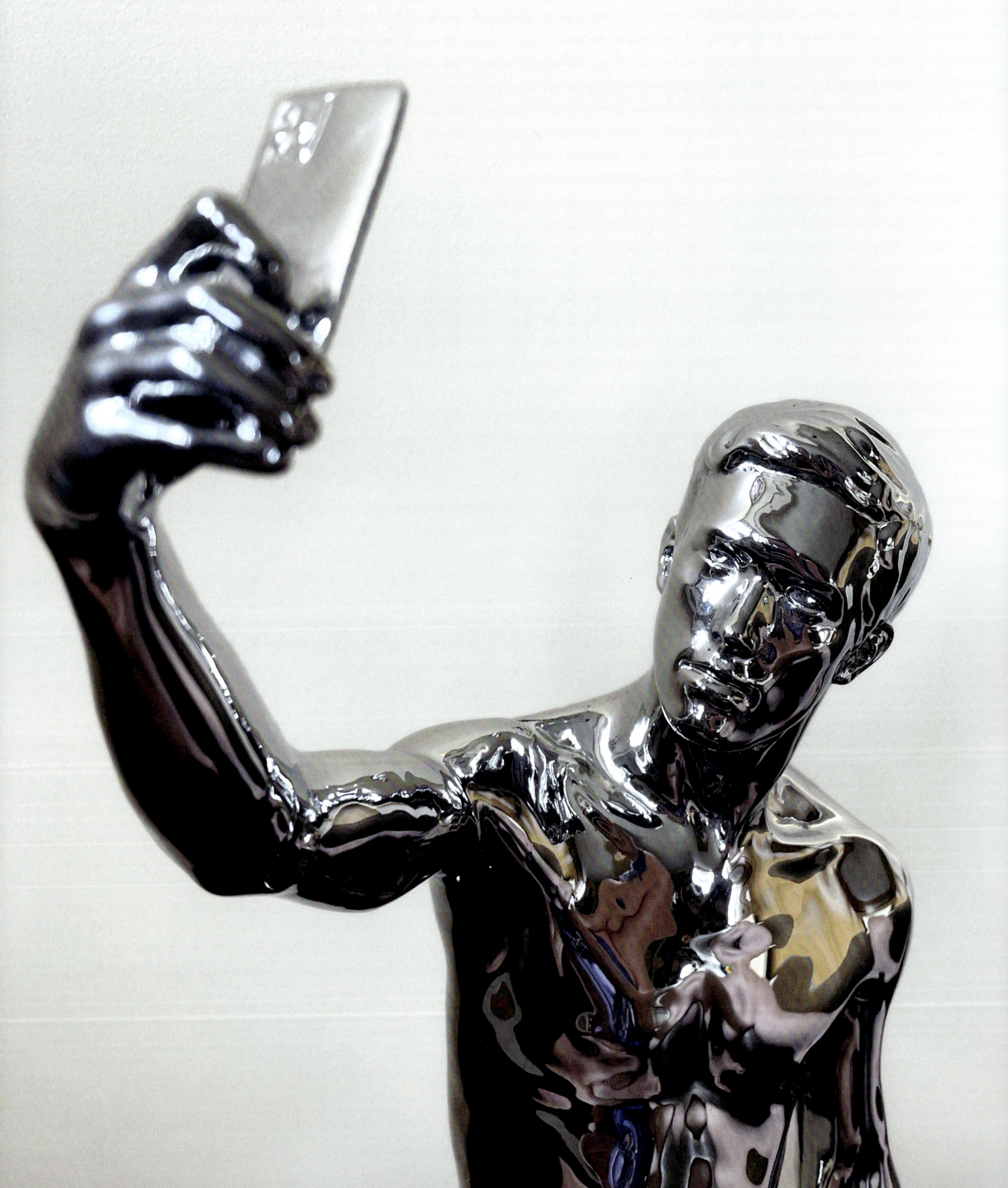

SELFIES

Artists have always been interested in themselves. The self-portrait has a long history, from the ancient Egyptian monuments to ancient Greek and Roman tomb statuary, through the Renaissance, and on through later art movements to the present day. Perhaps the modern 'selfie' starts to come into focus with the self portraits of Vincent van Gogh in the nineteenth century. He aimed to examine his physical likeness and his internal struggle for self. In the early twentieth century, Egon Schiele and Frida Kahlo were two exponents of the intense, unrelenting, unflattering self-portrait.

The birth of photography made it easier to document the upper classes, and with its relatively low cost, also the working people of the world; as Kodak and others brought out inexpensive cameras, such as the Kodak Brownie, the general populace could document their own lives. The next major step towards the selfie was the Polaroid, which became popular in the 1960s and '70s. Andy Warhol is perhaps its best-known proponent, taking more than 100,000 Polaroid snaps of New York's stars, including himself. Warhol's dressing up for the images he took has found its natural fruition online, where millions are having their fifteen minutes of fame.

Adam Smith said in his book *The Money Game* (1968): 'The first thing you have to know is yourself. A man who knows himself can step outside himself and watch his own reactions like an observer.' This is truly a difficult endeavour, and even with the help of the modern smartphone, with its camera and its associated selfie culture, many who now make a daily (or more) self-portrait, never stop to consider who it really is in that digital reflection.

The smartphone has made the modern selfie truly ubiquitous, and often unintentionally (or intentionally) graphic. I have written about the idea that we have all become porn stars, now that dating apps demand more and more content of an adult nature. Adult content tends to seep out, as many famous people can attest, and certainly has become a topic for contemporary artists. Even the simple act of posting, as self-promotion, has been deconstructed by artists in this chapter. The notion of the innocent or spontaneous 'perfect moment' in photographic form has long faded, as image-altering applications become freely available. AI can imagine in a few seconds what we looked like as a child, or will do as an old person, and then post it into an eternal digital space.

This new type of mirror reflects the state of popular culture and the self-obsession encouraged by the likes of Facebook and Instagram. Apps allow the sitter to place all sorts of flattering filters to make them appear less wrinkled, healthier or, in the case of Cindy Sherman, more surreal. Her current Instagram feed is like a sharpened pin in the bubble of self-deception and flattery. Younger artists such as J. D. Smith, Juno Calypso and Stuart Sandford also clearly dissect their contemporaries' fascination with the self.

Stuart Sandford, *Adlocutio (Sean Ford)*, 2021. Mirror-polished stainless steel, 53.5 × 19.5 × 16.5 cm (21⅛ × 7¾ × 6½ in)
Unique work + 1 AP

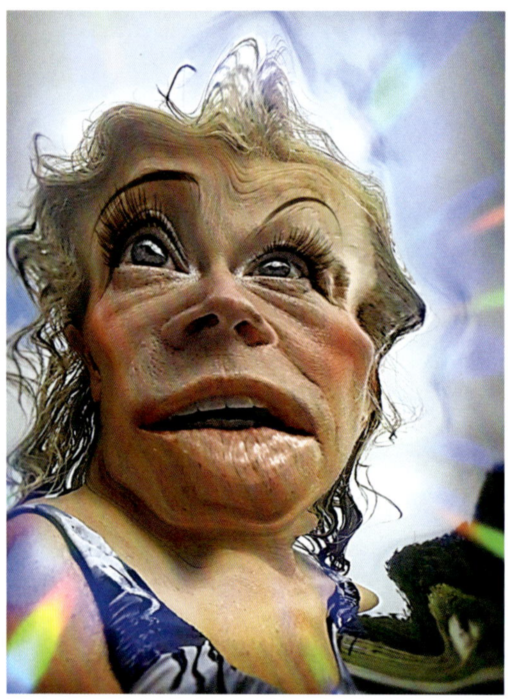

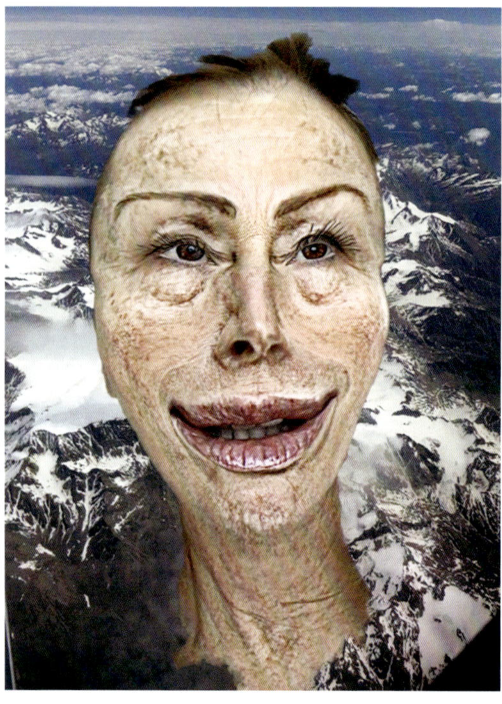

American artist **CINDY SHERMAN** (b. 1954) has long been fascinated by the performative nature of how to be a woman in a patriarchal world and the many roles required. From her early *Untitled Film Stills* (1977–80) to the many photographic iterations of her altered self, she has explored the world of costume and makeup to create startling images of what social norms of certain types of woman can, or might, or should look like. She does this by using her own face as a starting point. When she started to make her Instagram 'selfies' (2017) she used digital tools to alter her image, taking the process and the results forward into the digital selfie age. Sherman has said that 'I actually hate the idea of selfies', and 'I really kind of cringe at [the] thought' that many of the general public think of her as the 'queen of selfies'.

MATHIAS VEF is a German photographer who works with many post-processing systems and filters to develop complex and striking images. For his *Destitute of Myself* he started with a selfie image and then worked on it extensively using Adobe Photoshop to get the ghostly essence of an image. The multiple layering of himself as imagery creates visual and physiological depth. The image harkens back to views of large-scale photographic negatives that were used in commercial printing, though here he has only his image to market. Selfies are of course a form of self-marketing used on social media to increase personal brand awareness, and this series of works highlights that.

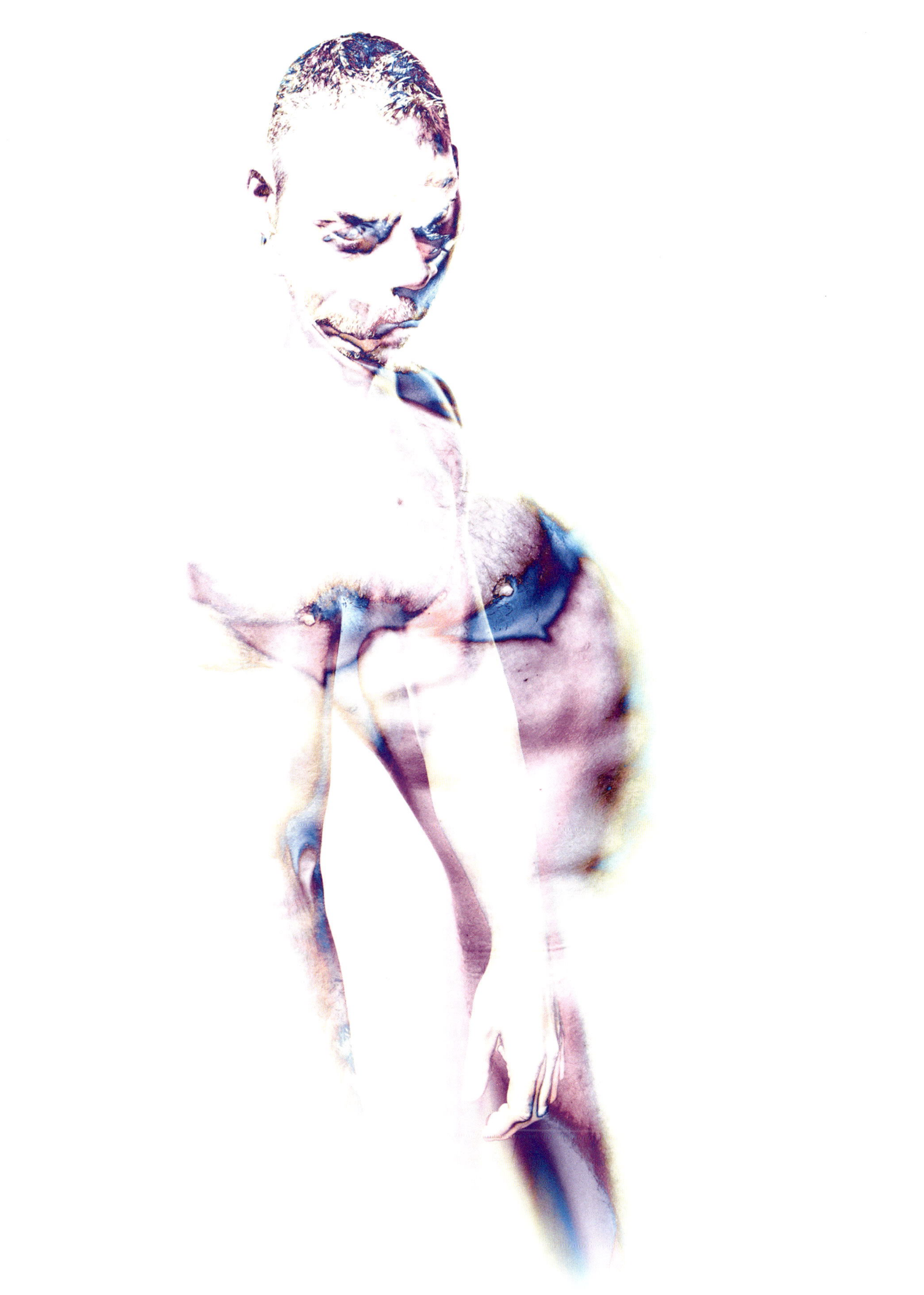

Artists have made self-portraits for hundreds of years, be they sculptures or, more commonly, paintings. The camera and now the cellphone have made the process much simpler. Canadian artist **AA BRONSON** (b. 1946), one of the founders of the group General Idea, has used reflective surfaces in his private and group work (see pp. 85–87). In *Mirror Sequences*, a series of photo pieces from 1969–70, Bronson documented himself using a number of small curved mirrors (below). We see the camera in front of his face as he frames his body, or parts of his body, and focuses the lens onto himself, as well as the many mirrors and reflections of his body. The layered work was made without filters or self-censorship. Bronson has returned to the documentation of self over the years, including with *Mirror Photo #7* (opposite) and in his daily Instagram feed.

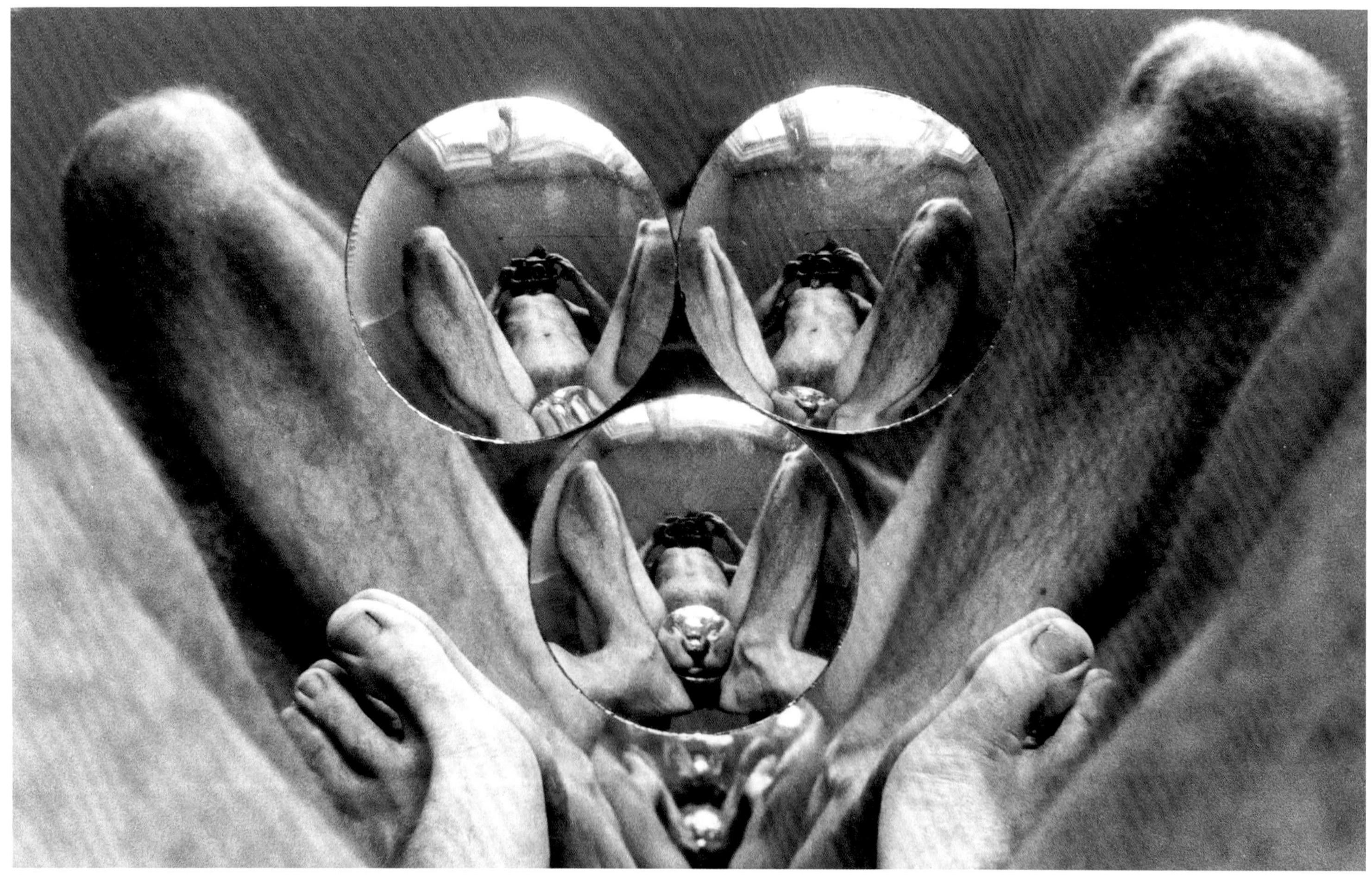

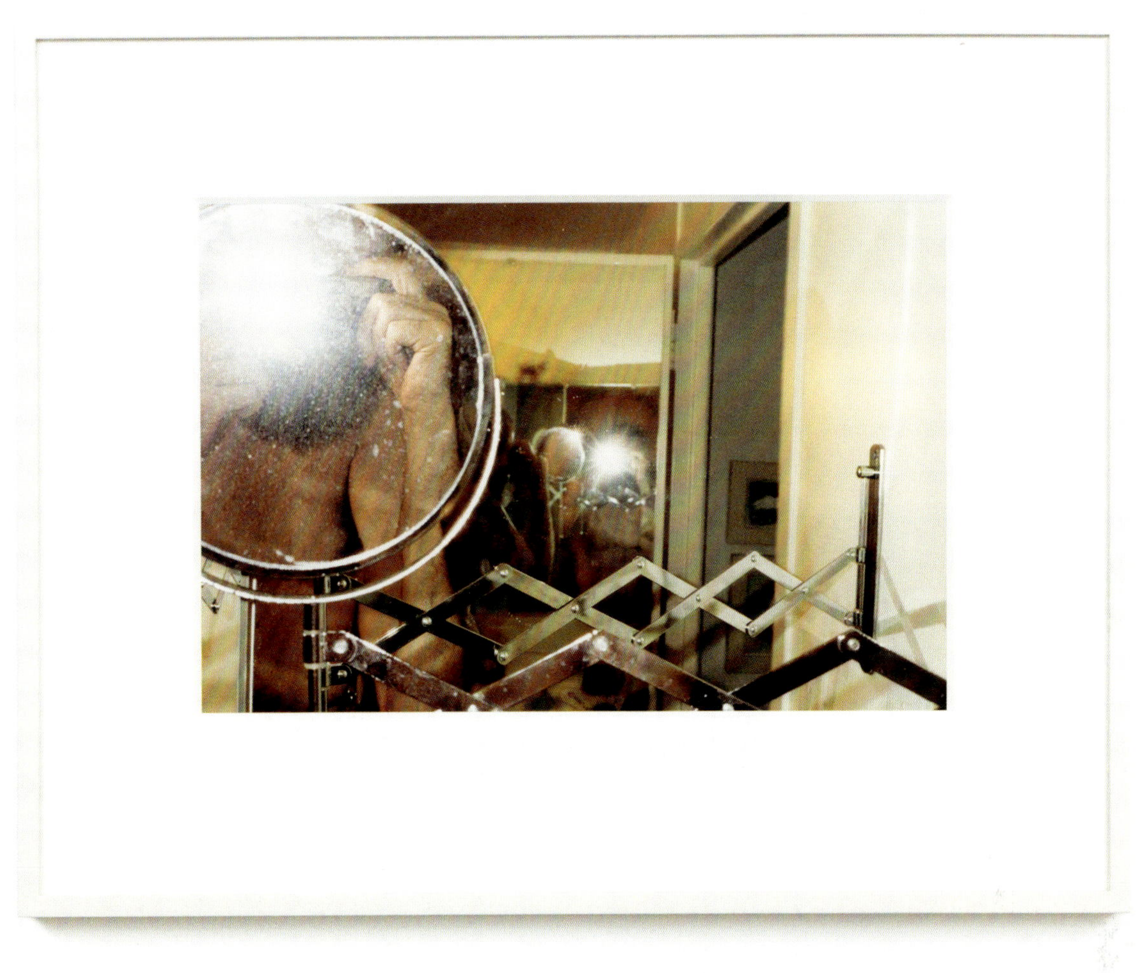

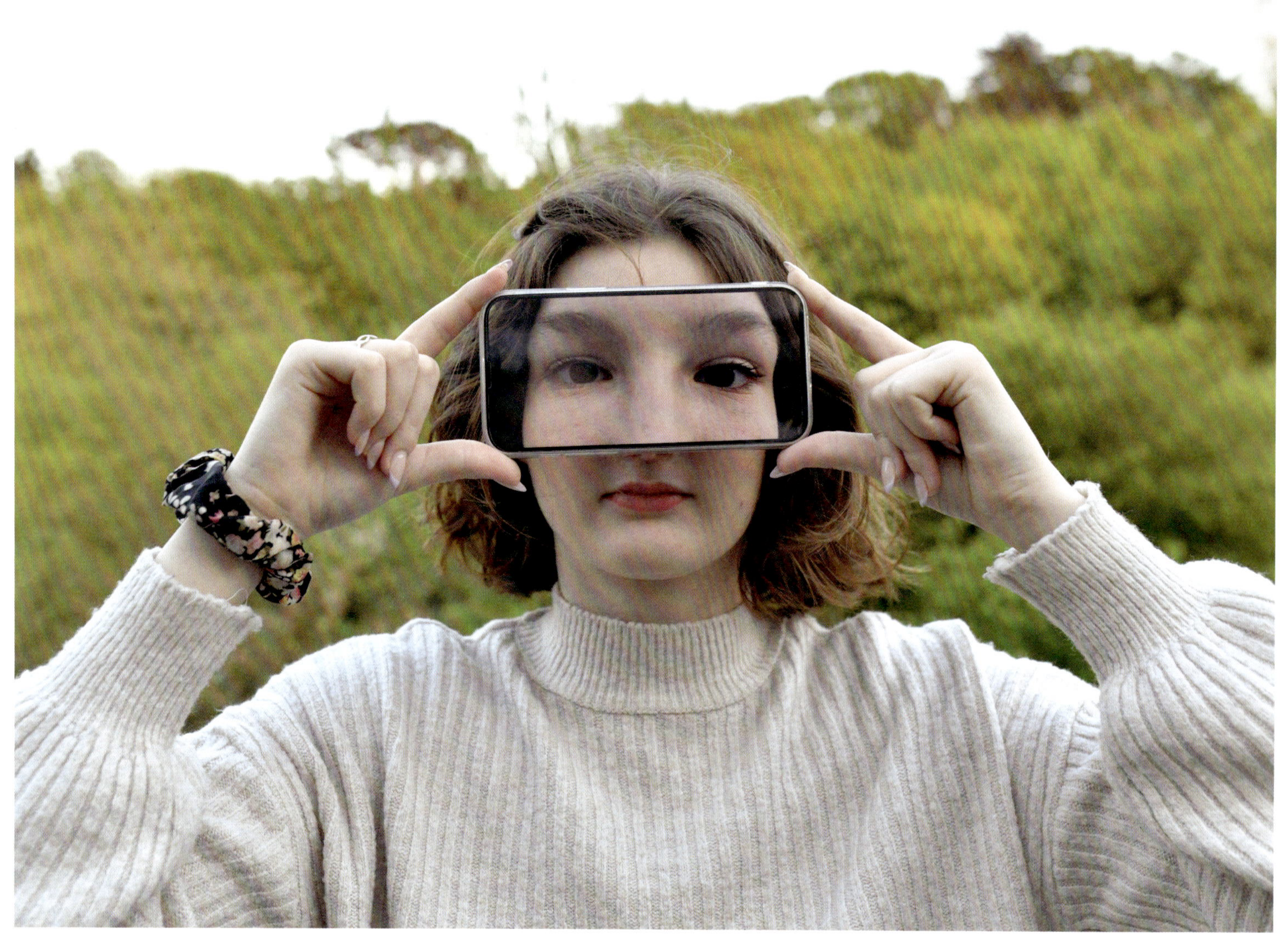

British photographer **TIM WILLCOCKS** has made a series of works called *The Screenface Ones*, where he contacted sitters on social media, then met them in the real world, to make a complex image involving their own digital device. He takes an initial image of them on their mobile phone or laptop and edits it on the device, as they will retain this image as another work. He then gets them to move the device into position and takes a final photograph, with a professional digital camera, which he allows the sitter to approve of or discard. He feels that the procedure, and photography as an art form in general, 'is essentially a collaborative process'. Willcocks leads the process and has a concrete idea of what the final image will look like before starting but knows that it is important for the sitter to be happy as the resultant image will become part of their online identity when he posts it.

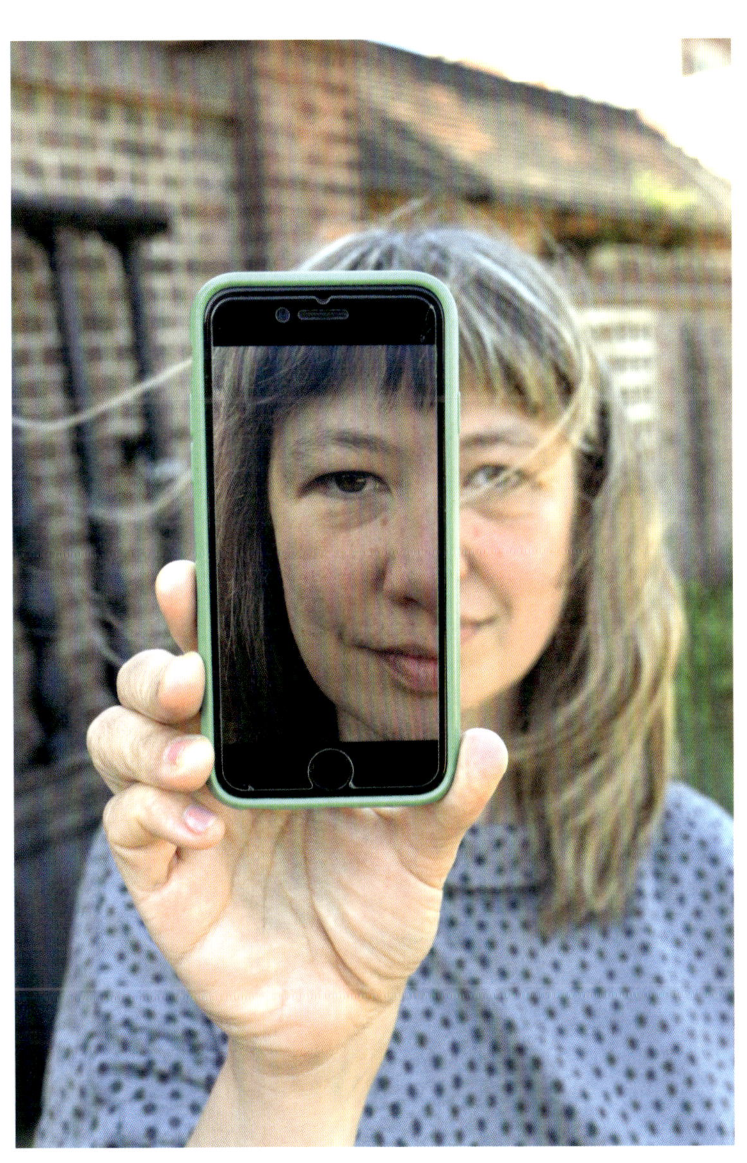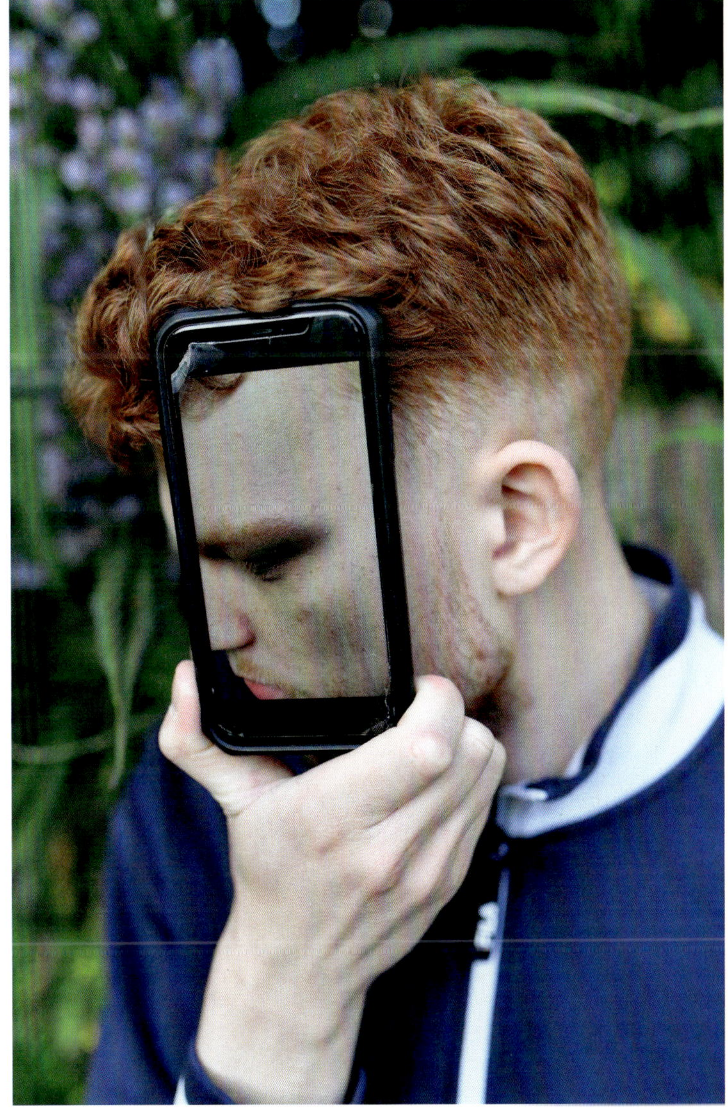

British artist **DAWN WOOLLEY** (b. 1980) has made a series of photographic works called *The Substitute* where she has replaced her physical body with that of a life-sized printed colour photograph of herself. These 'selfies' also include a living male figure who is in interaction with her. In *The Substitute (Jay Tunnel)* we see the live three-dimensional Jay laying on the cold tile floor of the entrance to a tunnel as he lovingly caresses Woolley's photographic face. Her double, her substitute, exists in two dimensions, like the compressed image of a real-time event into a photograph. We have a doubling of the process as well as a doubling of her as a person. In *The Substitute (bed16)* we see her in imagined coitus as her 2D burgundy-painted toe nails wrap around the real, 3D soles of her lover's feet. The viewer is two times the voyeur in these works. *The Substitute* reflects on how much viewers of selfies are on the outside.

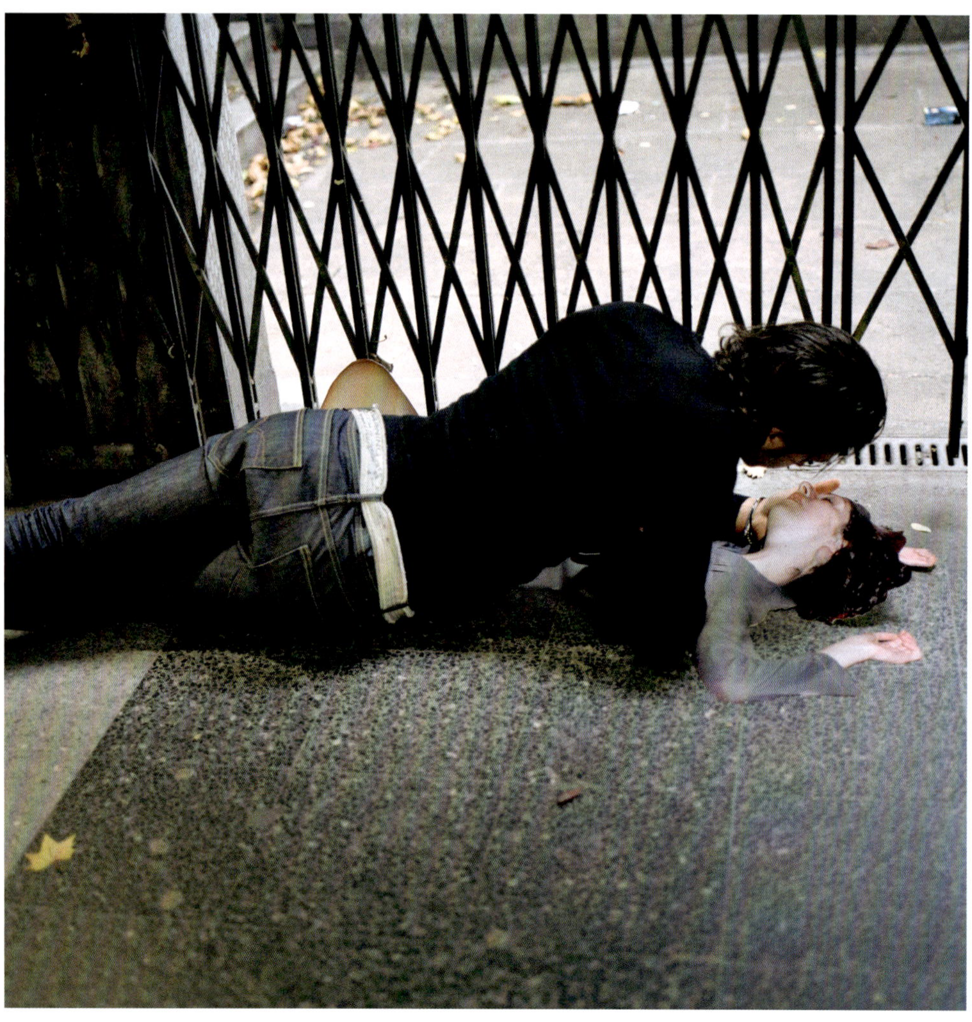

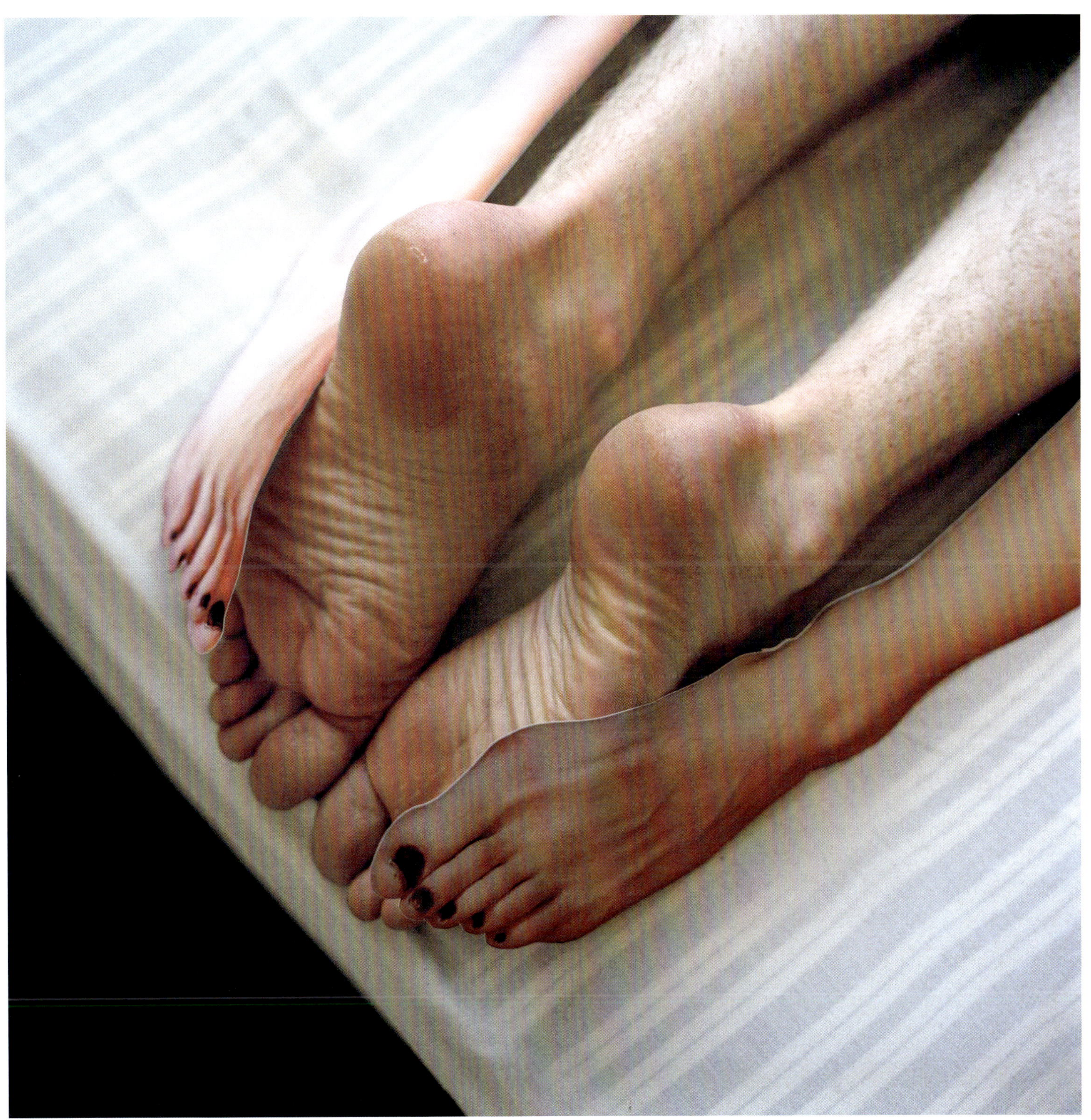

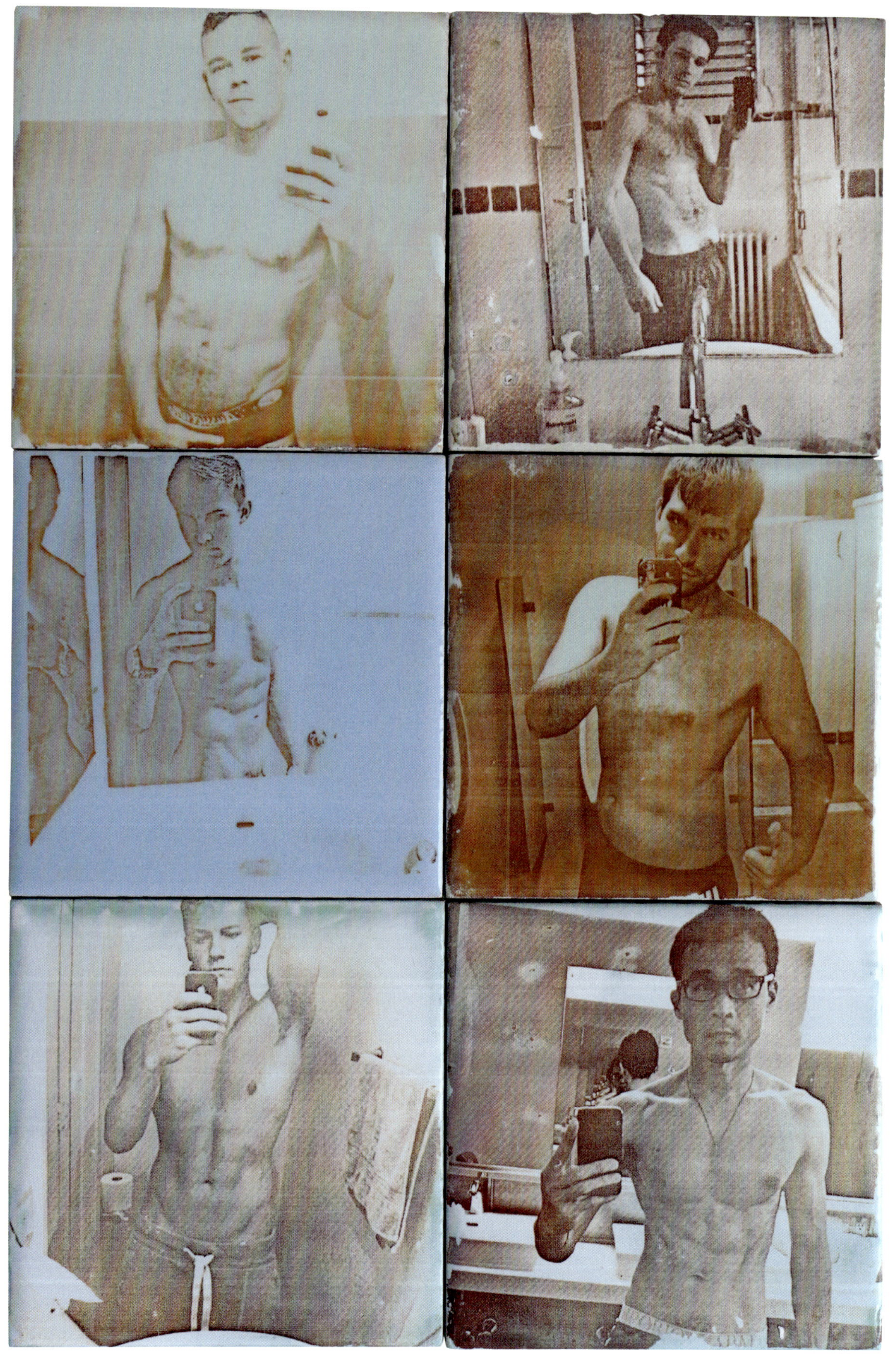

Spanish photographer **DAVID TRULLO**
(b. 1969) took to the internet to gather an
array of images of gay men taking selfies,
all bare-chested and always reflected
in bathroom mirrors, which they had
uploaded to the profile pages of their social
media accounts. Such images, clothed or
nude, are common on gay dating apps.
Each image of the edition (of five sets of
six) is a unique selfie, forming part of a
wide variety of body types, races and levels
of self-awareness. Trullo's project suggests
that the internet has, in a way, turned
everyone who uses it into Narcissus, who
didn't recognize his own reflection and
fell in love with it. In the myth he melted
away from the passion burning inside
him, and a narcissus sprang up in his
place – a daffodil flower, which looks like
a staring eye. Trullo's men are not so much
'narcissistic' in the exhibitionist sense,
but are visual messages to those on the
other side of the mirror/screen.

Belgian artist **DEBORA DE HAES** works
across many media, including photography,
digital imagery and painting. All her
works inspect the female body (often her
own) and through various lenses change
or expand on human flesh. In *Life is
possible only where life can exist*, she has
imagined what the cosmic Big Bang might
look like from a female perspective. 'The
position of my arm and hand is on that
location in time and space where life can
exist,' she says; in any other position the
universe as we know it would not have
come into existence.

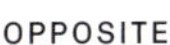

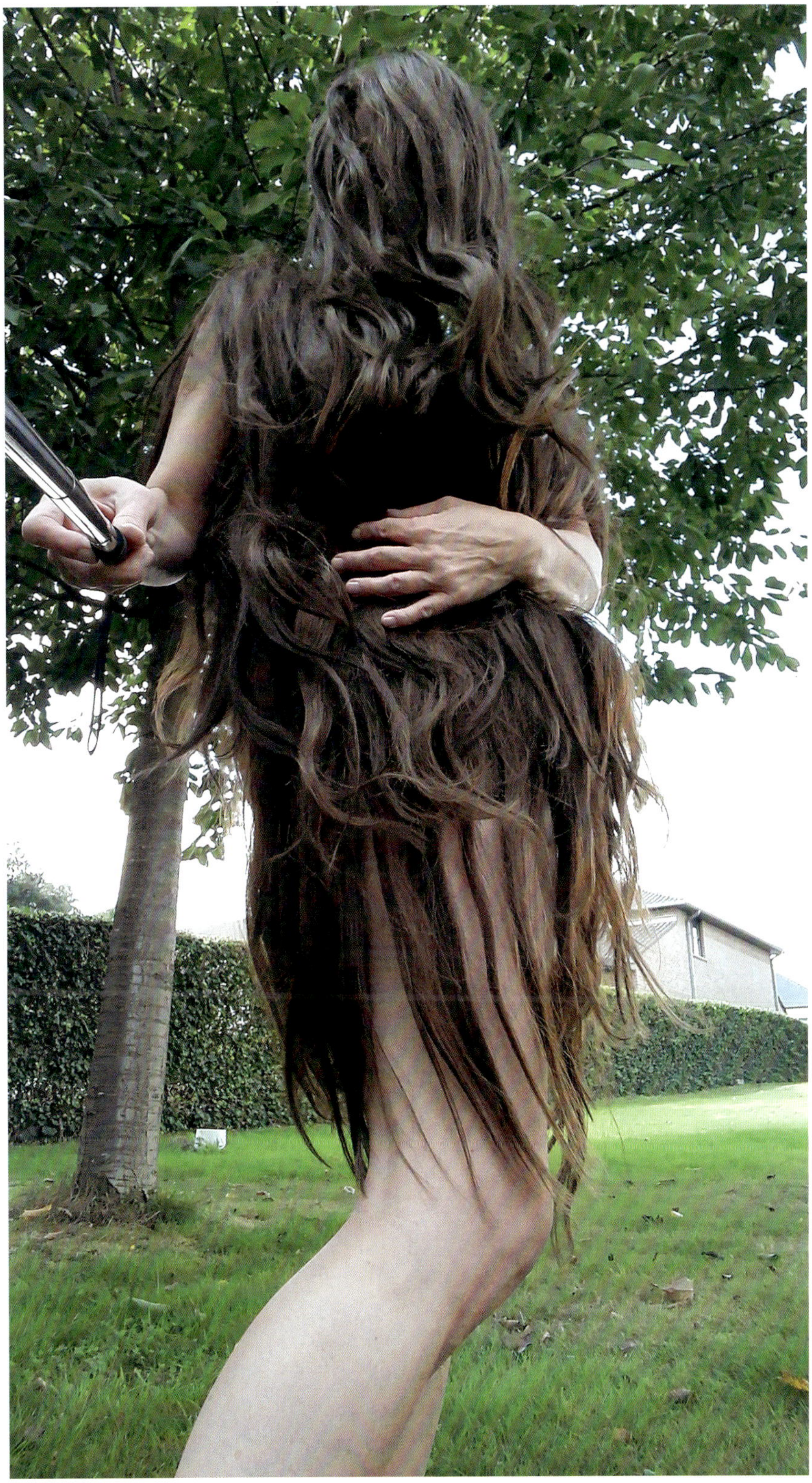

British artist **JUNO CALYPSO** (b. 1989) is a photographer who uses herself for the basis of fictional self-portraits. She has created the character of 'Joyce' as her stand-in. Calypso gained access to an American hotel to make a body of work by posing as a travel writer. The series is called *The Honeymoon*, and the hotel specializes in the assumed desires (heart-shaped bathtubs…) of romantic newlyweds, or those trying for a romantic getaway to rekindle lost flames of love. In many shots Calypso is masked in a facial wrap, pampering herself, in a mix of 1950s glamour and futuristic dread. In the end we never see the real 'Juno', any more than we see the real person in any self-conscious selfie. She says, 'My generation came of age at the same time as digital photography, the internet and the selfie. It was an awkward time to be alive'; and, 'All of my work essentially boils down to two things: desire and disappointment.'

Mirror, 2015
Digital image
Dimensions variable

OPPOSITE
The Honeymoon Suite, 2015
Digital print
152.4 × 101.6 cm (60 × 40 in)

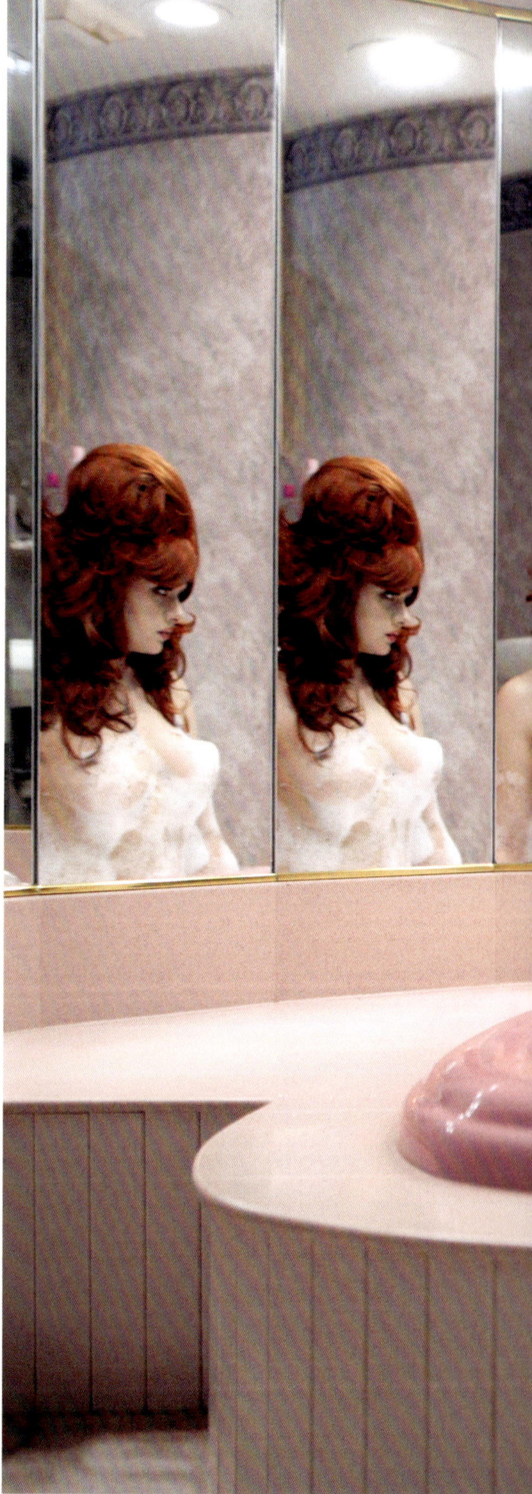

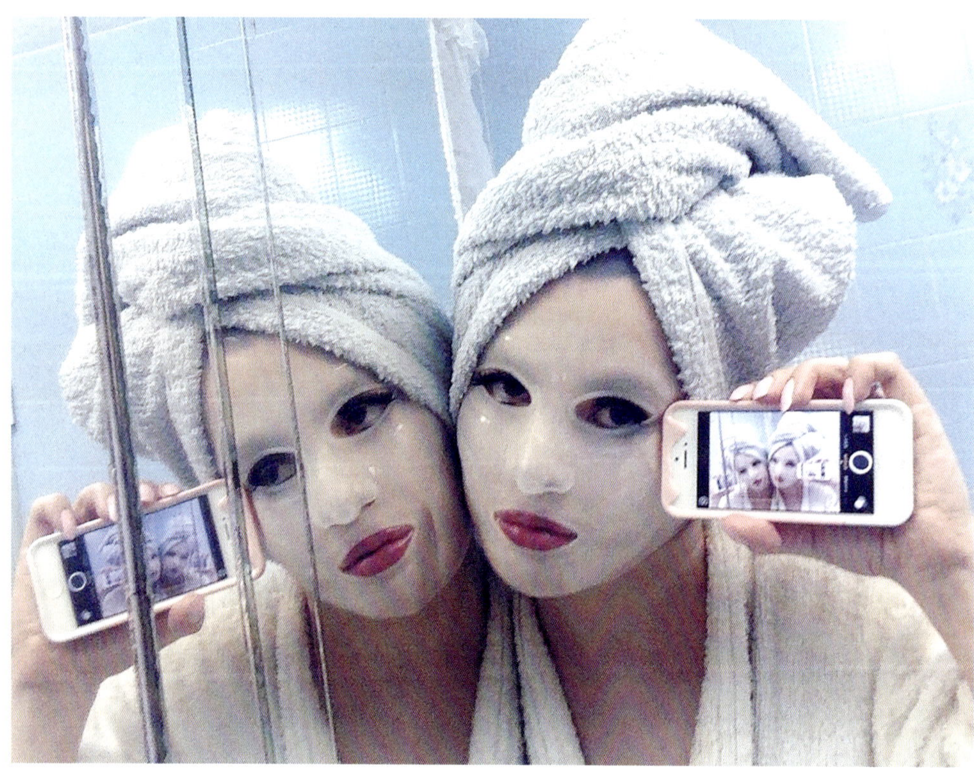

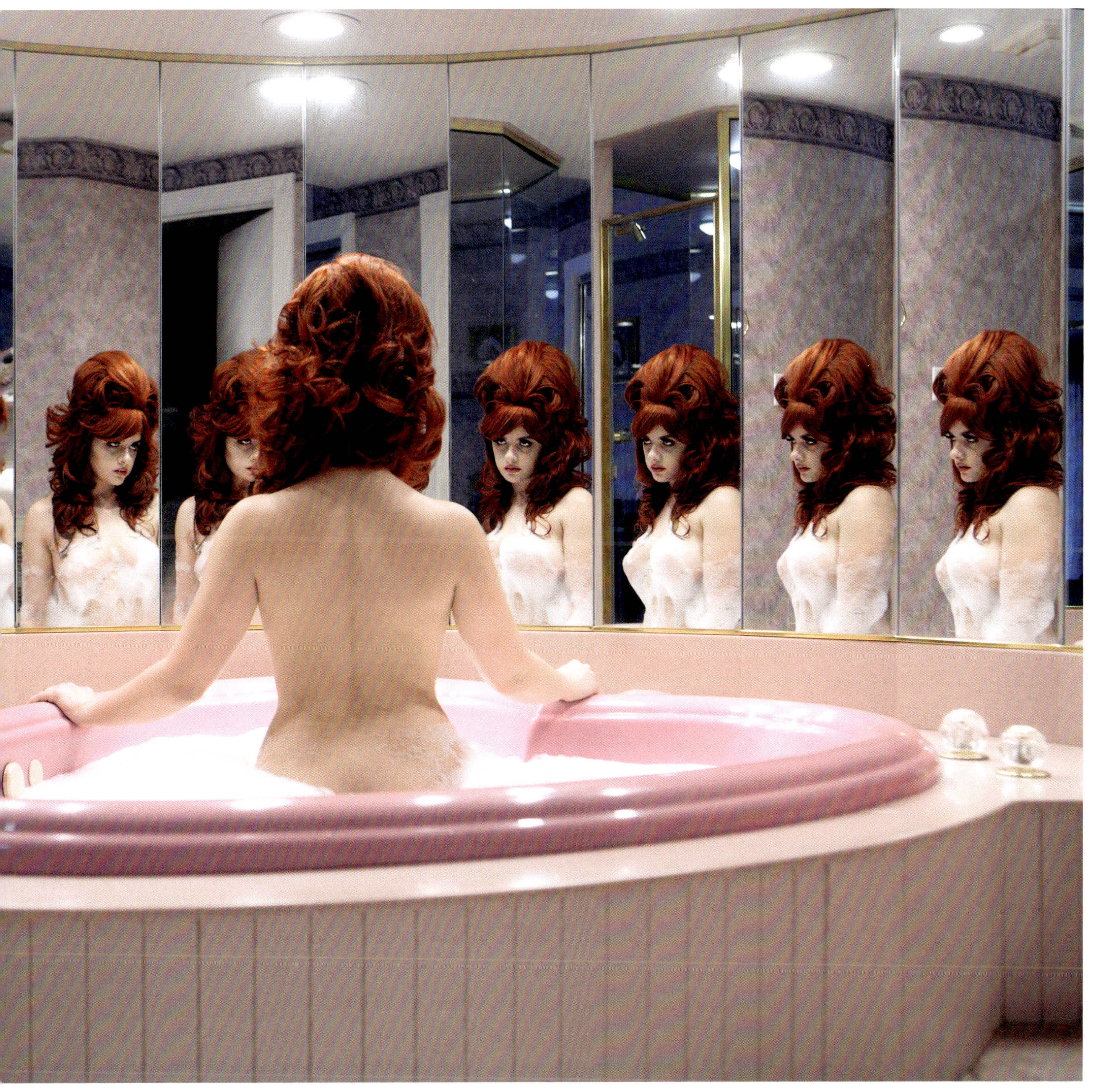

British artist **FINNIAN CROY**'s *Self-Portrait*s, taken seven years apart, reflect on coming of age and the nature of selfies in a generation influenced by social media. His use of the iPhone allows him to find his own gaze and return it to the viewer. Colour being central to Croy's work, he seeks environments to enhance an already existing feeling or emotion within an image. 'The contrast within these works could be seen to reflect the lightness and innocence of adolescents with heavier, richer tones of early adulthood.' In the earlier, blue image (below), he can be seen in two bathroom mirrors at once, his gaze directed at the viewer, not himself. In the orange bathroom (opposite) he looks squarely at those who behold him. The format is similar but he is visibly older, and in the eye seen bottom left, perhaps he could be winking to the viewer and his former self.

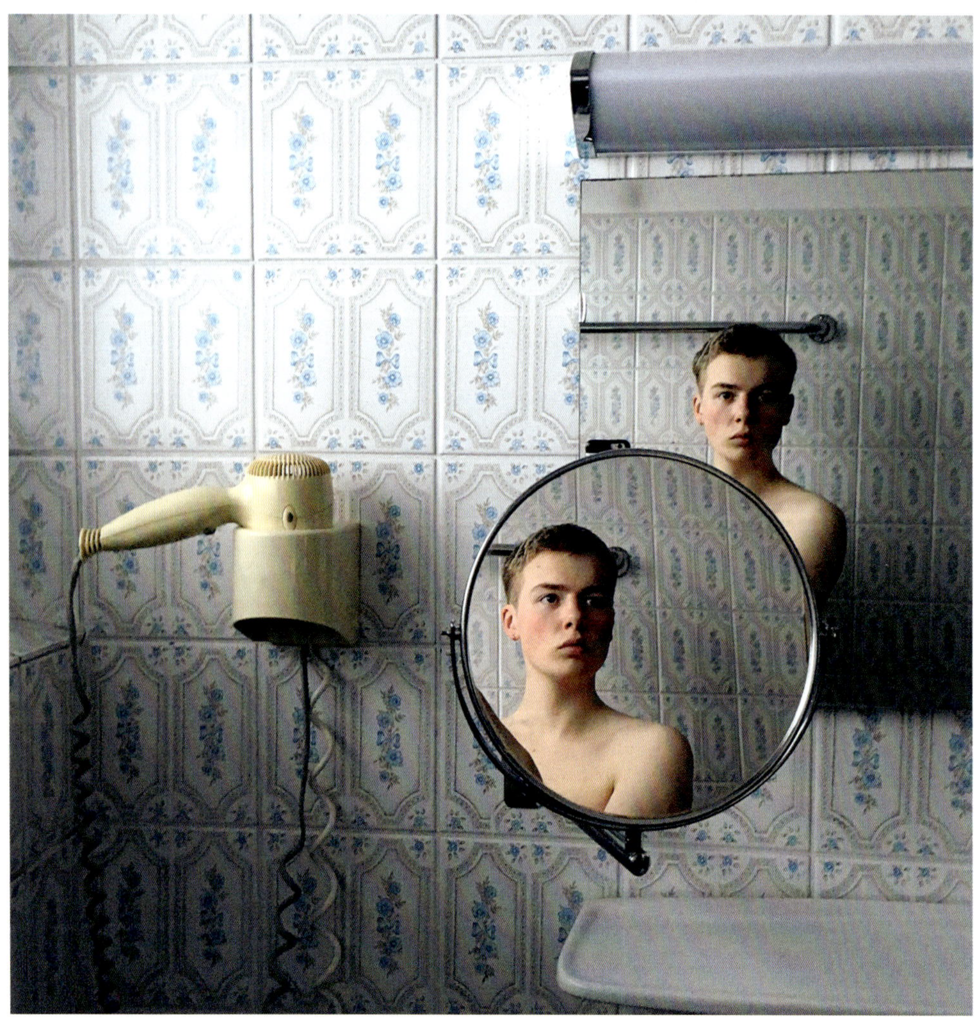

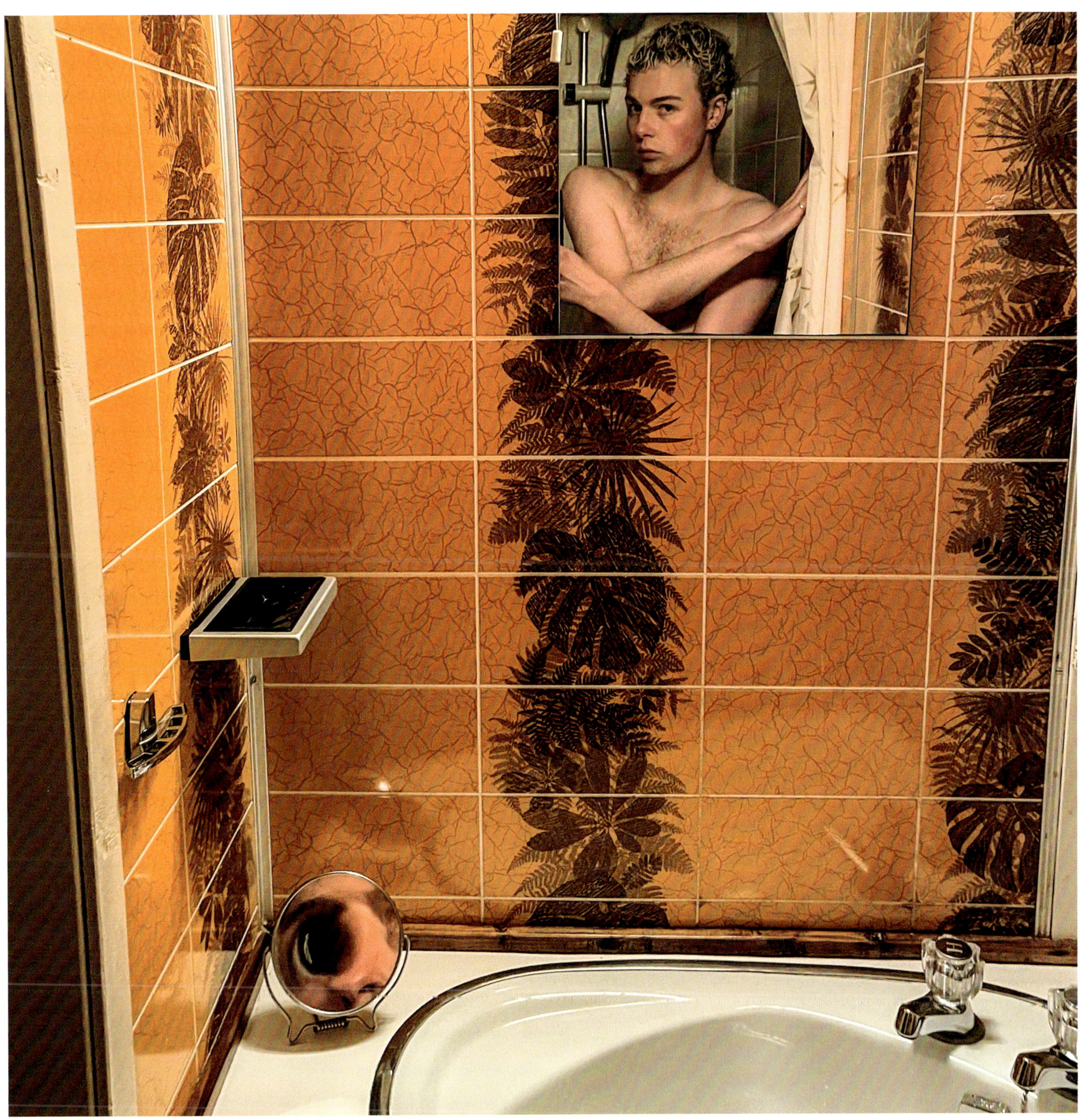

Romanian photographer **FELICIA SIMION** has said that she became interested in the Magnum photographers from the early age of thirteen, and her *Selfie in the park* certainly stands apart from traditional ideas of fast, if not instantaneous, cellphone selfies. She holds a round hand mirror and we see her looking down, away from our gaze; her eyes do not meet ours and she is lost in what appears to be self-reflection. She says that she situates her work '…somewhere near the thin line between reality and fiction, easily floating from one side to another. In the last couple of years, I have drawn inspiration from Cultural Anthropology, exploring themes such as family, identity, dynamics of tradition or body.'

Finnish painter **JUKKA KORKEILA** (b. 1968) looks into his work *Legend of Mt Paektu*, his face and that of North Korea's supreme leader Kim Jong Un merging into one with black spermatozoa converging on it. Korkeila says that 'when I paint a portrait of somebody else than myself, I inevitably incorporate part of myself to that portrait'. Korkeila often paints dictators, politicians and religious leaders in fictional compromising sexual situations. North Koreans hold Mount Paektu in great reverence; the sacred mountain is the highest spot along their border with China, and it is the focus of many myths. However, since the Kim family takeover of the country, traditional myths have been forcibly altered to include Kim Jong Suk (Kim Jong Un's grandmother), the mother of the revolution, as almost a goddess.

BELOW
Felicia Simion, *Selfie in the park*, 2017
Digital print
100 × 70 cm (39⅜ × 27⅝ in)

OPPOSITE
Jukka Korkeila, *Legend of Mt Paektu*, 2023
Acrylic on glass and digital print
40 × 37 cm (15¾ × 14⅝ in)

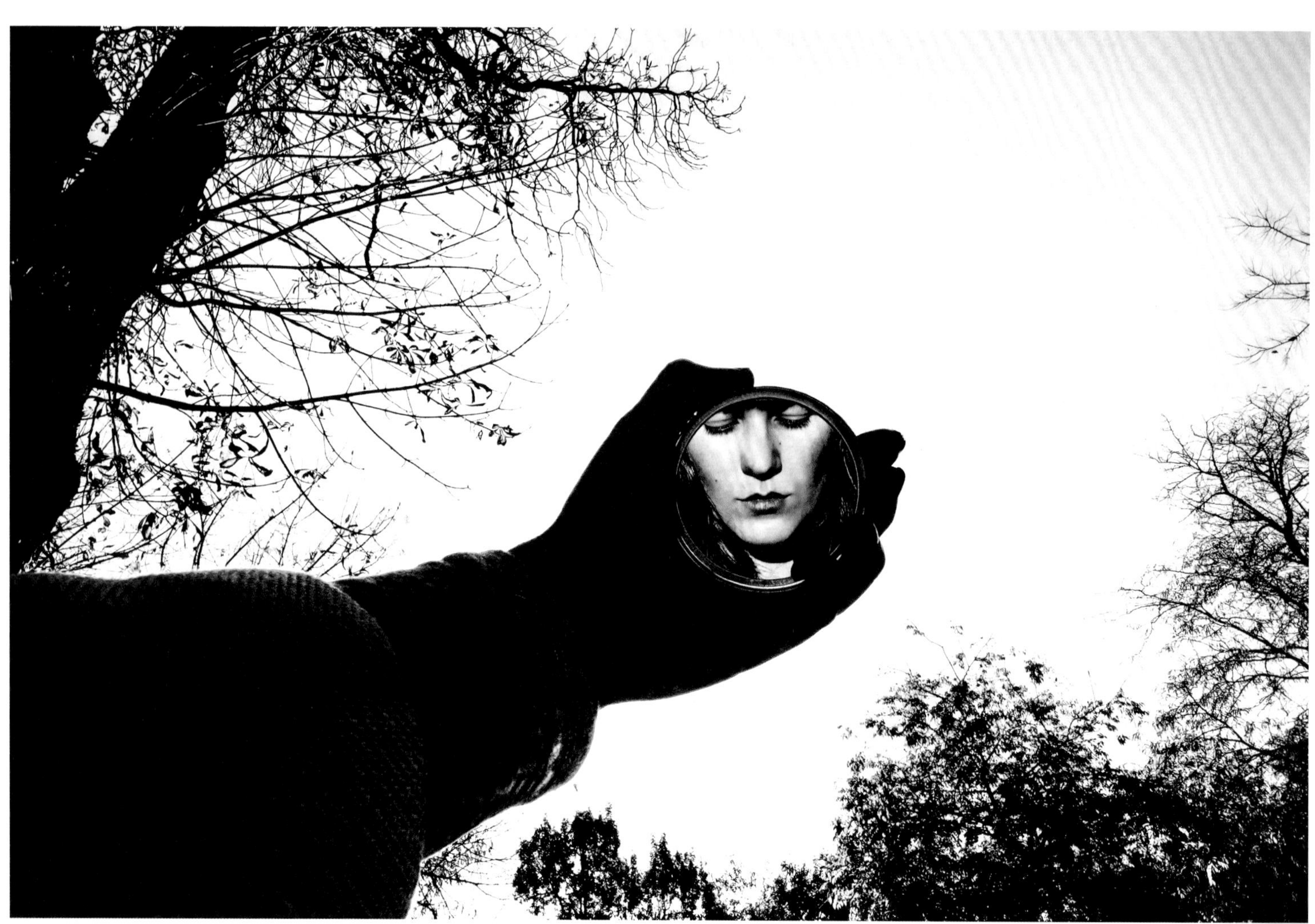

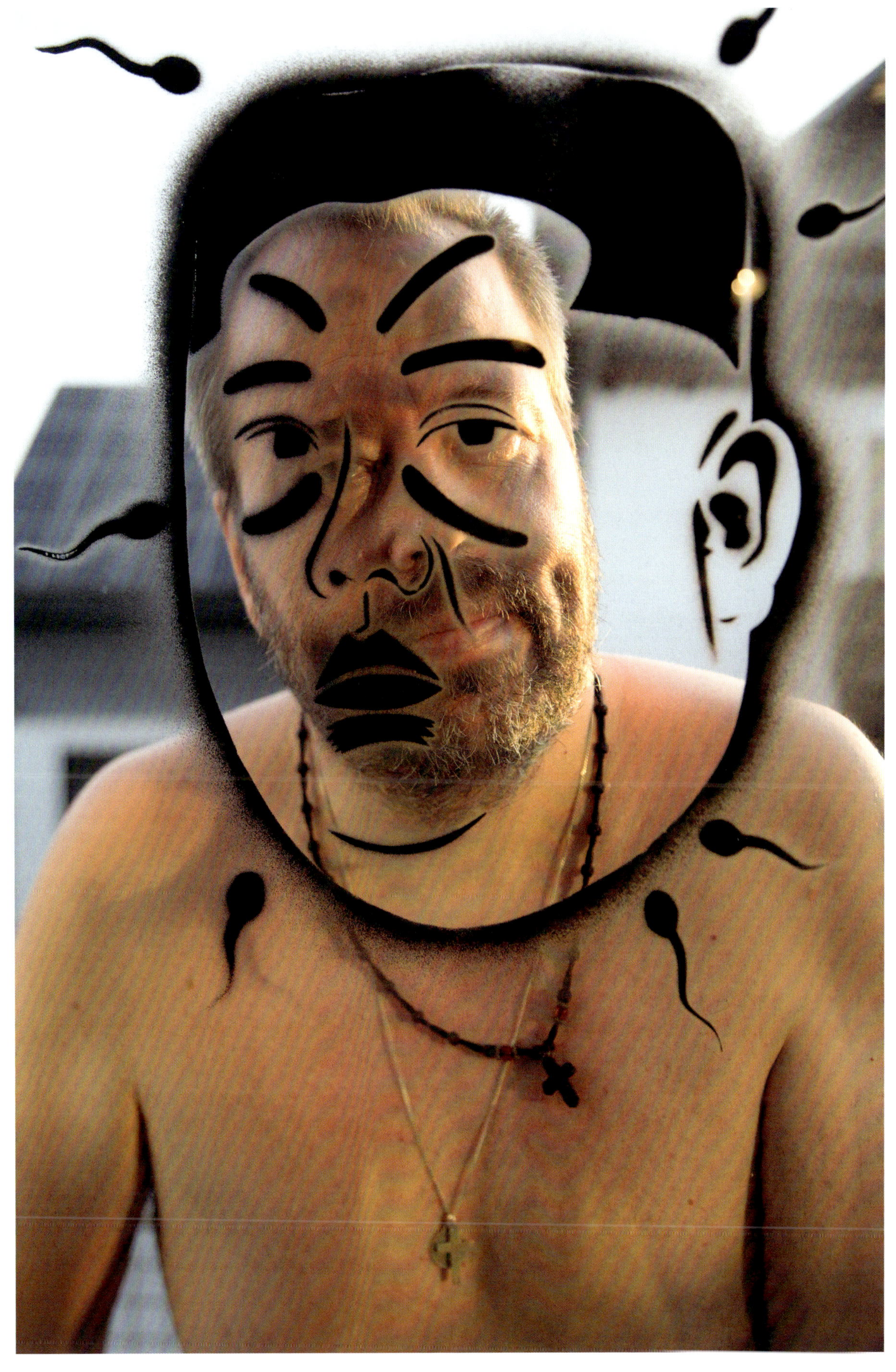

JEFF ZIMMER (b. 1970) is an Edinburgh-based American artist who works mainly with glass. In his large work *I'm Afraid of You* we see not only that work itself, but several of his framed glass dronescapes reflected within. The mirror work was included in 'Craft Scotland Selects: Glass' at the Open Exhibition at the Royal Scottish Academy. It is intended to eventually form part of a 'hall of mirrors…of all different shapes, sizes, vintages, styles…' as it reflects the viewer and the other works in the room, and its text is bold, accusatory and yet self-reflective. Is the large glass afraid of being broken, or is the artist afraid of the viewer, or is it for the viewer to be in a position of fear?

British-born Los Angeles-based **DAVID VAN EYSSEN** was a well-known new media creator when he became ill. He has said that 'During several years of cancer treatment, I took photographs of myself with my phone, recording surgeries and side-effects, and using the camera to confirm my existence'. In recovery, he has gone on to explore his self-portraiture practice. For his series *A Slim Volume of Poetry In No Particular Order* (overleaf), he temporarily installed and broke large mirrors across Los Angeles. These startling works hide as much as they document, and the viewer must work hard to seek him out. The violence stilled in the fractured image has a clear bodily parallel. In *DisAppearance* (opposite), with the use of AI, sections around the edges of four self-portraits were extended until the figures recede into an imagined vista.

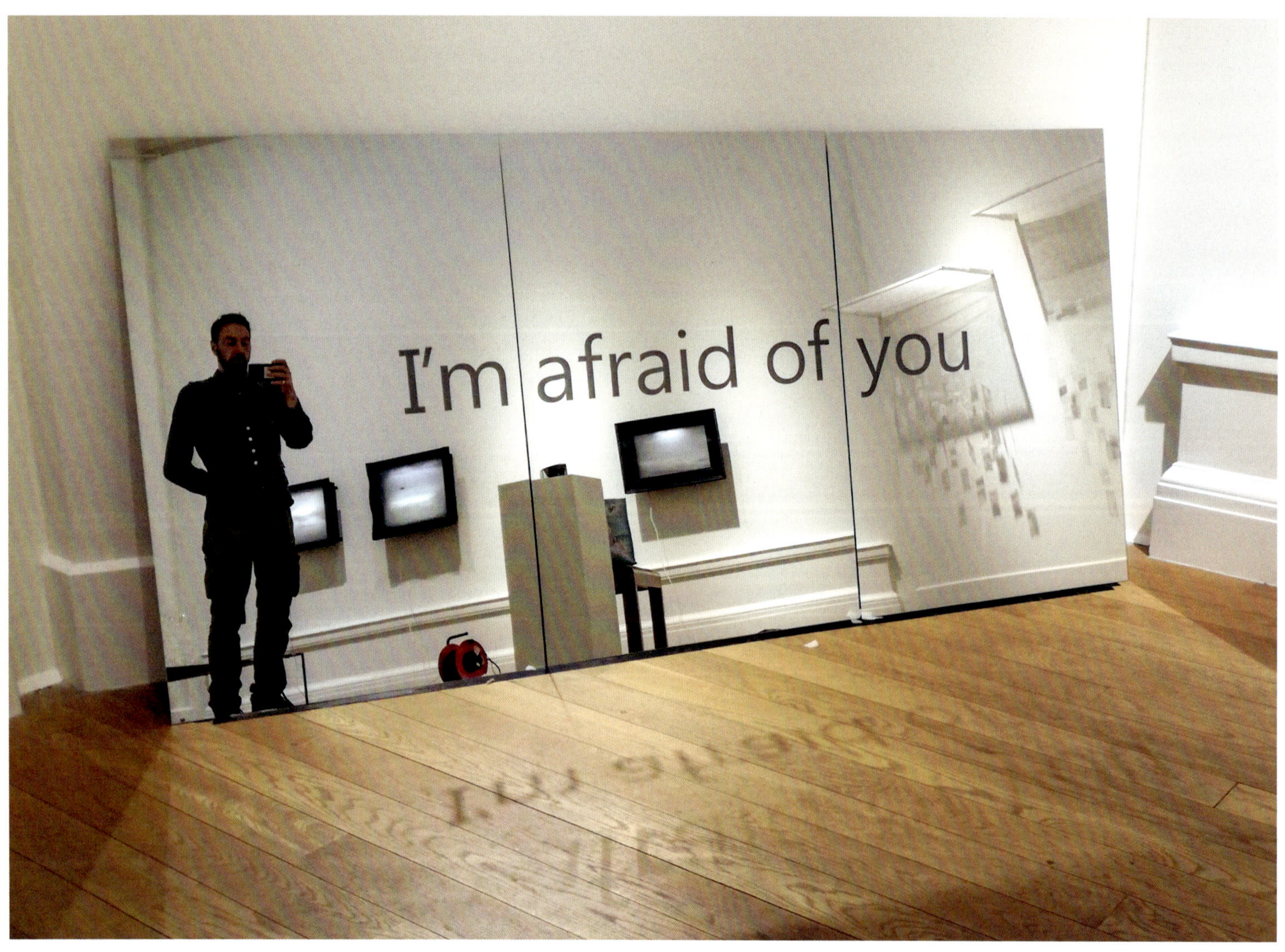

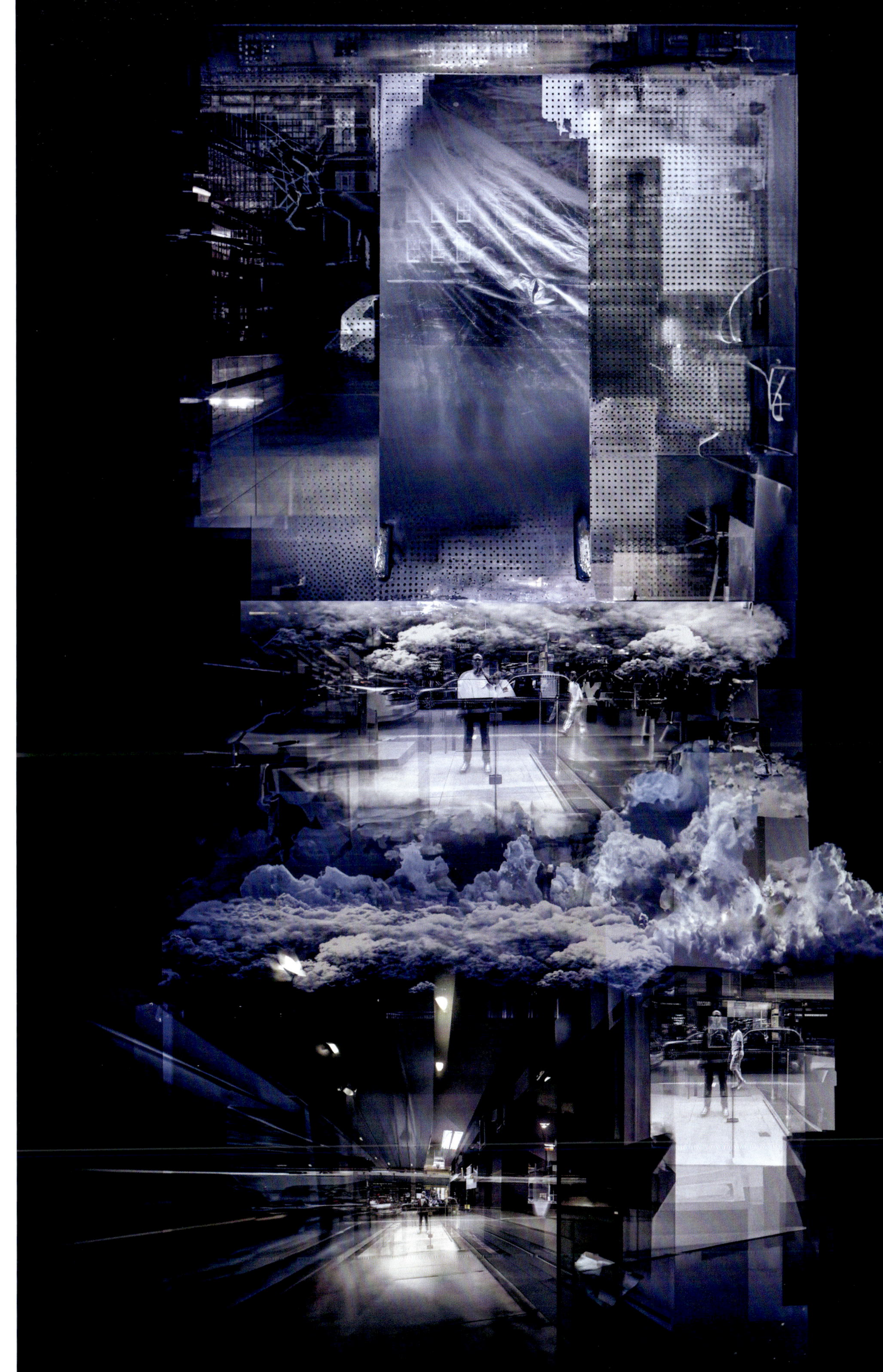

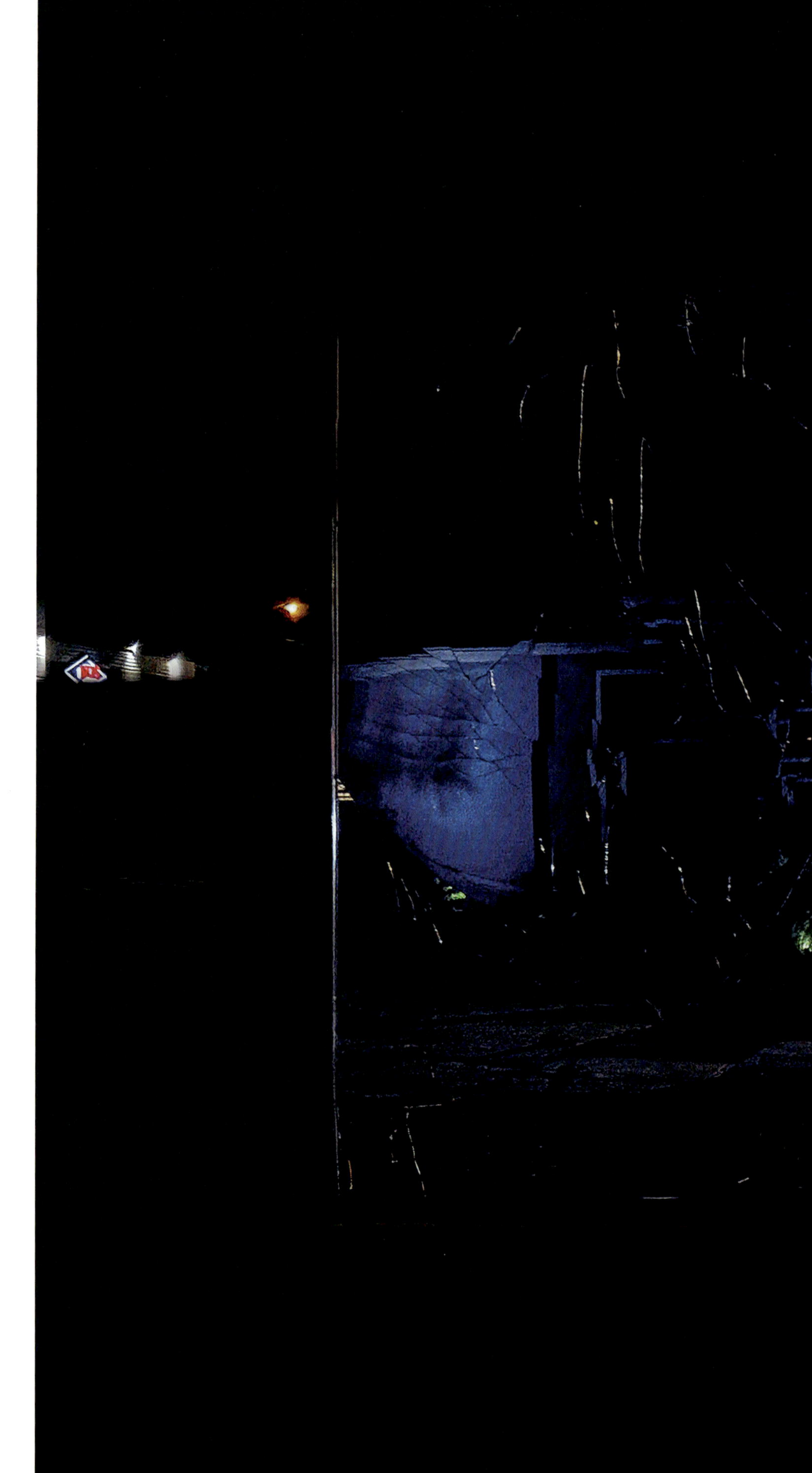

David Van Eyssen, *A Slim Volume of Poetry*
In No Particular Order Pt. III, 2022
Archival pigment print
63.5 × 48.3 cm (25 × 19 in)

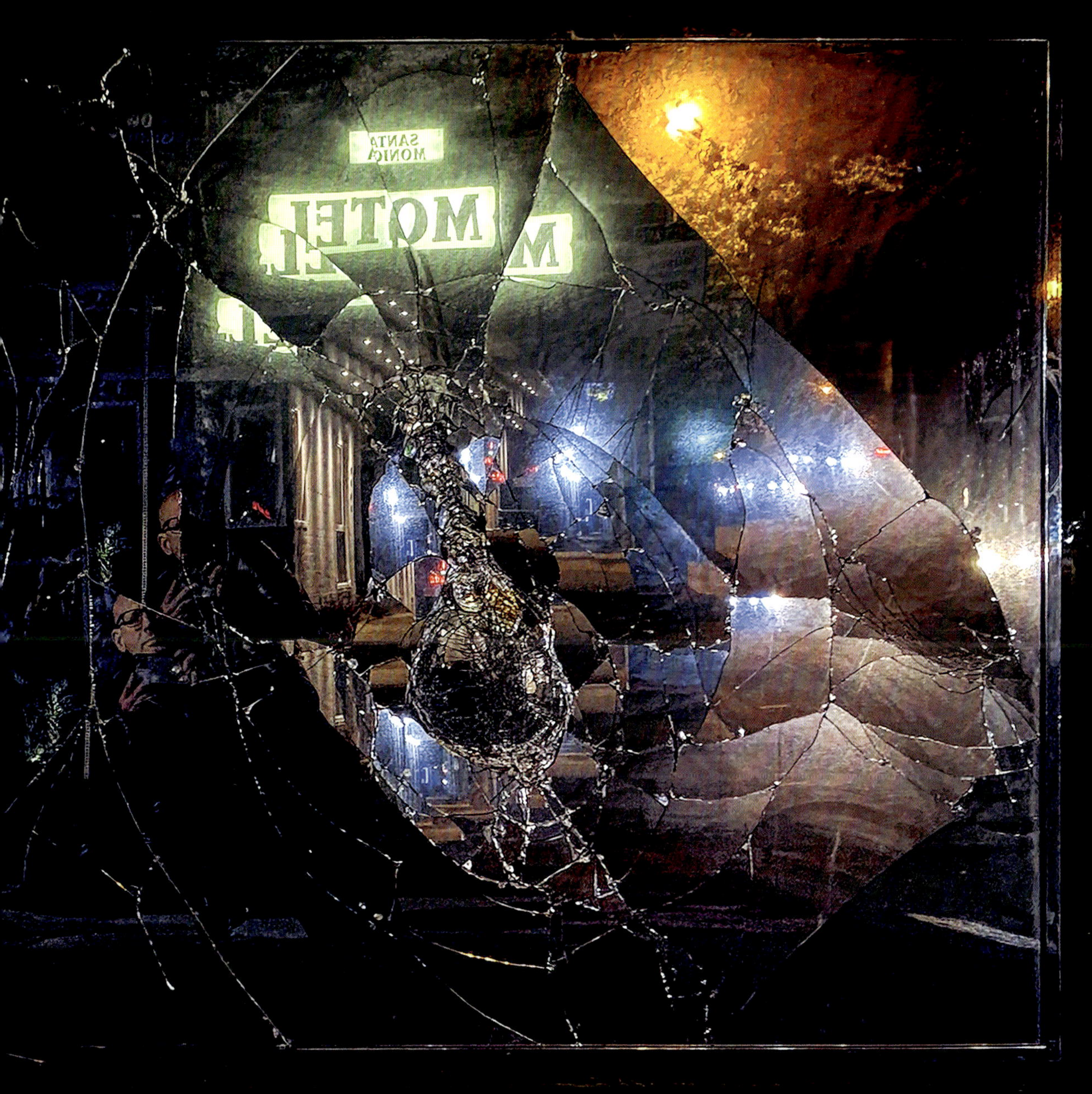

SANTA
MONICA
MOTEL

complements the double self-portraits they
make in their everyday life and post online.
The closeness and honesty of the images
mirrors their relationship to each other
and the viewer.

BELOW
Stav B and Anka Dabrowska, *Selfie*,
Kalymnos, Greece, Aug 2022
Digital image
Dimensions variable

OPPOSITE
John-Michael Parry, *Self-Portrait*, 2023
Digital image
Dimensions variable

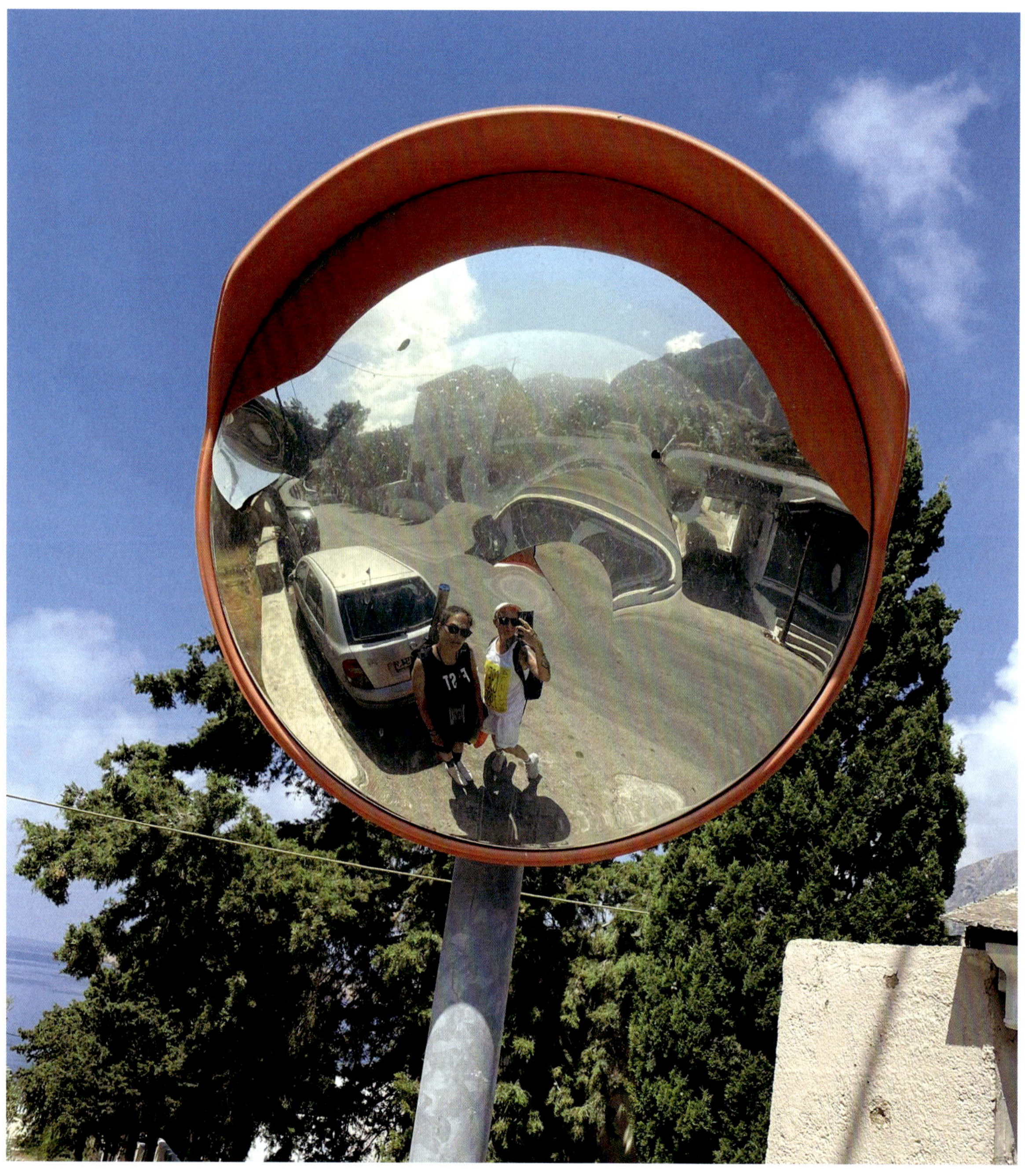

British artist **JOHN-MICHAEL PARRY**
is interested in body horror, time travel and
the ruin of our future culture, and makes
sculptures that look as if they were ancient
relics, but from centuries ahead of today.
His self-portraits attempt to disrupt his
own body, to split it up or fragment it, and
like atoms or neutrinos flying through space
and time, they are highly un-interactive.
His portrait reflected on the side of a car
sees him split into four, his gaze on his
phone, the means of capturing time. We can
barely make out what he looks like: he is a
relic of his current future self.

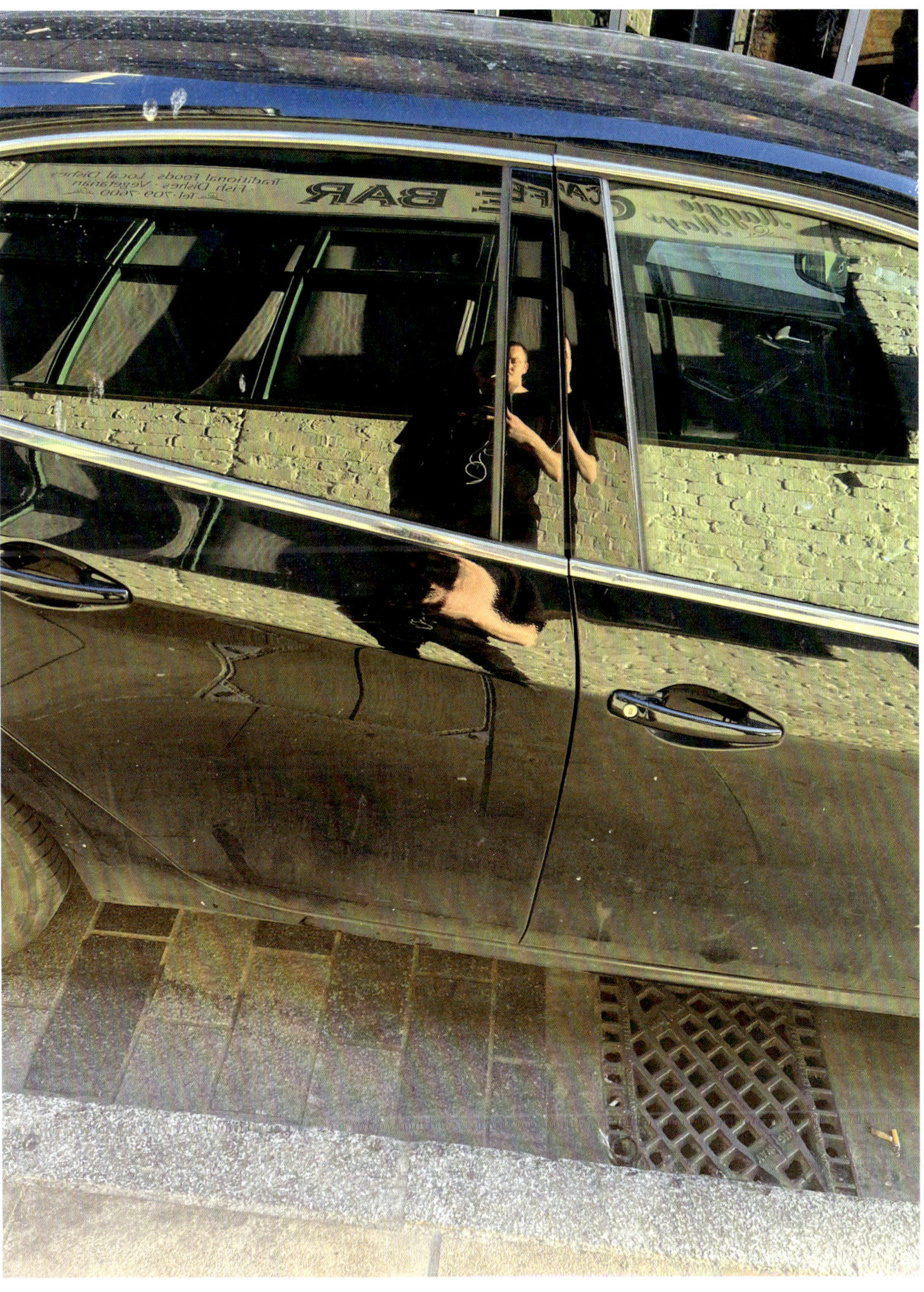

Born in Northern Ireland and now based
in the United States, **JONATHAN DAVID
SMYTH** (b. 1987) has been taking what he
calls 'Arm's-Lengths' since the mid-2000s,
believing these offer a more precise
portrayal of self-capture through phone
photography. Smyth's ongoing project of
self-documentation is titled *Just One More*,
a phrase he utters to his husband when
pausing to take yet another photo. While
at first glance Smyth's selfies might resemble
many others found online, they are highly
composed, utilizing the reflective façades
of the buildings he positions himself within.
They are often multilayered, capturing
both the urban landscape and Smyth as
a *flâneur* navigating it.

BELOW AND OPPOSITE
Just One More series (2012–present)
Digital image (iPhone)
Dimensions variable

BELOW LEFT
Chelsea, NYC, October 06, 2020, 2020

BELOW RIGHT
Pioneer Square, Seattle, February 24, 2020,
2020

OPPOSITE
West Chelsea, NYC, January 27, 2018, 2018

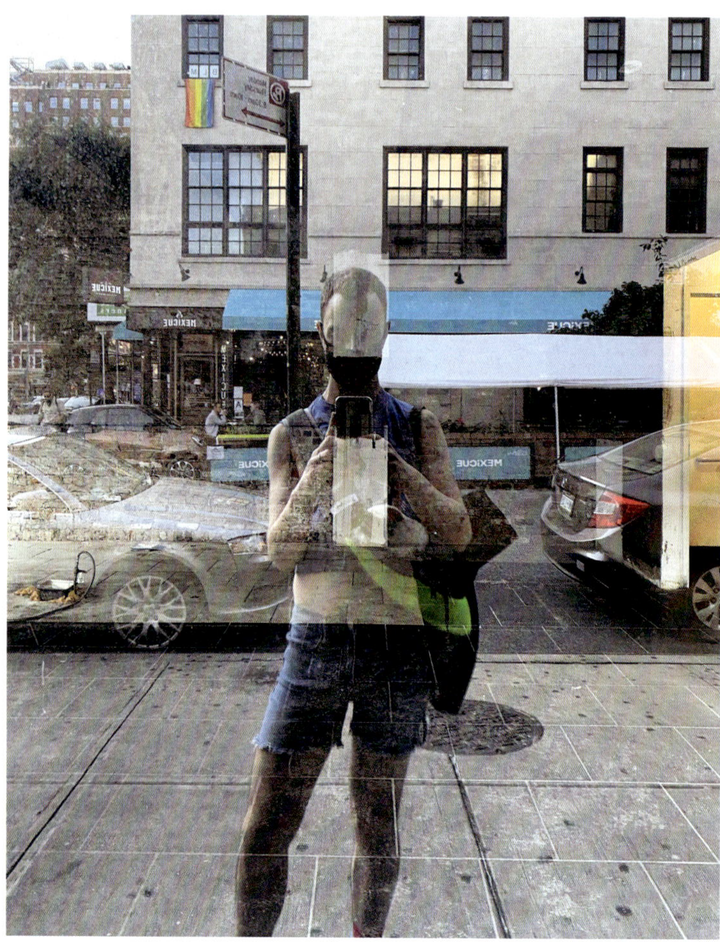

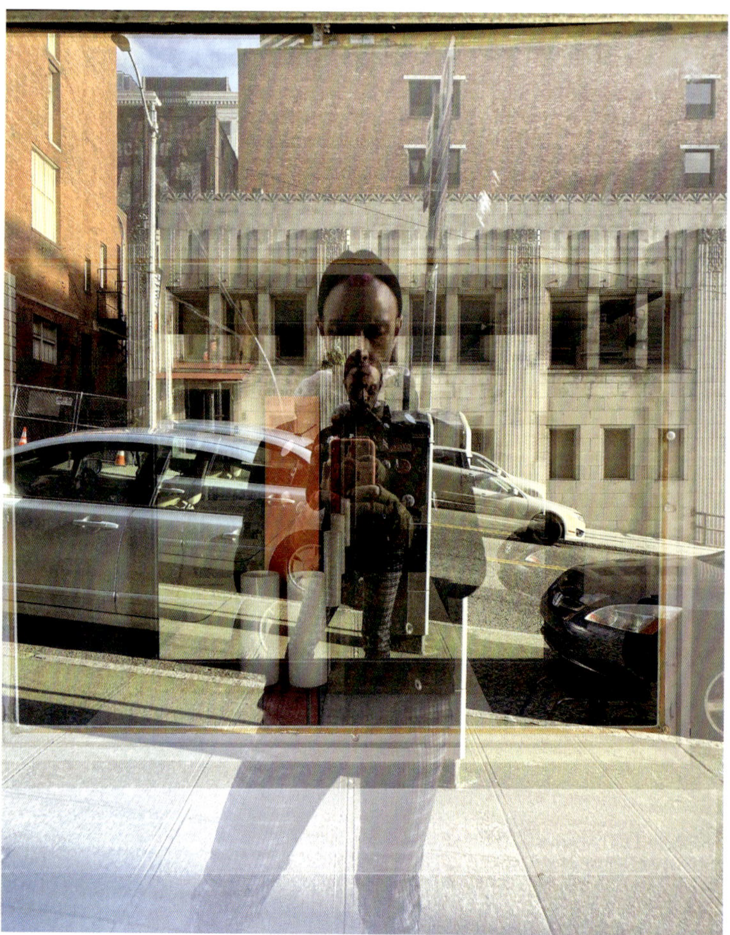

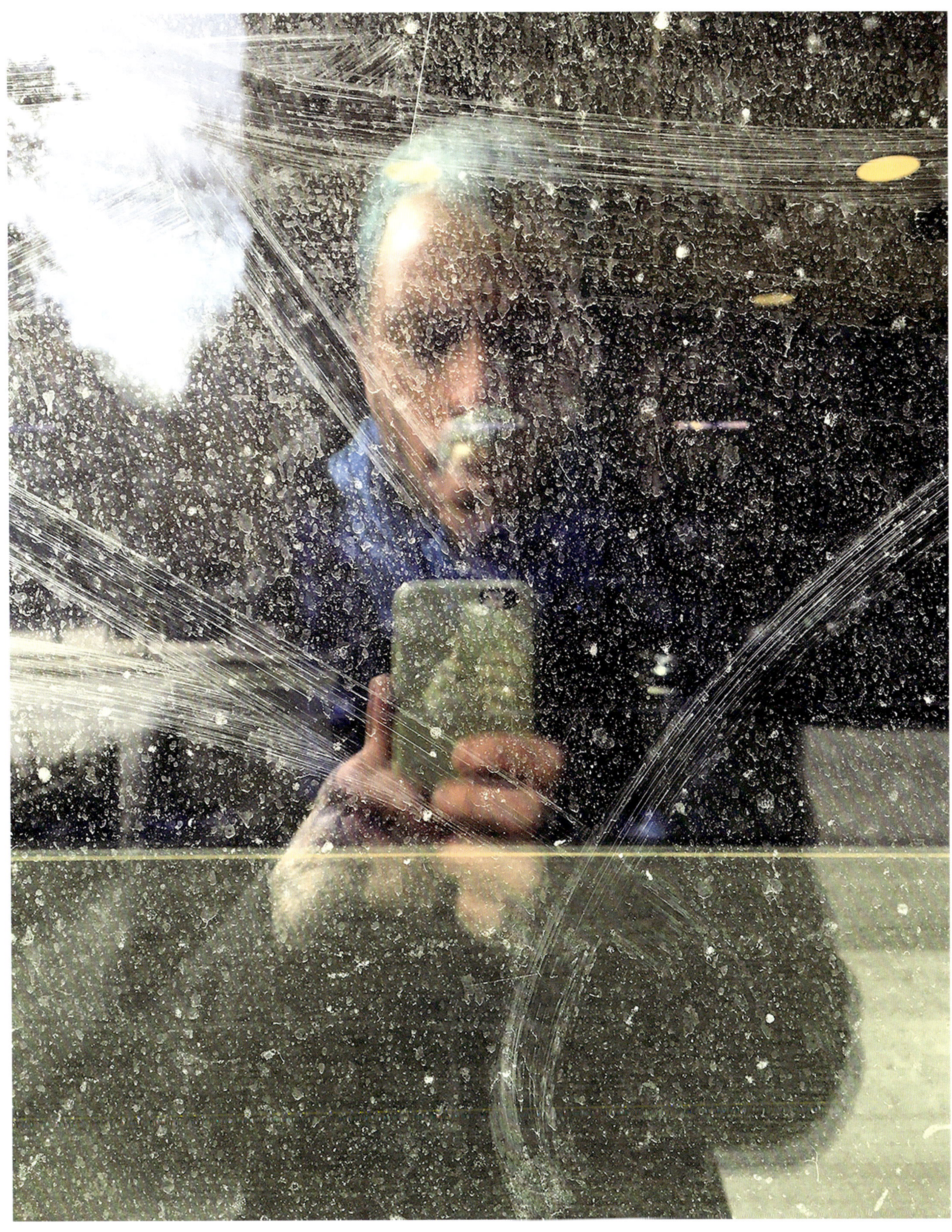

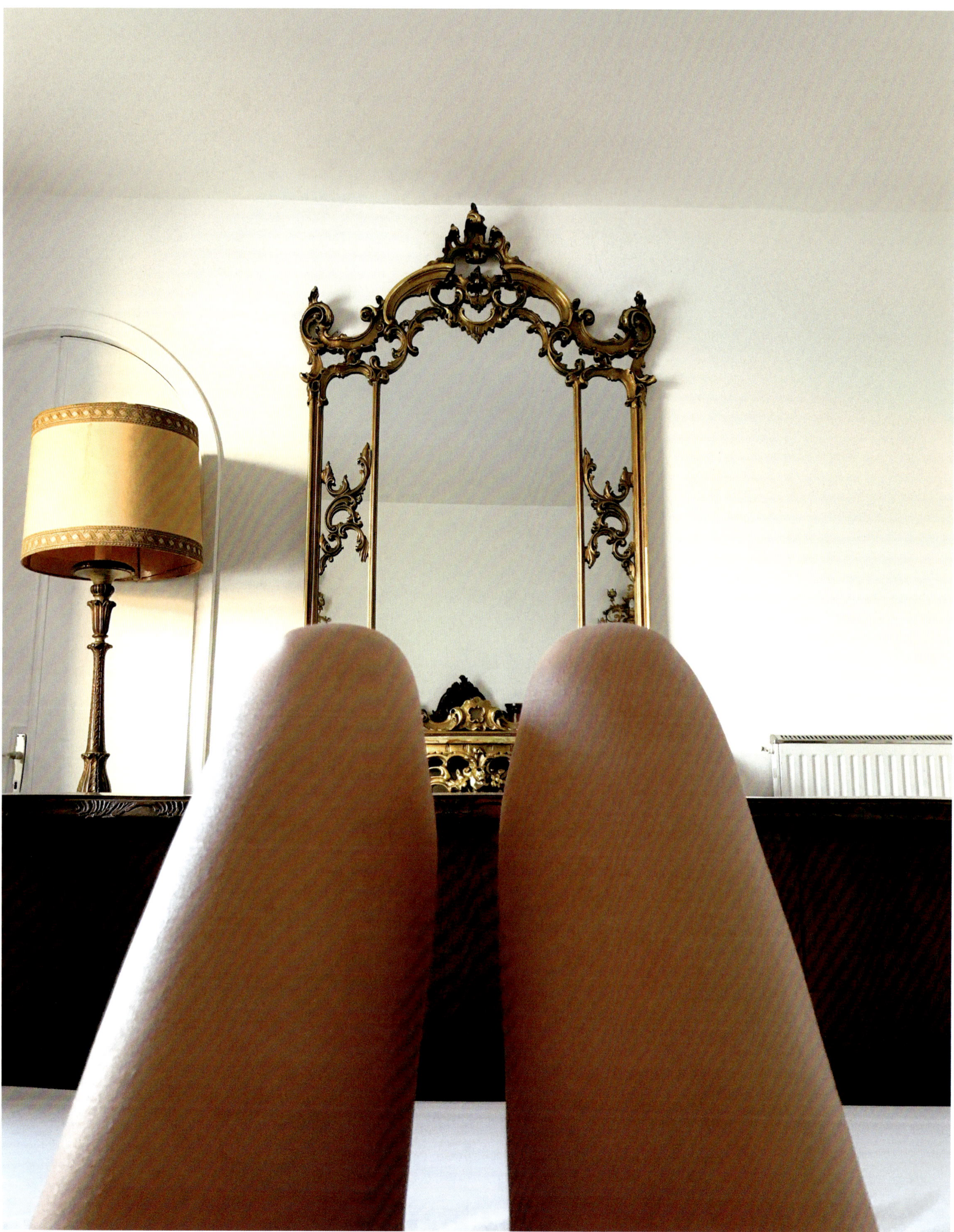

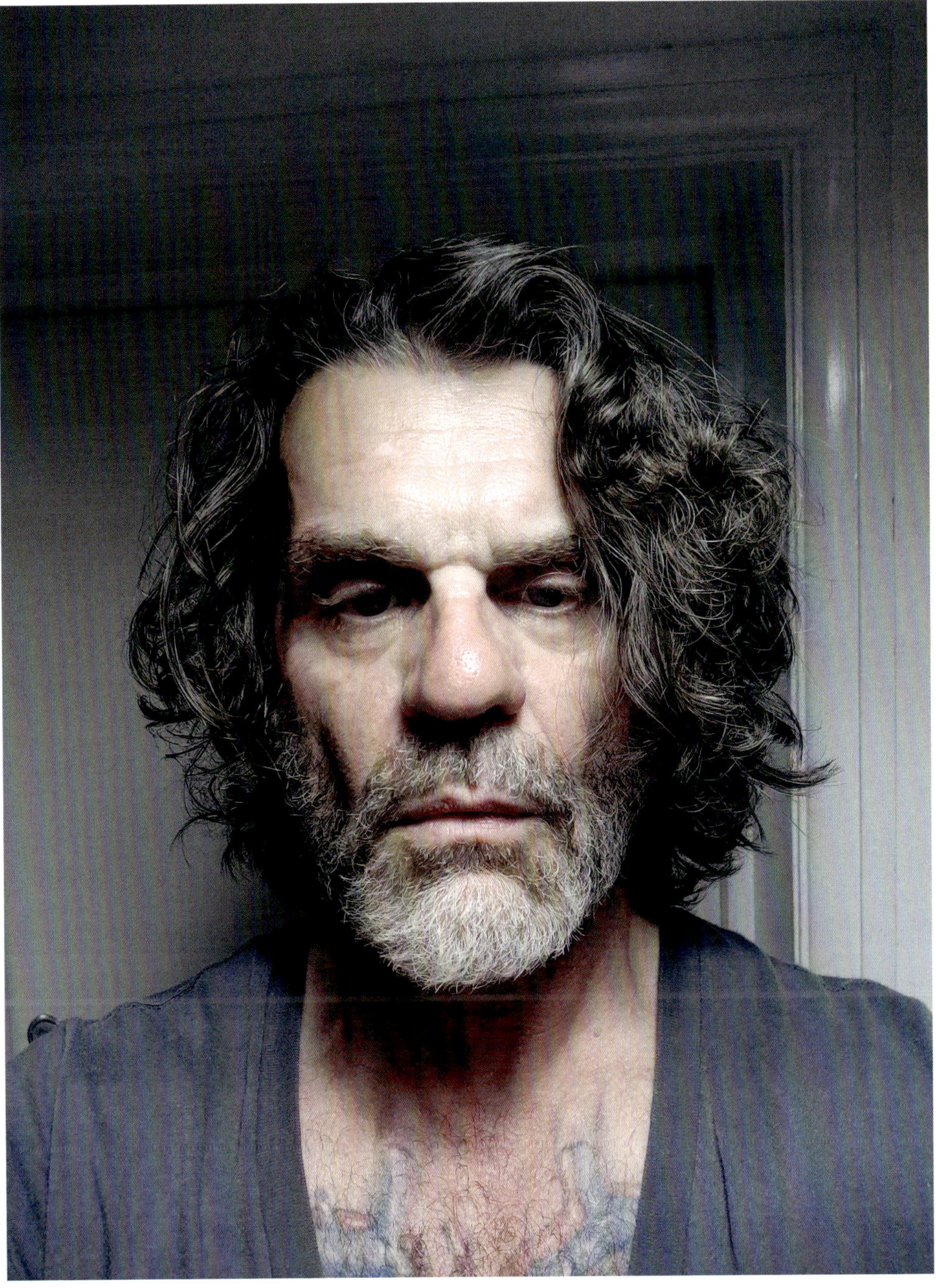

British-Israeli artist **MICHAL COLE** (b. 1974) has been examining the patriarchy in large-scale installations since the start of the #metoo movement. Her work was shown at the 'Objection' exhibition at the Pavilion of Humanity (Venice Biennale, 2017), a collaboration with Turkish artist Erin Onat. It featured 'a gentleman's' living room created from 27,000 used men's ties collected over many years. It took Cole and her team three years to hand sew the content of the room. Both artists come from countries where traditional roles for women are often strongly enforced. Cole has pushed back against these confines in many ways, including in her series of 'sausage knees' selfies taken from a low vantage point in surprising locations.

RICHARD SAWDON SMITH is a British photographer and academic who has used his own body as a site of medical, social and sexual history for more than thirty years. He has a vast array of 'selfies' taken with professional cameras that document his ongoing body art. His front has anatomical tattoos of veins, arteries and his heart, just visible in the photograph above, and his back is tattooed to look as if he has had invasive surgery. Sawdon Smith has documented his own medical journey (living long-term with HIV), and the effects that illness, medicine and time have had on him. The 2023 selfie was taken for his sixtieth birthday on a cameraphone without filters or studio lighting, and the honesty and rawness of the image is in harsh contrast to the many 'self-improved' shots posted on social media.

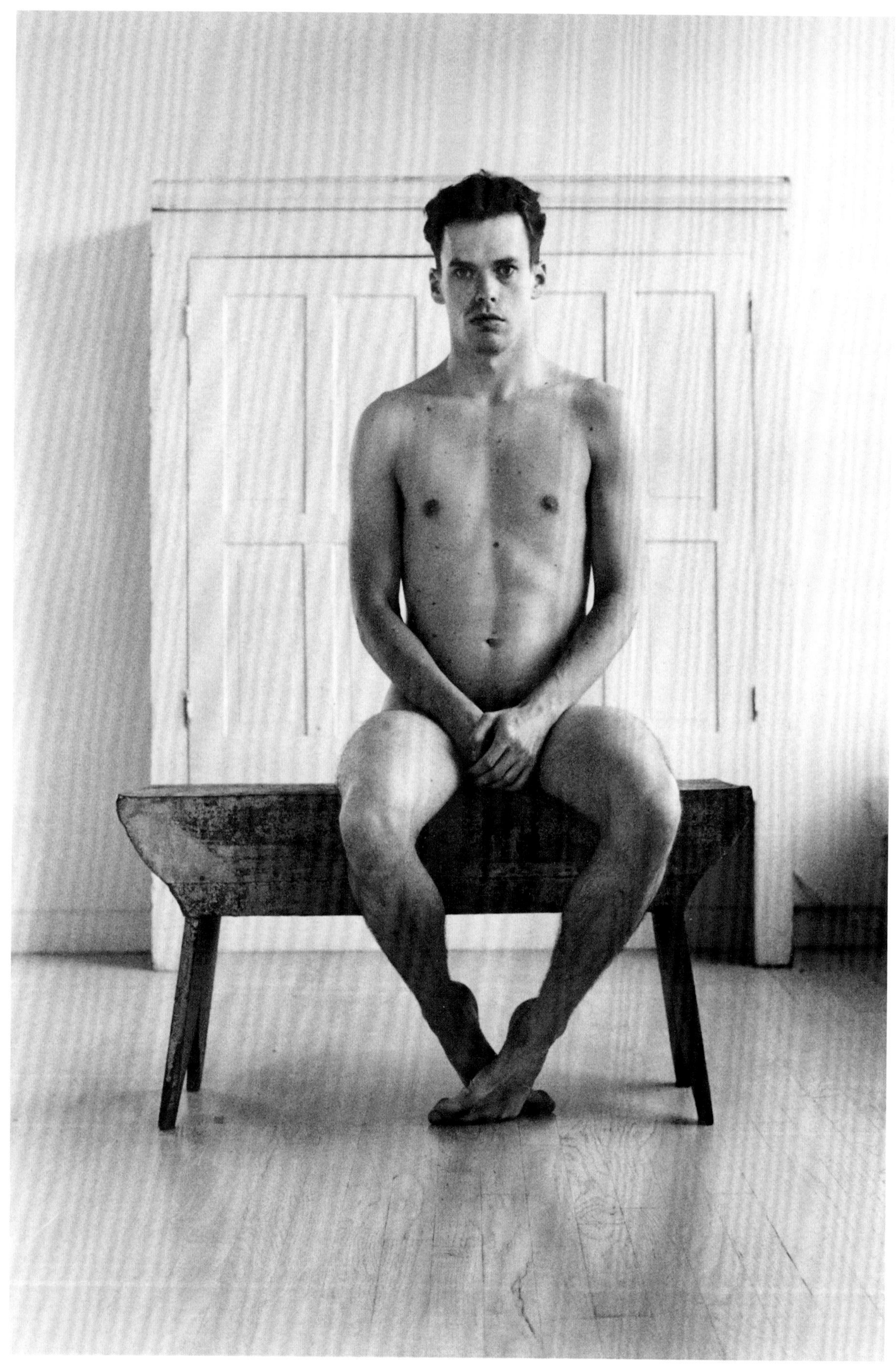

American artist **ERIC RHEIN** (b. 1961) moved to New York's East Village in 1980 and became part of the district's explosive arts scene, which sadly became one of the first to be hit by the HIV/AIDS crisis. Rhein has been open about his positive status and since 1987, with his diagnosis, he has made his own life the focus of his work. At the time, few who became infected expected to live for any extended period. His first self-portrait, *Seated* (opposite), was shot in 1992: he looks directly at the camera, naked and exposed. This became a model for further self-portraits over the following decades, thanks to life-saving medications. His selfie *Survival at 60* (below) positions the medicated body at the forefront of the image and again he stares out at the viewer. Rhein has said, 'If the names of those who died of complications from AIDS aren't spoken, their stories told, they'll be forgotten… documenting the shared overwhelming experience will ensure knowledge that we were here and our struggle mattered.'

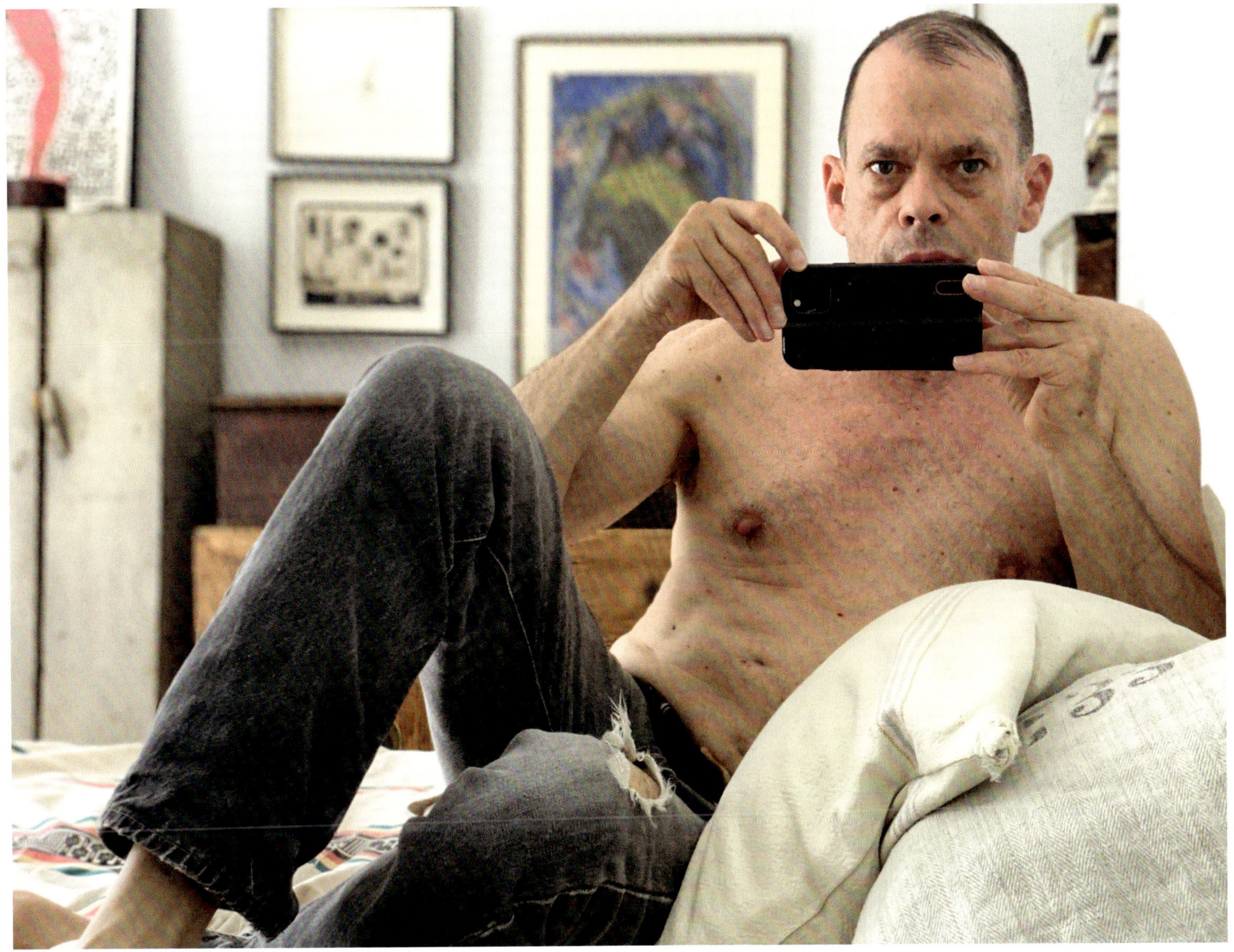

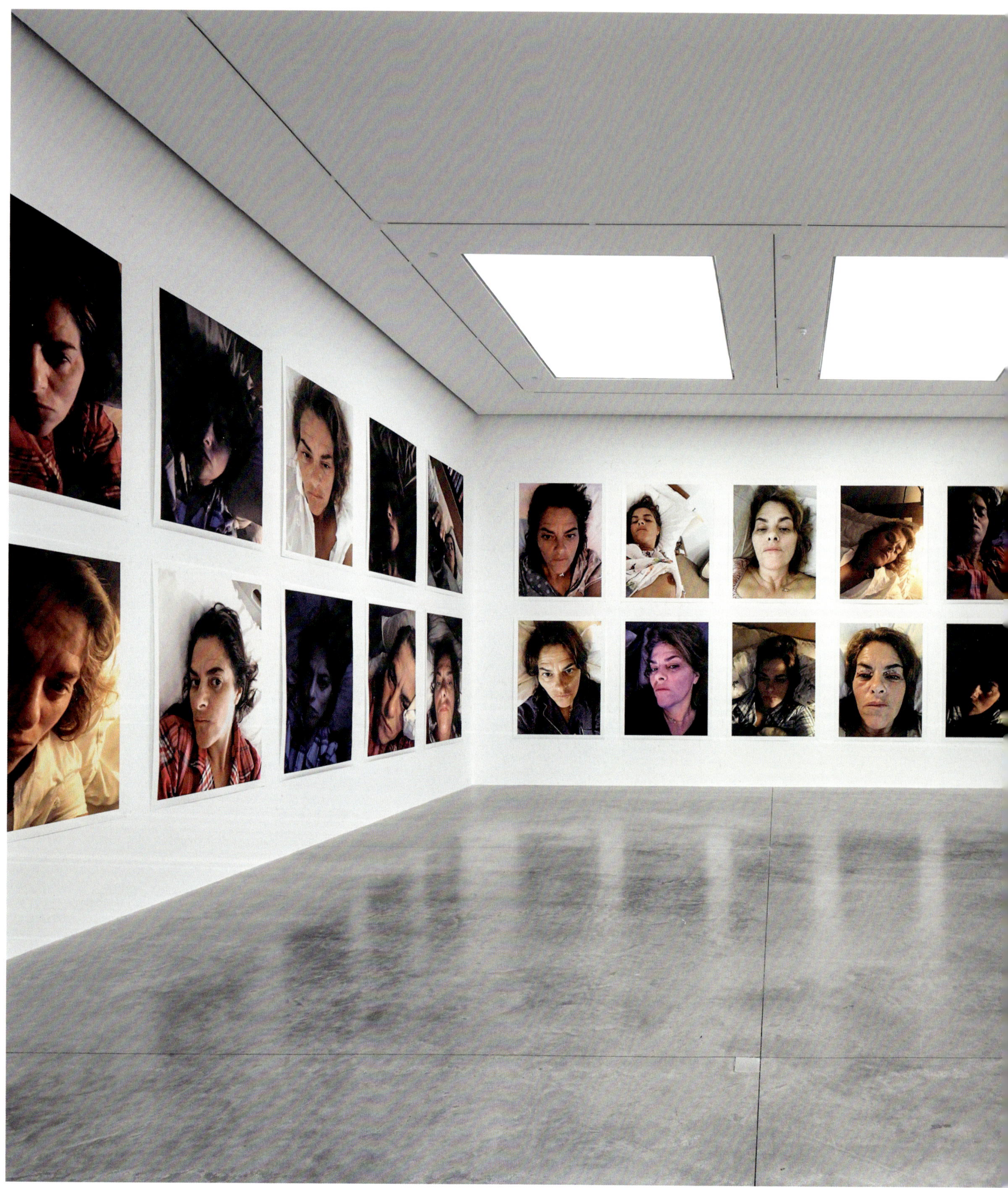

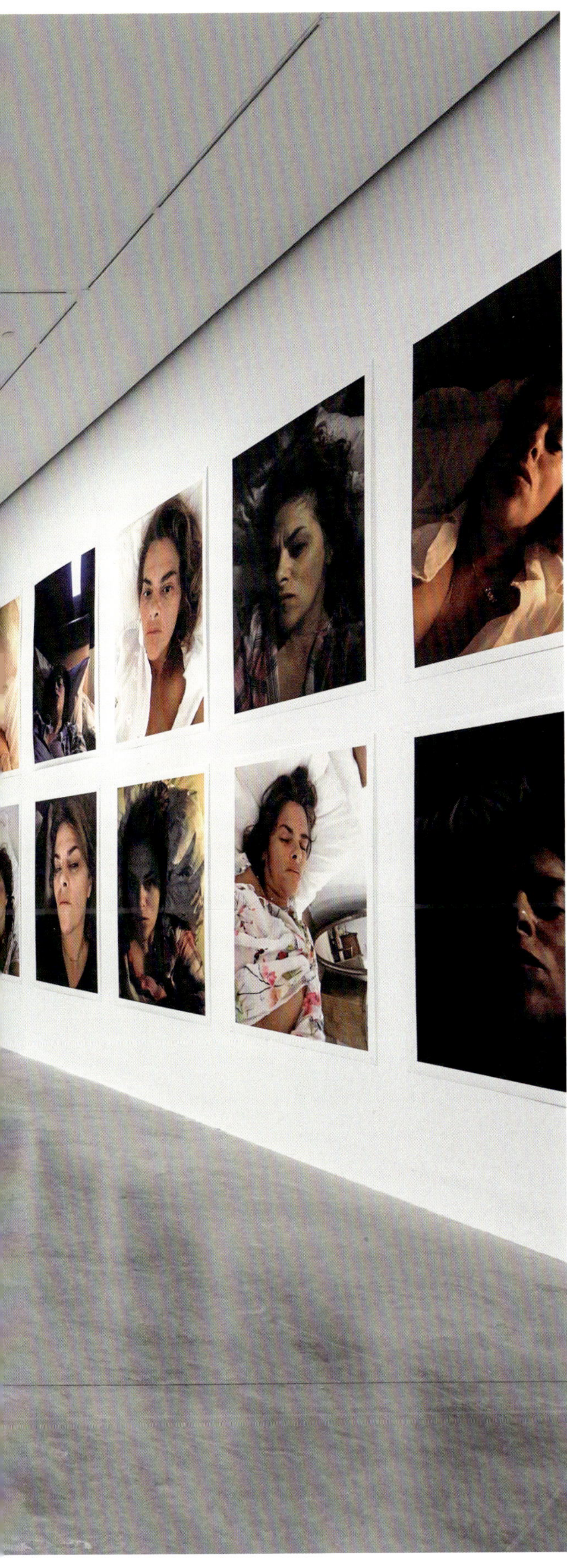

British artist **TRACEY EMIN**'s (b. 1963) exhibition 'A Fortnight of Tears' at London's White Cube gallery featured sculpture, painting, a film and her *Insomnia Room Installation*, the latter filled with fifty large prints of herself taken on her cameraphone in the middle of the night when she could not sleep. It is clear they have been taken over a period of time (four years), as her appearance changes radically across the images. In some details, the viewer can see evidence of her facial surgery, while other photographs document her recovery. She wears a myriad of different bedclothes, and the background of white sheets reflects one of her most famous works, *My Bed* (1998). Emin is clearly aware of the possible reading of the work as overly self-exposing or self-centred, but it seems evident that she is in on all the jokes that might be made and alludes to deeper thoughts on the project, describing it as 'like an early death from within'.

Insomnia Room Installation, 2019
Installation view: White Cube Bermondsey, London, UK
Giclée prints
Each: H 200 cm (79 in)

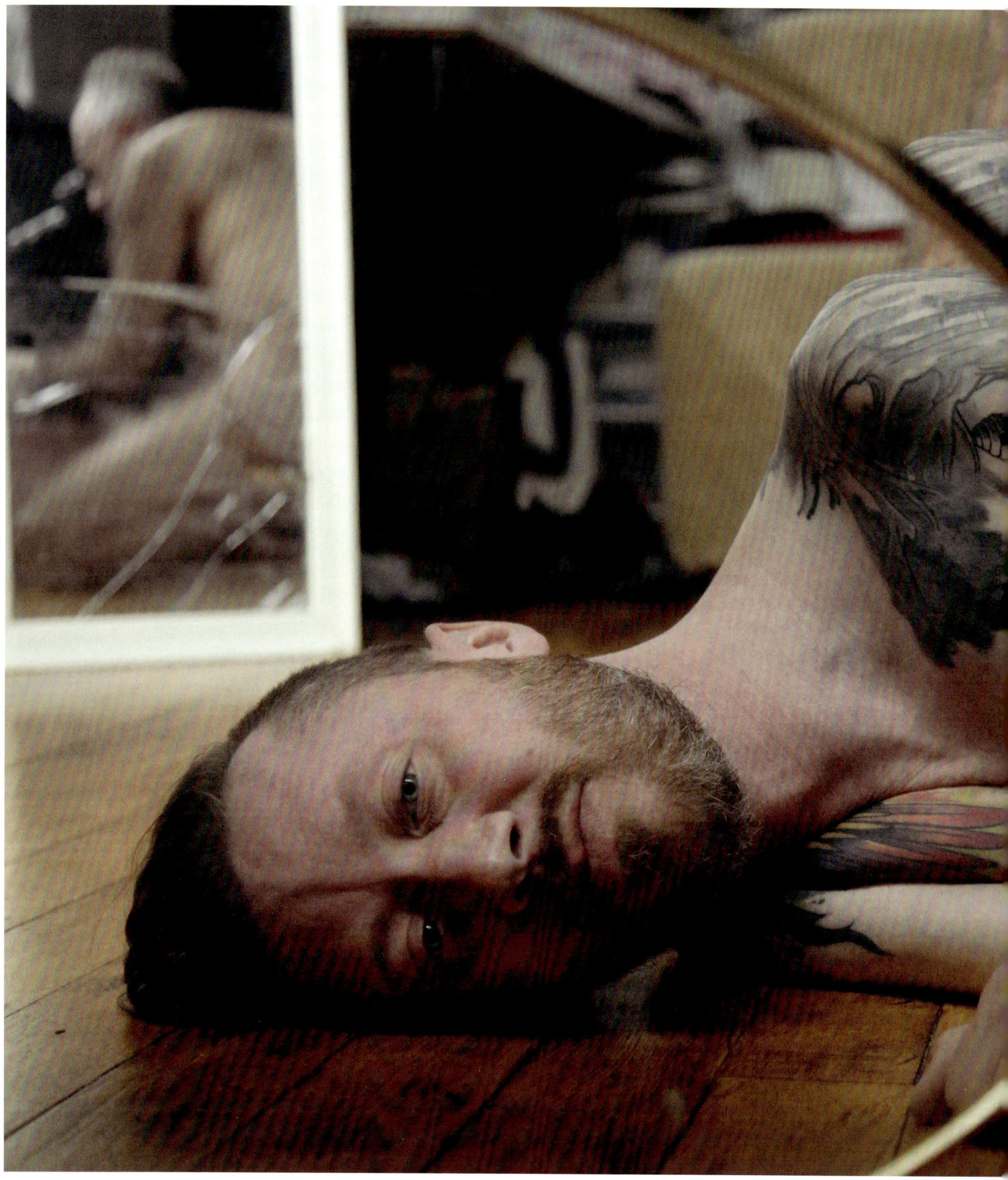

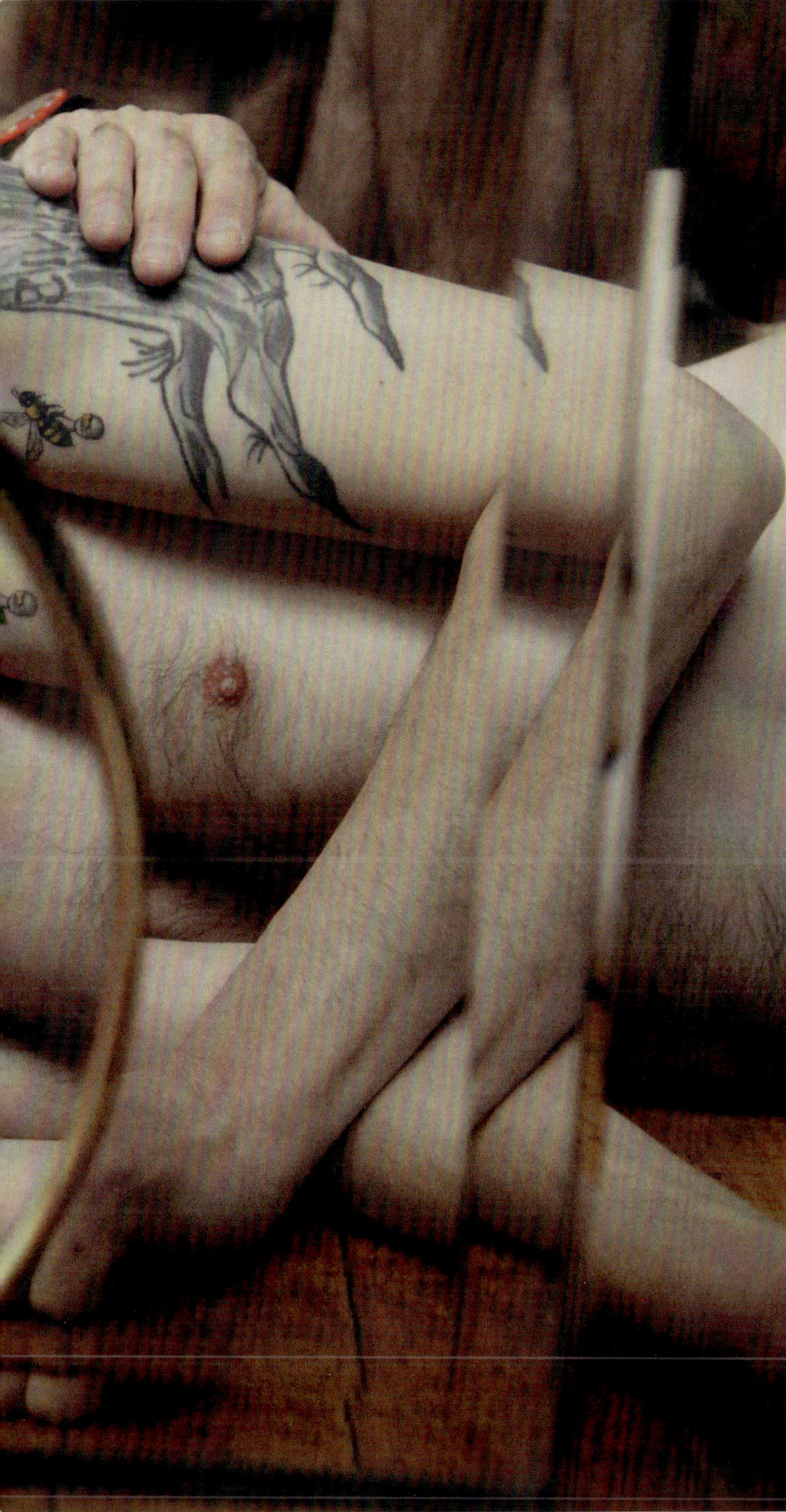

American artist **ROBERT SIEGELMAN** has produced a series of self-portrait images that see him nude accompanied by a younger male model. These men are often of a different race or are gender fluid, and almost always much younger than himself, but they are always involved in the image-making itself. We sometimes see Siegelman clearly reflected in a mirror or directly facing the camera, or we see his body in contact with the model, as in *The Model and The Photographer (Eddy)*, where Siegelman's face is hidden behind the camera. 'Older queer men often feel invisible and undesirable in a culture where youth is valued quite highly. This work is a layered portrayal of coming to terms with aging, body image and my own struggle with body positivity.' Equally the work foregrounds questions about power imbalance and consent.

The Model and The Photographer (Eddy), 2022
Digital image
Dimensions variable

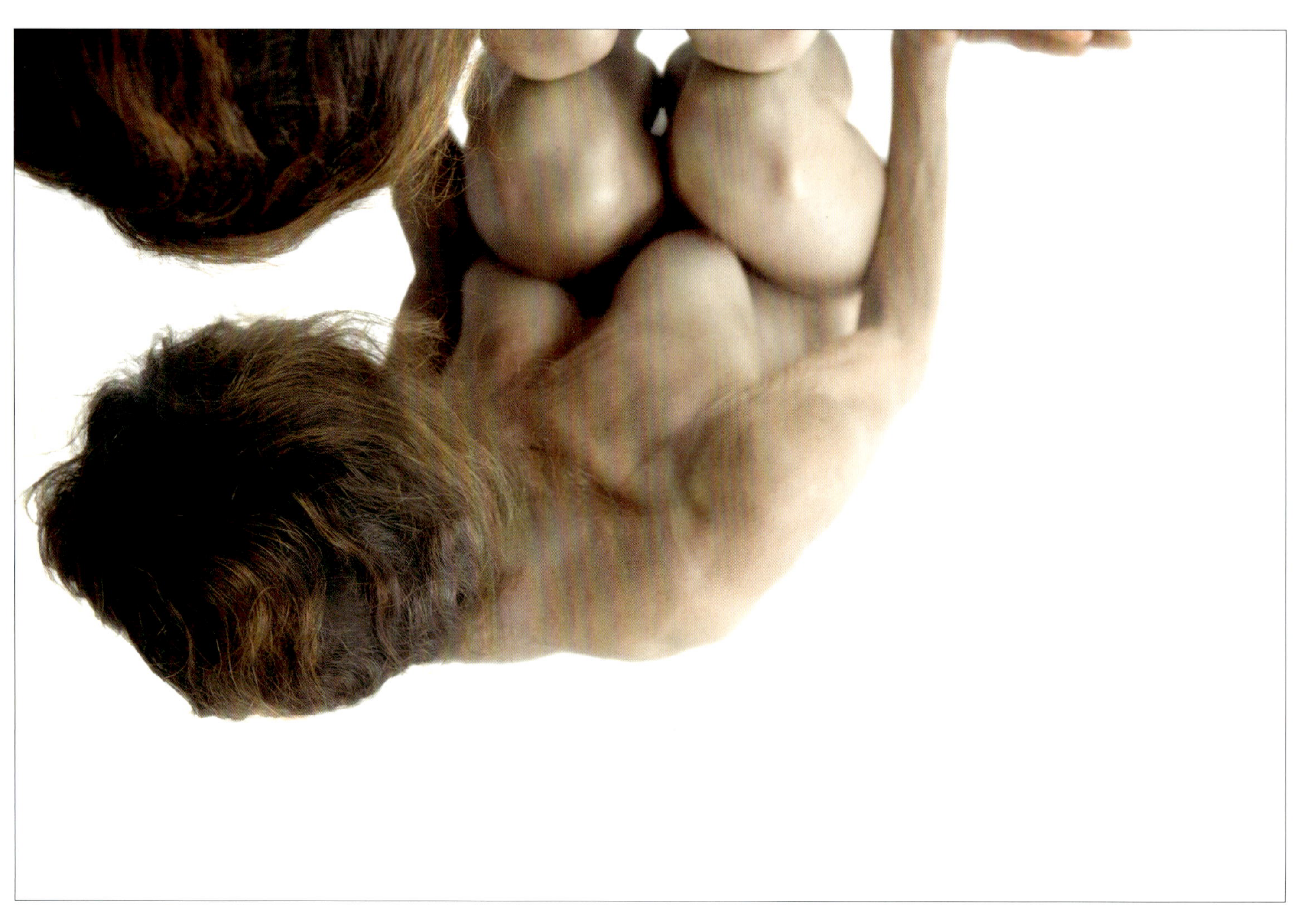

SUSAN SILAS, a Hungarian–American artist based in Brooklyn, New York, is engaged with the concept of embodiment and has often used herself as a subject. *AGING VENUS* (2018), based on a 3D scan of her body, is a 60-centimetre (24-inch) tall marble sculpture, loosely modelled after classical sculptures of Venus but presenting an older body as an idealized form. Silas's *MIRROR* series (2021), one of which is shown opposite, is a continuation of her explorations, creating a self and a reflection. The preparation for her video *TORSO* (shot in 2017) led to her arresting self-portrait (below). With the help of new digital technologies Silas is able to disrupt traditional binaries and create hybrid beings, as in the sculpture *Ode to Echo and Narcissus* (2019), where she combined her own body with that of her husband.

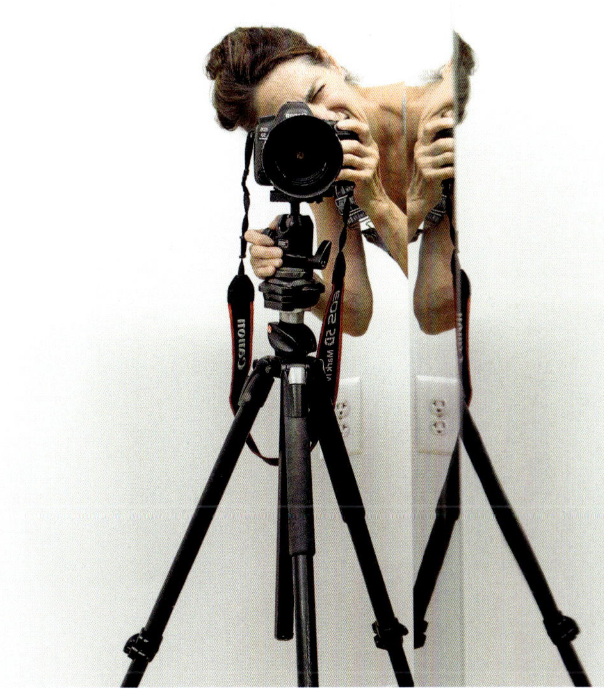

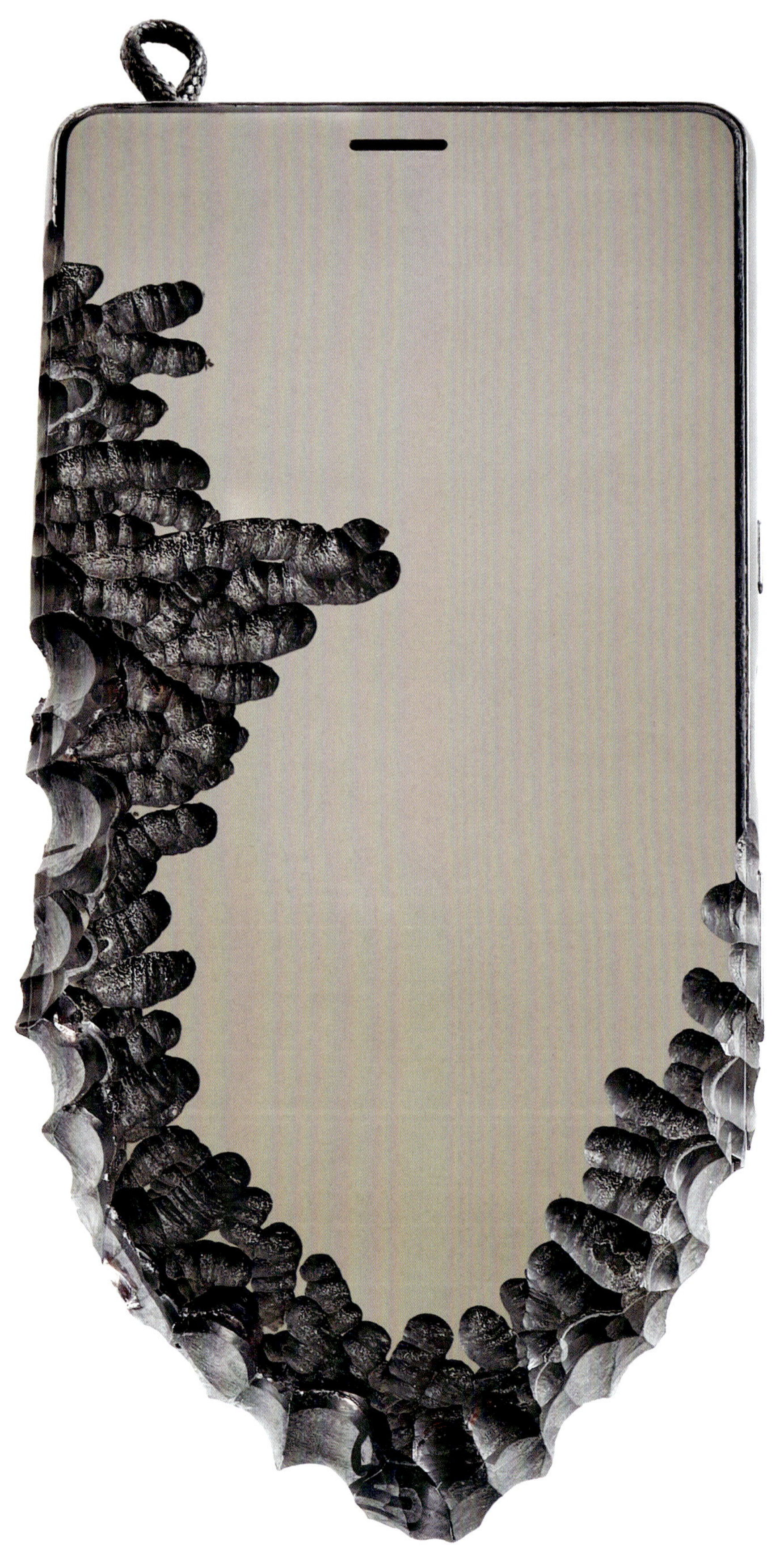

Polish artist **TADEUSZ JAŚKOWIAK**'s
(b. 1962) *Stone age smartphone* pendant
won the Gran Prix at the 29th Legnica
International Jewellery Competition,
STILL HUMAN?, in 2021, juxtaposing
the old and the new, in terms of both
technology and society. Here the digital
world is represented within an analogue
physical object that does not function
in the expected way. Jaśkowiak took
inspiration from Brian Aldiss's science-
fiction book *Hothouse* (1962), in which
the world is dominated by plants as
the Earth continuously faces the sun
on one side, leaving the other side in
darkness. Jaśkowiak has stated that this
sort of yin/yang approach encompasses
his smartphone as an object and on a
conceptual level. It reflects the viewer
like a traditional mirror but has no way
to digitally *capture* their image.

British artist **TIM ELLIS** (b. 1981) made
a cast of a BlackBerry cellphone, further
emphasizing the obsolescence of the
object. This type of mobile phone had at
one time been the state of the art in cellular
and online privacy. Ellis says: 'I saw the
handset as a mirror of the person using it,
an extension of themselves, a digital clone,
with more personal information readily
available in it.' However, the company
decided to get out of the market, stopping
all services in 2022, while keeping
customers' data 'as long as necessary…
When personal information is no longer
necessary or relevant, BlackBerry will
delete, destroy, erase, or anonymize
your data.' Customers' digital profiles
(including selfies) have been frozen,
or, in a way, cast in stone, with no real
prospect of being erased.

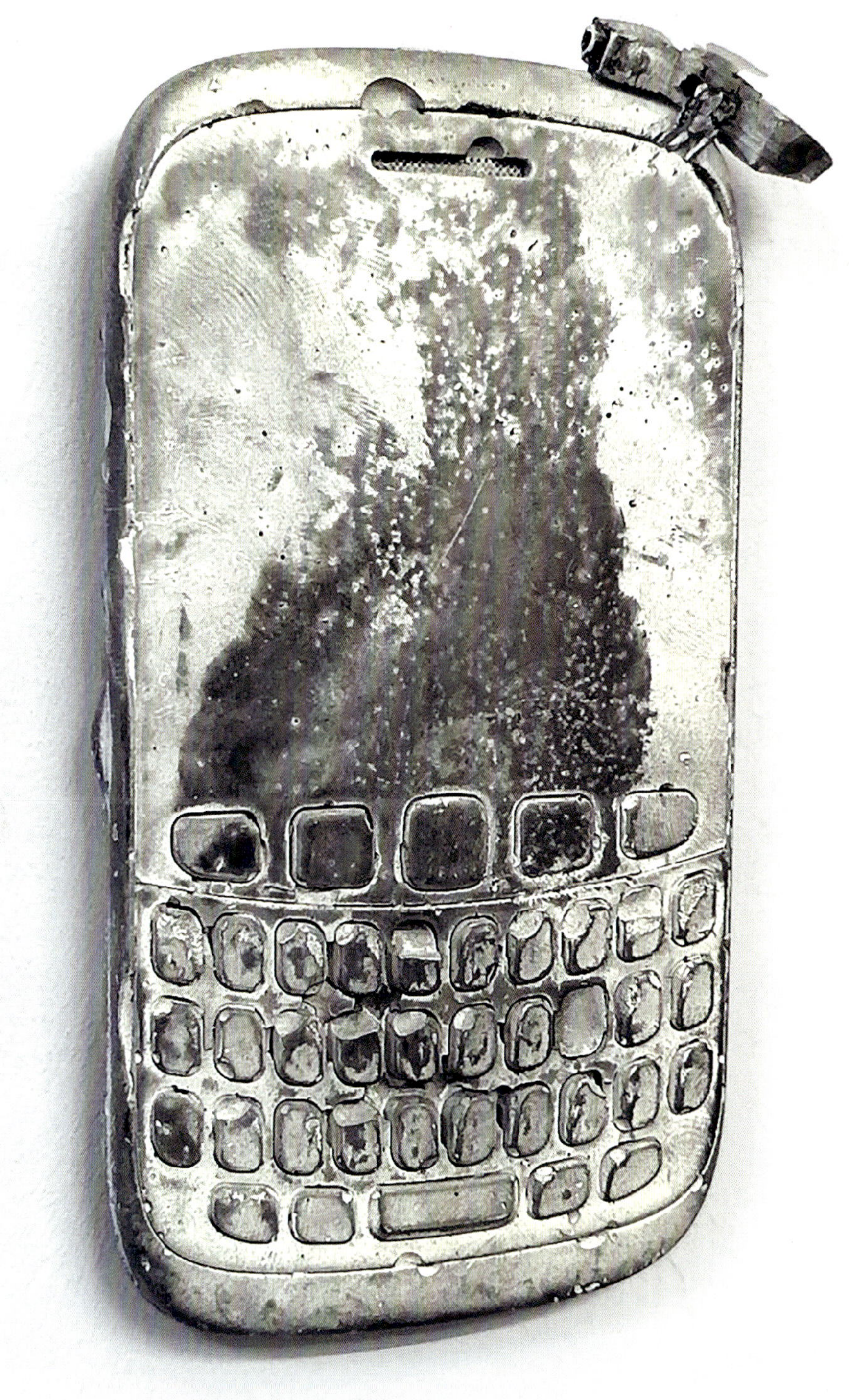

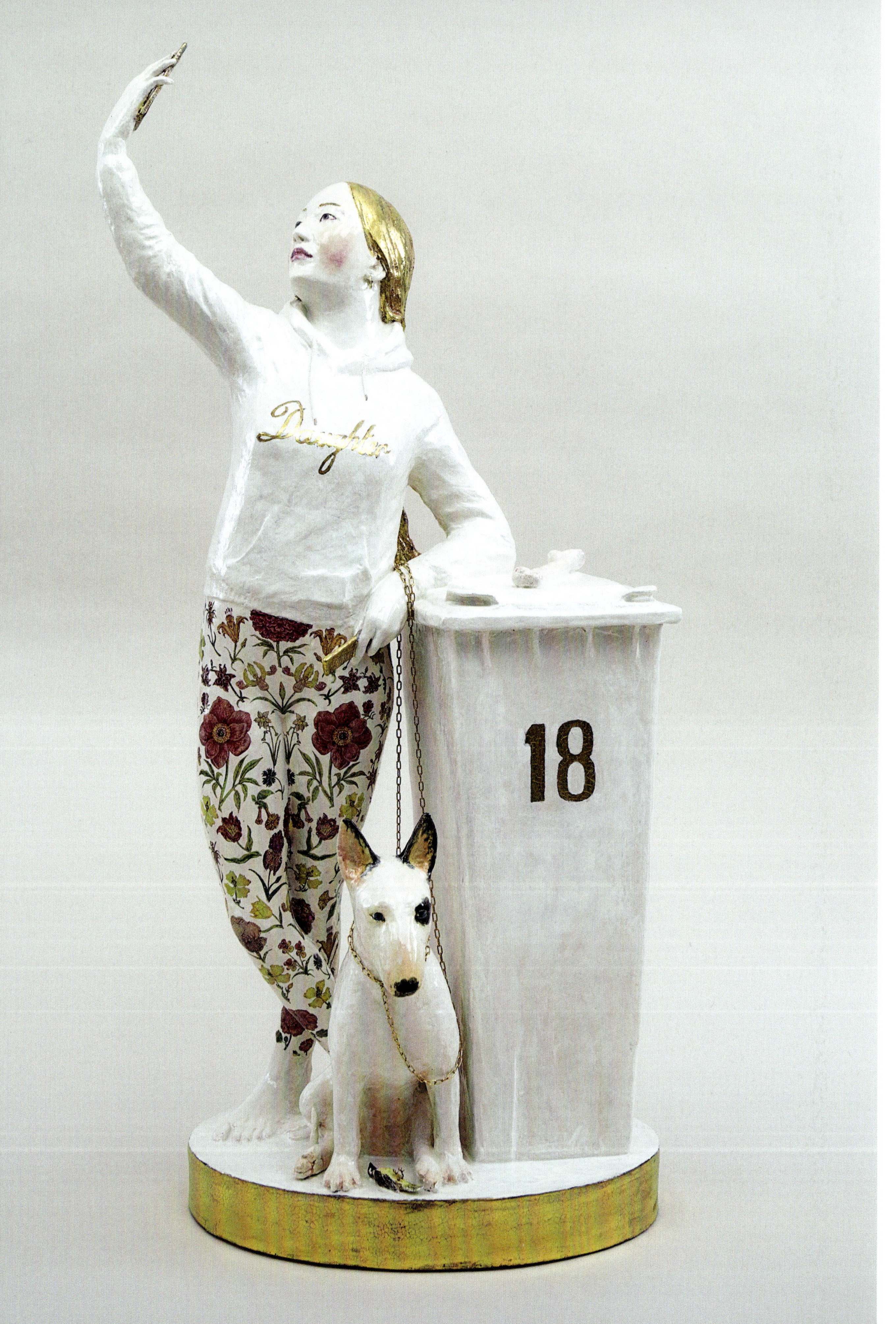

British sculptor **CLAIRE PARTINGTON** (b. 1973) has made a series of sculptures that takes everyday people you might meet on almost any London street and turns them into Renaissance beauties. In *Daughter* we see a young woman holding up her cellphone to take a selfie while out walking her dog. She has stopped to rest on a local council-provided rubbish bin and her dog seems to have killed a bird. She wears a hooded sweatshirt with 'Daughter' emblazoned across it in gold, and her porcelain-white skin could have been made by a Meissen craftworker. What makes the image truly striking is that when we see her picture in the cameraphone, her face is that of Botticelli's Venus.

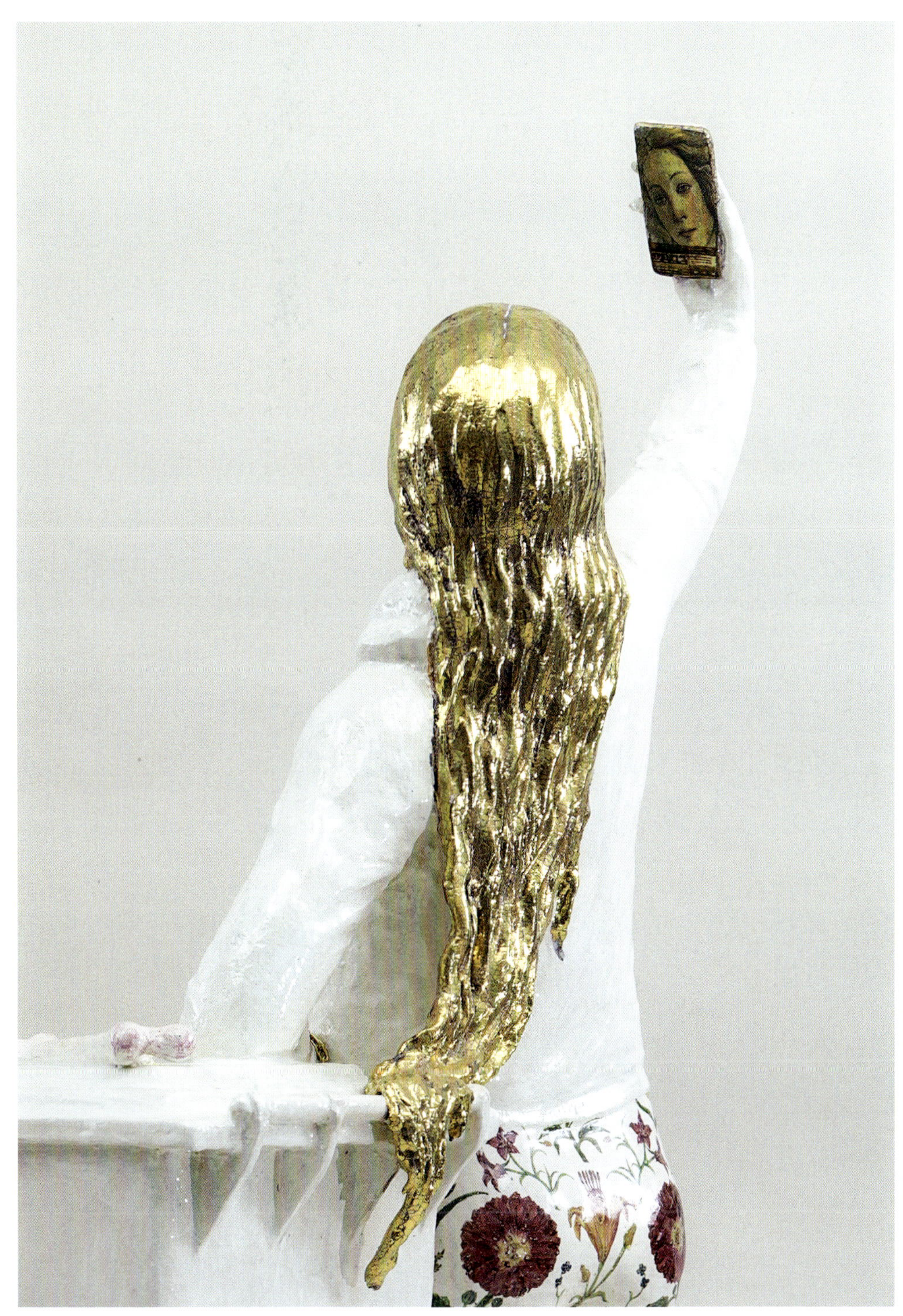

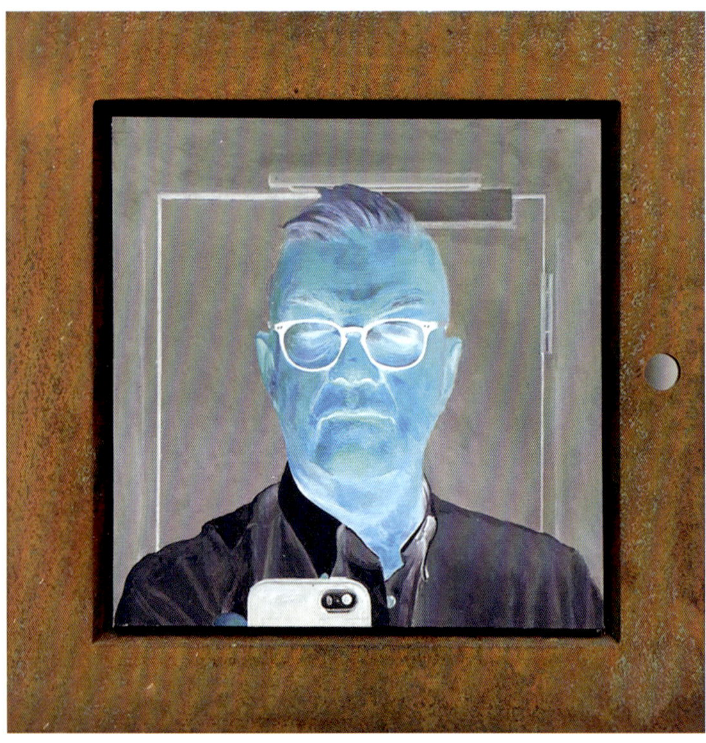

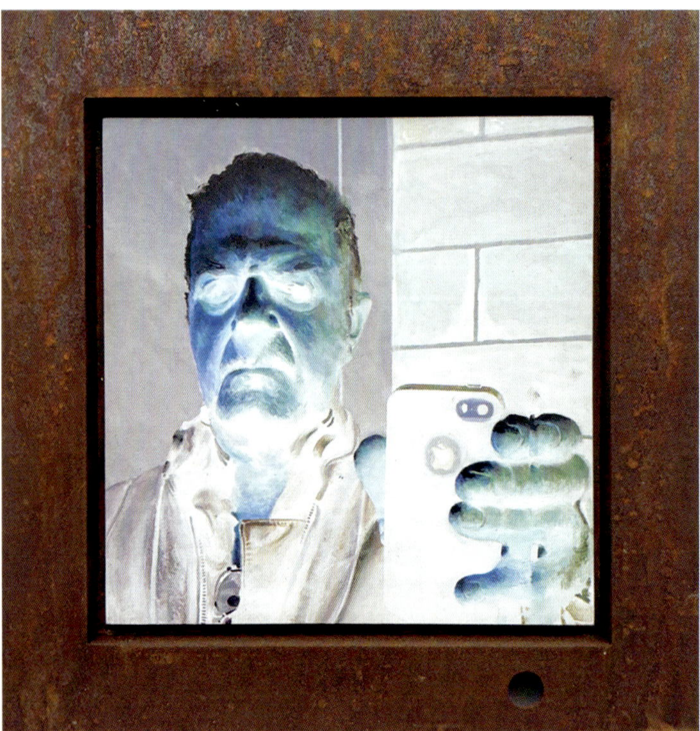

British artist **KEITH MILOW** (b. 1945) became engaged in an online exchange with a gardener that involved sending numerous selfies to each other. This led to Milow's series *Values*, which consists of portraits of the gardener, other friends and artists and a number of self-portraits, all painted and framed in an identical manner. Milow inverted the images to a negative view on his computer, and then painted the result on MDF. The images (left) can be re-inverted by using the 'classic invert' display feature on most mobile phones to startling, lifelike effect. In a kind of shorthand code for Milow, each frame has a hole in the metal at either the three or the five o'clock position, denoting respectively the traditional time of Christ's death or Thomas Becket's murder.

STUART SANDFORD is a British artist based in London, Los Angeles and Mexico City. He has made a series of sculptural images that often feature adult film stars in erotic poses that refer back to classical themes, such as his *Ouroboros*, where a flexible young man fellates himself, in editions of bronze, Carrara marble or stainless steel. In *Sebastian* (opposite) we see a fit youth in the process of taking a semi-nude selfie. He, like many who post similar images online, is wearing only a pair of tight briefs. We can see in the shadow that the camera's lens is erect as it documents the pouting young man. Other versions of the work exist in various sizes and materials (including white marble), and its replication mirrors what happens to online imagery, which can never be fully erased from the digital world.

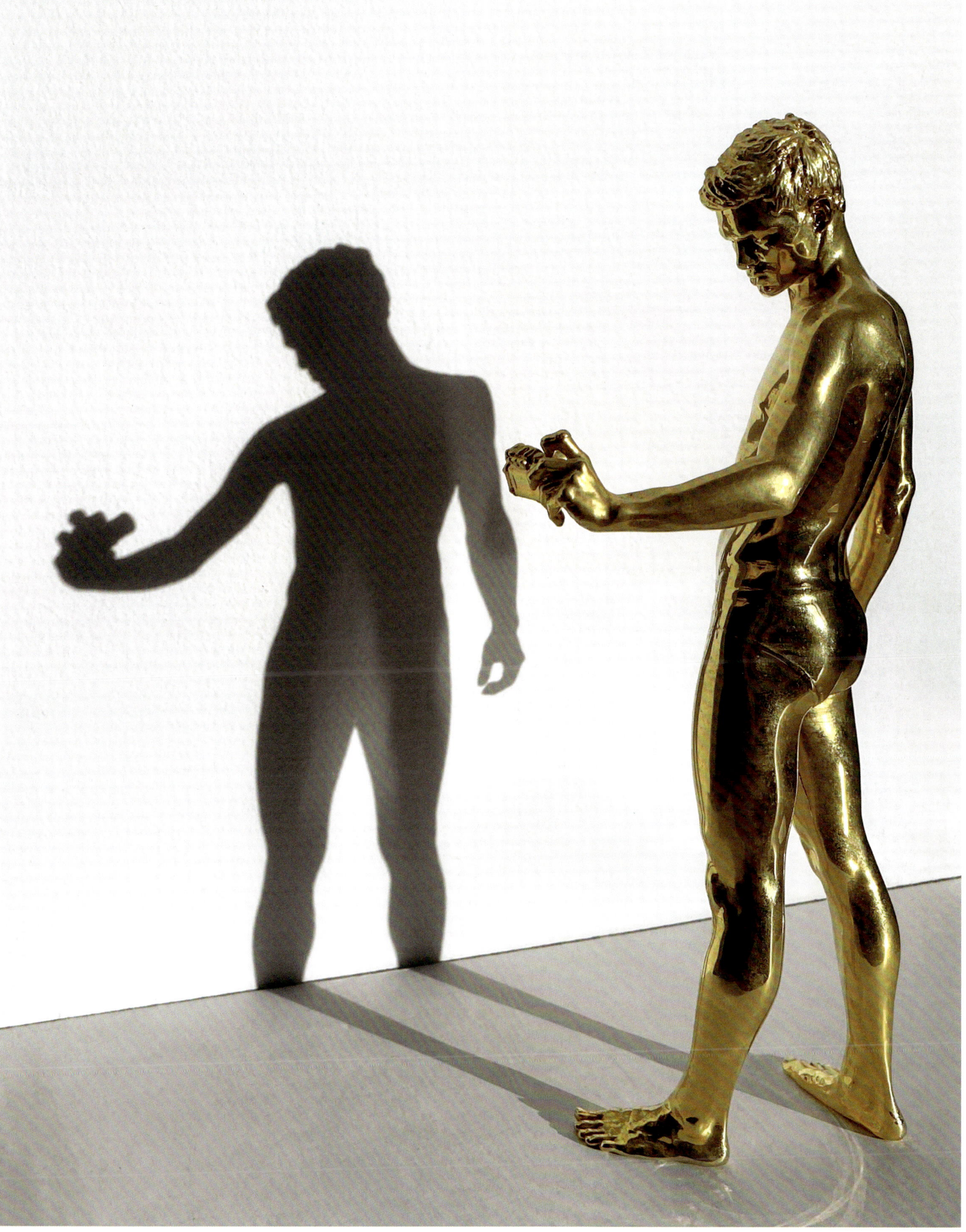

FRANKO B (b. 1960) is an Italian-born, London-based visual artist also working with performance. His late 1980s body-based and blood-letting work *I Miss You* is deservedly well known. Although he is not HIV positive, the UK press has frequently claimed that he is. He has continued to bring challenging live work to an often staid art world. *Reflecting Wounds* was performed in London, Venice and Stromboli in 2023. The selfie shown here was taken in London as he prepared to do a performance. The process of applying the mirrors is long and complex, with many hundreds of tiny mirrors glued directly to his face. The artist has said: '…*Reflecting Wounds* is about a journey through memory, history personal and collective, like many times in my works, the body, my body, and the body of the artist becomes a canvas, a sculpture, a poetry a sound also.'

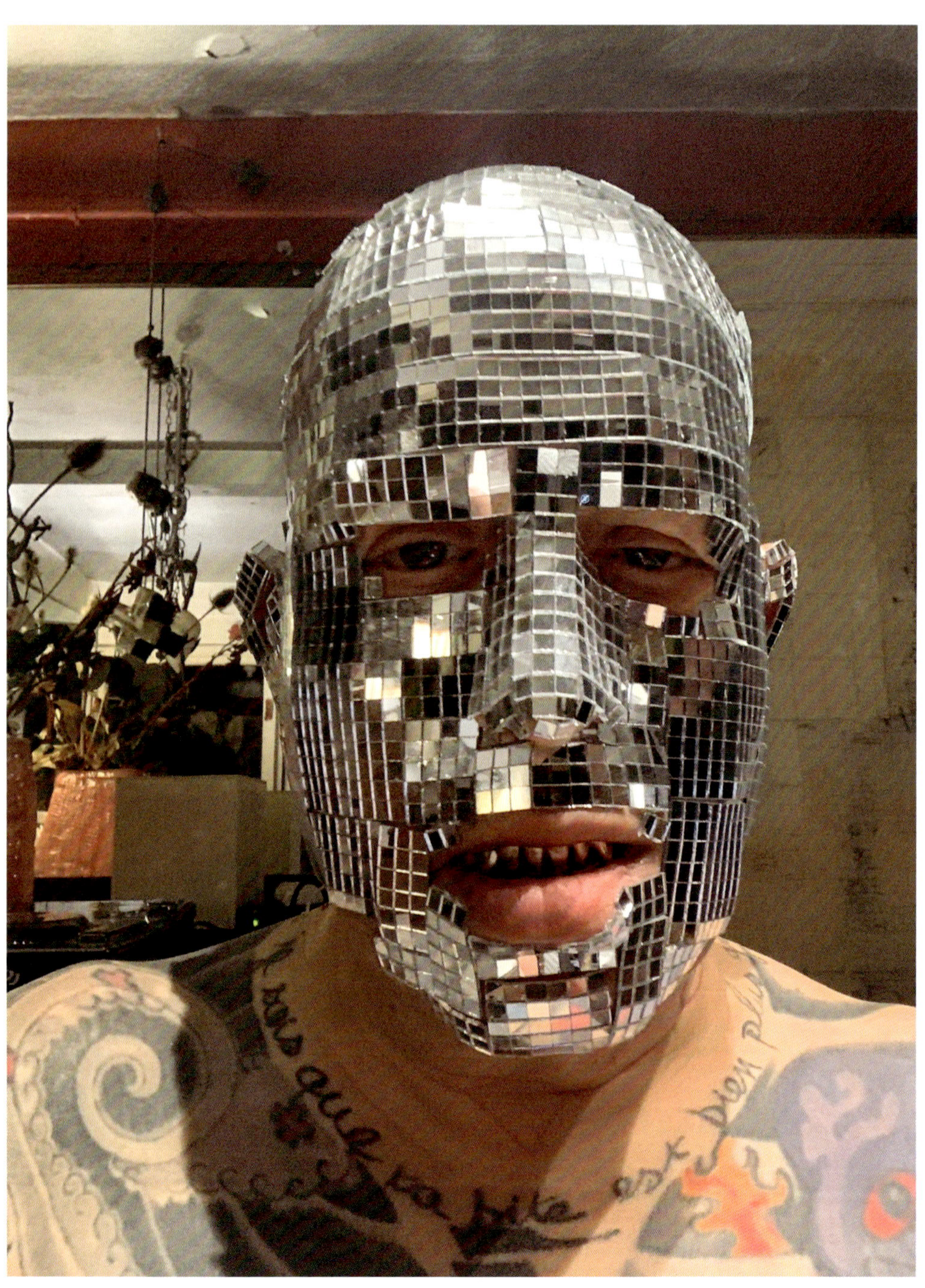

Reflecting Wounds, 2023
Digital image
Dimensions variable

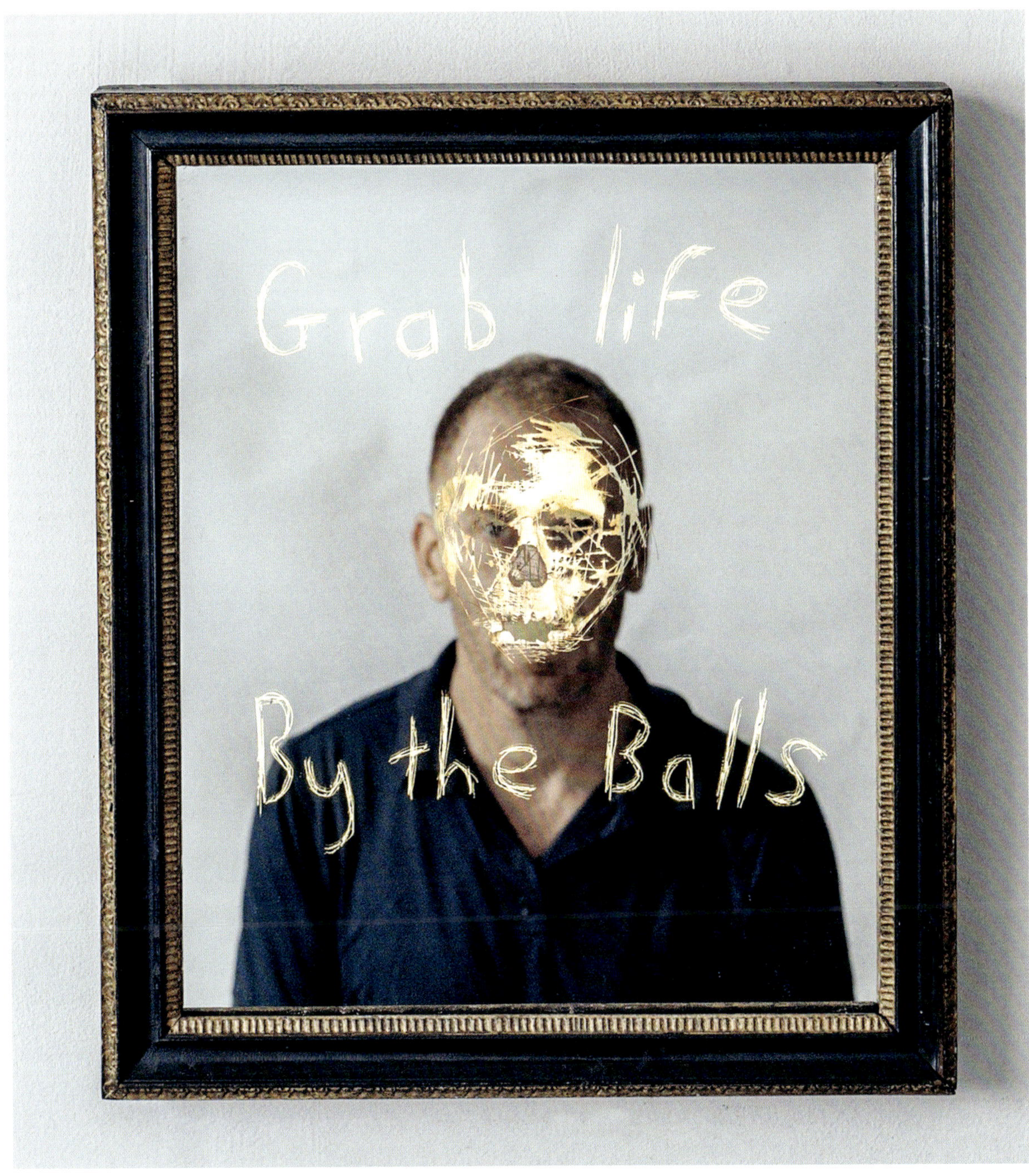

GRAB LIFE BY THE BALLS, 2016
Vintage framed mirror, etching
with LED light panel
48 × 39 × 3.5 cm (19 × 15⅜ × 1½ in)

London-based South African artist **GRAEME MESSER** made a series of physical mirrors that had texts scratched into their silvered surface so that the words could be illuminated from behind by LED lights. These phrases are a wry take on selfie culture. Messer encourages viewers to take a selfie looking into his mirrors, which say things like 'ME.ME.ME.ME.ME', or 'My Angel' with a halo added above head height. Other mirrors say 'Head Over Heels In Love' or 'Aim Lower' or 'Comparison is the thief of contentment'. In *GRAB LIFE BY THE BALLS* the illuminated text has an accompanying skull where the viewer's face fits in perfectly, in this case reflecting the artist's own selfie.

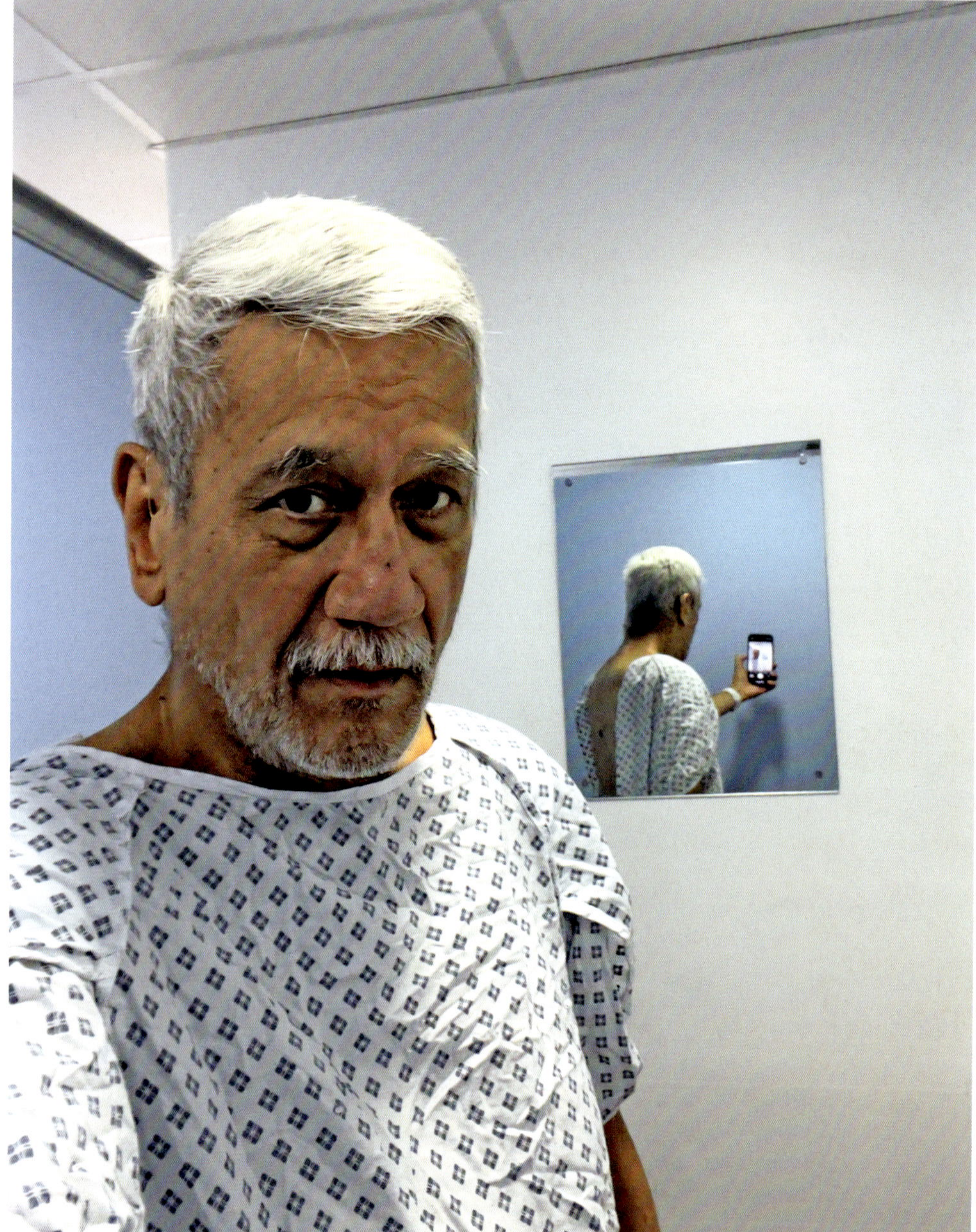

Indian-born Canadian–British photographer **SUNIL GUPTA** (b. 1953) has long turned the camera back onto himself in his work as an artist using a camera. Over many decades he has traced and documented how he and others from sexual and racial minorities have been seen by the wider culture as well as by themselves. In the mid-1990s Gupta contracted HIV, and he has also photographed his own medical journey and the way in which those with the disease are perceived. His recent selfie, taken at St Thomas' Hospital in London, where he lives, documents a recent health-care visit.

INDIA ROPER-EVANS is a Hungarian–British photographer who has been commissioned many times to take portraits of other artists, including Maggi Hambling, Antony Gormley and Marina Abramović, as well as the work of Ai Weiwei, Katharina Fritsch, Ernesto Neto and many others. Yet her ongoing series of selfies often does not feature her own face. She is invisible; we see the back of her head in a room of mirrors that reflect each other but not her face. We see parts of her, a hand or a leg in the bath or bedroom, and when we do see her from the front, her face is in dark shadow and again she cannot be

recognized. Even when she faces herself in a mirror to take her own photo, what we see is the phone in front of her face, and the rest of her studio hung with test pieces. She is and is not there in the majority of the images, though on occasion she does pop into view.

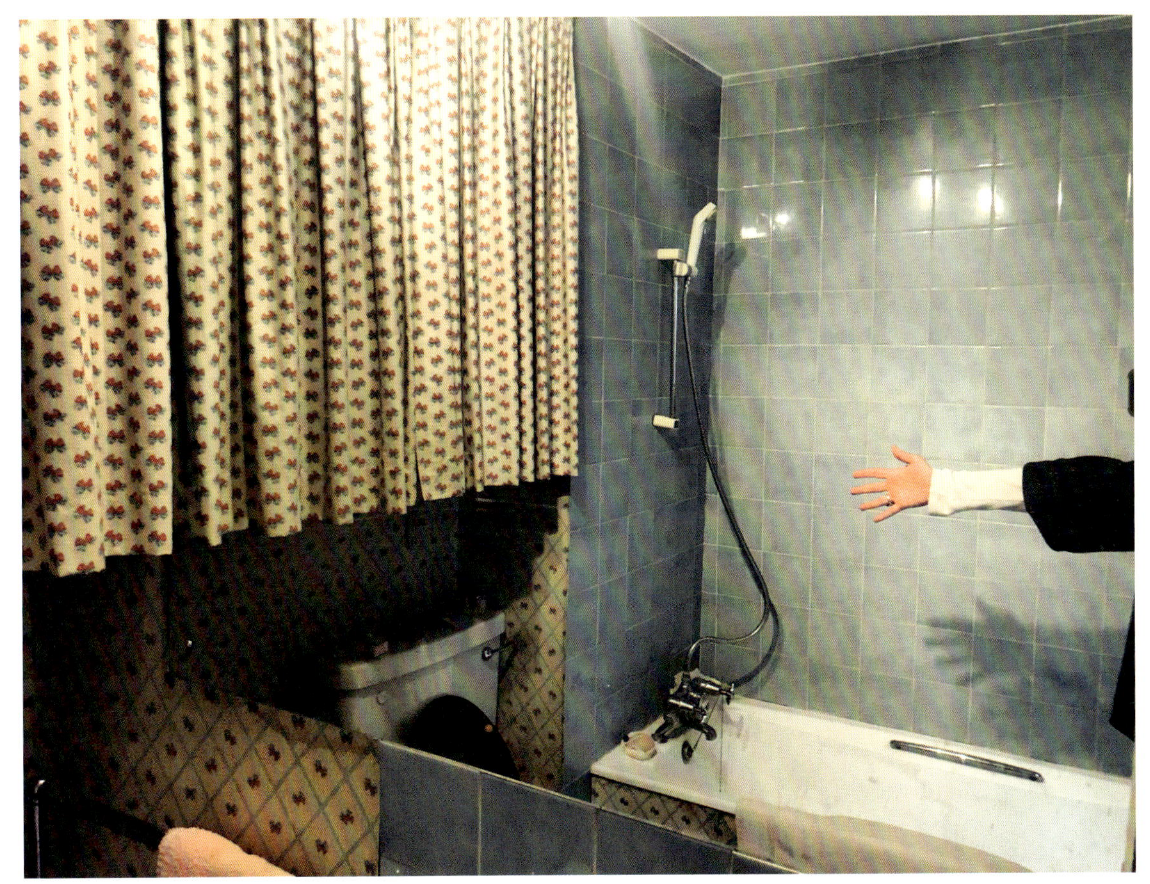

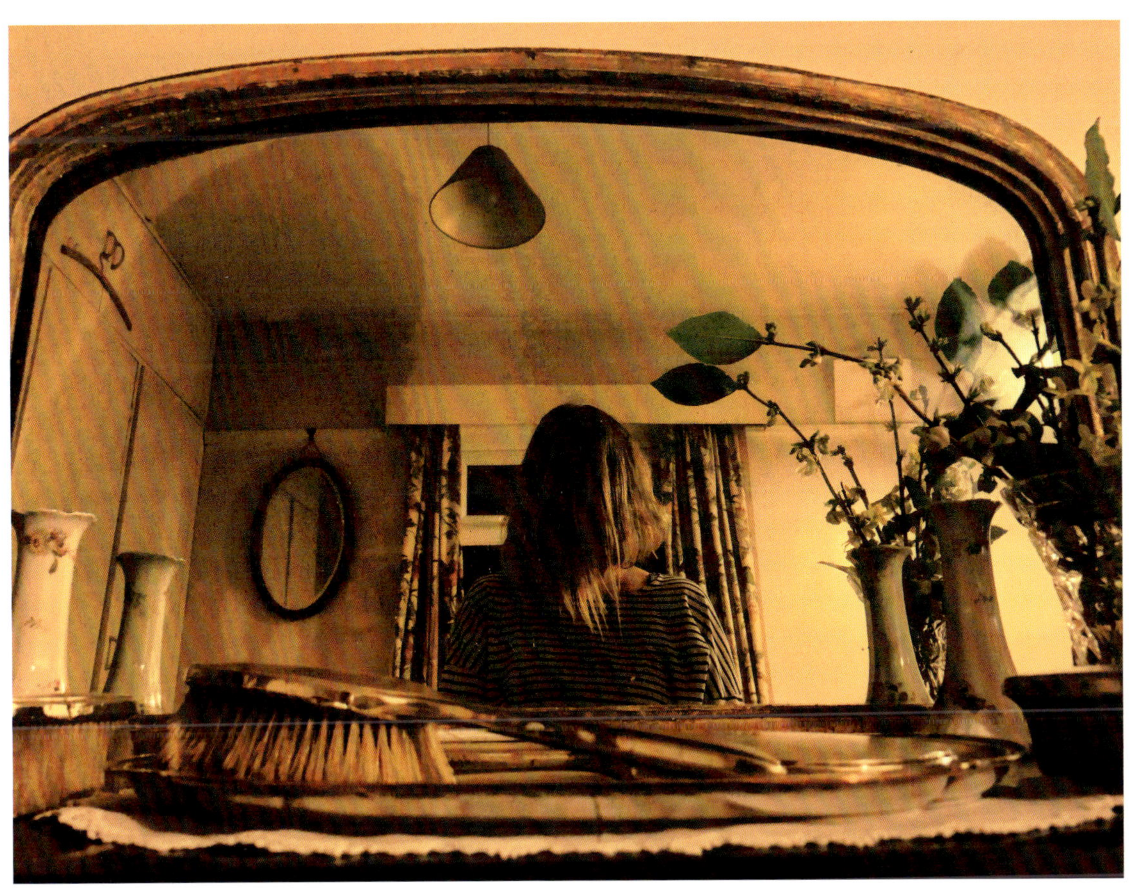

Catalan photographer **POL ÚBEDA HERVÀS** has made an arresting self-portrait image by absenting himself from it. He is there and he is not. We see his dirty white trainers at the edge of a cool blue pool, as well as a shadow reflection of his image. The self-portrait shows hints of the man, who appears to possibly have a beard, perhaps the only gendered part of the image. We see his shoes, and the pool's reflection, but the man himself is absent. Hervàs has said, 'My shadow is there but I have erased myself because I don't know who I am any more. The shoes remain simply as a reminder that there is something more than a shadow.' The image leads the viewer to question whether the subject is always absent in selfies.

I'm Not There, 2012
Giclée print on cotton paper
50 × 50 cm (19¾ × 19¾ in)

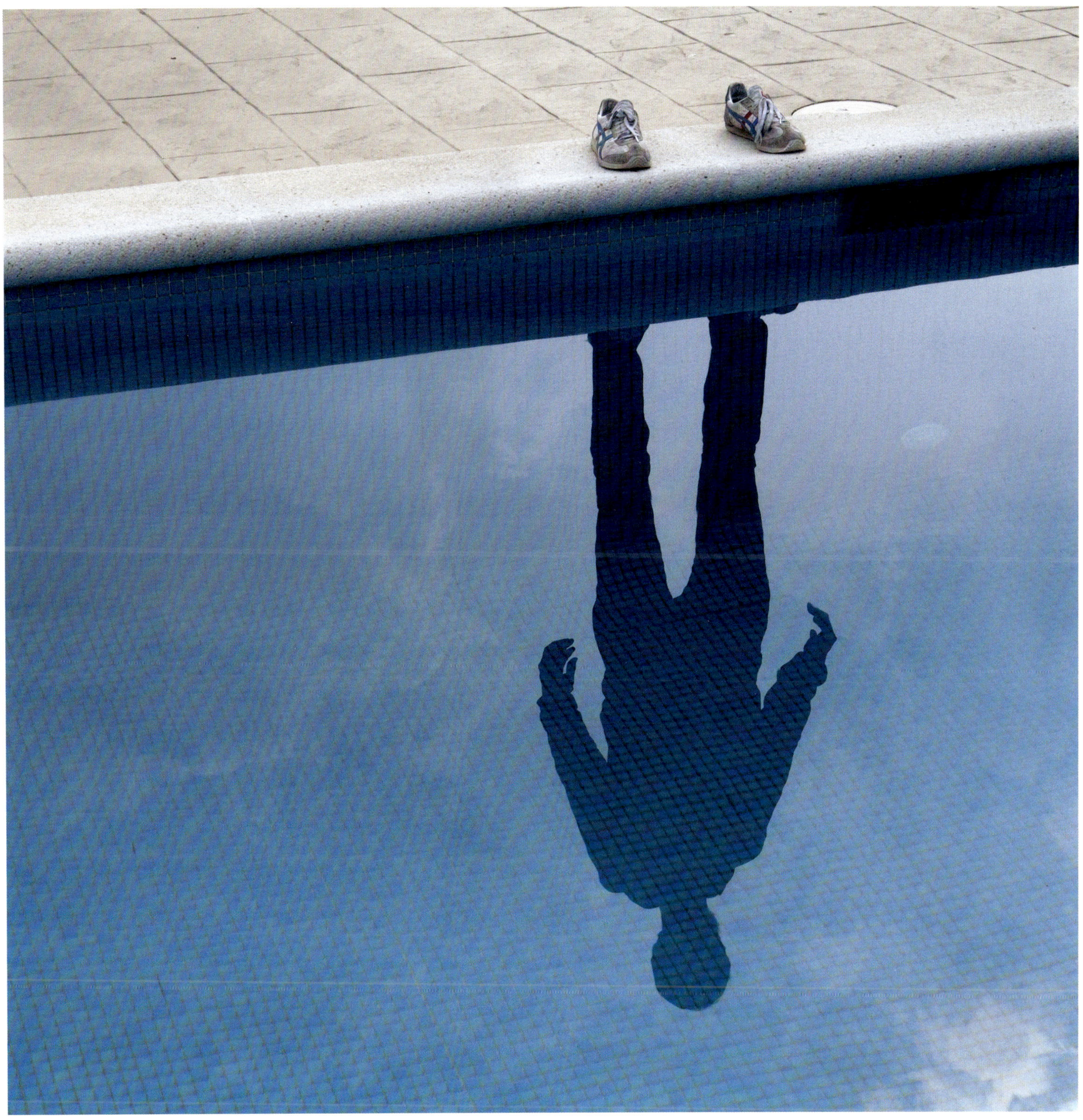

shirinabedinirad.com
dougaitkenworkshop.com
instagram.com/thekathrynandrews
kaderattia.de
gulerates.co.uk
franko-b.com
stavb.co.uk
barnabybarford.co.uk
tinebech.com
bigertbergstrom.com
peterbriggssculpture.com/accueil
aabronson.com
leebul.com
instagram.com/burrtomburr
instagram.com/janebustin
junocalypso.com
tony-cragg.com
michalart.com/about
matcollishaw.com
debcovell.com
instagram.com/finniancroy
ankadabrowskaart.com
deboradehaes.com
robertoekholm.com
olafureliasson.net
timellis.org
instagram.com/traceyeminstudio
fridaescobedo.com
amelie-esterhazy.de
instagram.com/teresita.fernandez
ursfischer.com
fransfranciscus.nl
instagram.com/mmichel_francois
philippfuerhofer.de
pollygould.co.uk
instagram.com/subodhguptastudio
https://paulhazelton.com
jeppehein.net
flickr.com/photos/polubeda
simonhitchens.com
instagram.com/andres_moreno_hoffmann
carlhopgood.com
jameshopkinsworks.com
shirinhosseinvand.com
anthonyjamesstudio.com
instagram.com/tadeusz.jaskowiak
isaacjulien.com
anishkapoor.com
andrewkearney.net
tarikkiswanson.com
saijakivikangas.com
instagram.com/jeffkoons
instagram.com/jukka_korkeila

remigijuskriukas.com
mischakuball.com
danielkukla.com
yayoi-kusama.jp/e/information
alicjakwade.com
ariklevy.fr
andrewlogan.com
zhengluart.com
shanamabari.com
instagram.com/krismartinofficial
dillonmarsh.com
stuartmayes.com
mentalklinik.com
instagram.com/graememesser
chandrikametivier.com
keithmilow.com
instagram.com/paulmorrisonstudio
robmulholland.org
studio.jonnyniesche.com
paglen.studio
angelaspalmer.com
instagram.com/johnmichaelparry
clairepartington.co.uk
traceypayne.co.uk
aliciapaz.com
annepeabody.com
instagram.com/simonperiton
michaelpetry.com
emmapeura.com
hubertphipps.com
suzypoling.com
sarahpucill.co.uk
fredrikraddum.no
thomasrentmeister.de
carlosrolon.com
ugorondinone.com
indiarophotography.com
instagram.com/premsahib
ericrhein.com
fabricesamyn.com
stuartsandford.com
richardsawdonsmith.com
yutasegawa.com
paulsepuya.com
instagram.com/cindysherman
yukoshiraishi.com
robertsiegelman.com
susansilas.com
feliciasimionphotography.com
jonathandavidsmyth.com
valeskasoares.net
instagram.com/mattiasmiele
superflex.net

sarahsze.com
matthewszosz.com
gorantomcic.com
mungothomson.com
kenjitoki.com
instagram.com/davidtrullo
gavinturk.com
csub.edu/~Svanderlip
davidvaneyssen.com
mathiasvef.com
santiagovelez.net
notvital.com
johanneswald.de
zhanwangart.com/en
megwebsterstudio.com
theiswendt.com
timwillcocks.com
woodeson.co.uk
markwoods-studio.com
dawnwoolley.com
robwynne.net
jeffxzimmer.com

Photo: Michael Richter **138–139** Courtesy Hubert G. Phipps. Photo: Hubert G. Phipps **140** © Arik Levy. Photo: © Arik Levy **141** Courtesy the Artist. Photo: Dai Ruoying **142–143** © The Donum Estate and the artist. Photo: Robert Berg **144–145** © Lynda Benglis/VAGA at ARS, NY and DACS, London 2024. Photo: Jonathan Nesteruk, courtesy Pace Gallery **146, 147** Photos: Simon Hitchens **148** Courtesy Paul Morrison Studio **149 T, B** Courtesy Angela Palmer. Photo: A C Cooper Ltd **150–151** © The Donum Estate and the artist. Photo: Robert Berg **152** © Gary Hume. Courtesy the artist, Sprüth Magers and Matthew Marks Gallery. Photo: Stephen White & Co. **153** © Simon Periton. Courtesy the artist and Sadie Coles HQ, London **155** © Katharina Fritsch/DACS, London 2024. Courtesy Matthew Marks Gallery **156** © Cerith Wyn Evans. Photo © Ueno Norihiro, Yokohama Triennale. Courtesy White Cube **157** Collection CNAP – Centre National des Arts Plastiques. Courtesy the artist and carlier | gebauer. Photo: Günther Lepkowski **158** Courtesy the artist and David Kordansky Gallery, Los Angeles. Photo: Flying Studio **159** Courtesy the artist and David Kordansky Gallery, Los Angeles. Photo: Fredrik Nilsen Studio **160 T, B** Courtesy Tove Nilson and Maribel Toral. Series 2018–ongoing **161** Photo: Rob Bohle. Courtesy Paul Derrez **162, 163** Courtesy the artist and greengrassi, London. Photos © Marcus Leith **164–165** Courtesy the artist and Lehmann Maupin. Photos: Matthew Herrmann **166–167** Courtesy Anthony James & Melissa Morgan Fine Art. Photo: Anthony James Studio **168, 169** Courtesy the artists. Photos: Emma Peura **170** Courtesy the artist **171** Photo: Courtesy the artist and Copperfield, London **172** Courtesy Imi Knoebel and Galerie Christian Lethert, Cologne. Edition published by Galerie Christian Lethert, Cologne. Photo: MOCA London **173** Photo: Matteo Piazza **174, 175** Photos: Poppy Woodeson **176** Collection: Göteborgs Konstmuseum. Courtesy Hans Alf Gallery. Photo: Julie Nymann **177** Courtesy the artist, Sies + Höke, Düsseldorf. Photographer Simon Vogel, Cologne **178–179** © Sherrie Levine. Courtesy the artist and David Zwirner **180–181** Courtesy Michael Petry and The Parsonage Gallery **182, 183** © Meg Webster. Courtesy Paula Cooper Gallery, New York. Photos: Steven Probert **184** © Ugo Rondinone. Courtesy the artist; Galerie Eva Presenhuber, Zurich; Esther Schipper, Berlin; Sadie Coles HQ, London; Gladstone, New York; Kamel Mennour, Paris; Kukje Gallery, Seoul. Photo: Andrea Rossetti **185** © Ugo Rondinone.

Courtesy the artist and Sadie Coles HQ, London. Photo: Stefan Altenburger **186** Photo: Cal Carey Photographer **188–189** Private collection. Photo courtesy the artist **190** Photo: Marc Renshaw **191** Courtesy the artist. Photo: Simon Regan **192, 193** Courtesy Goran Tomcic; Dimensions Variable, Miami; SomoS, Berlin. Photo: Francesco Casale **194** Courtesy the artist; 1301PE, Los Angeles; and Starkwhite, Auckland. Photo: Marten Elder **195** Courtesy the artist and Sarah Cottier Gallery, Sydney. Photo: Ashley Barber **196** Courtesy Galerie Greta Meert, Galerie Rolando Anselmi. Photo: Emile Rubino **197** Photo: Anne Peabody **198** Courtesy the artist. Photo: ©Markus Schneider **199** Courtesy Theis Wendt and Grimm Gallery. Photo: Noortje Knulst **200** Jon Gasca Collection, Spain. Courtesy the artist, Sies + Höke, Düsseldorf. Photo: Tino Kukulies, Düsseldorf **201** Courtesy König Galerie, Berlin, 303 Gallery, New York, and Galleri Nicolai Wallner, Copenhagen. Photo: Studio Jeppe Hein/Jan Strempel **202–203** Courtesy the artist; LaGuardia Gateway Partners; Public Art Fund, New York; 303 Gallery, New York; König Galerie, Berlin; Galleri Nicolai Wallner, Copenhagen. Photo: Nicholas Knight **204, 205** © Philippe Parreno. Courtesy the artist and Gladstone Gallery. Photo: David Regen **206–207** Photo courtesy the artist and Grey Cube Projects **208, 209** Photos: Cal Carey Photographer **210** Courtesy the artist. Photo: the artist **211** Photo: MOCA London **212** Photo: MOCA London **213** Courtesy the artist and Phillida Reid, London. Photo: Lewis Ronald **214 T, B** Private collection **215, 216–217** Courtesy Rob Wynne & GAVLAK gallery, Los Angeles and Palm Beach. Photo: Kelly McCormick **218** Courtesy the artist and Catharine Clark Gallery, San Francisco **219** Courtesy the artist. Photo: Marius Rudžianskas **220, 221** Courtesy Shana Mabari. Photo: Eric Minh Swenson **222, 223 BL, BR** Courtesy the artist **224** Photo: Uwe Seyl **225** Photo: Jörg Hejkal **226** V&A Collection. Courtesy the artist and The Victoria & Albert Museum. Photo: Kenji Toki **227** Courtesy the artist **228, 229,** Courtesy the artist **230–231** Courtesy Dillon Marsh **232–233,** Courtesy Murray Fredericks. Image Courtesy Hamiltons Gallery **234,** Photo courtesy of and from the collection of François Chappuis **236 T, B** © Cindy Sherman. Courtesy the artist and Hauser & Wirth **237** Courtesy the artist **238** Image © AA Bronson. Image courtesy the artist and Esther Schipper, Berlin **239** Image © AA Bronson. Image courtesy the artist and Esther Schipper, Berlin. Photo © Andrea Rossetti

240, 241 BL, BR Courtesy the artist. Photos: Tim Willcocks **242, 243** Courtesy Dawn Woolley **244** Photo: MOCA London **245** Courtesy Debora De Haes **246–247** Courtesy Juno Calypso/TJ Boulting Gallery. Photos: Juno Calypso **248, 249** Courtesy Finnian Croy **250** Courtesy Felicia Simion **251** Courtesy the artist. Photo: Jukka Korkeila **252** Photo: Jeff Zimmer **253, 254–255** Photos courtesy the artist **256** Courtesy Stav B and Anka Dabrowska **257** Courtesy John-Michael Parry **258 BL, BR, 259** Courtesy the artist. Photos: Jonathan David Smyth **260** Photo: Michal Cole **261** Courtesy the artist. Photo: Prof Richard Sawdon Smith **262, 263** Courtesy Eric Rhein **264–265** © Tracey Emin. All rights reserved, DACS 2024. Photo: © White Cube (Theo Christelis) **266–267** Courtesy Robert Siegelman **268, 269** Courtesy Susan Silas **270** Grand Prix of the Minister of Culture, National Heritage and Sport in the 29th International Jewellery Competition *STILL HUMAN?* International Collection of Contemporary Jewellery. Photo: The Gallery of Art in Legnica **271** Courtesy Tim Ellis **272, 273** © Claire Partington. Courtesy the artist. Photo: Claire Partington **274 T, B** Photos: KM **275** Photo courtesy of and from the collection of David Russell **276** Photo: Franko B **277** Photo: Suki Mok **278** Image courtesy the artist and Hales Gallery, Materià Gallery, Stephen Bulger Gallery and Vadehra Art Gallery. © Sunil Gupta. All Rights Reserved, DACS 2024. Photo: Sunil Gupta **279 T, B** Courtesy India Roper-Evans **281** Courtesy Pol Úbeda Hervàs

ACKNOWLEDGMENTS

This book is dedicated to my partner, Travis Barker

I would like the reader to note that the artist Hubert Phipps died during the production of the book, and would like to thank his family for their continued support in the use of an image of his in this book.

I would like to thank Constance Kaine for her continued support in my work and strong belief in my books.

I would like to thank all the participating artists, their gallery representatives and their staff, along with all the Thames & Hudson production teams. Particular thanks for all their help and diligence in the making of the book go to Paola d'Albore, Jonathan Abbott, Karolina Prymaka, Ilona de Nemethy Sanigar and Kirsty Seymour-Ure. I would like to thank the following for their support: Travis Barker and Devon Abts, Devin Borden and Robert Briscoe, Hiram Butler, Lee Cavaliere, Daniell Cornell, Cross Lane Projects, Roberto Ekholm, Germaine Franco, Gavin Greenaway, Juliane Jung, Rick Herron, Kristin Hjellegjerde, Marilyn Loesberg, Alec Longmuir, Donna MacMillan, Melissa Morgan, Bryan Mulvihill, Peter Otto and Gary Bracken, Parsonage Gallery, Joshua Pazda, Theresa Petry, John Powell, Eric Prince, David Robinson, Paul and Sara Robinson, Aaron Rosen, Rebecca Scott and Mark Woods, St Mary the Virgin Episcopal Church, Paul Stone, Christene and Michael Tashjian, Georges Tourtellotte, Vane Gallery, Chris Westbrook, Sammy Wood, Christopher Yeats, VOMA, Sandy Zane.

AUTHOR'S BIOGRAPHY

Michael Petry (b. Texas, 1960) studied at Rice University, Houston, and has a doctorate in Arts from Middlesex University. Petry is an artist and author, and is director of MOCA London. He co-founded the Museum of Installation and was curator of the Royal Academy Schools Gallery, both in London. Petry's books for Thames & Hudson include *Installation Art in the New Millennium: The Empire of Senses*, *The Art of Not Making: The New Artist Artisan Relationship*, *Nature Morte: Contemporary Artists Reinvigorate the Still-Life Tradition* and *The WORD is Art*. Most books included a touring exhibition that he curated, as with his *Hidden Histories: 20th century male same sex lovers in the visual arts* for the New Art Gallery Walsall. Petry was the first artist in residence at Sir John Soane's Museum in London, and recent one-man shows include 'The Touch of the Oracle' (Palm Springs Art Museum) and 'In League with Devils' (Henry Luce III Center for the Arts, Washington, DC). Petry's work has been shown in museums and international exhibitions, including 'Frontiers Reimagined' at the 2015 Venice Biennale.

First published in the United Kingdom in 2024 by Thames & Hudson Ltd, 6–24 Britannia Street, London WC1X 9JD

First published in the United States of America in 2024 by Thames & Hudson Inc., 500 Fifth Avenue, New York, New York 10110

EU Authorized Representative: Interart S.A.R.L. 19 rue Charles Auray, 93500 Pantin, Paris, France
productsafety@thameshudson.co.uk
interart.fr

A CIP catalogue record for this book is available from the British Library

Library of Congress Control Number 2024934205

ISBN 978-0-500-02620-5
02

Printed and bound in Canada by Transcontinental Printing